D0575104

NATIONAL UNIVERSITY
LIBRARY   SAN DIEGO

Handbook of Software Quality Assurance

Third Edition

Edited by

G. Gordon Schulmeyer, CDP

and

James I. McManus

Prentice Hall PTR
Upper Saddle River, NJ 07458
http://www.phptr.com

ISBN 0-13-010470-1

90000

9 780130 104700

Library of Congress Catalog-in-Publication Data

Handbook of software quality assurance / edited by G. Gordon
    Schulmeyer and James I. McManus. -- 3rd ed.
        p.   cm.
    Includes bibliographical references and index.
    ISBN 0-13-010470-1
    1. Computer software--Quality control.   I. Schulmeyer, G. Gordon.
II. McManus, James I.
QA76.76.Q35H36   1998
005.1--dc21   98-36662
                                                       CIP

Editorial/production supervision: *Nicholas Radhuber*
Interior formatting: *Vanessa Moore*
Cover design director: *Jerry Votta*
Cover design: *Anthony Gemmellaro*
Manufacturing manager: *Alexis Heydt*
Acquisitions editor: *Stephen Solomon*
Marketing manager: *Dan Rush*

© 1999 Prentice Hall PTR
Prentice-Hall, Inc.
A Simon & Schuster Company
Upper Saddle River, NJ 07458

Prentice Hall books are widely used by corporations and government
agencies for training, marketing, and resale.

The publisher offers discounts on this book when ordered in bulk quantities.
For more information, contact Corporate Sales Department, Phone: 800-382-3419,
Fax: 201-236-7141, Email: corpsales@prenhall.com

or write: Prentice Hall PTR
             Corporate Sales Department
             One Lake Street
             Upper Saddle River, NJ 07458

All rights reserved. No part of this book may be reproduced, in any form or by any means,
without permission in writing from the publisher. Chapter 13 copyright © 1998 by Quality
Assurance Institute®. Chapter 18 copyright © 1997 Boeing Company.

All Trademarks are the property of their respective owners.

Printed in the United States of America

10   9   8   7   6   5   4   3   2   1

ISBN 0-13-010470-1

Prentice-Hall International (UK) Limited, *London*
Prentice-Hall of Australia Pty. Limited, *Sydney*
Prentice-Hall of Canada, Inc., *Toronto*
Prentice-Hall Hispanoamericana S.A., *Mexico*
Prentice-Hall of India Private Limited, *New Delhi*
Prentice-Hall of Japan, Inc., *Tokyo*
Simon & Schuster Asia Pte. Ltd., *Singapore*
Editora Prentice-Hall do Brasil, Ltda., *Rio de Janeiro*

TRADEMARKS

The following trademarks are referenced within this book:

ANSI is a registered trademark of American National Standards Institute

Bell, UNIX, and AT&T are registered trademarks of American Telephone and Telegraph Co.

Teamwork is a registered trademark of Cayenne Software, Inc. (formerly owned by Cadre Technologies, Inc.)

COHESION, DECwindows, COBOL, and VMS arc registered trademarks of Digital Equipment Corp. (now Compaq Computer, Inc.)

Hewlett-Packard is a registered trademark of Hewlett-Packard Co.

RTM is a registered trademark of GEC Marconi Limited

Software Through Pictures is a trademark of Interactive Development Environment

SLATE is a registered trademark of TD Technologies, Inc.

IBM is a registered trademark and OS-land OS/2 are trademarks of International Business Machines Corp.

SUN and JAVA arc trademarks of Sun Microsytems, Inc.

FrameMaker is a registered trademark of Adobe Corp.

Windows 95, Windows 98, and Windows NT are registered trademarks of Microsoft Corp.

SQCpack® for Windows™ is a trademark of PQ Systems

CMM^SM is a service mark of the U. S. Government

CMM® is registered in the U. S. patent and trademark office

JMP® and SAS® are registered trademarks of SAS Institute, Inc.

QMX is a registered trademark of DPI Services

QED Scope™ for Windows™ is a registered trademark of Integrated Quality Dynamics, Inc.

Maestro II (V2.2) is a registered trademark of Softlab, Inc.

AppBridge is a registered trademark of Software Development Tools, Inc.

BPSimulator is a registered trademark of Technology Economics, Inc. (TEI)

TeamWare Flow (V1.1) is a registered trademark of TeamGROUP

Softest (V5.1) is a registered trademark of Bender & Associates, Inc.

Analyzer Case and Q/Artisan Version 2.5 are registered trademarks of Consult Corp.

PureDDTS (Release 3.3) is a registered trademark of Pure Atria

AISLE/QualGen & CISLE/QualGen are registered trademarks of Software Systems Design

PathMaker® and SkyMark™ are registered trademarks of SkyMark

ProcedureDesign™ is a registered trademark of MEGA International

For Jane
and
For Janice

Contents

Chapter 5   Software Quality Program Organization   115

By Emanuel R. Baker, Ph.D., and Matthew J. Fisher, Ph.D.

Chapter 6   Personnel Requirements to Make Software Quality Assurance Work   147

By Kenneth S. Mendis

Chapter 21   Software Safety and Its Relation to Software Quality Assurance   669

By Kenneth S. Mendis

Appendix   Glossary of Acronyms   681

Preface

*T*he software industry has witnessed a dramatic rise in the impact and effectiveness of software quality assurance recently. From its day of infancy, when a handful of software pioneers explored the first applications of quality assurance, to the development of software, software quality assurance has become integrated into all phases of software development.

This *Handbook of Software Quality Assurance* capitalizes on the talents and skills of the experts who deal with the implementation of software quality assurance on a daily basis. To have their accumulated knowledge at hand makes this Handbook a valuable resource. Each author, because of his special skills, talents, foresight, and interests, has contributed to the maturing process occurring in the field of software quality today.

What this *Handbook* brings to the reader then, is a collection of experiences and expectations of some of the best people in the field of software quality assurance. Because of their early involvement in software quality and because of their continued pursuit to discover improved methods for achieving better on the job software quality assurance, each author provides an insightful presentation of his personal involvement in software quality assurance.

The structure of this *Handbook* is relatively straightforward: twenty-one chapters covering many key areas of software quality assurance.

The first part of the *Handbook* sets the stage with a presentation of fundamental concepts and some historical discussion. Relevant terms are initially defined. Then the interaction of software quality assurance with several software specialty areas is covered. Next, the knowledge gained by the experts in the quality field is directed at software quality. A brief history and future direction of the standardization of software quality assurance follows. Organizational considerations for a software quality program are presented. The backbone of success in any enterprise—the people performing software quality assurance—is discussed in terms of how to identify, get, and keep those most suited for quality assurance. Chapter 7 discusses the recent American Society for Quality's exam process for Software Quality Engineer certification. "Quality is free"; how this dictum applies to software quality is the subject of "The Cost of Software Quality," discussed in Chapter 8.

The next set of chapters within this *Handbook* discuss quality techniques and opens with a discussion of inspections, the Pareto Principle, and software configuration management. This section continues with the Software Engineering Institute's Capability Maturity Model (CMM) for Software, which has had an enormous impact on software development, management, and quality since 1988. Chapter 12 covers the fundamentals of the CMM process and the relationship of the CMM to software quality assurance. Next follows a discussion of a very successful organization's implementation of the CMM Level 5 process and what this has meant to software quality. The use of both software quality Computer Aided Software Engineering (CASE) tools and the use of software quality metrics are necessary techniques in today's environment, and are covered in this section.

The final set of chapters within this *Handbook* emphasize applications relevant to software quality assurance. Practical SQA applications for mission-critical software and for commercial software are discussed. The application of statistical testing methods, software reliability, and software safety, areas of recent empahsis within software quality assurance, are also covered.

A brief summary of each chapter, highlighting its main thrust, is provided below for the reader to decide which topics are of immediate interest. If information is required from another chapter for additional insight, adequate cross-reference has been provided within each chapter and in the index.

Chapter 1 defines important terms relevant to this *Handbook*. More recent terms, such as those related to software quality assurance certification and TQM (Total Quality Management), are covered.

Chapter 2 discusses the relationship of software quality assurance with the various types of software, such as operating systems software, mission-critical software, real-time systems software, interactive software, and business software. The chapter also addresses the relationship of software quality assurance with other key areas, such as software configuration management. The Year 2000 (Y2K) Problem and the role of SQA is also discussed.

Chapter 3 is an overview of the contributions made and the roles played by the dominant figures in the Quality field. The individual contribution of the dominant quality experts—Ishikawa, Juran, Akao, Deming, Crosby, Shingo, and Taguchi—are assessed.

Chapter 4 traces the history of the process of standardization of software quality assurance. The Department of Defense, Federal Aviation Administration, North

Atlantic Treaty Organization, and Institute of Electrical and Electronic Engineers (IEEE) standardization activities are all covered. The future directions of standardization are given special emphasis because the thrust is to apply commercial standards, such as, EIA/IEEE 12207 to all government projects. This is a major philosophical shift and moves away from the former document-driven software development paradigm of the previous standards.

Chapter 5 presents a software quality organization. This chapter includes a discussion of what commercial organizations require to conduct software quality assurance and the impact of the CMM on software quality organizations. The role of assessing and measuring product quality during development and the controversy over the independence of SQA versus being part of the development organization are also presented in this chapter.

Chapter 6 discusses the personnel requirements for a good software quality engineer and how a software quality organization should deal with personnel issues such as training, roles for software quality engineers, paraprofessional possibilities, and career paths. The impact of the ASQ software quality engineer certification program is covered.

Chapter 7 lays out the requirements for the new software quality engineer certification program established by the ASQ (American Society for Quality). More specifically, the chapter deals with how you should prepare for the exam and what in the body of software quality knowledge is needed to pass the exam. The chapter also includes a recommended bibliography.

Chapter 8 deals with the assessment of the total cost of software quality and examines what input is required, the value added, and the expected output. Concerns such as major task elements, productivity, and potential misuse are evaluated. Also discussed are the "Price of Nonconformance" and the effect of budgetary constraints on the implementation of SQA.

Chapter 9 deals with the widely acclaimed use and application of inspections and the impact of conducting inspections during the software development cycle. The inspection process is described and numerous results of inspections are provided to give the reader a first hand picture of what to look for when evaluating inspection data. Emphasis is given to documentation inspections, inspection metrics, and the national software quality experiment, which captures inspection results across the country.

Chapter 10 looks at the role of software configuration management (SCM) and what that role implies for software quality and software development. Key issues discussed are staffing for SCM, the Configuration Control Board, auditing the SCM process, and allocating resources to perform SCM.

Chapter 11 applies the well-known Pareto Principle (80/20 rule) to the concerns and issues of software quality assurance. The impact and advantage of performing a

Pareto analysis is supported by two classic examples; one dealing with WWMCCS (World Wide Military Command and Control System), the other with the Federal Reserve Bank. How Pareto analysis is applied to defect prevention, its use in analysis of inspection data, and a unique aspect of how to compare Pareto charts are covered in this chapter.

Chapter 12 introduces the concepts behind the very influential Software Engineering Institute's Capability Maturity Model (CMM) for Software. The underlying concepts behind the CMM are discussed as well as the CMM's Key Process Area relationships to software quality assurance.

Chapter 13 examines the methods used by the Boeing Space Transportation Systems software organization in their pursuit of the coveted CMM Level 5—the Optimizing level. An organization operating at Level 5 understands its technology and processes and is constantly improving them. This chapter covers what it takes to be there.

Chapter 14 addresses Computer Aided Software Engineering (CASE) tools available for use by the SQA organization. This chapter provides insight into the environment for CASE tools, discusses where and how to find tools, and provides a look ahead in this very dynamic area.

Chapter 15 provides a survey of metrics proposed and currently used to determine the quality of the software development effort. Software quality metrics methodology, omnibus software quality metrics, software quality indicators, and some practical implementations are covered.

Chapter 16 discusses how to successfully perform the job of software quality assurance in a real development environment for mission-critical software programs. Discussions are based on lessons learned and success stories from practical applications in mission-critical software.

Chapter 17 discusses how to successfully perform the job of software quality assurance in a real development environment for commercial programs. Discussions are based on lessons learned and success stories from practical applications in commercial environments. These are contrasted with mission-critical environments.

Chapter 18 discusses the quality assurance of software in the Information environment. This chapter gives the results of the 1998 Quality Assurance Institute Information Processing Quality Assurance Survey. The chapter then explains software quality metrics and their implementation.

Chapter 19 is a treatise on the use of statistics as a means of achieving software quality control. This chapter provides a quantitative method of assessing the effectiveness of testing. The cornerstone of this method is the development of the Symbolic Input Attribute Decomposition (SIAD) tree. A number of practical implementations of the methodology are discussed.

Chapter 20 is updated, based on the events surrounding IEEE Project 982, which was established to enhance measurement of software reliability. It discusses many measures of software and their interrelationship with software quality and software reliability.

Chapter 21 deals with that aspect of software quality concerned with software safety. Covered are the various requirements related to software safety, what it takes to develop a software safety assurance program, and hazard avoidance and mitigation techniques.

Appendix A is a glossary of the acronyms used throughout this *Handbook*. Also included is an index. The index is a combined author and subject index.

Acknowledgments

The editors thank each and all of the contributors for their time, energy, and foresight in bringing to this *Handbook* an excellent collection of original papers. This collection provides, in a single source, a wide spectrum of experiences and issues of concern not only to software quality assurance, but also to the future of software development.

The editors also appreciate the patience and help of Bernard Goodwin, editor-in-chief, Stephen Solomon, acquisitions editor, and Nicholas Radhuber, editorial/production supervisor, Prentice Hall, without whose assistance and support this *Handbook* would not have been accomplished.

G. Gordon Schulmeyer
James I. McManus

Contributing Authors

Emanuel R. Baker, Ph.D., (Chap. 5) is president of Software Engineering Consultants, Inc. (SECI), a consulting firm based in Los Angeles, California, specializing in software engineering and training services. He has been a consultant in software engineering and software acquisition management since 1984. He has over 25 years of technical and managerial experience in the field of software development with specific emphasis on proposal development, software process assessments, software systems engineering, software configuration management, software quality assurance, software test,
software standards development, and acquisition management, as well as training in these disciplines. Prior to that, he was manager of the Product Assurance Department of Logicon's Strategic and Information Systems Division. In that capacity, along with his duties of managing the department, he also had responsibility for the contract to develop the Department of Defense software quality standard, DOD-STD-2168.

From 1962 to 1980, he was employed at TRW. In 1972, he assumed the position of section head in the Software Systems Engineering Department on the Site Defense Program, a landmark program in the development of standardized methodologies and practices for software development, configuration management, and quality assurance. Dr. Baker played an important role in the development of the standards and procedures utilized to implement these methodologies and practices. These standards and procedures later became the software development policies, standards, and procedures for the entire division. Later, he transferred into the Product Assurance area, playing an important role in the continuing development of software configuration management and quality assurance procedures used at TRW.

His last assignments at TRW were as assistant program manager for Product Assurance on the Site Defense Program and the Battlefield Exploitation and Tactical Assessment (BETA) Program.

Dr. Baker has authored and coauthored a number of papers and articles on software quality, configuration management, and software process assessments. He has conducted seminars in the U.S., Canada, Mexico, Australia, New Zealand, Israel, England, Italy, Sweden, Germany, and Spain on the topics of Software Quality Management, Total Quality Management for Software, and Software Process Assessments. In addition, he has appeared as a panelist at a number of conferences and workshops, speaking on the topic of software quality.

Dr. Baker is authorized by the SEI as a lead assessor for the CBA-IPI methodology. He has performed assessments for organizations in both the commercial and defense sectors, as well as Government agencies. He is also a member of the CMM Correspondence Group.

He has a B.S.M.E. from New York University and the M.S.M.E. from the University of Southern California. In addition, he holds a M.S. and a Ph.D. in education from the University of Southern California.

Chin Knei Cho, PhD, (Ch. 19) an internationally recognized expert in software engineering and quality assurance, is president of Computa, Inc. Dr. Cho has been staff scientist and chairman of the Singer Artificial Intelligence Committee and of the Ada Steering Committee at the Singer Company, with responsibilities for development of technologies in software engineering and quality assurance, computer performance evaluation, Ada software engineering, very large database management systems, and Picture Archiving and Communication System (PACS) for military, industrial, and medical applications.

He has served as director of software technology at International Software Systems, Inc. As systems engineer at the MITRE Corporation, he was responsible for software quality assurance during the development of the real time Automated En Route Air Traffic Control Testbed System (AERA) for the Federal Aviation Administration. Dr. Cho's many successful software projects include worldwide satellite tracking and data networking tools, operations research and management science projects, and design and development of management systems. He is the author of *An Introduction to Software Quality Control*, published by John Wiley & Sons, 1980, and translated into Japanese by Kindai Kagaku Sha, Tokyo, 1982. He also wrote *Quality Programming: Developing and Testing Software with Statistical Quality Control,* published by John Wiley & Sons in 1987.

Dr. Cho is an associate professorial lecturer in the Department of Electrical Engineering and Computer Science at George Washington University and also lectures in the Electrical Engineering Department and Department of Computer Science at the University of Maryland. He is a member of ACM and the IEEE Computer Society.

Dr. Cho holds a B.S. in Business Administration from National Cheng Kung University, an M.S. in Industrial Engineering from the University of Houston, and a Ph.D. in Computer Science from the University of Texas.

James H, Dobbins, CQA, (Chs. 8, 9, 20) is an internationally recognized expert in software quality and reliability management, with over 33 years experience in these and related disciplines. Prior to joining the faculty at Defense Systems Management College (DSMC) in October 1990, he was a professor of systems management at the National Defense University. His current responsibilities include that of course director of the Management of Software Acquisition Course (MSAC) and software management instructor in the Program Management Course.

Following his tenure of service as a communications officer in the U.S. Air Force (SAG), he had 21 years of service with IBM Federal Systems Division, participating in the development of numerous DoD and NASA programs. These included the Gemini Program, Apollo Program, Air Force satellite programs, and Navy Anti-Submarine Warfare systems. Following his service with IBM, he joined American Management Systems, Inc. as a principal of the company and director of Software Quality Engineering.

He is active in numerous professional organizations and has presented many invited papers at conferences throughout the world. He was a featured speaker at the Quality Assurance Institute national conference on quality measurement held in March 1992. As a senior member of the Institute of Electrical and Electronics Engineers (IEEE), he chaired the working group that developed the industry standard for software reliability management, IEEE Std. 982.1 and associated Guide 982.2.

In 1985, and again in 1986, he was chosen to participate in the French-American exchange of engineers and scientists program and visited France as a state guest to discuss his work in software reliability with several French companies, interfacing with the French Society for Industrial Quality Control and the French Standardization Society. He was a recipient of the NASA Apollo Achievement Award, and received a special Navy Letter of Commendation for his software test and evaluation effort on the LAMPS Program.

He has served as a consultant to NCR Corporation, UNISYS, RAND Corporation, and Time-Life Books. He authored *Software Quality Assurance and Evaluation*, published by ASQC Quality Press, three chapters of the *Handbook of Software Quality Assurance*, Van Nostrand-Reinhold Publishing Company (1987 and 1992), and one chapter of *Software Validation*, North Holland Publishing Company (1983). He is the author of one chapter of *Total Quality Management for Software* (1992), Van Nostrand-Reinhold, and three chapters of *Military Project Management Handbook* (1992), McGraw-Hill.

His biography has appeared in Marquis' *Who's Who in America, Who's Who in American Education, Who's Who in the South and Southwest, Who's Who in the East, Who's Who in the Computer Graphics Industry, Who's Who in Science and Engineering, Who's Who in American Law*, West's *Who's Who in U.S. Executives*, and *Personalities of the South*.

He holds a B.S. in Physics, an M.S. in Information Systems, and is an attorney-at-law licensed to practice law in Virginia and various Federal Courts. He received his certification as a Certified Quality Analyst from the Quality Assurance Institute, and has completed the training program conducted by the Software Engineering Institute required to conduct Software Capability Evaluations (SCE). He is a member of the talent bank of the United States Congress on the subjects of software quality and reliability, a member of ASQ, a Senior Member of IEEE, a member of the IEEE Computer Society, the Boston Computer Society, American Defense Preparedness Association (ADPA), Mathematical Association of America (MAA), MENSA, the Virginia State Bar, the Virginia Trial Lawyers Association, and the Association of Trial Lawyers of America.

Scott E. Donaldson (Ch. 10) is vice president with Science Applications International Corporation and has been in the computer field since 1974. He has a broad range of software engineering experience in the public, private, and commercial industries. This experience includes the design, development, implementation, technical management, and evaluation of computer systems application. Mr. Donaldson is the director of an SEPG helping a 350-person organization achieve SEI Level 3. He is also the deputy program manager for this $25+ million business. Together with Dr.  Stanley Siegel, he authored *Cultivating Successful Software Development: A Practitioner's View*, published in March 1997. Mr. Donaldson received a bachelor's degree in operations research from the United States Naval Academy and master's degree in systems management from the University of Southern California.

Andreas Felschow (Ch. 12) is an internationally recognized expert in software process improvement. He is the director of process improvement at Technology and Process Consulting, Inc. (TCP). His background includes the development of software process improvement products and services, quality assurance and testing on software products, and the development of a software error estimating program. He has been active in the field of software engineering for the past 17 years holding many positions in software development and software program management.

In his current assignment he manages the software process improvement and assessment services program. In this role he has helped establish TCP as a nationally recognized leading provider of process improvement services. He has developed the CMM profile method, which is used primarily as a non-intrusive assessment method that complements the CMM-Based Appraisal for Internal Process Improvement (CBA IPI) method. Mr. Felschow is authorized through the Software Engineering Institute to lead CBA IPIs. He also has developed a suite of software tools that automate many of the tasks within the CBA IPI method. This has benefited many organizations by reducing the cost of performing assessments and dramatically increasing the efficiency of data gathering and interpretation.

Mr. Felschow is very active in the Software Process Improvement Network (SPIN) where he has presented on several software process improvement topics. He has served on the SEI's CBA IPI advisory board and is a member of the ASQ.

Mr. Felschow holds a B.S. in Engineering from Virginia Tech, College of Engineering, in Blacksburg, Virginia and an A.S. in Oceanography from Florida Tech in Melbourne, Florida.

Matthew J. Fisher, Ph.D., (Ch 5) is currently a visiting scientist with the Software Engineering Institute (SEI). He is responsible for planning and coordinating work products for SEI's software acquisition project, including the Software Acquisition Capability Maturity Model (SA-CMM) and the Software Acquisition Improvement Framework (SAIF).

A civilian employee with the federal government for 30 years, Dr. Fisher has worked as a research engineer in computer technology and software, navigation systems, and software product assurance.

Dr. Fisher was the Army's representative to the Joint Logistics Commanders subgroup for Computer Resource Management, which is responsible for efforts to standardize computer resource policies and military standards within DoD. He is co-editor, with John D. Cooper, of *Software Quality Management* (Petrocelli Books, 1979). The author of more than 25 published technical papers on software quality, Dr. Fisher has lectured at numerous seminars.

He has an MSEE from the University of Pennsylvania and a Ph.D. from Drexel University. He is a member of Tau Beta Pi, Eta Kappa Nu, and Phi Kappa Phi honor societies.

Douglas B. Hamilton (Ch. 7) is currently a senior manager at Andersen Consulting in Northbrook, Illinois where he is responsible for methodology, estimating, and metrics development and deployment. He has more than 19 years of software development and software quality experience.

Prior to joining Andersen Consulting, Mr. Hamilton worked for Eli Lilly and Company in Indianapolis, Indiana. In this role he was involved in the company's methods initiative, covering both the tool investigation and selection, and was assigned program manager for the global implementation of methods and project management. Prior to this assignment, Mr. Hamilton had been the company's Software Engineering Process Group manager and consultant, conducting Software Process Assessments based on the Capability Maturity Model (CMM) from the Software Engineering Institute (SEI) at Carnegie Mellon University. He authored the *Configuration Management and Metrics Management Handbooks* which were used to derive standard business operating procedures.

Mr. Hamilton has presented nationally on the subjects of configuration management and metrics, served on the SEI working group to guide the direction of the CMM, served as a subject matter expert facilitator for multiple cross-industry groups that defined processes and metrics for Information Solution Delivery, Information Technology Planning and Management, and Data Resource Management, as well as teaching University-level Computer Science classes for over 10 years.

He is a Certified Software Quality Engineer (CSQE) as well as a Certified International Configuration Manager (CICM). He participated in the Certified Software Quality Engineer Certification Program for Job Analysis, Test Specification, Item Writing, and Item Review, and is the Chair for the Examination Review Committee. He is a member of the ASQ Certification Committee and continues to participate in the CSQE examination sustaining steps.

He holds both a B.A. (Indiana University) in Mathematics and Psychology and an M.B.A. (Indiana University) and is a member of ASQ and IEEE.

Mr. Hamilton can be reached at Andersen Consulting, 3773 Willow Road, Northbrook, IL 60062; (847)714-3306; fax: (847)326-3306; Internet: douglas.b.hamilton@ac.com

James H. Heil (Ch.16) is currently a technical manager at Telos Corporation Fort Monmouth Operations in the Management and Engineering Services Branch, supporting the Army Software Engineering Center (SEC) in areas such as Acquisition Risk Management, Software Best Practices, Software Standards, Process Improvement, Acquisition Reform, Software Assessments, and Army and CECOM policy reviews and updates.

Previously, he worked at MITRE Corp. (Ft. Monmouth) in the Software Engineering Center, primarily on the Crusader and Paladin Self-Propelled Howitzer Fire Control Systems software, as well as Software Standards (MIL-STD-498, IEEE-1498, EIA/IEEE 12207, etc.)

Earlier, Jim was a Software Development Manager and SQA Manager at ITT Avionics (in Clifton, NJ), and worked primarily on ECM software to protect Air Force, Army, and Navy aircraft.

He was chairman of the CODSIA industry Task Force for both MIL-STD-2167 and 2167A software standards, and the related handbooks. Jim also served on the industry working groups for both MIL-STD-498 and IEEE 1498/EIA 640 (since designated J-STD-016), and is now part of the review group for the U.S. version of ISO/IEC 12207. Previously, he was a software development manager at IBM Federal Systems Division and IBM Corporate Headquarters

Mr. Heil is past-Chairman of the NSIA Software Quality Assurance group, and has been active in the organization of NSIA and Data Management Association Conferences on Software Quality, Software Process Improvement, Software Acquisition, and Software Testing. He has participated in audits of other SQA organizations, as well as Software Capability Evaluations (SCEs). He was an invited participant at both Orlando II and San Antonio I Workshops on Software Standards sponsored by the Joint Logistics Commanders (JLC).

He holds a bachelor's degree in Mechanical Engineering and a master's degree in Electrical Engineering from New York University, a master's degree in Industrial Engineering and Operations Research from Ohio State University, and an M.B.A. degree from the New York Institute of Technology. He is a member of Tau Beta Pi, ORSA, ASQ, IEEE, and DPMA.

Thomas J. McCabe (Ch. 11) is president and CEO for McCabe & Associates, Inc. He is widely known as a consultant and an authority of software development, testing, and quality control methods. His company is a major supplier of software testing and re-engineering tools.

He has held a variety of high-level positions within the Department of Defense, accumulating extensive hands-on experience in the following areas: software specification, design, testing, maintenance, software quality assurance, compiler construction, optimization, operating systems, software acquisition, and project management.

Mr. McCabe is best known for his research and publication on software complexity (*IEEE Software Engineering Transactions*, December 1976) and by the complexity measure that bears his name. (This measure allows the quantification of the paths within a module, leading to an understanding of its complexity). He has personally developed and published a structured testing methodology now being adopted extensively both throughout the U.S. and internationally. He has developed advanced state-of-the-art courses in software quality assurance, structured testing, software specification and design, and software engineering, which he and his company present throughout the U.S., Canada, and Europe.

Mr. McCabe holds both a B.S. (Providence College) and M.S. (University of Connecticut) in Mathematics.

James I. McManus (Chs. 2, 14) is a principal engineer in the quality department at Northrop Grumman Corporation, Electronic Sensors and Systems Division (ESSD). As part of the Northrop Grumman team, Mr. McManus is QA Manager for one of the highly successful Air Defense Systems developed at ESSD. He is an active participant in extra-program activities to advise and promote compliance with ISO and SEI Standards. He has conducted internal assessments within the division and has promoted changes in software development processes. He also has promoted the tasking of

quality engineers to conduct requirements management activities on programs using databases (such as the relational database RTM by GEC Marconi and the object-oriented database SLATE by TD Technologies). Mr. McManus is a also a member of the Slate Users Group at Northrop Grumman, which supports use of the tool.

Mr. McManus has worked in the field of engineering and software since 1968. His experience covers aerospace engineering, underwater acoustics, research, simulation, structured methodologies, computer programming, software quality assurance, and consulting.

At Northrop Grumman ESSD (formerly Westinghouse) Mr. McManus was QA manager for a mobile satellite communication system. The program is operational today and is at the forefront of a new market in satellite communications.

Mr. McManus supervised a government research program to study the feasibility of implementing zero defect software. A prototype checking system was developed based on the standards of the day.

Earlier in his career Mr. McManus was director of consulting for McCabe and Associates, taught the McCabe SQA seminar, and consulted to several software organizations in the Baltimore-Washington D.C. area. He has worked for IBM, Vitro Laboratories, and the former Singer Link, Simulation Products Division.

Mr. McManus is a member of the American Society for Quality (ASQ). He is coauthor/editor of this *Handbook* (all editions) and coeditor of *Total Quality Management for Software* (First edition).

He has a master's degree and a bachelor's degree in Aerospace Engineering from the University of Maryland and a bachelor's degree in Engineering-Physics from Loyola College of Baltimore.

Kenneth S. Mendis (Chs. 6, 21) is manager of Automation Quality Assurance and Validation at Roche Carolina, Inc. He has over 20 years experience in design-proving activities involving a full range of system integration, quality assurance, and validation services for integrated computer systems.

Mr. Mendis has been responsible for developing and instituting software quality assurance and computer validation programs for real time Command and Control and Distributed Computer Systems. Mr. Mendis' computer quality assurance and validation techniques have been successfully applied to such programs as the Patriot missile; Command, Control and Communication systems for nuclear submarines and surface ships; Weather Radar Control Systems; and Air Traffic Control systems. More recently Mr. Mendis has applied this expertise to pharmaceutical and vitamin Distributed Control Systems both in the United States and Europe.

Mr. Mendis holds a B.S. degree in Engineering from Capitol College and an M.B.A. in Management from Bryant College. He is a graduate of the Advanced Manufacturing Management Program of Boston University School of Management. From 1981 to 1987 Mr. Mendis served as the founding chairman of the Software Quality Assurance Subcommittee of the National Security Industrial Association, a committee that today represents over 100 major defense contractors. Mr. Mendis has spoken before several professional organizations; among them the American Society for Quality (ASQ), the Institute of Electrical and Electronics Engineers (IEEE), the American Institute of Aeronautics and Astronautics (AIAA), Parenteral Drug Association (PDA), and the International Association for Pharmaceutical Technology. Mr. Mendis is also the published author of several technical articles on Software Quality Assurance and Management.

Lawrence E. Niech (Ch. 17) is the vice president of the Information Technology (IT) Product Assurance Organization at Automatic Data Processing (ADP)— the largest dedicated software service company in the United States.

At ADP he has successfully implemented effective quality & test processes on various products across multiple platforms (mainframe, PC, client/server) encompassing a wide range of technologies.

His previous positions have been at ITT Avionics, Singer-Kearfott (Guidance & Navigation Division) and Unisys Corp. He has played major roles in implementing first time or reengineering software quality assurance programs as an executive (ADP, Singer), engineer (ITT) and consultant (various commercial and defense companies).

Mr. Niech has published papers, presented tutorials, taught at the college level and lectured extensively in the areas of software engineering management, software quality assurance, software/hardware test engineering and computer programming.

He is a member of several national software societies where he has held key Chair positions.

Mr. Niech holds a M.B.A. from the Rutgers Graduate School of Management and a B.S. in Electrical Engineering from Rutgers, The College of Engineering.

William E. Perry, CQA, CSTE, (Ch. 18) is and has been executive director of the Quality Assurance Institute (QAI) since its inception. The Quality Assurance Institute was formed to provide leadership to the information systems industry in improving quality and productivity. Past experience includes 15 years with the Eastman Kodak Company in various MIS management positions. More recently, Bill ran an IBM users group.

Bill was appointed to the United States Department of Commerce, National Institute of Standards and Technologies, to serve as an examiner on the 1988 and 1989 board of examiners of the prestigious Malcolm Baldridge National Quality Award. He is also listed in *Who's Who in the Compuer Industry* and *Who's Who in America.*

A graduate of Clarkson College, Bill also holds his M.B.A. from Rochester Institute of Technology, and has a Master of Education degree from the University of Rochester. He is a New York State Certified Public Accountant, a Certified Information Systems Auditor, a Certified Internal Auditor, and holds certificates as a Certified Quality Analyst and a Certified Quality Examiner from the Quality Assurance Institute. He was a professor of data processing at Monroe Community College, a member of the board of directors of the American Federation of Information Processing Societies, and was committee chairman of the GUIDE International PL/1 Committee.

Bill is author of over 50 books dealing with quality assurance in the data processing field, as well as a series of video courses for both ASI and QAI. He is the primary author of the *QA Practices Manual, QA Manager's Handbook,* and the *Quality Assurance Skills Manual,* and is the author of Auerback Publishers' *Standard for Software Testing and Auditing Computer Applications.* He runs four major conferences each year in addition to teaching at numerous seminars and conferences. Over 25,000 students have attended his educational programs.

Contact him at: Quality Assurance Institute, Suite 350, 7575 Dr. Phillips Blvd., Orlando, FL 32819-7273, (phone) 407-363-1111, (fax) 407-363-1112.

G. Gordon Schulmeyer, CDP, (Chs. 1, 3, 4, 11, 15) has 37 years experience in management and information processing technology. He is president of PYXIS Systems International, Inc. [(410) 729-0416] which specializes in software process improvement and software quality and management. He was manager of software engineering at Westinghouse Electronic Systems Group, and was previously manager of software quality assurance, also at Westinghouse.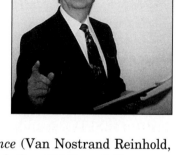

Mr. Schulmeyer is the author/editor of *Total Quality Management for Software* (Van Nostrand Reinhold, 1992), *Handbook of Software Quality Assurance* (Van Nostrand Reinhold, 1987 and 1992), *Zero Defect Software* (McGraw-Hill Book Co., 1990), and *Computer Concepts for Managers* (Van Nostrand Reinhold, 1985); and the forthcoming *Verification and Validation of Modern Software-Intensive Systems* (Prentice Hall, 1999). He has published numerous other papers and lectured on software and software-quality subjects. He was a panelist on DOD-STD-2168, Software Quality Evaluation at the October 1985 IEEE COMPSAC Conference. He has taken two long-term foreign assignments to provide information processing technology abroad.

Since 1968, Mr. Schulmeyer has been a holder of the CDP issued by the Institute for the Certification of Computing Professionals (ICCP). He is a member of the Association for Computing Machinery, IEEE Computer Society, and the American Management Association.

Mr. Schulmeyer is the 1992 recipient of the prestigious Shingo Prize, the First Prize for Professional Research, administered by the Utah State University College of Business. Mr. Schulmeyer received this award in May 1992 for his work in zero defect software—a first in the business sector.

He holds the following degrees: B.S. Mathematics Loyola College; J.D. Law University of Baltimore; and M.B.A. Management Loyola College.

Stanley G. Siegel, Ph.D., (Ch. 10) is an assistant vice president with Science Applications International Corporation and has been in the computer field since 1970. Since 1976, he has specialized in the area of software product assurance. Dr. Siegel is coauthor of the first textbook on software configuration management, *Software Configuration Management: An Investment in Product Integrity,* which appeared in 1980. He also coauthored a textbook on software product assurance that appeared in 1987. Together with Scott Donaldson, he authored *Cultivating Successful Software Development: A Pracitioner's View,* which was published in March 1997. Dr. Siegel is a member of an SEPG in an organization working on approximately forty software projects of various sizes. Dr. Siegel received a Ph.D. in theoretical nuclear physics from Rutgers University.

Gary B. Wigle (Ch. 13) is currently the senior principal engineer for software processes in Boeing's Defense and Space Group (D&SG) in Seattle, Washington. He is responsible for deployment of Software Engineering Institute (SEI) Capability Maturity Model (CMM) Level 4 and 5 processes to major programs in D&SG.

Mr. Wigle has been a leader in software process improvement over the past fifteen years at Boeing, with more than twenty-four years of experience in embedded software applications in the Air Force and at

Boeing. He was the Software Engineering Process Group (SEPG) lead for Space Transportation Systems (STS), as it accomplished a SEI CMM Level 5 rating. He has been a leader in the development of the Boeing software standards, guidelines, and model documents, in addition to many other process improvement efforts. He was also a lead instructor in software development processes at Boeing for many years.

He has had assignments in both the defense and commercial parts of Boeing, as evidenced by heavy involvement in the DOD-STD-2167 related activities and RTCA DO-178B activities. He was appointed as the Boeing representative to the Electronics Industries Association G-34 Computer Resource Committee 1984-1990 and served as chairman of the G-34 Software Engineering and Management Subcommittee for two years. He was also appointed as one of five members to the Methodology Technical Advisory Group for the Software Productivity Consortium, 1989–1990.

Prior to joining Boeing, Mr. Wigle served as a captain in the Air Force, as a software engineer for the Precision Location Strike System (PLSS) and the Low Altitude Navigation and Targeting by InfraRed at Night (LANTIRN) System Program Offices at Wright-Patterson AFB, Ohio. He worked as a team coordinator with contractor personnel to define requirements, formulate the government's position on acceptability of specifications and design reviews, and negotiate software acquisition policy with the prime contractor under severe budgetary and schedule constraints.

Mr. Wigle has a B.S. in Physics from the U.S. Air Force Academy and an M.S. in Systems Management from the Air Force Institute of Technology.

George Yamamura (Ch. 13) is the Software Engineering Process Manager of Boeing's Defense and Space Group (D&SG) in Seattle, Washington. He managed the Space Transportation Systems (STS) software development organization and its efforts leading to a SEI CMM Level 5 rating. He is also an instructor in the computer field at Renton Technical College.

Mr. Yamamura has thirty years of software experience in the space application field. During the past twenty years at Boeing D&SG he has supported the STS organization in developing on-board flight software and verification and validation environmental simulation software. He has worked on several successful proposals and programs, and has conducted a number of assessments and audits. He is currently managing the D&SG software engineering process group supporting Boeing programs and working on deployment of best practices.

His background covers orbital mechanics, flight analysis, numerical analysis, statistics, and software engineering and processes. Given his combined knowledge in these areas, he has successfully applied improvements to several software-intensive DoD programs. He has developed a proven formula for success that has achieved exceptional improvements. He has been invited to the Pentagon to brief the Undersecretary of Defense for Acquisition & Technology, and has provided support to other Air Forces facilities. He has written papers and given briefings at key software conferences, as well as to international executives from Europe.

He has a B.S. and a M.S. in Aeronautics and Astronautics from the University of Washington and a M.S. in Applied Mathematics from the University of Santa Clara.

Software Quality Assurance— Coming to Terms

G. Gordon Schulmeyer
PYXIS Systems International, Inc.

1.1 Introduction

What is software quality assurance (SQA)? This chapter addresses that question from the following points of view:

- What is software quality control?
- What is software reliability?
- What is software maintainability?
- What is software verification and validation (V&V)?
- What is SQA personnel certification?
- What is software test and evaluation (T&E)?
- What is software process improvement?
- What is ISO software certification?
- What is Total Quality Management (TQM) as related to software?

Each of the above items is treated separately, and its meaning in terms of quality is discussed from a practitioner's point of view. Comparative discussions ensue with a recommended position on each.

1.2 Quality—The Elusive Element

Still the best expository material in popular literature about quality occurs in Robert M. Pirsig's *Zen and the Art of Motorcycle Maintenance*. The difficulty of explaining quality is addressed in the following passage:

Any philosophic explanation of Quality is going to be false and true precisely because it is a philosophic explanation. The process of philosophic explanation is an analytic process, a process of breaking something down into subjects and predicates. What I mean (and everybody else means) by the word *quality* cannot be broken down into subjects and predicates. This is not because Quality is so mysterious but because Quality is so simple, immediate and direct. [1, pp. 224–225]

Further difficulties in coming to grips with quality are explained through the following dilemma exposed by Pirsig:

If Quality exists in the object, then you must explain just why scientific instruments are unable to detect it . . .
On the other hand, if Quality is subjective, existing only in the observer, then this Quality is just a fancy name for whatever you like . . .
Quality is not objective. It doesn't reside in the material world . . .
Quality is not subjective. It doesn't reside merely in the mind. [1, pp. 205–213]

To define quality, Pirsig turns from philosophy to reality in the following brief passage:

When traditional rationality divides the world into subjects and objects, it shuts out Quality. When you are really stuck, it is Quality, not any subjects or objects, that tells you where you ought to go.
By returning our attention to Quality it is hoped that we can get technological work out of the non-caring subject-object dualism and back into craftsmanlike self-involved reality again, which will reveal to us the facts we need when we are stuck. [1, p. 253]

David Garvin studied how quality is perceived in various domains, including philosophy, economics, marketing, and operations management. He concluded that "quality is a complex and multifaceted concept" that can be described from five different perspectives.

- The *transcendental view* sees quality as something that can be recognized but not defined.
- The *user view* sees quality as fitness for purpose.
- The *manufacturing view* sees quality as conformance to specification.
- The *product view* sees quality as tied to inherent characteristics of the product.

• The *value-based view* sees quality as dependent on the amount a customer is willing to pay for it. [2, p. 13]

In approaching the definition of quality from the "user view," some of the thoughts of J. M. Juran are appropriate:

The basic building block on which fitness for use is built is the *quality characteristic.* Any feature (property, attribute, etc.) of the products, materials, or processes which is needed to achieve fitness for use is a quality characteristic. [3, pp. 2–4]

Recognizing some of the same difficulties encountered by Pirsig and Garvin, Juran goes on to say:

Because the unqualified word "quality" has multiple meanings, it is risky to use it in unqualified form. [3, pp. 2–5]

Standards organizations have tended to refer to quality from the "manufacturing view" (meeting needs or expectations). The ISO standard ISO 8492 of 1986 defines quality as the totality of features and characteristics of a product or service that bears on its ability to satisfy stated or implied needs and appends that definition with the following note: In a contractual environment, needs are specified, whereas in other environments, implied needs should be identified and defined. [4, p. 3]

IEEE *Standard Glossary of Software Engineering Terminology*, however, does qualify the meaning of quality (as accepted by this *Handbook*):

The degree to which a system, component, or process meets (1) specified requirements, and (2) customer or user needs or expectations. [5, p. 60]

1.3 Software—The Basic Element

A starting point definition of software from the *Encyclopedia of Computer Science* is:

to describe the non-hardware components of the computer, in particular the programs that are needed to make the computers perform their intended tasks. [6, p. 1214]

The IEEE *Software Engineering Terminology Standard* immediately focuses a debate in the definition of software:

Computer programs, procedures, and possibly associated documentation and data pertaining to the operation of a computer system. [5, p. 66]

The use of the word "possibly," including associated documentation and data, says that some factions believe documentation and data should be included and others not. For the purpose of this *Handbook*, the term "software" derives from the definition of Matthew J. Fisher and William R. Light, Jr., in "Definition in Software Quality Management." Software is therefore defined as computer programs, procedures, and associated data and documentation pertaining to the operation of a computer system; where the subordinate definitions are:

> *Computer program* — a series of instructions or statements in a form acceptable to computer equipment and designed to cause the computer to execute an operation or operations.

> *Computer data* — a representation of facts, concepts, or instructions in a structured form suitable for acceptance, interpretation, or processing by computer equipment. Such data can be external to (in computer-readable form) or resident within the computer equipment.

> *Computer program documentation* — technical data, including program listings and printouts in human-readable form which document the requirements, design, implementation, and other details of the computer program. It also provides instructions for using and maintaining the computer program. [7, pp. 5–6]

1.4 Software Quality—The Attribute

A number of good definitions have been proffered for software quality. An appreciation of what software quality is may be garnered from an examination of each of these definitions. Moving from the more general to the more specific definitions should aid comprehension.

First, we have from Fisher and Light in "Definitions in Software Quality Management";

> The composite of all attributes which describe the degree of excellence of the computer system. [7, p. 7]

We have the "composite of all attributes" that usually include the "ilities" of reliability, maintainability, availability, and so on; but here the concept of "excellence" also enters into the software quality definition.

From Donald Reifer in his *State of the Art in Software Quality Management* and also from Fisher and Baker in "A Software Quality Framework" comes the following definition:

The degree to which a software product possesses a specified set of attributes necessary to fulfill a stated purpose. [8, p. 72; 9, p. 99]

This definition continues in the vein of a "set of attributes," but points out the added ingredient of fulfillment of "a stated purpose."

In *Software Quality Assurance and Measurement: a Worldwide Perspective*, there is a focus on the "stated purpose" and expansion to the "implied" needs of the customer:

. . . the totality of features and characteristics of a software product that bear on its ability to satisfy stated or implied needs. [10, p. 13]

Stephen Kan in *Metrics and Models in Software Quality Engineering* is clear about the requirements aspect in the definition of software quality:

. . . the role of the customers should be explicitly spelled out in the definition of quality: conformance to customers' requirements. [11, p. 4]

This definition of quality comes close to that of Philip B. Crosby in *Quality Is Free* as "conformance to requirements," [12, p. 5] which when extended to software quality becomes "conformance to software requirements." The problem encountered in this definition is: what are the software requirements? Are they the technical requirements defining only what the software should do? Or, do they also include the requirements (imposed by the contract) for software quality?

In *Testing Computer Software*, the authors state that software quality has inconsistencies regarding the requirements that need to be conformed to:

Some businesses make customer-designed products to order. The customer brings a detailed specification that describes exactly what he wants and the company agrees to make it. In this case, *quality* means matching the customer's specification.

Most software developers don't have such knowledgeable and precise customers. For them, the measure of their products' and services' quality is the satisfaction of their customers, not the match to a specification. [13, p. 59]

Watts Humphrey in *A Discipline for Software Engineering* focuses on software quality from the individual practitioner's point of view; so that he may improve his personal software process:

. . . you must recognize the hierarchical nature of software quality. First, a software product must provide functions of a type and at a time when the user needs them. If it does not, nothing else matters. Second, the product must work. If it has so many defects that it does not perform with reasonable consistency, the users will not use it regardless of its other attributes. [14, p. 272]

Peter J. Denning, in his article, "What is Software Quality?" in the *Communications of the ACM* presents his argument for software quality that is similar to Humphrey's position:

I have argued that software quality is more likely to be attained by giving much greater emphasis to customer satisfaction. Program correctness is essential but is not sufficient to earn the assessment that the software is dependable. [15, p. 15]

In "Cornering the Chimera," Geoff Dromey states that an ultimate theory of software quality is like the chimera (a mythical beast of hybrid character and fanciful conception) of the ancient Greeks. We are obliged, however, to strive to make progress, [16, p. 34] and so with that admonition, we derive the definition of software quality which applies in this *Handbook*:

Software quality is the fitness for use of the software product.

1.5 Software Quality Assurance—The Activity

J. M. Juran in his *Quality Control Handbook* defines quality assurance as:

Quality Assurance is the activity of providing to all concerned the evidence needed to establish confidence that the quality function is being performed adequately. [3, pp. 2–23]

Borrowing heavily on this base, the IEEE software engineering terminology *Glossary* uses the following definition for quality assurance:

Quality Assurance is a planned and systematic pattern of all actions necessary to provide adequate confidence that an item or product conforms to established technical requirements. [5, p. 60]

Because of the placement of this definition in the software-related glossary, it is the same as software quality assurance.

James Dobbins, a contributor to this *Handbook*, notes the difference between hardware and software in his definition of software quality assurance:

Unlike hardware systems, software is not subject to wear or breakage; consequently, its usefulness over time remains unchanged from its condition at delivery. Software quality assurance is a systematic effort to improve that delivery condition. [17, p. 108]

Fisher and Baker, who discuss the software quality program organization in Chapter 5 of this *Handbook*, tie their definition to the organizational aspect of responsibility for performance:

Software quality assurance is the functional entity performing software quality assessment and measurement. [9, p. 105]

Richard E. Fairley in his *Software Quality Engineering* course presented a more modern view:

. . . [software quality assurance] involves both process and product assurance. The basic charter of SQA is thus to assure that software projects fulfill their commitments to both process and product. [18, pp. 3–10]

Robert H. Dunn in *Software Quality Concepts and Plans* is concerned about the confusion of SQA with software quality programs, and provides his usual insight into the potential confusion:

The management of software quality programs is commonly called "software quality assurance" but the name is just about the only thing common to the management of software quality programs. This is understandable, since no two quality programs can be expected to address precisely the same purposes. Software quality assurance is actually somewhat of a misnomer, since software quality assurance does not assure the quality of software, but the effectiveness of a software quality program.

The distinction may seem overly fine, but it serves to rule out software quality assurance activities directed exclusively to testing, verification and validation activities, or the like. If we are to believe that software quality must be built into the product through the use of a process that itself has quality built in, then we must also accept the software quality assurance must be an aspect of all software development (and maintenance) activities. [19, p. 11]

Remember from the *Encyclopedia of Computer Science* that:

Software quality assurance should be applied throughout the development process. [6, p. 226]

In *A Guide to Total Software Quality Control* the emphasis is on the activities of software quality assurance, which are to:

- provide an independent review of the software development process, its products and the resources applied
- check for conformance to the selected standards for products and their documentation, and for procedures used for software development
- reduce the cost of correcting defects during tests and integration by finding the defects during requirements, design, and code reviews. [20, p. 121]

From Microsoft's Jim McCarthy, software quality assurance is the "QA" function for software development:

QA's principal function—and it is a principal function—is to continually assess the state of the product so the rest of the team's activities can be focused on development.

QA's ongoing assessment is integral to the act of software creation, not an *ex post facto* event. The goal of QA is to support the product development process by providing an ongoing induction of reality, which can't be exaggerated. The unrelenting natural tendency in software development organizations is to transmute hopes and wishes into peculiar reality distortion wishes. QA provides compensation for this nearly overwhelming urge. [21, p. 11]

Also, from Microsoft, Steve McConnell sees software quality assurance as a sequence of checklist activities:

- Have you identified quality characteristics that are important to your project?
- Have you made others aware of the project's quality objectives?
- Have you differentiated between external (correctness, usability, efficiency, reliability, integrity, adaptability, accuracy, and robustness) and internal (maintainability, flexibility, portability, reusability, readability, testability, and understandability) quality characteristics?
- Have you thought about the ways in which some characteristics may compete with or complement others?
- Does your project call for the use of several different error-detection techniques suited to finding several different kinds of errors?

- Does your project include a plan to take steps to assure software quality during each stage of software development?
- Is the quality measured in some way so that you can tell whether it's improving or degrading?
- Does management understand that quality assurance incurs additional costs up front in order to save costs later? [22, pp. 557, 558, and 569]

In this *Handbook*, the definition for software quality assurance is:

Software quality assurance is the set of systematic activities providing evidence of the ability of the software process to produce a software product that is fit to use.

1.6 Software Quality Control—The Action

We turn again to J. M. Juran for a general definition of quality control:

Quality Control is the regulatory process through which we measure actual quality performance, compare it with standards, and act on the difference. [3, pp. 2–11]

This definition is very reminiscent of "the control loop" provided in systems to ensure proper functioning of the system.

From the IEEE *Standard Glossary of Software Engineering Terminology* the definition for quality control is:

Note: This term has no standardized meaning in software engineering. At this time, use: A set of activities designed to evaluate the quality of developed or manufactured products. [5, p. 60]

Applying this general definition to software very nicely, Fisher and Light in their "Definitions in Software Quality Management" derive this definition:

Quality Control is the assessment of procedural and product compliance. Independently finding these deficiencies and correcting them assures compliance of the product with stated requirements. [7, pp. 13, 14]

According to Fisher and Light, quality control and quality design make up software quality management, where quality design involves participation in the insertion of quality attributes into the software development. [7, pp. 13, 14]

Software quality control is equated with software verification by Donald Reifer:

Software quality control is the set of verification activities which at any point in the software development sequence involves assessing whether the current products being produced are technically consistent and compliant with the specification of the previous phase. [8, p. 20]

Dr. Fairley's *Software Quality Engineering* course provides a list of elements for software quality control:

The following techniques provide an effective methodology for measuring and controlling software quality: work packages, peer reviews, root cause analysis, binary tracking, incremental development, technical performance measurement, systematic verification and validation. [18, pp. 2–31]

The following definition of software quality control is used in this *Handbook*:

Software quality control is the independent evaluation of the ability of the software process to produce a usable software product.

1.7 Software Quality Personnel Certification—The Recognition

The American Society for Quality (ASQ) and this *Handbook*'s definition of a Certified Software Quality Engineer is:

. . . a professional who has a comprehensive understanding of software quality development and implementation; has a thorough understanding of software inspection, testing, verification, and validation; and can implement software development and maintenance processes and methods. [23]

The requirements for a Certified Software Quality Engineer fall into three categories:

1. Education and Experience
2. Proof of Professionalism
3. Examination

The following is a high-level outline of the examination topics that constitute the body of knowledge for software quality engineering. Note that there are 160 questions probing the candidate's knowledge of software quality principles. For more details, refer to Chapter 7, *American Society for Quality Software Quality Engineer Certification Program*, of this *Handbook*:

1. General Knowledge, Conduct, and Ethics (24 Questions)
2. Software Quality Management (16 Questions)
3. Software Processes (24 Questions)
4. Software Project Management (16 Questions)
5. Software Metrics, Measurement, and Analytical Methods (24 Questions)
6. Software Inspection, Testing, Verification, and Validation (24 Questions)
7. Software Audits (16 Questions)
8. Software Configuration Management (16 Questions)

1.8 Software Reliability—Only One Error Left

Turning to the expert, J. M. Juran, for a definition of reliability for hardware/systems is a starting point.

> Reliability is the probability of a product performing a specified function without failure under given conditions for a specified period of time. [3, pp. 2–7]

Now we move to software reliability for a series of definitions that relate to software design quality:

> Software reliability is really concerned with software design quality. [24, p. 182]

> For software, reliability becomes a question of correctness, confidence, accuracy, and precision rather than the time to the next failure. [7, p. 9]

> [The] extent to which a program can be expected to perform its intended function with required precision. [25, p. 129]

The definition of software reliability in the *Encyclopedia of Computer Science* describes three distinct methods of estimating software reliability:

> The probability that a software fault that causes deviations from the required output by more than a specified tolerance, in a specified environment, does not occur during a specified exposure period. There are three distinct methods of estimating software reliability, namely, (1) on the basis of its failure history, (2) its behavior for a random sample of points taken from its input domain, or (3) the number of seeded and actual faults detected by the test team. Seeded faults are those that are deliberately inserted into the program at the start of the debugging phase, the details of which are withheld from the testing team. [6, p. 1242]

The IEEE *Standard Glossary of Software Engineering Terminology* ties the definition to "the ability of a system," stressing software as a subpart of the system (or a "component"):

The ability of a system or component to perform its required functions under specified conditions for a specified time. [5, p. 32]

Norman Schneidewind stresses the difference between hardware reliability (error occurrence) and software reliability (error detection):

The passage of time is related to error detection and not to error occurrence; the errors which are detected were made at a previous time. [26, p. 175]

For "Software Quality in Consumer Electronics Products" there is an unusual high emphasis on software reliability as explained below:

Many organizations make reducing defects their first quality goal. However, the consumer electronics business, by necessity, pursues a different goal: keeping the number of defects in the field at zero. Once they leave the showroom floor, the final destination of these products is unknown, so detecting and correcting a serious software defect would entail recalling hundreds of thousands of products. [27, p. 55]

Reliability, as defined in *Software Quality Assurance and Measurement: a Worldwide Perspective*, is very similar to the IEEE *Standard Glossary* definition, which relies upon the ISO standard:

A set of attributes that bear on the capability of software to maintain its level of performance under stated conditions for a stated period of time. [*ISO 9126 Software product evaluation: quality characteristics and guidelines for their use*] [10, p. 13]

Harking back to the pure reliability definition of J. M. Juran, the IEEE *Standard Glossary* provides the definition of software reliability which most closely meets the requirement of this *Handbook*:

The ability of the software to perform its required function under stated conditions for a stated period of time. [5, p. 32]

1.9 Software Maintainability—Keep Chugging Along

This is the traditional definition for hardware that J. M. Juran provides:

> Maintainability is (1) the use of conducting scheduled inspections and servicing, called serviceability, and (2) the case of restoring service after failure, called repairability. [3, pp. 2–8]

There is no clear relationship between serviceability and a counterpart in the area of software maintenance.

In the *Draft Glossary of Software Quality Terms* from RADC, the focus is on updating:

> The extent that it facilitates updating to satisfy new requirements. [28, p. 9]

From the *Encyclopedia of Computer Science* is:

> Software maintenance is the activity that addresses the correction of software errors and to remedy the inadequacies that may exist. [6, p. 1232]

Dunn and Ullman view the various perspectives of software maintenance:

> Maintenance **(corrective)**—correction of faults uncovered in a program; **(adaptive)**—the response to a change in the program's operating circumstances; **(perfective)**—enhancements of all kinds. [29, pp. 78, 79]

As one of the many "ilities" discussed by James McCall in the software measurement (metric) area, maintainability for software receives the following definition:

> Effort required to locate and fix an error in an operational program. [25, p. 129]

This definition is too narrow for what is being done with software under the name of software maintenance. Sixty to seventy percent of the expenditure for software is allocated to software maintenance rather than to new software development. In order to capture the activity that is being called software *maintenance*, the following definition from the IEEE *Standard Glossary of Software Engineering Terminology* is most appropriate:

Software maintenance is the process of modifying a software system or component after delivery to correct faults, improve performance or other attributes, or adapt to a changed environment. [5, p. 46]

This is the definition favored by this *Handbook*.

1.10   Verification and Validation (V&V)—On the Up-And-Up

There is crossover and confusion between verification and validation (V&V) and test and evaluation (T&E). In this section the elements of V&V are defined and how they fit together is discussed. The next section discusses T&E and its interrelationship with V&V.

It is usually the developing contractor's job to deliver a complete system; so, depending on its facilities and capabilities it could provide testing at all levels. The Atlas Missile Program hired an "independent software tester" to provide additional unbiased software test support in the late 1950s. This outside source, now called a validation and verification (V&V) contractor, performs the testing job which sometimes extends over the module, functional area, software system, and sometimes even the target system. [30, p. 275]

In a V&V paper, Robert Lewis gives a broad definition that includes the testing concepts within it:

Verification and Validation is the systematic process of analyzing, evaluating, and testing system and software documentation and code to ensure the highest possible quality, reliability and satisfaction of system needs and objectives. [31, p. 238]

The IEEE *Standard Glossary* focuses on the requirements aspects:

The process of determining whether the requirements for a system or component are complete and correct, the products of each development phase fulfill the requirements or conditions imposed by the previous phase, and the final system or component complies with specified requirements. [5, p. 81]

Verification and validation, as defined in EIA/IEEE DRAFT US 12207-1996, *Information Technology: Software Life Cycle Processes,* is only defined in the context of "independent" verification and validation:

Independent verification and validation (IV&V): Systematic evaluation of software products and activities by an organization that is not responsible for developing the product or performing the activity being evaluated. [32, p. 17]

A most succinct definition is provided by Barry Boehm. It, however, does not address the independence issue.

Verification is doing the job right and validation is doing the right job. [33, p. 728]

The process discussed above needs further breakout in definitions to clarify what verification is and what validation is. For each of these, the IEEE *Glossary* definition is given first and followed by the EIA/IEEE DRAFT US 12207-1996 definition. There is little difference between the definitions and all are acceptable within this *Handbook*:

Verification is the process of evaluating a system to determine whether the products of a given development phase satisfy the conditions imposed at the start of that phase. [5, p. 81]

Verification is the confirmation by examination and provision of objective evidence that specified requirements have been fulfilled. NOTE: In design and development, verification concerns the process of examining the result of a given activity to determine conformity with the stated requirement for that activity. [31, p. 16]

Validation is the process of evaluating a system or component during or at the end of the development process to determine whether it satisfies specified requirements. Contrast with: Verification. [5, p. 80]

Validation is the confirmation by examination and provision of objective evidence that the particular requirements for a specific intended use are fulfilled. NOTE: In design and development, validation concerns the process of examining a product to determine conformity with user needs. [32, pp. 15, 16]

The use of the term internal independent verification and validation (I^2V&V) may be considered a contradiction. According to Robert O. Lewis, software V&V Rule 1 is: V&V must be an independent, third-party activity. [31, p. 238] The independence of I^2V&V is immediately brought into question. Perhaps it is best approached by that portion of the IEEE *Standard Glossary* which states, "The degree of independence must be a function of the importance of the software." An examination of that definition would logically produce an independence of IV&V that means:

Importance	Independence
life critical	different company
organizational survival	different company (unless proprietary)*
very important	same company, separate organization*
important	same company, separate organization
trivial	same company, same organization

* Same company may subcontract to different company.

It is expensive to have independent V&V—up to 30 percent of the cost of development. [34, p. 60] For a task of any significant size this becomes very costly, so there is a strong desire to do the independent V&V internally; thus less costly, the I²V&V personnel can use the development community which helps reduce the cost, but the independence is less independent.

It should be noted that *Verification and Validation of Modern Software-Intensive Systems,* authored by G. Gordon Schulmeyer and Garth R. MacKenzie, is to be released by Prentice Hall. shortly after the release of this *Handbook*. Because of the close relationship between software quality and V&V, this V&V book answers many questions concerned with the quality of the software product and development involving modern technology and methods, such as client/server; internet/intranet; object-oriented methods; data warehousing; etc.

1.11   Test and Evaluation (T&E)—See How They Run

This section discusses test and evaluation (T&E) and concludes with a distinction between V&V and T&E.

The IEEE *Standard Glossary* defines testing in a rather broad manner:

Testing is the process of operating a system or system component under specified conditions, observing or recording the results, and making an evaluation of some aspect of the system or component. [5, p. 76]

Donald Reifer narrows the definition of software testing rather than the broad testing described above:

Software quality testing is the systematic series of evaluation activities performed to validate that the software fulfills technical and performance requirements. [8, p. 60]

"Evaluation," following the standard dictionary definition, means "to appraise," and "to appraise" means "to judge the quality or worth of."

Therefore software T&E is defined as *the process of exercising complete programs to judge their quality through the fulfillment of specified requirements.*

The difference between V&V and T&E is that V&V can be accomplished without testing the software (but usually is not). The essence of V&V rests in the traceability of requirements. First, verification can be accomplished through the tracing of requirements embodied in the development specification to the design specification, and finally to the units of code. Second, validation can be accomplished by a test closure traceability for which the entire set of requirements is formally established in an approved test plan and test procedures, and finally proven as valid at the various levels of tests. The essence of T&E is in the actual exercising of the computer programs during test. As each test is made and evaluated, the validation assurance which traces requirements to software under test can be checked off for each test until all tests have been passed.

1.12 Software Process Improvement—The Latest Wave

In "Defining Software Process Improvement," Szymanski and Neff focus on the "value added" portion of achieving improvement:

> Software process improvement is a deliberate, planned methodology following standardized documentation practices to capture on paper (and in practice) the activities, methods, practices, and transformations that people use to develop and maintain software and the associated products. As each activity, method, practice and transformation is documented, each is analyzed against the standard of value added to the organization. [35, pp. 29–30]

In "Defining Software Process Improvement," Szymanski and Neff go on to provide proposed steps of process improvement:

1. Prepare and document a flowchart of the entire process from beginning to end using conventional flowcharting notations.
   a. "Walkthrough" each activity in the flowchart
   b. Authenticate each activity observed using the ETVX (entry criteria, task, validation, exit criteria) approach or a similar model for documentation
   c. List the input and output of each activity
   d. Estimate the time involved to complete each activity
   e. Schedule each activity in its proper and natural sequence
   f. Identify the specific person or office responsible for each activity
2. Analyze each activity documented in the flowchart to determine if it is "value-added:"
   a. Eliminate any activity that detracts (cost, schedule, or quality) from the process
   b. Add any needed activity not previously identified in the flowchart

    c. Modify any activity that does not enhance customer satisfaction.

  3. On a continuous basis in a structured, repeatable fashion, identify ways to eliminate or modify non-value-added activities in the process Add any activities that would attach value to the process. [35, pp. 29–30]

From the *Encyclopedia of Computer Science* a basic concept of software process improvement is provided:

> Software process management is the effective use of available resources both to produce properly engineered products and to improve the organization's software engineering capability. One of these software engineering principles is that effective software engineering can be done only when the software process is effectively managed. [6, p. 1220]

The guidelines for effective software process management are:

(1) The production of quality software depends on the skill, support, training, and motivation of the software professionals.

(2) These professionals will typically perform as effectively as they can within the limitations of their organization's process.

(3) Management owns the process, and only management can initiate continuing process improvement.

(4) Process improvement must be treated as a priority activity with dedicated resources and management.

(5) While software design is an intellectual skill, software development also involves many routine activities to which traditional management methods can be applied. [6, p. 1221]

The leaders in software process improvement concepts in the United States have been the Software Engineering Institute (SEI) with the Capability Maturity Model (CMM) (see Chapter 12, *Understanding the Software Engineering Institute's Capability Maturity Model and the Role of SQA in Software Development Maturity*). The CMM and the related assessment and evaluations have provided a benchmark throughout the software industry to understand where they stand in relation to industry. Figure 1-1 provides a quick look at the advantages of becoming more mature. The figure shows the percentage of respondents who reported that their organization had "excellent" or "good" performance in the following areas: product quality, customer satisfaction, productivity, ability to meet schedules and budgets, and staff morale. There are now a rare few companies, such as Boeing Space Transportation Systems Software, that have achieved the optimizing Level 5. This means they are devoted to continuous software process improvement and know how to implement it as explained in Chapter 13, *SEI CMM Level 5: Boeing Space Transportation Systems Software*.

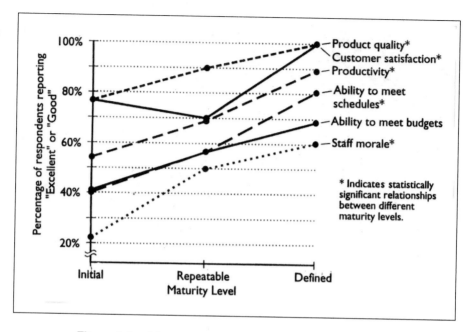

Figure 1-1 Advantages of higher maturity levels. [36, p. 35]

1.13 ISO 9000 Software Certification—Only the Best

Software Quality Assurance and Measurement: a Worldwide Perspective provides a summary of ISO 9000 and TickIT:

> In Europe, also increasingly, in Japan the pre-eminent quality standard to which people aspire is based around the international standard, ISO 9001. This general manufacturing standard specifies a set of 20 requirements (Table 1-1) for a quality management system, covering policy, organization, responsibilities and reviews, in addition to the controls that need to be applied to life cycle activities in order to achieve quality products. ISO 9001 is not specific to any market sector; the software 'version' of the standard is ISO 9000-3. The ISO 9000-3 standard is also the basis of the TickIT initiative that was sponsored by the UK Department of Trade and Industry. Companies apply to become TickIT-certified and they must be re-assessed every three years. [10, pp. 12, 13]

The publication, in June 1991, of ISO 9000-3 was significant for software quality because it provided an internationally accepted model for a software quality system. This standard is used as a basis document for quality system certification of software companies. The Japanese software industry anticipated that quality system certification would spread to software very quickly. Some companies are establishing software quality systems to conform to ISO 9000-3. It is expected that this will result in a broad awareness of the importance of software quality. It is also expected that adherence to a quality system will reduce the introduction of errors in the software process. [10, p. 114]

Kan has observed the following about ISO certification:

> Although many firms and companies are in the process of pursuing ISO 9000 registration, it is interesting to observe that many companies actually fail the audit during the first pass. The number of initial failures ranges from 60% to 70%. This is quite an interesting statistic and is probably explained by the complexity of the standards, their bureaucratic nature, the opportunity for omissions, and a lack of familiarity with what is actually required. From the software standpoint, we observed that corrective action and document control are the areas where most nonconformancies were incurred. [11, p. 47]

Mark Paulk of the Software Engineering Institute (SEI) says:

> Clearly there is a strong correlation between ISO 9001 and the CMM, although some issues in ISO 9001 are not covered in the CMM, and vice versa. The level of detail differs significantly; ISO 9001 is broadly written, covering 20 requirements; ISO 9000-3 interprets for software and the CMM covers 20 key process areas in detail.

> . . . the biggest difference between the two documents is the explicit emphasis of the CMM on continuous process improvement. ISO 9001 addresses only the minimum criteria for an acceptable quality system. See Table 1-1 for a comparison of ISO clauses and the CMM. Another difference is that the CMM focuses strictly on software, while ISO 9001 has a much broader scope that encompasses hardware, software, processed materials, and services. [37, p. 81] See Table 1-2 for how the CMM relates to the ISO document.

> . . . organizations should focus on improvement to build a competitive advantage, not on achieving a score—whether that is a maturity level or a certificate. The SEI advocates addressing continuous process improvement as encompassed by the CMM, but even then there is a need to address the larger business context in the spirit of TQM. [37, p. 82]

Table 1-1 Summary Mapping between ISO 9001 and the CMM [37, p. 78]

ISO 9001 Clause	Strong Relationship to CMM	Judgmental Relationship to CMM
4.1: Management responsibility	Commitment to perform Software project planning Software project tracking & oversight Software quality assurance	Ability to perform Verifying implementation Software quality mgmt.
4.2: Quality system	Verifying implementation Software project planning Software quality assurance Software product engineering	Organization process def.
4.3: Contract review	Requirements management Software project planning	Software subcontract mgmt.
4.4: Design control	Software project planning Software project tracking & oversight Software configuration management Software product engineering	Software quality mgmt.
4.5: Document and data control	Software configuration management Software product engineering	
4.6: Purchasing	Software subcontract management	
4.7: Control of customer-supplied product		Software subcontract mgmt.
4.8: Product identification & traceability	Software configuration management. Software product engineering	
4.9: Process control	Software project planning Software quality assurance Software product engineering	Quantitative process mgmt. Technology change mgmt.
4.10: Inspection and testing	Software product engineering Peer reviews	
4.11: Control of inspection, measuring, & test equipment	Software product engineering	
4.12: Inspection and test status	Software configuration management Software product engineering	
4.13: Control of nonconforming product	Software configuration management. Software product engineering	
4.14: Corrective and preventive action	Software quality assurance Software configuration management	Defect prevention
4.15: Handling, storage, packaging, preservation, & delivery		Software configuration mgmt. Software product engineering
4.16: Control of quality records	Software configuration management Software product engineering Peer reviews	
4.17: Internal quality audits	Verifying implementation Software quality assurance	
4.18: Training	Ability to perform Training program	
4.19: Servicing		
4.20: Statistical techniques	Measurement and analysis	Organization process def. Quantitative process mgmt. Software quality mgmt.

Table 1-2   CMM Related to ISO 9001 [37, p. 81]

Key Process Area	Not Satisfied	Fully Satisfied
Process change management		
Technology change management		
Defect prevention		
Software quality management		
Quantitative process management		
Peer review		
Intergroup coordination		
Software product engineering		
Integrated software management		
Training program		
Organization process definition		
Organization process focus		
Software configuration management		
Software quality assurance		
Software subcontract management		
Software project tracking and oversight		
Software project planning		
Requirements management		

Legend: ■ Practices directly addressed by ISO 9001 or 9000-3

▓ Practices that may be addressed by ISO 9001 or 9000-3

Practices not addressed by ISO 9001

1.14   Total Quality Management (TQM)—The Big Picture

Dunn and Ullman define Total Quality Management as:

> . . . a management approach to long-term success measured through customer satisfaction. TQM is based on the participation of all members of an organization to improving processes, products, services, and the culture they work in. . . .

The methods for implementing this approach are found in the teachings of such quality experts (see Chapter 3) as Philip B. Crosby, W. Edwards Deming, Armand V. Feigenbaum, Kaoru Ishikawa, and J. M. Juran.

At its core, TQM places responsibility for the quality of a process primarily with the owners of the process. This differs from the older notions of quality control in which quality control specialists were responsible for making sure that work was performed in accordance with established standards of quality. Under a TQM regimen, we do not depend on checking and testing to get quality. We expect the process owners to build quality into their work. [29, pp. 6-8]

Michael Hammer and Steven Stanton in *The Reengineering Revolution* compare TQM with reengineering:

Most companies undertaking reengineering today have some experience with total quality management. This can be helpful, or it can be a hindrance. TQM and reengineering share many characteristics, including a focus on customers, orientation toward processes, and a commitment to improved performance. There are, however, important differences between the two. TQM stresses incremental improvement through structured problem solving, whereas reengineering is about radical improvement through total process redesign. TQM assumes the underlying process is sound and looks to improve it; reengineering assumes it is not and seeks to replace it. [38, pp. 96, 97]

Stephen Kan provides a historical and philosophical framework for TQM:

TQM is a term that was originally coined in 1985 by the Naval Air Systems Command to describe its Japanese-style management approach to quality improvement. . . . The key elements of TQM are: continuous improvement; customer focus; process improvement; human side of quality; metrics, models measurements and analysis. [11, pp. 7 and 9]
   The TQM philosophy aims at long-term success by linking quality with customer satisfaction. Despite variations in its implementation, there are four key common elements of a TQM system: (1) customer focus, (2) process improvement, (3) human side of quality, and (4) measurement and analysis. [11, p. 10]

From a Department of Defense perspective, in a presentation entitled, "The View of Total Quality Management," Peter Angiola provided the following definition of TQM:

TQM is both a philosophy and a set of guiding principles that represent the foundation of a continuously improving organization. TQM is the application of human resources, and quantitative methods to improve the material and services supplied to an organization, all the processes within the organization, and the degree to which the needs of the customer are met, now and in the future. TQM integrates fundamental management techniques, existing improvement efforts, and technical tools under a disciplined approach focused on continuous process improvement. [39]

Philip Crosby provides his usual insight when he discusses "What Does TQM Mean?":

Actually, managing quality is a matter of establishing a clear policy on quality; assuring that everyone involved has a common practical education on the vocabulary and tools of the subject; and conducting an unending witness on the part of the management of the organization in insisting that we are going to do what we said we were going to do. TQM means that, but so does plain old "quality management." [40]

On the Internet, Richard Green provides some difference between software quality management and TQM:

TQM . . . often requires something akin to a religious conversion to introduce it. Fundamental changes in personal and professional attitudes are sometimes necessary, covering areas of the company's activities that lie outside the scope of quality standards. [41]

In *Software Quality Assurance and Measurement: a Worldwide Perspective* there is that emphasis on philosophy again:

TQM is an umbrella term for a philosophy that emphasizes shared responsibilities for quality. In TQM quality improvement is achieved by focusing on customer needs and streamlining the production process to eliminate defects and waste. TQM is characterized by activities such as process analysis using measurement, objective setting, root cause analysis of defects, problem solving and teamwork. [10, pp. 2, 3]

Richard Brydges in his introduction to *Total Quality Management for Software*, as particularized here for software, tries to come to grips with this multifaceted "methodology":

TQM must provide the focus for achieving "constancy of purpose." It ultimately facilitates continuous improvement through a collective vision of quality. A vision of quality that shifts from defect correction to defect prevention; from quality inspected into the software product to quality designed and built into the software product; from acceptable levels of defects to continuous process improvement; from approval of waivers to conformance to properly defined software requirements; from emphasis on cost and schedule to emphasis on quality, cost, and schedule. [42, p. xxxii]

There are those who criticize the TQM movement for not having a more standardized definition or concurrence on what TQM is. While the eclectic nature of the concept lends itself to such variations, it is more important to derive meaning and understanding through the process of definition and implementation. The insights, applications, and experiences cited throughout this *Handbook of Software Quality Assurance* provide a foundation of understanding software as applied to TQM from which to develop a definition that uniquely fits your organizational business strategy.

References

1. Pirsig, Robert M., *Zen and the Art of Motorcycle Maintenance* (New York: William Morrow & Co., 1974).
2. Portions reprinted, with permission, from Kitchenham, Barbara and Pfleeger, Shari Lawrence, "Software Quality: The Elusive Target." In: *IEEE Software* (New York: IEEE, January, 1996), © 1996 IEEE.
3. Juran, J. M. "Basic Concepts." In: *Quality Control Handbook*, Juran, J. M., Gryna, Frank M., Jr., and Bingham, Frank M., Jr., eds. (3rd ed. New York: McGraw-Hill Book Co., 1979).
4. Gentleman, W. M., "If Software Quality is a Perception, How Do We Measure It?" Institute for Information Technology, National Research Council of Canada, Ottawa, 1996.
5. Standards Coordinating Committee of the IEEE Computer Society, *IEEE Standard Glossary of Software Engineering Terminology*, IEEE-STD-610.12-1990 (New York: IEEE, 1991).
6. Ralston, Anthony and Reilly, Edwin D. (editors), *Encyclopedia of Computer Science* (3rd ed.), New York: Van Nostrand Reinhold Co., 1993).
7. Fisher, Matthew, J., and Light, William R., Jr., "Definitions in Software Quality Management." In: *Software Quality Management*, Fisher, Matthew J. and Cooper, John D., eds. (New York: Petrocelli Books, 1979).
8. Reifer, Donald J., *State of the Art in Software Quality Management* (Torrance: Reifer Consultants, 1985).
9. Baker, Emanuel R., and Fisher, Matthew J., "A Software Quality Framework." In: *Concepts, The Journal of Defense Systems Acquisition Management*, Moore, Robert Wayne, ed. Vol. 5, No. 4 (Fort Belvoir, VA: Defense System Management College, Autumn 1982).

10. Fenton, Norman; Whitty, Robin; and Iizuka, Yoshinori (editors). *Software Quality Assurance and Measurement: a Worldwide Perspective* (Boston: International Thomson Computer Press, Boston, 1995).

11. Kan, Stephen H., *Metrics and Models in Software Quality Engineering* (Reading: Addison-Wesley publishing Company, 1995), (extracted from pages 4, 7, 8, 47). © 1995 Addison-Wesley Publishing Company, Inc. Reprinted by permission of Addison-Wesley Longman, Inc.

12. Crosby, Philip B., *Quality Is Free* (New York: New American Library 1979).

13. Kaner, Cem; Falk, Jack; and Nguyen, Hung Quoc, *Testing Computer Software* (2nd edition). (Boston: International Thomson Computer Press, 1993).

14. Humphrey, Watts S., *A Discipline for Software Engineering* (Reading: Addison-Wesley Publishing Company, 1995), (page 272).© 1995 Addison-Wesley Publishing Company, Inc. Reprinted by permission of Addison-Wesley Longman, Inc.

15. Denning, Peter J., "What is Software Quality?" In: *Communications of the ACM*, Association for Computing Machinery (New York, Vol. 35, No. 1, Jan., 1992).

16. Portions reprinted, with permission, from Dromey, Geoff R., "Cornering the Chimera." In: *IEEE Software* (New York: IEEE, January, 1996), pp. 33–43, © 1996 IEEE.

17. Dobbins, James A., and Buck, Robert D., "Software Quality Assurance." In: *Concepts, The Journal of Defense Systems Acquisition Management*, op. cit.

18. Fairley, Richard E. , Ph.D., *Software Quality Engineering Course Notes*, presented 16 April 1997.

19. Dunn, Robert H., *Software Quality Concepts and Plans* (Englewood Cliffs: Prentice Hall, Inc., 1990). © 1990. Reprinted by permission of Prentice Hall, Inc., Upper Saddle River, NJ.

20. Clapp, Judith A. and Staten, Saul F., *A Guide to Total Software Quality Control* (Boston: The Mitre Corporation, 1992).

21. McCarthy, Jim, *Dynamics of Software Development* (Redmond: Microsoft Press, 1995), Reproduced by permission of Microsoft Press. All rights reserved.

22. McConnell, Steve, *Code Complete* (Redmond: Microsoft Press, 1993), Reproduced by permission of Microsoft Press. All rights reserved.

23. American Society for Quality Control Certified Software Quality Engineer Certification Brochure, 1996.

24. Kline, Melvin B., "Software and Hardware Reliability and Maintainability: What are the Differences." In: *1980 Proceedings, Annual Reliability and Maintainability Symposium*, 1980.

25. McCall, James A., "An Introduction to Software Quality Metrics." In: *Software Quality Management*, op. cit.

26. Schneidewind, Norman E, "The Applicability of Hardware Reliability Principles to Computer Software." In: *Software Quality Management*, op. cit.

27. Portions reprinted, with permission, from Rooijmans, Jan; Aerts, Hans; and van Genuchten, Michiel, "Software Quality in Consumer Electronics Products." In: *IEEE Software* (New York: IEEE, January 1996), © 1996 IEEE.

28. *Draft Glossary of Software Quality Terms*, Data & Analysis Center for Software (RADC), 8 November 1985.

29. Dunn, Robert H. and Ullman, Richard S., *TQM for Computer Software* (New York: McGraw-Hill Book Co., 1994).

30. Nelson, J. Gary, "Software Testing in Computer-Driven Systems." In: *Software Quality Management*, op cit.

31. Lewis, Robert O., "Software Verification and Validation (V&V)." In: *Software Quality Management*, op. cit.

32. EIA/IEEE DRAFT US 12207-1996, *Information Technology: Software Life Cycle Processes*.

33. Boehm, Barry, *Software Engineering Economics* (Englewood Cliffs, NJ: Prentice Hall, 1982). © 1982. Reprinted by permission of Prentice Hall, Inc., Upper Saddle River, NJ.

34. Dunn, Robert, *Software Defect Removal* (New York: McGraw-Hill Book Company, 1984).

35. Szymanski, David and Neff, Thomas, "Defining Software Process Improvement." In: *CrossTalk*, February, 1996.

36. Herbsleb, James; Zubrow, David; Goldenson, Dennis; Hayes, Will; and Paulk, Mark, "Software Quality and the Capability Maturity Model." In: *Communications of the ACM*, Vol. 40 No. 6, June 1997, ACM, New York, pp. 31–40.

37. Portions reprinted, with permission, from Paulk, Mark C., "How ISO 9001 Compares with the CMM." In: *IEEE Software*, (New York: IEEE, January, 1995). © 1995 IEEE.

38. Hammer, Michael and Stanton, Steven A., *The Reengineering Revolution* (New York: HarperCollins Publishers, Inc., 1995).

39. Angiola, Peter, "The View of Total Quality Management Presentation." Directorate for Industrial Productivity and Quality, Department of Defense, November 16, 1989.

40. Crosby, Philip B., "What Does TQM Mean?" In: *Quality Update* (Winter Park: The Creative Factory, Inc., November–December, 1989).

41. Green, Richard, "SQM or TQM: Where are we going?" In: SQM, issue 14, http://www.avnet.co.uk/tesseract/QiC/articles/Green/14.html.

42. Brydges, Richard, "Introduction: The Total Quality Concept." In: *Total Quality Management for Software,* Schulmeyer, G. Gordon and McManus, James I. (editors) (New York, Van Nostrand Reinhold, 1992).

## CHAPTER 2

How Does Software Quality Assurance Fit In?

James I. McManus
Northrop Grumman Corporation,
Electronic Sensors and Systems Division

2.1 Introduction

It is important to understand the role of software quality assurance (SQA) for different kinds of software development efforts and for several of the specialized functions that are required to support the development of software. Although the primary role of assurance does not change, a shift in emphasis is required in order to enhance the success of the development effort. This shift in emphasis is a matter of degree and is required to focus attention where developmental concerns and risks are of the highest priority.

The question of where to place the major thrust of the SQA effort can be answered by experience and by Pareto analysis; a methodology (see Chapter 11, *The Pareto Principle Applied to Software Quality Assurance*) which highlights where the most attention is needed. Based on historical records, Pareto analysis has consistently demonstrated what has come to be known as the 80/20 rule. The 80/20 rule states that roughly 80 percent of the problems are caused by 20 percent of the _____ (this is where SQA finds the root cause to fill in the blank). There are three advantages to consider about Pareto analysis. First, it is a value-added process, but often overlooked. If SQA does not do Pareto analysis, who will? Second, it focuses attention where it is needed most. If Pareto analysis is not done, what timely information, key to management's decision-making process, is missing. Third, if 80 percent of the problems can be solved by having to adjust only 20 percent of the resources, it is definitely worth a look.

Within this chapter, six categories of software have been identified; each requiring a shift in emphasis in the role of SQA. These categories are operating systems software, mission-critical software, real-time systems software, interactive software, business software, and business process reengineering and Y2K. The role of SQA within each of these categories is presented in terms of what distinguishes one software type from another. A set of recommendations highlights the unique items and concerns for SQA within each category. Note, as used herein, "recommendations" takes into consideration that not all recommendations will apply universally and it is anticipated that some tailoring would be required pending company strategy, policy, resources, size of program, etc. The recommendations are tied to the following phases of development as applicable: requirements, design, implementation, verification, and operation.

A common framework for SQA activities is provided here in the introduction for all six software categories. The individual discussions highlight extensions to this framework for unique areas requiring additional SQA emphasis within each software category.

Also discussed is the role of SQA with several software specialty areas. These are software configuration management (SCM), software maintenance, and independent verification and validation (IV&V).

Common Framework for Recommended SQA Activities

Requirements
- review requirements
- assure/sponsor internal reviews to eliminate ambiguities and uncertainties
- assure/sponsor internal reviews to define requirements in terms of their testability
  - –evaluate customer input
  - –participate in formal requirements reviews with the customer
- assure agreement on requirements assumptions
- assure use of the requirements volatility metric
  - –maintain system requirements database (as applicable)
  - –assure functional baseline (SCM establishes baseline)

Design
- review software design and requirements allocations to components
- promote peer inspections of design components (SQA follows-up on action item closure)
- participate in formal customer design reviews with the customer
  - –assure allocated baseline (SCM establishes baseline)
  - –assure that test procedures cover all testable requirements

Implementation

- review code against coding standards (source lines of code, complexity, templates, etc.)
- promote peer inspections of code and unit tests (SQA follows-up on action item closure)
  - —assure internal SCM for problem control and corrective action logs (SQA evaluates both corrective action effectiveness and areas for prevention)
  - —assure version control of development software prior to integration and test
  - —review software build plan and build readiness for test

Verification

- SQA reviews test procedures for requirements and functional coverage
- SQA validates test results (assure dry runs, build tests, Software CI tests, burn-in period, etc. as necessary—where CI = configuration item)
- assure SCM of test results, test records, redlines, corrective action records versus test problems, problem closure, etc.
  - —assure adequate regression testing as necessary
  - —assure readiness to release software to system test
  - —assure product baseline (SCM establishes baseline)
  - —assure adequate description exists of the released software version

Operation

- training as needed
- track key metrics (failure rates, functions which fail most frequently, nuisance problems, corrective action, etc.) and maintain database.

2.2 SQA and Operating Systems Software

Operating Systems software is a collection of programs written to coordinate the operation of all computer circuitry allowing the computer to run efficiently. [1, p. 85] Operating system software is composed of both control programs and processing programs. *Control programs* control the efficiency and effectiveness of the computer on which they reside. *Processing programs* control the efficient processing of programmer preparation.

The actual development of operating system software is an ongoing activity, with better versions of existing and, frequently, new operating systems being released by their manufacturers. These include the well known UNIX® by AT&T®, Windows 98® and Windows NT® by Microsoft, OS1™ and OS2™ by IBM®, and VMS® by Digital Equipment Corp., to name a few.

Although the development of operating systems software is similar to the development of applications software, the prime area of emphasis is different as noted by the following observation:

> With the knowledge that potentially millions of customers can receive delivery of products containing operating system software (take Windows 95, for example, as witnessed by the recent PC explosion), the greatest areas of emphasis are configuration *control* and *dependable* performance.

Manufacturers must diligently keep everything under strict configuration *control* prior to release of the new version. There is literally no room for error. Companies can go out of business if their products do not deliver. Customer perception is critical here. Once the customer perceives that a product does not measure up, the manufacturer can face a nightmare of returns, complaints, lawsuits, etc., not to mention the bottom line. To compound the problem further, it is not unusual to have multiple versions of operating systems in the hands of various customers simultaneously.

Note however, that this can be offset if the manufacturer can quickly resolve the problem and make available a reliable version of the software. Use of "alpha" and "beta" trial versions of new operating systems software for limited periods of time at no cost to potential customers is a good strategy to employ. This offers the advantage of reduced liability and provides an avenue for customer feedback critical to product enhancement and adaptability to users' needs.

This is precisely where SQA fits in. First, during the product development and test cycle, SQA must assure a solid configuration management and control process with appropriate baselines, detailed records of product problems, solutions, and performance. There must be a way to quickly define the state of the product, if the product experiences problems in the field. Second, also during product development and test, SQA must assure substantial testing and validation of the product against all marketable claims. This will reduce the risk of liability once the product is released. Third, again during development and test, if not sooner, SQA can initiate or assist investigating the potential of the proposed product for violation of existing patent or copyright infringement from a competitor; an area not to be taken lightly. Fourth, once the product is released, the role of SQA now shifts to evaluating customer satisfaction, suggestions, complaints, etc. This information is imperative for continuing product improvement and for potential future releases.

Recommendations (for operating systems software)

SQA top priority: software configuration *control* during development and after product release.

SQA second priority: assuring *dependable* product *performance* prior to release.

Requirements
- benchmark the competition
  - −assure no copyright infringement violations
- establish requirements based on firm marketing claims
  - −evaluate customer input
  - −consider platform versatility

Design
- promote peer inspections to assure the intended capability of the operating system

Implementation
- consider trial release prototype models (alpha, beta)
  - −assure SCM configuration *control* of prototype models and problem control/corrective action
  - −assure version *control* of alpha, beta models in the field

Verification
- assure operators/users manuals are up to date
- validate product *reliability* and *dependable performance*
- assure resolution of high priority problems to avoid customer dissatisfaction
- assure adequate regression testing as necessary
- assure readiness to release final product (beyond alpha/beta)

Operation (after product release)
- assure adequate packaging protection and any warranty prior to distribution
- follow-up customer suggestions, complaints, etc.
- measure customer satisfaction (surveys, hot-line, etc.)

2.3   SQA and Mission-Critical Software

Mission-critical software (also refer to Chapter 16, *Practical Applications of Software Quality Assurance to Mission-Critical Embedded Software*) is a term which has been generally reserved for software developed for the Department of Defense (DoD). What the name implies is software developed to execute on "mission-critical resources" as defined by DoD. "Mission-critical computer resources" include computers and services for the conduct of the military missions of the Department of Defense related to:

• Intelligence activities
• Cryptology activities related to national security
• Command and control of military forces
• Equipment integral to a weapon or weapons system
• Equipment critical to direct fulfillment of military or intelligence missions, but not routine administrative and business applications. [2, p. 38]

The Department of Defense often requires development of "embedded computers" that contain software that is

incorporated as an integral part of, dedicated to, or required for direct support of, or for the upgrading or modification of major or less-than major systems.

The most common definition of this term includes a broad spectrum of technologies from simple chips to computer systems with multiple processors. The use of "embedded computers" is also associated with an array of complex military operations and equipment. [2, p. 38] The term "embedded computers" has persisted in relation to "mission-critical computer resources," but the terminology is now considered passé.

Embedded software is that software which executes on embedded computers. Such software includes nonvolatile firmware. In accordance with IEEE Std. 729-1983, firmware is defined as an assembly composed of a hardware unit and a computer program integrated to form a functional entity whose configuration cannot be altered during normal operation.

Mission-critical software must be extremely reliable.

In today's military systems reliability requirements are defined at the upper limit of what can be achieved. On a scale of 0.0 to 1.0, reliability requirements are often quoted to be on the order of 0.9999 (more or less).

Consequently, for mission-critical software, SQA should be most concerned with software *reliability* and should focus on those activities which have the most impact on reliability.

Several factors enter into providing such high levels of reliability. First is the requirement for *excellent performance* on the part of the software developed. The software must execute for long periods of time without failure; this period is similar to what is defined as the Mean Time Between Failures (MTBF) in the world of hardware. Second is the element of *redundancy*; a completely redundant system provides a backup readily accessible to take over in case of primary system failure. Third is the use of replaceable parts (otherwise known as *spares*) which can be quickly replaced on-site with minimum downtime.

SQA needs to be concerned with all three factors noted above.

Excellent performance requires a concentrated, sophisticated, life cycle development effort. Mission-critical software requires detailed analysis and tradeoff analysis of requirements at the systems level. The critical point of focus is performance reliability. Down time essentially is unacceptable during any of the defined critical missions. The complexity of the system's operations and interfaces and the specific allocations of performance requirements to major software components requires dedicated front end evaluation. Rapid prototyping is highly desirable. In this type of environment, the customer is heavily involved on the front end of development. It is not uncommon during the requirements analysis phase that an independent verification & validation (IV&V) team live on-site at the contractor's facility.

SQA can play a major role in all these areas. The first role of SQA is to promote tighter controls on the front end of the life cycle to assure that performance reliability is extensively evaluated to reveal all facts about the system. Both internal systems requirements reviews and systems design reviews are required to solidify the functional baseline which may include derived requirements. Ambiguous, untestable, nonquantifiable, and assumed requirements are inadequate and are cause of real concern. Development should not proceed without resolving these uncertainties at the front end of the life cycle. In some cases SQA maintains the online database of the requirements, acts as the database administrator, and is the single point of contact for managing entry of requirements, requirements modification, and baselining, when approved. A key metric during requirements analysis is requirements volatility; a measure of how frequently requirements are changed. This can have serious consequences particularly after the set of requirements has been baselined. This metric is often required at customer monthly meetings.

Once the operational, functional, and performance requirements have been solidified, i.e., essentially agreed to by contractor and customer, and baselined, another follow-up role for SQA is to assure that requirements are verifiable—not an easy task. Verification itself is a requirement specified by customer-invoked high level specifications and usually encompasses inspection, analysis, demonstration, and test.

Test is the most common verification technique for software. Often an index, called the Verification Cross Reference Index (VCRI) or Matrix (VCRM), is required as a deliverable. The VCRI/VCRM traces each high level specification requirement to one or more of the four approved methods of verification.

Another role, often conducted under the purview of SQA, is the responsibility for modeling the system's software reliability. Early software predictions can later be evaluated during the operational phase; providing feedback to fine tune the original model.

Redundancy is also an area for potential problems. As noted above, a totally redundant backup system minimizes downtime, thus enhancing system reliability. If two identical systems are to be built, then SQA must assure that the backup system has the exact version of software as the primary system. Maintaining the version descriptions of course is an SCM function. A second caution for SQA is the growth of software during development of prototype systems. Predictions for sizing software are often exceeded since they are basically optimistic and can not account for all unknown problems, which of course require unforeseen workarounds. The problem being that if the primary system is inadequate to meet the unforeseen growth of software, in order to meet the requirements of the system, the tendency might be to place the overflow software on the redundant system. This will result in degradation of performance during backup mode, which may be totally unacceptable to the customer. SQA therefore needs to assure that this metric (the growth aspect of software) is closely monitored during development to provide management sufficient warning to reduce risk in this area.

Note, the use of redundant systems for reliability is not to be confused with requirements to maintain specified reserves, often quoted for mission-critical systems. Reserve requirements for memory, Input/Output channel utilization, and throughput are usually specified to allow for future growth after the system is delivered to the customer. In this case, SQA would assure that both sizing and timing of software components are monitored to assure that the reserve capacities are maintained throughout development.

Spares, usually associated with hardware, have software significance. Remember the term embedded software defined above; spares include replaceable boards which contain such software or may contain nonvolatile firmware which derives from software. These boards must be tested and verified at both component test and system test. It is SQA's role to verify the adequacy of these tests.

A well known example of reliability in mission-critical software is the space shuttle. The initial flight was delayed because one of five on-board computers did not agree with information supplied by the other four. This level of redundancy was required because of the requirement for safety of flight, safety of mission, and safety of personnel.

Recommendations (mission-critical software)

SQA top priority: software *reliability*.

Requirements
- review mission-critical system software requirements
- evaluate requirements for one or more *redundant* systems
- evaluate requirements for *spares*; particularly spare boards with embedded software or firmware
- evaluate requirements for software size and for reserve requirements
- evaluate the need for rapid prototyping
- promote tighter controls on the front end of the life cycle
- model mission-critical *software reliability* and provide early predictions

Design
- promote peer inspections of design components to assure the intended capability of the mission-critical system
- assure *redundancy* requirements are not violated at design
- assure results of trade studies are incorporated into the design (both components and interfaces)
- assure rapid prototype modeling (if implemented) of trade study recommendations

Implementation
- promote peer inspections of code and unit tests to monitor conformance with timing and sizing budgets
- monitor development for software growth versus resource capacity and reserve requirements
- assure definition of critical path items for mission-critical software and tie into build strategy

Verification
- verify *reliability* and *performance* at each level of test
- assure dry runs, performance metrics/budgets, reliability burn-in period, etc., as necessary)

Operation
- provide training for the customer
- track reliability performance metrics (failure rates, functions which fail most frequently, nuisance problems, corrective action, time to repair, etc.); maintain in database
- track operational reliability results against reliability model predictions for accuracy of earlier predictions and to improve the software reliability model during the next go-around

2.4   SQA and Real-Time Systems of Software

Real-time software is that software that controls a computer that controls a real-time system. A real-time system is one that provides services or control to an on-going physical process.[3, p. vii]

Software that executes in real-time is software that is subject to very strict performance requirements and constraints. Real-time software must interact with other external entities (other computer programs, terminals, subsystems, etc.) and execute all required processing in a real-time window. This software is therefore restricted by timing constraints, and, in many instances, also by sizing constraints. The software is usually complex and may exist in several forms such as firmware, assembly language, microcode, and a recompiled version of the developmental high order language (HOL) source code. With the advent of Ada 95 and ANSI® C++, many concurrent tasks associated with real-time can now be programmed in these HOLs.

Real-time tasks are performance-driven using timing and sizing allocations for various parts of the system (to include hardware and components, software and components, component-to-component interface times, and user-to-machine interface reaction times). Critical components and interfaces must be identified early on, thoroughly evaluated, and carefully followed. Timing and sizing estimates must be updated frequently during each phase of software development. The original estimates should be based on dependable models and simulations early in the life cycle to be subsequently transformed into real-time performance gradually as development progresses.

In order to keep real-time programs intellectually manageable, Niklaus Wirth recommends that they first be designed as time-independent multiprograms and that only after analytic validation they be modified in isolated places, where the consequences of reliance on execution time constraints are simple to comprehend and document. [4, p. 141]

The systems/software architecture needs to be defined early on as well to assure proper allocations of requirements and timing budgets between hardware and software. Early rapid prototyping is highly recommended here for large, complex, state-of-the-art, real-time programs to validate the overall hardware/software architecture and to identify critical functions, interfaces, and problem areas as soon as possible. Modeling and analysis also help to evaluate the impact of the selected hardware on software. Since hardware is difficult to undo later on, software may receive the brunt of unplanned, downstream, changes to account for unforeseen oversights in hardware selection. Of course, these late changes to software tend to increase software complexity which may adversely impact real-time performance.

It is noteworthy to mention the tradeoff between cyclomatic complexity (from McCabe of Chapter 11) and real-time. Normally the rule of thumb on complexity is to maintain design complexity at 7 or less and code complexity at 10 or less. This allows for growth during testing without affecting software maintenance adversely. However, for real-time systems, additional modules directly increase the overhead and correspondingly the time required to process those modules. Since time is not a luxury in real-time systems, complexity may have to be relaxed a degree. Note this is not a blank check to forget about complexity, but a caution to try to balance real-time constraints with complexity requirements. Planning for both at the outset is what is required. Extremely complex modules do not accept change very well.

Dynamic modeling also supports tradeoff studies. System/software design tradeoff studies should include interrupt processing as well as concurrent engineering techniques. Reliability, maintainability, availability, and logistic requirements should also be considered up front since they can not be added later.

To better implement the results of tradeoff studies, design should be simple not complex, flexible not rigid, and modular. This is necessary not only to accommodate changes, but to test the design early on in order to assure some measure of *efficiency* and optimized performance. The method of testing may be innovative and require several changes and iterations to verify fitness of the system/software design.

Real-time software is based on concurrent processing and on timed interrupts which are keyed to a priority assignment for each critical function. Although real-time processing also involves recovery processing and high systems/software reliability, the key to real-time processing is *efficiency*.

Therefore SQA has responsibility to ensure the overall efficiency of the real-time systems software.

For real-time systems, SQA needs to keep track of the "not-to-exceed" estimates of timing and sizing budgets for all system components, monitor results from trade-off studies and from rapid prototyping, track changes to the software as a consequence of trade studies, track the impact of software changes on the associated estimated timing budgets from modeling or reviews, evaluate the adequacy of concurrent processing and interrupt processing schemes to be provided by both the HOL and the targeted multiprocessors.

Finally, the rubber hits the road at test. Testing should be done in stages to allow for fine tuning where possible. Normally three levels of test apply: stand-alone tests to evaluate individual components, integration test to evaluate interfaces and integrated components, and system test. At each level of test the component(s) are evaluated to determine/validate actual timing versus not-to-exceed estimates. Real-time checking may be done by various timers and the computer(s), with the results monitored by SQA personnel. At system test, real-time values should meet estimates, if nothing was missed along the way. Of course, this is a matter of diligence at each step of the process and requires a team effort.

Since many components make up the real-time systems software, special attention must be given to SCM. Experience has shown that when real-time computer programs are integrated for the first time, at least one component fails its time constraint. By testing incrementally and closely controlling (a critical SCM function) the existing components and the new increments of software to be added, the team significantly enhances the probability of success for the real-time system.

If it seems that real-time programs are heavily weighted toward the front end of the life cycle, that is exactly right. This is where the program team can make it or break it. The front end task is actually a systems engineering job, covers both hardware and software, and is one of the most challenging efforts confronting the developer.

Peer inspections, reviews, audits, and documentation play a significant role in the success of real-time system software. Since real-time systems are steeped in analysis especially on the front end of development, additional reviews, peer inspections, audits and documentation will be required.

Recommendations (for real-time software)

SQA top priority: software *efficiency*.
Second priority: software *reliability*.

Requirements
- review real-time system software requirements

- evaluate requirements for concurrent processing and interrupt handling
- evaluate the software HOL for its ability to meet real-time concurrent processing needs
- evaluate requirements establishing "not-to-exceed" timing estimates for each function
- promote extensive analysis and tradeoff studies to optimize timing allocations
- promote use of rapid prototyping to model tradeoff recommendations
- promote tighter controls on the front end of the life cycle
- model real-time *software reliability* and provide early predictions

Design
- monitor the approved list of "not-to-exceed" timing estimates to assure they are not being exceeded
- promote peer inspections of design components to assure the intended capability of the real-time system
- monitor cyclomatic complexity of design modules to stay within tolerable limits
- promote tradeoff analysis of the systems/software architecture (to optimize concurrent and interrupt processing)
- track results of rapid prototyping for optimizing tradeoff study recommendations
- investigate shortcomings in hardware for impact of unplanned additional changes to software

Implementation
- monitor the approved list of "not-to-exceed" timing estimates to assure they are not being exceeded
- monitor processes that implement concurrent processing schemes
- promote peer inspections of code and unit tests;
  - to monitor conformance with "not to exceed" timing budgets, and
  - to monitor caps on cyclomatic complexity of code modules
- track the impact of software growth and changes on allocated timing budgets for software

Verification
- participate in dry runs to assure real-time performance

- monitor actual timing results during stand-alone, integration, and system level testing

Operation

- track real-time performance (real-time problems, functions which fail most frequently, nuisance problems, corrective action, etc.); maintain in database
- track real-time reliability results against reliability model predictions for accuracy of earlier predictions and to improve the software reliability model during the next go-around

2.5   SQA and Interactive Software

Interactive software is software that controls the interactive communication between person and machine. Interactive systems actively respond to human operator intervention; accepting and acknowledging commands and responding via some form of audio/visual alarm or some form of output via screen display or printout. In a general sense, all of the types of software discussed in this chapter are interactive to a greater or lesser degree.

There are many examples of interactive software systems. An airport surveillance radar system tracks and displays live aircraft data for an air traffic controller to monitor and respond to in real time. A missile fires at the precise moment the fire control system is given the command by the fighter pilot. Three-dimensional drawings are generated using interactive Computer Aided Design /Computer Aided Manufacturing (CAD/CAM) systems. A user demonstrates dynamic graphs using a Graphical User Interface (GUI) package. Users send and receive information across the Internet. A writer interacts with a word processing package on a Personal Computer (PC) to draft a document. Security systems respond to a trigger when someone enters the area and only deactivate upon human intervention (hopefully the homeowner).

Note, it is one thing to be a user of an interactive system; quite another to be the designer/developer. This section is concerned with both. Of course, development is relative here, since a developer can make use of an existing interactive system, such as a DEC Alpha display from Digital Equipment Corporation (now Compaq Computer), and incorporate it into the design of a new interactive product such as an air traffic control system.

2.5.1 Developer of Interactive Software

The developer of interactive software has two concerns: one is to provide the interactive capability; the other is the presentation or how to best present the system to the user. The interactive capability is what the system must accomplish, its *per-*

formance, in essence. The *presentation* is concerned with the human factors engineering aspects of the system; best described in terms such as "user friendliness" and "ergonomics."

SQA needs to be concerned with both the performance and the presentation aspects of interactive systems. For *performance,* SQA needs to assure that adequate requirements for the interactive system to be developed meet customer functional and performance needs. This requires meeting with the customer, agreeing upon requirements, and documenting and baselining the results. Things to consider are real-time constraints (such as responsiveness of the system), reliability requirements, sizing of the physical system to fit where the customer needs it (which may impact what computer is needed to fit into a given space and still execute the software), etc.

For *presentation*, note that in any of the examples above, the user may be faced with long hours of operation. Controls should be easy to reach; responses easy to read and interpret. What appears on the screen; how much information appears at any given time; how large the words, figures, and symbols are; how bright; what colors; color contrast; foreground versus background; how to make it easy for the user to find on the display what is most important and when to find it; all come into play. Any and all of these concerns are candidates for SQA consideration.

Take a far-fetched example: a real-time air traffic control system would require minimal interaction time if all the information could be displayed at once. However, the information would probably be so crowded that to find, decipher, and interpret what is most important at any given time would take so long that the real-time requirement could not be met. This suggests multiple reviews with the customer for input (requirements) and conducting tradeoff studies (design) early on to assure that at a minimum the highest priority information will be readily displayed and readable on the screen when needed. This might employ the use of menu-driven software, real-time graphical user interface software, alerts, etc.

Once the system/product has been developed, the customer may require training. In some cases training is highly interactive and may use sophisticated interactive software provided by simulators, etc. Training is imperative when safety is an issue. Two examples are training to operate a nuclear reactor and training a student pilot to fly a fighter aircraft. SQA can play a major role in assuring that the simulator is fully qualified prior to use.

Thus the primary areas of focus for SQA for interactive software are interactive performance (i.e., *responsiveness*) between person and machine and *presentation* to the user.

Note, in many cases the customer is the general public. If your company is developing a product to be marketed and distributed in stores across the country, one mechanism to use as a sounding board for what potential users would and would not prefer is the Internet, an interactive process in and of itself. The Internet provides a way for a company to solicit the likes and dislikes of users through the use of a survey form or questionnaire. As pointed out by Jakob Nielsen [5, p.111] a questionnaire of this sort needs to be pilot tested prior to its release on the Internet in order to assure that the kind and quantity of responses desired are actually achievable.

Recommendations (for developer of interactive software)

SQA top priority: *responsiveness and presentation.*

Requirements
- promote early, up-front meetings with potential users to assess customer needs
- evaluate requirements (or the need) for training to improve marketability and usability
- review interactive requirements for software
- promote analysis and tradeoff studies to optimize the person-to-machine interactions to include commands, responses, *responsiveness,* or response times, etc.
- promote analysis and tradeoff studies to optimize the *presentation* aspects of the person-to-machine interfaces and interactions to include menus, screen displays, data type, symbols, size of text, graphics, colors, etc.

Design
- promote peer inspections of design components to assure the intended capability of the interactive system for *responsiveness* and for on-screen *presentation* of data

Implementation
- conduct peer inspections of code and unit tests to assure compliance with design

Verification
- participate in dry runs to assure expected results
- monitor actual person-to-machine interactions, use of menus, performance of menu-driven commands, *responsiveness*, displays, etc.

Operation

- assure adequate training is available or is provided if contractually required
- track key metrics (problems, corrective action, etc.) and maintain database as applicable.
- note any improvements for next go-around

2.5.2 User of Interactive Software

Concerns for interactive software arise because of potential problems from users and abusers. The first of these is *intrusion*. In today's environment PCs and workstations are not only networked together via the company's intranet but now everyone has access to the World Wide Web via the Internet. Users not only send and receive mail but can also download software from the Internet. Who is to say the attachment (via electronic mail) does not contain a virus or that the software just downloaded from the Internet is not a virus? Companies today need protection from viruses, from sabotage, and from external hackers. Even with a firewall to lock out outsiders to protect proprietary information, employees can still get out on the Net and bring stuff in. With new breakthroughs in technology it will be hard to stay ahead of the onslaught.

The second concern is *legality*. There are legal ramifications associated with interactive software. These concern copyright protection and licensing agreements for well known vended software packages and commercial off-the-shelf (COTS) software. To illustrate this, just ask how many copies of Microsoft Word are in use within your division. Then ask how many licenses there are. If no one can answer this question or if there is a mismatch, there is a problem. SQA should know who controls such purchases and license agreements. One role for SQA is be on the look out for maverick copies and to promote their elimination. Just for the record, there are hefty fines and possible imprisonment for use of illegal copies of others' software. This is a serious issue for SCM, the system administrator, and the legal department among others. The following cannot be overstated—all software must be controlled.

A third concern is *information export violation*. Note, this is not meant as an SQA task but as a caution to be shared equally by every employee in the organization. Because of recent events in certain foreign countries regarding pirating of U.S. technology, new laws now govern exports of U.S. products that contain state-of-the-art technologies in software. These laws require U.S. companies to formally request an export license from the U.S. government to conduct business with certain foreign countries. Until your company is granted such a license, you as an individual can not divulge any information that would be considered sensitive or detrimental to the safeguarding of U.S. technologies to any person from that country. The simple act of conversing can be a violation in that conversing with a foreigner is a form of information export. This is very serious and infractions can lead to fines and/or imprisonment. Many companies are conducting training sessions to inform employees of the seriousness of this situation.

Just for illustration: your company wins a contract to build a radar system for a foreign country not yet on the approved list. Your company files for an export license. While waiting for approval of the export license from the U.S. government, the customer requests that representatives from their country work at your facility on a daily basis. As a measure of good faith you agree. Situation: your employees come face to face with in-country representatives every day. The customer reps are anxious to learn about the new system and ask many questions in meetings, in hallways, at lunch, etc. Employees must be extremely cautious in this environment not to say anything that would be in violation of the export laws.

Export violations can occur in several ways, including verbal conversation, teleconference, papers lying around on your desk while unattended, not picking up your fax papers immediately, via interactive software on the PC you forgot to shut down on your way out to lunch, the intranet, etc.

This is similar to the way classified information is treated for many government programs. However, in this case the technologies are resident in commercial products, and represent proprietary information and intellectual property owned by the company. If this information falls into the wrong hands, your competitive edge may soon be gone.

A fourth concern facing SQA today is the increasing number of third-party software vendors who sell COTS software packages that execute on various manufacturers' PCs or which may be targeted as a major component for a product we are developing for our customer. These software packages do not come with any *guarantees* and are not necessarily approved by any manufacturer's internal quality assurance department prior to release. A role of SQA here is to protect one's own corporation from any misuse or misrepresentation on the part of a vendor by requiring proof of performance. A demonstration and an adequate trial period should be required of any vendor at the time of purchase to determine fitness for a purpose.

The important issue here is *control*.

Recommendations (for user of interactive software)

SQA top priority: *control*.

Requirements
- enforce the writing and release of authorized procedures to define required practices to:
  - *safeguard* proprietary information and guard against *intrusion* from outsiders
  - prevent use of unauthorized, *illegal* copies of COTS and *licensed* software

– prevent *information export violations*

• require demos and certificates of conformance or *guarantees* from vendors at time of purchase

Implementation

• promote a grace period for anyone to turn in unlicensed copies of vended products; (no questions asked during grace period)

• follow up on the above requirements

• monitor *conformance* to the above procedures in practice on the job.

• enforce proper *control* through functional & departmental groups responsible for controls.

• evaluate practices for prevention of the above problems

• assure *version control* of all COTS and vended software

• recommend a COTS database to record the status of all purchases of licensed products and monitor licenses for expiration dates

Verification

• follow up on corrective action as applicable

• audit COTS database for currency

2.6 SQA and Business Software

The primary application of software in the business environment is that of information resources (IR) or information systems (IS). Chapters 17 and 18 cover methods of quality assurance for business software.

The role of the SQA person, in support of information systems, is to perform an audit of information systems to determine the adequacy of procedures, security of the system, adequate documentation, whether the ledgers are accurate and up-to-date, and that the system is functioning properly.

The primary method of auditing information systems is through the use of software tools to aid the information systems auditor. There are many such tools available, but these are not the focus of this chapter. However, the recommendations which follow in this section are all predicated upon the premise that an adequate toolset is available to and is used by the auditor.

The information systems auditor should prepare for the audit by generating a checklist to highlight key issues and concerns for each area to be audited. Checklists provide several advantages. First, checklists provide consistency from one audit to the next so that the person(s) audited knows what to expect time after time. Checklist results also show change where a process has either improved or degraded. The auditor can establish trends over a period of time and make recommendations to the information resource manager or the resident systems software specialist as applicable.

Auditors of information systems may also refer to past audits to prepare for an upcoming audit (for instance to review any past action items), or to assess and evaluate the history of existing files or current processes associated with the information systems. Prior audit information, however, should only be considered as supplementary in preparing for the audit. The company should have existing procedures which lay the ground rules for conducting business, for maintaining corporate ethics, etc. These should be subject to the audit as well.

For business software, then, SQA personnel must ensure the accuracy of software records and the *dependability* of its daily operation as their primary focus.

This is accomplished mainly through comprehensive reviews and audits, maintaining metrics, and monitoring operation. Because a high percentage of business software is in the operational/maintenance phase, daily operation is critical. This software must therefore be dependable and reliable. If the system crashes, immediate recovery is imperative. The information systems auditor and the resident system software specialist must work together to fix the problem, restore operation, find the root cause, conduct trend analysis and look for ways to prevent future operational failures. The importance of maintaining accurate configuration records of the software failures, new or modified software releases, and associated documentation is a must. Consequently, the information systems auditor must assure that a good SCM function is in place. Any problems with existing baselines must be thoroughly documented. The auditor would then follow up with the resident systems software specialist to verify the fix. The auditor must also monitor testing of any new information system releases to verify operational performance. The auditor also has responsibility to review software configuration records and documentation to assure that they reflect the current versions and status of all information resources for the system.

Recommendations (for business software)

SQA top priority: *accuracy of records*.
Second priority: *dependability of daily operation*.

Requirements
- review information systems procedures for areas to be audited
- normal operational procedures
- procedure in case of system degradation or crash
- recovery procedures

- review prior audits for any action items, etc.
- generate or update audit checklists as needed
- baseline any changes to requirements that require new/modified design

Design
- promote peer inspections of new/modified design components for new releases
- assure proposed design changes are approved
- assure that test procedures provide adequate and thorough coverage of what the information system must do prior to test

Implementation
- monitor operation of the information system as scheduled
- conduct audits
- assure version control of existing software and any new or modified software

Verification
- assure SCM of current released software versions
- participate in dry runs of new releases to verify operability and assure expected results
- assure readiness to release the new or modified information system

Operation
- monitor daily operation as needed
- track key metrics (problems, corrective action, etc.); maintain in database as applicable
- note improvements for next go-around

2.7 Business Process Reengineering and Y2K

2.7.1 Year 2000 (Y2K) Problem and Legacy Software

In the last few years, one of the most significant software problems of our time has emerged in what has come to be known as the "Y2K" or Year 2000 problem. This problem concerns what are known as *legacy* programs. *Legacy* programs are software programs that have been in existence for some time, are completely operational today, execute with no problem, but are doomed to fail after the turn of the century. Since many businesses have legacy software that is both "date" and "interest rate" sensitive, it is imperative that such software be fixed during this century. Imagine buying your spouse a $10.00 Christmas gift on Dec. 15, 1999. One month later, about the middle of January, the year 2000, you may wind up in divorce court when your spouse receives a bill for well over $320,000,000.00. This is not as ridiculous as it seems. After midnight Dec. 31, 1999, all computer programs roll the year, symbolized by '99, to the year '00. But the computer does not recognize '00 as the year 2000 and computes interest compounded monthly for every month from the year 1900. That's a whopping 100 years of compounded interest. Loosely applying the rule of 72, at 18 percent interest per year, on a $10.00 purchase, even with round off for simplicity, this comes to well over $320,000,000.00.

The Y2K problem is in the software. The obvious solution is to replace the two-digit year with a four-digit year. But this is not as easy as it seems. Many programs, originally written in COBOL, now exist in executable form only. In many cases the original source code is nonexistent and the original programmers are long gone. Consequently, software engineers may be unable to find the two-digit codes buried throughout their programs. Even if source code exists, how accurately does it agree with the current version of the executable code used in daily practice? The bottom line is that there is much work to do and little time to do it. There are many unfixable programs today that may be put to rest on the last day of this century.

What is worse is that this problem is compounded globally because the Y2K problem permeates all kinds of business software. Consider the financial markets, banks, credit card businesses, anyone who sells on credit, anyone who buys on credit, mortgage institutions, Social Security, Medicare, other government agencies, Government bond issues not yet at maturity, and the list goes on and on. Essentially everyone is at risk. According to Minda Zetlin [6, p. 11], the estimated cost to fix the Y2K problem is in excess of $600 billion worldwide.

The following table, Table 2-1, which can be found on the Internet [7], is a snapshot in time of where the federal government agencies are in terms of meeting the deadline for Y2K compliance.

TABLE 2-1   Y2K Status of Government Agency Compliance (May 15, 1998) [7]

Government Agencies	Number of Systems	Number Compliant	Percent Compliant	No. being Replaced	No. being Repaired	No. being Retired
Agriculture	1080	430	40%	271	317	62
Commerce	472	343	73%	57	72	0
Defense	2,803	812	29%	255	1,566	170
Education	14	4	29%	2	8	0
Energy	411	149	36%	131	119	12
HHS	289	98	434%	62	129	0
HUD	63	31	49%	11	21	0

Interior	91	37	41%	11	43	0
Justice	197	57	29%	10	130	0
Labor	61	21	34%	18	22	0
State	64	24	38%	27	13	0
Transportation	630	237	38%	69	297	27
Treasury	323	125	39%	46	150	2
VA	11	2	18%	0	9	0
AID	7	1	14%	2	4	0
EPA	61	40	66%	5	14	2
FEMA	47	29	62%	11	7	0
GSA	58	39	67%	10	9	0
NASA	158	79	50%	6	69	4
NRC	7	2	29%	2	3	0
NSF	21	10	48%	1	6	4
OPM	118	40	34%	12	64	2
SBA	42	19	45%	0	23	0
SSA	308	284	92%	1	22	1
Total:	**7,336**	**2,913**	**40%**	**1,020**	**3,117**	**286**

2.7.2 SQA and Business Process Reengineering for Y2K

Although not strictly a reengineering issue, the severity of fixing the Y2K problem may be the catalyst for many companies to rethink and reengineer their entire business process. As defined by Hammer and Champy,

> "Reengineering is the fundamental rethinking and radical redesign of business processes to achieve dramatic improvements in critical, contemporary measures of performance, such as cost, quality, service, and speed." [8, p. 32]

Several Y2K companies (that is, companies that provide Y2K solutions, such as Viasoft [9], ZITEL [10], Peoplesoft [10], Keane [10], etc., to name a few) may offer reverse-engineering and reengineering solutions.

Reverse-engineering to fix the Y2K problem is viable if all two-digit date codes can be found in all key programs and the task is completed prior to the year 2000. If this is not viable, which is highly likely for some COBOL legacy programs (where, as noted above, the vulnerable company no longer has in-house expertise and no source code), then reengineering may be a valid alternative solution.

The benefits of reengineering go beyond Y2K and aim at long term market leadership, quality products and services, profitability, and success. It is also worth noting that, because of the high cost associated with fixing Y2K, the added cost for reengineering in this case may be reduced to a non-issue. It is expected that large organizations will spend tens to hundreds of millions of dollars to make their programs Y2K compliant [9]. See Table 14-2 (Chapter 14) for a sample list of tools which reference a representative reengineering tool.

Obviously not all programs will be Y2K compliant. A temporary solution to buy time (about another 60 years) is to change the two-digit date fields to hexadecimal [11]. This may be viable for organizations that need more time, assuming again that all date fields, in whatever form, can be found and fixed.

This opens a new door for SQA. SQA should conduct an internal survey (via a Y2K questionnaire [12]) to determine the need for Y2K compliance. All programs identified should be prioritized as either mission-critical (must be fully operational by the year 2000), necessary (can do without on a temporary basis but must have as soon as possible), or no longer needed. An integrated product team (IPT) may be necessary with SQA as the possible lead. The IPT needs to evaluate potential solutions to include reverse-engineering of existing programs, reusing where it makes sense, making or buying replacement programs, or reengineering the process. The selection of special Y2K-oriented tools also needs consideration. A tool classification scheme for Y2K issues is presented by David Sharon [13]. Also to be decided is whether to implement the solution(s) strictly in-house or to find and contract qualified Y2K specialists—decisions not to be taken lightly. Findings and recommendations then need to be presented to management for final decision and funding of the effort.

For those organizations already in the midst of implementing a Y2K solution, SQA needs to monitor the process to assure strict version control of changes in new software releases. SQA also needs to determine conformance to schedule in meeting Y2K compliant milestones. Finally, SQA must assure that the final Y2K software release duplicates all functions and results of the original programs being replaced.

> For Y2K, SQA personnel must enforce strict *version control* of prior versions and performance versus updated programs and performance. SQA must also monitor the Y2K process for *timeliness,* be it reverse engineering, reengineering, etc.

> For Reengineering, SQA must enforce *Process Control*.

Recommendations (for business process reengineering and Y2K)

SQA top priority: *version control* of software programs and changes.
Second priority: *timeliness* of meeting schedule and milestones.

Requirements
- review current system requirements, states, and modes of operation
- normal operational requirements
- system performance characteristics
- system output
- review degraded modes of operation and recovery procedures
- assure proper tool selection
- baseline existing system software

Design
- assure use of formal reverse-engineering and/or reengineering methodologies for Y2K
- promote peer inspections of reverse-engineered or reengineered design for Y2K
- assure proposed design changes are controlled and documented
- assure that test procedures provide adequate and thorough coverage of system capability for Y2K compliance

Implementation
- monitor Y2K implementation process for *timeliness* against schedule and milestones
- assure version control of existing software and any new or modified software

Verification
- assure SCM of current released software versions and performance results
- verify that results duplicate or exceed results of programs being replaced or superseded.
- verify Y2K compliance (assure performance of Y2K compliant systems using post year 2000 trial dates prior to the year 2000)

Operation
- monitor break-in period for newly released Y2K compliant programs/systems
- track key metrics (problems, corrective action, etc.) to assure desired performance
- maintain database as applicable
- note improvements for next go-around

2.8   SQA and Software Configuration Management

Software configuration management (SCM) (See Chapter 10) is extremely important to all of the categories of software discussed above. SCM is referred to in several of the process phases (requirements through operation) cited for each category. These references highlight the significant impact that SCM processes have throughout the total life cycle. The primary functions of SCM are identification, control, and status accounting. The intent of these functions is to maintain and track changes to the functional, allocated, and product baselines, requirements specifications and other documentation; provide software version descriptions; track change requests, problem reports, and records of resolution; provide configuration control board (CCB) minutes, etc. The role of SQA is to assure that these practices are executed properly throughout the life cycle as necessary.

The role of SCM is of the highest priority when the final software product has been approved and sold to a customer. It is a simple fact of life that software is subject to change. Changes required after a product has been developed are of the highest concern. This concern is multifaceted:

- any rework is costly [14, p. 40]
- resources spent on rework are lost to new projects
- if changes are not identified and controlled accurately, the version or versions of software that exist will become untraceable due to unknown, unaccounted fixes
- the ripple effect due to a single change can be very time-consuming to trace and, if all of the secondary affects are not accounted for, they probably will show up as future changes
- even if a good SCM function exists, a system can still diverge when subjected to ever increasing numbers of changes

The role of SCM is critical when environments of extreme change exist. The divergent system is the worst case, in which each change begets two or more new changes. When this occurs, closure can never be obtained until the number of new changes starts to decrease as the program progresses. When such a situation exists, SQA can conduct Pareto analysis and trend analyses to determine the reason(s) for the increasing number of changes. Additionally, SQA personnel must also assure that each new correction actually resolves a known problem and that the impact of the change on other system functions is traced, tested, and verified to eliminate or minimize any ripple effect.

The importance of doing the job right during development is never more obvious then when things go wrong in production or in the operations and maintenance phase. A primary goal of SQA, then, is to make unnecessary and to prevent downstream changes by assuring that early developmental life cycle processes find the problems. This is where peer inspections come into play.

If changes are required early in the life cycle of a software product's development, it is SQA's responsibility to assure that an adequate SCM function is in place at that time to control those changes from inception to closure. These changes then are to be identified, controlled, and subject to status accounting by the SCM function. Regardless of when such changes occur, all changes must be individually approved by the CCB.

Changes should be logged and maintained as part of the software library. The role of SQA is twofold here. First, SQA should audit library control procedures to assure that required change reports, versions of software, documentation, etc. are identified and controlled as part of the library function. This also includes how library items will be accessed. Second, SQA should audit the contents of the library to assure that all versions, baselines, and revisions are up-to-date and that library records reflect the latest status of its contents. This is a process compliance issue.

2.8.1 Y2K Configuration Control

As noted in Section 2.7 above, the key to success in implementing Y2K compliance is to measure the performance and output of the proposed compliant program(s) against the original baseline performance.

This requires strict version control of all changes to each new software release and strict monitoring and documenting of variances in performance. The Y2K problem may be the ultimate challenge for SCM. There can be no deviations in performance regardless of function changeover and there is essentially no time relief.

2.9 SQA and Software Maintenance

Software maintenance, defined in Chapter 1, includes fixing software, enhancing software, or adapting software after delivery. Studies conducted by Bennet Lientz uncovered three major software quality problems related to software maintenance :

1. Adequacy of application system design specifications.
2. Quality of original programming of the application system.
3. Quality of application system documentation. [15, p. 277]

These problems must be corrected prior to any maintenance activity. Therefore, according to Lientz, the SQA person must investigate all three problem areas to ensure system adequacy before maintenance activity proceeds. An aspect of business software (Section 2.6) is that most businesses have resident system software specialists who "maintain" the system software for the local computer environment. Here, "maintain" means to investigate local system software problems and inform and work with the manufacturer's personnel to achieve resolution of problems. "Maintain" also means to know enough to answer local system software inquiries. Lastly, "maintain" means the traditional software maintenance of correcting or enhancing the local, unique version of the system software.

These activities of the system software specialists make it clear that the SQA person must be primarily concerned with control (SCM) and testing (error discovery) of the system software under maintenance. As discussed in Section 2.8 (SCM), all maintenance changes must be approved by formal configuration control board (CCB) action. If a CCB does not exist, it is in the interests of quality that one be formed to provide adequate review, analysis, and approval of the change. This must occur to formally accept any rework, regression test, and verification of the change when implemented.

In the event that major requirements or design changes are required during the maintenance phase, the software modification to the system should be treated the same as during development with the exception that formal change control is required. Note, during maintenance the customer often presides over the CCB. As mentioned at the start of this section, software documentation often is a major problem in maintenance. Consequently, SQA personnel must review the affected configured documents to assure that the approved requirements and design changes are fully documented in the approved updated specifications and that the new version of the modified software is correctly identified. Lastly, reviews and audits are to be conducted by SQA personnel as in development to cover all items affected by the proposed changes.

During maintenance, SQA assumes the role of keeping records of operational failures and associated downtime whenever software failures occur. This task is particularly worthwhile if SQA performed the task of modeling software reliability during the development stages, as recommended for mission-critical software (Section 2.3) and real-time software (Section 2.4). SQA should document and compare actual reliability results against reliability model predictions. Actual results can be used to fine tune the reliability model for the kind of software product the company is most likely to develop on a continual basis.

To jump start this task, SQA should review the field report for any changes required to capture the failure data for software problems. During operation, these incoming field reports would be used to separate hardware and software problems. For software, SQA would identify the particular software function at fault (an item that should be recorded on the incoming field report). In some cases the failed item is a spare board. The software on the board should then be identified to permit follow-up evaluation. All this is an attempt to capture and define the actual operational reliability of the system software. Reliability items should include parameters such as the following: Mean Time Between Software Failures (any failure), Most Prevalent Software Function(s) That Failed, Downtime Due To Software Failures, Corrective Action Taken, Prevention Needed. A histogram plot would readily show the frequency of the most prevalent software failures and the total number of failures for each software function over time. These records would be extremely beneficial in explaining the software reliability of the product. Over the long haul, trends could be established to determine where improvements are needed and to show where improvements have been made.

2.9.1 Y2K and Maintenance

For the Y2K problem (See Section 2.7 above), maintenance can be difficult. It is not uncommon for legacy program operators and specialists to practice partial maintenance during normal operation. In other words, only a part of the system is subject to maintenance. The part of the system not subject to maintenance literally has little or no visibility. What's worse is that this non-maintained part has been left alone for so long, chances are no one currently working the job has knowledge of how it does what it does. This makes it all the more complicated to perform assessments and reverse-engineering activities needed to make the system Y2K compliant.

In this regard, automated tools can play a significant role in maintaining and controlling the conduct of Y2K maintenance activities. These tools, as noted by Newcomb and Scott [16], should support a four-phase adaptive maintenance process: Inspection (date domain modeling/searching), Assessment (impact of change), Correction (make compliant), and Test (verify compliance). Adaptive maintenance "involves changes to software necessitated by modifications in the software's operational environment." [16] Newcomb and Scott originally developed a set of Y2K maintenance tools for COBOL programs. At the time of this writing, they are in the process of converting the tool set to be used on programs written in Ada®, FORTRAN, Natural, Jovial, and CMS-2.

2.10 SQA and IV&V

IV&V (see Chapter 1) activities are to independently verify, validate, and certify that the products produced comply with approved requirements and satisfy customer needs. In an Internal IV&V (I2V&V) team the contractor/developer takes on the role of IV&V agent.

IV&V was only discussed in Section 2.3 for the category of mission-critical software. This was done primarily since DoD is normally the agent requiring IV&V, if at all. A major thrust of the IV&V team is to trace all A-Specification requirements to a method of verification and validation. These methods include inspection, analysis, demonstration, and test. Note, for purposes of this discussion analysis includes simulation and modeling. All requirements are accounted for normally in the form of a very detailed Verification Cross Reference Matrix (VCRI). The VCRI traces each A-Spec requirement to its assigned method of verification. The IV&V team then has responsibility to verify each requirement either individually or by group as applicable.

   If IV&V is imposed, SQA personnel would review the VCRI and prepare to monitor IV&V testing when conducted by the IV&V agent. The testable requirements would be traced to test procedures, which are also subject to SQA review and formal approval prior to test. SQA may participate in tracing the requirements to test procedures. SQA auditors would then witness the test to verify the results. SQA personnel would ensure that each test was repeatable and that each test followed the approved test procedure. Each entry in the test procedure is checked to status the expected result versus the actual result, with a note made of any discrepancies or redlines.

2.11   Summary

The question of how software quality assurance fits in to the world of development and maintenance has been answered to some degree in this chapter. The role of SQA has been discussed in terms of the different stress points one would find for the different categories of software presented. Although other categories of software exist, the five categories selected should cover a broad enough spectrum to assist the SQA person in defining the primary areas of focus for their particular type of software program. Table 2-2 indicates the degrees of SQA emphasis required for the different categories of software programs presented in this chapter.

TABLE 2-2   SQA Emphasis

Categories of Software	Area of Emphasis for SQA	SQA Attention to	Related Areas of Emphasis
1. Operating Systems Software:	Primary - Configuration Control Secondary - Dependability	Baseline Control Version Control Change Control Alpha/Beta Trials	Maintain Customer Focus Track Maintenance Problems Assure Marketing Claims Prevent © Infringement
2. Mission-Critical Software:	Primary - Software Reliability	Requirements Definition Baseline Control Rapid Prototyping Early Tradeoff Studies Promote Peer Inspections	Monitor Sizing Budgets Monitor Software Growth Support IV&V as Necessary Model SW Reliability Check Spares Impact on SW Evaluate Training Needs

3. Real-Time Software:	Primary - Efficiency
	Secondary - Software Reliability
		Requirements Definition
		Baseline Control
		Rapid Prototyping
		Early Tradeoff Studies
		Promote Peer Inspections
			Monitor NTE Timing Budgets
			Track Throughout:
			  - Processing, IO channels,
			  - Concurrent Processing,
			  - Interrupt Processing
			Model SW Reliability

4. Interactive Software: • developer of	Primary - Responsiveness and Presentation	Requirements Definition Early Tradeoff Studies Promote Peer Inspections	Assure User Satisfaction Assure Human Factors Assess Need for Training

• user of	Primary -Control	Assure Version Control
		Assure COTS Inventory
			Assure Procedures:
			  - Prevent © Infringement
			  - Assure Licensed COTS SW
			  - Assure Vendor Guarantees
			  - Prevent Info. Export
			    Violation

5. Business Software:	Primary - Accuracy of Records
	Secondary - Operational
	        Dependability
		Audit for Detail
		Certify All Releases/Mods
		Assure SCM &
		  Version Control
			Assure Backup Operation
			Assure Recovery of System
			Maintain Metrics for Trends

6. Business Process Reengineer. and Y2K:	Primary (Reengineering)
	  - Process Control
	Primary (Y2K) -VersionControl
	Secondary - Timeliness
		Monitor Radical
		  Improvement,
		Apply Metrics to Evaluate
		  Process
			Business Unit Relevance
			Grow the Business
			SEI Advancement per SEI
			  CMM
			Value Added Beyond Y2K

References

1. Mandell, Steven L., *Computers and Data Processing* (St. Paul: West Publishing Co., 1979).

2. Becker, Louise G., "Military Computers in Transition: Standards and Strategy." In: *Concepts, The Journal of Defense Systems Acquisition Management*, Vol. 5, No. 4, Moore, Robert W., ed., (Fort Belvoir, VA: Defense Systems Management College, 1982).

3. Glass, Robert L., *Real-time Software*. (Englewood Cliffs, NJ: Prentice Hall, 1983).

4. Wirth, Niklaus, "Toward a Discipline of Real-time Programming." In: Glass, Robert L., op. cit.

5. Nielsen, Jakob, "Let's Ask the User." In: *IEEE Software*, May/June 1997, pp. 110–111.

6. Zetlin, Minda, "Countdown To Trouble." In: *Management Review*, The American Management Association, May 1997, p. 11.

7. U.S. Office of Management and Budget, "5th Quarterly Report—Progress of Year 2000 Conversion," May 15, 1998. Sponsored by the Chief Information Officer's

(CIO) Committee on Year 2000. Maintained by the General Services Administration's (GSA) Office of Governmentwide policy; Internet address: http://www.cio.gov/598rpt.html

8. Hammer, Michael, and Champy, James, *Reengineering the Corporation* (Harper Collins Publishers, 1993).

9. Vecchio, Dale, "A Strategy of Time" (A WHITE PAPER. (Supplement to *Software Magazine*) (Viasoft, Inc., 1997).

10. Smith Barney, Inc., The YTK Index of 18 stocks—listed daily on the American Stock Exchange. (May 9, 1997).

11. Keegan, Robert R., "Y2K Fix for the Little Guy." In: *IEEE COMPUTER*, Vol. 10, No. 7, p. 9, July 1997.

12. "Y2K Questionnaire." In: *Consortium Quarterly*, The Software Productivity Consortium, p. 14, December, 1996.

13. Sharon, David, "Year 2000 Tool Classification Scheme." In: *IEEE Software*, July/August 1997, pp. 107–111.

14. Boehm, Barry W., *Software Engineering Economics* (Englewood Cliffs, NJ: Prentice Hall, 1981).

15. Lientz, Bennet P., "Issues in Software Maintenance." In: *Computing Surveys*, Vol. 15, No. 3 (September 1983).

16. Newcomb, Philip H., and Scott, Melvin, "Year 2000 Inspection, Assessment, Correction, and Testing." In: *CrossTalk The Journal of Defense Software Engineering*, pp. 10–14, November 1996.

General References

Burrell, Claude W., and Ellsworth, Leon W., *Quality Data Processing* (Tenafly, NJ: Burrell Ellsworth Associates, 1982).

Glass, Robert L., *Software Reliability Guidebook* (Englewood Cliffs, NJ: Prentice Hall, 1979).

Perry, William E., *Effective Methods of EDP Quality Assurance* (Wellesley, MA: Q.E.D. Information Sciences, Inc., 1981).

Wright, Bruce J., *How to Audit and Control Computer Systems* (Sandy, UT: Wright & Associates, 1981).

Fagan, Michael, "Productivity Improvement Through Defect-Free Development." Handout at the American Society for Quality (ASQ) sponsored presentation, Baltimore MD, 26 March 1997.

## CHAPTER 3

Software Quality Lessons from the Quality Experts

G. Gordon Schulmeyer
PYXIS Systems International, Inc.

"Quality is never an accident; it is always the result of intelligent effort."

— *John Ruskin*

3.1 Introduction

The time has come for personnel performing software quality assurance to apply the teachings of the quality experts. What important lessons learned in the past are the eminent quality experts telling us? The results achieved in Japan by following the lead of such significant quality thinkers literally mandate that the western world turn toward the example set by the Japanese to learn about quality.

In general, the quality concepts put to use in Japan have not been accepted in the western world, though the trend is changing. Identifying the quality concepts that the Japanese have capitalized on so successfully and applying them to computer software development is a significant step that needs to be taken.

The principles of the quality experts generally have not been applied to software development. The issue of applying other people's approaches (i.e., the experts) to a different problem (i.e., software) could be raised and should be addressed. The generic nature of "quality" production is applicable whether the product be automobiles, stereos, or computer software.

Although production lines—being machine-intensive, repetitive, and resulting in many units—and computer software—being people-intensive, intellectual, and resulting in one software system—do differ; the transition of quality principles is reasonable. A fundamental principle of transition training is learning from other people's experience, and so the software development and software quality assurance personnel may learn from the quality principles covered in this chapter.

This chapter looks to the works of Kaoru Ishikawa, Joseph M. Juran, Yoji Akao, W. Edwards Deming, Genichi Taguchi, Shigeo Shingo, and Philip Crosby. Certainly, in the United States the trio of Deming, Juran and Crosby are the real leaders. [1, p. 47] This trio of gurus seem to agree on certain basic points. They believe that until top management gets permanently involved in quality, nothing will work. They set little store in robots, automation, and other gadgetry. They have little use for quality circles except as an adjunct to other methods. [2, p. 30] The fundamental message of all three gurus is basically the same: Commit to quality improvement throughout your entire organization. Attack the system rather than the employee. Strip down the work process—whether it be the manufacturing of a product or customer service —to find and eliminate problems that prevent quality. Identify your customer, internal or external, and satisfy that customer's requirements in the work process and the finished product. Eliminate waste, instill pride and teamwork, and create an atmosphere of innovation for continued and permanent quality improvement. [1, p. 48] This chapter highlights some major points from these U. S. quality experts and their Japanese counterparts with conclusions applicable to software development.

The works of these contributors each contain important quality messages that are applied to software development. Typically, quality applications to software development have been supplied by software specialists. However, the concepts available that address quality production must now be used for the production of quality software. The definition of quality quoted in Chapter 1 from Philip Crosby is: to conform to requirements. [3] The logical extension of that definition to software quality is: to conform to software requirements and to provide useful services. [4] This parallels the definition provided in Chapter 1 ("the fitness for use of the software product"), although it is somewhat more narrow in scope.

First is a look to Japan with the six major features of quality as seen by Kaoru Ishikawa. Second is Joseph M. Juran's three ways for the western world to meet the Japanese quality challenge. This is followed by a look at Quality Function Deployment (QFD), commonly called the "House of Quality," of Dr. Yoji Akao, as applied to software by Dr. Tadashi Yoshizawa.

Then, we review the statistical methods to achieve quality control provided by W. Edwards Deming, along with an application of his 14 points to software development. The goal of reduced variability in production of Genichi Taguchi through online quality control and off-line quality control are covered. The zero quality control methods of Shigeo Shingo with source inspections and the *poka-yoke* system are applied to software development. Finally, the implementation concepts successfully incorporated at International Telephone & Telegraph (ITT) by Philip Crosby are discussed.

Figure 3-1 is a simple diagram, borrowed from Joseph M. Juran, that graphically portrays what all the excitement is about concerning quality.

This chart, which compares results for Japan and the western world since 1950, illustrates the impact of quality taught by the experts. Japan, originally behind the western world in quality, took heed of the quality concepts and principles proposed by the quality experts. The western world had been the quality leader, but ignored the quality concepts and fell behind. This is further amplified by the fact that from 1970 to 1980 the U. S. share of world high technology exports (excluding agricultural chemicals and plastics and synthetic materials) dropped an average of 3.5 percent, according to the Department of Commerce.

The chart shows us that Japan listened to these quality experts for management concepts, while the western world did not. For software in the 1990s the western world (led by the United States) has a relatively superior position in software quality similar to that which existed in the 1960s for overall product quality. The point of this paper is that as cost and importance of software development increases through the years, the western world does not want a duplication of the relative product quality loss in software. Therefore, the software development community must heed the warnings from the past and follow the advice of the quality experts.

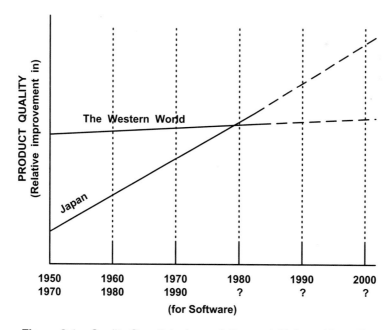

Figure 3-1   Quality Growth in Japan & the west. [Adapted from 5]

3.2   Kaoru Ishikawa

To explain the quality "miracle" in Japan, Kaoru Ishikawa gives six features of quality work there.

- Companywide quality control
- Top management quality control audit
- Industrial education and training
- Quality Circles (QC) activities
- Application of statistical methods
- Nationwide quality control promotion activities [6]

Companywide quality control means that all departments and all levels of personnel are engaged in systematic work guided by written quality policies from upper management. The consequence of this point to software quality is that the software developers are committed to producing a quality product guided by software development management ("upper management") trying to achieve the same objective. This is how to build quality into the software product.

A quality control audit team of executives visits each department to uncover and eliminate any obstacles to the productivity and quality goals. Normally, this auditing of software is placed in the hands of the software quality experts, but periodically an executive audit team is required to evaluate software quality. Directed conversations with the users of the software product, software quality management, and workers, and the software development management and workers will uncover much that the executive audit team could act upon.

Education and training in quality control must be given to everybody in all departments and at all levels, because companywide quality control requires participation by everyone involved. The initial training has to take place within the software quality assurance organization so that software quality personnel, per Kaoru Ishikawa's advice, will "train ourselves before we are fit to train others." Then, the quality organization can provide a concentrated, intensive software quality training program to be attended by software developers and their managers. This is a necessary, but not sufficient, way to develop quality software. Education about how to develop "quality" software solidifies the awareness and discipline necessary for meeting that objective. The teachers in this arena should be the software quality personnel who also carry out the evaluation functions on a daily basis. Software quality personnel as the teachers bring uniformity to the effort by providing knowledge common to all quality software development.

A Quality Circle (QC) is "a small group (which met) voluntarily to perform quality control within the workshop to which they belonged." [7] Quality circles originated in Japan in the early 1960s as part of a drive for quality and a critical economic need to overcome a reputation for cheap, poorly made goods. W. Edwards Deming and J. M. Juran introduced the concepts of statistical quality control and quality management to the Japanese. Dr. Ishikawa, merging these two disciplines, created a system called quality control circles. In 1961, a series of exploratory meetings were sponsored by the Union of Japanese Scientists and Engineers (JUSE) under the leadership of Dr. Ishikawa, an engineering professor at the University of Tokyo. The objective was to develop a way for hands-on workers to contribute to the company. In 1962, the first circle was registered with JUSE, and a total of 20 circles were registered and operating by the end of the year. Since that time, QC techniques have been taught to and applied by the entire Japanese work force. Today, there are an estimated one million quality circles in Japan with over ten million members. [8, p. 5]

The QC traditionally has been applied to the manufacturing process, and recently has been used to enhance some management and professional (engineering) quality. The software developers could use the QC as another tool to guide the production of quality software. The QC provides a forum to discuss software production problems.

The QC frequently uses Ishikawa diagrams to highlight influential factors. Ishikawa diagrams are usually drawn to identify control points, the ingredients, including people, materials, machines, organization, processes, etc. [9] Using Ishikawa's "fishbone" cause and effect diagram provides a useful tool to find the cause(s) of the software production problem(s) and the resolution(s) to it(them).

Figure 3-2 is a sample Ishikawa diagram that explores the possible causes of a slipped software development schedule. Each of the probable causes is written onto the "fishbone" in relation to the major control points of manpower, machines, methods, and materials (the four Ms). The group then reviews all the possible causes in detail to determine the most likely ones. Those which are most likely are circled and receive the appropriate attention. In the sample "insufficient development computers" is the most likely cause of software development being behind schedule.

Statistical methods for quality control include the Pareto analysis, cause and effect diagram, stratification, check sheet, histogram, scatter diagram, and the Shewhart control chart. Thomas McCabe has advocated the use of Pareto analysis to software quality techniques, which is further explored in Chapter 11. Suffice it to say that these various statistical concepts were so influential in Japan through the guidance of W. Edwards Deming that they brought about "the quality revolution." Each of these statistical methods may provide help to the software developer and a few are explored in the Deming section in this paper. Since the details of these methods are sufficiently covered in various textbooks, they are not covered here.

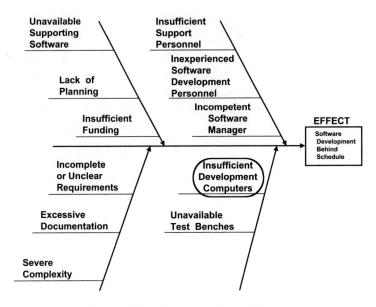

Figure 3-2   Sample Ishikawa Diagram.

Nationwide quality promotion activities peak in Japan in November—Quality Month—when the Deming Prize is awarded. The Deming Prize is used to advertise the company's products because it instills such a high degree of customer confidence that the consumer can be sure of a quality product. Why not stimulate quality interest in software by awarding an annual award for special quality achievement in software? Why not stimulate quality interest more locally by providing incentives in contracts for measurable software quality achievements? This type of awareness continually reinforces the quality concepts for software developers.

3.3   Joseph M. Juran

To meet the challenges of the solid Japanese campaign for quality achievement shown in Figure 3-1, Joseph M. Juran prescribes the following:

- Structured annual improvements in quality
- A massive quality-oriented training program
- Upper management leadership of the company's approach to product quality [5]

In the early 1950s the Japanese faced a grim reality. No alarm-signal is as insistent to industrial managers as inability to sell the product. Since their major limitation was quality, not price, they directed their revolution at improving quality. They learned how to improve quality, became proficient at it, and are now reaping the rewards of their efforts. Their managers are equally at home in meeting current goals and in making improvements for the future. [5]

This story of the Japanese electronics industry with transistor radios, for example, illustrates the dedication to annual improvements in quality that exists in Japan. The results of this commitment are shown in Figure 3-1.

There is a grim reality in software development that quality needs immediate attention and can stand improvement yearly. Too many software systems never meet their requirements, either because development overruns financial or time budgets or because the user is unsatisfied. Software management must plan for and make this same total commitment to quality software improvements from within. Software managers must not only be technically aware, but they also need to be committed to annual improvements in quality.

To accomplish these annual quality improvements Joseph M. Juran advises that a team:

- study the symptoms of the defects and failures
- develop a theory on the causes of these symptoms
- test the theory until the cause(s) is known
- stimulate remedial action by the appropriate department(s) [5]

Software quality assurance personnel are beginning to identify and categorize the defects in the software (see Chapters 9 and 20). As error identification matures, the steps required for annual quality improvements can be applied to software development.

Defects can be separated into those that are worker-controllable and those that are management-controllable. The latter are defects that cannot possibly be avoided by workers. Whether a certain defect should be regarded as a worker-controllable defect or a management-controllable defect depends on the extent to which the following conditions are met:

- the worker knows what he is to do
- the worker knows the result of his own work
- the worker has the means of controlling the result

If all three conditions are met and the work is still defective, the worker is responsible. However, if one or more of the conditions has not been met, this is a management-controllable defect. [10]

W. Edwards Deming made two relevant points on the responsibility for defects which apply to software development (substitute software developer for "worker"):

> To call to the attention of a worker a careless act, in a climate of general carelessness, is a waste of time and can only generate hard feelings, because the condition of general carelessness belongs to everybody and is the fault of management, not of any one worker, nor of all workers. [11]

Many managers assume they have solved all the problems once they have brought worker-controllable defects under control. They are, in fact, just ready to tackle the most important problems of variation, namely, the *management-controllable* causes. [12]

During software development many worker-controllable defects can be controlled by software developers. However, there is a wide class of defects in software because the developer does not know what he/she is supposed to do. This occurs because of the inevitable intertwining of specification and implementation. In more direct wording the problems are that during the software development (the implementation), the requirements (the specification) are continually being changed. Many times the software developer is continually engineering something new, without the benefit of frozen requirements.

Contrary to claims that the specification should be completed before implementation begins ("worker knows what he is supposed to do"), there are two observations that the two processes must be intertwined. First, limitations of available implementation technology may force a specification change. That is, the hardware hosting the computer software may require software work-arounds because of hardware limitations. Second, implementation choices may suggest augmentations to the original specification. That is, as more is accomplished, more is learned, making it reasonable to augment with a better approach than what was originally specified.

It is only because the already-fixed and yet-to-be-done portions of this multistep system development process have occurred unobserved and unrecorded that the multistep nature of this process has not been more apparent. [13] This is especially true of the large software development for prototype systems where the entire system is pushing technology of hardware and software. In most of these systems the hardware does not even exist to test the software, but is under concurrent development with the software.

That "the worker (software developer) knows the result of his own work" in software can be very immediate and sometimes humbling for the worker who made a "stupid mistake." For he/she receives the results immediately from the computer exactly as he/she commanded, whether correctly or incorrectly. On the other hand are the subtle errors that are not found for years. This is a worker-controllable defect, but one where "the worker does not know the result of his/her own work." Quality software development must continually resolve to remove this type of error.

In software development "the worker has the means of influencing the result." Assuming a reasonable task assignment, the worker is directly involved in the production of the result (computer program) and is the first to see that result. Consider as one example a situation where the worker looses that influence, for example, when the computer is unavailable. It is usually not worker-controllable to make the computer available.

To summarize this discussion of the annual quality improvements suggested by Joseph M. Juran it is clear that software developers must first know where they stand before setting up a program for improvement. In this specialty area to know where one stands from a quality viewpoint is essential. From a quality viewpoint this means that the defects (errors) must be identified and the causes determined. Only when this is accomplished is movement toward quality improvement possible.

To date, selective training in quality sciences in the western world has been largely confined to members of the specialized quality departments, which constitute only about five percent of the managerial and specialists forces in the companies. In contrast, the Japanese have trained close to 100 percent of both their managers and specialists in the quality sciences.

This massive quality-oriented training program carries the education and training nostrum of Kaoru Ishikawa to its logical conclusion. Joseph M. Juran points out that common quality training needs to include:

- the universal sequence of events for improving quality and reducing quality-related costs (creation of beneficial change)
- the universal feedback loop for control (prevention of adverse change)
- tundamentals of data collection and analysis [5]

Particular training for software developers in quality disciplines should include design reviews, reliability analysis, maintainability analysis, failure modes and effects analysis, life cycle costing, quality cost analysis, concepts of inspection for design and code, etc.

An example of Japanese upper management commitment to quality is an observation made by Lennart Sandholm to the International Quality Control conference held in Tokyo in 1978. Sandholm noted that almost half of the Japanese participants at the conference were from upper management—presidents, general managers, division heads, and directors. At conferences held in Europe or the United States almost all participants are from the quality profession—quality assurance engineers, reliability engineers, quality managers, etc. There are few senior managers. [14]

W. Edwards Deming also observed that in Japan top people in the companies took hold of the problems of production and quality. All the reports showing successful implementation of quality principles quoted in his paper were written by men with the rank of president of the company, managing director, or chairman of the board. [15]

Dr. Deming said, "All of top management came, not only to listen, but to work. They had already seen evidence from their own engineers that what you've got is this chain reaction. As you improve the quality, costs go down. You can lower the price. You capture the market with quality and price. Americans do not understand it. Americans think that as you improve quality, you increase your costs." [16]

The need for upper management leadership stems from the need to create major changes, two of which include annual improvements in quality and a massive quality-oriented training program already discussed above. The recommended step for western upper management is to perform a comprehensive companywide quality audit to understand what needs to be done.

An organizational weakness in the western world is the <u>large</u>, central Quality Department with numerous functions of quality planning, engineering, coordination, auditing, inspection, and test. In Japan most of these quality-oriented functions are carried out by line personnel (who have the necessary training to carry out such functions). The Japanese do have quality departments, but they are small in terms of personnel and they perform a limited array of functions: broad planning, audit, and consulting services. Upper management quality audits evaluate the effectiveness of the organization and only upper management has the authority to institute the necessary changes.

For the software development process, senior software management is the upper management. The commitment, then, of senior software management to producing quality software is necessary to accomplish that objective. Also, putting responsibility for software quality in the software development department is a correct posture for senior software management to enforce. The most obvious benefit of this posture is the close awareness of software quality brought to the software development organization.

3.4   Yoji Akao

In the early 1970s, Dr. Yoji Akao performed the first applications of Quality Function Deployment (QFD) in Japan to address the issue of meeting all customer requirements; i.e., making the customer happy. To accomplish this he devised a matrix of customer requirements versus technical product specifications; that when portrayed had a "roof" appearance to the matrix, hence the popular name of "House of Quality." Shortly after Dr. Akao's development of the tools and techniques of QFD, Dr. Tadashi Yoshizawa applied QFD to software. [17, p. 1] Software QFD is a front-end requirements solicitation technique, adaptable to any software engineering methodology, that quantifiably solicits and defines critical customer requirements. [18, p. 42]

QFD provides voice to the user, which then should provide views from three user or customer perspectives (known as Kano):

1. What the users can verbally express (normal requirements),
2. What they silently take for granted they will get (expected requirements), and
3. What the developers can anticipate will truly excite the users (exciting requirements).

This, in turn, has the following effects:

- Increases user communication
- Identifies critical success factors
- Prioritizes user influence
- Requirements traceability
- Prioritizes features and functions
- Reinforces front-end emphasis
- Identifies release candidates
- Provides basis for schedule reduction [19, pp. 51, 52]

QFD is quite different from traditional quality systems, which aim at minimizing negative quality (such as defects). With these systems the best you can get is zero defects—which is not good enough. The absence of a negative does not make a positive. In addition to minimizing defects, we must also maximize positive quality— that is, value. Just because there is nothing wrong with the software does not mean there is anything right with it from the customer's perspective. It does not mean it has any value to the customer. [17, p. 2]

It is significant that all of the organizations that utilize software QFD also use quality policies based on TQM in other areas of the organization. [18, p. 45]

3.5 W. Edwards Deming

W. Edwards Deming is the guiding consultant for the application of statistical methods to quality control as laid out by Walter A. Shewhart. The Japanese Union of Scientists and Engineers (JUSE)'s Board of Directors established the Deming prize to repay Deming for his friendship and kindness. [20, p. 37] Deming declared:

(The) economic and social revolution, which took hold in Japan, upset in fifteen years the economy of the world, and shows what can be accomplished by serious study and adoption of statistical methods and statistical logic in industry, at all levels from the top downward. The statistical control of quality is the application of statistical principles and techniques in all stages of production, maintenance, and service, directed toward the economic satisfaction of demand. [15]

Statistics have been proven to have wide application in many different aspects of business, which would lead one to believe that there are many different statistical theories. However, Dr. Deming cleared up this point:

Rather than a separate and distinct theory for probability for process-control, another theory for acceptance sampling, another for reliability, another for problems of estimation, another for design of experiment, another for testing materials, another for design of studies for statistics, another for engineering, there is instead one statistical theory. [12]

This statistical theory may be applied in many ways to software development. Some proven statistical methods for software are covered next.

This body of statistical knowledge has a variety of applications to the production of quality software. *An Introduction to Software Quality Control* [21] by Chin-Kuei Cho compares a statistical sampling method for testing of software to a statistical sampling method for manufactured products. It is usually impossible to test every input to a computer program. By using Dr. Cho's sampling method a broad range of input values *never previously considered* can be evaluated. Chin-Kuei Cho further discusses these concepts in Chapter 19 of this *Handbook*.

The analysis of errors either for type of error or cause of error will help control errors. An accepted method of error analysis in software quality assurance is the use of the *inspection technique*. Both design and code error types are categorized in a post-inspection analysis which leads to a determination of the cause of the error. James Dobbins covers the direction and details of this method in Chapter 9 of this *Handbook*.

The statistical technique called seeding models covered in Chapter 20 helps to estimate the total number of errors actually in the computer program. This technique helps to baseline the defects in the software so that quality improvements can be made.

Important observations made by W. Edwards Deming:

Mr. Harold Dodge of Bell Telephone Labs said, "You can not inspect quality into a product." He meant that you must build quality: you must make the product so that it has quality in it, if you want quality. Quality is not built by making a great number of articles, hoping that some of them will be good, and then sorting out the bad ones. [12]

Even 100 percent inspection using automatic testing machines doesn't guarantee quality. It's too late—the quality is already there. [22, p. Q31]

These remarks apply directly to the production of quality software. The test and evaluation phase of software development is too late to retrofit quality into the software. The software has to be built with quality foremost from the beginning.

In addition to the statistical knowledge, W. Edwards Deming professes that everyone learn a common method of attacking and describing problems. This commonality of method is essential if people from different parts of the company are to work together on quality improvement. The method is referred to as the P-D-C-A approach (Plan-Do-Check-Analyze and Act), and is usually represented as the Deming Circle (see Figure 3-3).

When the president visits the various operations of the company to discuss their performance, he/she comes prepared to discuss intelligently how well each operation is doing and what can be done to improve the system by reading the P-D-C-A information ahead of time. This approach should be contrasted with the usual "management by exception" approach under which, when things go wrong, the manager then tries to figure out what is wrong and what to do about it. [6]

A significant step can be taken when senior software management use the Deming Circle in conjunction with the software development cycle so that each development phase is subject to the P-D-C-A approach. This method focuses attention as the development proceeds and so allows time to "act" when required.

"Plan - Do - Check - Analysis / Act"

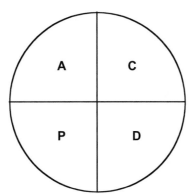

Figure 3-3　The Deming Circle.

This Deming Circle has been used by the Software Engineering Institute as a model for a method for continuous software process improvement using the Capability Maturity Model. This model is called IDEAL, an acronym for Initiating, Diagnosing, Establishing, Acting, and Leveraging. [23, p. 81]

The quality approach of Deming is a management approach for continuous improvement of quality. Richard Zultner has adapted Deming's 14 points for management, seven deadly diseases, and obstacles to quality to software development. Table 3-1 contains the Fourteen Points for Software Development, Table 3-2 contains the Seven "Deadly Diseases" for Software Managers, and Table 3-3 contains the Obstacles to Software Quality.

The following common principles drawn from Deming's fourteen points are being applied in excellent companies:

1. Recognize the entire work force as thinking people, not just management, but everyone.
2. Encourage software developers to identify errors, propose solutions and solve problems in the work place. In other words follow Dr. Deming's advice and DRIVE OUT FEAR.
3. Promote teamwork by eliminating the "we vs. they" attitude; such as, between coders and testers. In a typical organization, management and the employees are divided into two camps—stop that.
4. Make everyone a shareholder in the future of the company, which seems to be a guiding principle in the success of Microsoft.
5. Establish "pride" in workmanship and products.
6. Concentrate on prevention. [24, pp. 1465, 1466]

Deming's point 4 states, "End the practice of awarding business on price tag alone." When awarding business based solely on the price tag, other important "rules of nature," such as quality and schedule, are ignored. If consumers made every purchase based on the lowest price, they might soon go broke repairing and replacing piles of cheap, shoddy merchandise. As consumers, people consciously or subconsciously base their buying decisions on a tradeoff between quality and price. Shouldn't the software products purchased by businesses and governments also be purchased based on such a tradeoff? [25]

Dr. Deming says that it is a bad supposition that it is only necessary to meet specifications. For example, Zultner relates that a programmer learns, after she finishes the job, that she programmed very well the specifications as delivered to her, but that they were deficient. If she had only known the purpose of the program, she could have done it right for the purpose, even though the specifications were deficient. [26]

Table 3-1   The Fourteen Points for Software Managers [28]

1. Create constancy of purpose for the *improvement* of systems and service, with the aim to become excellent, satisfy users, and provide jobs.

2. Adopt the new philosophy. We are in a new age of software engineering and project management. Software managers must awaken to the challenge, learn their responsibilities, and take on leadership for change.

3. Cease dependence on mass inspection (especially testing) to achieve quality. Reduce the need for inspection on a mass basis by building quality into the system in the first place. Inspection is not the answer. It is too late and unreliable—it does not produce quality.

4. End the practice of awarding business on price alone. *Minimize total cost.* Move toward a single supplier for any one item or service, making them a partner in a long-term relationship of loyalty and trust.

5. Constantly and forever improve the system development process, to improve quality and productivity, and thus constantly decrease the time and cost of systems. Improving quality is not a one-time effort.

6. Institute training on the job. Everyone must be well trained, as knowledge is essential for improvement.

7. Institute leadership. It is a manger's job to help their people and their systems do a better job. Supervision of software managers is in need of an overhaul, as is supervision of professional staff.

8. Drive out fear, so that everyone may work effectively. Management should be held responsible for faults of the organization and environment.

9. Break down barriers between areas. *People must work as a team.* They must foresee and prevent problems during systems development and use.

10. Eliminate slogans, exhortations, and targets that ask for zero defects, and new levels of productivity. Slogans do not build quality systems.

11. Eliminate numerical quotas and goals. *Substitute leadership.* Quotas and goals (such as schedules) address numbers—not quality and methods.

12. Remove barriers to pride of workmanship. The responsibility of project managers must be changed from schedules to quality.

13. Institute a vigorous program of education and self-improvement *for everyone.* There must be a continuing training and education commitment to software managers and professional staff.

14. Put everyone to work to accomplish the transformation. The transformation is everyone's job. Every activity, job, and task is part of a process. Everyone has a part to play in improvement.

Copyright © 1988 by Zultner & Co. Reprinted with permission.

Finally, House Speaker Newt Gingrich in his course on Renewing American Civilization sums up his understanding of Deming's principles. The five pillars of American civilization are:

1. the historic lessons of American civilization,
2. personal strength,
3. entrepreneurial free enterprise,
4. the spirit of invention and discovery, and
5. quality (containing six core principles) as defined by W. Edwards Deming.

Following is an abstraction of Mr. Gingrich's understanding of those six core principles of quality based upon his time spent with Dr. Deming:

1. The consumer, not the bureaucracy, defines value.
2. The producer invents value.
3. To improve future results, you must improve the process.
4. People have intrinsic motivation. They want to do a good job.
5. Every person, process, and system is part of an interdependent larger system.
6. Continual learning is the basis for continual improvement. [27, pp. 25–29]

Table 3-2   The Seven "Deadly Diseases" for Software Quality [28]

1. Lack of constancy of purpose to plan systems that will satisfy users, keep software developers in demand, and provide jobs.

2. Emphasis on short-term schedules—short-term thinking (just the opposite of constancy of purpose toward improvement), fed by fear of cancellations and layoffs, kills quality.

3. Evaluation of performance, merit rating, and annual reviews—the effects of which are devastating on individuals, and therefore, quality.

4. Mobility of software professionals and managers. Job hopping makes constancy of purpose, and building organizational knowledge, very difficult.

5. Managing by "visible figures" alone—with little consideration of the figures that are unknown and unknowable.

6. Excessive personnel costs. Due to inefficient development procedures, stressful environment, and high turnover, software development person-hours are too high.

7. Excessive maintenance costs. Due to bad design, error ridden development, and poor maintenance practices, the total lifetime cost of software is enormous.

Copyright © 1988 by Zultner & Co. Reprinted with permission.

Table 3-3   The Obstacles to Software Quality [28]

1. Hope for instant solutions. The only solution that works is knowledge—solidly applied, with determination and hard work.

2. The belief that new hardware or packages will transform software development. Quality (and productivity) comes from people, not fancy equipment and programs.

3. "Our problems are different." Software quality problems aren't unique—or uncommon.

4. Obsolescence in schools. Most universities don't teach software quality —just appraisal techniques.

5. Poor teaching of statistical methods. Many software groups don't have good statistical-oriented training in quality or project management.

6. "That's good enough—we don't have time to do better"—but time will be spent later to fix the errors. Doing the right things right the first time (and every time) is fastest.

7. "Our quality control people take care of all quality problems." Quality is management's responsibility, and cannot be delegated. Either management does it, or it does not happen.

8. "Our troubles lie entirely with the programmers." Who hired the programmers? Trained them (or not)? Manages them? Only management can do what must be done to improve.

9. False starts with quality (or productivity). Impatient managers who don't understand that quality is a long term proposition quickly lose interest.

10. "We installed quality control." Quality is a never-ending daily task of management. Achieve consistency (statistical control)—then continuously improve.

11. The unmanned computer —such as a CASE package used without solid knowledge of software engineering.

12. The belief is only necessary to meet specifications. Just meeting specifications is not sufficient. Continue to improve consistency and reduce development time.

13. The fallacy of zero defects. Constant improvement doesn't end with zero defects (all specs met). The mere absence of defects is no guarantee of user satisfaction.

14. Inadequate testing of prototypes. The primary purpose of testing prototypes is to learn— and then apply that knowledge to a robust production system.

15. "Anyone that comes to help us must understand all about our systems." Software managers may know all there is to know about their systems and software engineering— except how to improve.

Copyright © 1988 by Zultner & Co. Reprinted with permission.

3.6   Genichi Taguchi

Dr. Taguchi has been using and teaching methods to reduce variability at Bell Labs and throughout Japan, Taiwan, and India from 1955 through 1980. The Taguchi Method shows techniques for reducing variability in products and processes at the design stage, thus enhancing their ability to overcome the many uncontrollable

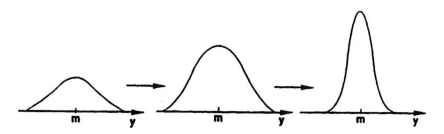

Figure 3-4   Off-line quality control. [29]
Copyright © 1988 American Supplier Institute, Inc. Reprinted by permission of
American Supplier Institute, Inc., of Dearborn, Michigan (U.S.A).

changing conditions in production. In the U. S. these methods are taught by the
American Supplier Institute, Inc., [29] which has given permission to use the material in this section.

Off-line quality control, as shown in Figure 3-4, attempts to reduce product or
process variability by controlling noise factors and control factors. Noise factors are
items categorized as outer noise—environmental conditions such as thermal, mechanical, electrical, customer misuse; inner noise—deterioration such as wear and embrit-
tlement; and piece-to-piece variation. Control factors are items categorized as
(increase robustness—change location and robustness); (adjust location—change location); (increase robustness—change robustness); and (reduce cost—change neither).

The application of off-line quality control to software development would place
development variables under control factors. This applies the analogy to the software
development process for the production of software units. The key control factors for
software development are personnel, software tools, methodologies (i.e., object-oriented design, structured analysis, structured programming, etc.), workstations, languages, database management systems, work areas, and desk layout. The measurement of these factors would be elements in the matrices resulting in signal-to-noise
(S/N) ratios that would provide indications of what controls need to be applied.

Even after optimal production conditions have been determined, Dr. Taguchi
says that the following remain:

- Variability in materials and purchased components
- Process drift, tool wear, machine failure, etc.
- Variability in execution
- Measurement error
- Human error

These sources of variability are dealt with by quality control during normal
production by online (real time) quality control (Figure 3-5), which is truly feedback

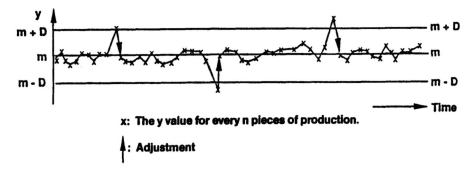

x: **The y value for every n pieces of production.**

↑: **Adjustment**

Figure 3-5 Online quality control. [29]
Copyright © 1988 American Supplier Institute, Inc. Reprinted by permission of
American Supplier Institute, Inc., of Dearborn, Michigan (U.S.A).

control. There are three online quality control techniques: measurement and disposition, prediction and correction, and diagnosis and adjustment. *Measurement* is made on every product (100 percent is Taguchi's philosophy) and a *disposition* of deliver, scrap, or repair is made. To control variable quality characteristics in a production line, measurement is made every nth unit. From the measurement, the average quality of the next n units is *predicted*. If the predicted value deviates from a target value by more than specified limits, *corrective action* is taken by adjusting a controllable variable. A manufacturing process is *diagnosed* at a constant interval. When normal, production continues; otherwise, the cause of the abnormality is investigated, and *adjustment* to the abnormality is made.

Online quality control applies to software development when a company has a defined, repeatable process. Such a process is subject to measurement, prediction, and diagnosis. In fact, online quality control methods are exactly right to provide insight into how to constantly improve the process, as described for a Level 5 organization in Chapter 13.

3.7 Shigeo Shingo

Dr. Shigeo Shingo has written a book, *Zero Quality Control: Source Inspection and the Poka-yoke System.* [30] The English translation is copyrighted by Productivity, Inc., and much of the following information in this section is provided with their permission.

The book's title refers to three critical and interrelated aspects of quality control. As taught by Shigeo Shingo, Zero Quality Control (Zero QC) is the ideal production system—one that does not manufacture any defects. To achieve this ideal, two things are necessary.

Poka-yoke (in English, "mistake-proofing"), looks at a defect, stops the production system, and gives immediate feedback so that we can get to the root cause of the problem and prevent it from happening again. *Source Inspections* looks at errors before they become defects and either stops the system for correction or automatically adjusts the error condition to prevent it from becoming a defect. Using *poka-yoke* devices and source inspection systems has enabled companies like Toyota Motors to virtually eliminate the need for statistical quality control (SQC), which has been the very heart of quality control in this country for years. [30, p. v,vi]

The author, in his book *Zero Defect Software* [31, p. 33], has followed many of Shigeo Shingo's ideas as applied to software development. The primary elements of the zero defect software method are the software development process chart and its associated activities checklist, inspections and zero defects software checklists, *poka-yoke* (software tools) methods, and the importance of the concept of an internal and external customer.

Error prevention and detection techniques at predefined checkpoints are basic to the zero defect software method. In defining a zero defect software program, a distinction must be made between an "error" and a "defect."

An "error" is an unwanted condition or occurrence which arises during a software process and deviates from its specified requirement.

A "defect" is that specific kind of unwanted condition or occurrence which has defied all attempts (inspections, reviews, walkthroughs, tests, and corrective action measures) to be eliminated during development and so is delivered to the customer.

Inspection methods are based on discovering errors in conditions that give rise to defects and performing feedback and action at the error stage so as to keep those errors from turning into defects, rather than stimulating feedback and action in response to defects. Every product, whether it be a document or work product of software development, has an informal review to check its integrity which is the self-checking by the worker who produced it. This also takes place whenever a work product is updated, which happens frequently during software development. This is called source inspection.

If this work product is to be handed off to another, this is the time to get that other person—the internal customer—into the process. The receiver has a vested interest in what he or she is going to have to work with and so will be critically sure that this is a good product. This is called a successive inspection.

Jim McCarthy of Microsoft has described an inspection method inherent in the software development at Microsoft as follows:

The ratio is usually something like six developers, two or three QA people, one program manager, and two documentation people. The ratio varies all over Microsoft and will probably be slightly different for your team, too. But you are not going to get away with many more than two developers for every one QA person. The QA group is in charge of shipping the software. The first place we look when a product is late is QA. Are there enough of them? Are they adequately empowered? Did they get a vote on the design? Are they caught up with development, or are they lagging substantially? Do they raise red flags promptly and efficiently? Are their expectations being met? Are there dozens of small "contracts" or handshake dates between development and QA? [32, p. 39]

How is *poka-yoke* (mistake-proofing) applied to the zero defects software program? Throughout the process, software tools need to be incorporated to automate the process and the inspection thereof. These software tools will make the process more "mistake proof."

Inherent in the zero defect software program is the need for consistency. Checklists, as applied to products and processes, will reveal where consistency can be or, more importantly, needs to be stressed. When such consistency is desirable, new tools can be integrated into the process to reinforce the "expected" level of achievement. [31, p. 38]

3.8 Philip Crosby

In his book *Quality is Free*, Philip Crosby lists the five maturing stages through which quality management evolves as:

- Uncertainty
- Awakening
- Enlightenment
- Wisdom
- Certainty

These are shown in the Quality Management Maturity Grid in Table 3-4. The Measurement Categories in the Grid include management understanding and attitude, quality organization status, problem handling, cost of quality as a percent of sales, quality improvement actions, and a summation of company quality posture. Drawing upon the Quality Management Maturity Grid as a guide the Software Quality Assurance Measurement Category is added to produce Table 3-5. The quality maturity stages established by Philip Crosby are examined below in relation to the production of quality software.

In the stage of uncertainty there are a number of deeply rooted "facts" that "everybody knows" about software quality:

1. Quality means goodness; it cannot be defined.
2. Because it cannot be defined, quality cannot be measured.
3. The trouble with quality is that American workers don't give a damn.
4. Quality is fine, but we can't afford it.
5. Data Processing is different—error is inevitable. [33]

Table 3-4(a)   Quality Management [3]

Measurement Categories	Stage 1: Uncertainty	Stage 2: Awakening
Management Understanding and Attitude	No comprehension of quality as a management tool. Tend to blame quality departments for "quality problems."	Recognizing that quality management may be of value but not willing to provide money or time to make it all happen.
Quality Organization Status	Quality is hidden in manufacturing or engineering departments Inspection probably not part of organization. Emphasis on appraisal or sorting.	A stronger quality leader is appointed but main emphasis is still on appraisal and moving the product. Still part of manufacturing or other.
Problem Handling	Problems are fought as they occur; no resolution; inadequate definition; lots of yelling and accusations.	Teams are set up to attack major problems. Long-range solutions are not solicited.
Cost of Quality as % of Sales	Reported: unknown Actual: 20%	Reported: 3% Actual: 18%
Quality Improvement Actions	No organized activities. No understanding of such activities.	Trying obvious "motivational" short-range efforts.
Summation of Company Quality Posture	"We don't know why we have problems with quality."	"Is it absolutely necessary to always have problems with quality?"

Table 3-4(b)   Quality Management (continued)

Stage 3: Enlightenment	Stage 4: Wisdom	Stage 5: Certainty
While going through quality improvement program, learn moreabout quality management; becoming supportive and helpful.	Participating. Understand absolutes of quality management. Recognize their personal role in continuing Emphasis.	Consider quality management an essential part of company system.
Quality department reports to top management, all appraisal is incorporated andmanager has role in management of company.	Quality manager is an officer of company; effective status reporting and preventive action. Involved with Consumeraffairs and special assignments.	Quality manager on board of directors. Prevention is main concern. Quality is a thought leader.
Corrective action communication established. Problems are faced openly and resolved in an orderly way.	Problems are identified early in their development. All functions are open to suggestion and improvement.	Except in the most unusual cases, problems are prevented.
Reported: 8% Actual: 12%	Reported: 6.5% Actual: 8%	Reported: 2.5% Actual: 2.5%
Implementation of the 14-step program with thorough understanding and establishment of each step.	Continuing the 14-step program* and starting Make Certain program*	Quality improvement program is a normal and continued activity.
"Through management commitment and quality improvement we are identifyingand resolving our problems."	"Defect prevention is a routine part of our operation."	"We know why we do not have problems with quality."

* Names of specific programs used to make a quality improvement.

Table 3-5   Software Quality Management Maturity Grid [Adapted from 3]

Measurement Category	Stage 1: Uncertainty	Stage 2: Awakening	Stage 3: Enlightenment	Stage 4: Wisdom	Stage 5: Certainty
Software Quality Assurance (SQA)	There are five quality "facts" that software development believes.	SQA is called upon in crisis situations.	The SQA Plan is written first as the "driver" to the software development effort.	SQA management and software development mgmt. are working together to produce quality software.	Quality software is produced on time within cost every time.

Among software developers there usually will be agreement about these quality "facts," especially the inevitability of errors in software. Education is required to dispell these erroneous "facts," better identified as mindsets.

When education is completed there is usually lip service given to quality where people will say "yes" from their minds while they feel "no" in the pits of their stomachs. They will pay lip service to quality without really realizing it. [33] They will say they want quality but will continue to judge performance solely by schedule and budget.

There seems to be an implied assumption that the three goals of quality, cost, and schedule are all conflicting; all mutually exclusive. It is not true. Significant improvements in both cost and schedule can be achieved *as a result of focusing on quality*.[34] Fundamental to W. Edwards Deming's teachings is that the only way to increase productivity and lower cost is to increase quality.[9]

Often, it is company policy to supply exactly what a customer orders every time. This may seem too elementary to be important, but it is important. Remember that software quality is "to conform to requirements and to provide useful services" to the customer. Too often companies place the emphasis on making the shipment, whether it's right or just close to right. [35]

Some cost will be incurred from the massive educational and procedural reworking effort that will be required. Each project will have to relearn what it really takes to achieve quality software production. To effectively increase quality the SQA person has to get into the "barrel" with software development to see that the relearning takes place on every project.

In Stage 2, the Awakening stage of software quality, the only times that SQA personnel are looked toward are times of crisis for the software development activity. One crisis during Stage 2 is customer assaults on the integrity of the software development activities. SQA personnel can contribute by acting as a buffer to absorb these assaults. Usually this takes the form of special intensive quality investigations into the software development resulting in a report to the customer. There is value to be gained by highlighting the quality perspective of the software development.

Another crisis in software development is the software documentation trap. Software documentation is usually a deliverable item along with the computer programs, but due prior to the computer programs. Often the format and content requirements are so stringent that the computer programs are neglected in order to meet these documentation requirements. The SQA person is ultimately requested to perform a detailed software documentation audit which leads to the establishment of a checklist which may quickly be fulfilled. The checklist makes it much easier for the software development team to meet the format requirements.

Philosophically, the Enlightenment stage occurs when it is understood that SQA contributes in a meaningful way to the role of software development management. Quality goals and objectives must be established first as a matter of corporate policy and then must be enforced through management involvement, procedural policy, and universal commitment. In essence, the quality role becomes a management role in which software quality principles and objectives are upheld at the start of the contract by software management, and development practices are driven by the quality objectives of those developing the software.

In the typical case of a software development project the requirements are imposed on the contractor to produce plans for software development, software configuration management, and SQA. The usual organizational alignments are such that each of these plans is developed independently by software development, configuration management, and SQA.

Because of this planning process each organization has its "job" to do and goes on to do it. When organizational interactions are required to implement the plans, each of the organizational elements tolerates the activities of the others. Seemingly, the quality of the software under development is being assured by SQA personnel through its use of planned tools, techniques, and methodologies.

Contrary to the usual practice of writing the Software Development Plan before or concurrent with the SQA Plan, there is a strong case for requiring the SQA Plan to be written first. For software development to "build quality in" the Software Development Plan, written by and subscribed to by the software development team, must follow the concepts included in the SQA Plan.

The SQA Plan should be the first document written in a software development project. The SQA Plan has to tell more than the usual implementation auditing techniques. It must set the tone for those developing the software and espouse the quality principles inherent in producing quality software. These software quality principles may vary on different software development projects, so the particular software quality principles for this project are written into the SQA Plan.

With the "guidance system" in place for quality software, then software development can write the software development plan following the principles in the SQA Plan. Only in this manner can software development write a software development plan that has quality inherent in the product.

The Wisdom stage occurs when it is realized that software quality can only be built-in. And must be the management objective of the software development management and software quality assurance management teams! Since software development management is responsible for making the decisions for planning the project, software quality assurance management must contribute to this up front decision making process. Software quality assurance personnel must be an active participant in the entire software development effort. This concept is strongly reinforced by James I. McManus in Chapter 2.

Throughout the software development cycle the software development management can produce quality software and the software quality assurance management can ensure the quality of that product. As a result of putting increased emphasis on the *quality* of everything we do, we're beginning to realize some very significant gains—*as a result of*, not in place of or instead of other performance measures. [18] In software, often there is a subcontractor producing software that must integrate with the overall software system. By emphasizing the quality of that subcontractor provided software, the quality of the overall software system gains.

In the Certainty stage the objective of software development management and software quality management of producing quality software on time within cost everytime is possible. The guidance given by the quality experts as applied to the development of quality software in this chapter should help lead to this objective.

3.9 Conclusion

This paper applies the overall quality principles of leaders in the quality revolution to the specialty area of software quality. These principles lead to a philosophy about the application of what may appear to be remote principles to the reality of producing quality software.

Kaoru Ishikawa has laid a quality framework of six features, each of which have applicability to development of quality software. Joseph M. Juran's three methods for meeting the Japanese quality challenge all have applicability to the production of quality software. The QFD concepts of Dr. Yoji Akao, because of their focus on customer satisfaction, also show applicability to software quality. Statistical methods and the Deming Circle taught by W. Edwards Deming have very specific application to software reliability and quality. Also, Dr. Deming's 14 Points are applicable to software development. The Taguchi Method of reduction in variability of production is applied to the production of software. Shigeo Shingo's zero quality control applies source inspection for the zero defect software methodology. Software quality can be shown as progressing through the five maturing stages of Philip Crosby's Quality Management Maturity Grid.

These experts have been responsible for a revolution in world economics brought about by attention to quality. The state of computer software will improve significantly by applying these revolutionary quality principles to the development of software. The groundwork has been surveyed in this chapter, but there is so much to learn and apply from each expert that it is hoped others will expand the scope of their work and apply their teachings to the quality of software development. The key message from Juran, Deming and others in the quality movement is that long-term improvement only comes about from systematic study and action, not from slogans or arbitrary objectives. [36, p. 95]

This chapter started with a quotation: "Quality is never an accident; it is always the result of intelligent effort." It concludes with a philosophical quotation from Robert Persig about the necessity of understanding quality in order to use it:

> A real understanding of quality doesn't just serve the System, or even beat it or even escape it. A real understanding of quality *captures* the System, tames it and puts it to work for one's own personal use, while leaving one completely free to fulfill his inner destiny. [37]

References

1. Oberle, Joseph, "Quality Gurus: the Men and their Message." In: *Training*, January, 1990.
2. Main, Jeremy, "Under the Spell of the Quality Gurus." In: *Fortune*, August 18, 1986.
3. Crosby, Philip. *Quality is Free* (New York: New American Library Inc., 1979), pp. 32–33.
4. Tice, Jr., George D. "Management Policy & Practices for Quality Software." In: *ASQC Quality Congress Transactions*, Boston, (American Society for Quality Control, Inc., 1983). Reprinted by permission.
5. Juran, Joseph M. "Product Quality—A Prescription for the West, Part I: Training and Improvement Programs." In: *Management Review*, (copyright J.M. Juran, June 1981).
   "Product Quality—A Prescription for the West, Part II: Upper-Management Leadership and Employee Relations." In: *Management Review*, (July 1981).
6. Ishikawa, Kaoru. "Quality Control in Japan." 13th IAQ Meeting, Kyoto, 1978.
7. "General Principles of the QC Circles." *QC Circle Koryo* (Tokyo: JUSE, 1980).
8. Aubrey, II, Charles A. and Felkins, Patricia K., *Teamwork: Involving People in Quality and Productivity Improvement* (New York: American Society for Quality Control, 1988).
9. Tribus, Myron. "Prize-winning Japanese Firms' Quality Management Programs Pass Inspection." In: *AMA Forum, Management Review* (February, 1984).

10. Juran, Joseph M. "Quality Problems, Remedies and Nostrums." In: *Industrial Quality Control*, Vol. 22, No. 12, pp. 647–653 (Copyright American Society for Quality Control, Inc., June 1966). Reprinted by permission.

11. Deming, W. Edwards. "On Some Statistical Aids Toward Economic Production." In: *Interfaces*, Vol. 5, No. 4, p. 8, August 1975.

12. Deming, W. Edwards. "What Happened in Japan?" In: *Industrial Quality Control*, Vol. 24, No. 2, p. 91 (Copyright American Society for Quality Control, Inc., August 1967). Reprinted by permission.

13. Swartout, W. and Balzer, R. "On the Inevitable Intertwining of Specification and Implementation." In: *Communications of the ACM*, Vol. 25, No. 7, July 1982, pp. 438–440, (Copyright Association for Computing Machinery, Inc., 1982). Reprinted by permission.

14. Sandholm, Lennart. "Japanese Quality Circles—A Remedy for the West's Quality Problems?" In: *Quality Progress*, February 1983, pp. 20–23 (Copyright American Society for Quality Control, Inc., 1983). Reprinted by permission.

15. Deming, W. Edwards. "My View of Quality Control in Japan." In: *Reports of Statistical Application Research, JUSE*, Vol. 22, No. 2, p. 77, June 1975.

16. Gottlieb, Daniel. "The Outlook Interview: W. Edwards Deming, U.S. Guru to Japanese Industry, Talks to Daniel Gottlieb." In: *The Washington Post*, p. D3, January 15, 1984.

17. Zultner, Richard E., *CQE, Quality Function Deployment (QFD) for Software*, (Princeton: Zultner & Company, 1992).

18. Haag, Stephen, Raja, M. K., and Schkade, L. L., "Quality Function Deployment: Usage in Software Development." In: *Communications of the ACM, Association for Computing Machinery*, Vol. 39, No. 1, New York, January, 1996.

19. Zells, Lois, *Applying Japanese Total Quality Management to U.S. Software Engineering* (Washington, D.C.: ACM, 1991).

20. Noguchi, Junji, "The Legacy of W. Edwards Deming." In: *Quality Progress*, December, 1995.

21. Cho, Chin-Kuei. *An Introduction to Software Quality Control* (New York: John Wiley & Sons, 1980).

22. Deming, W. Edwards. "It Does Work." In: *Quality*, A Hitchcock publication, August 1980. Reprinted by permission.

23. Paulk, Mark C. et al, *The Capability Maturity Model: Guidelines for Improving the Software Process* (Reading: Addison Wesley Longman, Inc., 1995), (adapted from page 81), ©1995 Addison-Wesley Publishing Company, Inc. Reprinted by permission of Addison-Wesley Longman, Inc.

24. Hansen, Captain Richard L., "An Overview to the Application of Total Quality Management." Aeronautical System's Division, U.S. Air Force, 1990.

25. Windham, Jeff, "Implementing Deming's Fourth Point." In: *Quality Progress* (December, 1995).

26. Zultner, Richard, CQE, "SPC for Software Quality." In: *NSIA Software Quality Conference* (Alexandria 1989).

27. Gingrich, Newt "Renewing American Civilization, Pillar Five: Quality as defined by Deming." In: *Quality Progress* (December, 1995).

28. Zultner, Richard, "The Deming Way—A Guide to Software Quality (Adapted by Richard Zultner)." Brochure from Zultner & Co., 12 Willingford Drive, Princeton, NJ 08540, Copyright © 1988 Zultner & Co., Reprinted by permission.

29. Taguchi Method One Day Seminar, 10 August 1988, Copyright © 1988 American Supplier Institute, Inc., 15041 Commerce Drive South, Dearborn, MI 48126, (313) 336-8877, Reprinted by permission of American Supplier Institute, Inc. of Dearborn, Michigan (U.S.A.).

30. Shigeo Shingo, *Zero Quality Control: Source Inspection and the Poka-yoke System,* English translation (Portland: Productivity Press, P.O. Box 13390, Portland, OR 97213-0390, (800) 394-6868, 1986). © 1986 by Productivity Press. Reprinted by permission.

31. Schulmeyer, G. Gordon, *Zero Defect Software* (New York: McGraw-Hill Book Company, 1990).

32. McCarthy, Jim, *Dynamics of Software Development* (Redmond: Microsoft Press, 1995). Reproduced by permission of Microsoft Press. All rights reserved.

33. Burrill, Claude W. & Ellsworth, Leon W. Quality Data Processing, *The Profit Potential for the 80's* (New Jersey: Burrill-Ellsworth Associates, Inc. 1982), p. 176.

34. Walter, Craig. "Management Commitment to Quality: Hewlett-Packard Company." In: *Quality Progress*, August 1983, p. 22, Copyright American Society for Quality Control, Inc., Reprinted by permission.

35. Turnbull, Don. "The Manual—Why?" In: *Quality*, August 1980, p. Q5.

36. Fowler, Priscilla and Rifkin, Stan, *Software Engineering Process Group Guide.* Software Engineering Institute Technical Report (Pittsburg: CMU/SEI-90-TR-24, September, 1990). Special permission to use excerpts from *Software Engineering Process Group Guide*, CMU/SEI-90-TR-24 © 1990 by Carnegie Mellon University, in *Handbook of Software Quality Assurance* is granted by the Software Engineering Institute.

37. Persig, Robert M. *Zen and the Art of Motorcycle Maintenance* (New York: William Morrow & Co., 1974), p. 200.

Standardization of Software Quality Assurance— Where Is It All Going?

G. Gordon Schulmeyer
PYXIS Systems International, Inc.

"Ruth made a big mistake when he gave up pitching,"
said the baseball expert (?) Tris Speaker in 1921.

4.1   Introduction

Many software engineers have said, "You can't apply standards or controls to something as creative as developing software." There are some so-called "experts" still saying this. This chapter addresses not those standards specifically, but the standardization of software quality assurance (SQA), which ensures that there is discipline and control in the software development process via independent evaluation.

A point-counterpoint discussion of the value of standards in improving the quality of software is presented in the *Communications of the ACM* with Schneidewind and Fenton: Schneidewind says that there are many examples of standards improving software product quality: Space Shuttle, World Wide Web, and Local Area Networks, whereas Fenton says that he found no evidence that software standards improve the quality of the resulting software products cost-effectively. Software engineering standards pose unique problems: software standards overemphasize process; many software standards aren't standards; it is impossible to measure conformance to software standards; many software standards prescribe, recommend, or mandate the use of technology that has not been validated objectively; and many software standards are simply too big. [1, pp. 22, 23] I have seen standards applied successfully, whereas previous implementation and quality assurance without standards was inadequate. In fact, Roger Pressman says that once an organization has decided to institute software quality assurance, a plan should be developed and standards should be required. [2, p. 588]

A lot has occurred in the field of software-related standards since the previous edition of this *Handbook*. Most significant is the Department of Defense's (DoD) move toward the adoption of commercial standards. In 1994, Secretary of Defense William J Perry released "DoD Policy on the Future of MILSPEC," which states,

"...use performance and commercial specifications and standards in lieu of military specifications and standards, unless no practical alternative exists to meet the user's needs."

A large defense contractor has received a blanket change for the entire organization to replace the DoD MIL-Q-9858 quality system with the commercial ISO 9000 quality system. This move to commercial standards is seemingly motivated by the understanding by DoD in software acquisition that commercial standards can be cost-effective.

If DoD (or any organization) wants a successful standardization program, standardization authorities must recognize that they have two objectives: develop or adopt usable standards and convince users and developers that the standards are usable. If the first objective is not realized the second will not be either. Without the second objective, the first is useless.

Usable standards development requires the participation of practitioners. It must be based on the system requirements. If a specific use for a piece of information cannlot be stated, it cannot be considered usable for standardization. Development of usable standards means cooperation and teamwork with actual systems. If no practitioners are actually using a standard that has been developed, it ain't[*] a standard.

Adoption of usable standards implies that the standards are already in use somewhere. They may be industry, government, or standards-organization sponsored. Usability is a function of quality, but the real measure of usability is widespread acceptance and implementation. Standardization may require compromise where the most widespread standard is "not as good" as its less widely used competitor or the one developed in-house.

A most awakening idea is that there may be no one standard for any particular concept or representation of that concept. Instead, there may be several. The best standardization programs choose the "best" standards by reviewing them all against mission activity and system requirements. It is entirely conceivable that more than one representation of the same concept could be adopted to meet differing mission requirements. [3, p. 27]

In 1994, the DoD moved away from a separate, but parallel, software quality assurance standard; such as, DOD-STD-2168, to defining software quality assurance

---

[*] "Ain't" is a well-understood, generalized representation for a concept whose more preferred representations are "am not," "are not," and "is not." As a generalization, ain't is a more "standard" term than any of its substitutes.

requirements within MIL-STD-498 (*Software Development and Documentation*). Another representation of this basic concept has been carried forward into EIA/IEEE 12207, *Information Technology: Software Life Cycle Processes*, which is the proposed international life cycle software process standard that DoD is in the process of modifying for its use.

First, within this chapter, a historical review of the software quality-related standards is provided to place the issues in perspective. Some of the historical data that is captured in tabular form for ease of inspection is provided in the Appendix to this chapter. With the brief history provided, there is a quick move to a discussion of the commercial standard(s) that take the place of the former government standards for software quality assurance activities. Then, there is a comparison table of the requirements for software quality assurance that have been applied throughout the brief history of software quality assurance's standards. There are some concluding remarks.

4.2 Historical Perspective

Table 4-1 provides a chronological list of software quality-related standards and plan guidelines. It lists 32 of the major ones, but does not claim to be all-inclusive.

The preponderance (22 of 32) of those listed were established by DoD, driven by the high defense expenditure on weapons systems of which an ever increasing percentage was allocated to software development. Fourteen of these (3, 6, 7, 9, 11, 12, 14, 15, 17, 19, 22, 24, 26 and 29) are plan guidelines or outlines usually employed in conjunction with a standard.

Five items from the list in Table 4-1 are IEEE planning standards with four of them being outlines for SQA plans. Each of the SQA plan outlines is an update from the previous version; the dates are 1980, 1981, 1984, and 1989.

There was one standard provided rather early (1977) by the FAA and updated in 1987 that includes a complete software quality program. Similarly, there was one standard for a complete program provided by NATO in 1981 with the issuance of the allied quality assurance publication (AQAP-13).

The first major standard was MIL-S-52779[*], which has had significant impact on software quality standards. Every following standard and plan guideline was influenced strongly by this landmark standard. That influence is shown in Section 4.4, where the various standards are compared.

Items 30 to 32 represent the latest era for software quality standards. The software quality sections are placed as an integral part of the software development standard on the supposition that quality needs to be built into the product, not considered a separate activity.

---

[*] MIL-S-52779 was originally published as an appendix to MIL-Q-9858, *Quality Program Requirements*, before being issued as a stand-alone document.

TABLE 4-1   Chronological List of Software Quality-Related Standards and Plan Guidelines

Ref. No.*	Reference Name	Title	Date	Sponsor	Appendix Table
1	MIL-S-52779	*Software Quality Program Requirements*	5 Apr. 1974	Army	
2	FAA-STD-018	*Computer Software Quality Program Requirements*	26 May 1977	FAA	
3	DI-R-2174	*Software Quality Assurance Plan*	29 Nov. 1978	Navy	
4	MIL-STD-1679	*Software Development*	1 Dec. 1978	Navy	
5	MIL-S-52779A	*Software Quality Program Requirements*	1 Aug. 1979	Army	
6	ANSI-IEEE-STD 730	*IEEE Trial-Use Standard for Software Quality Assurance Plans*	Jan. 1980	IEEE	
7	(U)-E-759/ESD	*Software Quality Assurance Plan*	20 May 1980	Air Force	
8	AQAP-13	*NATO Software Quality Control System Requirements*	Aug. 1981	NATO	
9	ANSI/IEEE-STD 730-1981	*IEEE Standard for Software Quality Assurance Plans*	13 Nov. 1981	IEEE	
10	MIL-STD-SQAM	*Software Quality Assessment and Measurement*	1 Oct. 1982	DoD/JLC	
11	R-DID-126	*Software Quality Assessment and Measurement Plans*	1 Oct. 1982	DoD/JLC	
12	DI-R-X105	*Software Quality Assurance Plan*	Undated (1982)	DoD/JLC	
13	DOD-STD-1679A	*Software Development*	22 Oct. 1983	Navy	
14	DI-R-2174A	*Software Quality Assurance Plan*	22 Oct. 1983	Navy	
15	IEEE-STD-730-1984	*IEEE Standard for Software Quality Assurance Plans*	30 June 1984	IEEE	
16	DOD-STD-2168	*Software Quality Evaluation Program (draft)*	26 April 1985	DoD/JLC	
17	DI-MCCR-80010	*Software Quality Evaluation Plan (draft)*	4 June 1985	DoD/JLC	
18	DOD-STD-2167	*Defense System Software Development*	4 June 1985	DoD/JLC	4-6
19	IEEE-STD-983-1986	*IEEE Standard for Software Quality Assurance Planning*	20 Feb. 1986	IEEE	4-7
20	FAA-STD-018a	*Computer Software Quality Program Requirements*	30 Sept. 1987	FAA	
21	DOD-STD-2167A	*Defense System Software Development*	29 Feb. 1988	DoD/JLC	4-8
22	DI-MCCR-80030A	*Software Development Plan*	29 Feb. 1988	DoD/JLC	
23	DOD-STD-2168	*Defense System Software Quality Program*	29 Apr. 1988	DoD/JLC	
24	DI-QCIC-80572	*Software Quality Program Plan*	29 Apr. 1988	DoD/JLC	
25	DOD-HDBK-287A	*A Tailoring Guide for DOD-STD-2167A*	11 Aug. 1989	DoD/JLC	
26	IEEE-STD-730-1989	*IEEE Standard for Software Quality Assurance Plans*	17 Aug. 1989	IEEE	4-9

27	MIL-HDBK-286	*A Guide for DOD-STD-2168*	14 Aug. 1990	DoD/JLC	
28	DOD-STD-2168A	*Defense System Software Quality Program (draft)*	6 Aug. 1991	ARMY	
29	DI-QCIC-80572A	*Software Quality Management Plan (draft)*	6 Aug. 1991	ARMY	
30	MIL-STD-498	*Software Development and Documentation*	5 Dec. 1994	DoD	4-10
31	IEEE-STD-1074	*IEEE Standard for Developing Software Life Cycle Processes*	26 Apr. 1996	IEEE	
32	EIA/IEEE 12207	*Information Technology - Software Life Cycle Processes*	14 June 1996	EIA/IEEE	4-11

Reference numbers 10, 11, 12, 16, 17, 27, 28, and 29 had been proposed in draft form when this paper was first written (some disappeared, but others became standards).

Reference numbers 3, 6, 7, 9, 11, 12, 14, 15, 17, 22, 24, 26 and 29 had been written as outlines for plans.

4.3 Commercial Standards

4.3.1 MIL-STD-498

DoD issued MIL-STD-498, Software Development and Documentation on 5 Dec. 1994. The consolidation of DOD-STD-2167A (mission-critical) with MIL-STD-7935 (information systems) standards resulted in a single life cycle standard—MIL-STD-498. MIL-STD-498 was intended to correct some concerns with DOD-STD-2167A; such as,

- Perceived preference for waterfall development model
- Compatibility with incremental and evolutionary development models
- Dependence on formal reviews and audits
- Compatibility with Ada and object-oriented methods
- Distinction between requirements and design
- Emphasis on preparing documents
- Use of CASE tools [4, p. 14]

Table 4-10 in the Appendix to this chapter contains the paragraph outline of software quality assurance within MIL-STD-498. It is brief, but focused on building quality into the software; and it has only an interim two year approved life. MIL-STD-498 also has related requirements dealing with:

- Handling of critical requirements
  - Safety assurance (see Chapter 21, *Software Safety and Its Relation to Software Quality*)

–Security assurance

–Privacy assurance

–Assurance of other critical requirements

• Software product evaluation

–In-process and final software product evaluations

–Software product evaluation records

–Independence in software product evaluation

But, why discuss MIL-STD-498 in this section entitled Commercial Standards? This standard did two significant things that affect software quality assurance. The first is the integration of the software quality requirements within the body of the standard, instead of a separate standard as had been the case. The second is that for software MIL-STD-498 is the jumping-off standard to the commercial standard adoption. So, much study and many comparisons have been based on MIL-STD-498 which is useful in our discussion of standardization of software quality.

4.3.2 IEEE-STD-1074

From the introduction to *IEEE-STD-1074, IEEE Standard for Developing Software Life Cycle Processes*:

This is a standard for the processes of software development and maintenance. This standard requires definition of a user's software life cycle and shows mapping into typical software life cycles, but it is not intended to define or imply a software life cycle of its own. This standard applies to the management and support processes that continue throughout the entire life cycle, as well as aspects of the software life cycle from concept exploration through retirement. [5, p. iii]

The software quality management process, Section 3.3 of the IEEE-STD-1074, requires the following basic software quality activities:

1. Plan software quality management
2. Define metrics
3. Manage software quality
4. Identify quality improvement needs.

4.3.3 ISO / IEC 12207

According to Dr. Raghu Singh, editor of ISO/IEC 12207, this international standard on software lifecycle processes was created to establish a common international framework to acquire, supply, develop, operate, and maintain software. ISO/IEC

12207 was proposed in 1988 and published in August 1995. ISO/IEC 12207 describes the major component processes of a complete software lifecycle, their influences with one another, and the high-level relations that govern their interactions. [4, p. 14]

To further the rather complex history of 12207, we call upon the expertise of Moore and Rada, who relate that the IEEE and the Electronics Industry Association (EIA) initiated a joint project to create a commercial replacement for MIL-STD-498. This effort produced one standard with two names: IEEE Trial Use Standard 1498 and EIA Interim Standard 640. Since both the IEEE and the EIA produced the standard, the American National Standards Institute (ANSI) issued it under a third name, ANSI Joint Standard 016 (J-STD-016-1995) (Figure 4-1). Tables 4-2 and 4-3 provide the fundamental changes between MIL-STD-498 and J-STD-016-1995.

The international standards committee developed a standard called ISO/IEC 12207. Whereas J-016 placed requirements on only the development process, 12207 specified four additional primary processes—acquisition, supply, maintenance, and operation—as well as eight supporting and four organizational processes. Although 12207 is useful in organizational or individual contexts, its conformance requirement specifically applies to the relationship between an acquirer and a supplier in the development, maintenance, or operation of software.

ISO 12207 is expected to become an important standard for international commerce in software because it provides a common framework of terminology and process structure for acquirers and suppliers in different countries. Many countries are moving toward the adoption of 12207 as a national standard. Nevertheless, there are some obstacles to use, particularly in the U.S. The standard does not provide a set of data descriptions for recording information essential to software development. The standard provides no way for an organization to assert that its own internally institutionalized software development methods conform to 12207.

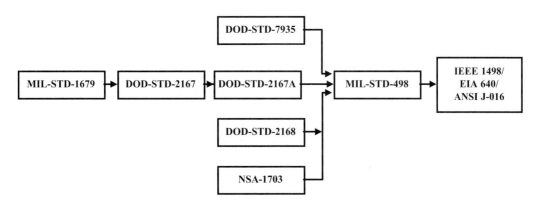

Figure 4-1 Convergence of defense life-cycle standards. [Adapted from 6, p.18]

Table 4-2   Terminology Changes Between MIL-STD-498 and J-STD-016-1995 [9, p.13]

1. Computer software configuration items are now software items.

2. Hardware configuration items are now hardware items.

3. Support concept is now support strategy.

4. Fielding is now distribution.

5. Software support is now software maintenance.

6. Privacy is now privacy protection.

7. Requirements analysis is now requirements definition.

8. Sections are now clauses, paragraphs are subclauses, subparagraphs are subordinate clauses, and appendixes are annexes.

9. Data Item Descriptions (DIDs) are now software product descriptions found in annexes to the standard. The standard is intended to be tailored by the deletion of inapplicable tasks (specific parts of processes) when applied to a particular contract. Additional requirements may be placed in a contract.

Table 4-3   Requirements Changes Between MIL-STD-498 and J-STD-016-1995 [9, p.13]

1. Added mandatory (binding) annex that requires tailoring.

2. Allows developer to reference software practices, as well as standards, for software development in the software development plan.

3. Added requirement to ensure each element of the software development environment performs its intended function prior to use.

4. Added a traceability tasking clause that clarifies traceability is both upward and downward.

5. Added requirement to update the system and software descriptions to match the approved "as built" system and software.

6. Removes default application to deliverable software; standard now applies to all software on the project whether deliverable or not.

7. Deleted default time limit; i. e., duration of the contract, for record keeping and retention or other items (software development library and software development files). (The acquirer must specify how long records must be kept—may be shorter or longer than the duration of the contract.)

8. Deleted requirement to obtain approval for any language not specified (If the contract is silent, the developer is free to use any language unless other provisions or laws apply).

9. Deleted reuse requirements to
    • Use reusable software that resulted from identifying software for reuse: developer now tasked only to identify and evaluate for potential reuse
    • Identify opportunities for reuse and evaluate their benefits and costs
    • Interpret the standard when reusable software is incorporated according to Appendix B, where Appendix B changed from mandatory [binding] to informative

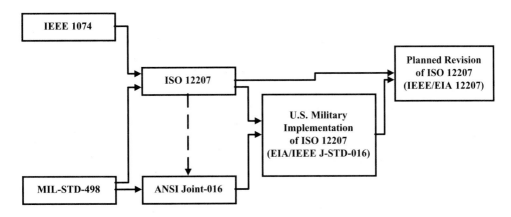

Figure 4-2 Harmonization of U.S. and international life-cycle standards. [Adapted from 6, p.18]

To effectively participate in the international software market, the U.S. must determine how to reconcile or "harmonize" ANSI Joint Standard 016, IEEE Std 1074, and ISO 12207. That effort is underway. The fundamental principles behind the three standards are not dissimilar; ANSI J-016 was influenced by 12207, which was in turn influenced by 1074 and by J-016's predecessor (Figure 4-2). The transition path for the large number of U.S. stakeholders in the 2167/498/J-016 family of standards will be the EIA/IEEE J-STD-016. [6, pp. 17, 18] That is the *tactical* standard that provides a continuing reference for organizations that have invested in software processes created under prior military standards. An important difference from the military standards, though, is that this standard is properly applied through voluntary adoption rather than contractual imposition.

The first step is an IEEE ballot on a standard that adopts 12207. The second step is to create a U.S. industrial implementation of 12207. The U.S. version will provide an organizational mode permitting its internally adopted processes for software development, maintenance, and operation to meet all requirements of the U.S. 12207. IEEE/EIA 12207 will be the strategic standard that addresses the following objectives:

- represent the best commercial practices
- be suitable for application to the complex requirements of defense acquisition, and
- be compatible with those of the emerging global marketplace for software

It is an adaptation of the international standard, ISO/IEC 12207, and provides a basis for organizationwide adoption of software processes suitable for commercial and defense projects that serve both domestic and international customers. [7, p. 6]

In this transition to commercial standards, the advantages provided by ISO/IEC 12207 have been discussed by Perry DeWeese at the Data Processing Management Association–sponsored 1996 Software Acquisition Management Conference. [8] He points out that a common framework for the life cycle of software is established to acquire, supply, develop, operate, and maintain software; as well as to manage, control, and improve the framework. The standard integrates supporting processes (documentation, configuration management, quality assurance, verification and validation, joint reviews, audits, and problem resolution) into the software process. It supports the use of integrated product and process development and integrated product teams. A summary list of benefits includes:

- Integrated systems/software solution
- Efficient utilization of project personnel
- Enhances SEI process maturity capability
- Quality products at lower costs
- Organizational focus for process improvement
- *Quality management* included in the organizational process

4.3.4 498 / 12207

Because of the transition to 12207, it is a worthwhile effort to compare MIL-STD-498 and ISO/IEC 12207. The following activities in MIL-STD-498 correspond to processes in ISO/IEC 12207:

1. Software configuration management (configuration management and audit)
2. Software quality assurance
3. Software product evaluation (verification and validation)
4. Joint technical and management reviews
5. Corrective action (problem resolution)
6. Project planning and oversight (management)
7. Establishing a software development environment (infrastructure) [4, p. 14]

The requirements in ISO/IEC 12207 simply allow developers to use data in CASE storage or format to document their work, but do not explicitly encourage this, as the requirements in MIL-STD-498 do.

ISO/IEC 12207 defines the joint review process flexibly as "a process for evaluating the status and products of an activity on a project as appropriate. Joint reviews are at both the project management and technical levels and are held together throughout the life of the contract." Here, the standard allows for reviewing the results of planning and engineering work in their natural, technical form.

ISO/IEC 12207's treatment of documentation and CASE tools is more suitable for most development methods than requirements in older standards like DOD-STD-2167A. ISO/IEC 12207 has no standard deliverable data. ISO/IEC 12207 is a suitable standard for Rapid Application Development where sophisticated integrated CASE tools play a critical role. In its un-tailored form, it poses less of a risk of creating accidental, excessive documentation requirements in contracts than does MIL-STD-498. [4, p. 18]

Another big difference between ISO/IEC 12207 and MIL-STD-498 is that the requirements in the international standard are at a much more general level than those in the military standard. In fact, ISO/IEC 12207 says in paragraph 1.5 that it "describes the architecture of the software life cycle processes, but does not specify the details of how to implement or perform the activities and tasks included in the processes." [4, p. 15]

Draft EIA/IEEE 12207, *Information Technology—Software Life Cycle Processes*, 14 June 1996, will be the U.S. implementation of the international ISO/IEC 12207 standard, *Software Life Cycle Processes*. This version of the standard augments ISO/IEC 12207's development process and supporting processes, with requirements and clarifying or elaborating notes from MIL-STD-498, *Software Development and Documentation*, December 1994. Future versions of the standard are intended to provide additional requirements to implement the acquirer, supplier, operation, and maintenance processes of ISO/IEC 12207. Those activities of the maintainer that are the same as those of a developer are covered in this version of the standard.

4.3.5 498 / CMM

MIL-STD-498 "establishes uniform requirements for software development and documentation" and is focused on the development of a specific piece of software on a project. The key words that describe MIL-STD-498 are *software* and *project*.

The SEI's CMM (see Chapter 12) is "a framework that describes the key elements of an effective software process," and it "describes an evolutionary improvement path" for that process. The CMM is focused on process improvement in an organization, and its key words are *organization* and *process*. [10, p. 4]

The summary of these concepts follows:

	CMM	MIL-STD-498
Scope	organization	project
Focus	process	software

Table 4-4 provides the relationship for software quality assurance between that CMM key process area and the supporting MIL-STD-498 paragraphs. Parenthetical paragraphs only provide general support to the CMM activity. The specifics of how a project intends to reflect the CMM are found in the project's SDP, the key document under MIL-STD-498 software development.

Table 4-4   Relationship between Software Quality Assurance CMM and MIL-STD-498 Paragraphs [adapted from 10]

Key Process Area Activity (paraphrased)	Supporting MIL-STD-498 Paragraph	Comments
Software Quality Assurance		
1. Documented procedure for SQA plan preparation	(5.16)	Check proposed SDP for procedure
2. Perform SQA activities in accordance with SQA plan	5.1.6, 5.16	Check proposed SDP for SQA activities
3. Participate in preparation and review of SDP, standards, and procedures	(5.16)	MIL-STD-498 encourages an IPT that includes SQA group
4. Review software engineering activities for compliance	5.16.1.a	
5. SQA audits software work products	5.16.1	
6. SQA reports its results to products software engineering group	(5.16.2)	Records are kept. Check proposed SDP for dissemination of records
7. Documented procedure to handle deviations in products and activities	5.16.1.b, 5.17	
8. Periodic reviews between the project SQA and the customer SQA		Check proposed SDP for SQA reviews

4.4 Comparison of Requirements

The chart in Table 4-5 provides a matrix of the various software quality activity subject matters versus the standards and DIDs. It is a chart showing in which standards or DIDs the subjects are covered.

Most of the subjects have been taken from DOD-STD-2168 and DI-QCIC-80572 because they portray the most complete software quality activities. Then, the other standards and DIDs have been checked off where they conform. Finally, some few subjects were in early standards and DIDs, but not in DOD-STD-2168 or DI-QCIC-80572, so they have been included.

TABLE 4-5   Comparison of Requirements

Software Quality Standards & DIDs

Subject Matter	MIL-S-52779	FAA-STD-018	DI-R-2174	MIL-STD-1679	MIL-S-52779A	ANSI/IEEE STD 730	(U)-E-759/ESD	AQAP-13	ANSI-IEEE STD 730-1981	MIL-STD-SQAM	R-DID-126	DI-R-X105	DOD-STD-1679A	DI-R-2174A	IEEE STD 730-1984	DOD-STD-2167	DOD-STD-2168	DI-MCCR-80010	DOD-STD-2167A (draft)	DOD-STD-2167A	DI-MCCR-80030A	DI-QCIC-80572	MIL-HDBK-286	DOD-HDBK-287A(drafft)	MIL-STD-498	EIA/IEEE 12207
Organizational Structure	X	X	X	X	X	X		X	X			X	X	X	X		X	X	X	X	X	X	X	X	X	X
Personnel Required				X									X	X			X	X	X	X	X	X		X	X	X
Resources Required				X			X			X			X	X			X	X	X	X	X	X		X	X	X
Schedules		X		X							X	X	X				X	X	X	X			X		X	X
Evaluation Procedures, Methods, Tools & Facilities (tools, techniques & methods)	X	X	X	X	X	X		X	X	X		X	X	X	X	X	X	X	X	X	X		X		X	X
Evaluation of Development Processes	X	X	X	X	X	X	X		X	X	X	X	X	X	X	X	X	X	X	X			X		X	X
Configuration Management	X	X	X	X	X	X	X	X	X	X			X	X	X	X	X	X	X	X			X		X	X
Software Development Library	X	X		X	X	X	X	X	X				X		X	X	X	X	X	X			X		X	X
Documentation Reviews	X	X	X	X	X	X	X	X	X	X	X	X	X	X	X	X	X	X	X	X			X		X	X
Evaluation of Media Distribution	X	X		X	X	X			X	X	X		X		X	X	X	X					X		X	X
Storage & Handling	X	X	X		X	X			X	X	X			X	X	X	X	X	X				X		X	X
Evaluation of Non-Deliverables				X							X						X	X	X				X		X	
Evaluation of Risk Management				X								X					X	X	X	X	X	X			X	X
Subcontractor Controls	X	X	X	X	X	X	X	X	X	X			X	X	X	X	X	X	X	X	X	X		X	X	X
Reusable Software Controls (Supplied Material)								X									X	X	X	X	X		X			X
Records		X		X	X	X			X	X			X		X	X	X	X			X	X	X	X	X	X
Corrective Action	X	X	X	X	X	X	X	X	X	X	X		X	X	X	X	X	X	X	X			X		X	X
Quality Evaluation Reports		X	X	X					X	X	X		X	X		X	X	X	X	X	X		X		X	X
Certification		X	X					X	X	X			X					X	X	X			X			X
Software IV & V Contractor Interface				X									X		X			X	X	X	X				X	X
Government Facility Review	X	X		X	X								X					X	X	X			X		X	
Quality Cost Data																			X	X	X					X
Activities Evaluation (Reviews & Audits)	X	X	X	X	X	X	X	X	X	X	X	X	X	X	X	X	X	X	X	X	X		X		X	X
Products Evaluation	X	X	X	X	X	X		X	X	X	X	X	X	X	X	X	X	X	X	X			X		X	X
Software Test & Evaluation	X	X	X	X	X	X	X	X	X	X	X	X	X	X	X	X	X	X	X	X			X		X	X
Acceptance Inspection				X				X		X	X		X		X	X	X	X	X	X			X		X	
Installation & Checkout																X	X	X		X			X		X	X
Code Reviews			X	X	X	X			X	X	X	X	X	X	X	X	X	X	X	X					X	
Deviations & Waivers										X									X							
Work Tasking, Authorization, & Instructions	X	X		X	X	X		X	X				X	X	X											
Accommodations & Assistance								X																		
Evaluation Criteria																			X	X	X		X		X	X
Transition to Software Support																			X	X					X	X
Safety Analysis																			X	X						X
Software Development File																			X	X	X			X	X	X
Nondevelopmental Software																			X	X		X		X	X	

4.5   Conclusion

A consideration not previously discussed in this chapter is raised by James Dobbins [11, pp. 49, 50] when he relates that there is nothing inherently wrong with systems developed based upon Total Quality Management (TQM) or continuous process improvement. Many multinational companies, such as Boeing, developed internal standards based on the military standards, and then sought to improve the standard even further as their software development processes matured. The software development systems based on these internal, commercial standards, and improved over the years have proved to be good systems.

It is hoped that this survey of standards provides the reader with a better perspective of what is available and where to find it. Much work has been done since the 1970s to standardize software quality requirements, and an introduction to these is provided herein with the emphasis on the 1990s consolidation to commercial standardization.

References

1. Portions reprinted, with permission, from Schneidewind, Norman F. and Fenton, Norman, "Do Standards Improve Quality?" In: *IEEE Software* (New York, IEEE, January, 1996) © 1996 IEEE.
2. Pressman, Roger S., *Software Engineering: A Practitioner's Approach* (3rd edition), (New York: McGraw-Hill Book Co., 1992).
3. Ham, Gary A. and Mann, Douglas D., "If Nobody Uses It, It "Ain't" a Standard." In: *CrossTalk*, June 1998.
4. Gray, Lewis, "ISO/IEC 12207 Software Lifecycle Processes." In: *CrossTalk*, August, 1996.
5. IEEE, IEEE STD-1074, *IEEE Standard for Developing Software Life Cycle Processes* (New York: IEEE, 1996).
6. Moore, James W. and Rada, Roy, "Organizational Badge Collecting." In: *Communications of the ACM*, Vol. 39, No. 8, August, 1996.
7. Moore, James W., DeWeese, Perry R., and Rilling, Dennis, "U.S. Software Lifecycle Process Standards." In: *CrossTalk*, Vol. 10, No. 7, July, 1997, pp. 6–8.
8. DeWeese, Perry R., "U.S. National Software Standard; Transition to Commercial Standards." In: *Software Acquisition Management Conference*, Data Processing Management Association, 8 October, 1996.
9. Sorensen, Reed, "MIL-STD-498, J-STD-016, and the U.S. Commercial Standard." In: *CrossTalk*, June, 1996.
10. Sorensen, Reed, "MIL-STD-498 and the CMM: How Do They Relate?" In: *CrossTalk*, November/December, 1995.
11. Dobbins, James H., "Adequacy of ISO 9000 Certification for DOD Weapon System Software Development Contractors." In: *Program Manager*, March-April 1996, pp. 42–51.

General References

IEEE/EIA 12207.0-1996, *Software Life Cycle Processes*, March 1998.

IEEE/EIA P12207.1 (Draft) *Guide for Information Technology: -Software Life Cycle Processes, -Life Cycle Data*, 11 February 1997.

IEEE/EIA 12207.2-1997, *Software Life Cycle Processes—Implementation Considerations*, April 1998.

FAA-STD-018a, *Computer Software Quality Program Requirements*, 30 September, 1987.

IEEE, ANSI/IEEE STD 730-1981, *IEEE Standard for Software Quality Assurance Plans* (New York: IEEE, 1981).

IEEE, IEEE STD-730-1984, *IEEE Standard for Software Quality Assurance Plans* (New York: IEEE, 1984).

IEEE, IEEE STD-983-1986, *IEEE Standard for Software Quality Assurance Planning* (New York: IEEE, 1986).

IEEE, IEEE STD-730-1989, *IEEE Guide for Software Quality Assurance Plans* (New York: IEEE, 1989).

IEEE, *IEEE Trial-Use Standard for Software Quality Assurance Plans* (New York: IEEE, 1980).

IEEE, *IEEE P-1061/D21, Standard for a Software Quality Metrics Methodology (draft)* (New York: IEEE, 1990).

IEEE, IEEE STD-1074, *IEEE Standard for Developing Software Life Cycle Processes* (New York: IEEE, 1996).

ISO 9001, *Quality Systems—Model for Quality Assurance in Design, Development, Production, Installation, and Servicing* (Geneva: International Organization for Standardization, 1994).

ISO 9000-3, *Quality management and quality assurance standards - Part 3: Guidelines for the application of ISO 9001 to the development, supply and maintenance of software* (Geneva: International Organization for Standardization, 1991).

North Atlantic Treaty Organization AQAP-13, Allied *Quality Assurance Publication—NATO Software*.

Quality Control System Requirements (Washington, D.C.: NATO International Staff—Defense Support Division, 1981).

U.S. Air Force, (U)-E-759/ESD, *Data Item Description—Software Quality Assurance Plan* (Washington, D.C.: NAVMAT 09Y, 1980).

U.S. Air Force, AFSCP Pamphlet 800-14, *Software Quality Indicators* (Andrews Air Force Base, D.C., Headquarters AFSC, 1987).

U.S. Air Force, AFSC Pamphlet 800-43, *Software Management Indicators* (Andrews Air Force Base, D.C., Headquarters AFSC, 1990).

U.S. Army, MIL-S-52779, *Military Specification—Software Quality Assurance Program Requirements* (Washington, D.C.: NAVMAT 09Y, 1974).

U.S. Army, MILS-52779A, *Military Specification—Software Quality Assurance Program Requirements* (Washington, D.C.: NAVMAT 09Y, 1979).

U.S. Army, DOD-STD-2168A, *Defense System Software Quality Program (draft)*, 6 August, 1991.

U.S. Army, DI-QCIC-80572A, *Software Quality Management Plan (draft)*, 6 August, 1991.

U.S. Dept. of Defense, DOD-STD-2168 (draft), *Military Standard— Software Quality Evaluation Program* (Washington, D.C.: NAVMAT 09Y, 1985).

U.S. Dept. of Defense, MIL-Q-9858A, *Quality Program Requirements*, 16 December, 1963.

U.S. Dept. of Defense, MIL-STD-498, *Software Development and Documentation*, 5 December, 1994.

U.S. Dept. of Transportation, FAA-STD-018, *Federal Aviation Administration Standard-Computer Software Quality Program Requirements* (Washington, D.C.: Government Printing Office, 1977).

U.S. Joint Logistics Command, DI-R-X 105 (draft), *Data Item Description—Software QualityAssurance Plan* (Washington, D.C.: NAVMAT 09Y, 1982).

U.S. Joint Logistics Command, DI-MCCR-80010 (draft), *Data Item Description— Software Qualityy Evaluation Plan* (Washington, D.C.: NAVMAT 09Y, 1985).

U.S. Joint Logistics Command, DOD-STD-2167 (draft), *Military Standard—Defense System, Software Development* (Washington, D.C.: NAVMAT 09Y, 1985).

U.S. Joint Logistics Command, MIL-STD-SQAM (draft), *Proposed Military Standard Software Quality Assessment and Measurement* (Washington, D.C.: NAVMAT 09Y, 1982).

U.S. Joint Logistics Command, DI-MCCR-80030A. *Data Item Description—Software Development Plan* (Washington, D.C.: NAVMAT 09Y, 1988).

U.S. Joint Logistics Command, DI-QCIC-80572, *Data Item Description—Software Quality Program Plan* (Washington, D.C.: NAVMAT 09Y, 1988).

U.S. Joint Logistics Command, DOD-STD-2168, *Military Standard—Defense System Software Quality Program* (Washington, D.C.: NAVMAT 09Y, 1988).

U.S. Joint Logistics Command, DOD-STD-2167A, *Military Standard—Defense System Software Development* (Washington, D.C.: NAVMAT 09Y, 1988).

U.S. Joint Logistics Command, MIL-HDBK-286, *Military Handbook—A Guide for DOD-STD-2168 Defense System Software QualityProgram* (Washington, D.C.: NAVMAT 09Y, 1990).

U.S. Joint Logistics Command, DOD-HDBK-287A, *Military Handbook—A Tailoring Guide for DOD-STD-2167A* (Washington, D.C.: NAVMAT 09Y, 1989).

U.S. Navy, DI-R-2174, *Data item Description—Software Quality Assurance Plan* (Washington, D.C.: NAVMAT 09Y, 1978).

U.S. Navy, DI-R-2174A, *Data Item Description—Software Quality Assurance Plan* (Washington, D.C.: NAVMAT 08Y, 1983).

U.S. Navy, DOD-STD-1679A, *Military Standard—Software Development* (Washington, D.C.: NAVMAT 09Y, 1983).

U.S. Navy, MIL-STD-1679, *Military Standard—Weapon System Software Development* (Washington, D.C.: NAVMAT 09Y, 1978).

Appendix

Tables From Standards

TABLE 4-6   DOD-STD-2167 Software Quality Requirements Outline

4.3 General Software Quality Requirements
Contractor shall build in quality by:
a) Maintaining standards
b) Implementing a complete development process
c) Maintaining a software quality evaluation process
  5.1.l.le   Prepare Software Quality Evaluation Plan:
    1) Evaluate development plans, standards, and procedures
    2) Evaluate compliance with (1)
    3) Evaluate software development products
    4) Implement reporting system
    5) Implement corrective action system

5.8 Software Quality Evaluation
Contractor shall establish and implement procedures to:
1) Evaluate software requirements
2) Evaluate software development methodologies
3) Evaluate software development products
4) Provide feedback to effect software quality improvements
5) Perform corrective action with controlled software
 5.8.1 Software Quality Evaluation—Activities:
  5.8.1.1   Contractor shall perform necessary planning.
  5.8.1.2   Contractor shall conduct internal reviews to evaluate compliance to standards. The internal reviews shall be:
   5.8.1.2.1 Evaluation criteria for reviews are:
    a) Adherence to required format
    b) Compliance with contractual requirements
    c) Internal consistency
    d) Understandability
    e) Technical adequacy
    f) Degree of completeness appropriate to the phase
   5.8.1.2.2 Internal reviews—all phases
    a) SDP, SSPM, SCMP, and SQEP*
    b) Evaluate:
     1) Software configuration management
     2) Software development library
     3) Documentation control
     4) Storage and handling of project media
     5) Control of non-deliverables
     6) Risk management

(continued)

TABLE 4-6   DOD-STD-2167 Software Quality Requirements Outline (continued)

       7) Corrective action

       8) Conformance to all approval standards and procedures

[5.8.1.2.3 through 5.8.1.2.8. Internal reviews during the phases: Software Requirements Analysis, Preliminary Design, Detailed Design, Coding and Unit Testing, CSC Integration and Testing, CSCI Testing.

Review of the following documents and activities during these phases: OCD, Requirements, SRS, IRS(s), STLDD, STP, CSOM, SUM(s), CSUM, CRISD, SDDD, IDD(s), DBDD(s), STD, SDF, Unit tests, Integration tests, SPM, FSM, Source code, STPR, CSCI testing, STRs, SPS, VDD.

Review the documents and activities for the following: (1) criteria in 5.8.1.2.1, (2) consistency, (3) understanding, (4) traceability, (5) testability, (6) appropriateness, (7) adequacy, (8) accuracy, (9) compliance, and (10) correctness. Also, monitor CSCI testing to ensure that (1) current controlled code is used, (2) testing is conducted in accordance with approved test plans, description and procedures, and (3) includes all necessary retesting.]

5.8.1.3	Ensure all products are available for formal reviews and audits.
5.8.1.4	Ensure all products are available and all procedures performed and documented to support acceptance inspection.
5.8.1.5	Evaluate installation and checkout.
5.8.1.6	Evaluate software or documentation for completeness, technical adequacy, and compliance.
5.8.1.7	Evaluate and certify commercially available, reusable, and Government furnished software.
5.8.1.8	Prepare and maintain written quality records.
5.8.1.9	Prepare quality reports showing results and recommendations.
5.8.1.10	Implement a corrective action system.
5.1.8.11	Collect quality cost data.

5.8.2 Software Quality Evaluation—Products

5.8.2.1	Prepare and maintain quality evaluation records.
5.8.2.2	Prepare and maintain quality reports.
5.8.2.3	Certify compliance with the contract of each contract line item.

5.8.3 Independence sufficient to perform evaluation activities as required.

All acronyms are defined in Appendix A, this *Handbook*.

Table 4-7   IEEE 983-1986 Guide for Software Quality Assurance Planning Outline

3.   Contents of Software Quality Assurance Plan

   3.1 Purpose

   3.2 Reference Documents

   3.4 Documentation

   3.5 Standards, Practices, and Conventions

TABLE 4-8 DOD-STD-2167A Software Quality Requirements Outline

4.4 Software product evaluation
    4.4.1 Independence in product evaluation activities
    4.4.2 Final evaluations
    4.4.3 Software process records
    4.4.4 Evaluation criteria

5.x.4 Software product evaluations
where x = 1 System requirements analysis/design
      = 2 Software requirements analysis
      = 3 Preliminary design
      = 4 Detailed design
      = 5 Code and CSU testing
      = 6 CSC integration and testing
      = 7 CSCI qualification testing
      = 8 System integration and testing

For each x there is a list of products being evaluated and an evaluation criteria table provided.

TABLE 4-9   IEEE STD 730-1989 Outline

3.   Software Quality Assurance Plan
    3.1   Purpose (Section 1 of the Plan)
    3.2   Reference Documents (Section 2 of the Plan)
    3.3   Management (Section 3 of the Plan)
        3.3.1   Organization
        3.3.2   Tasks
        3.3.3   Responsibilities
    3.4   Documentation (Section 4 of the Plan)
        3.4.1   Purpose
        3.4.2   Minimum Documentation Requirements
            3.4.2.1   Software Requirements Specifications (SRS)
            3.4.2.2   Software Design Description (SDD)
            3.4.2.3   Software Verification and Validation Plan (SVVP)
            3.4.2.4   Software Verification and Validation Report (SVVR)
            3.4.2.5   User Documentation
            3.4.2.6   Software Configuration Management Plan
        3.4.3   Other
    3.5   Standards, Practices, Conventions, and Metrics (Section 5 of the Plan)
        3.5.1   Purpose
        3.5.2   Content
    3.6   Reviews and Audits (Section 6 of the Plan)
        3.6.1   Purpose
        3.6.2   Minimum Requirements
            3.6.2.1   Software Requirements Review (SRR)
            3.6.2.2   Preliminary Design Review (PDR)
            3.6.2.3   Critical Design Review (CDR)
            3.6.2.4   Software Verification and Validation Plan Review (SVVPR)
            3.6.2.5   Functional Audit
            3.6.2.6   Physical Audit
            3.6.2.7   In-Process Audits
            3.6.2.8   Managerial Reviews
            3.6.2.9   Software Configuration Management Plan Review (SCMPR)
            3.6.2.10 Post Mortem Review
        3.6.3   Other
    3.7   Test (Section 7 of the Plan)
    3.8   Problem Reporting and Corrective Action (Section 8 of the Plan)
    3.9   Tools, Techniques, and Methodologies (Section 9 of the Plan)
    3.10 Code Control (Section 10 of the Plan)
    3.11 Media Control (Section 11 of the Plan)
    3.12 Supplier Control (Section 12 of the Plan)
    3.13 Records Collection, Maintenance, and Retention (Section 13 of the Plan)
    3.14 Training (Section 14 of the Plan)
    3.15 Risk Management (Section 15 of the Plan)

Table 4-10   MIL-STD-498 Software Quality Outline

Software quality assurance

      Software quality assurance evaluations

      Software quality assurance records

      Independence in software quality assurance

Table 4-11   EIA/IEEE 12207 Quality Outline and Related Annex L

Quality Assurance Process

      1) Process implementation

      2) Product assurance

      3) Process assurance

      4) Assurance of quality systems

Annex L   (Informative)   Software product evaluations

1 Scope

This annex identifies criteria that may be used for software product evaluations, and contains a suggested default set of definitions for the evaluation criteria. This annex is informative only, provided to aid in using this standard.

2 Software product evaluations

Suggested software products that may undergo software product evaluations are listed.... Evaluations of system-level products are to be interpreted as participation in these evaluations. Some of the criteria are subjective. Because of this, there is no requirement to prove that the criteria have been met; the requirement is to perform the evaluations and to identify possible problems for discussion and resolution.

3 Criteria definitions

The following subclauses provide definitions for the evaluation criteria that may not be self-explanatory. The criteria are listed in alphabetical order.

    3.1 Accurately describes (an item)

    This criterion, applied to user/operator/programmer instructions and to the "as built" design and version descriptions, means that the instructions or descriptions are correct depictions of the software or other item described.

    3.2 Adequate test cases, procedures, data, results

    Test cases are adequate if they cover all applicable requirements or design decisions and specify the input to be used, the expected results, and the criteria to be used for evaluating those results. Test procedures are adequate if they specify the steps to be

(continued)

Table 4-11   EIA/IEEE 12207 quality outline and related annex L *(continued)*

followed in carrying out each test case. Test data are adequate if they enable the execution of the planned test cases and test procedures. Test or dry run results are adequate if they describe the results of all test cases and show that all criteria have been met, possibly after revision and retesting.

3.3 Consistent with indicated product(s)

This criterion means that: (1) no statement or representation in one software product contradicts a statement or representation in the other software products, (2) a given term, acronym, or abbreviation means the same thing in all of the software products, and (3) a given item or concept is referred to by the same name or description in all of the software products.

3.4 Contains all applicable information in (a specified annex)

This criterion uses annexes E through J to specify the required content of software products, regardless of whether a deliverable document has been ordered. Allowances are to be made for the applicability of each topic in the annex. The formatting specified in the annex (required subclause structure and numbering) are not relevant to this evaluation.

3.5 Covers (a given set of items)

A software product "covers" a given set of items if every item in the set has been dealt with in the software product. For example, a plan covers the SOW if every provision in the SOW is dealt with in the plan; a design covers a set of requirements if every requirement has been dealt with in the design; a test plan covers a set of requirements if every requirement is the subject of one or more tests. "Covers" corresponds to the downward traceability in the requirements, design, and test planning/descriptions in annexes E through J.

3.6 Feasible

This criterion means that, based on the knowledge and experience of the evaluator, a given concept, set of requirements, design, test, etc. violates no known principles or lessons learned that would render it impossible to carry out.

3.7 Follows Software Development Plan

This criterion means that the software product shows evidence of having been developed in accordance with the approach described in the Software Development Plan. Examples include following design and coding standards described in the plan. For the Software Development Plan itself, this criterion applies to updates to the initial plan.

3.8 Internally consistent

This criterion means that: (1) no two statements or representations in a software product contradict one another, (2) a given term, acronym, or abbreviation means the same thing throughout the software product, and (3) a given item or concept is referred to by the same name or description throughout the software product.

3.9 Meets delivery requirements, if applicable

This criterion applies if the software product being evaluated is deliverable and has been formatted for delivery at the time of evaluation. It focuses on the format, markings, and other provisions specified in the contract, rather than on content, covered by other criteria.

3.10 Meets SOW, if applicable

This criterion means that the software product fulfills any Statement of Work provisions regarding it. For example, the Statement of Work may place constraints on the operational concept or the design.

3.11 Presents a sound approach

This criterion means that, based on the knowledge and experience of the evaluator, a given plan represents a reasonable way to carry out the required activities.

3.12 Shows evidence that (an item under test) meets its requirements

This criterion means that recorded test results show that the item under test either passed all tests the first time or was revised and re-tested until the tests were passed.

3.13 Testable

A requirement or set of requirements is considered to be testable if an objective and feasible test can be designed to determine whether each requirement has been met.

3.14 Understandable

This criterion means "understandable by the intended audience." For example, software products intended for programmer-to-programmer communication need not be understandable by non-programmers. A product that correctly identifies its audience, and is considered understandable to that audience meets this criterion.

Software Quality Program Organization

Emanuel R. Baker, Ph.D.
Software Engineering Consultants, Inc.

Matthew J. Fisher, Ph.D.
Software Engineering Institute (SEI)

5.1   Introduction

The relationship between the quality of a software product and the organization responsible for that product is multidimensional. This relationship depends upon many factors, including the business strategy and business structure of the organization, available talent, and resources to produce the product. It also depends upon the combination of activities selected by the organization to achieve the product quality desired. To reduce the dimension of this problem, let's consider the following precepts.

First, consider the definition of software product quality.[*] Software product quality is defined as, "The degree to which a software product possesses a specified set of attributes necessary to fulfill a stated purpose." [1] As explained in the referenced work, this definition implies that "Quality is everybody's business." When we consider how software development projects are organized, this translates to: "Quality is affected by many, but effected by few." Virtually everyone working on the project, from the program/project manager (PM)[**] on down to the most junior member of the staff, affects the quality of the software product; however, only those actually producing the product (the developers performing the requirements analysis, design, and coding) build quality into it. Because of this, the person ultimately responsible for the quality of the software product is the PM—the "manager of quality" for the system produced. It is the PM's responsibility to integrate the efforts of

---

[*]   This is different than the definition of software quality which appears in the Software Acquisition Capability Maturity Model [2]. The definition that appears there states, "Software quality is the degree to which a system or a system component meets specified requirements." Under this definition, a system is regarded as a product, a process, or any other object.

[**] A program/project manager is an individual assigned the management responsibility for developing or providing a software product or service.

"the many" and "the few" and bring them to bear on the development effort to accomplish the quality objectives. The PM may, of course, delegate the authority for this function, but, ultimately, he or she is responsible. The facts that the manager has the ultimate responsibility for the software product quality and development groups build quality into the products are often overlooked.

Second, there is a method for structuring the project to manage and control the product quality, and that is to implement a software quality program (SQP). The SQP has three critical elements, which will be described below. Each of these elements spawns a series of tasks. The PM must determine the allocation of these tasks to the available personnel or organizations supporting the program, express them in an SQP plan, and obtain the commitment of the supporting organizations. The main topic of this chapter is how organizations could be structured to implement the SQP and achieve the quality objectives.

5.2   Software Quality Program Concepts

The software quality program is the overall approach to influence and determine the level of quality achieved in a software product. It consists of the activities necessary to:

- establish requirements for the quality of a software product
- establish, implement, and enforce methodologies, processes and procedures to develop, operate, and maintain the software
- establish and implement methodologies, processes, and procedures to evaluate the quality of a software product and to evaluate associated documentation, processes, and activities that impact the quality of the product

Figure 5-1 illustrates the elements of the SQP.

The foundation of the software quality program is not how well one can measure product quality nor the degree to which one can assess product quality. While these are essential activities, they alone will not achieve the specified quality. Software quality cannot be tested, audited, evaluated, measured, or inspected into the product. Quality can only be built in during the development process. Once the quality has been built in, the operating and maintenance processes must not degrade it. It is that understanding that lays the basis for the software quality program.

The foundation of the SQP stems from the definition of software quality. It is the concept that product quality means, in effect, compliance with its intended end use, as defined by the user or customer. Does the software do what it is supposed to do? In other words, does it meet correctly specified requirements? The consequence of this concept is that product requirements are really quality requirements. These include the software functional and performance require-

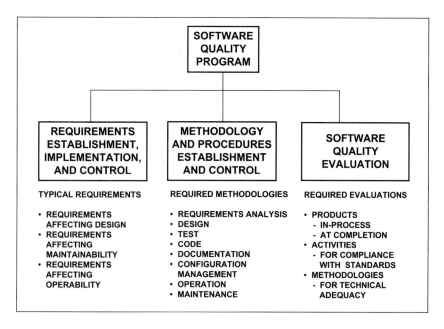

Figure 5-1   Software quality program elements.

ments, and also include requirements for maintainability, portability, interoperability, and so on. Software requirements are, in fact, the requirements for the quality of the software.

Figure 5-2 illustrates the elements of the software quality program and how it affects software quality. The interaction of the SQP with the other parts of the project elements as depicted in the figure is necessarily complex. The involvement is at all levels of the project organization and takes place throughout the project's life. In some cases, the SQP directs the other activities; in other circumstances, it can only influence those activities. In any case, all the project activities, in some way, affect software product quality.

The software quality program covers both technical and management activities. For instance, if we look at the element of the SQP concerned with methodologies for software development, enforcing these methodologies (in order to build quality into the software) is a management activity, while the specification of the methodologies is a technical activity.

5.2.1   Establishment of Requirements

The first element of the software quality program is the establishment of the requirements for the software to be produced on the project. As previously pointed out, the requirements for the software are, in fact, the requirements for the quality

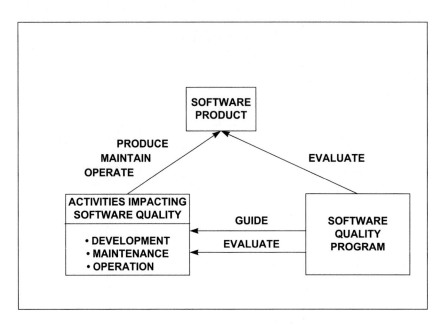

Figure 5-2   What creates quality software?

of the software. Consequently, the requirements must accurately reflect the functionality, performance, etc., that the customer or user expects to see in the software. This
activity includes not only defining the requirements but also includes baselining (formalizing) them, as well.

However, merely defining and formalizing the requirements are insufficient.
Changes to the product requirements, after they have been baselined, must also be
controlled. Furthermore, the baselined software requirements must be enforced, in
other words, implemented as stated, and in full. The developers must not be allowed
to unilaterally deviate from implementing them. Failure to implement the requirements as stated can result in software products that do not meet user needs and
requirements. The resultant impact on software product functionality and performance will range from negligible to severe (see Chapter 11, *The Pareto Principle
Applied to Software Quality Assurance*). Deviation, intentional or otherwise, may not
always cause significant problems, but the potential is clearly always there.

The process of defining and establishing the requirements and controlling
changes to them involves interfaces with the other two elements of the SQP: establishment of methodologies and quality evaluation. Two kinds of interfaces with the
establishment of methodologies exist. One has to do with the methodology for performing requirements analysis. To illustrate, the use of data flow analysis or object-
oriented analysis to define requirements results from the establishment of one or the

other methodology for performing requirements analysis. The second has to do with baselining requirements and controlling changes to them. This process, or methodology, is known as a "configuration management process." This is a management methodology implemented to

- prevent uncontrolled changes to baselined items
- improve the likelihood that the development effort will result in quality software, and that software maintenance will not degrade it

The interface between this element of the SQP and the software quality evaluation element is concerned with the evaluation of the requirements. As pointed out in Chapter 11, total compliance with requirements does not guarantee quality software. If the requirements have not been properly defined, and errors exist in them, then compliance with requirements will produce software that does not satisfy the intended end use. Clearly, requirements must be evaluated for adequacy while they are being developed.

5.2.2   Establishment of Methodology

The second element of the SQP pertains to the establishment, implementation, and enforcement of methodologies for the development, operation, and maintenance activities for the software product.

There is a very strong link between software quality and the processes used to develop it. The quality of the software product is very much dependent on the quality of the process used to develop it. If the processes in use by a software development organization are not well defined or organized, the quality of their software products will not be predictable or repeatable from project to project. The relationship of software quality to the degree of process definition has been characterized by the Software Engineering Institute (SEI) at Carnegie Mellon University in a Capability Maturity Model[SM] (CMM) [3]. Five levels of maturity are described by the CMM (see Chapter 12). The levels, their names, and the characteristics which describe when the organization has reached that level are identified below.

- **Level 1 — INITIAL.** Chaotic, ad hoc. Few, if any, organized procedures exist within the organization. Not even the most rudimentary procedures for project planning or management are likely to exist—nor are they likely to exist for configuration management or quality assurance. Success of development projects is very much dependent on key individuals.

[SM] The Capability Maturity Model is a service mark of the Software Engineering Institute.

- **Level 2 — REPEATABLE.** Development process is intuitive, rather than codified; however, procedures for project planning and management, configuration management, and quality assurance exist and are implemented. Success of development projects, however, is still very much dependent on key individuals, and not on process. In times of crisis, established procedures tend to be abandoned.
- **Level 3 — DEFINED.** Procedures and tools for software development exist and are implemented. Processes are codified and followed for all projects. When faced with a crisis, the organization continues to use the defined process.
- **Level 4 — MANAGED.** Minimum basic process measurements have been established. A process database and the resources to manage it have also been established. Resources to gather and maintain the data have been established. Process measures are used for corrective action and to establish quality goals for software products.
- **Level 5 — OPTIMIZING.** Process measurements are being taken and entered into the process database. The process database is being used to fine-tune and optimize the development processes, evaluate new technologies, and analyze processes to prevent defects.

A methodology, called the CMM-Based Appraisal for Internal Process Improvement (CBA-IPI), has been developed by the SEI to determine the level at which software development organizations are functioning. This assessment methodology is an update of the original assessment methodology, called the Software Process Assessment (SPA), which was first reported upon back in 1987 [4, 5]. As of October 1997, 688 organizations had been surveyed. Of these organizations, 62 percent were found to be functioning at Level 1, and 19.6 percent at Level 2 [6]. This means that approximately 85 percent of the organizations surveyed do not have well-established, codified software development processes. Data gleaned from various sources indicate that the Japanese software industry is achieving defect rates two orders of magnitude better than those of the "best in class" U.S. companies [7]. One reason why the Japanese are achieving such low defect rates, based on reviews of the Japanese software industry conducted in 1984 and 1989, is because of their emphasis on understanding and improving the software development process. The same report also indicates that many of the Japanese companies are operating at Levels 3, 4 and 5, whereas only 15 percent of U.S. companies are operating at Level 3 or above.

From the foregoing, it can be seen why establishment of methodologies is such an important element of the Software Quality Program.

Establishment of the methodologies refers to the definition of the methodologies to apply to the development, operation, and maintenance efforts. Implementation of the methodologies is accomplished by codifying them in the form of standard practices and procedures, and training the organization in how they are to be used. Implementation of the methodologies may be facilitated by the acquisition of tools compatible with the methodologies and the standard practices and procedures. Enforcement is accomplished through the commitment of corporate management. Management must consistently and unequivocally require the application of the selected methodologies from project to project, and under all conditions of schedule pressure. (This does not preclude tailoring the methodologies to be consistent with the unique characteristics of the various projects. Nor does this preclude the acquisition, development, or use of different methodologies; but, the appropriate scheduling of their introduction must be observed.) Some tools, such as automated process environments, can facilitate the enforcement of the methodologies and the associated standard practices and procedures; however, such environments have been developing slowly, and are not likely to be commercially available for some time.

"Development," as used here, refers to the requirements definition, design, and test phases of the project and the documentation produced during these phases. Development procedures refer to those needed to define how to establish requirements and to design, code, test, and document the software: utilization of structured analysis, implementing object-oriented design, the use of software development folders [8], coding standards to be implemented, configuration management, and the like.

"Operation" refers to production or operational usage of the software. Quality can be affected by improper operation of the software system or by inadequacies in instructions contained in the user's manual. Chapter 11 illustrates this point quite well. It describes a situation where the software was apparently correctly designed and implemented, but the instructions in the user's and operator's manuals were not properly written. A large number of abnormal terminations occurred because the software was not correctly operated. Reference 1 points out that "quality is in the eye of the beholder." If the software doesn't operate the way that the user of the system expects, it will not be perceived as quality software. As the example in Chapter 11 shows, this can occur even when the software has been properly designed and coded, that is, the software product complied with the requirements.

The "maintenance" activities pertain to those activities that occur after development has been completed and a baseline has been established for the software (code, design, documentation). At this point, acceptance testing has been completed and the software is ready for operational or production usage. If adequate procedures have not been established to handle software maintenance, the quality initially built into the software product may suffer degradation. For example, inadequate change control procedures or inadequate definition of procedures to fix the code in the event of a failure, would result in such degradation.

As of 1998, the process for selecting the methodologies to apply is based on experience, intuition, literature search, and common knowledge. No formalized techniques exist for specifying methodologies.

5.2.3   Evaluation of Process and Product Quality

The third element pertains to those activities necessary to evaluate the software development process and the resultant products. This element is referred to as the software quality evaluation (SQE) program. SQE is a set of assessment and measurement activities performed throughout the software development cycle to evaluate the quality of software products and to evaluate associated documentation, processes, and activities that impact the quality of the products. "Assessment" pertains to qualitative evaluation while "measurement" pertains to quantitative evaluation.

The "set of evaluation activities" refers to the actions (such as reviews, assessments, test, analysis, inspections, and so on) that are performed to determine that technical requirements have been established, and that products and processes conform to these established technical requirements, and, ultimately, to determine software quality. These activities vary as a function of the phase of the development cycle, and they can be performed by several organizations, some or all of which may be within a program manager's immediate organization. The set of evaluation activities are generally documented in project plans, software development plans, project-specific software quality procedures, and/or company quality plans and related software quality procedures.

In the case of the products, determination of the state of the software can be performed by comparing the products against pre-established criteria. However, evaluation of product quality is difficult, especially since the definition of software quality is hard to express quantitatively within the current state-of-the-art. A large volume of research has been directed toward the establishment of quantitative definitions of quality, for example, software reliability. We see much of this effort expressed in terms of software metrics. Numerous definitions for software metrics have been proposed and applied to specific cases. However, the software development community has not come to a common agreement in the selection and use of these metrics for the measurement of software quality. Nonetheless, efforts to establish a "menu" of typical process and product measures, together with guidelines on their selection and use, have been ongoing. One such effort resulted in the development by the Defense Department's Joint Logistics Commanders of a guidebook on the use of measurement, called "Practical Software Measurement." [9] The guidebook presents very useful information, but, like the selection of methodologies, the determination of what measures are useful for any specific organization is still not a cookbook solution. Moreover, in some cases it may even be more useful for certain organizations to develop their own measures—measures that are specific for their own environment and product lines.

On the other hand, the technology is available to establish and enforce various forms of meaningful quality criteria. The approach is relatively straightforward: Establish criteria based upon measurable entities; entities that lend themselves to validation during software development. As long as the project believes that these criteria reflect the type of quality it desires ("quality is in the eye of the beholder"), it can use them to gauge the quality. For example, the metric of cyclomatic complexity is a measurable entity. If the project believes that software exhibiting some level of cyclomatic complexity is high quality software, than this metric is adequate for the project to use to determine the product quality.

The evaluation program also includes assessment and measurement of the software development process and the activities/methods making up this process. It may be that the process is being properly implemented, but the products are not achieving the desired level of quality. Such evaluations are a check against the initial analysis done prior to the start of the development, that is, during the methodology selection process discussed above. Such concepts are embodied in the CMM, that is, the improvement of product quality through process corrective action and/or the continuous improvement of the processes used to produce the product. Continuous improvement is achieved by focusing on the processes, and using product evaluations as indicators of process adequacy (see, for example, Reference 10). This evaluation may be implemented by examining interim software products, such as initial specifications, or the products that result from the process itself, such as Software Development Folders. The state of the practice as a whole within the organization may also be examined by having a CBA-IPI performed to identify institutionalized processes that need improvement.

Generally, the basis for determining which process to implement has been to look at a candidate process or set of processes and compare the proposed process against established development practices and methodologies. The assumption is that if the process has been shown to produce "high quality software" in the past, then proper implementation of the process will result in a high quality product. This argument is somewhat misleading. There has been no conclusive demonstration of a definite link between the process selected for the software development and the resultant quality of the software product itself. Establishment of such links has been more heuristic or intuitive rather than analytical. For example, Ada promotes information hiding which, in turn, should make the software more adaptable. But, the actual cause and effect link has not, as yet, been clearly demonstrated.

An often confused aspect of SQE is the role of Software Quality Assurance (SQA) organizations in performing these evaluations and assessments.

SQA in and of itself is not an organized discipline with a single, unambiguous meaning. The confusion seems to stem from two sources: the functional definition of

SQA, and organizational aspects of SQA. These two sources are not usually independent when it comes to implementation.

The functions that constitute SQA are usually defined by the organization. And, the functional assignments vary considerably from organization to organization. The differences stem from misconceptions, legacy approaches from hardware quality control, and, simply, the definitions of SQA promoted by the SQA community.

Historically, SQA has been incorrectly interpreted by some as the primary means to achieve software quality. This originates from an inspection-oriented approach to software quality, rather than a total quality approach. As noted earlier, the facts that the manager has the ultimate responsibility for the software product quality and development groups build quality into the products are often overlooked. Some individuals believe that it is the software quality assurance groups that are responsible for the quality of the product. Often SQA people are referred to as the "quality" people, as if they are the sole "effectors" and "affectors" of the quality. This is obviously not true. They are indeed participants, but the responsibility is not solely theirs. But the misconceptions that derive from such statements and definitions of SQA are promulgated and never adequately resolved. Here, for example is one definition of SQA:

> *software quality assurance:* (1) A planned and systematic pattern of all actions necessary to provide adequate confidence that a software work product conforms to established technical requirements. (2) A set of activities designed to evaluate the process by which work products are developed or manufactured. [11]

The first part of the definition implies "any and all actions" taking place in a development project. Based on the definition of quality and responsibility for product quality noted above, this definition implies that every action or activity on a project falls under the functions of SQA. This may be considered correct until it comes to the assignment of these actions solely to an SQA organization. One also usually asks the questions What is adequate? What is adequate confidence? To whom is this confidence provided? Definition two relegates SQA to examination of the process (which may be close to the hardware usage). But the two definitions taken together are conflicting and lead to misconceptions and incorrect assignments of responsibilities. In one case, the definition focuses exclusively on determining the quality of the product, and in the other, on evaluating the process. Note that the two aspects are *not* combined in a single definition. Note also that the second definition (which is also a software quality assurance definition) includes manufacturing.

Compounding this problem is the difference in approaches to SQA from company to company. SQA to one organization may mean a checklist approach to assure the development process is proceeding as expected, while other organizations assign many SQE activities to the SQA organization. In many commercial organizations, SQA means only testing. This is the only SQE function performed within those organizations, and is the primary responsibility of the SQA group.

A further consideration is that SQA organizations are not the only organizations performing all evaluations defined by SQE as necessary to verify and validate that the software products, as well as the processes producing that software, meet all requirements. We find that in many organizations, a large number of personnel from other parts of the organization are performing many of the process and work product evaluations. This is not a reflection on the expertise or adequacy of SQA, but an acknowledgment of the fact that SQA can't possibly possess the expertise to be proficient in all technical disciplines that may be involved in producing the organization's software products. It would be cost-prohibitive to do so.

From an organization aspect, then, the term SQA often has been identified as a specific functional entity within a development organization or within a government agency, i.e., an SQA group. In many cases, the group is assigned tasks labeled as SQA functions, based solely on the organization's definition of SQA and, usually, the complement of skills of the group designated to carry out these functions. Thus, if an SQA entity exists in a corporate structure and, let us say, the capability of this group is more or less limited to a checklist function, then a program manager may mistakenly conclude that the effort performed by this SQA group is sufficient to satisfy all the quality evaluation or SQE needs of his or her program. This situation may preclude vital measurements (or tests) on critical software modules.

Because of nonuniform interpretation of SQA functional entity responsibilities from organization to organization, conflict arises about the performance of it. As a result, very often the implementation of "quality assurance" falls by the wayside. Some evaluations may be overlooked and not performed. Many times software developers successfully promulgate an image of an SQA organization as ill-equipped to do so. More often, organizational charters circumscribe what assessments and measurements are actually performed by the SQA entity, leaving other equally valid and significant evaluations to fall through the cracks.

The point to be learned from this is that SQE and SQA are not necessarily synonymous. A clear, unambiguous definition of SQA does not exist. To avoid ambiguities and misunderstandings, our concept of a Software Quality Program focuses in on the facts that SQE is a set of activities and SQA is a functional entity within an organization. The Software Quality Program concentrates on ensuring that all the necessary evaluations are performed, rather than on who does them. The degree of SQE performed by an SQA organization is related to an SQA organization's competence (and independence) to perform those activities and, to a large extent, the size of the company.

What is crucial to any software development project is the definition and implementation of the activities necessary to assess and measure the quality of the software products produced by that project, in accordance with the requirements established for the project. When the SQE activities have been defined, the assignment of these activities to specific organizations is a management prerogative. Where SQA organizations have the capability to perform many or most of the SQE activities, these can be assigned to the SQA organizations.

5.3   Organizational Aspects of the Software Quality Program

Each of the elements of the SQP discussed above involves a number of organizations or functional entities within a company. The discussion that follows describes the functions or activities these organizations perform in the implementation of the SQP. It also explores how these organizations interact to implement the SQP.

Often the functions that will be described are not necessarily performed by separate organizations, but may sometimes be performed by different individuals within a single organization. For instance, within an MIS department, the responsibility for some of the SQP functions may be shared between the data administrator, database administrator, and quality administrator. In consideration of that, for convenience, the word "organization" will be used to refer to both actual organizations and to the situation where the functions are performed by separate individuals within an organizational entity, rather than separate organizations.

5.3.1   Organizational Relationships for the Software Quality Program

Requirements Definition. A number of organizations participate in establishing, implementing, and controlling the software quality requirements (for example, the functional and performance requirements). The kinds of organizations that are involved will depend on the type of software under development. To illustrate, the kinds of organizations that will be involved in this effort for data-intensive systems, such as MIS applications, will be very different from the kinds of organizations that will be involved for engineering applications, such as an inertial navigation system. Nonetheless, the activities that occur in establishing, implementing, and controlling the requirements, and the sequence in which they occur, will be effectively the same for all types of applications (with minor variations).

The typical sequence of events is as follows:

1. Define the system requirements.
2. Review and approve the system requirements (using in-process reviews as well as a formal review).
3. Baseline the system requirements.

4. Allocate the system requirements to hardware and software elements (subsystems) of the system.
5. Define the hardware and software subsystem requirements.
6. Review and approve the subsystem requirements (using in-process reviews as well as a formal review).
7. Baseline the subsystem requirements.
8. Define the processing requirements for the individual software applications.
9. Review and approve the processing requirements (using in-process reviews as well as a formal review).
10. Baseline the processing requirements.

Where the system is reasonably uncomplicated, subsystems may not exist. Consequently, for that situation, the steps associated with subsystem requirements definition and baselining may be eliminated.

The foregoing is not intended to characterize the requirements development process as occurring in any kind of software development waterfall model. For example, as the system requirements are being developed, the allocation of the system requirements may sometimes have begun, even though the definition of all the system requirements has not been completed. Furthermore, there may be some iteration back and forth between the system requirements development and the subsystems' requirements development to make sure that the requirements make sense. In any event, there always has to be some amount of "crawling before you learn to walk," that is, some kinds of activities must precede other activities, even if the precedent activity hasn't been completed. The intent of the foregoing is only to show the general flow of events in defining software requirements.

In developing the system requirements, a number of organizations are involved. For engineering or scientific applications, although systems engineering takes the lead for developing the requirements, software engineering organizations should be involved in a cooperative effort to jointly develop the system requirements and define the allocation of them to software elements. The using organization must also be involved in order to assure that the system requirements reflect what is needed in the production system. Where the software is developed under contract, such customer (user) involvement may be difficult to achieve without affecting the contract costs and/or schedule.

For MIS or similar applications, a number of entities are also involved. The development of the system requirements should be the primary responsibility of the using organization and specified in a user specification, which defines the functionality of the system (and does not specify how it is to be implemented in software). In many instances, the using organization may obtain assistance from the software development organization in order to ensure that the requirements are expressed correctly and unambiguously, in a manner that developers can understand, and in a manner that from which the developers can generate detailed processing requirements. The participation of the user is essential in order to ensure that the requirements are responsive to the user's needs. In parallel to this, as the user specification is being developed, preliminary processing and database design requirements are being developed by the MIS organization. Within the MIS organization, this process could involve system analysts, data analysts, and the data administrator.

A formal review should occur after the system requirements have been defined and documented, to baseline the system requirements specification (in accordance with procedures established by the configuration management group). For engineering/scientific systems, this review could involve:

- project management personnel from the user and/or customer organization
- system engineering
- major subsystems engineering (including software engineering)
- configuration management and quality assurance groups
- various groups concerned with operating, fielding, and supporting the system

For MIS systems, the review could involve:

- project management and user personnel
- MIS development organization (system analysts, data analysts, and data administrator)
- MIS configuration management and quality assurance administrators

After the formal review is successfully completed, the configuration management group is then charged with the responsibility for overseeing the control of the documented requirements to prevent unauthorized changes to them.

In developing the processing requirements for the software, there are also a number of organizations involved. For engineering or scientific applications, the software engineering organization should take the lead for developing the processing requirements. The systems engineering organization should be involved in the effort to ensure that the system requirements have been correctly allocated to the software and are being implemented, and to satisfy themselves that the software requirements are traceable to the system requirements. The using organization should also be involved in order to make sure that the software requirements reflect what is needed in the production system. Where the software is developed under contract, again, the using organization becomes the customer (or is represented by another agent acting on their behalf, for example, the Air Force Material Command acquiring aircraft systems for the operating commands), and such involvement may be difficult to achieve without affecting the contract costs and/or schedule.

For MIS or similar applications, the development of the detailed software processing and database requirements should be performed by the MIS development organization. Within the MIS organization, this process typically involves system analysts, data analysts, and the data administrator. The user organization is also involved, insofar as they have a role to play in verifying that the processing requirements reflect the functionality they want in the system.

A formal review for the software requirements should also be held. It is quite similar to the formal review for the system requirements. It should occur after the software processing requirements have been defined and documented. The software requirements specification should then be baselined in accordance with procedures established by the configuration management group. For engineering/scientific systems and for information systems, this review may involve the same participants enumerated above for system requirements reviews.

After the formal review is successfully completed, the configuration management group is then charged with the responsibility for overseeing the control of the documented requirements to prevent unauthorized changes to them.

The manager and subordinate managers responsible for software engineering (or MIS development) are accountable for implementing the requirements as established and for assuring that they are not changed in an unauthorized manner. The quality assurance group may be responsible for monitoring the configuration management process to verify that no unauthorized changes have occurred.

For this element of the Software Quality Program, then, as noted above, we see that numerous groups are active in establishing, implementing, and controlling the software quality requirements for engineering/scientific applications and information systems.

Methodology Definition. Establishing and implementing methodologies to develop the software and maintain its quality include establishing the methodologies themselves and institutionalizing them in the form of standard practices and procedures. These methodologies, practices, and procedures cover a wide number of areas. They include requirements analysis, documentation, design, coding, test, configuration management, installing and operating the software, and software maintenance.

In implementing this element of the SQP, interactions occur with a number of organizations. Software engineering must be involved in the definition process since they will be the ultimate users of the methodologies, standards, procedures, and associated tools (if applicable). An interface with the quality evaluators exists. From time to time, changes are made to the specified methodologies and implementing documentation and tools. This occurs under two conditions:

1. The specified methodologies, documentation, or tools aren't producing the required levels of quality, or

2. New methodologies have become available which will materially improve the quality of the product.

Once the changes have been made to the processes, they must be monitored to determine if, in fact, improvements have been made. The determinations of methodology adequacy result from product and process evaluations. The personnel performing software quality evaluations typically provide the raw data for evaluating existing, new, or modified methodologies and tools, while software engineering personnel generally do the analyses of the data or of the methodologies. The project manager must be consulted regarding the adoption of new methodologies and/or tools to determine if such changes will negatively impact productivity, schedule, and/or cost for that project. Operations personnel, such as software librarians and database administrators, must be consulted to determine the effect on operations. Personnel must be assigned the task of producing standards and procedures for implementing the methodologies and using the tools in a manner compatible with the established standards. Clearly, company management must be involved in this element of the SQP because of the investment in personnel to staff the function, as well as approval or disapproval for the acquisition of new methodologies, and tools to implement the methodologies.

Again, the multidisciplinary nature of the Software Quality Program is evident. One can deduce from this that many organizations are involved in establishing and implementing the methodologies for development and maintenance and producing standard practices and procedures for these functions. In organizations that have adopted the CMM as the model for process improvement, the function of coordinating these activities is often assigned to a Software Engineering Process Group (SEPG). We will discuss their role in more detail later in this chapter.

Software Quality Evaluation. Finally, we come to software quality evaluation, or SQE. Activities involved here cover the establishment of standard practices and procedures for performing evaluations and also for implementing these evaluations to determine (1) the quality of software products and (2) the adequacy of the processes impacting the quality of the products. Any evaluative undertaking that requires reasoning or subjective judgment to reach a conclusion as to whether the software product or process meets requirements is considered to be an assessment. It includes analyses, audits, surveys, and both document and project reviews.

On the other hand, measurement encompasses all quantitative evaluations, specifically, tests, demonstrations, metrics, and inspections. For these kinds of activities, direct measures can be recorded and compared against pre-established values to determine if the software meets the requirements. Accordingly, tests for unit level, integration, and software application level performance can be considered as measurement activities. Similarly, the output of a compare program or a path analyzer program can also be considered measurement.

The number of organizations involved in performing SQE can be large. Considering that SQE includes analytical as well as measurement activities, it is easy to see that SQE is a discipline that encompasses engineering as well as support groups. For example, analyses may be performed by systems engineering or a software engineering group. Tests may be performed by an integration test team or an independent software test group (or both), possibly with a quality assurance group monitoring. In some companies, the quality assurance group does testing as well.

Project reviews may include project management, and the system engineering, software engineering, configuration management (see Chapter 10, *Software Configuration Management—A Practical Look*), and quality assurance groups. Certainly a quality assurance entity would participate in and conduct audits. The configuration management and quality assurance groups would be involved in document reviews as would the system and software engineering groups.

In any event, it can be seen that the activities involved in SQE require the talents of almost all groups participating in the development process.

To complete this discussion of SQE, it is imperative to introduce the concept of independence. Relative to SQE, independence implies performance of the software quality evaluation by an organization (or individuals) different from the organization (or individuals) that has produced the products or documentation, or that execute the processes and activities being evaluated.

In some cases, independence of quality evaluators is also extended to preclude them from establishing the criteria against which the project's outputs are being gauged. Such preclusion helps reduce the perception of promoting self interest (or the potentiality for it), as might occur with the use of an outside verification and validation (V&V) agent. The V&V agent's performance might be evaluated on the basis of the number of problems found (as has been done, in some cases), rather than on their ability to demonstrate that the software performs as required. Under those circumstances, it's in the best interest of the V&V agent to find as many problems as possible—meaningful or not. Evaluators with a hidden agenda can hardly be considered independent. By removing from them the responsibility for establishing the evaluation criteria, such problems cannot arise. It should be the PM or the corporation that decides how the project should be gauged, not the software quality evaluator. The criteria for the evaluations must be based on the requirements for the product, hence the importance of establishing good requirements, and ensuring that the user's or customer's needs are accurately reflected in the requirements documents.

Independence, as a concept, has two aspects. One is independence exercised within an organization, such as the use of test team comprised of individuals different from those who designed and developed the code. The second form of independence is perhaps, the most stringent. Here, independence is exercised by employing agencies totally outside the project organization, for example, an independent V&V agent from outside the organization producing the software product. Either way, the notion of independence is applied to reduce errors resulting from oversight due to extensive familiarity with the product being evaluated.

One effort within independent SQE is the collection of the objective evidence that technical requirements have been established, products and processes conform to technical requirements, and that software products meet the specified quality requirements. This may mean that one organization does a specific measurement or assessment, but another organization establishes the criteria for measurement and assessment, verifies that the measurement and assessment has been performed, and impounds the data for eventual use in certifying the product or service. "Objective evidence" includes such items as audit reports, certified test data sheets, V&V reports, resolved software trouble reports, and the like.

The point stressed here is that the activities described as software quality evaluation are very often performed as an independent activity which can take many forms: independent organizations within a structure, independent agency within the corporation, and/or independent contractor acting on behalf of the corporation. Decisions as to the application of independence, the degree of independence to apply, and the types of independent agencies to employ are a function of a number of variables. Examples of key variables entering into these decisions are the size and complexity of the software project, corporate policy, available funds, and criticality of software to its end use (e.g., human safety, destruction of equipment, severe financial loss, etc.).

5.3.2 Mapping Software Quality Program Functions to Project Organizational Structures

Numerous organizational structures can be applied to implement a software quality program. The important point is the allocation of the associated tasks to corporate organizations available to the PM. (We make an assumption here that a PM exists. A PM typically is responsible to a higher level organization, which may be at the corporate level, and which has overall responsibility for one or more projects. This organization provides general guidance by means of policies that impact each individual project.) This allocation of the associated tasks depends upon several interrelated factors. Obviously, one factor is the business structure and guidance established by the corporation or by the PM to accomplish the project. The structure and guidance given to the PM eventually reduces to authorized funding and permissible execution control within the corporate structure, both of which limit the flexibility the PM has to conduct projects. Another factor is the extent of the tasks and the availability of personnel to perform these tasks.

In many cases, the corporation has predetermined responsibilities for its elements, thereby predetermining the allocation of tasks. This *a priori* assignment of tasks does restrict the PM in how he or she mobilizes a particular project. It is recommended that instead of imposing corporate assignment upon the project, that the PM be allowed to structure the project. This recommendation is especially applicable to the software quality program, which involves the coordination of so many disciplines. One way a PM can help insure this coordination is to appoint a software quality manager (SQM) to his or her staff (see Section 5.4 and Figure 5-4).

If we assume that most, if not all, necessary resources and talent are usually available for the program manager's execution of the SQP, the PM's task reduces to coordination of assigned activities. If the necessary resources and talent are not available, the PM must secure these through negotiation with company management.

The purpose of delegating a software quality manager is to support the PM in providing quality on the project and, more importantly, making the quality program more visible to the rest of the PM's organization. The quality manager does this by ensuring that a software quality program is planned as part of the overall software development process, by insuring that the SQP is implemented, and by keeping the PM informed and on track with the overall software development. Based upon the definition of quality (i.e., including functionality, performance, and other quality attributes), the software quality manager has the responsibility for planning and coordinating all the disciplines involved in the project. In this context the SQM is the technical lead for the project. Again, based upon the definition and implications of software quality noted earlier in this chapter, the term software quality manager does not imply that the individual is from the SQA group, as is sometimes incorrectly assumed by SQA groups (and others, as well), or that the individual is only managing the SQA portion of the project. The SQM has a much broader responsibility, especially in the coordination of all the activities that "build" quality into the product, not just simply testing for it.

Planning. The software quality manager must be an integral part of the program planning to ensure that the software quality program is addressed. He or she must play a very active role in this effort, setting up all the steps to follow in executing the software quality program, including those in the SQE effort.

Important in performing this role is the development of the software quality program plan. This can be either a major subset of the software development plan, or may be a separate document that is referenced within the software development plan. In any event, the vital task of the software quality manager during the planning phase is to produce this plan.

The SQM must work very closely with all participants in the project in order to generate the SQP plan, specifically, to ensure that:

1. the SQP plan is produced;

2. the SQP plan is complete and the elements of the SQP are integrated into the total management plan;
3. the plan contains realistic schedules;
4. the plan describes assignment of responsibilities and designates necessary authority to the appropriate performing organizations;
5. expected program outputs are specified; and
6. criteria for successful completion of tasks are stipulated.

It is important that project personnel understand how the SQP will affect them and what they are expected to input to the program. This interface definition is particularly sensitive for the assessment and measurement portion of the SQP. No one, especially in engineering, appreciates others constantly reviewing, testing, and analyzing their work. So it is important to establish what the SQE effort consists of and how it may be structured to alleviate or reduce this sensitivity.

During software development, the software quality manager uses the result of the SQE effort to track the progress of the software quality program against the program plan. A primary concern is not simply to determine compliance with the plan, but, more important, to determine if application of the planned SQP will achieve the quality, or, if the plan must be changed, to affect the desired quality.

Requirements Definition. During the process of establishing the software requirements for the project, the software quality manager must have the authority to represent the PM. Here, he or she actually manages the process. As indicated earlier, a number of organizations (or functions within an organization) may be involved in defining and establishing functional and performance requirements. These may include software engineering, user organizations, system engineering, etc. Other groups, such as those representing human factors or maintenance, must have a chance to participate in the requirements definition process in order to ensure that their needs are also reflected in the requirements documentation. The kinds of groups involved will depend on the type of application under development. As the number of these groups increases, the job of establishing the requirements becomes more and more difficult. Having the software quality manager coordinating or managing this process for the PM simplifies control to insure that requirements are established and that they are quantitative, testable, complete, and so forth.

The SQM can use several methods to accomplish this process, orchestrating the various groups involved. For example, he or she may depend totally upon the software engineering group or MIS development group to both specify the processing requirements and perform checks (assessments) as to their adequacy. On the other hand, the SQM may use some groups to define the requirements, and other groups to perform the evaluations. In some cases, the evaluations may be split between the developers and the evaluators. For instance, the assessment for traceability might be performed by the software developers, instead of other designated evaluators, utilizing the traceability capabilities embedded within the computer aided software engineering (CASE) tool being used to develop the requirements. Whoever is assigned to make these evaluations is designated in the SQP Plan.

As pointed out previously, there is an interface between the requirements definition element and the SQE element of the SQP. Requirements development involves a strong interplay between requirements analysis and SQE. The requirements must be evaluated as they are being developed to make sure that the job is being performed completely and correctly. The SQM utilizes those personnel designated in the SQP Plan to make such assessments (perform SQE). The two functions are buffered from each other by the SQM (see Figure 5-3). This technique provides some independence and is normally quite effective in reducing sensitivity on the part of those whose products (or efforts) are being assessed. The quality manager uses the outputs of the assessments to:

- ensure that the evolving requirements are modified where necessary
- assist in revising the process of establishing requirements

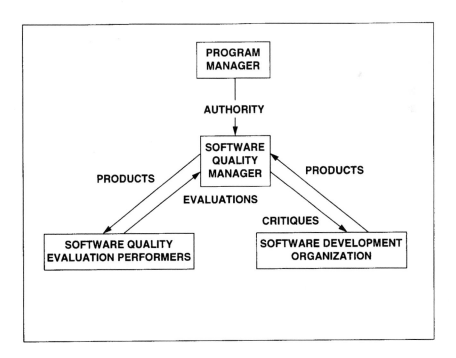

Figure 5-3   Nonsensitive interface for SQE.

- assist in changing methodologies used in this process
- enforce the procedures originally planned for this part of the SQP

Communication between the two elements can be conducted totally through the software quality manager.

Methodology Definition. As with the requirements portion, the second element of the SQP is easy to accomplish within the project structure by assigning the job to the software quality manager. There are really three parts to this job: establishing the methodologies to be used for the project, enforcing the methodologies, and modifying the selected methodologies, when necessary.

One way in which the accomplishment of this element of the SQP can be facilitated is by establishing a Software Engineering Process Group[*] (SEPG) [3, 12]. An SEPG typically is a corporate asset that evaluates methodologies for use by the organization and supports each project in selecting appropriate methodologies. It is the focal point for the methodology element of the SQP. Its main function is to serve as the initiator, sustainer, and evaluator of process change. Based on data collected through the SQE element of the SQP, the SEPG determines if the established processes for software development and maintenance are satisfying the quality requirements, especially in the form of product quality. If they are not, the SEPG researches other available methodologies to determine a suitable replacement. It also evaluates new methodologies as they become available to determine their applicability to the company's products, and their capability to meet quality criteria. If the introduction of a new methodology can effect a material improvement in product quality, the SEPG may recommend its introduction. In making this recommendation, it examines the impact of introducing the new methodology to determine if that will create excessive disruption, and significantly degrade the execution of the development or maintenance processes in ongoing projects.

At the very outset, the applicability of the established methodologies, techniques, and tools for the software to be developed on the project is determined. If an SEPG exists within the company, the software quality manager must consult with that function in order to adequately carry out this assignment. The methodologies, which are established by the SEPG, are established for use throughout the entire organization according to the different types of software products produced by the organization. It may be necessary to modify these methodologies to suit the unique requirements for the software to be produced on this project. The SQM, in conjunction with the SEPG, makes this determination and oversees the modifications, if

---

[*]   In MIS organizations, it may be known as the MIS Standards Committee. It may be known by other names as well, in other organizations, but its functions are essentially the same, no matter what it it called. For ease of reference, it will be referred to as the SEPG.

required. These modifications will be reflected in the form of project-specific modifications to the standards and procedures.

When an SEPG does not exist, the SQM must assume much of the responsibility and coordination effort that the SEPG would have performed. In establishing methodologies to use in order to achieve the desired quality attributes for the software, the SQM must bring to bear a wide range of disciplines, not just software engineering. The intent of this effort is to select those software engineering methodologies which offer the best promise of producing a software product meeting all the specified requirements—an extremely difficult process due to varying maturity in available software engineering techniques. The software quality manager must further assure that the interfacing disciplines (e.g., software engineering, testing, configuration management, etc.) are communicating with each other and coordinating on the methodologies to be employed on the project to assure that they are mutually compatible.

Once the project is started, the SQM is responsible for enforcing the implementation of the methodologies. This is accomplished by setting policy and monitoring the development, operation, and maintenance activities to verify that the policy is being followed. Enforcement often depends upon an assessment or measurement of products and development, operation, maintenance activities, creating an interface between this element of the SQP and the SQE element of the SQP. Products include preliminary and final versions of documents and preliminary software releases. Since methodologies are procedural in nature, other kinds of products may be used to evaluate whether the methodologies are being properly implemented in the development activities. For example, software development folder audit reports and reports of walkthroughs may be used to determine if the developers have followed the prescribed methodologies.

The methodologies established for the project must also be evaluated during the life of the project to determine if they are, in fact, achieving the desired results. They must be modified if they are not. The basic information on which a decision to modify the methodologies is based are the results of software quality evaluation. These adjustments (or corrective action of the processes) are initially at the project level; however, if it is determined that the corporate process is deficient, the corporate SEPG would take on the task of enterprisewide corrective action or long term improvement of the process.

Process measures can be used to make this determination. For the most part, such measurement activities have been limited to an after-the-fact evaluation, based on measurements of final work product quality (i.e., the resultant product of some specific development activity, such as a requirements specification). Thus, the utility of the information has been effectively restricted to "lessons learned" to be used on the next similar project. However, a measurement program cam be implemented to examine trends in the process effectiveness during a development effort. This effectiveness may be determined by analyzing cost, schedule, and earned value trends as a resulting from the process, as well the quality of interim products generated during development (for example, as determined from the results of a design or a code walkthrough).

Because of the interfaces that exist between this element of the SQP and SQE element of the SQP, it becomes readily evident that the software quality manager is the most logical individual to assign as the one responsible for ensuring that this job is properly accomplished on the project.

Software Quality Evaluation. The software quality manager is also responsible for the implementation of the SQE program. The software quality program plan should have defined the totality of assessment and measurement activities and assigned these to the appropriate performing organizations. Clearly, the SQA organization can be a major performer, and as indicated previously, a number of other organizations are likewise involved. Accordingly, it is essential that the SQM completely and totally define the tasks and performers.

SQE is the major instrument defining the health of the product and hence the project. Through the evaluations performed, the PM can determine if his or her product will satisfy the customers' or user's needs within cost and within schedule. Because of the number of organizations involved in the SQE process, coordination of the results of this process is an essential role to be performed by the SQM.

Whatever decision management makes, it must be sure that all SQE activities have been assigned to an organization competent to perform that function and, where independence is specified, to an organization with the proper detachment as well.

5.3.3 Example Implementations of the Software Quality Program

To varying degrees, the principles discussed in this chapter are slowly coming into practice. A number of organizations have begun to incorporate the elements of the SQP, including the SEPG, into the structure of their software development organizations.

Although many organizations have implemented SEPGs, and do many of the SQP activities described in this chapter, what is still lacking in most organizations is the coordination of the elements of the SQP, and the coordination of the SEPGs (when they do exist) with the elements of the SQP.

Clearly, a major determinant as to how the SQP is to be implemented is the size of the organization. A small organization, comprised of a number of small projects, cannot implement the SQP in the same way that a large organization would. This section discusses strategies for implementing the SQP, based on the experience of these organizations. It also discusses the implementation of the SEPG concept.

Software Engineering Process Group Role. Many companies have begun to adopt the SEPG concept. It is an important factor in successful implementation of the second element of the Software Quality Program, the establishment of methodologies. As pointed out earlier, the SEPG is the focal point for methodology selection and evaluation. Many of the companies that have been assessed by the SEI, or that have been trained by the SEI to perform self-assessments, now use SEPGs. This has come about as an outgrowth of the assessment results. Some of these organizations have established SEPG structures without having an assessment performed. They were established because these organizations recognized that the function performed by such a group is vital for the production of quality software and, consequently, to the success of the organization. Many MIS departments have established Standards Committees that perform many of the same functions that an SEPG does.

Reference 3 describes strategies for the implementation of SEPGs into the organizational structure. Organizational size is taken into account in the strategies discussed.

Large Projects. Clearly, the easiest organization structure to describe is that which exists for large projects in organizations producing a good number of engineering or scientific applications. "Large," as used here, is qualitative. It refers to organizations having approximately 40 or more developers with at least some projects that involve four or more developers. These should not be taken as hard and fast numbers, but rather as a rough threshold values to distinguish between large and small.

Figure 5-4 illustrates one organizational concept. In this example, the organization is producing a number of software applications that are embedded in a hardware system. Each application is being developed by a team of developers, and the number of developers in any one team ranges from eight to thirteen. Each team is headed by a software project leader who, in turn, reports to the assistant project manager (APM) for Software Development.

In this structure, the software quality manager, or project software quality manager (PSQM) as this person is called, is responsible for planning the performance of the SQP and documenting the output of the planning effort in the appropriate plans, coordinating the activities of the performers of the SQP activities, and monitoring their performance to verify that it is being performed properly.

For the requirements element of the SQP, the organizations involved in the requirements definition effort include Systems Engineering, Software Development, and Logistics. The Logistics organization participates in the definition of the maintainability and software supportability requirements for the operational software. In this structure, the PSQM is responsible for coordinating and integrating the requirements definition activities of these areas of the project. The PSQM, as can be seen from the figure, also coordinates with the configuration manager with regard to establishing the baseline for the requirements.

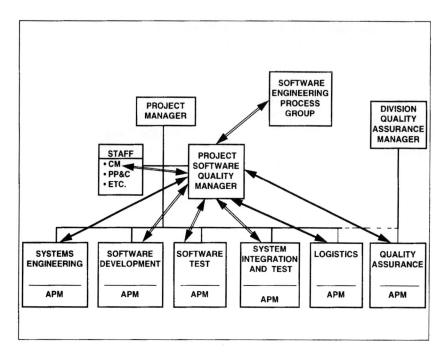

Figure 5-4   Large project organization example.

To establish and maintain the methodologies to be utilized on the project, the PSQM coordinates with the SEPG. The SEPG is responsible for coordinating with the other organizations within the company with regard to establishing the methodologies in general usage and for determining their effectiveness. (Its position on the chart has no significance with respect to hierarchy or importance. Its position is only intended to show that, as an enterprisewide resource, it is outside the organizational structure for the project).

Software quality evaluation is performed by Quality Assurance, Software Test, System Integration and Test, and Software Development. The PSQM coordinates and monitors the performance of the software quality evaluation elements of the SQP. The functions that each organization performs in support of the quality evaluation element of the SQP is documented in the Software Quality Evaluation Plan (SQEP) document. Feedback of the evaluation results into the development, operations, and maintenance activities and products is provided for in the SQEP. The coordination and monitoring of the feedback process is another function performed by the PSQM.

Because the PSQM is a staff function to the project manager, he has a direct line of communication to him to ensure that all project staff members comply with the requirements of the SQP. In the event of a noncompliance that cannot be resolved directly with the individual or organization involved, the PSQM can call on the project manager to enforce compliance. This type of a project structure can also deal effectively with recalcitrant project managers. Direct lines of communication also exist with the Quality Assurance organization, and these lines can be used to resolve any such conflicts.

Another organizational structure that has been effective is the integrated product team (IPT). The intent of the IPT concept is to ensure effective communication of project-critical information between all members of the team. This is often accomplished through colocation of the team members. IPTs will often include customer representatives to encourage rapid resolution of contractual issues, as well as speedy clarification of requirements-related questions.

IPTs may exist at various levels. For instance, if we examine Figure 5-5, we see that IPTs exist at the system, segment, and subsystem level. Since software exists at each of these levels, a SQM could exist at each level shown. For instance, one would exist at the Space Segment level, and one could likely exist for each one of the subsystems comprising the Space Segment. Furthermore, if the lower level subsystems were sufficiently large and complex. IPTs could exist at lower levels. An SQM would be a member of each of these IPTs, as well, if each had a significant software component.

Small Organizations. Small organizations face a totally different picture when it comes to implementing the elements of the SQP. In this situation, a number of conditions may exist. Two example situations are: (1) the company may be a one-project

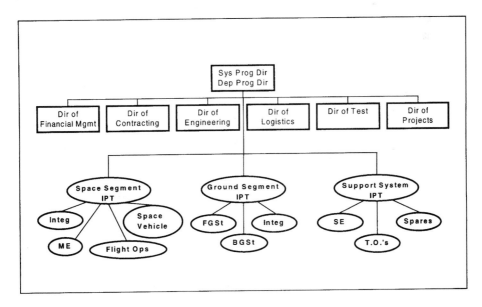

Figure 5-5   Sample integrated product team structure.

company, or (2) the company may be working entirely on a number of small projects. MIS organizations in many companies are an example of the latter. Figure 5-6 is an example of how one MIS department organized to implement the SQP.

Within the MIS Department, the MIS Standards Committee fulfills the function of the SEPG. It is comprised of key members of the department including the MIS quality administrator, and representatives of the development, system resources, data administration, and configuration management areas of the department. Because of the size of the department, none of the members is assigned full-time to the Standards Committee to do its work.

The MIS quality administrator reports administratively to the MIS manager, and is an employee of that department. By company policy, the MIS quality administrator is deputized to act on behalf of Corporate Quality Assurance to ensure that the provisions of the corporate quality program are carried out. The MIS quality administrator has a responsibility to Corporate Quality Assurance to provide periodic reports on the activities of the MIS Quality Program. Note that in this case the quality administrator is not independent. The intent of independence is achieved, however, through a reporting channel to Corporate Quality Assurance and periodic audits by Corporate Quality Assurance to ensure that the provisions of the applicable policies and procedures are being correctly implemented.

In this structure, the MIS quality administrator acts more as a coordinator and monitor with respect to the SQP functions. The responsibility for defining require-

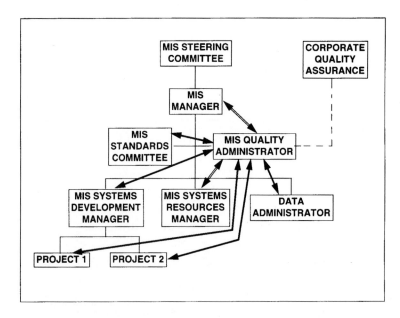

Figure 5-6   Small organization example—MIS organization.

ments is shared between the user community and the project. Requirements definition is performed in accordance with the procedures defined in the MIS Standards Manual, and the individuals responsible for performing this task, the outputs they produce, the informal and formal reviews to be held, and the schedule for the entire activity is documented in the Software Development Plan (SDP) for the project. The MIS quality administrator monitors the activity to ensure that it is being performed as prescribed by the MIS Standards Manual and the SDP. Any conflicts regarding implementation that cannot be resolved directly with the development or user project leaders are raised with the MIS Systems development manager for resolution.

The responsibility for the methodology element of the SQP is vested in the MIS Standards Committee. They perform the function of the SEPG. The MIS quality administrator is a member of the MIS Standards Committee and ensures that this function is being properly executed. The project-specific modifications, if applicable, to the standardized methodologies are documented in the SDP. Project-specific adaptations to the standards and procedures are also identified in the SDP. The MIS quality administrator is a signatory party to the SDP and, consequently, can coordinate and monitor the application of this aspect of the SQP to the project.

The SQE element of the SQP is handled in a unique way by this company. A typical project size is approximately three to four developers. Because of the size of the entire organization, and the size of the projects, only two people, the MIS quality administrator and one assistant, are dedicated full-time to quality program tasks. Each project has its own part-time quality evaluator, and this person is also a part-time developer. He or she is responsible for performing the quality evaluations. Where necessary, the quality evaluators can call on other resources elsewhere within the MIS Department or within the affected user community to assist in the quality evaluations. For instance, in performing a quality evaluation of a requirements specification for a payroll program, the quality evaluator can call on personnel within Accounting to assist in the review of the document.

The results of each evaluation are documented on a quality evaluation record. These are entered into a log and into a database. Both are available online. A major function performed by the MIS quality administrator is auditing each individual project for compliance with the SQEP and the standards and procedures specific to SQE contained in the MIS Standards Manual. Since the SQEP contains the definition of the SQE tasks to be performed, the person responsible for performing it, and the schedule for its performance, the MIS quality administrator uses it to determine when to perform the audits. The database is queried to determine if a record exists of a given evaluation's performance. The MIS quality administrator has the authority to review the record and can spot check the product itself to ensure that the review was performed in accordance with the approved procedures. The MIS quality administrator can also participate in a review performed on an activity or product.

Another responsibility assigned to the MIS Quality Administrator is the audit of the configuration management functions. The configuration management functions are distributed to various projects. The development baseline is under the control of the development project leader, which results in another interface with the project leader, and the production baselined is under the control of the MIS Software Configuration Control Board, which is chaired by the MIS manager. Changes to the applications software, corporate and project data dictionaries, and databases are handled by the librarian, data administrator, and database administrator, respectively, and their functions are audited by the MIS quality administrator.

Audits performed on the MIS area by Corporate Quality Assurance determine if these functions are being properly performed by the MIS quality administrator.

5.4   Summary

In organizing to implement the Software Quality Program, several concepts must be kept in mind.

First, it must be emphasized that the foundation for the organization is tied to achieving the requisite quality in the software product. One must understand what software quality is and the technical aspects of specifying, designing, and testing for it. Software quality is achieved with proper software design and implementing appropriate processes. Quality cannot be achieved by "assuring" and testing the product.

Second, the ideas associated with software quality lead to the software quality program. General principles of such a program have been discussed. Three elements of the Software Quality Program were described in some detail; these elements interact not only with each other but also with all other project activities. This interaction is extremely complex, occurring at many levels within the software project and throughout the project's life.

From the perspective of the software quality program, an organization can be derived based upon corporate structure (controlling policies) and available talent. It is recommended that the PM be allowed to structure his or her own project organization without the restriction caused by *a priori* corporate organizations. The PM needs to recognize and understand the SQP. Given this understanding, the PM allocates tasks of the SQP to those with appropriate talent. Because of its broad nature, the SQP requires a range of disciplines including software engineering as well as evaluation expertise. It is recommended that a software quality manager be appointed who is steeped in this expertise and in the methodologies needed to achieve software quality.

References

1. Baker, Emanuel R., and Fisher, Matthew J., "A Software Quality Framework." In: *Concepts—The Journal of Defense Systems Acquisition Management*, Moore, Robert Wayne, ed.; Vol. 5, No. 4 (Autumn 1982) (Fort Belvoir, VA: Defense Systems Management College, 1982).

2. Ferguson, J.; Cooper, J.; Falat, M.; Fisher, M.; Guido, A.; Matejecek, J.; Marciniak, J.; Webster, R. "Software Acquisition Capability Maturity Model (SA-CMM^{SM})" Version 1.01, *CMU / SEI-96-TR-020*, December 1996.

3. Paulk, Mark C.; Weber, Charles V.; Curtis, Bill; and Chrissis, Mary Beth. *The Capability Maturity Model: Guidelines for Improving the Software Process* (New York: Addison-Wesley, 1995).

4. Humphrey, W. S. and W. L. Sweet. "A Method for Assessing the Software Engineering Capability of Contractors." *Technical Report CMU / SEI-87-TR-23*. Software Engineering Institute, Carnegie Mellon University, September 1987.

5. Humphrey, W. S. and Kitson, D. H. "Preliminary Report on Conducting SEI-Assisted Assessments of Software Engineering Capability." *Technical Report CMU-SEI-87-TR-16*. Software Engineering Institute, Carnegie Mellon University, July 1987.

6. Report, *Process Maturity Profile of the Software Community: 1997 Update*, Software Engineering Institute, Carnegie Mellon University, October 1997.

7. Yacobellis, Robert E. *A White Paper on U.S. vs. Japan Software Engineering*, January 1990.

8. Ingrassia, Frank S., "The Unit Development Folder (UDF); An Effective Management Tool for Software Development." In: *Tutorial; Software Management*, Reifer, Donald J. ed., third edition, (Washington, DC; IEEE Computer Society Press, 1986).

9. Joint Logistics Commanders Joint Group on Systems Engineering, *Practical Software Measurement*, Version 2.1, 27 March 1996.

10. Schulmeyer, G. Gordon and McManus, James I., ed., *Total Quality Management for Software*, (New York: Van Nostrand Reinhold Company, Inc., 1992).

11. IEEE Standard 610.12, *Glossary of Software Engineering Terminology*, 1990.

12. Humphrey, Watts S. *Managing the Software Process*, (New York: Addison-Wesley, 1989).

## CHAPTER 6

Personnel Requirements to Make Software Quality Assurance Work

Kenneth S. Mendis
Roche Carolina, Inc.

6.1   Introduction

Obtaining qualified engineers and keeping them motivated in what they are doing is a problem most of the engineering disciplines have been facing for some time. The problem is compounded when we focus on the software engineering discipline. At the level of software quality assurance (SQA), we find ourselves battling with the software developers for the few software engineers who are available.

To be effective and contribute to a project's success in a manner that is professionally acceptable, the SQA organization must be staffed with qualified software engineers. In addition, these individuals must also possess the credentials that make them good quality assurance representatives. Achieving any of the promised benefits of SQA is directly related to an organization's ability to staff the operation. Some of the issues the manager will be confronted with are engineer motivation, career training, and recruiting techniques.

Former Department of Defense (DoD) standards for software development (DOD-STD-1679A and DOD-STD-2167) and their companion handbooks (MIL-HDBK-286 and DOD-HDBK-287) of the 70s and 80s, and the more recent MIL-STD-498 Software Development and Documentation, have now been replaced by the commercially available Software Life Cycle Process standard defined in ISO/IEC 12207. Additionally, ISO 9001 and the ISO 9000-3 Guidelines for the application of ISO 9001 process requirements to the development, supply, and maintenance of software, is also beginning to influence the software development and quality decisions of many organizations. Also along these lines is the Code of Federal Regulations that direct the Food and Drug Administration (FDA) as it monitors food production, the development of medical devices, the medicines we take, and other FDA-relevant consumer products and services. Each standard defines a structured approach for developing software, and with that approach comes the need to staff positions within the organization to enforce the plans that have been set in motion. Unfortunately, the glamour and challenges provided by a developing environment attracts the interest of the majority of software engineers. This leaves SQA with a limited number of qualified personnel from which to choose.

More recently the Defense Logistics Agency (DLA) has developed and introduced an approach to software quality assurance. The procedure, known as the Single Process Initiative (SPI) for In-Plant Quality Assurance, replaces the current Contractor Quality Assurance Program and makes use of continuous improvement tools and problem solving techniques to examine the adequacy of a contractor's process to continuously produce conforming products and to identify opportunities for product improvements.

The concept of SPI includes management commitment, people development, quality excellence, and user satisfaction. Implementation of SPI embraces techniques that use process and product quality to evaluate the quality of an organization's software products. SPI focuses on working with the software developers, working with the software users, and working with contracting agencies to produce a product that meets the users' needs. It means working as a team to measure and continuously improve the process. How does the SQA engineering staff face these challenges?

6.2 Facing the Challenge

Why consider Software Quality Assurance? A review of warning letters issued by the U.S. Food and Drug Administration to firms in the U.S., Europe, and Asia, as a result of formal inspections, highlighted the weakness of firms to adequately institute a Software Quality Assurance program that assures proper software design, development, testing, documentation, and change control. In most cases reviewed, FDA actions usually had a negative impact on the validation status of the computer system and on a firm's bottom line.

Imagine the impact on the Gulf War if the United States Army had to wait to validate the performance of its Patriot missiles after installation in a war zone. What if the computer control and guidance system had not been validated to do what it was supposed to do every single time, i.e. intercept and destroy incoming enemy missiles? Or in another instance, picture yourself several hundred feet below sea level sitting in front of a computer terminal in the submarine command and control center ready to fire a missile. What if the installed guidance software used to deliver the missile had not been validated? Think of the destruction it would cause if it ended up somewhere hundreds of miles from its intended target! SQA played an important part in the outcome of the Gulf War.

If the process of computer quality assurance can land men on the moon and bring them back safely, defend a country against external attack, help pilots land safely at our busiest airports during a blinding snow storm, then why not apply such a trustworthy methodology to all of your software development efforts?

Our academic institutions today do not provide the required training for SQA engineers. By an SQA engineer is meant a software engineer trained in the disciplines of software quality assurance. Today, little or no training is provided in the techniques of software design review, good software documentation, or software reliability and maintainability. Training is also inadequate for software attributes such as the use of program design languages, top-down development, object-oriented methods, and structured programming techniques, which are used to assess and measure the progress of software development. About the only way an individual becomes knowledgeable of SQA principles and disciplines is by hands-on work-related experience, which only makes the SQA staffing problem even more difficult.

Individuals involved in developing, staffing, and maintaining an SQA organization within their organization are familiar with the daily battles of SQA staffing. It is not uncommon to search through countless resumes and interview hundreds of applicants in an effort to find those individuals who would make good SQA engineers. In many instances, if an applicant is technically acceptable, then he or she still lacks those special attributes that turn a software engineer into a software quality assurance engineer. Therefore, recruiting and hiring qualified personnel to staff SQA positions is expensive and time consuming.

Thus, before the organization proceeds on a recruiting campaign, it is necessary to define and set priorities for those issues and positions that are critical to the success of the SQA function, The organization must consider the following factors:

- Is it possible to promote from within and train individuals to fill the openings?
- Can contract employees help fill the organization's needs and, if so, in what capacity should these employees be utilized?
- Should the recruiting effort be national, regional, or local?
- What does it take to attract qualified trained individuals to your company?
- What does an organization do to retain its qualified staff?

Another problem that one has to face is how to hold the qualified individuals' interest and motivation in job assignments. Developing and outlining career paths is another important factor in the problems facing SQA staffing. Indeed, in my opinion, the most serious problem a manager faces is preventing his or her department from becoming a stepping stone to other opportunities within the organization. The SQA department, if it is to develop into an effective organization dedicated to assuring a product's software quality, must consist of professionals both seasoned in software and dedicated to quality, and capable of providing guidance, training, and quality-consciousness within the organization.

Lastly, top management support is of prime concern. The lack of top management support or lack of a clear understanding of SQA's needs is perhaps the major issue confronting most SQA organizations today. To properly staff the organization, management must clearly understand the problems of personnel and assurance goals and be willing to address them. Support and understanding must go hand in hand; one without the other is ineffective.

6.3   Organization Structure

In April, 1979 the Software Management Subgroup of the Joint Coordinating Group on Computer Resource Management (JCG, CRM) sponsored a Joint Logistics Commanders software workshop. One of the key findings of the workshop stressed the difficulties facing the implementation of SQA, such as the lack of a well-defined and consistent set of requirements, differences in SQA approaches across the various branches of the services and industry, and the unavailability of a good source of experienced personnel. Almost two decades later this requirement continues to be a concern within organizations.

Experience has shown that independence is the key to success in implementing SQA programs. The SQA organization should be situated in the overall organization so that it always reports to the same level as the department that it must evaluate and audit. The SQA organization must have the organizational status and access to top management as do the other functions. Figure 6-1 shows how this concept may be instituted within an organization and how the assurance function can use its position within an organization to achieve its goals and objectives.

An industry survey conducted by the National Security Industrial Association in 1983 and a 1995 assessment by the American Society for Quality (ASQ) reveals that the typical SQA organization possesses the following attributes:

- The SQA organization is located within the quality assurance organization.
- SQA is staffed with people who possess approximately one to five years of software engineering experience.
- The person in charge of the SQA organization has over five years of software experience and is a middle manager within the organization.
- The career path for these individuals is into development and management.

The SQA function, established to evaluate the software development effort, must possess the objective and authoritative controls required. An SQA function that

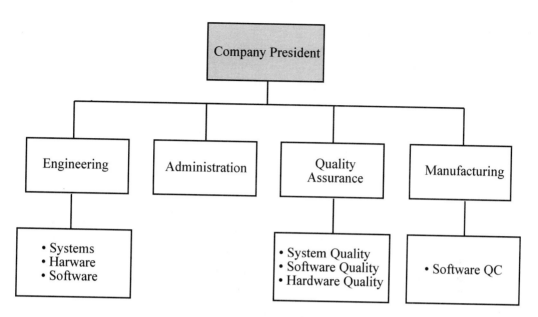

Figure 6-1   Organizational structure.

reports to the development organization lacks the independence needed to get the job done properly. Moreover, the members of the development organization are by first love software designer/programmers, therefore making their quality tasks secondary in nature. An organizational structure of the type shown in Figure 6-1 allows itself to develop the SQA engineers into a position of responsibility, leadership, and independent management reporting. It is from here that the SQA engineer derives a perceived responsibility that allows him or her to translate that into getting the job done right.

A common problem of many organizations arises from appointing project-related software engineers as SQA personnel. These individuals function as senior staff members within the project organization, directing and managing the SQA effort of the project, while reporting to project management. A shortcoming of this approach is that if SQA is relatively new and not completely defined, its implementation varies sharply from individual to individual trying to enforce it—particularly those with a loyalty divided between the project and assurance.

Experience has shown that to establish any new discipline within an organization, a central motivating force is needed. Fragmented efforts are diluted and end up being ineffective. In my own experience, project-related SQA activity generally lacks depth and maturity. All too often, the SQA activity functions as a workhorse of the developer performing tasks for the developer.

SQA will work effectively only if all project SQA personnel report to a single SQA manager. This organizational posture allows for specialization—all personnel meeting the needs of the project, as well as uniformity—all projects meeting the same minimum acceptance criteria. Members of the SQA staff should have relatively high technical expertise and a thorough knowledge of good software and quality assurance practices. The manner in which the staff is organized depends largely on staff size, estimated work load, and personnel skills.

6.4   Identifying Software Quality Assurance Personnel Needs

A ten-step process to identify SQA personnel needs is shown graphically in Figure 6-2. The process is presented sequentially with each step using the results of the previous step to build upon the next. What is particularly important about this process is that it is established on a Total Quality Management (TQM) foundation. Using a team from within the organization together with continuous improvement techniques and buy-in by the organization and those involved in developing the system, "personnel requirements to make software quality assurance work" is treated as an integral part of the organization's staffing activity. The ten-step process will assure the organization that the individuals selected will require minimal effort to train and integrate into the organization. The process is based on W. Edward Deming's circle (Plan-Do-Check-Act) and on the fact that a successful computer system is achieved only if QA is built into the design, development, and release process.

6.4.1 Step 1: Identify the Team

When formulating this approach, first consider how you intend to answer these questions. What is the person supposed to do in SQA? What are the required qualifications for the position? How will you know if the solution will meet the needs of the organization and the project? Who is the responsible individual(s) for monitoring progress? How will I know if the results were a success or a failure? To get the answers to these and other questions use the team approach to develop solutions. Do this by convening past and present software development process owners. The team leader should be someone who has prior experience in computer system development combined with a strong background in software quality assurance, software/system engineering, and an expertise in post-development software support. This person must understand today's computer software development, testing, quality assurance, and change management methodologies. He or she must possess skills that foster teamwork and he or she must understand the requirements for computer systems development. The technique of team dynamics depends on working relationships and the fact that each team member brings a specialized expertise during the selection process and that these team members are capable of critiquing and providing the needed expertise to develop the solution.

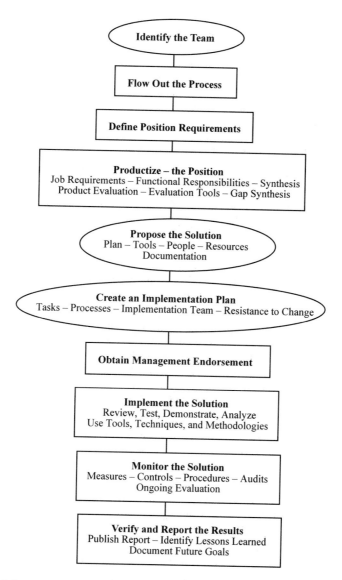

Figure 6-2   Ten-step process to identify SQA personnel based on Deming's Circle.

6.4.2 Step 2: Flow Out the Process

Before beginning the selection process tasks it is helpful to first flow out the computer system development process and the quality assurance tasks associated with the process, if not already done so. Interview developers and process owners. Determine what processes and functions are under computer control and monitoring and which are not. Prioritize each task, assigning a high priority to those tasks critical to product quality and personnel safety. Using the process, develop a plan that outlines those processes that need to be implemented in order to assure a quality software product.

6.4.3 Step 3: Define Position Requirements

The next task that will be handled by the team is to develop the position requirements—job descriptions. At a minimum, address the following topics: identify and define qualifications and position tasks, evaluate the design process and determine current results, compare current results to requirements and expectations, and identify problems to solve and opportunities for improvement. Process capability requirements and problem identification and management are the building blocks that help define if the position requirements can be met.

6.4.4 Step 4: Productize the Position

This task is associated with determining what engineering documentation will be required to support the position. Productization can be grouped into four steps: requirements analysis, functional analysis, synthesis, and solution. Although represented sequentially, these steps are interacting and interdependent. Each step not only feeds the next step but also provides new considerations for the previous step. The outcome of this step will be a job description and the tasks associated with the requirements of SQA.

6.4.5 Step 5: Propose the Solution

This step requires that the plans, tools, people, and resources be documented. Proposing the solution also means determining the cost and benefits associated with implementation. In proposing the solution also consider the following:

- **Describe the Proposed Solution**
    - create the new process flowchart
    - identify appropriate in-process and outcome measures
    - identify change in techniques; resources; information
    - determine people aspects; roles, training, interactions

- **Cost and Benefits**
    - estimate the costs
    - estimate the savings
    - identify performance improvements
    - identify customer benefits

6.4.6 Step 6: Create an Implementation Plan

In addition to those items discussed in step 5 the team should develop an implementation plan that also addresses the following:

- The SQA process to be implemented
- Identify and plan for resistance to changes
- Establish implementation team

6.4.7 Step 7: Obtain Management Endorsement

For the solution to be successful management buy-in is crucial. In order to secure this approval consider the following tasks during this step:

- Prepare a presentation for management
- Present the solution to management
- Present the solution to those affected (after obtaining management approval)

6.4.8 Step 8: Implement the Solution

The implementation phase begins with a briefing that explains the goals and objectives of the SQA solution. Implementation is the responsibility of the team (quality, development, and manufacturing) responsible for producing and using quality software. A team approach is recommended because SQA should be viewed as a task that involves both developer and user.

6.4.9 Step 9: Monitor the Solution

The responsibility of the team during this step is to assure that the solutions that have been developed are consistent throughout all phases of the development effort and that in-process product and process audits, evaluations, controls, and procedures are being used to assure adherence to the plan. The solution monitoring process may consists of three activities: a capability audit, a product compliance audit of documentation, and problem identification and management.

6.4.10 Step 10: Verify and Report the Results

At the conclusion of predefined intervals management should be briefed on the findings and should be given an opportunity to offer evidence or to refute any finding. Following the completion of each validation task, an exit interview shall be conducted with process owners to debrief them of the validation team's findings. The findings and recommendations should be published in a validation report and made available to process owners and cognizant personnel affected by the validation findings. Follow-up investigations of validation findings should be conducted by the validation team or their representatives to verify that corrective actions have been implemented.

6.5   Characteristics of a Good SQA Engineer

As mentioned earlier, the shortage of software professionals makes recruiting software engineers into the quality assurance profession a difficult task. Two factors appear to work against SQA:

- developing software is far more attractive to the software engineer, and
- the career path for someone in the development environment is clearly more attractive.

Dunn and Ullman [1] suggest that, in the past, software engineers have commanded salaries substantially greater than those of quality engineers. This is a differential that appears to be diminishing and should be eliminated by all organizations developing software on any significant scale. Then the subtler prestige and glamour aspects can be addressed. If an organization is willing to take the time, it can probably find suitable candidates within its wage and salary guidelines. But time is money, and the longer it takes to hire the talent required, the longer it takes to bring the SQA function up to the engineering level now required to produce quality software products. More recently the new incentive by companies to have SQA engineers certified by the ASQ as Certified Software Quality Engineers (CSQE) makes selecting qualified SQA engineers easier. Built on topics that constitute the "Body of Knowledge for Software Quality Engineers," CSQEs are certified on their body of knowledge in Software Quality Management, Software Process, Software Metrics, Measurement, and Analytical Methods, Software Inspection, Testing, Verification, and Validation, Software Audits, and Software Configuration Management. Refer to Chapter 7, *ASQ Software Quality Engineer Certification Program,* for more details about the certification process.

What makes a good software quality assurance engineer? Consider the following characteristics:

- The individual who seems to work the best appears to have spent approximately three to five years developing software. This individual recognizes the limited involvement he or she has had in the total developmental effort, and now wants a bigger piece of the pie. SQA clearly will provide this opportunity. This is an opportunity to get system and managerial exposure in a relatively short period of time. It is to the SQA manager's advantage to point this out to a prospective new hire. However, finding such an individual with the necessary qualifications, as listed below, can be difficult and may require a national recruiting policy.

- The experienced software engineer who has seen it all and has survived the software battles. This individual can truly contribute to improving software development methodologies, being inherently familiar with the existing developing techniques and capable of assuming a position of leadership in a very short time. However, I must caution the reader that lack of motivation may sometimes be a problem for individuals in this group.

- The individual seeking to advance to management or a program manager's position clearly is a good candidate. It is within the SQA organization that one learns how to deal with people, learns about design and development approaches and techniques, and how to manage and report on software development projects—some of the attributes one would look for when recruiting for a management position.

- A good SQA engineer must possess good communication skills. This is especially true if he or she is to be effective in performing SQA duties. As we are well aware, software engineers at times can be an unfriendly breed of professionals, very possessive of their work, and always protecting what they have designed as confidential. An SQA engineer has to be able to deal with this and win the trust and respect of software design engineers. Communication skills play a vital role in this regard; the individual should be skillful in expressing ideas both orally and in writing.

- An academic background in computer science is essential. Over the years many individuals who possess a degree in education or the liberal arts have made the switch to software. They were hired as programmers and function in this capacity. I have found that for the most part their ability in the software engineering field is limited to that of being programmers rather than being effective in design. These individuals work well under the supervision of a good software designer. They do, however, make poor SQA engineers.

- The individual who will succeed as an SQA engineer must be willing to meet and accept new challenges, and be able to carry out independent research and analysis assignments that deal with analysis of the techniques used to develop software. Such an individual must be capable of evaluating software development methodologies with an eye to improving software productivity and performance.

- The introduction of Total Quality Management tools such as continuous improvement. and problem solving techniques places additional demands upon the SQA engineer (see Reference 2, *Total Quality Management for Software*). For the first time SQA engineers are now being called upon to help establish and manage the cultural environment and monitor performance improvement goals set by the development organization, therefore requiring the SQA engineer to sharpen the needed people development skills.

6.6 Training the Hardware QA Engineer

Training the hardware QA engineer is one method of obtaining and retaining good SQA engineers. Some hardware QA engineers of yester-year may now be in a very unmotivated position because of obsolescence in hardware engineering. Selecting those individuals willing to be retrained in software engineering is the first step. Such individuals will tend to stay within the SQA field the longest. Furthermore, they bring to the function the needed expertise to deal with designers and managers, a quality that is learned over years of on-the-job training.

A hardware QA engineer requires a number of years of training to become an effective SQA engineer. However, the return on this type of investment is, in my opinion, the surest method of developing a staff of good qualified engineers in software quality. This approach to SQA staffing allows for a permanent core within the function, essential if the SQA activity is to survive as a long-range objective of the company.

Training of hardware QA engineers in software should follow one of two paths. The engineer should be encouraged to pursue a degree in computer science. Also, in-house training and learning by example should be pursued, with job assignments utilizing newly learned skills. Today's highly technological advances in the computer engineering field mandates that these individuals obtain the required academic training before releasing them to perform SQA work.

6.7 Training the Software Engineer

The optimal approach—the one the author has found to work the best with software engineers—is the mentor approach to training in the SQA discipline. A mentoring SQA is a teacher or an advisor, someone who has worked in SQA for a number of years. This individual is charged with teaching the software engineer the principles of SQA engineering. This technique to training works well with recent college graduates. Selective training is needed if this approach is to be applied to the more experienced software engineer.

The basic principle under the mentor approach to staffing is to hire software engineers into the SQA organization and to assign them to an experienced SQA engineer. The mentor's responsibility will be to outline a program of task training and to closely monitor the new hire's work output. This mentor–new hire relationship gives the new hire access to someone who will provide guidance and leadership during the learning phase. For this approach to training to work, it is imperative that a training plan exist. An example of such a plan is outlined below.

The following steps will be taken to indoctrinate new personnel into the software quality assurance team:

- Describe the organization surrounding the project to which the new hire is to be assigned, and explain what each department does and how it interacts with the other departments. As a minimum, the departments to be discussed should include the following:
  - System engineering
  - Software engineering
  - Software configuration management
  - Data management
  - Software integration
  - Software quality assurance
  - Software test
- Indoctrinate the new hire in the use and availability of existing tools and how to utilize tools to their full potential.
- Assign as reading assignments project-related software development plans, software quality assurance plans, and software configuration management plans. The objective in these assignments is to orient the new hire in the company's software development and quality assurance process.
- Define SQA's involvement in the development process and monitor compliance by establishing entry and exit criteria associated with the respective development phases as outlined in Figure 6-3. The reviews of the program technical approach include a requirements review, design reviews that include preliminary and critical reviews, and documentation reviews. During the build and test phases reviews include test readiness and test exit reviews, and prior to release and use, the conduct of physical and functional reviews.

The benefits to be derived from such a program are twofold. The new hire has easy access to someone who is capable of guiding him or her in the performance of work assignments. Most important, the new hire is able to learn first-hand from someone who has been through the process and knows all of its ups and downs. The organization must be willing to devote a minimum of one calendar year to such a training program before the individual can be utilized effectively as a junior contributor within the organization.

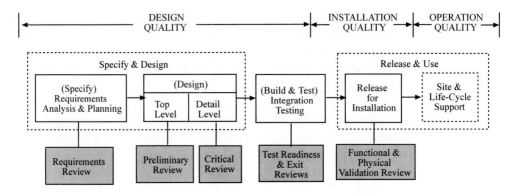

Figure 6-3   Software development with in-process SQA reviews.

6.8   Rotating Software Engineers

Rotating software engineers through the SQA function is an approach that brings to the software QA function bright and capable software professionals. They should be expected to serve a minimum of at least one year within the SQA function. But the following problems will have to be worked out before such an approach to SQA engineering will benefit the organization:

- There exists a shortage of qualified software professionals within the software development environment. A software manager would be hard-pressed to release a good software engineer to SQA, if he or she is facing a manpower problem that could impact schedule completion of a project. In many instances the tendency is to release those individuals who are poor performers.

- A rotating SQA policy requires support from upper management to become effective and not to end up as a dumping ground for the bad programmer or software engineer. The choice of who makes the rotation into the SQA section should be mutually agreed to by all concerned. Motivating the software engineer to participate willingly in such a program is necessary, and the only sure means of accomplishing this is to institute a promotional policy that gives special consideration to individuals who have already served as SQA engineers. The same policy should also hold true for one being considered for a manager's position in software engineering.

   The author knows of three organizations that have tried such a program: IBM, Raytheon, and ITT. The benefits these organizations have derived from such a program have been limited to how successful they have been in retaining the services of the individuals that participated in the rotation program. Because the majority of those participating in the program were recent college graduates all companies reported that many participants had left for assignments in other companies. For a rotation policy of this type to succeed as a means of increasing the awareness of SQA within an organization, what is needed is a core of resident SQA experts to learn from so as to continue the smooth operation of the SQA function. Furthermore individuals selected to participate in the program should have between three and five years of industry experience, therefore reducing the possibility of their departure after the rotation assignment.

6.9 New College Graduates

The recent college graduate is ideal for certain specialized tasks within the SQA organization. Today's SQA organizations are evolving from a labor-intensive approach to a more computerized approach to quality software (see Chapter 14). Such a transition requires developing SQA tools to perform tasks that were once manually performed, hence the transition from a labor-intensive approach to QA to an automated approach. Based on the author's experience, the recent college graduate is an excellent source of expertise to perform some of the tasks needed to orchestrate such a transition.

It is a well-known fact that the interest and professional development of recent college graduates in computer science tends to follow the following broad guidelines. First, the graduate seeks out programming tasks and appears to find satisfaction in the activities associated with such a task. After a short period, from three to six months, his or her interest focuses on the challenges provided with being involved in software design. Some time later in terms of career growth, task assignments in software architecture become appealing. Employing a recent college graduate to perform SQA tasks at the onset has been proved to be a poor management decision, and the organization runs the risk of losing that employee because of a lack of interest in the work assigned.

The procedure that appears to work best is to combine programming tasks with SQA tasks. Obviously the mixture of programming and SQA tasks must be tailored to the needs of both the organization and the individual. During the first six months of a college graduate's employment, a 60/40 ratio of programming tasks to SQA tasks seems to work well. The benefits to be derived from such a mixture are many, but most of all the recent college hire's perception is that of performing a constructive task. He or she is also able to observe the benefits of these efforts while the benefits to be derived from purely SQA tasks are more subjective and therefore a demotivator.

Orienting the new hire to the SQA methodology employed by the organization is an important training procedure that must not be ignored. Typically the SQA training process takes somewhere between one and two years before such an individual should be allowed to make independent SQA decisions without supervision. This orientation should involve exposure to overall company policies and procedures as well as the specific software tools and techniques employed by the organization to develop software.

6.10   SQA Employment Requisitions

Recruiting, hiring, and training software engineers in quality assurance can be very expensive and time-consuming. It would be wise for the SQA organization to define and set priorities for key positions in the form of job descriptions and responsibilities (see Appendix to this chapter). Before proceeding, the organization should consider these issues:

- Is the organization located in an area that can provide a local pool of software quality people? Should recruiting policy be national, regional, or local, considering that the degree of staff turn-around is directly related to where the new hire comes from? Can contract employees help and how best can they be utilized? Can the company promote from within and train individuals to fill SQA openings?
- What tasks should be assigned to a new SQA organization?

Whether SQA personnel are acquired from within or outside of the company, care must be given to distinguishing between software professionals and paraprofessionals. Job descriptions for these individuals should be documented to inform the placement office of the specific tasks they will be called on to perform and the backgrounds needed to sustain these tasks. Furthermore, the careful allocation of tasks between professionals and paraprofessionals will determine the attrition rate the organization will experience. Typical professional job titles within the SQA function are:

- software quality assurance manager
- engineer software quality assurance
- software reliability engineer
- software configuration management specialist
- software safety engineer

The SQA manager is typically responsible for supervising the operation of the SQA section through planning and directing the utilization of personnel. This position in the organization also requires that counseling and guidance be given to company management in matters pertaining to the quality and reliability of software products developed or purchased. From a global viewpoint, the SQA manager must set the framework that will dictate the use of a software development methodology that lends itself to quality software. The engineering reliability and configuration staff supporting this effort will provide the technical expertise necessary to assure that the objectives of the QA effort are achieved and maintained. Specific duties of the SQA function should include but not be limited to the following:

- Provide SQA support and improve upon the existing SQA system.
- Develop SQA tools that sense software problems during the design, development, and life cycle phases.
- Keep management aware of the quality status of software development projects during the design, development, and life cycle phases.
- Monitor the continuing needs and requirements of the SQA program and implement them.
- Participate in software design reviews, testing, configuration control, problem reporting and resolution, and change control.
- Provide inputs to technical and cost proposals relative to the company's participation in computer software quality.
- Audit, monitor, evaluate, and report on subcontractor software development efforts.

Many of the tasks within the SQA function can be performed by individuals who are paraprofessionals. It would be to the benefit of the organization to use these individuals to perform those tasks. This category may include the following positions:

- software librarian aide
- senior software librarian
- software quality assurance engineering assistant
- software quality engineering assistant
- software quality assurance aide

The role of these paraprofessionals can be viewed as assisting the professionals in achieving the SQA objectives defined by management. Work assignments are, in many instances, related to performing tasks that have been defined in detail by the professionals assigned to the SQA function. The manager employing the services of such paraprofessionals should realize that, properly trained and with formal education, these individuals could in the future make excellent SQA professionals.

6.11   What to Expect from Your SQA Engineering Staff

Members of the QA staff should have a relatively high level of technical expertise and a thorough knowledge of good software quality assurance policies. The manner in which the staff is organized depends largely on staff size, estimated work load, and personnel skills. Several alternatives are suggested:

- Each SQA staff member could be specialized to perform one task for all software products.
- Each SQA staff member could perform all software QA tasks associated with a particular product.
- The SQA organization could act as a team in which all members would cooperate in performing the QA tasks.

If it is properly staffed and organized, you can expect the following from your SQA organization:

The ability of the staff to work independently. If your staff and organization are to grow and meet the demands placed upon them, the individuals assigned to perform SQA tasks must possess an understanding of and involvement in their assigned projects. This understanding and involvement is achieved if the system requires their independent involvement and participation. The part-time SQA engineer is ineffective and does little to improve the quality and reliability of the software product. Productivity with minimum supervision is achieved only if the policies and procedures in place lend themselves to a team approach to quality assurance. Productivity with supervision does not permit individuals the freedom to develop into professionals who function independently.

Ability to devise new and improved methods to perform SQA tasks. The discipline of SQA is relatively new, and the whole process is being transformed from an approach that is labor-intensive to one that can be automated. The SQA engineer must be expected to develop the necessary tools, techniques, and methodologies to accomplish tasks that have been assigned.

Good judgment and objectivity in approaching problems. It is imperative that the SQA engineer be able to apply good judgment and objectivity when dealing with other members of the software development team. These attributes are important, because the SQA engineer must have the support of the software development team to function effectively. If an SQA engineer alienates himself or herself from the development team, the SQA function is no longer contributing to the team's effort.

Communication skills for a better understanding. The SQA engineer must possess good communication skills. Skill in expressing ideas both orally and in writing are crucial; for example, when communicating SQA review and audit findings to the software development team, or making presentations to upper management. Since most findings are of a negative nature, challenge provided by the developing environment to these findings will require considerable skill to get the message across. Furthermore, SQA is frequently called upon to present its needs and requirements to the developers. Good communication can make this job easier.

Technical competence and knowledge of the project are imperative. An SQA staff (or member or portion of the staff) not knowledgeable about software development cannot support the objectives of the SQA organization. Moreover, these individuals cannot provide the expertise needed to perform the software QA tasks that the position will demand. Such individuals will therefore not be able to complete assignments rapidly or at all without compromising standards of quality.

6.12   Developing Career Paths

A software quality assurance organization without engineering-defined career paths will not survive the tests of time and effectiveness. It is essential that SQA engineers have the opportunity to ascend the corporate ladder. One of the disadvantages of some corporate organizational structures is that many of the SQA organizations exist within a hardware matrix organization, which limits the career paths for the software professionals within the product assurance organization. It is imperative that the organization recognize this critical shortfall and take steps to remedy it in order to permit the SQA function to develop into an essential and capable factor in software development.

What should be done? Obviously, if the organization is to survive, career paths from SQA to other disciplines within the organization must exist, such as SQA engineers becoming lead software engineers or SQA management moving into software development management. Specifically, a dual ladder system must exist: this allows highly competent technical employees to continue their career growth without assuming management responsibilities. It also allows management-oriented engineers to climb organizational ladders and assume management responsibilities. (In fact, one of the *Handbook*'s editors moved from manager of Software Quality Engineering to manager of Software Development Engineering. Another example, at the same firm, occurred when an experienced software quality engineer transferred into Software Systems Engineering.) This parallel structure bridges the gap between engineering and management. The organization's main goal, however, for such an approach to staff development, must be to allow engineers to progress up the ladder without becoming managers, if they desire not to.

6.13   Recommendations

The organizational environment plays a decisive role in how successful the software quality assurance function will be. Success can be measured only in terms of a team of dedicated individuals contributing in a supportive posture to a project. To give this success its best chance, the following recommendations are offered:

- The salaries of the SQA engineers should be generally competitive and specifically in line with those of software development engineers.
- Project-related SQA functions are dysfunctional and present too many problems. A central, independent SQA function driving all projects is a more effective method to achieve SQA goals.
- A rotating SQA policy should be used as a long-range plan only after a core of experienced SQA individuals already exists. The rotation program is not a recommended approach to starting up an SQA function.
- Responsibilities of SQA must be clearly defined and firmly supported by corporate management.
- The best approach to starting an SQA function is to first create a position within the corporate organization for an SQA manager, then promote or hire an individual to fill that position.
- The SQA organization should be situated in the corporate organization so that it always reports to the same level as the department that it must evaluate and audit.

References

1. Dunn, Robert, and Ullman, Richard, *Quality Assurance for Computer Software* (Englewood Cliffs, NJ: Prentice-Hall, 1983).
2. Schulmeyer, G. Gordon, and McManus, James I., *Total Quality Management for Software* (New York: Van Nostrand Reinhold Co., Inc., 1992).

General References

Arthur, L. J., *Measuring Programmer Productivity and Software Quality* (New York: John Wiley & Sons, 1984), pp. 12–35.

Mendis, Kenneth S. "A Software Quality Assurance Program for the 8Os." In: *ASQC Technical Conference Transactions* (1980), pp. 379–388.

Mendis, Kenneth S., "Software Quality Assurance Staffing Problems." In: *ASQC Technical Conference Transactions* (19831), pp. 108–112.

Ryan. J. R. "Software Product Qualitv Assurance." In: *Proceedinqs of the National Computer Conference* (1981). pp. 393–398.

Appendix

Typical Software Quality–Related Job Descriptions

Software Quality Assurance Manager

Experience required:	Eight years software related experience, three years in SQA, one year management experience.
Education required:	B.S., Computer Science, Information Technology or related technical discipline MBA or M.S. in Software Engineering highly desirable.

Duties: Manage the SQA organization. Provide personnel to support the projects that require SQA activities. Do strategic planning for the SQA organization. Interview and hire SQA personnel. Inform upper management of the status of SQA and its activities across the projects supported. Monitor the SQA portion of proposals and estimates. Provide management interface with software engineering and software process organizations. (Refer to Sections 6.5 and 6.10).

Engineer Software Quality Assurance

Experience required:	Four years software related experience, one year in SQA.
Education required:	B.S., Computer Science, Information Technology or related technical discipline.

Duties: Perform SQA activities on the projects. Participate in software design reviews, testing, configuration control, problem reporting and resolution, and change control. Audit, monitor, evaluate, and report on the software subcontractor activities. Assist in the interviewing of SQA personnel. Produce write-ups and estimates for the SQA portion of proposals. Interface with software engineering, software configuration management, and the software process organizations. (Refer to Sections 6.5 and 6.10).

Software Reliability Engineer

Experience required: Four years software related experience, one year in SQA or reliability engineering.

Education required: B.S., Computer Science, Statistics or related technical discipline.

Duties: Perform the reliability calculations for the software projects that require them. Utilize the software reliability tools available on the PC to perform the calculations. Advise the other software quality engineers on the meaning of and results of the software reliability calculations are for the project.

Software Configuration Management Specialist

Experience required: Four years software related experience, one year in SQA or software configuration management.

Education required: B.S., Computer Science, Software Engineering or related technical discipline.

Duties: Perform the software configuration management functions for the project. This includes software identification, configuration control, configuration status accounting, and configuration audits. Coordinate these activities with software development and SQA. Review subcontractor's software configuration management activities. Orient the software-related personnel on projects as to the software configuration management requirements. Evaluate and support software configuration management tools for the project.

Software Saftey Engineer

Experience required: Four years software related experience, one year in SQA, software safety or human factors.

Education required: B.S., Computer Science, Software Engineering or related technical discipline.

Duties: Perform the software safety functions for the project. This includes the evaluation of human factor, human-machine interface, and life-critical functions of the software. Coordinate these activities with software development and SQA. Review subcontractor's software safety activities. Evaluate and support software safety tools for the project.

Software Librarian Aide

Experience required: None.

Education required: AA degree in computer-related field, or computer
technical school diploma, or high school diploma with
proven competency in PC software.

Duties: Assist the software configuration management person on the project in
performing the software library duties. These duties include both the hard
copy library management and the electronic library control. Handling the
releases and baselines of the software and documents are an integral part
of these function. Keeping access control is a critical function to be performed.

Senior Software Librarian

Experience required: Two years as a software librarian aide.

Education required: AA degree in computer-related field, or computer
technical school diploma, or high school diploma with
proven competency in PC software.

Duties: Handle the software library duties for the project. These duties include
both the hard copy library management and the electronic library control.
Handling the releases and baselines of the software and documents are an
integral part of these function. Keeping access control is a critical function
to be performed.

Software Quality Assurance Engineering Assistant

Experience required: One year as a software quality engineering assistant.

Education required: AA degree in computer-related field, or computer
technical school diploma, or high school diploma with
proven competency in PC software.

Duties: Handle administrative activities for the SQA engineer on the project.
Place information into the SQA tool used for the project to report deficiencies. Be the interface to the SQA tools in use on the project. Where necessary keep the SQA hard copy project book on SQA findings. Assist in test
witnessing. Fill out SQA evaluation reports where appropriate. Interface
with software configuration management as necessary.

Software Quality Engineering Assistant

Experience required: One year as an SQA aide.

Education required: AA degree in computer-related field, or computer technical school diploma, or high school diploma with proven competency in PC software.

Duties: Handle administrative activities for the SQA engineer on the project. Place information into the SQA tool used for the project to report deficiencies. Be the interface to the SQA tools in use on the project. Where necessary keep the SQA hard copy project book on SQA findings. Assist in test witnessing. Fill out SQA evaluation reports where appropriate. Interface with software configuration management as necessary.

Software Quality Assurance Aide

Experience required: None.

Education required: AA degree in computer-related field, or computer technical school diploma, or high school diploma with proven competency in PC software.

Duties: Handle administrative activities for the SQA engineer on the project. Place information into the SQA tool used for the project to report deficiencies. Be the interface to the SQA tools in use on the project. Where necessary keep the SQA hard copy project book on SQA findings.

American Society for Quality (ASQ) Software Quality Engineer Certification Program

Douglas B. Hamilton, CICM, CSQE
Andersen Consulting LLP

7.1   ASQ Background

The American Society for Quality (ASQ), formerly the American Society for Quality Control (ASQC), is a society of individual and organizational members dedicated to the ongoing development, advancement, and promotion of quality concepts, principles, and techniques. ASQ's vision is to be the world's recognized champion and leading authority on all issues related to quality.[1]

The origin of ASQ goes back to the United States' entry into World War II, which greatly increased demand for war supplies and the need for weapons perfection. The U.S. War Production Board sought help in improving production and quality from those skilled in applying statistical methods. As the prominence of quality control grew, representatives from different factories and industries responsible for the quality of manufactured products formed groups in various parts of the country to share information. In 1946, 17 local quality control societies formed the American Society for Quality Control. ASQ has grown to more than 130,000 individual members and membership is open to anyone interested in quality.

ASQ is governed by an elected board of directors and their mission is to "facilitate continuous improvement and increased customer satisfaction by identifying, communicating, and promoting the use of quality principles, concepts, and technology; and thereby be recognized throughout the world as the leading authority on and champion for quality."

ASQ members belong to one of 246 local sections, which are organized geographically to serve members and community needs on the local level. Located throughout

---

1. ASQ Web Page http://www.ASQ.org

the United States, Canada, and Mexico, sections provide ASQ members with the opportunity to meet others interested in quality to discuss common issues and concerns and to share ideas. Sections hold monthly meetings and many sections also provide members with a newsletter that includes articles about quality-related issues and information about certification, conferences, and training courses. Many sections also provide outreach to their community and are involved with local businesses, schools, and government agencies promoting quality concepts.

ASQ members may also join a division or a technical committee that serves the needs of members involved with specific industries and applications. For example, the Software Division provides specialized training, information, and professional programs for those interested in applying quality principles to the field of software development. The Software Division has responsibility for the following activities and services:

- Developing the software quality engineer certification program
- Sponsoring the annual International Conference on Software Quality
- Co-sponsoring the World Congress on Software Quality
- Publishing a quarterly newsletter
- Maintaining liaison with national and international standards bodies such as ANSI and ISO
- Interacting with other professional software organizations such as IEEE and the Association for Computing
- Cooperating with academia to make educational resources available to the software quality profession
- Reviewing tools and techniques for improving the quality of software products

7.2   ASQ Certification Program

The ASQ certification program was developed to recognize individuals who have demonstrated proficiency within a specific area called the *Body of Knowledge*. In the 25-plus years of the certification program, more than 55,000 professionals have become certified in one or more of the following seven certification areas:

- Mechanical Inspector Certification—Designed for those who, under professional direction, can evaluate hardware documentation, perform laboratory procedures, inspect products, measure process performance, record data, and prepare formal reports.
- Quality Auditor Certification—Designed for those who understand the standards and principles of auditing and the auditing techniques of examining, questioning, evaluating, and reporting to determine quality systems adequacy.

- Quality Engineer Certification —Designed for those who understand the principles of product and service quality evaluation and control.
- Quality Manager Certification—Designed for those who understand quality principles and standards in relation to organization and human resource management.
- Quality Technician Certification—Designed for those who can analyze quality problems, prepare inspection plans and instruction, select sampling plan applications, and apply fundamental statistical methods for process control.
- Reliability Engineer Certification—Designed for those who understand the principles of performance evaluation and prediction to improve product/systems safety, reliability, and maintainability.
- Software Quality Engineer Certification—Designed for those who understand software quality development, implementation, inspection, testing, verification, and validation, and can implement software development and maintenance processes and methods.

The ASQ membership identifies the certification program as one of the most important activities of the Society and the program has become a marketplace requirement for quality professionals.

7.2.1 What is Certification?

Certification is a formal recognition that an individual has demonstrated proficiency in a subject at a point in time. ASQ certification requires education and/or work experience in a specific field and demonstrated knowledge through the successful completion of a written examination. Certification is NOT a license or registration. It is peer recognition of competence because the certified individual has passed an examination developed by industry subject matter experts covering the most important aspects of a specific professional area.

7.2.2 Why Become Certified?

For an individual, certification can be an important step in career advancement. Certification helps to ensure that professional skills are kept current, provides credibility in a job interview, and can lead to higher pay and faster career growth. Leonard Turi, owner of TMS Consulting Services, Inc., states: "Certified candidates are requested for more interviews and placed on consulting jobs sooner and for longer duration."[2] This is not to say that individuals without certification cannot get a job, but companies are increasingly looking for highly qualified candidates and the impact of making a wrong hiring decision can be detrimental.

2. *Chicago Tribune*, February 9, 1997, Carol Kleiman

For organizations, the global business environment requires the maximum utilization of technology to remain competitive. Companies need a tool to accurately assess and choose the best Information Technology (IT) professionals to help an organization reach its goals and objectives. Many organizations are turning to certification as a way to help make hiring and promotion decisions. Over 125 companies have formally recognized ASQ certification as a way to ensure their workforce is proficient in the principles and practices of quality. Supporting certification also demonstrates a commitment to quality and an investment in the future of these highly skilled employees.

An International Data Corp survey of more than 250 Information Technology managers found definite advantages to having certified personnel. Although it is difficult to quantify the benefits of certification, most IT managers surveyed believe that certified personnel are worth higher salaries, almost $10,000 per year over non-certified personnel.[3]

People would not think of having surgery performed by a doctor who failed to pass the board exam or go to an attorney who has been disbarred. Yet, we do not hesitate to place the successful utilization of technology and survival of companies in the hands of IT professionals who may or may not have demonstrated any degree of competence. Certification provides a professional badge of competence and a mark of excellence.

7.2.3 What is a Certified Software Quality Engineer (CSQE)?

The ASQ definition of a Certified Software Quality Engineer is "a professional who has a comprehensive understanding of software quality development and implementation; has a thorough understanding of software inspection, testing, verification, and validation; and can implement software development and maintenance processes and methods."

7.2.4 What Qualifications are Necessary to Become a CSQE?

The requirements for a Certified Software Quality Engineer fall into three categories:

1. **Education and Experience**
   The candidate for certification must have eight years of on-the-job experience in one or more of the Body of Knowledge topics (see Section 7.5, What is in the Body of Knowledge?). At least three of those years must have been in a decisionmaking, technical, professional, or management position. Up to five years of the eight-year experience requirement will be waived if the

---

3. Info Canada, June 1996

candidate has completed a degree from a college, university, or technical school with accreditation recognized by ASQ.

2. **Proof of Professionalism**
   Proof of professionalism may be demonstrated by one of the following: membership in ASQ, registration as a Professional Engineer, or signatures of two ASQ members verifying the candidate's qualifications as a practitioner of quality.

3. **Examination**
   The successful candidate must pass a four-hour written examination. Each examination consists of 160 multiple-choice questions that cover all topics in the Certified Software Quality Engineer Body of Knowledge.

7.3   How Is the Certification Exam Developed?

The process for establishing a new ASQ certification is a multistep process spanning several years.

The chart in Figure 7-1 depicts the steps necessary to develop a new ASQ certification examination. This chart is followed by a detailed explanation of each step.

7.3.1   A. Proposal for New Certification

Initiation of a new ASQ certification requires a sponsoring group. Usually a Division or Technical Committee within ASQ is that sponsoring group. The sponsoring group must document how their new proposed certification meets each of the following seven criteria:

1. The discipline shall be a unique area of quality technology generally practiced in the quality profession. This involves addressing how this proposed certification is substantially different from any existing examination.
2. The discipline shall be generic in nature, generally applicable to the production of any product by any process and/or to the rendering of any service.
3. The discipline shall have a substantial and authoritative Body of Knowledge in the public domain describing proven principles and practices of the technology. A draft bibliography is developed to identify available sources of the discipline.
4. The discipline shall be consistent with ASQ objectives, policies, and procedures.
5. Training in the principles and practices of the technology shall be readily available on a geographically dispersed basis. This could be addressed by a list of available training.

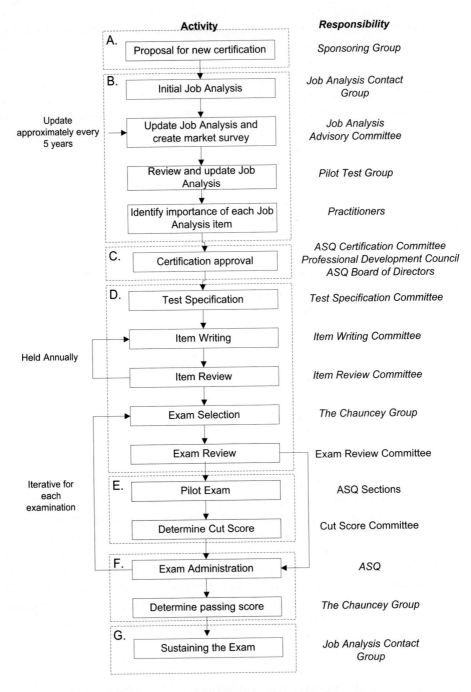

Figure 7-1   Certification development process.

6. The area of technology shall have the commitment and active support of one or more ASQ Divisions or Technical Committees with the capacity of providing adequate testing criteria for proficiency in the technology.
7. There must be a definable and continuing market and a justified need on a broad geographic basis for certification. This would include the projected market size, market growth and percentage of the market that is expected to pursue the new certification. This information may be gathered by conducting a market research analysis.

The ASQ Certification Committee may give tentative approval for the Division/Technical Committee to proceed with the next step, or they may request additional information before approval is given.

7.3.2   B. Job Analysis

The Job Analysis defines the major tasks that a certified individual would be expected to be able to perform and the associated knowledge and skill set. Conducting the initial Job Analysis is the responsibility of the Division/Technical Committee proposing the new certification.

Several groups are necessary to complete the Job Analysis:

Job Analysis Contact Group. This committee consists of 10–12 individuals who are considered industry experts in the discipline of the new certification. Telephone interviews are conducted by The Chauncey Group (a subsidiary of Educational Testing Service) to obtain their input for the initial Job Analysis Survey instrument.

Job Analysis Advisory Committee. This committee consists of 10–12 experienced practitioners in the discipline of the new certification and meets for two days to review and revise the Job Analysis survey. A supplemental document is created with market survey questions that will provide evidence of a demand for the certification.

Pilot Test Group. This committee consists of five to six experienced practitioners in the discipline of the new certification and meets to review the draft Job Analysis Survey for clarity of directions, time required to complete the survey, and understanding of the survey rating process that will be used to determine the importance of each item.

The final version of the Job Analysis Survey is sent to a randomly selected group of 1000–2000 practitioners in the discipline of the new certification. These practitioners include members of the ASQ Division/Technical Committee, attendees at related conferences, or members of other related professional societies. Their responsibility is to provide professional opinion on the level of importance of each item as a necessary part of the certification discipline.

The Chauncey Group analyzes the responses received from the surveys and issues a preliminary report that indicates whether each item in the questionnaire should be included in the Body of Knowledge for the certification, excluded from the Body of Knowledge, or is marginal. Members of the Job Analysis Advisory Committee and the Executive Committee of the Division/Technical Committee review these results and make a final recommendation for inclusion or exclusion of each item in the certification Body of Knowledge.

The Chauncey Group then issues a final report describing the Job Analysis process, the method of data analysis, and a summary of the results including inclusion/exclusion recommendations for the Body of Knowledge. The ASQ Certification Committee reviews this report and then determines the final content of the Body of Knowledge.

7.3.3   C. Certification Approval

Upon completion of the Job Analysis, the Division/Technical Committee updates its proposal on how the certification meets the seven criteria for a new certification. A representative of the Division/Technical Committee presents the proposal to the ASQ Certification Committee. If approved, the representative presents the certification proposal to the Professional Development Council. If the new certification is approved, the representative will present the proposal to the ASQ Board of Directors. When approval is given by the ASQ Board of Directors, the certification becomes an official ASQ Certification and the ASQ national assumes future responsibility for the certification.

A key point to note is that up until this time, all expenses incurred by the participating practitioners are covered by their respective organizations or the individual. This highlights the initial industry and individual support necessary for a new ASQ certification. From this point forward, participant expenses are reimbursed by ASQ, but individuals who participate in the exam development process volunteer their time.

7.3.4   D. Creating the Examination

Several steps are necessary to create the initial examination and some of these steps are repeated for subsequent examinations, as shown in the chart.

Test Specification.   This committee consists of 10–12 experienced practitioners in the discipline of the certification. This group takes the results of the Job Analysis and creates the Body of Knowledge for the certification. They also define the mechanism for administering the examination. This includes the number of questions that will be included in the examination, the distribution of these questions over the Body of Knowledge, the format of the examination (for example, multiple choice questions, short answer questions, or a combination) and the mechanism for delivery (paper and pencil or computerized testing). The Test Specifications are used for all examinations that occur until the Job Analysis is updated and a revised Body of Knowledge developed.

Item Writing. This committee consists of 25–35 experienced practitioners in the discipline of the certification. This group is responsible for writing the actual examination questions. This is a very tedious activity because each question must test a specific area of the Body of Knowledge and have not only a correct answer (key), but also three viable incorrect answers (distracters) that someone without the specific knowledge could possibly select as a correct answer. For each question, a written justification must be documented explaining why the key is the correct answer as well as why the distracters are incorrect. In addition, specific references in the literature must be documented that support the topic being tested to show that this information is publicly available in the literature to a person taking the examination.

Not only must the chairperson for this committee find 25–35 willing volunteers, but must also make sure there is representation for each of the areas in the Body of Knowledge. The large committee is divided up into smaller groups, each concentrating on a specific area of the Body of Knowledge. It is not unusual for a question to take several hours to write, review with other experts in the group, rewrite, and obtain sign-off by each person in the small group. This committee demands a large commitment from the participants, since the sessions take place on Friday, Saturday, and Sunday. The group leaves on Sunday feeling very exhausted! Item writing sessions are typically held annually to ensure that the questions available for the examination are kept current.

Item Review. This committee consists of 12–14 experienced practitioners in the discipline of the certification. This group reviews each examination question for wording, accuracy, and validity. Approved questions are added to the pool of available examination questions. Unapproved items may be discarded or flagged to be returned to the next Item Writing Committee for rework. Item Review meetings are held after each Item Writing session.

Examination Selection. Prior to administering each examination, The Chauncey Group selects questions for the examination from the question pool. The mix of questions is based on the distribution of questions over the Body of Knowledge as defined in the Test Specification.

Examination Review. This committee consists of 10–12 experienced practitioners in the discipline of the certification. This group reviews the examination's accuracy, consistency, and validity. Each member must take the exam and answer each question as well as noting any concerns and comments. In the committee meeting, the group goes through the examination question by question. This group can change the wording of the question, change the wording of the answers, or replace the question with another one from the pool that tests the same area of knowledge.

7.3.5 E. Initial Examination Development

The following two steps are executed only for the first examination:

Pilot Examination. When a new certification is created, a Pilot Examination is administered. Typically, 20–25 pilot sites will be selected from the list of ASQ Sections who have volunteered to sponsor the pilot. These examinations are graded and statistically evaluated. However, the Cut Score Committee will meet and determine the passing grade prior to completion of the grading cycle.

Determine Cut Score. This committee consists of 10–12 experienced practitioners in the discipline of the certification. This group meets to recommend a written standard of minimum competency for the certification based on the Body of Knowledge and a recommended minimum passing score for the examination.

7.3.6 F. Examination Administration

Typically, certification examinations are administered twice a year. ASQ certification staff are responsible for the administration of the examination. They screen potential candidates based on the certification requirements. Local ASQ Sections provide sites and proctors for the examination.

Determine Passing Score. The Chauncey Group scores the examination and runs statistical validation checks on each examination question. Statistically questionable items are reviewed. The Cut Score is statistically adjusted for each subsequent examination based on it's difficulty. In this way, the same passing standard is maintained for each exam. Based on the established passing score, individuals who passed the examination are awarded certification. Individuals who do not meet the minimum passing score are given a report that indicates areas of the examination where they did well and areas where they need improvement.

7.3.7 G. Sustaining the Examination

The ASQ Certified Software Quality Engineer bibliography (see Section 7.6, ASQ Certified Software Quality Engineer Bibliography) is updated occasionally to reflect new publications that provide information about topics in the Body of Knowledge.

The Job Analysis Process is repeated approximately every five years to ensure that the certification continues to reflect the state of the practice in the discipline. As a result, the content of the Body of Knowledge could change.

7.4 How Should You Prepare for the Exam?

An "Application for Certification as a Software Quality Engineer" must be completed and mailed approximately two months before the date of the examination. The fee for taking the exam is as follows:

1. ASQ Member — North America $ 90.00
2. ASQ Member — outside North America $120.00
3. Nonmember — North America $195.00
4. Nonmember — outside North America $225.00

The best approach to prepare for the examination is to review the Certified Software Quality Engineer Body of Knowledge and identify specific topics on which to focus your studies. Then review the bibliography provided for each topic in the Body of Knowledge and identify key references that should be used for study. Begin your preparation well in advance because of the extensive breadth and depth of the topics. Waiting until the last minute will only bring on frustration and confusion. As the examination date gets closer, make sure your reference materials are organized so you can locate information quickly.

Refresher courses are also available to help you prepare for the examination. These courses are not sponsored nor endorsed by ASQ. Attending a refresher course does not ensure that you will pass the examination. Also, be aware that a refresher course may not be covering the exact topics on the examination. Anyone offering a refresher course cannot participate in the question writing nor the examination review so they do not have any "inside" information as to the specific content. The majority of each examination is new, so past questions do not reflect future questions on any given version of the examination. Refresher courses may be helpful to motivate early study and review, but be aware that they do not replace individual preparation.

7.4.1 What Reference Materials Can Be Used During the Exam?

The Certified Software Quality Engineer examination is open-book and your personal notes from preparation and materials from refresher courses are allowed. However, material containing sample questions and answers are not allowed. Any reference materials taken into the examination room must be made available to the proctor for review. Reference materials cannot replace having an understanding of the material. The average time to answer each question is 1 ½ minutes (four hours for 160 questions); therefore, there will not be time to dig through reference material for many answers.

Calculators may be used during the examination, but laptop computers are not allowed.

7.5   What Is In the Body of Knowledge?

The following is a high-level outline of the topics that constitute the Body of Knowledge for Software Quality Engineering.[4, 5] Note: the number in parentheses following the title of each major topic (see I–VIII below) represents the number of questions for that section of the exam, totaling 160, and does not represent the number of items listed below; these items represent areas from which questions may be taken.

   I. GENERAL KNOWLEDGE, CONDUCT, AND ETHICS (24 questions)
      A. Standards
         1. Domestic and international standards and specifications (e.g., ISO 9000, IEEE, Human Factors and Ergonomics Society, graphical user interface guidelines)
         2. Software quality and process initiatives, ventures, and consortia (e.g., SEI, SPICE, bootstrap, ESPIRIT)
      B. Quality Philosophies and Principles
         1. Benefits of software quality
         2. Quality philosophies (e.g., Juran, Deming, Crosby)
         3. Prevention vs. detection philosophies
         4. Software Total Quality Management principles and applications
         5. Organization and process benchmaking (i.e., identifying, analyzing, and modeling best practices)
      C. Organizational and Interpersonal Techniques
         1. Verbal communication and presentation
         2. Written communication
         3. Effective listening
         4. Interviewing
         5. Facilitation (e.g., team management, customer-supplier relationships)
         6. Principles of team leadership and facilitation

---

4. ASQ CSQE Certification Brochure, Item B0110.
5. CSQE Certification Chair, Linda Westfall.

      7. Meeting management

      8. Conflict resolution

      9. Organization and implementation of various types of quality teams

  D. Problem-Solving Tools and Processes

      1. Root cause analysis

      2. Tools (e.g., affinity diagram, tree diagram, matrix diagram, interrelationship digraph, prioritization matrix, activity network diagram)

      3. Risk management (e.g., project, product, process)

      4. Problem-solving processes

  E. Professional Conduct and Ethics

      1. ASQ Code of Ethics

      2. Conflict of interest issues for a software quality engineer

      3. Ethical issues involving software product licensing

      4. Legal issues involving software product liability and safety (e.g., negligence, customer notification, recall, regulations)

II. SOFTWARE QUALITY MANAGEMENT (16 questions)

  A. Planning

      1. Product and project software quality goals and objectives

      2. Customer requirements for quality

      3. Quality and customer support activities

      4. Issues related to software security, safety, and hazard analysis

  B. Tracking

      1. Scope and objectives of quality information systems

      2. Categories of quality data and their uses

      3. Problem reporting and corrective action procedures (e.g., software defects, process nonconformances)

      4. Techniques for implementing information systems to track quality-related data

      5. Records and data collection, storage, maintenance, and retention

  C. Organizational and Professional Software Quality Training

      1. Quality training subject areas (e.g., inspection, testing, configuration management, project management)

      2. Available training resources, materials, and providers

      3. Professional societies, technical associations, and organizations for software quality engineers

III. SOFTWARE PROCESSES (24 questions)

  A. Development and Maintenance Methods

      1. Software development procedures

      2. Life cycle or process models (e.g., waterfall, spiral, rapid prototyping)

      3. Defect prevention, detection, and removal methods

      4. Requirement analysis and specification methods (e.g., data flow diagram, entity-relationship diagram)

      5. Requirements elicitation methods and techniques (e.g., quality function deployment, joint application development, context-free questioning, needs analysis, focus groups)

      6. Software design methods (e.g., structured analyses and design, Jackson design methods, Warnier-Orr methods, object-oriented)

      7. Issues related to reuse, reengineering, and reverse engineering

      8. Maintenance processes (e.g., reengineering, reverse engineering, change management, retirement)

   B. Process and Technology Change Management

      1. Software process and technology change management theory and methods

      2. Process maturity model

      3. Software process assessment and evaluation techniques

      4. Software process modeling (e.g., entry and exit criteria, task definition, feedback loops)

      5. Software environments (e.g., development methodologies, tools, data, infrastructure)

      6. Barriers to the implementation or success of quality improvement efforts and quality systems

IV. SOFTWARE PROJECT MANAGEMENT (16 questions)

   A. Planning

      1. Project planning factors (e.g., quality, costs, resources, deliverables, schedules)

      2. Project planning methods and tools (e.g., work breakdown structures, documentation, forecasting, estimation)

      3. Goal-setting and deployment methodologies

      4. Maintenance types (e.g., corrective, adaptive, perfective)

      5. Software maintenance and adaptability program planning

      6. Supplier management methodologies

   B. Tracking

      1. Phase transitioning control techniques (e.g., reviews and audits, Gantt charts, PERT, budgets)

      2. Methods of collecting cost of quality data

      3. Cost of quality categories (e.g., prevention, appraisal, internal failure, external failure)

      4. Cost, progress, and deliverable tracking (e.g., status reports, life cycle phase reports)

    C. Implementation
  1. Project management tools (e.g., planning, tracking, cost estimating, reporting)
  2. Methods of reporting cost of quality data
  3. Tradeoffs involved in product release decisions (e.g., cost, quality, schedule, customer, test sufficiency, stability)

V. SOFTWARE METRICS, MEASUREMENT, AND ANALYTICAL METHODS
(24 questions)
    A. Measurement Theory
  1. Goal, question, metric paradigm for selecting metrics
  2. Basic measurement theory and techniques
  3. Definitions of metrics and measures
  4. Designing measures
  5. Psychology of metrics (e.g., how metrics affect people and how people affect metrics)
    B. Analytical Techniques
  1. Issues involving data integrity, completeness, accuracy, and timeliness
  2. Basic statistical concepts and graphical techniques for analysis and presentation of software data (e.g., distributions, confidence intervals, statistical inference)
  3. Quality analysis tools (Pareto chart, flowcharts, control charts, check sheets, scatter diagrams, histograms)
  4. Sampling theory and techniques as applied to audits, testing, and product acceptance
    C. Software Measurement
  1. Prediction techniques of future maintainability
  2. Applications of measurements to process, product, and resources
  3. Commonly used metrics (e.g., complexity, reliability, defect density, phase containment, size)
  4. Software quality attributes (e.g., reliability, maintainability, usability, testability)
  5. Defect detection effectiveness (e.g., cost, yield, escapes, customer impact)

VI. SOFTWARE INSPECTION, TESTING, VERIFICATION, AND VALIDATION
(24 questions)
    A. Inspection
  1. Inspection types (e.g., peer reviews, inspections, walk-throughs)
  2. Inspection process (e.g., objectives, criteria, techniques and methods, participant roles)

    3. Inspection data collection, reports, and summaries

    4. Methods for reviewing inspection efforts (e.g., technical accomplishments, resource utilization, future planning)

B. Testing

    1. Types of tests (e.g., functional, performance, usability, stress, regression, real-time response)

    2. Test levels (e.g., unit, integration, system field)

    3. Test strategies (e.g., top down, bottom up, automated testing, I/O first, beta testing, black box, white box)

    4. Test design (e.g., test cases, fault insertion and error handling, equivalence class partitioning, usage scenarios, customer defect reports)

    5. Test coverage of code (e.g., branch-to-branch, path, individual predicate, data)

    6. Test coverage of specifications (e.g., functions, states, data and time domains, localization, internationalization)

    7. Test environments (e.g., tools and methodologies, test libraries, drivers/stubs, equipment compatibility test laboratories)

    8. Test documentation (e.g., test plans, logs, test designs, defect recording, test reports)

    9. Test management (e.g., scheduling, freezing, resources, dependencies, analysis of test results)

    10. Methods for reviewing testing efforts (e.g., technical accomplishments, resource utilization, future planning, risk management)

    11. Methods for testing supplier components and products

    12. Methods for testing the accuracy of customer deliverables including user documentation, marketing and training materials

    13. Traceability mechanisms (e.g., system verification diagrams)

C. Verification and Validation (V&V)

    1. V & V planning procedures

    2. Methods for reviewing V & V program (e.g., technical accomplishments, resource utilization, future planning, risk management, impact analysis of proposed changes)

    3. Methods for evaluating software life cycle products and processes (e.g., physical traces, documentation, source code, plans, test and audit results) to determine if user needs and project objectives are satisfied

    4. Methods for performing requirements traceability (e.g., requirements to design, design to code)

    5. Methods for evaluating requirements for correctness, consistency, completeness, and testability

    6. Methods for evaluating interfaces with hardware, user, operator, and other software applications

      7. Methods for evaluating test plans (e.g., system, acceptance, validation) to determine if software satisfies software and system objectives

      8. Methods for evaluating the severity of anomalies in software operation

      9. Methods for assessing all proposed modifications, enhancements, or additions to determine the effect each change will have on the system

      10. Methods for determining which V & V tasks should be iterated based upon proposed modifications and enhancements

VII. SOFTWARE AUDITS (16 questions)
    A. Audit Types
      1. Performing internal audits (e.g., quality system, product, process, project, customer)
      2. Performing external audits (e.g., supplier qualifications, certification of supplier systems, auditing testing done by independent agencies
      3. Functional and physical configuration audits
    B. Audit Methodology
      1. Purpose, objectives, frequency, and criteria of the overall audit program and individual software audits
      2. Procedures, tools, and issues related to conducting audits in specific areas (e.g., software development, project management, configuration management)
      3. Audit steps (planning, preparation, execution, reporting, corrective action, verification, follow-up)
      4. Audit process (e.g., objectives, criteria, techniques and methods, participant roles)
    C. Audit Planning
      1. Audit team member responsibilities
      2. Management (auditee and auditor) responsibilities concerning audits
      3. Hosting external audits
      4. Audit program development and administration
      5. Auditing requirements (e.g., industry and government standards)

VIII. SOFTWARE CONFIGURATION MANAGEMENT (16 questions)
    A. Planning and Configuration Identification
      1. Technical and managerial factors that guide software product partitioning into configuration items and components
      2. Release process issues (e.g., supporting multiple versions, feature vs. corrective releases, hardware and software dependencies
      3. Liberty control procedures
      4. Configuration identification methods (e.g., schemes, reidentification, naming conventions, versions and serialization, baselines)

    5. Configuration management tools

B. Configuration Control, Status Accounting, and Reporting

    1. Documentation control (e.g., issuing, approval, storage, retrieval, revision)

    2. Patching issues (e.g., testing, traceability, source updating)

    3. Tradeoffs between cost, cycle time, and integrity of software product and rigor and formality of change control process

    4. Source and object code control procedures

    5. Software configuration/change control board processes

    6. Techniques for assessing impacts of proposed software changes

7.5.1 Sample Questions

The following examples are intended to provide a general overview of question types that appear on the CSQE certification examination.

1. Which of the following reviews are required in order to ensure proper tracking of software between phases of a project?

    I. Product feasibility
    II. Software requirements
    III. Software design
    IV. Acceptance test

    a. I and II only
    b. II and III only
    c. I, II, and III only
    d. II, III, and IV only

    Answer: d

2. What happens to the relative cost of fixing software errors from the requirements phase through the test phase?

    a. It decreases linearly
    b. It remains fairly constant
    c. It increases linearly
    d. It increases exponentially

    Answer: d

3. When an audit team concludes that a finding demonstrates a breakdown of the quality management system, the finding should be documented as:

    a. a minor nonconformance
    b. a major nonconformance
    c. a deficiency
    d. an observation

    Answer: b

4. According to Crosby, it is less costly to:

    a. let the customer find the defects
    b. detect defects than to prevent them
    c. prevent defects than to detect them
    d. ignore minor defects

    Answer: c

5. Which of the following is LEAST likely to be used during software maintenance?

    a. Software project management plan
    b. Customer support hot line
    c. Software problem reports
    d. Change control board

    Answer: a

6. An effective software development environment consists of tools that:

    a. are freestanding and free from access by other tools
    b. have different user interfaces for each tool depending on the development phase supported by each tool
    c. allow maximum flexibility while maintaining security and traceability
    d. are integrated, linked to other tools, and have common user interfaces

    Answer: d

7. A software firm has just signed a contract to deliver an inventory tracking/online transaction system for use by 500 entry clerks. The client has demanded a schedule of rigorous checkpoints but the requirements for the project are poorly defined. Which of the following would be most suitable as a development model?

   a. Spiral
   b. Top-Down
   c. Rapid Prototyping
   d. Waterfall

   Answer: c

8. Which of the following is NOT an accepted code inspection technique?

   a. Domain analysis
   b. Item-by-item paraphrasing
   c. Mental code execution
   d. Consistency analysis

   Answer: a

9. The defect density for a computer program is best defined as the:

   a. ratio of failure reports received per unit of time
   b. ratio of discovered errors per size of code
   c. number of modifications made per size of code
   d. number of failures reported against the code

   Answer: b

10. When a company evaluates its own performance, it is conducting what type of audit?

    a. First-party
    b. Second-party
    c. Third-party
    d. Extrinsic

    Answer: a

11. The primary task of the Change Control Board (CCB) is to:

    a. define change procedures
    b. approve or disapprove changes to software products
    c. evaluate cost and schedule impact of changes
    d. authorize personnel to implement change

    Answer: b

12. A module includes a control flow loop that can be executed 0 or more times. The test that is most likely to reveal loop initialization defects executes the loop body:

    a. 0 times
    b. 1 time
    c. 2 times
    d. 3 times

    Answer: b

7.6 ASQ Certified Software Quality Engineer Bibliography

7.6.1 I. General Knowledge, Conduct, and Ethics

Standards
> ANSI/ASQ Q91-94
> ISO 9000-3 Guidelines

TICKIT Guidelines
The Team Handbook (Scholtes; Joiner Assoc.) ISBN 0-9622264-0-8
Quality Planning & Analysis (Juran & Gryna; McGraw-Hill) ISBN 0-07-033183-9
Software Quality Engineering (Deutsch & Willis; Prentice Hall) ISBN 0-13-823204-0
Software Quality Manual (Boyer; Globe Engineering Documents) ISBN 0-91-270286-9

7.6.2 II. Software Quality Management

Out of the Crisis (Deming; Quality Press) ISBN 0-911379-01-0
Metrics and Models in Software Quality Engineering (Kan; Addison-Wesley)
> ISBN 0-201-63339-6
Managerial Breakthrough (Juran; McGraw-Hill) ISBN 0-07-034037-4
Assessment and Control of Software Risks (Jones; Prentice Hall) ISBN 0-13-741406-4
Handbook of Software Quality Assurance (Schulmeyer & McManus; Van Nostrand
> Reinhold) ISBN 0-442-00796-5

Software Quality Concepts & Plans (Dunn; Prentice Hall) ISBN 0-13-820283-4

7.6.3   III. Software Processes

Managing the Software Process (Humphrey; Addison-Wesley) ISBN 0-201-18095-2
A Manager's Guide to Software Engineering (Pressman; McGraw-Hill)
    ISBN 0-07-050820-8
Software Engineering, A Practitioner's Approach (Pressman; McGraw-Hill)
    ISBN 0-07-050783-X
ACM Communications (May 1995, vol. 38 #5)

7.6.4   IV. Software Project Management

Metrics and Models in Software Quality Engineering (Kan; Addison-Wesley)
    ISBN 0-201-63339-6
Software Engineering Productivity Handbook (Keyes; Windcrest/McGraw-Hill)
    ISBN 0-07-911366-4
Software Engineering Concepts (Fairley; McGraw-Hill) ISBN 0-07-019902-7
Software Engineering, A Practitioner's Approach (Pressman; McGraw-Hill)
    ISBN 0-07-050783-X

7.6.5   V. Software Metrics, Measurement, and Analytical Methods

Metrics and Models in Software Quality Engineering (Kan; Addison-Wesley)
    ISBN 0-201-63339-6
*IEEE Guide for the Use of IEEE Standard Dictionary of Measures to Produce
    Reliable Software* (IEEE)
Software Engineering, A Practitioner's Approach (Pressman; McGraw-Hill)
    ISBN 0-07-050783-X
Software Quality Concepts and Plans (Dunn; Prentice Hall) ISBN 0-13-820283-4
Handbook of Software Quality Assurance (McManus; Van Nostrand Reinhold)
    ISBN 0-442-00796-5

7.6.6   VI. Software Inspection, Testing, Verification, and Validation

Testing Computer Software (Kaner, Falk, Nguyen; Van Nostrand Reinhold)
    ISBN 0-442-01361-2
The Art of Software Testing (Myers; John Wiley & Sons) ISBN 0-471-04328-1
Software System Testing and Quality Assurance (Beizer; Van Nostrand Reinhold)
    ISBN 0-442-21306-9
Managing the Software Process (Humphrey; Addison-Wesley) ISBN 0-201-18095-2

7.6.7 VII. Software Audits

Quality Audits for Improved Performance (Arter; Quality Press) ISBN 0-87389-263-1
Software Quality Assurance and Evaluation (Dobbins; Quality Press)
    ISBN 0-87389-059-0
Standards
       # 1028-1988: Standard for Software Reviews and Audits (IEEE)
       Guide to Software Quality Management System Construction & Certification
          (TICKIT) ISBN 0-9519309-0-7
       Guidelines for Auditing Quality Systems (ANSI)

7.6.8 VIII. Software Configuration Management

Software Configuration Management (Babich; Addison-Wesley) ISBN 0-201-10161-0
A Manager's Guide to Software Engineering (Pressman; McGraw-Hill)
    ISBN 0-07-050820-8
Standards:
       #1042-1987: Guide to Software Configuration Management (IEEE)
       #828-1990: Standard for Software Configuration Management Plans (IEEE)
       Managing the Software Process (Humphrey; Addison-Wesley)
          ISBN 0-201-18095-2
       Software Configuration Management: An Overview (Osborne; National
          Computer Systems Lab) NIST Special Publication 500-161

7.7 Recertification

ASQ has a Maintenance of Certification program that requires recertification every three years, beginning from the date you were originally certified. It is necessary to accumulate 18 recertification units during the three-year period. Recertification units are earned by participating in activities in the field in which you are certified that maintain your expertise. These activities include professional employment, continuing education, attending conferences and workshops, teaching, or publishing articles or papers.

If you are unable to accumulate 18 recertification units, it will be necessary to pass the examination again in order to be a Certified Software Quality Engineer.

Since the Body of Knowledge and bibliography for Software Quality Engineering can change over time, always contact ASQ for the latest information.

For questions about the ASQ Certification program, call the Certification Department at ASQ headquarters, 800-248-1946 (United States, Canada, and Mexico) or 414-272-8575.

References

1. ASQ Web Page http://www.asq.org.
2. Kleiman, Carol, "Certified is the magic word in qualifying computer specialists." In: *Chicago Tribune*, February 9, 1997.
3. King, Julia, "Are there big benefits in certification?" In: *Info Canada*, June 1996.
4. ASQ Certified Software Quality Engineer Certification brochure, Item B0110.
5. Author's Note: Special thanks to Linda Westfall, CSQE Certification Chair, for contributing certification exam development information contained in this chapter.

## CHAPTER 8

The Cost of Software Quality

James H. Dobbins, CQA
Defense Systems Management College

8.1 Introduction

The discipline of quality has been the focus of a paradox. The slogan "Quality is Free" [1] is ever before us, in books, posters, slogans, and other media input. Yet the perpetual question asked by all program managers whenever a quality goal is required or suggested is, "What is it going to cost me?" It is as if everyone speaks of quality being free, but no one believes software quality is free. The real issue is one of investment, not cost.

It is time to examine the question of the cost of software quality and to draw some conclusions which, it is hoped, will enable the program managers to ask the correct questions about the cost of software quality, recognizing that the net value of a software quality investment is in terms of costs avoided. The investment in software quality, like any investment, has an immediate cost, with an expected net payback. The worth of the investment is determined by the value of the gain realized. If the gain realized from the quality investment is sufficient, then the net result is positive. To make this assessment, quantitative methods of evaluation are necessary.

8.2 Concepts of the Cost of Software Quality

The concepts of the cost of software quality have to be understood before the activities and measures related to the cost of software quality can be addressed in meaningful terms. Traditionally, the cost of quality, with its roots in hardware analysis, focused on failure-related issues and activities. These included spoilage, defects, or the effort required to bring an item into, or back into, conformance with a set of requirements. The costs were usually tracked as the costs of scrap, rework, and repair. The costs were largely limited to labor and materials, and were often tracked in terms of their percent of total production cost, or percent of total sales volume.

Today, we recognize the cost of quality as being those segmented in terms of error prevention, appraisal (or product and process evaluation), and failure-related activities. The drive is to minimize the failure-related activities by making the proper level of investment in the prevention and evaluation activities. The categories of the cost of software quality and how they relate to each other must be understood in terms of the activities comprising each category and the measures describing and evaluating the cost of each of the software quality activities.

8.2.1 Visibility

A key consideration in any analysis of the cost of quality is visibility. The only reason for undertaking the analysis is to gain the visibility needed to make the enlightened decisions that result in highly effective software engineering processes producing high quality software products and their improvements. It is the visibility gained from cost of quality analysis that enables the project personnel to focus their attention on those activities which discover, and correct, the root causes of software defects. This root cause analysis allows the project personnel to determine how the development processes can be improved to prevent further defects. This visibility also provides the vehicle for excellent communication across all functions supporting the project, regardless of the organizational structure. The activities and resultant measures that provide the visibility are diverse, and are conducted across the life cycle phases. They can include inspections, audits, tests, vendor surveys, subcontractor audits, proposal evaluations, cost analysis, incorporation of CASE tools (Chapter 14, *Software Quality Assurance CASE Tools*), and any of several other such activities.

8.2.2 The Nature of Quality

A prerequisite to any meaningful discussion of the cost of software quality is an understanding of the nature of software quality. One of the impediments to a true understanding of cost of quality analysis, and identification of quality activities and measures, is the set of traditional "baggage" that comes with the term quality. This traditional view is founded in several myths, including the following:

- quality is defined by the producer, not the customer,
- quality relates only to the final product,
- software development is the biggest contributor to defects,
- improving quality always costs more money,
- quality is the responsibility of the Quality Assurance Department.

The real story behind quality is that

- the customer (user) defines quality,
- quality is determined by every process, support function, and subproduct,
- software defects are traceable to the requirements as a major contributor, and can occur during any life cycle phase,
- improving quality will result in a lower life cycle cost,
- quality is everyone's job, on every task they perform.

8.2.3 Why is There a Cost to Software Quality?

The cost or, more accurately, the investment, of software quality for activities conducted is rooted in the requirement to assure that the developed product meets the approved requirements. The nature and size of the investment involved will be determined by several diverse elements. Some of these are:

- the requirements imposed by the buyer and whether or not the contract is a government contract with specific activities mandated by standards and regulations,
- the kinds of technologies used,
- the kind of product being developed,
- the internal development environment,
- the project budget,
- the degree to which repeatable processes and measures are incorporated into the everyday working practices of the developers,
- the domain knowledge possessed by the development team.

The objective of a cost of software quality analysis is not to reduce the cost, or investment, of software quality, but to make sure that the costs expended are the right kinds of costs and that the maximum benefit is derived from that investment. This requires a level of management understanding which recognizes the need for, and economic advantage of, error prevention in the early phases as opposed to error detection and correction during the later test phases. This cannot be accomplished without a management team sufficiently sophisticated and educated in the concepts, processes, and measures necessary for error prevention and process evaluation, and possessed of the wisdom to put into effect the activities needed to reap the maximum rewards for the investment.

As has been noted, the traditional view of the cost of quality, inherited from the hardware production disciplines, revolved around failure-related activities. These costs were typically discussed in terms of scrap, rework and repair. Very little attention was given to defect prevention. More recently the hardware producers have adopted the concepts of Total Quality Management, and the focus has shifted to the same kinds of concepts that are relevant to the cost of software quality. The major categories of emphasis have shifted to include prevention and evaluation, and not just failure. By shifting the emphasis from failure to prevention and evaluation, significant return on the quality investment, the Quality Return on Investment (QROI), can be realized.

8.2.4 Activity Assessment

In any assessment of quality, the question of cost can be quantified in terms of those activities that are done or not done. Things that are done can be costed in terms of the labor hours and material expended in those tasks, and the cost benefit of doing those activities. Things that are not done can be costed, perhaps not as definitively, in terms of the impact of their not having been done, or not having been done at the right time. In either case, measurements have to be established by which management can evaluate both the activities and their effects.

In order to determine the activities to be performed, and therefore budgeted, an assessment must be made of the labor hours to be expended, any material resource costs, any costs related to the software equivalent of "scrap and rework," and the schedule impact on the life cycle phases during which the activities are performed. The value-added benefit derived from these activities is evaluated in terms of process improvement, personnel skills improvement, product quality at delivery, overall project cost, impact on total project schedule, total manpower and material resources, warranty costs, competitive advantage in the marketplace and the post-delivery software maintenance costs.

In any analysis of activity, the effects of the activities must be measured for quality impact. If there is no impact on product quality, the value of the activity is zero. There must be a set of determinants which drives the questions asked and which focus the issue on the benefits derived. There must be a relationship between the objectives of the project and the activities performed.

8.3   Input

Input to the cost of software quality analysis are the base elements necessary to conduct the analysis. This includes the requirements for data, material, customer needs, costs related to training, resources needed to support the process, and the procedures and standards required or followed.

8.3.1 Data

In order to perform a task which is to be measured as a cost of quality, the relevant data must be observable or measurable. This may be data directly observed,

derived from analysis, provided by the customer, gathered as a result of the performance of some other task, provided as the output of another project, or data necessitated by the physical aspects of the project itself (such as the requirements of a
nuclear energy project which are a function of the nuclear process itself). The data
must be categorized as to whether it is related to error prevention activity, evaluation activity, or related to failures that occur at various life cycle phases. Once the
determination is made regarding the data required, the cost of obtaining that data
can be determined by the process chosen to obtain the data.

8.3.2 Material

Any requisite material needed for the task must be determined. This may be
the acquisition of a personal computer for analysis of the data to be obtained, or it
may be something as simple as the forms necessary for recording data or activity
results. In any case, the material involved has a cost of purchase or a cost of creation. The cost is determinable as long as the material is identifiable and available.

8.3.3 Customer Needs

The needs of the customer are among the lesser identifiable parameters of the
set of input requirements for quality assessment. It is not uncommon for customers
to have an overall idea of their needs, but they may lack the specific details about
requirements which they need to communicate to the developer. It is very important
to determine the project requirements, and the allocated software functional requirements. There is little doubt that software requirements that are not well defined or
are constantly changing have a significant impact on the product quality and
adversely affect the development processes. Each identified requirement must be
measurable and testable. If it is not measurable and testable it is not a true requirement. If not, there can be no pass-fail criteria for determining whether the requirement has been met. Customers must also understand the difference between requirements and desirements. Customers often want everything, but they are only willing
or able to pay for a portion of what they desire.

The way in which the requirements are specified can have a quality determinant and associated cost of its own. If written in prose, there will be a quality impact
different from the impact of requirements written in a structured requirements definition language. The quality analysis activity will likewise be quite different. The
quality cost is not the cost of writing the requirements, but the cost of: error prevention processes employed in the requirements generation process, requirements
volatility, investments made in training or CASE tools to better produce requirements, and the difference in product production cost when the requirements are produced in different ways.

8.3.4 Training

Quality activities often require training in certain process techniques. The type of training, the extent of the training, the travel, if any, required for obtaining or providing the training and the resources which must be expended to conduct or receive the training are all elements whose costs can be determined. The training must also be evaluated in terms of whether it is a one-time event or a continuous requirement.

The benefit derived from the software training in terms of process and product quality must be compared to the prior cost of not performing the activities, plus the cost of the training. In software development, how the beneficial cost of training is to be measured, and over what time period, has to be determined. This is not as easy as it might first appear. Training is given to people, and when people are trained there is an initial skill benefit. However, there is often a long-range educational benefit derived from the application of that new skill in solving the problems of the tasks needed by the project.

8.3.5 Resources

The cost of resources required for providing or obtaining the necessary input data or material or training must be determined. The cost of facility resources for these elements must be determined in terms of space, utilities, and other overhead impacts. Management involvement in all of these activities is a resource which must be accounted for but one which is often overlooked.

8.3.6 Procedures

Any activity probably will be done in accordance with some set of requirements, and therefore will be, or should be, in response to a set of procedures. If the procedures are not already available, they must be created and the cost of that creation recorded.

8.3.7 Standards

In many instances, the activities associated with the product production will have to conform to the requirements of certain standards. These standards may be government, industry, or internal. If an activity is performed only because a standard is invoked, and not because it would be done anyway, the cost of that activity must be considered a cost of quality. However, this must be assessed realistically. If the activity is treated as pure cost, and is not offset by benefits derived, the manager is saying that the activity has no cost benefit, but is done only because of the standard. If the standard imposes activity but adds no quality, the standard must be questioned.

Alternatively, if the processes required by the standard add quality, but the activity associated with the standard would be done anyway as part of the normal development process even if the standard was not in place, then there is no added cost due to the standard.

8.4   Value-Added Actions

For each type of input, there must be a value-added activity associated. Value-added activities are those which add value to the product itself or to the process of producing that product. The value added can be in terms of increased quality of the product, positive impact on processes or procedures implemented in the production, and activities that lower the production cost without impacting product quality.

Overshadowing all of these activities are the customer needs. Clearly, there may be a compelling case for a defect-free product. Associated with this, of course, are the costs related to attempting to achieve such a state of quality. Other customer needs may include systems that are "man-rated" (i.e., systems in which people are an active part of the system) or that will affect personal safety, such as the manned spaceflight projects or some nuclear applications or weapons systems. But there may be many instances where a defect-free system is desirable but quite unnecessary. The degree of reliability of the system must be optimized on the basis of cost, schedule, resources, and available technological skills. It is important for the customer, as well as the contractor, to understand what the realistic needs are for the system under contract.

8.5   Output

The output of the cost of software quality analysis is the result of the application of the quality-related processes and activities. The output is affected by the product, related services, and information.

8.5.1 Product

The product produced by the development activities will have a level of performance that is determined in part by the degree to which it is free of defects and is maintainable. The product will have performance requirements which will or will not be met depending in part on whether or not the input necessary is available and whether or not the value-added actions have been performed. The product will have a reliability, however acceptable or unacceptable, which should be optimized based on all of the determining factors of cost, schedule, resources, and technology. The customer may desire a system with proven reliability of 100 percent, but can seldom afford the activity it would take to reach such a goal.

8.5.2 Services

The output of the value-added actions may be in the form of a service performed for other departments or agencies. While not the product to be delivered, the service may be necessary for the product to be produced with the requisite level of quality. For example, performance of formal design and code inspections [2] may be a non-deliverable service, but the impact on the product quality can be significant. Document inspections are another form of quality service performed which tend to assure the customer that the product delivered—the document—is as defect-free as the implemented procedure will allow.

It is worthy of note that the inspection process used in software is different from inspection of hardware. In hardware, the product is sample inspected to look for flaws in the production. Various things (such as loose or cold solder joints, missing fasteners, and the like) are identified, the product is pulled from the line, and the defective product is returned for rework: it is a failure-related activity.

In software, the inspection process is both a defect detection process and a defect prevention process. Software is an intellectual activity performed only once, and recorded. It is not mass produced, using new pieces each time, but merely copied as needed. The inspections are conducted at each step in the software life cycle to make the software product the best it can be at that time. It is an in-process activity which is largely analytical. Software is the recording of the thought process of the designer and programmer, and inspections are essentially a group analysis and validation of the work of the author, performed while the product is in the various stages of being developed.

8.5.3 Information

Information is often the result of quality activities, even though the information itself is nondeliverable. This may take the form of quality analysis reports, such as the analysis of the design and code inspection data, or audit reports wherein the quality performance or activity or product of another group or department is assessed. Information may take any of several other forms, and any which are quality-related activities are part of the cost of quality.

8.6 Total Cost of Quality

In assessing the total cost of quality, all of the questions that many program managers fail to ask must be asked. When the program manager, who does not understand the real elements of quality, asks what the cost of an activity will be, he is asking what the specific cost of the performance of the activity will be, not the resultant impact of doing or not doing the task. If the task costs one amount, but the result of performing that task saves another amount, the real cost is the difference between the two, not the initial cost of the activity. However, it is never this difference about which the uneducated program manager is seeking information. If the real answer is a negative cost, and if the program manager does not really understand these relationships, he or she will be tempted to ask for a cut in budget for that activity since the total cost is perceived as a negative.

Because the program manager may not be conversant enough in quality processes to ask the real question or to assess the real impact of performing a quality activity, it is necessary to provide a means for assessing the real cost of quality on a project and offer the complete picture to the program manager to ensure that the proper questions are asked and the proper evaluations conducted.

To do this, each department should go through a quality assessment activity analysis, gather the proper data, and present the true picture to the program manager. Once the true picture is presented, and the program manager is brought up to speed, the process has the opportunity to work and the task of performing the quality activities is encouraged.

8.7 Activity Analysis

In going through a process of quality cost analysis, there are four major steps. They are:

1. List all MAJOR activities
2. For each activity:
   - List all input: What? From where?
   - Determine value added: Why do?
   - List all output: What? Where?
3. For each activity:
   - Determine customer requirements
   - Determine supplier requirements
   - Determine measurements
4. For each activity:
   - Analyze measurement requirements
   - Determine level of effort: Estimate cost of effort.
   - Divide cost into categories

To accomplish this, a form should be used by each person in the department so that the activities associated with the product production may be assessed for quality cost/benefit/impact. This is not as intuitively simple as it may seem.

The activities must first be identified. A brief general description must be provided for each major activity in order to properly assess that activity. This may be done through the use of a form such as that shown in Figure 8-1. This is a very simple form, which can be used in multiple copies if the list of activities will not fit on one page; it is easily scanned to determine the number of activities as well. This form prioritizes the activities, and can be used to group the activities by number, by type of activity, or other such pertinent classification.

The next step is to determine the requisite information for each of these tasks in terms of input required and value added by the performance of that activity. The output for the activity must also be determined. An example of a form for this purpose is shown in Figure 8-2. The advantage of the form is the removal of the guesswork involved and a clear indication of where vital information is missing. Each activity should have a separate form of its own for this purpose.

The work required to complete such an analysis may not be as simple as it seems, however. The "Impact If Not Done" part of the form is not always easy to specify, especially in terms of a cost element. The answer to this question may be an educated evaluation based on data from past projects.

The next step is to determine the answers to the requirements questions. Figure 8-3 shows a form for recording such information, but the information for large projects may reference another document. The output requirements must be determined and, finally, the measurements must be identified, which will show whether the requirements are met.

Department Activity Analysis

Department Name: ______________________________

Department Number: ______________________________

Function Name: ______________________________

General Description of Work (Major Activities):

____

____

____

____

____

____

Manager's Signature **date** **phone**

____

Figure 8-1 Department activity analysis.

Department Value Added Analysis

Department Name: _____

Department Number: _____

Activity: _____

Prepared by: _____

INPUT:

WHAT: _____

_____

FROM: _____

_____

VALUE-ADDED WORK ACCOMPLISHED

Why Do? _____

_____

Value Added: _____

_____

Impact if Not Done: _____

_____

_____

OUTPUT:

WHAT: _____

_____

TO:

_____

_____

Figure 8-2   Department value-added analysis.

Department Requirements Activity Analysis

Department Name: _____

Department Number: _____

Activity: _____

Prepared by: _____

AGREED INPUT REQUIREMENTS:

_____

_____

_____

_____

AGREED OUTPUT REQUIREMENTS:

_____

_____

_____

_____

_____

_____

_____

MEASUREMENTS:

_____

_____

_____

_____

Figure 8-3   Department requirements activity analysis.

To identify a set of measurements that is going to prove the requirements are met may necessitate considerable investigation. The arena of software measurements is just reaching a stage of development where companies are becoming comfortable with the idea of software quantification.

The assessment process developed by the Software Engineering Institute (SEI) at Carnegie-Mellon University, [3] and which is now being used by the Department of Defense as one of the contractor source selection criteria, has a five-step scale for assessment. At Level 1, "the contractor has ill-defined software engineering procedures and controls . . . the organization does not consistently apply software engineering management to the process, nor does it use modern tools and technology." [4]

It is not until an organization reaches Level 3 that meaningful metrics become part of the normal software engineering process, and are used by management in decisionmaking. In the initial studies conducted, 86 percent of the companies assessed by SEI were at Level 1. Because of this, the measures, if any, which are selected by the contractor may not necessarily be understood or acceptable to the customer. Each measure selected must be identified, justified, and documented.

It is advisable for contractors to develop sets of measures for each development stage of the software life cycle rather than one measure at the very end of the development or test phase. This will afford the development management a means for continual assessment and correction throughout the software development process. In addition, if the company is a defense contractor, the revised DODI 5000.2-R [5], released 15 March 1996, mandates the use of metrics in the software development process. The Department of Defense will no longer have the option of deciding whether or not to require contractors to incorporate metrics into their software engineering environment.

The measurement selection process is one which should be governed by several factors, such as the input data requirements, the availability of support software to make the necessary computations or evaluations, the ease with which the results can be understood and evaluated by management, and the amount of information contained in the measurement result. It is clear that a measure which only indicates that a problem exists is far less valuable than one which indicates that a problem exists and also why it exists. All too often, measurement tools provide lengthy printouts of data, but the data are not converted to information, and especially not information that can be quickly and easily understood and utilized by management. In some instances, the measurement tool output is so involved, the company that developed the tool requires that one of their employees be always available, and paid, to interpret the results. Perhaps this approach is why so many managers have struggled with implementation of software metrics.

Once the activity analysis, i.e., the activities, input requirements, output requirements and measurement requirements have been determined, then the final set of questions must be asked. As is seen in Figure 8-4, for each activity, the manager (either the SQA and/or program manager) must determine whether the measurement is possible now, if it is possible at all, and whether the activity should be measured: It may cost more to perform the measurement than to accomplish the task.

The activity itself must be costed in terms of the man-hours required to perform the task. The activity may be purely a quality activity, it may be an activity which is only partially a quality activity, or it may be a totally nonquality activity.

The cost of quality should then be categorized in terms of prevention activity, appraisal activity, or failure activity (see Figure 8-4).

Department Quality Activity Cost Analysis

Department: _____

Activity: _____

Prepared by: _____

MEASUREMENT ANALYSIS

IS ACTIVITY MEASURED NOW?   ❏ NO   ❏ YES

CAN THIS ACTIVITY BE MEASURED?   ❏ NO   ❏ YES

SHOULD ACTIVITY BE MEASURED?   ❏ NO   ❏ YES

LEVEL OF ACTIVITY

ESTIMATED HRS/WK SPENT ON THIS ACTIVITY: _____

IS ACTIVITY A "COST OF QUALITY"?

❏ NO   ❏ YES   ❏ PARTIALLY

ESTIMATED "COST OF QUALITY" HRS/WK SPENT ON THIS ACTIVITY:

_____

COST OF QUALITY CATEGORIES

PREVENTION: HRS/WK: _____   COST: _____

APPRAISAL: HRS/WK: _____   COST: _____

FAILURE: HRS/WK: _____   COST: _____

TOTAL: HRS/WK: _____   COST: _____

Figure 8-4   Department quality activity cost analysis.

8.8 Focus

Once these actions have been completed, the department manager has the information necessary to go to the program manager and present a true picture of the real cost of producing a quality product. The focus should be on the cost to analyze problems and the cost to redo the task.

8.8.1 Software Quality Assurance

The analyses tasks provide the means for identifying errors in the system and for prioritizing the errors for corrective action. The attention is on the means to accurately identify nonconformances, and this requires that the employees get involved in the task. Involving the employees in a quality process to this degree builds up their quality awareness—the key to quality program success.

The result of the analysis process must be documented and presented to those who have to make decisions based on the information.

8.9 Task Elements

8.9.1 Non-Cost of Quality

In making the assessments discussed, the nonquality portion of tasks has to be determined. To do this, the manager or employee must decide if the task is purely design, development, fabrication, documentation, assembly, process, creation, or upgrade.

Any of these, done the first time, is a nonquality task element. They are tasks which would be done just to get the product out the door, regardless of quality considerations. But note well the phrase "done the first time."

8.9.2 Cost of Quality

Task elements, which are part of the cost of quality, are generally grouped into two classifications and three categories. The classifications are Conformance and Nonconformance. The categories are Prevention, Appraisal, and Failure. They are cataloged according to the relationship that exists between the categories and the classifications. Prevention and Appraisal are under the Conformance classification and Failure is under the Nonconformance classification. These relationships can be tabularized, as shown in Table 8-1.

In performing the Conformance activities, care must be taken to distinguish between the work of others and of oneself. The review and checking methods may be the same if all is done in-house. However, if the work is done by a subcontractor, then the methods and the cost elements may be quite different.

Table 8-1   Categorizing Task Elements

Conformance		Non-Conformance
Prevention	**Appraisal**	**Failure**
Training	Inspection	Rework
Planning	Testing	Service
Simulation	Audits	Modification
Modeling	Monitoring	Expediting
Consulting	Measurement	Recall
Qualifying	Verification	Correction
Certifying	Analysis	Retest
		Error Analysis

When this activity of categorization and classification is accomplished, an overall Quality Activity Analysis can be performed. This can be done using a simple form designed for that purpose, such as that shown in Figure 8-5. On this form the summary of the information gathered can be collected in one place, making it easier to present it to the program manager and providing the means for making the case for quality activity.

As an example, the form in Figure 8-5 has been filled out for a software development department. In this example, approximately two-thirds of the total department cost is a cost of quality. If these data points are maintained regularly, and if they are summarized on an annual basis, the annual costs can be determined, as shown in Figure 8-6. Here the data shows that of the $288,000 dollars spent as a cost of quality, $186,000 was spent on fixing problems. Clearly, this can be attacked by the introduction of error prevention activities and by the introduction of methods and techniques for detecting and removing, early in the development cycle, errors that do slip by.

It has been estimated, for example, that removal of an error after delivery to the field may typically cost as much as 80 times the cost of removal during software design. If the time expended and the costs incurred by performing cost of quality activity are the result of poor production or design processes or procedures, then the failure-related cost of quality can be reduced in proportion to the degree to which the design and production processes and procedures are improved. This reduction in the cost of quality can be measured and, if related to the production and design activity, can afford a means of assessing the effectiveness of the improvements made.

Department Quality Activity Analysis

Department: _____

Date: _____

ACTIVITY	NCOQ	CONFORMANCE		NONCONFORMANCE	TOTAL
		PREV	EVAL	FAILURE	
PROGRAM DESIGN	616				616
DESIGN REVIEWS		63	42		105
CODE	432				432
CODE REVIEWS		57	36		93
UNIT TEST			329		329
INTEG TEST			458		458
SYSTEM TEST			379		379
CONFIG MGMT			273		273
PROBLEM SOLVING				184	184
REWORK				123	123
RETEST				167	167
TOTAL HRS	1048	120	1517	474	3159
% OF TOTAL	33.2%	3.8%	48%	15%	

Figure 8-5 Department quality activity analysis.

ESTIMATED ANNUAL COSTS

	HOURS	DOLLARS	%
NON-COST OF QUALITY	10,272	312,000	52
COST OF QUALITY	9,408	288,000	48
TOTAL ANNUAL COST	19,680	600,000	

CATEGORIES OF COQ

	HOURS	DOLLARS	%
PREVENTION	960	30,000	5
EVALUATION	2,304	72,000	12
FAILURE	6,144	186,000	31
TOTAL YEAR	9,408	288,000	48

Figure 8-6   COQ activity analysis.

8.10   Potential Misuse

As is true of most good things, the Cost of Quality Analysis, once published, can be misused. The cost of quality is not a normal financial program activity. Few finance departments have anything resembling a cost of quality analysis as is described here. The typical finance or cost analysis department in all likelihood knows the total cost of a software quality assurance department, but that cost is not the actual cost of performing quality assurance. Conversely, the cost of quality analysis is not a financial program. It is not a substitute for an existing accounting system.

The misuse of the cost of quality analysis is typically related to the focal point of the analysis. There is a tendency to place too much emphasis on the "cost" and not enough on the failure elements of the analysis. The "cost" is just a means of bringing attention to bear on the failure elements and their effect on the program. There is no need for absolute and infallible accuracy to the last dollar as is required in accounting departments.

There is a requirement for understanding the impact of the failures and the cost picture is the most convincing means of conveying that impact. This is not to say that the figures are erroneous or unimportant. The failures do give life to the cost elements; it is a question of focus. The focus should be on the failures and what can be done to prevent them. Developing the cost should be a means of tracking the effectiveness of the failure reduction program.

The figures should also not be used to compare departments or functions for the purpose of punishment. Again, the emphasis should be on failure removal from software being developed, with emphasis on trends within a department or function. If the trend is in the correct direction, then the process is working. If it is working, don't break it; improve it. If the focus and trend analysis is on defect prevention, this in itself will have a significant leverage on quality costs. If the focus is on cost alone, it is likely that very little will be accomplished.

8.11 Productivity

Closely allied to the cost of quality, and intimately related to the failure elements, is the question of productivity. Here again, the questions asked are seldom the correct questions. The program manager or the customer is most likely to track productivity in terms of the number of lines of code generated per unit of time. This is usually expressed in terms of lines per labor month. This measure, in itself, is counterproductive and encourages the development departments to overlook or eliminate quality tasks and procedures which they should be performing. If productivity is examined in conjunction with the cost of quality analysis, then the emphasis will be on lines produced correctly per labor month. For example, if a programmer produces 1,000 lines in one month, and 900 have to be corrected, then the programmer's productivity should really be measured as 100 lines per month, or even less depending on how many lines have to be added per line corrected. If another programmer produces 500 lines in a month, but only 100 have to be corrected, then that programmer's productivity is 400 lines per month, or four times the productivity of the other, supposedly the more prolific programmer.

This emphasis on productivity as a measure of correctly produced products requires considerable customer and manager education. It is often the combination of customer perception and manager ignorance of true programmer productivity which drives the definition, the measure, the reporting scheme, the schedule, and the overall program cost. Many contracts have built-in incentive fee awards, and if productivity is correctly assessed, this will afford a means of establishing an incentive fee award, which is truly meaningful. This concept can be applied to software production, and to those related elements upon which correct production depends, such as functional specifications. If the specification is produced quickly, but is full of defects, then the programmer productivity will be impaired. If the specification is produced with a minimal percent of defects, then that has a positive impact on the programmers' productivity and should be encouraged with incentives.

The foregoing aspects of productivity should be incorporated into a cost of quality analysis. It is these peripheral activities that can be major elements of the cost of quality and that can be most effective for improving cost and productivity.

8.12 Major Components

When the activities of software development are being assessed, along with the related cost components and the output, it is helpful to understand the differences between the software activities themselves and the software development attributes. The software activities are shown in Table 8-2, which gives the typical software development activities, the related cost components, and the output. These can be used as a basis for performing a cost of quality analysis for a software development department.

Table 8-2 Software Activities

Activity	Related Cost Component	Output
System Definition	• SW Requirements Definition	• SW Sys. Requirements Spec.
	• SW System Description	• SW Sys. Description Document
	• SW Development Planning	• SW Development Plan
	• Engineering Change Analysis	• Eng. Change Proposals
Software Design	• Functional Design	• Functional Design Spec.
	• Program Design	• Program Design Spec.
	• Test Design	• Test Design Spec.
	• Software Tools	• Data Analysis
	• Design Evaluation	• Evaluation Report
Software Development	• Module Development	• Module Libraries
	• Development Testing	• Test Documents
	• Problem Analysis & Correction	• Program Modification
Software System Test	• Test Planning and Design	• Test Procedures
	• Integration and Test	• Integration Library
		• Test Reports
System/Acceptance Test	• Test Support	• Test Library
	• Test Planning and Design	• Test Documents
	• Test Media Control	• Delivered System

Operational Support	• System Operation Support	• Assistance; Modification
	• Training	• Training Manuals, Courses
	• Site Deployment Support	• Logistic
General Support	• Project Management	• Development Decisions
	• Configuration Management	• Procedures; Configuration Control
	• Software Cost Engineering	• Cost Analysis
	• Software Quality Assurance	• Quality Evaluation Reports
	• Administrative Support	• Administrative Activities

Table 8-3 shows the relationship of software attributes (denoted as Design Objectives) to Design Practice. The various Design Practices (Top Down Architecture, Module Size, etc.) and the Attributes (Reliability, Accuracy, etc.) most impacted by the design practice are noted. Design Practices are defined along the left-hand side of Table 8-3. Attributes are denoted as Design Objectives, found across the top of the table. This table, when used in conjunction with Table 8-1, can help formulate a program of reduction of quality costs by emphasizing activities that will have the most significant impact on the "ility" which requires the most attention.

8.13 Conclusion

The Cost of Quality itself may be zero, but only if the proper activity, based on clear analysis, is performed. Quality is free provided that the effort is made to perform failure reduction tasks and to seek ways and means to move the failure prevention, detection, and removal activity closer to the front end of the development process. The closer to the front the failure removal activity is accomplished, the greater the impact and the more significant the cost reduction. It is only in this way that the cost of performing quality will become less than the cost of not performing quality tasks. Quality costs can be properly evaluated only in terms of the impact created when they are not incurred. It is that impact cost that will drive home the point that quality itself truly can be free.

TABLE 8-3 Software Attributes for Design

Design Practices	Design Objectives					
	Reliability	Accuracy	Testability	Maintainability	Change	Growth
Top Down Architecture	X		X			
Module Size			X	X		
Low Complexity	X		X	X	X	
Structured Programming	X	X	X	X	X	X
Statement Grouping			X	X	X	
Symbolic Parameterization			X	X	X	X
Uniform Naming Convention			X	X	X	X
Module Listing Convention			X	X	X	X
Reserve			X			X
Timing and Sizing Analysis	X		X			X
Accuracy Loss Monitoring		X	X			
Low Number of SW Paths	X		X	X	X	
Design Optimization		X				X
Minimize Dynamic Mods	X		X	X	X	

References

1. Crosby, Philip, *Quality is Free* (New York: McGraw-Hill Publ. Co., 1979).
2. Fagan, Michael E., "Design and Code Inspections to Reduce Errors in Program Development." In: *IBM Systems Journal*, Vol 15, Number 3, July 1976.
3. Humphrey, W. S., Sweet, W. L., *A Method for Assessing the Software Engineering Capability of Contractors*, Software Engineering Institute, Carnegie-Mellon University, Preliminary Version, Technical Report ESD-TR-87-186, September 1987.
4. Ibid; page 23.
5. "Mandatory Procedures for Major Defense Acquisition Programs (MDAPS) and Major Automated Information Systems (MAIS) Acquisition Programs." DODD 5000.2-R (March 15, 1996).

Inspections As an Up-Front Quality Technique

James H. Dobbins, CQA
Defense Systems Management College

9.1 Introduction

Ever since the publication of Michael Fagan's paper [1] on the design and code inspection process, inspections have been used as a quality improvement and cost reduction technique. There has been considerable discussion as to whether or not inspections are necessary and whether or not they are any different or any better than walkthroughs. After considerable time expended in performing inspections and after collection of data from many inspections on a wide variety of projects, it has become apparent that the use of design and code inspections during development is one of the most productive activities that a software development team can employ. In spite of the initial reluctance most software developers exhibit when the inspection process is first imposed, software developers enthusiastically perform inspections as a routine part of their development once they become aware of the increase in their productivity and in the correctness of their product which they achieve through inspections.

Program managers initially question the cost-effectiveness of program inspections and the impact they will have on milestone schedule deliveries. However, once a program manager has had firsthand experience with properly conducted inspections, and understands the implications of early defect removal as opposed to costly error correction during tests, the value added by the application of inspections will become more than apparent.

Over the years, since inspections were first begun, the process has been examined and training methods have been streamlined, but the fundamental process and the requirements for the proper conduct of an inspection remain essentially the same as described in Fagan's paper. An overview of the inspection process is provided in this chapter. The emphases of this chapter will be the lessons that have been learned through application of the process; how management can gain a measure of control over software projects, through proper analysis of the data collected; how to anticipate the results which should be obtained through application of inspections, with examples of application and analysis; and the impact the inspection process should have on any test program. Current practices will be surveyed, and speculation as to the impact software technology improvements might have will be pursued.

9.2   The Inspection Process

There are both primary and secondary purposes for conducting inspections. The primary vs. secondary categorization has more to do with the process of conducting the inspections than the net impact of having done inspections.

9.2.1 Primary Purpose

The Inspection, whether design or code, has only one primary purpose; that is, to remove defects as early as possible in the development process. The purpose of the inspection preparation and meeting is to

1. identify potential defects during preparation and validate them at the meeting;
2. validate the fact that identified items are actual defects;
3. record the existence of the defect; and
4. provide the record to the developer to use in making fixes.

It is not the intent of the inspection process to find solutions to identified defects, although not finding solutions is extremely difficult for some people. The fact that a defect exists will be sufficient cause to search for a solution. However, the time of the inspection process preparation and meeting is to be used to identify and record the existence of defects. It is the sole responsibility of the author to define the solution. It is also in the province of the author to request, outside the inspection process, assistance in finding a solution.

Therefore, one of the most difficult tasks many moderators face is keeping the discussion centered on finding defects and away from discussing solutions. In some cases, the mere identification of the defect may be sufficient also to state the solution, but in most cases this is not true and the inspection process will be unreasonably lengthened if the solutions are pursued when the defects are identified. It is also a usurpation of the right of the author to fix his or her own defects.

9.2.2 Secondary Purposes

The secondary purposes resulting from the inspection process are

1. to provide traceability of requirements to design;
2. to provide a technically correct base for the next phase of development;
3. to increase programming quality;
4. to increase product quality at delivery;
5. to achieve lower life cycle cost;
6. to increase effectiveness of test activity;
7. to provide a first indication of program maintainability; and
8. to encourage entry/exit criteria software management.

These secondary purposes are all part of the net effect of performing inspections properly and professionally. The fact that they are secondary purposes does not in any way diminish their importance to the overall software development effort.

If the inspections are performed properly and according to the procedures described, and limited to that, then these secondary benefits will occur naturally. Some of the secondary purposes will be achieved directly as a result of the inspections, and others will be achieved by the inspections working in concert with other activities. In other words, inspections are not the sole cause, but they are a significant—and in some cases a primary—cause of the secondary purposes being achieved.

9.2.3 Inspection Phases

The moderator of an inspection is responsible for the entire inspection process for the software product. There are six distinct inspection phases: planning, overview, preparation, inspection meeting, rework, and follow-up.

Planning. The planning phase is that phase during which the moderator establishes the conduct and progress for the entire inspection. This requires that the moderator

- assure the identification of the inspection team;
- assure that the team members will be able to adequately prepare for the inspection;
- assure that the materials to be inspected are available and conform to standards;
- determine whether the entry criteria have been met (usually in the form of a checklist);

- determine the need for an overview;
- assure that the place for the inspection meeting is available and reserved for the inspection;
- schedule the inspection meeting time and place;
- give all inspection team members and other interested parties notice of the inspection meeting time and place; and
- assign the role of *reader* to a selected member of the inspection team.

Some of these tasks may be accomplished by someone other than the moderator, and often the author will actually schedule the meeting place, pass out the materials, and other such tasks. However, it is still the responsibility of the moderator to assure that these tasks are accomplished.

Overview. An overview meeting is an educational meeting usually conducted prior to a design inspection. It is a short meeting in which the author of the product to be inspected gives the inspection team members, and others who will be interfacing with the author's product, a brief description of the software, what task is being performed, how it will perform that task, what interfaces are to be active, and a description of the interface functions. Such a meeting provides insight to the inspection team members and makes their job easier. It also provides other software developers who will interface with this program the opportunity to learn how the interface will be handled and, if necessary, identify any problems with the described approach. If there are any significant problems in violation of the entry criteria, the inspection can be postponed until after the problems are addressed.

The overview meeting is held at the beginning of the preparation phase and it is at this meeting, if held, that the moderator gives the inspection materials to the inspection team members and also gives them the inspection meeting notice. Otherwise, the moderator assures that the materials are distributed to the team members at the beginning of the preparation phase. The moderator may not do the actual distribution, but the moderator does have the responsibility to assure that the distribution is made.

Whether an overview meeting is held or not is at the discretion of the moderator. This is the only discretionary phase, all other phases are mandatory.

Preparation. The preparation phase begins when the inspection team members receive the inspection materials and the notice of the inspection meeting. Everything needed for the inspection should be provided to the inspectors at one time, at least five working days in advance of the inspection meeting. This lead time is to give the inspectors the opportunity to properly examine the materials and record any discrepancies found. Since each inspector has other responsibilities, the lead time is to allow them to perform their assigned tasks and also to prepare for the inspection meeting. The notice of inspection also includes the minimum estimated time required to prepare for the inspection—based on the size and complexity of the item(s) under review. As a rule of thumb, it is expected that the inspection team members will spend at least as much time preparing for the inspection as is required for the inspection meeting. Inspection meeting sessions should not exceed two hours each.

During this phase, the reader prepares to present the material to the inspection team. The reader makes particular note of any difficulty in understanding the design, code, or commentary. Each inspector examines the material for all possible defects. The defects are recorded on the inspection-defect log form, which is included in the inspection package provided to each inspector by the moderator. Each inspector also keeps track of his or her preparation time and records it on the inspection-defect log form.

Inspection Meeting. The inspection meeting is that phase of the inspection process during which the team members come together to discuss the discrepancies they have detected. The moderator is responsible for the proper conduct of the meeting and for assuring that the team members approach this task in a professional manner. The reader is responsible for presenting the product to the team in a logical and orderly manner so that discussion of the material and discovery of any inherent defects is not hindered.

During this phase, the moderator calls the meeting to order, records the preparation time for each team member, and directs the reader to begin the discussion.

As defects are identified, they are discussed and recorded. Particular attention is paid to previously undetected defects which are discovered as a result of the discussion and interaction between the team members. Also important is verification that items identified for discussion are true defects. The defects are then recorded by each team member, the defect type is noted, and, at the end of the inspection meeting, the defects are counted.

During the inspection meeting, to assure that the team members conduct themselves in a professional manner, the moderator at a minimum holds the participants to only one discussion at a time, sees to it that they address problems in an objective, professional, and as impersonal a manner as possible, and reinforces the intent that the person whose product is being inspected is being helped, not criticized.

As noted, the activity during the meeting is limited to finding defects, not solutions. It is the responsibility of the author to find the solutions. If a defect is a type that repeats itself, the team need discuss it only once. When the defect is encountered again, there need only be a reference back to the original defect detection point, and a note made that the same defect is repeated at this point. When summarizing defects, the moderator counts a defect once for each occurrence.

When defects are repeated in a product, the team should wait until the reader gets to the place each repeated defect is found before mentioning its repetition. The fact of repetition should not be mentioned when the first defect is found. To do so will distract from the flow of the material presented by the reader and tend to place unwarranted emphasis on this one defect or defect type.

When the inspection meeting is over, the moderator collects the individual defect logs from the team. If the moderator is able to ascertain from the meeting that a reinspection will or will not be required, it is announced then. If the defects will have to be examined first, then the moderator should do this in a timely manner.

When the inspection team has been dismissed, the moderator summarizes on the defect summary log form the defects found, records the preparation and inspection time, notes the author, department (or subcontractor company name), notes the requirement for a reinspection, whether this inspection was a reinspection or not, notes the type of inspection, and sends a copy of the data to the author and to the software quality engineering (SQE) department.

Rework. During the rework phase, the author examines the defects found and makes the necessary corrections. After the corrections are verified, the author discusses the corrections with the moderator. If the moderator determines that a reinspection is required, the author begins preparation for the reinspection.

Follow-Up. The follow-up phase is that activity engaged in by the moderator to assure that all of the defects detected during the inspection have been corrected. The moderator is responsible for the activity in this phase, and the inspection is not completed until the follow-up phase has been completed by the moderator.

The moderator has the responsibility to assure that each defect has been corrected. This verification is done in person, not by phone. If necessary, the moderator brings a member of the inspection team to assist in the verification process. The fix date (or the date when the fix is verified), is noted on the defect summary log. When verification is complete, the moderator sends a copy of the summary log to SQE with the notation that this is a fix notification. When this last task is accomplished, the task of the moderator for the inspection is completed, and the inspection itself for the software product is also completed.

9.2.4 Inspection Types

There are three types of inspections typically performed. These are high-level design inspection (I_0), low-level design inspection (I_1), and code inspection (I_2).

High-Level Design Inspection (I_0). During the high-level design phase, the overall design for a module or function is produced. This stage commences with the issuance of the relevant software requirements or performance specification, the interface design specification(s), and ends with the completion of the I_0 inspection. In this stage, the high-level architecture of the software is determined and recorded in the initial software design specification. This high-level design information is examined during the I_0 inspection. For each function, the design specification will provide

- the source of the design (new, other contract, etc.)
- a graphical presentation of the function allocation to hardware resources
- a graphical presentation of function flow
- a description of scheduling, timing, and synchronization
- a definition of interfaces
- the process of decomposition
- the design definition as follows:
  - retained modules: reference to the existing preliminary (i.e., high-level) design specification, as applicable
  - modified modules: reference to the existing preliminary (i.e., high-level) design spec, where applicable, and a narrative description of the changes
  - new modules: high-level description of the interfaces and processing

During the I_0, the high-level design information is further expanded to include a description of each new task/module, including interfacing and processing. An I_0 is held for each new function. For the retained and modified modules, an inspection plan is written by the software developer to define the scope of requirements for any additional I_0 inspections. These requirements are based on the anticipated extent of modification.

Resource utilization estimates are generated during this design phase and are collected and maintained by the system engineering organization, with the software development organization periodically providing input. The system engineering organization reviews and approves the high level design specification and the I_0 material to assure compliance with the baseline documentation.

All six phases of the inspection process (with the possible exception of the overview phase) are conducted for each I_0.

Purpose — I_0 inspections are conducted to formally examine the software product to verify that the functional design at the task level is a correct expansion of the software requirements or performance specification at the functional mode level. A mode-level function may be classification, tracking, and so forth. Verification is performed by identifying the allocation of software requirements identified in the requirements specification to processes and tasks. A single I_0 is typically performed for each mode.

Low-Level Design (I_1). The low-level design, or what is more commonly called *detailed design* or *module design*, reflects back on the overall design objectives. Key objectives considered in designing the software are

1. accuracy with high performance;
2. reliability and fault-tolerance, enabling the system to continue to perform in the event of hardware intermittent failures or other unexpected occurrences;
3. flexibility to accommodate change and growth;
4. easy testability; and
5. that it be readily maintainable.

Key features of the design process that facilitate the achievement of these objectives are described in Table 9-1.

Detail module design is developed and I_1 inspections are held for all modules which meet any of the following criteria:

1. new module development;
2. any change to the external interface or function of an existing module;
3. a structural change in an existing module; and
4. a 40 percent or greater change in the source lines of code (SLOC) in an existing module. This percentage presumes that the size requirements as specified in the military standards are adhered to. In the case of unrestricted module size, where the module is large, this percentage criterion may not be proper.

To improve maintainability, each new module, member, or subroutine process is self-documenting, as follows:

- It contains a prologue, or preamble, which describes the routine function, inputs, outputs, revision levels, and process flow.
- Comments for each section are blocked and delineate the routine into logical segments and describe the function of each segment.
- Inline comments clarify specific statements.

Purpose — The objective of I_1 is to stepwise refine the I0 design to an intermediate level before translation to the target language code is authorized. All interfaces between processes, tasks, and procedures are defined to the field or bit level. The level of decomposition must be sufficient to show the highest level of control structure for each procedure and the operations performed on the inputs and outputs. This does not, however, necessarily define completely all the control structures and internal data structures.

Table 9-1   Relationship of Software Design Practices to Design Objectives

Design Practices	Design Objectives					
	Reliability	Accuracy	Testability	Maintainability	Change	Growth
Top Down Architecture	X		X			
Module Size			X	X		
Low Complexity	X		X	X	X	
Structured Programming	X		X	X	X	X
Statement Grouping			X	X	X	
Symbolic Parameterization			X	X	X	X
Uniform Naming Convention			X	X	X	X
Module Listing Convention			X	X	X	X
Reserve			X			X
Timing and Sizing Analysis	X		X			X
Accuracy Loss Monitoring		X	X			
Low Number of Software Paths	X		X	X	X	
Design Optimization		X				X
Minimize Dynamic Mods	X		X	X	X	
Emphasis on Design Reviews	X	X	X			

All six phases of the inspection process (with the possible exception of the overview phase) are conducted for each I_1.

Only after the successful completion of the I_1 inspection, and any required reinspections, can the module coding process begin. Managers have the responsibility to assure that no code begins on a module until the successful completion of the design inspection for that module. This is a technical and product quality decision and should not be controlled by schedule. The portion of the design specification for the software design that has completed the I_1 phase should be updated and completed by the end of that inspection.

Code Inspections (I_2). A code inspection (I_2) is held for all new code or code from another task being modified to meet the requirements of the new task or contract. The code inspection is not performed until after there has been an error-free compilation. All six phases of the inspection process (with the possible exception of the overview phase) are conducted for each I_2. In some cases where there is a very minor program trouble report (PTR) fix, the lead software developer may decide not to hold an I_2 inspection. There should be a person designated with the responsibility to make this judgment and this decision should be a purely technical decision, not one driven by schedule.

Purpose — The code inspection will serve the following purposes before the program test functions proceed:

1. Verification that the code conforms to the requirements specification, design specification, and interface design specification requirements for operational software.
2. Confirmation that the design has been correctly converted to the target language.
3. Verification that the code conforms to the requirements where there may be online interfaces.
4. Early audit of code quality by the software developer's peers.
5. Early detection of errors.
6. Verification that the code meets level-to-level module interface requirements.
7. Review of module test specification, which is provided with the inspection materials package.
8. Verification that the module test specifications (module test plan) are necessary and sufficient to test the requirements specified for that module and are reviewed during the design inspection (I_0 and I_1).
9. Verification that the proper test tools and test environment have been identified and are available.
10. Verification that the test dependencies are correct and the module is testable based on the dependencies.
11. Decision whether to allow module test (unit test) to begin.
12. Verification that the software product conforms to the contract or internal standards and conventions.

Code inspections for each software module are typical of the pass/fail events which serve as milestones in software development schedules.

The result of a successful code inspection should be compiled code which conforms to the high-level design, low-level design, and software requirements or performance specification.

Only after successful completion of the code inspection can the module test begin.

9.2.5 Inspection Defect Types and Definitions

The inspection defect logs and design/code inspection summary logs used by the inspectors and the moderator require the categorization and typing of defects found.

The types of defects and their definitions follow:

Design defect:	function description does not meet the requirements specification.
Logic defect:	logic is missing, wrong, or extra information.
Syntax defect:	does not adhere to the grammar of the design/code language defined.
Standards defect:	does not meet the software standards requirements. This includes in-house standards, project standards, and military standards invoked in the contract.
Data defect:	missing, extra, or wrong data definition or usage.
Interface defect:	incompatible definition/format of information exchanged between two modules.
Return code / message defect:	incorrect or missing values/messages sent.
Prologue / comment defect:	the explanation accompanying the design/code language is incorrect, inexplicit or missing.
Requirements change defect:	change in the requirements specification which is the direct and proximate reason for the required change in the design or code.
Performance improvement defect:	code will not perform in the amount of time/space/CPU allocated.

9.2.6 Inspection Initiation

Inspections are initiated upon the completion of software design, either high- or low-level, or upon the completion of the first clean compilation of code. Developers should not spend any time doing desk-checking of the product if these conditions have been met.

There is always the feeling that doing desk-checking saves time, and minimizes exposure of one's mistakes. In most instances, no time is really saved since the inspections must be held and the inspection team will still have to review the material. In addition, in desk-checking, the only eyes, experience, and talent being applied to the product are those of the author. Often, this is insufficient. The whole idea is to make good use of the variety of backgrounds, experiences, and talents of the entire team to get a full, rigorous, and thorough examination of the product. Having it done twice, or more, by the author does not really accomplish much other than to alleviate some imaginary wounds to his or her pride.

The negative exposure the author receives from the inspection process is not nearly as great as it might seem to be at the time of the inspection. The inspectors do not really care how many defects are found. They are there to do a job, do it professionally, and then return to their assigned tasks. They are not going to spread out upon the office gossip line the number of defects everyone has in his or her product. Even if they did, the number of inspections held is so great that the numbers of defects would soon blend in everyone's mind to the point of becoming commonplace.

The real negative exposure occurs when the inspections are not held properly. If the defects are not found in inspections, they must be found in test. If found in test, they are recorded on a PTR or other equivalent form and entered into some database. Usually, everyone on the project has access to the database and all of the errors assigned to one individual are there for everyone to see. They also cost more to fix, require Configuration Control Board action, and take longer to implement and retest.

9.2.7 Inspection Prerequisites

The requirements for the proper conduct of an inspection are as follows:

- a team of technically competent, trained inspectors
- a trained moderator
- proper planning and distribution of materials
- a good professional attitude
- full preparation prior to the inspection meeting
- completed design or cleanly compiled code
- updated resource requirements

The training required is that which should be provided by the SQE department for moderators and inspectors. SQE also should have a course available for managers describing the inspection process and how it can be used to help achieve their project and department goals.

9.2.8 Inspection Teams

Establishing the Team. The moderator has the responsibility of identifying the inspection team. In the day-to-day activity, the moderator may not always personally select/identify the team members, but the moderator is responsible for assuring that the team is identified, that the team make-up is proper, and that the required materials are distributed.

In establishing the team, care should be taken to pick those who are willing and able to contribute in a positive and professional manner. Care should also be taken to avoid overloading good inspectors. Unless unusual conditions dictate otherwise, no one should be involved in inspecting the work of others more than 25 percent of his or her time. Otherwise, the inspector will either not have time to properly prepare for an inspection or, conversely, will have his or her own work suffer as a result.

The inspection team should be limited to no more than five people unless special conditions warrant an increase.

Inspection Team Members and Duties. Inspection team members include the moderator, the author, and, depending on which type of inspection, individuals from the system engineering organization, the software integration and test (SWIT) organization, other developers, and SQE.

Responsibilities of the Moderator — The moderator has certain well-defined responsibilities during an inspection.

Prior to the Inspection Meeting
1. Complete the SQE training course.
2. Determine whether the entry criteria for this level of inspection have been met.
3. Work with the author to establish the team membership:
   - System Engineering Personnel for I_0
   - Possibly System Engineering for I_1 or I_2
   - Developers with related design or interface knowledge
   - SWIT personnel
   - SQE personnel
4. Preview the material for conformance to standards.
5. Assure the team size and mix is proper.
6. Assure there are at least five working days of preparation.
7. Assure proper materials are distributed.

During the Inspection Meeting
1. Assure adequate attendance.
2. Assure adequate preparation; if not, postpone to a later time.
3. Lead the inspection meeting.
4. Log defects (if not already on inspectors' defect logs) and all open items.
5. Require reinspection for major defects, specification changes, or greater than 50 defects per 1,000 source lines of code (KSLOC).

After the Inspection Meeting
1. Review results with the author.
2. Provide the manager with an estimate-of-rework completion data.

3. Eliminate duplicate defect log entries and send the inspection summary to SQE.
4. Add the inspection summary and detail report to the software quality notebook kept by the departments or authors.
5. Verify correction of all defect log entries.
6. Add the completion notice to the software quality notebook and send copy to SQE.
7. Log open items in the software quality notebook or in the open issues log.

Responsibilities of the Author — The author also has well-defined responsibilities, both before and after the inspection meeting.

Prior to the Inspection Meeting
1. Prepare material to address all inspection level checklist items. Include as appropriate :
   • requirements specification or section
   • high-level design
   • low-level design
   • clean compilation of code
   • defect logs
   • result of prior inspections
   • updated resource utilization estimates
2. Review material with moderator for completeness.
3. Provide cover page listing material identified, including:
   • major function or process
   • all referenced packages
   • procedures or modules listing
   • SLOC count estimate vs. allocated resources
   • CPU estimates vs. allocated resources
   • memory and I/O estimates vs. allocated resources
   • any flows which might aid the inspectors
4. Prepare for the Overview if one is to be held.
5. Work with moderator to schedule time and place for meeting.
6. Work with moderator to establish team membership.
7. Produce materials distribution package in timely manner.

After the Inspection Meeting
1. Complete all rework required.
2. Verify fixes will correct problem and not cause any additional problem.
3. Verify to moderator that changes have been made.

Responsibilities of the Reader

1. Guide the team through the material during the meeting; paraphrase or verbalize the review material.
2. Present material with clarity and understanding.
3. Note any items difficult or impossible to understand.
4. Be able to tie-back to specification or design.
5. Fulfill normal inspector responsibilities.

Note: the reader should not be the author.

Responsibilities of All Inspectors

1. Attend the SQE training class.
2. Thoroughly review all material against the checklist.
3. Assure understanding of function; consult with author if necessary.
4. Record detected defects on inspection defect log form prior to the inspection meeting.
5. Record the inspection-meeting preparation time.

Responsibilities of the Manager — While not a part of the inspection team itself, the manager has an important role in assuring the success of the inspection process. (Note: the constraint that managers not attend inspections is where the term "peer" inspection arises). The manager's responsibilities are as follows:

1. Establish schedules that allow adequate review time and resulting follow-up. Preparation and rework time must be scheduled with the same attention as the inspection meetings themselves.
2. Assure all team members are aware of inspection procedures.
3. Meet with moderator and author to review open items and obtain rework estimate.
4. Monitor individual inspection time, to
   - assure sufficient inspection preparation time
   - assure sufficient inspection meeting time
   - assure particular individuals are not overloaded
5. Review SQE defect summary report for defect trends and perform defect-trends analysis.

The software developer's schedule should indicate when the actual rework from an inspection is complete, not when the inspection meeting is held. In addition, any open items which remain unresolved should prohibit the inspection from being considered complete, or the item should be logged in a highly visible action-item database.

9.3   Lessons Learned

After several years of performing inspections on a variety of different programs ranging in size from 60,000 lines to in excess of 4,000,000 lines, it has become evident that the most effective way to perform inspections is to utilize *only* personnel trained in the proper conduct of inspections.

It is likewise clear that the only way inspections can be effectively utilized as a management development technique is to perform inspections on 100 percent of all new code developed. Experiments have been tried in which inspections are performed on a selected basis according to program size, complexity, or function, and even software developer experience. In each case, the conclusion reached is that the process should be applied to all code.

9.3.1 The Psychological Factor

In order to properly conduct inspections, software developers must be trained in the psychology of inspections as well as the mechanics of the process. This is particularly important to the success of a project because inspections, by their very nature, cause people to become defensive. If people have a particular physical makeup that prevents them from becoming star athletes, they can accept this physical limitation. But in programming, the situation is somewhat different. No one wants to admit that someone else thinks more efficiently than he or she does. Every program that has been written is nothing but an extension of some person's mental process displayed on a printout.

There is a creative pride in the results which are subjected to inspection. The primary purpose of an inspection is to find every possible defect in the program. The working peers of the software developer are the ones who are engaged in this detailed search for defects. The roles people must play in the inspection process are critical to its success, but can lead to many difficulties if not properly understood. On the one hand, there is a software developer who takes great pride in the creative endeavor which is placed before the inspectors, and on the other hand, there are a group of associates who are attempting to use every available technique at their disposal to find as many flaws as they can.

Without the proper psychology being employed, the inspection process could be a total disaster. The personnel involved must understand the sensitivity of the author and the natural tendency to be defensive about one's own work. Without proper training, the inspectors will not possess the proper techniques, or sensitivity, for error detection necessary to allow the author to leave the inspection feeling as if he or she has been helped rather than crucified.

One particularly sensitive aspect of inspections is the recording and dissemination of the data. The results of every inspection should be recorded. The data that results from each of these inspections must be summarized and analyzed so that the most effective use can be made of the process. This means that information will be provided to the management team so that proper decisions can be made, yet it must be done in such a way that any individual software developer will not feel intimidated or degraded. Inspections will work only if the software developers feel at ease with the way the data collected is being used. This means that the resultant information must not be used by management as a club to hold over the head of any software developer.

9.3.2 Make Inspections Impersonal

To accomplish this, the data must be provided to management in such a way that the result of any individual inspection is not discernible in the summary data. With a properly prepared summary, the visibility into the inspection process which management requires to make proper decisions can be made available without having to repeat the result of any individual inspection. Managers should, therefore, not participate personally in the inspection process and should not attempt to obtain results of individual inspections.

If the software developers feel comfortable with the inspections, the benefits are significant. If they feel threatened by the process, the results are virtually worthless. In an experiment to test the impact of management's presence, managers were told to attend the inspections. As soon as the managers began to participate, the number of errors detected by the inspection team per KSLOC decreased significantly and the number of recommendations and suggestions by the inspection team went up correspondingly. When the managers stopped attending, the suggestions went away and the recorded defects returned to normal. Analysis of the results indicated that this was not any sort of conscious conspiracy on the part of the software developers, but rather a clear example of human nature at work. Most people are reluctant to expose their own failures or those of their fellow workers to those who are in a position of authority over them.

9.3.3 Inspectors Limit to Small Groups of Peers

Inspections were designed to be entirely a peer-group process and should remain that way. As mentioned above, the number of people involved in any one inspection should also be limited. Groups of various sizes have been tried as experiments, and the conclusions reached indicate that an inspection should never be conducted by more than five individuals. The author of the product always participates. There should also be an attempt to provide a proper mix of disciplines at inspections, with the mix driven by the type of inspection conducted. In addition to the designer and the implementer, during design inspections the engineers who wrote the software specification should participate; during code inspections, the test engineers should participate.

9.3.4 Make Data Collections Consistent

Data collection during inspections is critical to both the software developers and to the management team. Consistency in the data collected is likewise important. If a standard set of data collection forms is used, and if the process is conducted by those who have been properly trained, then a historical database can be generated that will provide the management team with the necessary insight into how well the inspections are being conducted and, more importantly, the impact of any change in software technology which has been introduced. If each project is allowed to collect whatever data there was in whatever form happens to be at hand or convenient, then the availability to the management team of any sort of comparison between contracts or between time periods is out of the question. For valid comparisons, the necessity is a standard set of data collection forms, a standard format for data presentation, and a standard method for training software developers in how to conduct inspections.

9.4   Requirements Inspections

The practice of design and code inspections is no more static than the discipline of software quality assurance itself. These practices are constantly under review and their effectiveness is continually examined. The process as a whole, and each of its parts, is also under consideration for automation. Which parts of the inspection process, if any, will be automated have not yet been determined. With continuing advances in technology and with the widespread use of personal computers, both individually and tied to a central system, it is natural to expect that any process as critical to the success of software development as properly conducted inspections will be a subject of major interest. The more we can automate, the more we can free the participants in software to concentrate on matters not inherently amenable to automation.

9.4.1 R_0 Inspection

The success of the design and code inspection process has prompted hardware design engineers to adapt it for hardware design, especially in disciplines such as very large scale integration (VLSI) and very high speed integration circuits (VHSIC). The system engineers who produce software requirement specifications are also adapting the technique. It has been identified as the R_0 inspection, which is analogous to the high-level design inspection being taken one step backward in time. It is important to understand that this step can only be effectively taken if implemented in conjunction with other improvements in software technology, such as the use of a structured language for the requirements document. It would be difficult or impossible to move the inspection practice back to the requirements stage if the requirements were still written in prose. The foregoing is just one example of the interrelationship of many of the subdisciplines, techniques, and measurements (see Chapter 20, *Software Reliability Management*) being developed to address the overall discipline of software quality assurance.

As technology progresses, the improvements currently being made will impact all which has gone before, including the inspection process. For example, the development of Ada, a compilable design language, eliminates the need for I_2 inspections. With the increasing use of distributed systems in real-time applications, the inspection process may correspondingly change to implement techniques for detection of an entirely different group of defects from those now commonly found.

The more requirements documents inspections, R_0, are done, the less testing will be required as a primary error detection and removal process. The knowledge gained from these processes will enable the practitioners of software quality assurance to determine the types of errors which are made, where they are introduced, and why they are introduced. This inevitably leads to effective error prevention techniques and tools.

All of this can be accomplished, but only if there are sufficient data on which to make judgments, and a consistent set of data obtained from well-recognized processes affording a common means of communication between disciplines and between persons actively involved in the field.

9.5 Specifications Inspections

Inspections provide a degree of visibility into the early development process, which is particularly useful in making early schedule and milestone decisions. By proper use and interpretation of inspection data, managers are able to gain useful insight into the level of correctness of the developing system and can make such critical decisions as whether they should halt development, better formulate specifications, or cancel the project altogether.

9.5.1 The Problem of Software Specifications

One of the areas in software development most in need of attention is the generation of clear, unambiguous software specifications. A software development manager confronted with specifications that are incomplete, inconsistent, vague, or inaccurate has no way of determining the real extent of the problem without some measure of its impact on the software developers. Through proper application of inspections, the specification document is examined along with the software design which is the primary object of the inspection. By an examination of not only the software design but also that which was the determinant of the design (the specification document), defects inherent in the specification document itself can be detected and recorded.

If the specification defects are tracked as a separate and distinct item on the inspection report, multiple benefits result. The software developers will not feel that they are being criticized for having to make a change in the design or code because the error is in the specification itself, not in the software developer's thought process. The managers have a means of assessing the impact of the specification defects and are able to make critical management decisions effecting the workload of the software developers. If a given functional area of the specification has significant problems, and these problems are evident from the number of changes required in the software because of requirements problems, the manager will have sufficient information at his or her disposal to address the issue with higher-level management, or perhaps even halt work on one or more functional tasks until the requirements have been more fully determined. These decisions must be backed by hard evidence and cannot be made purely on the basis of instinct or software developer complaints.

9.5.2 Recording Inspections

Because of the rigor required by the proper conduct of inspections, software defects are recorded, analyzed, and reported. Specification defects are counted and the changes necessary to correct the defects within the software, per KSLOC, are computed, thereby providing management with a measure of the modification density required in the software because of specification errors. This independent assessment of requirements defects is a useful aid to software developers as well.

Software defects are tracked by density and by type. The most common defect types are tracked independently and the density of each is determined separately from the total defect density. Each program module is separately inspected three times and the data for all three inspections recorded. The data for a given function is reported as a summary of the data of the module(s) performing that function, and the totality of functions is reported as a summary of the entire project.

The management team can then assess the software by major function and by project. Different levels of management will examine the reports for different reasons. Program managers are primarily concerned with project summary information and with information comparing one project with another. Line managers are primarily concerned with the functional data for which they are responsible. Managers who are conversant with the inspection process know that it should only be used as a positive management tool and never to intimidate software developers. Line managers examining inspection data look for functional areas that are particularly error-prone, and they look for specific types of problems at different levels of inspection. During design inspections, the most predominant areas of interest necessarily will be design errors and functional specification defects; therefore design defects should be uncovered at this inspection with a greater frequency per KSLOC than other defect types, such as language errors or standards errors. During code inspections, it is expected that design errors will be minimal and that commentary or interface errors will predominate.

9.5.3 Benefit of Structured Languages

If a design language is not used on the project, and the design is done using flowcharts or other such devices, then inspections at the design stage will be virtually impossible and problems that should be detected at this stage will have to be uncovered during code inspections. Inspections, therefore, encourage the use of structured design languages such as PDL for business or scientific programs or Ada. Program managers from projects that have used inspections during several development efforts universally conclude that the use of structured design languages in combination with inspections is the most powerful set of development tools that can be employed to assure a high-quality product.

9.6 Documentation Inspections

Tom Gilb [2] comments that current document quality control mechanisms are a farce. Totally ineffective review and approval processes for design and requirements also are the norm. Inspections are generally malpracticed by most organizations. However, there is an inspection method that can be applied to any written document. The document undergoing inspection is checked against related documentation by a team of people who are assigned specific roles relevant to the task, for example, customer focus, security aspects, consistency, and identifying excess extras. Any specific document defects are logged and later resolved. Attempts are also made to identify generic defect causes and improve the overall systems process.

9.6.1 Improvements

Tom Gilb provides a list of improvements for the document quality control function as applied to inspections.

- Separate the document quality control functions of inspection from the GO/NO GO approval functions of a review. Reviews should have numeric entry criteria to guarantee the craftsmanship of the documents they evaluate. That level should be 100 times better than now, at say, maximum 0.2 major defects remaining per page.
- Focus initially on upstream inspections (such as I_0, I_1) that involve management and their staff, not on code. The misinformation that inspections are for coders and not managers is a plot to sabotage our systems. TRW long since proved for command and control systems that 62 percent of all defects that escape testing to live environments originate before coding in the design stages.

- Evaluate any type of inspection at all times for profitability. If it is not profitable, tune it to be so or dump it.

- Inspection, using intelligent sampling of documents, is cost effective. This should preferably be carried out in the documents' early stages of production. It should certainly be carried out prior to accepting them. Brute force defect removal by going through entire large documents, code, or test cases should be avoided.

- Recognize that inspection is only effective when you give checkers adequate time to find defects. You cannot force the pace, because effectiveness drops off to less than 1 percent rapidly. You must experiment to establish the rate of checking (in-house with your documents) that best finds your major defects. You must stick with that rate no matter what your hurry, even if you have to take smaller samples to stick to it. A military aircraft manufacturer reported that the optimum rate was 0.2 to 0.3 defects per page (of 600 words noncommentary) per hour per checker. They also reduced their error flow from over 20 major defects per page to about one per page in 18 months. The appropriate senior management level must be informed enough about this "optimum checking-rate" phenomenon and demand that middle managers respect it. Right now, inspection is receiving invalid criticism because of the lack of appreciation of this. If you are in a hurry, you will use optimum checking rates. Inspections, including the Defect Prevention Process, done properly will more than double productivity (Raytheon, factor 2.5 in four years and factor 2.7 in six years.)

- There must be a numeric exit criterion from every document production process. The allowed economic level of major (future cost in test or field use at 9.3 hours each vs. one hour to fix at inspection) defects must not exceed about 0.2 per page. It is normally today two orders of magnitude greater, and we pay in blood for it in testing and operation. When will we try to manage intelligently and "listen to the numbers," as Deming put it?

- Recognize that there are many aspects and objectives for inspection for which defect removal is not primary. It is not a garbage removal exercise. Far more important are the measurable powerful aspects of on-the-job training in good practices, the continuous improvement of practices capability (Defect Prevention Process, CMM Level 5—(See Chapter 13, *SEI CMM Level 5: Boeing Space Transportation Systems Software*), the ability to measure document and process quality (including the ability to sample at early stages of document production and correct a serious defect injection situation before a large document is produced), and the order of magnitude reduction in maintenance costs.

- The Defect Prevention Process has a 15-to-1 payback and avoids 50 percent of all defects normally injected during the first year and first project in which it is used, 70 percent avoidance within two or three years. Defect detection has an average ratio of 9-to-1 payback for invested time and is capable of removing 95 percent of injected defects before first test. Note that these two inspection methods are not alternatives, but intrinsically complimentary. The U.S. space shuttle has led the way in showing the technical capability of defect detection and prevention.

- Lessons learned show that effective training of people to lead inspection teams takes a week of training followed by certification (just like pilots), on-the-job coaching, and follow-up of performance numbers (just like Olympic athletes). Proper training is essential.

- Management needs to learn that inspection needs to be planned and managed as a long-term measurable process improvement (CMM Levels 4 and 5 should partly come *before* CMM Level 3). Management needs to set long-term numeric goals for people productivity, for lower rework costs, for reliability, and for project timeliness. They must expect proper implementation of inspections to achieve what history has shown that it is capable of doing. Inspection is not a technical issue. It stands and falls with good senior technical management (well above project leader level). [2]

9.7   Inspection Metrics

Michael Fagan in his "Advances in Software Inspections" notes that experience from 1976 to 1986 has shown that software inspections are a potent defect detection method, finding 60 to 90 percent of all defects, as well as providing feedback that enables software developers to avoid injecting defects in future work. [3, p. 50]

Project managers who gather and use inspection information effectively can better

- allocate resources
- control conformance to procedures
- determine the quality of inspected software
- measure the effectiveness of inspections
- improve them

AT&T Bell Laboratories established a measurement system that defines nine metrics to help plan, monitor, control, and improve the code inspection process, which brought them to achieve better than 70 percent defect removal efficiencies. This section is a review of these findings at AT&T Bell Laboratories. [4] Although this practice has been applied specifically to code inspections, it is felt that it is generally applicable to all types of inspections.

9.7.1 Goal-Question-Metric

Bell Laboratories has made one of the best uses of the Goal, Question, Metric (GQM) paradigm in arriving at the metrics to use for their code inspection process. GQM is a systematic approach to translate measurement needs into metrics. One begins by clearly identifying measurement goals, then posing specific questions—in measurable terms—whose answers fulfill the goals. Finally, one enumerates the metrics, the answers to those questions (Table 9-2).

Table 9-2　　Goals, Questions, and Metrics for Code Inspections

Goal	Question	Metric
Plan	How much does the inspection process cost?	Average effort per KLOC
	How much calendar time does the inspection process take?	Average effort per KLOC
Monitor & Control	What is the quality of the inspected software?	Average faults detected per KLOC
		Average inspection rate
		Average preparation rate
	To what degree did the staff conform to the procedures?	Average inspection rate
		Average preparation rate
		Average lines of code inspected
		Percentage of reinspections
	What is the status of the inspection process?	Total KLOC inspected
Improve	How effective is the inspection process?	Defect removal efficiency
		Average faults detected per KLOC
		Average inspection rate
		Average preparation rate
		Average lines of code inspected
	What is the productivity of the inspection process?	Average effort per fault detected
		Average inspection rate
		Average preparation rate
		Average lines of code inspected

9.7.2 Nine Metrics

This GQM paradigm led to the nine metrics and their related data items described as follows:

1. **Total noncommented lines of source code inspected, in thousands (KLOC).**

$$\text{Total KLOC inspected} = \frac{\sum_{i=1}^{N} LOC\ inspected_i}{1,000}$$

where N is the total number of inspections.

2. **Average lines of code inspected.**

$$\text{Average LOC inspected} = \frac{\text{total KLOC inspected} \times 1,000}{N}$$

where N is the total number of inspections.

3. **Average preparation rate.**

$$\text{Average preparation rate} = \frac{\text{total KLOC inspected} \times 1,000}{\sum_{i=1}^{N} \dfrac{preparation\ time_i}{number\ of\ inspectors_i}}$$

where N is the total number of inspections. To compute preparation rates for a single inspection, use this computation with N = 1. An unweighted average of preparation rates was rejected because it does not account for differences in the sizes of individual inspections.

4. **Average inspection rate.**

$$\text{Average inspection rate} = \frac{\text{total KLOC inspected} \times 1,000}{\sum_{i=1}^{N} inspection\ duration_i}$$

where N is the total number of inspections. To compute the inspection rate for a single inspection, use this computation with N = 1. An unweighted average of inspection rates was rejected because it does not account for slow inspections rates on small inspections.

5. Average effort per KLOC.

$$\text{Average effort per KLOC} = \frac{\displaystyle\sum_{i=1}^{N} inspection\ effort_i}{\text{total KLOC inspected}}$$

where N is the total number of inspections and where

$$inspection\ effort_i = preparation\ time_i$$
$$+ (number\ of\ particpants_i \times inspection\ duration_i)$$
$$+ rework\ time_i$$

This metric does not include the effort for the inspection's planning and fol-low-up phases because experience has shown that their effort is small and does not warrant the cost of collecting the data.

6. Average effort per fault detected.

$$\text{Average effort per fault detected} = \frac{\displaystyle\sum_{i=1}^{N} inspection\ effort_i}{\displaystyle\sum_{i=1}^{N} total\ faults\ detected_i}$$

where N is the total number of inspections. As with the average effort per KLOC, this effort computation includes only time spent by the inspection team preparing for the meetings, holding the meetings, and correcting the detected faults.

7. Average faults detected per KLOC.

$$\text{Average faults detected per KLOC} = \frac{\displaystyle\sum_{i=1}^{N} total\ faults\ detected_i}{\text{total KLOC inspected}}$$

where N is the total number of inspections. As with the average effort per faults detected, this effort computation includes all types of faults to emphasize the importance of all fault severities.

8. Percentage of reinspections.

$$\text{Percentage of reinspections} = \frac{\text{number of reinspections dispositions}}{\text{number of inspections}} \times 100$$

where number of reinspection disposition = number of inspection disposition of type reinspect + number of inspection dispositions of type inspect rework.

9. Defect removal efficiency.

$$\text{Defect removal efficiency} = \frac{\displaystyle\sum_{i=1}^{N} \text{total faults detected}_i}{\text{total coding faults detected}} \times 100$$

where N is the total number of inspections.

9.7.3 Data Items

The data items that make up these equations are collected for each individual inspection. Most data can be gathered at the inspection meeting and entered into the database. The data should be validated and access to it restricted to guarantee its quality and integrity. Tools and methods such as automated code counting, data-entry validation, and independent validation help ensure that the data is accurate. Because the data is contributed by the development staff, management should not have access to it to evaluate staff performance.

Inspection meeting date. The calendar date of an inspection meeting.

LOC inspected. The number of noncomment lines of source code inspected. Computing the lines of code inspected is complicated by such things as how to count statements that span many lines, and macro expansions. Projects often use a code counting tool to ensure consistency. Other problems arise when the inspection team must inspect modified code. The team must count new, changed, and deleted lines of code, as well as the additional lines related to the modification, as identified by the author. The important consideration is consistency.

Number of participants. The number of people participating in the inspection meeting, including the inspectors, moderator, recorder, reader, and author.

Number of inspectors. The number of people participating as inspectors— including the recorder, reader, and author only if they prepared for the inspection and assumed a second role as inspector.

Preparation time. The total time the inspectors spent preparing, not including the time spent by the moderator and the author in planning. However, it does include their time if they prepared for the meeting as inspectors. Traditionally, the moderator asks participants at the beginning of the meeting for a spoken account of their preparation time. However, to obtain data less likely to be influenced by peer pressure, we have participants write down their preparation time for submission to the moderator.

Inspection duration. The total time spent inspecting the code. A typical inspection meeting should not last more than two hours, so several meetings may be necessary to complete an inspection. Inspection duration is the total time spent in all meetings.

Total faults detected. The total number of faults at the inspection. In all computations, use the total number of faults and do not classify faults by severity. Classification by severity (for example, major versus minor, or observable versus nonobservable) diminishes the importance to inspectors of detecting certain faults. They pay less attention to identifying currently insufficient faults that may become important after code modification or maintenance.

Rework time. The time spent by the author correcting the faults detected in the inspection. It is collected by the moderator from the author after rework is complete.

Inspection disposition. At the end of an inspection, the moderator assigns an inspection disposition. (If multiple meetings are required for a code unit, the disposition is assigned at the end of the last meeting.) There are three possible dispositions.

1. *Accept.* If the nature and number of faults warrant it, the moderator, with input from the inspection team, decides it would not be cost-effective to reinspect the code unit or to inspect the rework. Usually, the moderator verifies (desk-checks) the rework from the inspection.
2. *Inspect rework.* It is cost-effective for the inspection team to inspect the rework.
3. *Reinspect.* The moderator, with input form the inspection team, decides it would be cost-effective to reinspect the entire code unit. Faults were likely missed because the code had so many faults, and the rework will be so significant that the code unit essentially will be rewritten.

Total coding faults detected. The total number of faults detected in the inspection process, plus the faults identified in the inspected code during subsequent unit, integration, function, and system testing, plus faults detected by customers. A single fault may cause multiple failures, and a single failure may be caused by more than one fault. Each distinct fault should be counted.

9.8 National Software Quality Experiment

Don O'Neill says that there is a surge of interest to install inspection processes because:

- Quality has become a national goal. The quest permeates industry, government and academia.
- Software engineering is maturing, and measurement is the foundation for higher states of maturity. The Software Engineering Institute's software process improvement program (see Chapter 12, *Understanding the Software Engineering Institutes's Capability Maturity Model (CMM) and the Role of SQA in Software Development Maturity*) places substantial importance on inspections as a way to stimulate that process improvement.
- Consumers are specifying tougher quality assurance standards and implementing them contractually.
- Major corporations are adopting market-driven strategies and laying down very aggressive quality goals. [5, p. 13]

Through 1992, the benchmark year, there have been 27 inspection labs in which 327 trained participants conducted inspection sessions. A total of 90,925 source lines of code have received strict and close examination using the packaged procedures of the lab. There have been 22,828 minutes of preparation effort and 5,464 minutes of conduct time expended to detect 1,849 defects (Table 9-3). An analysis of these results is given in Table 9-4.

Of these 1,849 defects, 242 were classified as major and 1,607 as minor (Table 9-5). It required 12.3 minutes of preparation effort on the average to detect a defect. To detect a major defect required 94.3 minutes of preparation effort. On the average, 0.99 thousand source lines of code were examined for each inspection conduct hour. There were 2.6 major defects detected in each thousand lines and 17.6 minor defects.

Table 9-3 National Software Quality Experiment Results [6, p. 12]

PREP. EFFORT [MIN]	CONDUCT TIME [MIN]	MAJOR DEFECTS	MINOR DEFECTS	SIZE [SLOC]	PAGES	PARTICIPANTS
22,828	5,464	242	1,607	90,925	244	327

Table 9-4 National Software Quality Experiment Results Analysis [6, p. 14]

	Organization						
	All	H	I	J	K	L	M
Minutes of preparation effort per defect	12.3	7.8	10.1	15.0	11.3	21.6	26.3
Minutes of preparation effort per major defect	94.3	75.2	112.1	102.7	80.3	122.0	117.6
Major defects per KSLOC	2.6	2.4	1.8	2.98	3.6	3.9	3.5
Minor defects per KSLOC	17.6	20.4	18.3	19.0	22.2	18.1	12.3
KSLOC per conduct hour	0.99	1.34	1.04	0.63	0.60	1.12	1.26

Table 9-5 National Software Quality Experiment Defects Analysis [6, p. 15]

	TOTAL %	MISSING %	WRONG %	EXTRA %	TOTAL %
DEFECT TYPE RANKING					
Documentation	41.36				
– Major		0.80	0.16	0.08	1.04
– Minor		21.84	15.52	2.96	40.32
Standards	22.08				
– Major		0.32	.80	0.0	1.12
– Minor		6.24	13.52	1.20	20.96
Logic	11.28				
– Major		1.36	3.28	0.32	4.96
– Minor		2.00	3.20	1.12	6.32
Performance	5.92				
– Major		0.40	1.04	0.08	1.52
– Minor		1.20	1.60	1.60	4.40

9.8.1 Common Issues

Analysis of the issues raised in the experiment to date has revealed common problems that recur from session to session. Typical organizations that desire to reduce their software problem rates should focus on preventing the following types of defects:

- **Loss of control.** Software product source code components are not traced to requirements. As a result, the software product is not under intellectual control, verification procedures are imprecise, and changes cannot be managed.
- **High defect rates.** Software engineering practices for systematic design and structured programming are applied without sufficient rigor and discipline. As a result, high defect rates are experienced in logic, data, interfaces, and functionality.
- **Maintainability impact.** Software product designs and source code are recorded in an ad hoc style. As a result, the understandability, adaptability, and maintainability of the software product are directly impacted.
- **Reuse impact.** The rules of construction for the application domain are not clearly stated, understood, and applied. As a result, common patterns and templates are not exploited in preparation for later reuse. [6, pp. 4–5]

9.9 Examples of the Payoff

9.9.1 AT&T Bell Laboratories [4]

The measurement system described in Section 9.7 helped AT&T Bell Laboratories reduce the cost of removing faults with code inspections by 300 percent compared with testing alone. The measurements also showed a 70 percent defect removal efficiency.

9.9.2 Bell Northern Research [7]

One finds approximately one defect for every person-hour invested, which is two to four times faster than detecting code errors by execution testing. Statistics show that each defect in software released to customers and subsequently reported as a problem requires an average of 4.5 person-days to repair. On average, one person-hour of code inspection avoids 33 person-hours of subsequent maintenance effort (assuming a 7.5 hour workday).

9.9.3 General Experience [8, p. 23]

Carl R. Dichter says that all inspections of more than 1,000 lines of tested code found problems that testing did not. These inspections were cheap—three inspectors looked at all the code, using about one hour per thousand lines of code, and yet they each discovered defects that would have cost much more to fix later.

9.9.4 Large Satellite Communications System [9]

This project took place in 1993. The environment consisted of 330,000 SLOC on five target platforms with many Commercial Off-The-Shelf (COTS) products.

The inspection process was handled as follows:

- developers deliver code to subcontractor moderator team
- subcontractor schedules inspection meeting
- developers and subcontractors review code
- inspection meeting
- subcontractor delivers inspection meeting minutes to developers
- developers correct errors
- subcontractor delivers final report

Results include 73 inspection meetings on 83,500 SLOC in 1,540 code units during a four-month period. The total number of issues recorded was 2,760 (1,180 major and 1,580 minor). Labor hours were 4,150 for subcontractors, including start-up, and 480 for developers.

Cost savings calculations were made based on the following formulas:

Cost savings = cost to find and fix during test − cost to find and fix using
inspections prior to test

Cost savings = $ 1 million

where,

Cost to find and fix during test = 2,760 issues × 1 hr/issue ×
developer's costing rate × cost multiplier

where,

Cost multiplier used is 5 and × is the multiplication operator

where,

Cost to find and fix using inspections prior to test =
(4,150 subcontractor hours × subcontractor costing rate) +
(480 developer hours × developer costing rate) +
(2,760 issues × 1 hr/issue × developers costing rate)

9.9.5 Hewlett-Packard [10, p. 56]

Hewlett-Packard derived the 1993 estimated savings of $21.5 million (Table 9-6) using the formula:

Estimated $ savings/year = % total costs saved × rework % × efficiency factor (0.4) × total engineering costs

where,

Percentage of total cost saved: Percentage for a work product component only. It peaks at 100%.

Rework percentage: An internal HP software development cost model estimates total rework at 33%. It is broken down into the work product components shown in Table 9-6.

Efficiency factor: Assume 40 percent for 1993.

Total engineering costs: Assuming 3,500 R&D software engineers at a cost of $150,000 per engineering year, total cost is $525 million.

Maximum possible savings from inspections: Total engineering costs ($525 million) times the rework percentage (33 percent) times the efficiency factor (60 percent) equals $105 million. (Some of this will be saved through other engineering techniques, so while this is a theoretical maximum, the practical maximum will be somewhat less. Also, while inspections substantially reduce costs, they do not totally eliminate them. HP uses a 60 percent efficiency factor to simulate these combined effects.)

Total savings: The sum of the savings from four major work products. Take the increase in the percentage of different types of inspections (for example, our 1993 survey showed design inspections had increased 33.8 percent), multiply it by how much the total cost ($525 million), you assume the rework of a work product accounts for (11 percent in the case of design) and multiply that by an assumed 1993 efficiency factor of 40 percent. So 1993 design savings are:

$$33.8\% \times (11\% \times \$525 \text{ million}) \times 0.4 = \$7.81 \text{ million}$$

These are very rough calculations, but they give a way to translate extent of adoption measure to companywide savings.

Table 9-6   Estimated Yearly Savings Attributable to Hewlett-Packard Software Inspections
[10, p. 56]

Work Product	Estimated starting point	Estimated 1993	Percentage total cost saved	Rework percentage	Estimated $ savings per year
Specification	1%	29.5%	28.5%	17%	$10,175,000
Design	1%	34.8%	33.8%	11%	$7,808,000
Code	5%	42.3%	37.3%	4%	$3,133,000
Test plan	1%	17.1%	16.1%	1%	$338,000
Total				33%	$21,454,000

9.9.6 Raytheon [11]

Inspection, as Tom Gilb defines it (shown with a capital "I"), consists of two main processes: the Defect Detection Process (DDP) and the Defect Prevention Process (DPP). A major defect is a defect that, if it not dealt with at the requirements or design stage, will probably have an order-of-magnitude or larger cost to find and fix when it reaches the testing or operational stages. On average, the find-and-fix cost for a major defect is one work hour upstream, but nine work hours downstream. DDP finds up to 88 percent of existing major defects in a document on a single pass. This alone is important, but DDP actually achieves greater benefit by teaching software developers. They go through a rapid, individual learning process, which typically reduces the number of defects they make in their subsequent work by two orders of magnitude.

In addition, DDP can and should be extended to support continuous process improvement. This is achieved by including the associated DPP, which is capable of at least 50 percent (first year, and first project used on), to 70 percent (second or third year) defect frequency reduction, and over 90 percent in the longer term. It has also shown at least a 13-to-1 ratio return on investment. It is the model for SEI CMM Level 5.

Raytheon provides a good case study. In six years (1988 to 1994), using DDP combined with DPP, Raytheon reduced rework costs (costs of dealing with preventable errors) from about 45 percent to between 5 and 10 percent, and had a 7.7-to-1 return on investment. They improved software productivity by a factor of 2.7-to-1, reduced negative deviation from budget and deadlines from 40 percent to near zero, and reduced error density by about a factor of three.

Following are some key tips from Gilb about how to improve your Inspection process and how to begin to achieve the kind of results Raytheon did:

- Know your purpose for using Inspection.
- Measure Inspection benefits.
- Make intelligent decisions on what you choose to inspect.
- Focus on finding the major defects.
- Apply good practice when leading Inspections.
- Other decisions include whether to log minors, whether to continue checking, and what is the likely optimum checking rate.
- Ensure you have provided adequate training and follow-up.
- Give visibility to your Inspection statistics and support documentation.
- Continuously improve your Inspection process.

9.9.7 Litton [12, pp. 2–4]

Litton chose a summary table (Table 9-7) from a representative project to show its inspection results. They maintain similar tables for each project. The total inspection effort for this project is distributed as follows:

preparation effort = 28%
inspection meeting effort = 40%
rework effort = 34%

Other projects are showing similar proportions. An overall inspection efficiency of 30 percent has been realized.

The net return of investment of tracking inspection success using:

Net return = Found defects ×
              Average effort to fix defects in test –
              Inspection effort

resulted in 20,206 person-hours, with an average inspection savings of 64 person-hours. Approximately 73 percent of all inspections have produced positive returns; i.e., 214 of the 320 inspections saved time.

Other findings include that recent data suggest that the 30 to 50 pages per hour inspection rate should be decreased for optimal inspection return. Four to five inspectors seems the optimal number of inspectors. The data suggest that a preparation time of 1.5 to 2.0 optimizes the defect detection rate. During design and coding about 3 percent of total project effort was used for inspections on one project.

Table 9-7   Litton's Project Inspections Summary Statistics [12, p. 3]

Subject Type	No. of Inspc.	Total Defects	Total Major	Inspection effort (person hours)	No. of pages	LOC	Defects/ Page	Defect Removal Effectiveness (major defects/ person hour)
Rqmts. Descrpt (R_0)	21	1243	89	328	552	0	2.25	0.272
Rqmts. Aysis (R_1)	32	2165	117	769	1065	0	2.03	0.230
H. L. Design (I_0)	41	2398	197	1097	1652	0	1.45	0.180
L. L. Design (I_1)	32	1773	131	955	1423	28254	1.25	0.137
Code (I_2)	150	7165	772	4612	5047	276422	1.42	0.167
Test Proc (IT_2)	18	1495	121	457	1621	0	0.92	0.265
Change Request	24	824	27	472	1579	340	0.52	0.057
Other	2	57	4	27	31	781	1.84	0.150
Grand Total	**320**	**17120**	**1518**	**8716**	**12970**	**305797**	**1.32**	**0.174**

9.9.8 Bull HN Information Systems [13]

The lessons Bull HN Information System's Major Systems Division learned were from metrics collected from more than 6,000 inspection meetings over three years (Table 9-8). They found that four-person teams were twice as effective, and more than twice as efficient, as three-person teams. The team found that they uncovered 19 defects per KSLOC for newly inspected code; seven defects per KSLOC for reinspected code; and four defects per KSLOC when inspections were held for code that had already been unit tested. This led to the conclusion in this environment that inspection should take place prior to unit testing. The team also found that it was important to control the amount of material that is inspected—document pages should be limited to about 15 and the presentation rate for code should be less than 200 LOC per hour to be effective.

Table 9-8   Bull HN Information Systems' Inspection Data from 1990 to 1992 [13, p. 39]

Data Category	1990 (May to Dec.)	1991	1992
Code inspection meetings	1,500	2,431	2,823
Document inspection meetings (anything other than code insp)	54	257	348
Design document pages inspected	1,194	5,419	6,870
Defects removed	2,205	3,703	5,649

References

1. Fagan, Michael E., "Design and Code Inspections and Process Control in the Development of Programs." In: *IBM-TR-00.73*, June 1976.
2. Gilb, Tom, "Requirements-Driven Management: A Planning Language." In: *CrossTalk*, June 1997, pp. 18–24.
3. Portions reprinted, with permission, from Fagan, Michael E., "Advances in Software Inspections." In: *IEEE Transactions on Software Engineering*, Vol. SE-12, No. 7, July 1986, pp. 744–751. © 1986 IEEE.
4. Barnard, Jack and Price, Art, "Managing Code Inspection Information." In: *IEEE Software*, March 1994, pp. 59–69.
5. O'Neill, Don, "Software Inspections: More Than a Hunt for Errors." In: *Software Quality Improvement Conference Proceedings*, 21 November 1991.
6. O'Neill, Don, "National Software Quality Experiment." In: *Fourth International Conference on Software Quality Proceedings,* October 1994.
7. Portions reprinted, with permission, from Russell, Glen W., "Experience with Inspection in Ultralarge-Scale Developments." In: *IEEE Software*, January 1991, pp. 25–31. © 1991 IEEE.
8. Dichter, Carl R., "Two Sets of Eyes." In: *UNIX Review*, Vol. 10, No. 1, June 1987, pp. 19–23.
9. Schulmeyer, G. Gordon related personal awareness of project, 1998.
10. Portions reprinted, with permission, from Grady, Robert and van Slack, Tom, "Key Lessons in Achieving Widespread Inspection Use." In: *IEEE Software*, July 1994, pp. 46–57. © 1994 IEEE.
11. Gilb, Tom, "Optimizing Software Inspection," In: *Internet Surfing*, 1998.
12. Madachy, Raymond J., "Measuring Inspections at Litton." In: *Software Quality*, Issue 4, Vol. 2, July 1996, pp. 1–10.
13. Portions reprinted, with permission, from Weller, Edward F., "Lessons From Three Years of Inspection Data." In: *IEEE Software*, September 1993, pp. 38–45. © 1993 IEEE.

Software Configuration Management—A Practical Look*

Stanley G. Siegel, Ph.D.
Science Applications International Corporation

Scott E. Donaldson
Science Applications International Corporation

10.1   It Is Raining—Where Is an Umbrella?

In providing motivation for their book *Principles of Software Engineering and Design* the authors tell the following short story: [1]

> When the Verrazano Narrows Bridge in New York City was started in 1959, it was estimated to cost $325 million and was to be completed by 1965. It was the largest suspension bridge ever built, yet it was completed in November 1961, on target and within budget . . . Would anyone care to base his or her reputation on such predictions for a large-scale software development project?
>
> Software is often delivered late. It is unreliable. It is expensive to maintain. . . . Why can engineering be so exact while software development flounders?

---

* This chapter is an update to a chapter that appeared in both the first and second editions of this book. William E. Bryan and Stanley G. Siegel coauthored this chapter in the first two editions. The current update has been slightly modified to incorporate revised figures and some accompanying text. This chapter presents fundamental engineering principles that still hold and are gaining wider acceptance within the software industry.

Since the first appearance of this chapter in 1987, the SCM discipline has achieved greater prominence within the software industry. One reason for this greater prominence is due to the work done at the Software Engineering Institute (SEI) at Carnegie Mellon University in Pittsburgh, Pennsylvania. In particular, the growing acceptance of SEI's Capability Maturity Model (CMM)^{SM} for software has helped to sensitize the industry to the importance of SCM for reducing software development risk (see Paulk, M. C., and others, *The Capability Maturity Model: Guidelines for improving the Software Process*, Reading, Mass: Addison-Wesley Publishing Company, 1995). [2] Also international workshops, conferences, and seminars have been established that address the need for SCM. In addition, since the appearance of the first SCM text book in 1980, [3] a number of other SCM books have been published.

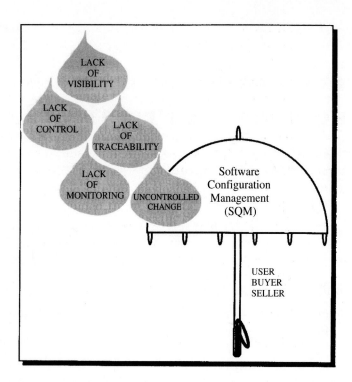

Figure 10-1 Why software development flounders—and the role of software configuration management.

Our response to the last question is illustrated in Figure 10-1.

The raindrops in the figure pour down on many software projects and their archetypical participants—the user, buyer, and seller. These problem raindrops are the following:

- *Lack of Visibility.* Unlike the engineering of bridges (suspension or otherwise), the development of software involves the "crafting" of something that is inherently difficult to see (we formally define software below). This lack of visibility tends to confound management (how can you manage what you cannot see?) and confuse project participants (especially on large projects where different organizations develop different pieces of software).

- *Lack of Control.* Because software development is often characterized by a lack of visibility, this development often spins out of control—how can you control what you cannot see? Schedules slip and budgets overrun because management simply lacks the means to assess what has been accomplished (and at what cost) and what remains to be done.

- *Lack of Traceability.* Contributing to software project misfortunes is a lack of linkage between project events. This linkage—or traceability thread—provides management the means for reexamining events when projects encounter unexpected happenings (such as sudden budget changes or key personnel losses) and for rationally determining how best to proceed. Lacking this thread, projects already going out of control spin yet further out of control.

- *Lack of Monitoring.* Because of lack of visibility and traceability, management lacks the means to monitor project events. Management is thereby hampered in its ability to make informed decisions—and again schedules slip and budgets overrun.

- *Uncontrolled Change.* Software, as its name implies, is highly malleable. This malleability, when coupled with a lack of visibility and control, leads to uncontrolled change—changes made without the knowledge of management and other key project participants. The effects of these changes frequently compound, consuming project resources while the participants who have been kept in the dark try to sort out these effects with (or without) the help of those who made the changes.

The raindrops in Figure 10-1 are turning into a cloudburst that threatens to wreak havoc with both military and commercial applications. Our military systems have become critically dependent on software, and concern is increasing that systems simply will not perform when they are needed. For example, the U.S. Air Force has recognized that SCM is a key element in reducing software systems development risk. [4]

Why can't we in the software industry turn out products that work right, are delivered on time, and are within budget? Is it because we don't understand what it takes to achieve these objectives? Or is it because we don't know how to manage costs? Our contention is that some of us probably don't understand what it takes to achieve these objectives, but most of us simply aren't willing to commit to meeting them.

In this chapter we offer some insight into what it takes and what it costs to provide software configuration management on a project as an important part in achieving overall software quality. Our orientation is toward the practical with specific suggestions, based on our experience, for raising the visibility of the software development process and infusing it with traceability, thereby bringing it under control. We take a candid look at some practices (such as using configuration control boards to manage the testing cycle) that our experience indicates are necessary to incorporate into the software development process to ward off the rain shown in Figure 10-l. We also look at some good business reasons for paying the price in time, effort, and budget to incorporate proactive activities into the software development process. Our approach is the following:

- We define the configuration management discipline and explain its crucial role in the production of working software.
- We then describe several real-world considerations needed to convince management (particularly top management) of the value of software configuration management and the subsequent need to implement it on software projects.

10.2   Software Configuration Management Overview

In this section, we present an overview of our concept of software configuration management. Our purpose is to establish the context for the discussion given in the next section, which presents real-world considerations for applying configuration management.

Software configuration management provides a means for visibly, traceably, and formally controlling the evolution of software. What is being controlled? Software configurations. What is a software configuration? To answer this question, we first need to define the concepts of *configuration* and *software*.

The concept of configuration is defined in Figure 10-2 (definition taken from *Webster's New Collegiate Dictionary* [1979]) together with a simple hardware example (i.e., a car). When it comes to cars, bicycles, lawnmowers, and other hardware items, the utility of this concept is widely accepted.

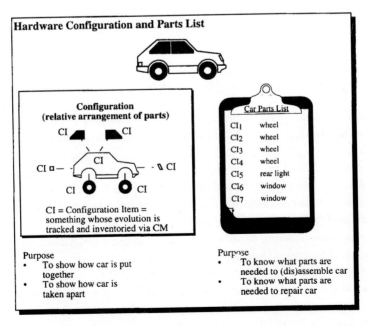

Figure 10-2   The concept of configuration.

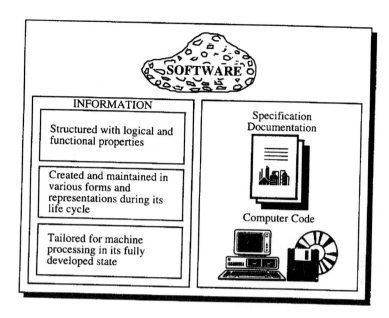

Figure 10-3 A concept of software.

A parts list and exploded parts diagram like those shown in Figure 10-2 serve as a set of instructions for assembling the hardware and for acquiring replacement parts when the hardware malfunctions and breaks down. It is interesting to note that, while we expect to receive "documentation," such as that shown in Figure 10-2, when we pay as little as tens, hundreds, or thousands of dollars for hardware "systems," such as cars or lawnmowers, some of us are willing, without question, to pay hundreds of thousands or even millions of dollars for software systems without such documentation.

Figure 10-3 defines our concept of software. [5] Classically, software has been looked upon as computer code (or programs) that, once installed on computer hardware, makes the hardware do its intended job. However, the software concept used in this chapter is more panoramic than the software concept generally used elsewhere.

In this chapter, *software* is therefore formally defined as: Information that has the following three distinguishing characteristics:

- Structured with logical and physical properties
- Created and maintained in various forms and representations during the software systems development life cycle
- Tailored for machine processing in its fully developed state

As shown in Figure 10-3, we use a sponge to represent software. A sponge is used throughout the chapter to portray software's susceptibility to change. Note that our concept of software encompasses not only computer code but also predecessor documents such as design specifications, software system concept papers, and requirements specifications.

As becomes evident in this chapter, our panoramic concept provides a unified view of certain software management support processes that generally appear in different, sometimes disparate, contexts in the software management world. We feel this unified view simplifies the task of controlling software development and maintenance. We illustrate this point as follows:

Consider, for example, the result of defining as software a design document that specifies the logic to be incorporated into computer code. The two processes—one of determining whether the design in such a document conforms to a user requirements document, and the other of determining whether computer code (operating in an environment approximating the user's operational environment) conforms to a user requirements document, are fundamentally the same. Both processes are software comparison exercises. The first comparison is generally referred to as a "design review" in the literature, while the second comparison is generally referred to as "acceptance testing." By defining software as more than just computer code, we can formulate and apply a relatively small set of principles that applies to any stage of the software life cycle. Thus, by thinking of document reviews and testing as essentially the same process (i.e., auditing), it is easier to train staff and control software development and maintenance.

It follows from Figures 10-2 and 10-3 that a *software configuration* is a relative arrangement of software parts. (The term *baseline* is often used synonymously for *configurations*.) This concept of software configuration is depicted in Figure 10-4, where we show an "exploded-parts" diagram of a multipiece software system.

Figure 10-4 also prompts the following question: What are the software analogues to the wheels, rear light, and windows shown in Figure 10-2? The answer to this question follows from our definition of software. Examples of software parts, include the following:

- 300-page specification document
- three-sentence paragraph in a design document
- a single FORTRAN, COBOL, Ada®, PL/1, C, C++, or assembly language statement[1]
- recording of a computer program on a magnetic medium
- sequence of instructions executing in computer hardware
- keystroke recorded in the memory of a programmable calculator

---

1. Ada is a registerd trademark of the Department of Defense.

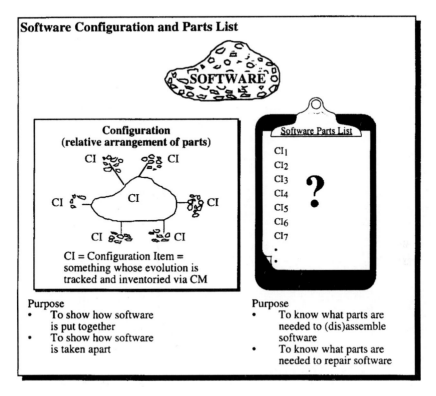

Figure 10-4   The concept of software configuration.

Basically, a software part can be any piece of information with the three characteristics listed in Figure 10-3. The key consideration regarding this concept is that software project participants should formally agree to a parts list (by a mechanism called the configuration control board (CCB), which we describe in Section 10.3) and maintain this agreement until the project participants formally agree to alter this parts list (also by a configuration control board).

Figure 10-5 depicts our concept of software configuration management. Elaborating on our earlier statement, we can define software configuration management as the integrated application of the four functions shown in Figure 10-5 for visibly, traceably, and formally controlling software evolution.

More specifically, the four software configuration management functions and the purpose of each are the following:

1. *Identification*, whereby each software part is physically labeled. In the figure we show three labels being attached to a software product (i.e., CI_1, CI_2, and CI_3 where CI stands for Configuration Item).

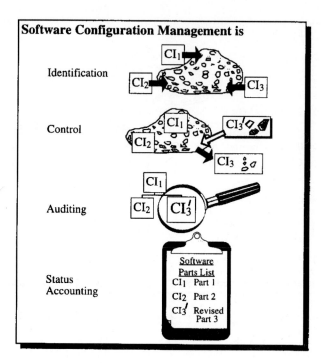

Figure 10-5   The four functions of software configuration management.

2. *Control*, whereby proposed changes to software parts are reviewed, then subjected to the agreement of project participants, and finally incorporated into the currently approved software configuration. In Figure 10-5, part CI_3' is shown replacing part CI_3. This transition is a two-step process. The first step is a review by the CCB of (1) the cost and schedule needed to effect the transition from part CI_3 to part CI_3' and (2) the impact of this transition on the other parts in the configuration. The second step is CCB approval (or rejection or postponement) of the transition from part CI_3 to part CI_3'.

3. *Auditing*, whereby approved changes are checked to determine that they have been implemented. In Figure 10-5, the auditor examines the software product to determine whether part CI_3' has been incorporated. More generally, auditing seeks answers to the following two questions:

     a. Is software evolution proceeding logically? The process of answering this question is termed verification. Consider, for example, the sequential development of a requirements document, an operational concept document, design document, and computer code. In verification, the auditor seeks answers to the following questions:

- Does the operational concept logically follow from the requirements specification?
- Does the design logically follow from the concept?
- Does the working code logically follow from the design?

b. Is software evolution proceeding in conformance with requirements for the software? The process of answering this question is termed validation. In terms of the example in 3a above, this question is asked three times, as follows:

- Is the operational concept congruent with the requirements specification or, if not, what are the incongruities?
- Is the design congruent with the requirements specification or, if not, what are the incongruities?
- Is the computer code operating on the intended host hardware congruent with the requirements specification or, if not, what are the incongruities?

4. *Status accounting*, whereby all of the approved parts of a software configuration are accounted for. In Figure 10-5, the status accountant updates the software parts list to reflect the transition from part CI_3 to part CI_3'. More generally, status accounting seeks answers to the following two questions:

a. What happened on a software project? (e.g.,what happened to the discrepancies between software code and software requirements—were these discrepancies included in a test [i.e., audit] report?)

b. When did an event happen on a software project? (e.g., when was a software design update approved by the CCB?)

The status accounting function provides a corporate memory of project events that supports accomplishment of the other three configuration management functions. This corporate memory also serves as an experience bank whose contents can be exploited on other projects, to avoid repeating past mistakes and to capitalize on the successful approaches.

In the previous section, we indicate that many software projects suffer from a lack of visibility and traceability. Now that we have described the four component functions of configuration management, we can indicate in specific terms how configuration management helps to raise the visibility of software projects and infuse them with traceability. Table 10-1 lists some of the ways each of the four configuration management functions helps to achieve visibility and establish traceability on a software project. This table thus provides insight into the protective nature of the software configuration management umbrella shown in Figure 10-1.

Table 10-1   How the Four Configuration Management Functions Infuse Visibility and Traceability into a Software Project

FUNCTION	👁 VISIBILITY 👁	👣 TRACEABILITY 👣
Identification	• User/buyer/seller can see what is being/has been built/is to be modified. • Management can see what is embodied in a product • All project participants can communicate with a common frame of reference.	• Provides pointers to software parts in software products for use in referencing. • Makes software parts and their relationships more visible, thus facilitating the linking of parts in different software products and in different representations of the same product.
Control	• Current and planned configuration generally known. • Management can see impact of change. • Management has option of getting involved with technical detail of project.	• Makes baselines and changes to them manifest, thus providing the links in a traceability chain. • Provides the forum for avoiding unwanted excursions and maintaining convergence with requirements.
Auditing	• Inconsistencies and discrepancies manifest. • State of product known to management and product developers. • Potential problems identified early.	• Checks that parts in one software product are carried through to the subsequent software product. • Checks that parts in a software product have antecedents in requirements documentation.
Status Accounting	• Reports inform as to status. • Actions/decisions made explicit (e.g., through CCB meeting minutes). • Database of events is project history.	• Provides history of what happened and when. • Provides explicit linkages between change control forms.

Having overviewed software configuration management, we can now examine some considerations governing the practice of the software configuration management discipline in the real world.

10.3 Real-World Considerations

This section presents some practical considerations involved in the establishment and practice of software configuration management (SCM). We discuss several aspects of configuration management, as shown in Table 10-2.

Table 10-2 Real-World Considerations in Software Configuration Management

SUBJECT	ESSENTIAL CONSIDERATION
Management Commitment	Management commitment to the establishment of checks and balances is essential to achieving benefits from SCM.
SCM Staffing	Initial staffing by a few experienced people quickly gains the confidence and respect of the other project team members.
Establishment of a CCB	As a starting point in instituting SCM, periodic CCB meetings provide change control, visibility, and traceability.
CM During the Acceptance Testing Cycle	CM integrated within the acceptance testing cycle maintains a visible and traceable product ready for delivery to the customer.
Justification and Practicality of Auditing	Although auditing consumes the greater part of the SCM budget, it has the potential of preventing the waste of much greater resources.
Avoiding the Paperwork Nightmare	The buyer/user and seller should agree on the paperwork needed to achieve a mutually desirable level of visibility and traceability.
Allocating Resources among CM Activities	Cost versus benefits must be evaluated for each individual project in determining the allocation of limited SCM resources.

We begin with a discussion of the importance of management commitment to SCM. Next, we present some ideas on the staffing of the SCM organization. We describe the mechanics of what we feel is the most important element of SCM—the configuration control board—in terms of its membership, organization, and procedures. This description is followed by a discussion of the integration of SCM into an area of much importance in the development and maintenance cycle—acceptance testing. Then we present our views on the problems of coping with the high resource consumption of auditing and of avoiding the paperwork nightmare of SCM. Finally, we provide some insights into how to allocate SCM resources among the SCM functions.

10.3.1 Management Commitment to Checks and Balances

How does one go about establishing a software configuration management program in his or her organization? One way might be by leading a software development coup—dazzle upper management one day with guarantees of software success and send in the storm troopers the next day, ready to control and discipline software development. Management by fiat and manifesto are necessary—after all, the poor developers don't yet realize how much they need SCM. Monitor every action by the developers and have them prepare a report on every effort—plenty of traceability here and tremendous visibility. If upper management becomes uneasy with the approach, guarantee them long-range success and share some of your visibility with them.

Is this approach practical? Hardly. Its only guarantee is a high turnover rate on the software engineering staff. A much better approach is to proceed gradually and convincingly. Let's consider some practical steps to take in instituting SCM in an organization.

First of all, start at the top. If SCM is to become successful, the software project manager and his or her boss need to commit to some form of checks and balances with respect to the activities of the software product developers (see Figure 10-6).

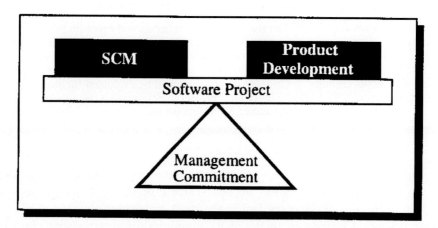

Figure 10-6   Keeping a software project on an even keel requires management commitment to checks and balances on product development—such as those provided through SCM.

In the absence of this commitment, software configuration management has little likelihood of being effective. Without management commitment to back up the SCM organization, SCM efforts will be eroded and eventually ignored altogether. Checks and balances are needed to give management a perspective of the software development process other than that of the developers. Developers quite naturally have one viewpoint of the products they develop, the software configuration management personnel another. After all, these two groups have different goals and objectives. Provision of these checks and balances immediately increases the visibility to management of the software development process. One raindrop deflected already! We repeat, upper management commitment to the establishment of checks and balances is essential to achieving benefits from SCM.

How do you convince management to make such a commitment? There are several ways to achieve this goal. One way is to hire, or be fortunate enough to already have aboard, managers who have experienced firsthand what can go wrong on software projects. Such managers are generally receptive to alternative approaches to software development and should be sensitive to the intrinsic value of checks and balances. They can readily perceive the benefit to them of a different perspective and of increased visibility into the project. Obtaining a commitment for the establishment of checks and balances on the developers from such managers as these should be relatively easy.

If your organization is not fortunate enough to have such experienced managers, obtaining an upper management commitment is a more difficult task. They must be sold at project outset on the benefits of the SCM checks and balances, and also honestly informed of their liabilities. The latter are readily perceived as the expenditure of additional resources—time and money. The benefits of SCM are the warding off of the raindrops shown in Figure 10-1. All four SCM functions provide increased visibility and traceability, as shown in Table 10-1. With this increased visibility and traceability, management can establish control and provide adequate monitoring of a software development or maintenance project. And, as a final benefit, SCM can control change—after all, control is the underlying purpose of SCM.

Unfortunately, upper management often cannot objectively weigh the intangible benefits versus the tangible liabilities of providing SCM on software development projects. Knowing that they must spend time and money to perform SCM, they want to know the potential savings to be achieved through performance of SCM. We contend that, although SCM costs time and money, it increases the likelihood that even greater amounts of time and money will not be required to recover from a software disaster.

The literature contains many accounts of software disasters. The scope of these disasters is so great as to constitute a crisis in the software industry. DeMarco, for instance, concludes from a multiyear survey he conducted of over 200 projects that 15 percent of all software projects never deliver anything, and overruns of 100 to 200 percent are common. [6] We do not contend that all these disasters result from a lack of SCM. However, it is clear that too little visibility and/or traceability (both of which can be attributed at least in part to a lack of SCM) account for some of these disasters. On the other side of the coin, the literature does contain some accounts showing a correlation between the application of SCM and software project success. [7] Our experience in the software industry has convinced us that the application of SCM is a necessary (though not sufficient) condition for software project success.

10.3.2 SCM Staffing

Staffing of the software configuration management organization with properly qualified people is extremely important to getting started in SCM (see Figure 10-7). Without qualified people to perform the SCM functions, the most comprehensive approach to SCM, backed by fully committed top-level management, will most likely fall short of helping to achieve the desired software products. If the people are available, the SCM team should be staffed initially with a few highly experienced (and thus probably highly paid) individuals rather than a larger number of less experienced people.

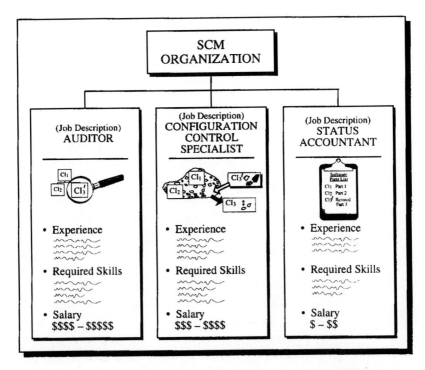

Figure 10-7   What kinds of people staff a proficient SCM organization?

Generally, the SCM team is viewed as a group of antagonists by the other project team members. To reduce antagonism and to enhance the likelihood that checks and balances will not be circumvented, a few experienced people will get the SCM task quickly off on the right foot and gain the confidence and respect of the other project team members. It is important to build the image that the SCM team has the objective of helping the other project team members achieve the overall team goals, that they are not a group of obstructionists and criticizers constantly harping on shortcomings, aberrations, and trivia. These experienced people generally will need to have the technical and diplomatic skills to analyze the developers' output from a broad perspective and to tactfully present the observed discrepancies and potential dangers perceived as development progresses.

Important qualifications of these people are the ability to see congruence between software products and the ability to perceive what is missing from a software product. With these abilities, the SCM team member, freed as he or she is from the responsibilities of detailed design and development, can observe how change to the software system is visibly and traceably being controlled.

Need all SCM personnel be skilled programmers and analysts? No, these particular skills are not a necessity by any means, although personnel performing software configuration auditing should be technically skilled. Table 10-3 presents some recommended qualifications that members of the SCM team should possess to perform the four SCM functions.

One can conclude from Table 10-3 that the job requirements for an SCM specialist are demanding. The SCM specialist is challenged to take a broad, comprehensive viewpoint in his or her tasks, while paradoxically being meticulous as to details in all work.

10.3.3 Establishment of a CCB

With management support and a cadre of CM personnel, how should you begin exercising SCM? We advise starting simply (particularly if your management remains somewhat skeptical of the benefits of SCM). Then, as confidence in the value of SCM grows, gradually expand the scope of SCM activities.

As a starting point, if you do nothing else, establish periodic meetings of a configuration control board (CCB). Why start with CCB meetings? We feel that the control function is central to the performance of SCM, and the CCB is the heart of the control function. (A CCB meeting is not an alternative for the project status meeting; it may have many of the same participants as the project status meeting, but its purpose and focus are quite different.) The CCB meeting is a mechanism for controlling change during the development and maintenance of software (another raindrop deflected!).

Table 10-3   Configuration Management Functions and Personnel Qualifications

FUNCTION	PERSONNEL QUALIFICATIONS

Identification	• Ability to see partitions.
	• Ability to see relationships.
	• Some technical ability desirable:
	  – System engineering orientation
	  – Programming

Control	• Ability to evaluate benefits versus cost. • System viewpoint (balance of technical/managerial, user/buyer/seller). • An appreciation of what is involved in engineering a software change.
Auditing	• Extreme attention to detail. • Ability to see congruence. • Ability to perceive what is missing. • Extensive experience with technical aspects of system engineering and/or software engineering.

Status Accounting	• Ability to take notes and record data.
	• Ability to organize data.
	• Some technical familiarity desirable but not required:
	  – System engineering orientation
	  – Programming

Remember that change is indigenous to, and continual on, a software project and includes both unplanned change (caused by discrepancies, requests for enhancements, and changes in environment) and planned change (the planned succession of software products providing an increasing level of detail in the development of a software system). The CCB infuses sustained visibility into this process of change throughout the system life cycle. The likelihood that problems will go unnoticed or unresolved is thereby reduced. The CCB also infuses traceability into the process of change, thereby increasing maintainability of the software.

Membership. CCB members should be drawn from all organizations on the project team. After all, a prime purpose of the CCB is to increase visibility on the project. The CCB should include policymakers, since it is a decisionmaking body, whose decisions might impact project budget or schedule. But the CCB must also include technical specialists, whose opinions are needed to reach decisions on technical issues. Certainly, the project manager should be a member of the CCB. However, the leaders of software and hardware engineering groups for the project should also be active members, with the type and number of additional engineers participating dependent upon the issues on the CCB agenda. Also, the leaders of both the SCM and the quality assurance (QA) teams for the project (if your company has separate SCM and QA organizations) should be members of the CCB.

Note in the foregoing the underlying assumption is that all CCB members are from the seller's company. However, equivalent personnel from the buyer's organization should also be members of the CCB. These personnel include the buyer's project manager, technical people (both hardware and software), and CM and QA representatives. Further, user personnel should also attend CCB meetings. The inclusion of buyer/user personnel on the CCB may seem ill-advised to many readers. After all, who wishes to air one's dirty linen before a customer? Our response is that everyone on the project team will benefit from the visibility that derives from having user, buyer, and seller representation on the CCB. The goal of the entire project team should be the satisfaction of user needs. Airing problems and successes at CCB meetings keeps the entire project staff informed as to the status of the project, facilitates reallocation of resources to problems, and helps keep the project on track, on schedule, and within budget.

Decision Mechanism. With the recommended variety of representatives on the CCB, the question arises as to how decisions are made. A natural suggestion is to give each CCB representative one vote with the majority vote effecting a decision. This exercise in democracy allows all views equal consideration and makes all CCB members a part of the decision-making process. CCB members are motivated to participate in and contribute to the board meetings.

This mechanism does have its drawbacks, however. One consideration is that a specific definition of majority vote must be made. What constitutes a quorum? Should it be a strict majority? A plurality? Two-thirds of those present and voting? A much more important consideration, though, is that this decisionmaking mechanism tends to introduce politics into the CCB. Members may tend to vote in blocks, e.g., buyer versus seller or developers versus SCM personnel. When this tendency develops, the number of representatives that an organization has on the CCB becomes more important than what the CCB is trying to do.

At the other extreme, all decisionmaking authority could be put in the hands of a single person, for example, the buyer's project manager. This arrangement, of course, fosters decisionmaking and allows flexible consideration of priority in making decisions. It appears, in the case of naming the buyer's project manager as the single voter, to be a reasonable choice, since he or she is the person who has ultimate responsibility for the project. On the other hand, this arrangement could stifle the interest of the other CCB members in the meetings. Why should they take an interest when they can't vote and feel their opinions don't count? Another decisionmaking mechanism is to seek a consensus of the representatives on the CCB, that is, informal (nonvoting) agreement by most of those present. This method is relatively expeditious and certainly allows all viewpoints to be expressed and considered. A fault of the method, though, is that if a consensus of the board cannot be reached, the board does not make a decision. To prevent the board from bogging down in such cases, an escape mechanism should be provided. For example, if the board cannot reach a consensus in a reasonable period of time, then the buyer's project manager unilaterally should make the decision on the matter at hand (because the buyer put up the funds to develop the software).

Chairing the Board. Another issue related to the formation of a CCB is who should serve as chairperson of the board. A number of individuals could be designated in the precept for the CCB or selected by the CCB. Table 10-4 lists some candidates and the rationale as to why they might be so designated. Note that some of these candidates may not participate in the decisionmaking process but rather simply preside over the meetings.

For example, a CCB organization that we have observed in successful operation over a long period of time involves the following:

> The CCB secretary serves as the CCB chairman, keeping the meeting on track and recording its decisions. Decisions are generally made on a consensus basis. However, where consensus cannot be reached, the buyer's project manager makes the decisions in matters regarding cost and priority of effort, and the seller's project manager makes the decisions on technical matters within the cost and priority constraints.

CCB Minutes. An important aspect of CCB meetings is the configuration status accounting function of recording and publishing minutes of each meeting. These minutes give visibility to the decisions of the CCB and, through approval or modification at the next meeting, ensure that the decisions of the CCB are correctly recorded. The minutes provide traceability through stating what happened and when. Every entry in the minutes should be specific and precise so that there is no margin for misinterpretation. When action is to be taken, the minutes should specify who is to take the action and when the action should be completed. The names of all attendees at the meeting should be recorded as well as the names of all board members absent. The minutes should be distributed not only to all attendees but also to upper-level management of the buyer and the seller, to permit management to track what is happening on the project. (The format and content of CCB minutes are subsequently discussed in this section under *Avoiding the "Paperwork" Nightmare.*)

Table 10-4   Candidate CCB Chairpersons

TITLE	RATIONALE FOR CHOICE
Seller's Project Manager	• Responsible for project development and maintenance. • Most technically competent of managerial personnel.
Buyer's Project Manager	• Ultimately responsible to the user for the end product. • Puts up money for the project.
A Subordinate to the Buyer's Project Manager (e.g., a Deputy)	• On a large project, the project manager is generally a planner (as opposed to a day-to-day supervisor). He or she is therefore generally far separated from the project details, thus may delegate this responsibility to a deputy or other subordinate.
Seller's CM Representative	• CM is his or her prime responsibility and the CCB is the focal point of configuration management.
Buyer's CM Representative	• CM is his or her prime responsibility and the CCB is the focal point of configuration management.
CCB Secretary	• Serves as an orchestrator but not as a decision maker. • Functions similarly to presiding officer of U.S. Senate.
Consultant from Outside the Project	• Unbiased orchestrator with no responsibility for implementation of any decision.
Jointly, Seller's and Buyer's Project Managers	• Two most responsible persons on CCB. • Buyer and seller both represented as orchestrators. (In case of disagreement, buyer's project manager should have ultimate authority, because buyer is putting up the money for the project.)

Regarding the amount of detail to include in CCB meeting minutes, the following considerations apply:

- The basic purpose of the minutes is to provide the CCB decisionmakers the information needed to make intelligent, informed decisions regarding how the program should proceed. Since memories tend to fade over time, the amount of detail needed depends, in part, on CCB meeting frequency—more frequent meetings generally imply a need for less detail.

- The seller project leader, in concert with the customer project leader, may choose to use CCBs as a forum for doing some product development (e.g., specify user-friendly requirements in testable terms). In this case, the CCB minutes can contain considerable detail. Such detail often expedites product completion since these details can be directly coordinated with the customer at the CCB. Then, this agreed-upon material can be directly incorporated into the product to be delivered.

- For programs that are planned to span a year or more, the amount of detail included in CCB minutes should be governed by the risks associated with personnel turnover. More detailed minutes will facilitate transitions associated with seller project turnover, and will lessen the impact of technical staff turnover.

Preparation of minutes of CCB meetings is not for the purpose of formality, but rather for clarity and completeness. Format and style are less important than content and precision. Further, CCB minutes are necessary for small projects just as they are for large projects. They eliminate such later comments as, "I thought someone else was going to take action on that issue," or, "I don't remember that being decided on." People often leave meetings with conflicting ideas as to what has been agreed on, and the results of this natural confusion can be disastrous. The preparation of minutes helps to avoid such problems.

10.3.4 SCM During the Acceptance Testing Cycle

Software configuration management is most important, and often neglected, during the phase immediately preceding handover of the system to the user. The developers have completed coding and unit testing the software modules and have integrated those modules into a software system. Delivery and installation dates are fast approaching. During the time remaining, a test team is formed to check out the system as thoroughly as time allows. Typically, the testers exercise the system a few (four to eight) hours each day by executing a previously prepared set of test procedures. Of course, they will find at least a few troubles and duly report them to the developers. The developers, in turn, will scurry to locate the bugs in their programs causing the problems. Once the bugs have been located, the code is corrected, the system is rebuilt, and the software system is returned to the testers.

This cycle is repeated until delivery day arrives. At this point, an acceptance test is usually conducted to demonstrate to the buyer and users that the system delivered fulfills the contractual requirements. This acceptance test can be conducted at the seller's plant prior to shipping, at the user's site after installation, or at both places. (The reader who desires a fuller description of this testing cycle than what follows should see reference 8.) [8]

10.3.5 Why SCM is Necessary

SCM is essential to elevate the visibility of, and to thread traceability into, the testing cycle. This cycle is characterized as a time of frequent and rapid change to the software code. Problems are reported, solutions are found, code is modified, documentation is (or should be) updated, and the system is rebuilt.

It is not difficult to lose control during such a period. Problems may be overlooked and go unreported. Even reported problems may be lost in the shuffle and never corrected. Solutions may be incorrect or unworkable or may give rise to other problems. Solutions might not be adequately tested to verify that they have resolved problems without harmful side effects. Corrected code can be lost or may not be included in new system builds. Documentation may not be updated. Even the fact that documentation needs correcting may even be overlooked.

Control of the change process throughout the testing cycle is essential as the system evolves to its operational state. Visibility must be provided as to the status of the software throughout this period. Traceability has to be established so that the operational system can be maintained. In view of the definition of configuration management given earlier, it is easy to see why SCM is essential during the testing cycle.

10.3.6 CCB Role During the Testing Cycle

How is configuration management integrated into this testing cycle? Actually, as shown in Table 10-5, all four functions of CM come into play throughout the testing cycle. Let's take a closer look at the testing cycle (shown in detail in Figure 10-8), concentrating on how configuration management is injected into the process. As in other phases of the development cycle, the CCB plays a central role in the testing cycle.

The CCB should meet at two points during the cycle. The first kind of CCB meeting should occur whenever the developers turn software over to the testers, while the second should occur immediately following each test period. (For the moment, let us assume that the testing cycle consists of alternating periods of development/problem resolution and of testing. Subsequently, we discuss another practical approach involving overlapping periods of development and testing.) These CCB meetings establish configuration control over the testing cycle, as we will explain.

The Software Turnover CCB Meeting. A CCB meeting is held at the beginning of the testing cycle, at which time the developers present a set of source code modules and a release note to the CCB. The release note lists all the modules turned over—a "parts list" that identifies the configuration of the software. The

developers also present a list of all known discrepancies (with respect to requirements and/or design) in the modules turned over. These discrepancies are accepted
by the CCB and logged (a function of configuration status accounting). The CCB
places the code modules under control and establishes them as a baseline (another
identification function). Recall from our discussion of Figures 10-2 and 10-3 that a
baseline is a relative arrangement of software parts as embodied in a software product. We label this baseline as the development baseline (the name is clearly arbitrary). Based on the known discrepancies of the development baseline and the
CCB's perception of the relative importance of the functions within the release, the
CCB establishes priorities and areas of particular concern for testing, and selects a
date for termination of the test period. The minutes of the CCB meeting are published and disseminated.

Table 10-5   Configuration Management Activities During the Testing Cycle

FUNCTION	CM ACTIVITIES IN SUPPORT OF TESTING
Identification	• Preparation of release notes (lists of changed software modules). • Identification of development baseline.* • Identification of incident reports. • Identification of operational baseline.*

Control	• CCB meetings:
	  – Establishment of development baseline.*
	  – Assignment of testing and incident resolution priorities.
	  – Establishment of turnover dates.
	  – Approval of audit and test reports.
	  – Approval of incident report resolutions.
	  – Establishment of operational baseline.*

Auditing	• Comparison of new baseline to previous baseline. • Assurance that standards have been met. • Testing (verification and validation) of software system. • Extensive experience with technical aspects of system engineering and/or software engineering.
Status Accounting	• Logging and tracking of incident reports. • Publication of CCB minutes.

*See Figure 10-8

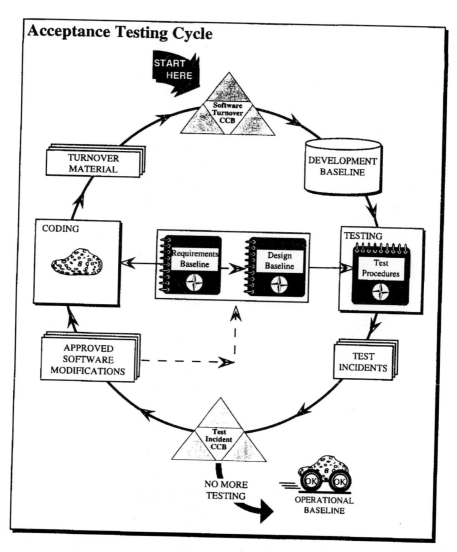

Figure 10-8 SCM and the testing cycle—iterating from the design baseline to the operational baseline with a development baseline created and controlled through CCB action. The cycle continues until the CCB determines that the development baseline incorporates the specifications of the requirements and design baselines (or approximations to these specifications). The resultant development baseline becomes the operational baseline.

Building the software system from the development baseline should be a configuration management function. Prior to building the system, SCM personnel perform a comparison (i.e., an audit) of the source code in the new development baseline with the source code in the immediately preceding development baseline (if any; clearly there will be no preceding development baseline on the first iteration of the testing cycle for a new product). The results of this comparison make visible all changes that have been made to source code from one baseline to the next. The next step in this audit is to verify that the changes detected in the comparison process are all approved by the CCB. Another part of this audit is to compare the source code modules that have changed since the last development baseline was established to the standards adopted for the project. These standards might require, for example, certain commentary in the code and proper identification of the changes to the code modules. The findings of the audit are documented in an audit report, which is presented to the next meeting of the CCB. The testers perform their tests using a documented set of test procedures. These test procedures specify a step-by-step set of operator actions. For each operator action, the reason for the action and the results expected from the action are documented. The test procedures are derived from two basic sources—the set of requirements for the project (requirements baseline) and the detailed design specifications for the software (design baseline). In performing the tests, the testers are assessing whether the development baseline logically follows from the design baseline and whether the development baseline is congruent with the requirements baseline. In the description of auditing in our SCM overview, we described the former process as verification and the latter process as validation. Thus, the testers are performing verification and validation, which are the fundamental processes of configuration auditing.

The results of this audit/testing are documented in a test report, which is akin to an audit report. This test report is presented at the next meeting of the CCB for approval (see Figure 10-8). Individual discrepancies uncovered by this form of audit are documented in test incident reports. These incident reports (IRs) are logged by the configuration status accounting function and tracked until they have been resolved and all approved actions arising from them have been completed.

The Test Incident CCB Meeting. The second kind of CCB meeting during the testing cycle occurs, as indicated in Figure 10-8, when the testers have executed the test procedures and written test incident reports. At this meeting the CCB considers the audit report on the development baseline, the test report on the just-completed testing period, the discrepancies uncovered by the audit, and the incident reports resulting from the testing. On the first iteration of the testing cycle, the number of problems made visible is likely to be substantial, and the CCB probably will decide to continue the testing cycle.

The problems are presented to the developers for investigation and recommendation of changes to be made to the software (code and/or documents) and, possibly, the test procedures. The CCB also sets a date for beginning the next iteration of the testing cycle.

As a result of this meeting, the CCB approves modifications to the computer source code and possibly to baselined documents (such as the requirements baseline or the design baseline—see Figure 10-8). The developers make the required software (source code and/or documentation) changes; if necessary, the testers make the required test procedure changes. These changes are packaged into turnover material for the next iteration of the testing cycle.

On the established date, the next iteration of the testing cycle begins with the repetition of the software turnover CCB meeting described above. At this meeting, the responses of the developers to the IRs and the discrepancies in the audit report are presented to the CCB. The release note for this meeting lists the software that has been changed since the last testing cycle began. If the CCB approves the recommended resolutions presented by the developers, the development baseline is updated with the changed software. The testers next audit the changed modules in the updated development baseline as they did on the preceding iteration. On this and subsequent iterations, the testers confirm that the problems whose resolutions have been approved by the CCB have actually been solved. In addition, the testers repeat the test procedures to ensure that the approved changes have not introduced new problems.

Terminating the Testing Cycle. At the CCB meeting following testing, the CCB will formally close out any problems whose satisfactory resolution has been demonstrated by testing. At each iteration of the testing cycle, the number of outstanding problems within the system should be reduced. When the number of remaining problems converges to only a few or possibly no problems remaining, the CCB will establish the software as an operational baseline, and delivery can be effected. Any remaining problems, still tracked and controlled, can be corrected through field changes or in the next release.

If a firm delivery date is reached before this convergence point, the software can still be delivered together with a list of known discrepancies. This delivery of a still-defective product can be done because of the visibility as to the state of the software system that the testing process provides. Usually the seller has the contractual responsibility to correct these outstanding defects.

Notice how, throughout the testing cycle, SCM has continuously maintained control, has elevated the visibility of the testing cycle, enabling the project team to be aware of the status of the configuration at all times, and has threaded traceability of how the end-product has been achieved into the testing cycle. Visibility, traceability, and control have been achieved through the pervasive application of configuration management.

Concurrent Development and Testing: An Alternative Cycle. As previously stated, the foregoing description is based on an alternating sequence of development/resolution periods and testing periods. It is also possible to successfully use another scheme, in which the development/resolution periods and test periods are concurrent. In this scheme, the development group uses the computer system on one shift, and the test group uses the computer system on a second shift. A brief CCB meeting generally is held each day between the two shifts. At these meetings, the CCB performs the same functions as at both CCB meetings in the sequential scheme as previously described. Incident reports arising from testing are introduced at the daily CCB meeting. Changed software code is released only periodically, however, perhaps weekly or every two weeks. Otherwise, the testing cycle remains the same.

This concurrent scheme allows increased utilization of resources at the expense of some inconvenience to the project staff due to the two-shift workload. It doubles the utilization of the project computer system (assuming that the luxury of two available computer systems is lacking). It also allows both the development group and the test group to be working continuously, and it puts the observed problems into the hands of the developers for resolution at an earlier point—daily, rather than at the end of a test period. Configuration management is even more important to maintaining control under this scheme because of the high, concurrent activity level. Since SCM is integrated into the testing cycle, the benefits of control, visibility, and traceability are obtained, and a product that can be maintained is achieved.

10.3.7 Justification and Practicality of Auditing

The conduct of auditing can be a heavy consumer of configuration management resources. Auditing is the most technical and also the most labor-intensive of the SCM functions. It requires an ability to understand and relate details, and to perceive not only what is present in a software product, but also what is missing from it. As a result, the most experienced (and thus, generally, the most expensive) SCM personnel generally are assigned to the auditing task. It is not difficult to see why auditing can consume such a large part of the SCM budget. (This specific SCM auditing activity is not to be confused with the auditing of the entire SCM process by software quality assurance personnel as discussed elsewhere in this handbook.)

In light of the potential high cost of auditing, management may well question the expenditure of valuable resources on this function (see Figure 10-9). This questioning is particularly likely to happen at project initiation, when a project manager is liable to say the following, as hypothesized by Boehm:

> Don't worry about that specification paperwork. We'd better hurry up and start coding, because we're going to have a whole lot of debugging to do. [9]

This questioning may also occur in the latter stages of a development, when the harried project manager is likely to reason as follows:

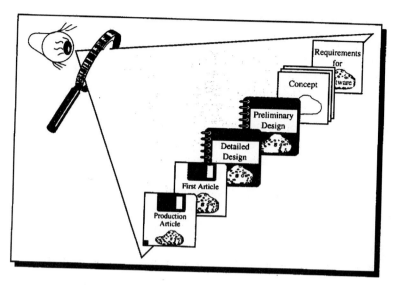

Figure 10-9   Paying an auditor to see what is (and is not) there—is the experiment worth it?

Look, I don't need anyone to tell me that I have problems. I know what my problems are—we are falling behind in our design and coding. I can hire two or three programmers for the cost of one auditor. That's where I need to spend my limited resources.

Often, the result of such reasoning is a sudden termination of auditing activities and a swarm of programmers coding as rapidly as possible. Such an approach can be extremely shortsighted. While the creation of gobs of code may seem productive on the surface, it can be very unproductive if the wrong code is produced and some customer requirements are left unaddressed. Elimination of auditing is generally false economy.

Likely Payoff. Auditing pays for itself through the avoidance of larger, unnecessary expenses. Boehm has indicated that savings of up to 100:1 for large projects and 4–6:1 for small projects can be achieved by finding (through verification and validation) and fixing problems early in the life cycle. [10] Through verification, we avoid wasting resources on the development of inconsistent products (such as a detailed design that is inconsistent with a preliminary design); through validation, we avoid wasting resources on the development of something that has not been asked for (e.g., including in a design document a capability that has no antecedent in a user's requirements specification).

Can we ever really be sure that the audit approach will save time and money? No, we cannot be certain. After all, auditing may not uncover latent problems, or there may not be any problems to uncover. Further, there is no guarantee that all discrepancies or flaws detected through auditing will be accepted and corrected. The best that we can say is that money spent on auditing may result in saving more money over the life of a project.

Of course, there are circumstances in which auditing is necessary, even though it is accepted *a priori* that time and money may not be saved. We may have a sufficiently complex system under development whose failure would result in calamitous consequences (e.g., a missile system). Or we may be developing a system whose failure would result in serious political consequences (e.g., an election outcome prediction system or a national space project). In these circumstances, the value of auditing is that it provides assurance that a software product works, as opposed to its value in reducing overall project costs.

Audit Compromises to Reduce Costs. There are times project management appreciates the value of auditing but, owing to budget constraints, must limit the amount of auditing that can be performed. There are two basic compromises that can be made to reduce expenditures for auditing. One of these compromises is to reduce the depth of each audit but still to audit each baseline. This approach maintains a degree of traceability with some loss of visibility. The second compromise is to eliminate one or more audits. Here, visibility is maintained, but traceability is impaired. If this latter approach is taken, the prime candidate for omission is the baseline established on completion of installation. This baseline is generally little changed from the baseline established at the end of the testing cycle. The most important baselines to be audited, which should never be omitted from audit, are the first baseline established (errors ferreted out here are much cheaper to repair than those discovered in later phases) and the first baseline containing code (this baseline is the first that has multiple representations, all of which must be congruent).

Both of the compromises indicated above increase project risk. They raise the likelihood that potentially serious discrepancies may not be detected. Further, extraneous and possibly costly items in software may not be detected. Certainly, visibility or traceability is diminished. Management (i.e., both user/buyer and seller) must decide whether these risks are acceptable, taking budget factors into account.

Coping with Numerous Software Products. Another resource problem connected with auditing often occurs at the end of a phase of the software development cycle. Here, usually a number of software products are delivered by the developers at approximately the same time. For example, at the end of the design phase, the developers may produce detailed design specifications, a user's manual, a data specification document, and possibly other documents. Not only must all these documents be audited at about the same time, but often several of these documents are voluminous in size. To exacerbate the problem, a limited amount of time is frequently provided to the auditors to review these documents. To maintain progress on the project, generally the time between the publication of the documents and the establishment of the baseline is kept relatively brief. How to audit all these documents in these circumstances with limited resources is indeed a problem.

There are a number of ways to cope with this problem. One is to bring extra auditors onto the project for a brief period to alleviate this peak demand. Unfortunately, the extra resources are rarely available when most needed. Another solution to this problem is to stretch out the period during which auditing is performed, for example, by performing preliminary audits on draft documents. This tactic allows the auditors not only a longer period over which to audit but also allows them to become familiar with the documents, thus facilitating their audit of the final documents. This tactic also provides preliminary input to the document developers, which allows them to improve documents before producing the final versions.

It is possible and often practical to conduct only a partial audit prior to establishing a set of products as a baseline, and then to continue the audit to a greater depth after the baseline is established. The partial audit concentrates on establishing the basic validity of the baseline (e.g., by determining whether all paragraph headings in, for instance, a design document have antecedents in a requirements specification). Using the results of this partial audit, the CCB can establish the baseline subject to the satisfactory completion of the audit. The developers can then proceed from this provisional baseline into the next phase of the project, knowing that, in all likelihood, only minor adjustments need be made when the full audit is completed. When establishing the baseline, the CCB also can direct the auditors to concentrate on particular issues of concern to the board. Auditing indeed consumes resources. However, the payoff in these resource expenditures is the avoidance, through early discovery of incongruities among software products, of consuming even greater amounts of resources.

10.3.8 Avoiding the "Paperwork" Nightmare

A criticism often leveled against SCM is that the primary product of its application is paperwork and more paperwork (see Figure 10-10). (Our definition of "paperwork" encompasses both hard copy and electronic copy.) It is true that the output of SCM functions is "paper," as follows:

- *Identification* produces parts lists
- *Control* produces CCB minutes and a multitude of forms pertaining to software changes—incident reports, prepared documentation modifications, patches to fielded code, and so forth

- *Auditing* produces discrepancy reports and test incident reports
- *Status accounting* archives and disseminates the paper produced by the other three SCM functions

Thus, unbridled application of SCM can precipitate literally mountains of "paper" which, in turn, can impede (or, in the extreme, stop) project progress.

Figure 10-10   Some typical SCM "paperwork."

A guiding principle whose application can serve to keep paperwork in check is the following:

> The buyer/user and seller should iteratively agree on how much and how frequently paper is needed to achieve a mutually desirable level of visibility and traceability.

To see how this principle works, we consider some of the paperwork associated with CCB meetings—CCB minutes. Of all the SCM paper produced on a project, these minutes are probably the most fundamental elements in establishing and maintaining a visible trace of project activities. For CCB minutes, the above principle translates into the following particulars:

- Begin with an outline and format such as that shown in Table 10-6.
- Use this format at the first few CCB meetings to generate minutes.
- Because the minutes from one meeting should serve as the basis for conducting the next meeting, it should become clear to the meeting participants which

topics are useful to the participants and how much detail should be recorded for each topic.

- In this manner, the format and content of the CCB minutes should evolve to accommodate the needs of the CCB participants, thus, by definition, avoiding unnecessary paperwork.

Table 10-6 Sample Format for CCB Minutes

| [Your Organization's Name and Logo] | **CCB MINUTES** | <u>Date</u>
<u>Identification Number</u> |

<u>List of Attendees and Organizational Affiliation</u>

1. Purpose of Meeting

 – Agenda
 – Adoption of minutes from preceding CCB

2. CCB Actions

 – Software parts labeled/relabeled
 – Baselines reviewed/changed/established
 – Disposition of change control forms
 – New/unresolved/unscheduled issues

3. Discussion of CM Audits

 – Discrepancies reviewed
 – Plan for resolution of discrepancies

4. Items for Subsequent CCB Meetings

 – Actions items
 – Agenda for next meeting
 – Time and place of next meeting

<u>Distribution List</u>

A by-product of the above process is the paring down of other paperwork associated with the conduct of CCB business. Specifically, the primary business of the CCB is the review and approval of software changes. This review and approval process, to be performed in a visible and traceable manner, needs to be supported by paperwork to accomplish the following tasks:

- To document incidents which may indicate problems with software code that is being tested prior to operational use or is in operational use.
- To document CCB-approved changes to software code.
- To document CCB-approved changes to software other than code (e.g., design specifications) and software-related documentation (e.g., user's manuals—documentation that describes in user language how to use software systems).
- To document requests for enhancements or new capabilities upon which the CCB must act.

The number and format of the forms needed to perform the above tasks can be agreed upon and defined during CCB meetings in a manner similar to that used to refine the format and content of CCB minutes. A starting point for defining these forms can be found in Reference 8, Chapter 4.

Avoiding the paperwork nightmare can thus be achieved through negotiation on the part of project participants on the form and content of project correspondence. The focus of this negotiation should be the CCB, through which the bulk of this paperwork flows. Judicious use of electronic tools is a further means to alleviate this flow, by regulating paper in response to specific needs.

10.3.9 Allocating Resources Among CM Activities

It is frequently necessary to make hard decisions regarding the percentage of already highly limited resources that should be parceled out to each of the SCM functions. Unfortunately, we are not aware of any general principles governing how these difficult decisions should be made (see Figure 10-11).

The particulars of individual projects often establish the deciding factors. Politics may dictate what SCM can and cannot do. For example, some software project managers simply do not want detailed audits of software products developed prior to code—they would rather wait until code testing to find out what the developers have been doing. We will therefore illustrate some of the tradeoffs involved with making such decisions by working through the following example based on a typical business-world situation.

Example of Allocating Resources Among CM Activities. Suppose that you have just been put in charge of a software development effort that is just getting started. Suppose further that your past experience with software projects has convinced you of the need for and importance of SCM. Finally, suppose that your management is (1) primarily interested in keeping project costs to an absolute minimum and (2) is unfavorably disposed toward "overhead functions" such as SCM. You are therefore placed in a position of reducing SCM to a bare minimum. After presenting various SCM proposals to your management, the guidance you receive is that you are permitted to fund only one of the following activities:

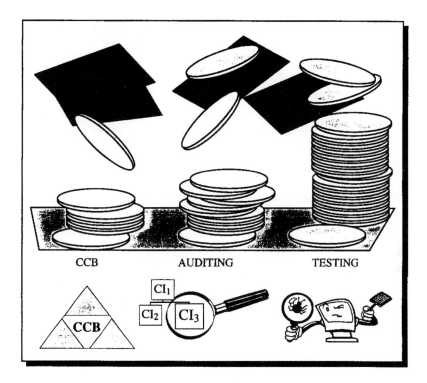

Figure 10-11   Where should limited resources be allocated to SCM activities?

1. Weekly configuration control board meetings attended by yourself and the buyer/user to review project progress and to consider proposed software changes.
2. Development and execution of written test procedures to determine buyer/user acceptance of the coded software that you are responsible for developing. The coded software is assumed to be exercised in an environment that either is identical to or approximates the actual user environment.
3. Audits of selected software products (such as the functional specification, design documents, and code).

Given the above scenario, how would you make your selection?

Table 10-7 lists the advantage and disadvantages associated with the above three SCM activities. Which activity you select depends upon how much weight you (or your boss) give to these advantages and disadvantages. This table thus illustrates typical tradeoffs associated with allocating resources to various CM activities and (qualitatively) the types of paybacks offered in return for resources invested. The table also indicates the manner in which SCM activities complement one another, thus suggesting that their integrated application is really necessary if working software products are to be achieved on time and within budget.

To see in more quantitative terms some of the cost-versus-benefit tradeoffs involving SCM activities, consider the following extension to the previous example:

Suppose that you estimate that it would cost $25,000 for each of the three activities. Suppose further that your management gives you $40,000 and allows you to fund any combination of the three activities. With this budget constraint, indicate how you would reallocate funds to these activities, and indicate how you would change their scope to reflect this reallocation.

Table 10-8 indicates one way to respond to the resource allocation and scope issues raised above. This table and the preceding one offer a specific example of the cost versus benefits associated with specific SCM activities.

Table 10-7 Tradeoffs in Deciding Which SCM Activities to Fund

ACTIVITY	ADVANTAGE 👍	DISADVANTAGE 👎
1. Weekly CCB Meetings	Sustained visibility forced on buyer/user/seller, which reduces the likelihood that problems will go unnoticed too long.	Does not provide definitive determination that delivered software code is doing what it is suppose to do.
2. Development and Execution of Test Procedures	Provides the most definitive indication (of all three activities) of the degree to which the final software product (i.e., the operating code) is doing what it is supposed to do.	A one-shot exercise late in product development cycle, whose application may be insufficient (or too late) to adequately deal with problems.
3. Audits of Selected Software Products	Provides an indication (long before testing) of potentially costly deviations from requirements (and design), thereby allowing corrective action to be taken at reduced schedule and cost risk to the project.	Probably conducted less frequently than the first activity, thus providing less visibility and thereby increasing the likelihood that problems will go unnoticed (or will be noticed later and thereby be more costly to rectify).

Table 10-8 Funding SCM Activities—Reallocation and Rescoping Considerations

ACTIVITY	ORIGINAL ALLOCATION	REALLOCATION	RESCOPING
1. Weekly CCB Meetings	$25,000	$18,000	Reduce frequency of meetings slightly (maybe to three per month).
2. Development and Execution of Test Procedures	$25,000	$12,000	Reduce depth and breadth of testing.
3. Audits of Selected Software Products	$25,000	$10,000	Audit to a lesser depth or do fewer audits (concentrating on initial software products).

10.4   Summary

Software configuration management offers the buyer, user, and seller protection against the myriad problems that often beset software development and maintenance projects—problems that, if left unaddressed, can easily spell project disaster. To address these problems, the four SCM functions—identification, control, auditing, and status accounting—must be practiced in, and indeed integrated into, the software development process throughout the project life cycle.

Establishment of an SCM program on a software project of any size is practicable and economically justifiable. Management commitment to installing the checks and balances provided by SCM is of paramount importance. An SCM program should be established gradually, molded to the organization and functions of the company and its projects and to available personnel. An early endeavor should be the establishment of a configuration control board periodically meeting to maintain change control for the project. Other areas of importance for SCM are the conduct of audits of the software products, particularly early in the life cycle, and of acceptance testing of the completed software code prior to its delivery to its users.

In this chapter, we have made a number of practical suggestions for implementing an SCM program. With the installation of such a program, a large measure of protection will be provided to a project through an increase in visibility and traceability, through the establishment of project control and change control, and through provision of a capability to monitor project events. The end result is an increased likelihood of developing software systems that satisfy user needs and that are delivered on time and within budget.

References

1. Zelkowitz, M. W., Shaw, A. C., and Gannon, J. D., *Principles of Software Engineering and Design*. (Englewood Cliffs. NJ: Prentice Hall, 1979), pp.1–2.
2. Paulk, M. C., et al, *The Capability Maturity Model: Guidelines for Improving the Software Process*, (Reading, Mass: Addison-Wesley Publishing Co., 1995).
3. Bersoff, E. H.; Henderson V. D; and Siegel, S. G., *Software Configuration Management: An Investment in Product Integrity,* (Englewood Cliffs, NJ: Prentice-Hall, Inc., 1980).
4. Software Technology Support Center (STSC) Document, "Software Configuration Management Technology Report." Hill Air Force Base, Utah, 84056, September 1994. See also references included therein.
5. Donaldson, S. E., and Siegel, S.G., *Cultivating Successful Software Development: A Practitioner's View*. (Upper Saddle River, NJ: Prentice Hall PTR, 1997), pp. 3–4.
6. Demarco, T., *Controlling Software Projects*. (New York: Yourdon Press, 1982).
7. Johnson, D. I., and Brodman, J. G., "Realities and Rewards of Software Process Improvement." In: *IEEE Software*, Vol. 13, No. 6 (November 1996), pp. 99–101.
8. Donaldson, S. E., and Siegel, S.G., *Cultivating Successful Software Development: A Practitioner's View*. (Upper Saddle River, NJ: Prentice Hall PTR, 1997), pp. 238–262.
9. Boehm, B. W., "Verifying and Validating Software Requirements and Design Specifications." In: *IEEE Software*, Vol. 1, No. l (January 1984), pp. 75–88.
10. *Ibid.*

The Pareto Principle Applied to Software Quality Assurance

G. Gordon Shulmeyer
PYXIS Systems International, Inc.

Thomas J. McCabe
McCabe & Associates, Inc.

11.1   Introduction

Concentrate on the vital few, not the trivial many. This admonition borrowed from quality consultant J. M. Juran (see Chapter 3) epitomizes the Pareto Principle as he applied it to quality management. Thomas J. McCabe has extended this Pareto Principle to software quality activities.

The Natural Law of Software Quality says that Pareto's Principle holds true, especially in software systems: 20 percent of the code has 80 percent of the defects—find them! Fix them! Remember from Fred Brooks' analysis of the development of OS/360 for IBM Corporation: 4 percent of OS/360 had over 60 percent of the errors. Similarly, on a reusable software library; two of the first 11 modules (20 percent) had *all of the errors.* Twenty percent of the code requires 80 percent of the enhancements—find them by looking into enhancement logs to find out where most changes occur. Externalize the changes in data or decision tables. [1, p. 51]

Barry Boehm is widely respected in the measurement community for his work at TRW. One of the top ten metrics from Boehm is that software phenomena follow a Pareto distribution:

- 20 percent of the modules consume 80 percent of the resources
- 20 percent of the modules contribute 80 percent of the errors
- 20 percent of the errors consume 80 percent of repair costs
- 20 percent of the enhancements consume 80 percent of the adaptive maintenance costs
- 20 percent of the modules consume 80 percent of the execution time
- 20 percent of the tools experience 80 percent of the tool usage [2, p. 130]

Simply put, Pareto analysis is a statistical method to identify the minority of agents that exert the greatest effect. The translation of Pareto methods from hardware-oriented quality analyses to those of software quality is another sign of the origin of software quality assurance in the traditions of quality management. [3, p. 169]

This chapter explores many aspects of the Pareto Principle and each aspect is then related to software. It is during the software development cycle that the application of the Pareto Principle pays off. Softare Quality Assurance (SQA) personnel should know how to apply the Pareto Principle during the software development cycle, which is what this chapter is all about. SQA personnel should note that use of the Pareto Principle promotes a win-win situation for SQA, for the program, and for the company.

First, a brief historical background is provided to set the stage. Then, two specific examples undertaken by McCabe & Associates, Inc,. for the World Wide Military Command & Control System (WWMCCS) and the Federal Reserve Bank are covered in some detail. These have become classic examples of the use of Pareto analysis. The various ways that the Pareto Principle can apply to software and the results of those applications are discussed.

Some extensions of the Pareto Principle to other fertile areas previously exposed by J. M. Juran are defect identification, inspections, and statistical techniques. Each of these areas is discussed in relation to software and its probable payoff in better quality.

For defect identification in software, some of the common symptoms of defects in software are uncovered, and suggestions as to the basic causes of defects in software are provided.

Inspections have been a mainstay in the factory to ensure the quality of the product. That inspections have been applied to software is well known, but tying inspections to the Pareto Principle is not well understood. So, the explanation of that phenomenon is also covered in this chapter.

The use of statistical techniques based upon error types is explored in relation to software. The frequency of error types in software and the use of statistics for software quality are covered.

A unique application of Pareto analysis in comparing Pareto charts, recently discussed by Ron Kennett, [16] is also covered.

11.2   Historical Background

J. M. Juran is the father of the Pareto Principle in quality management. He coined the terms *vital few* and *trivial many* as applied to the Pareto Principle. Fundamentally, the Pareto Principle stresses concentration on the vital few, not the trivial many.

The historical development of the Pareto Principle illuminates its application to software quality. The oldest application of the idea of the vital few (the "exception principle" for management decisionmaking) is provided by Juran in his book, *Managerial Breakthrough*. [4, p. 49]

> The principle is very old. An early example is charmingly related in the Old Testament. Following the exodus of the Israelites from Egypt, their leader Moses found himself the sole judge of the disputes which arose among the people. The number of such disputes was enough to make this solitary judge a bottleneck in decision making. In consequence, the people "stood by Moses from the morning into the evening," waiting for Moses to make decisions. Moses' father-in-law, Jethro, saw this spectacle and ventured advice. (For which Jethro has become regarded by some as the first consultant on record.)
>
> *Jethro's advice:* "And thou shalt teach them ordinances and laws, and show them the way wherein they must walk, and the work they must do." (Exodus 18:20)
>
> *Translated into modern management dialect:* "Establish policies and standard practices, conduct job training, and prepare job descriptions."
>
> *Jethro's advice:* "Moreover thou shalt provide out of all the people able men, such as fear God, men of truth, hating covetousness, and place such over them, to be rulers of thousands, and rulers of hundreds, rulers of fifties and rulers of tens." (Exodus 18:21)
>
> *Translated into modern management dialect:* "Set up an organization; first-line supervisors to have 10 subordinates; second-line supervisors to have five subordinates, etc.; appoint men who have supervisory ability."
>
> *Jethro's advice:* "And let them judge the people at all seasons; and it shall be that every great matter they shall bring unto thee, but every small matter they shall judge: so it shall be easier for thyself, and they shall bear the burden with thee." (Exodus 18:22)
>
> *Translated into modern management dialect:* "Institute delegation of authority; routine problems to be decided down the line, but exceptional problems to be brought to higher authority."

Next, a quantum time jump to the 1940s when Joseph Juran noticed that the concept, that a vital few members of the assortment account for most of the total effect, and contrariwise, the bulk of the members (the trivial many) account for very little of the total effect, was universal. He named the phenomenon "the Pareto Principle" (after the Italian economist, Vilfredo Pareto [1848–1923]) which has endured.

Juran later footnoted in his *Quality Control Handbook* that it was a mistake to name it the Pareto Principle. [5, pp. 2-17, -18] Pareto quantified the extent of inequality or nonuniformity of the distribution of wealth, but had not generalized this concept of unequal distribution to other fields. In fact, the First Edition of the

Quality Control Handbook by Juran illustrates cumulative "Pareto" curves which rightfully should have been identified with M. O. Lorenz, who had used curves to depict concentration of wealth in graphic forms.

McCabe & Associates, Inc. has been giving seminars on software quality assurance since 1978. It is during these seminars that Thomas McCabe introduced the application of the Pareto Principle to software quality. The Pareto Principle is presented in light of Juran's contribution to overall quality and then made specific for software quality in the *SQA Survey Book* [6, pp. 153–154] and the *SQA Seminar Notes* [7, p. 11] accompanying the seminar. The actual application of the concept of Pareto analysis to software quality in two real examples (WWMCCS and Federal Reserve Bank), as conducted by McCabe and Associates, Inc. is explored below in some detail.

11.3   WWMCCS—Classic Example 1

The example cited is from an actual study of quality assurance conducted by Thomas McCabe in 1977 for WWMCCS (World Wide Military Command and Control System). [6, p. 154–156] At that time WWMCCS was a large network of thirty-five Honeywell H6000's with a specialized operating system and hundreds of user application programs. The WWMCCS ADP Directorate is the organization responsible for WWMCCS software acquisition, integration, and testing. The quality assurance program was for the WWMCCS ADP Directorate organization. The following are examples of ways in which the Pareto Principle was applied to that organization.

11.3.1 Manpower

This heading represents internal WWMCCS ADP Directorate personnel expenditures. The first task was to identify the different functions performed in the WWMCCS ADP Directorate (e.g., planning, scheduling, task preparation, demonstration test, integration, stability testing, regression testing, and so on) and then analyze the WWMCCS ADP Directorate personnel expenditure on each task. The few functions that Pareto analysis determined as consuming 80 percent of the manpower were identified as strong candidates to be placed "under the microscope" to determine the reasons for this consumption. The goal was to reduce personnel expenditures by reducing the number of people required to complete the task without diminishing the quality of the complete job. In doing this, one could distinguish between technical and managerial manpower. This yielded two initial distributions for quality assurance which resulted in identifying two distinct classes of internal WWMCCS ADP Directorate functions.

A chart similar to the one in Table 11-1 aids in the analysis. The statistics assume a three-month time frame.

Table 11-1   Hours Expended on Personnel Tasks

Personnel Tasks	Hours Expended	% of Hours Expended	Cumulative Hours Expended	Cumulative % of Hours Expended
*Managerial Personnel**				
scheduling	600	43	600	43
"crisis reaction"	300	21	900	64
planning	200	14	1100	78
decision making	150	11	1250	89
contract administration	100	7	1350	96
controlling	30	3	1380	99
"task preparation"	20	1	1400	100
*Technical Personnel**				
software purchase analysis	2500	25	2500	25
planning	2000	20	4500	45
contract administration	1500	15	6000	60
integration	1200	12	7200	72
stability testing	1000	10	8200	82
regression testing	1000	10	9200	92
demonstration tests	500	5	9700	97
"crisis reaction"	300	3	10000	100

* Assumes three management & 22 technical

For managerial personnel note that scheduling and "crisis reaction" required over half of the expended time, and for technical personnel note that software purchase analysis and planning utilized just under half of the expended time. A particularly interesting WWMCCS ADP Directorate function in the table is "crisis reaction." It is informative to determine how much of the personnel resources this category actually consumed and then see which type of "crisis" was most frequently repeated and most costly. The "crisis reaction" function for managerial personnel turned out to be significantly expensive. So, a key point is that a program should be directed at more careful planning and coordination.

For a simpler graphic representation of the data shown in Table 11-1, see Figure 11-1.

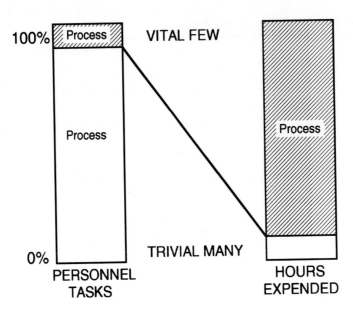

Figure 11-1   Pareto Principle simplified (adapted from reference 4, p.47).

11.3.2 Cost of Contracts

This category of examination is concerned with the internal software quality of a WWMCCS release. There are two steps in applying the Pareto Principle to the quality of the product. First, the WWMCCS ADP Directorate decides how to define quality—this could be done by prioritizing the software quality factors (metrics) listed in Table 11-2, and selecting a subset of the factors as an operational definition of quality, as shown in Table 11-3. The hurdle rates shown in Table 11-3 are the values set up-front that must be achieved during the measurement of these factors in the development phases when the evaluation (count) is made.

Once the definition of quality is agreed upon, the second step is to apply it to the different modules, software documentation, and software development notebooks, which are components or packages in a WWMCCS release. That is, the quality of each of the components of the WWMCCS release is analyzed. This results in a "quality distribution" through which Pareto analysis can identify the critical components.

11.3.3 By Release

Analyze the various historical releases processed by the WWMCCS ADP Directorate and rank their quality. By identifying and analyzing the releases with the poorest quality, some pitfalls can be avoided, and the beginning of a corrective program formed. Analyzing the best quality releases will likely result in positive principles to follow that would become part of a standards program.

Table 11-2   List of Software Quality Factors *

CORRECTNESS	RELIABILITY	EFFICIENCY
INTEGRITY	USABILITY	MAINTAINABILITY
TESTABILITY	FLEXABILITY	PORTABILITY
REUSABILITY	INTEROPERABILITY	

* See Chapter 15 for definitions of quality factors.

Table 11-3   Example Hurdle Rates for Selected Software Quality Factors

Software Quality Factor	Hurdle Rate*
Correctness	97%
Reliability	95%
Maintainability	95%
Useability	90%
Testability	85%

* *Hurdle Rate*—the values set up-front that must be achieved during the measurement of these factors in the development cycle phases when the evaluation (count) is made.

The "moving mountain" phenomenon occurs with the issuance of new releases. This phenomenon refers to a graphical representation of the number of defects in a software system plus new defects that are uncovered in a new release. The basic graph, Figure 11-2, shows defects being removed over time with a software system.

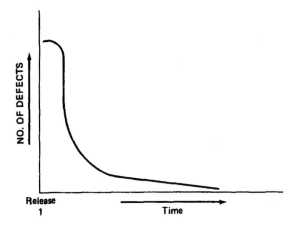

Figure 11-2   Software release defects.

The "moving mountain" occurs when the basic graph is drawn for each *new release* of the software system on the same graph, as shown in Figure 11-3.

With a graph, such as Figure 11-3, it becomes easy to recognize that release 4 is rather good in comparison to releases 1, 2, and 3. It even seems likely that one is better off by remaining with release 1, but of course release 1 lacks the enhancements incorporated in releases 2, 3, and 4.

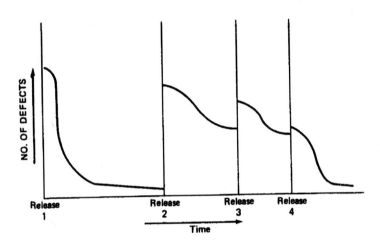

Figure 11- 3   "Moving mountain" software releases defects.

11.3.4 By Function

Analyze the "quality" of various WWMCCS ADP Directorate functions. The first step is to list the various WWMCCS ADP Directorate functions as under Manpower discussed above. Second, determine which of the functions lead to the most problems and direct the corrective program at these troublesome functions.

A chart similar to Table 11-4 aids in the "by function" analysis of problems. The statistics assume three months time. Implicit in this approach is that Pareto analysis is applied recursively within individual functions to determine which of the substeps have the most problems. A chart such as Table 11-5 aids in the "by function" analysis of problems.

Also resulting from this approach is the formulation of internal "quality criterion" to be applied to each of the internal WWMCCS ADP Directorate functions.

It should be noted that the functions of the various vendors can be analyzed in a similar manner. In this case, the program would monitor the quality of the functions performed by the various vendors.

Table 11-4   Problems Encountered by Personnel Functions

Personnel Tasks	Problems Encountered	% of Problems Encountered	Cumulative Problems Encountered	Cumulative % of Problems Encountered
Managerial Personnel				
contract administration	10	48	10	48
"crisis reaction"	8	38	18	86
scheduling	2	9	20	95
decision making	1	5	21	100
planning	0	0	21	100
controlling	0	0	21	100
"task preparation"	0	0	21	100
Technical Personnel				
software purchase analysis	110	42	110	42
contract administration	58	22	168	64
integration	40	15	208	79
"crisis reaction"	25	9	233	88
planning	15	6	248	94
stability testing	7	3	255	97
regression testing	5	2	260	99
demonstration tests	4	1	264	100

11.4   Federal Reserve Bank — Classic Example 2

The example cited is from another actual study of quality assurance conducted by McCabe & Associates in 1982 for the Federal Reserve Bank. [8] As part of a functional management program to improve the operations of the General Purpose Computer Department of the Federal Reserve Bank of New York, and to establish a departmental quality assurance program, McCabe & Associates was asked to conduct a software quality assurance study. The scope of the study, the analysis process, and the conclusions are stated below.

The scope of this effort was restricted to the ongoing operations and related interfaces of the General Purpose Computer Department of the Federal Reserve Bank of New York and how the quality of those operations might be improved.

Table 11-5   Problems Encountered by Personnel Subfunctions

Personnel Tasks	Problems Encountered	% of Problems Encountered	Cumulative Problems Encountered	Cumulative % of Problems Encountered
Managerial Personnel				
contract administration:				
monitor contract fulfillment	5	50	5	50
receive contract	2	20	7	70
resolve contractual conflict	2	20	9	90
discover contractual conflict	1	10	10	100
close out contract	0	0	10	100
send out contract	0	0	10	100
"crisis reaction":				
system crashes	5	56	5	56
loss of best analyst	2	22	7	78
previously unplanned customer presentation tomorrow	1	11	8	89
system late for delivery	1	11	9	100
boss needs report by tomorrow	0	0	9	100
Technical Personnel				
software purchase analysis:				
program to aid in vendor analysis	50	45	50	45
package history check	45	41	95	86
vendor history check	10	9	105	95
benchmark conduct	4	4	109	99
"perfect" package cost too much	1	1	110	100
contract administration:				
contractor disputes	30	52	30	52
contractor inadequate	20	34	50	86
contractor delivers late	7	12	57	98
monitor contract fulfillment	1	2	58	100
letter recommending cancellation	0	0	58	100

Specifically related to the project development cycle, the nature and extent of General Purpose Computer Department involvement in the following phases was investigated:

- Project Proposal (Stage I)
- Development Schedule
- Resource Requirements for:
  - Acceptance Testing
  - Production Operations
- Design Phase (Stage II)
  - Data Conversion Plan
  - Acceptance Test planning
  - User's Guide Review
- Implementation Phase (Stage III)
  - Completion Criteria for "Runbooks"
  - Completion Criteria for Operator/User Training
- Post-Implementation (Stage IV)
  - Post-Implementation Review
  - Post-Implementation Evaluation

Further, the effort was limited to those software quality factors directly affecting the General Purpose Computer Department as currently chartered. The primary factor for this project was *usability*.

Attributes, or criteria, as developed by McCabe & Associates and others[*] associated with the usability factor, are as follows:

- Operability—Those attributes of the software that determine operation and procedures concerned with the operation of the software.
- Training—Those attributes of the software that provide transition from the current operation or initial familiarization.
- Communicativeness—Those attributes of the software that provide useful input and output which can be assimilated.

Of these criteria, operability and training were considered to have impact on the General Purpose Computer Department, with communicativeness impacting mainly the user.

---

[*] William E. Perry, *Effective Methods of EDP Quality Assurance* (Wellesly, MA: Q.E.D. Information Sciences, Inc., 1981).

The metric for stating requirements and measuring the accomplishments of the above criteria is the number of occurrences of program failures (ABENDS in the General Purpose Computer Department environment) attributable to operator error.

Other, or secondary, software quality factors that have a high positive relationship with usability are *correctness* and *reliability*. These features were not analyzed in as much depth as the primary factor, usability.

The process used to conduct the analysis consisted of three major components:

- an analysis of the process used by the General Purpose Computer Department in accepting new or modified applications and placing them in production
- an investigation of the classes of errors occurring
- an investigation of the causes of the errors

The analysis of the General Purpose Computer Department acceptance and production process was divided into two parts: (1) the introduction and acceptance of new or modified applications, including documentation, training, testing activities, as well as General Purpose Computer Department participation in the development process; and (2) running the applications in production including acceptance of user inputs, job setup and scheduling, and delivery of output. In both cases, the analysis included studying input, procedures, output, supporting documentation, and error reporting and correction procedures.

The investigation of the classes of error occurrence dealt with objective errors, i.e., those causing reruns of a portion or all of the application, and also subjective errors, i.e., those which, while not causing reruns, contributed to inefficiency and lack of management control. In this investigation, formal error (ABEND) reports were analyzed using the Pareto technique to determine which classes of errors occurred most frequently and had the most severe impact on operations and/or the user.

The final and most detailed analysis was aimed at determining potential causes for the various types of errors. Specifically, an attempt was made to attribute the cause of failure to one of the following areas: system design, operating procedure, training, or documentation.

Part of the document review consisted of a review of a typical set of application operations documents called "runbooks." The payroll system was chosen as an example of a large system, frequently run, and considered to be of below-average quality. The payroll system is normally run 90 times a year, sometimes as often as three times in a single week. The system consists of 23 jobs (and hence 23 runbooks) in three major categories: prepayroll processing, payroll processing, and postpayroll processing. Each runbook contains about 20 pages of information (460 pages total), and an average of eight control cards in a plastic pouch (177 cards total). These 23 jobs are set up, including reading in the control cards and mounting at least one tape for each job, each time payroll is run. The setup is done manually and the payroll system ABENDs approximately every other time it is run. In addition, sometimes the attempted rerun also ABENDs. The ABENDs are almost always caused by human error in setup or processing. The conclusion reached was that the runbook procedure is largely a manual process. Thus, it is excessively error-prone.

The most detailed step in the analysis process was to review the file of General Purpose Computer Department Incident (ABEND) Reports of the past year. This file consisted of a stack of completed ABEND forms. The origin of the form is described below.

When a job or job step is unable to complete normally, for whatever reason, the job is suspended by the system and the operator is notified with a diagnostic code. This event is called an ABEND and the codes provided are ABEND CODES. Upon the occurrence of such an event, the operator fills out the top portion of a General Purpose Computer Incident Report and notifies the shift production support analyst. The analyst is provided the report and any supporting documentation, such as printouts. The analyst then takes action to diagnose and correct the error and initiate a rerun of the job, if appropriate. The analyst then completes the ABEND form as to corrective action and disposition.

The review of the ABEND file was performed using Pareto-type analysis to identify which of the potentially many error types were most frequent and thus impacted most severely on productivity and quality. The analysis yielded a relatively small number of error types, and an even smaller number of classes of errors which occurred with dominating frequency. A disturbing aspect of the analysis was that of the 1536 forms reviewed, 21 percent of the forms had no information entered as to cause of error and another 21 percent were unclear as to cause, although job disposition was given; there remained only 58 percent of the file for meaningful analysis. The result of this analysis is provided in Table 11-6.

What can be inferred from the analysis is that a relatively small number of error types (nine) have occurred during the last year. Six of these types comprising 78 percent of the total can be classified as human errors on the part of either the operator or the user, as shown in Table 11-7.

The other significant error class was hardware or system errors. These are primarily tape read errors which are corrected by varying the drive off-line or switching drives. The large proportion of human error could be attributable to one or more of the following:

- poor human factors design of the application
- inadequate training of operators and users

- inadequate performance aids for the operators and users, i. e. runbooks, checklists and automated tools

These human errors relate directly to the usability factor discussed earlier. In fact, these errors are the metric measurement for the operability and training criteria.

Table 11-6   ABEND Analysis

CORRECTIVE ACTION	NUMBER	% of TOTAL	% of SAMPLE
Changed JCL Card	195	11.6	22
System error (hardware/tape/system)	154	10	17
Return to user	127	8.3	14
Changed procedure	115	7.4	13
Override file catalogue	115	7.4	13
Incorrect job setup	97	6.3	11
File not found (late mount)	41	2.6	5
Contact programmer	23	1.5	3
Restored and rerun (error not found)	14	0.9	2
Sample Total	882	58.0	100
No information	324	21	
Insufficient information	330	21	
Total	1536	100	

Table 11-7   Rate of Human Errors Inferred from Analysis

JCL card in error	22%
User input in error	14
Procedure JCL in error	13
File catalogue/designation in error	13
Job improperly set up	11
Tape not mounted on time	5
Total	78%

With regard to the software quality factors and their criteria, as discussed above, the following conclusions may be drawn:

- The usability of the software application being run in production by the General Purpose Computer Department must be considered low. The per-shift rate of 1.6 ABENDS represents a high resource cost and an unpredictable and disruptive environment.
- The operability criteria in particular is not being adequately met by systems development, as evidenced by the high error rate, i. e. every other run for payroll. Nor are operability requirements being fed to system development during the project development cycle.
- The involvement of the General Purpose Computer Department in the project development cycle is minimal. No requirements for the usability of systems are fed in on a formal basis and review of development documentation is informal and inadequate.
- There exists an opportunity to reduce the number of error-prone human procedures through the use of installed packages, such as APOLLO and ABENDAID and SCHEDULER. Other related quality factors such as correctness and reliability appear to be satisfactory. This judgment is based on the lack of user complaints and the relatively infrequent need to call for programmer assistance. However, it should be noted that no evidence could be found that these factors were formally and rigorously tested prior to entering production.

The impact of the above findings and conclusions upon the operation of the General Purpose Computer Department can be characterized as follows:

The 1536 ABENDS, plus an estimated additional 384 (25 percent) errors not causing ABENDS, create an extremely disruptive environment. As has been stated, this is approximately two ABENDS per shift, with at least one application ABENDing every other time it is run. Some recoveries and reruns require more than a day to accomplish.

In financial terms, the recovery and rerun procedures require an estimated 65 percent of the production support personnel resources of the Central Support Division. The dollar value of these services is approximately $150,000 annually or 20 percent of the Division's budget. This cost can also be stated as 6 percent of the General Purpose Computer Department salary budget. If this 6 percent were extended to the entire General Purpose Computer Department budget, the dollar value would be $390,000 annually. If the useful life of an average application is five years, this would amount to almost $2 million merely to deal with operational errors over a five-year period. Probably most important is the consideration that as applications become more complex and database-oriented, the ability of the production support team to maintain processing may be exceeded.

11.5   Defect Identification

Defect identification is a fertile area for Pareto analysis in the software field. Some examples from other fields are first identified; then how this information points to other useful tools in software is explained using these examples, then demonstrations are provided for the software field. The extensions discussed in this section are the concepts of common symptoms, basic causes of defects, and cost of defects.

Table 11-8 shows the estimated cost of various types defects in a foundry. The most costly defects are the pits. Pareto analysis highlights this highest cost item.

The list of defects in Table 11-8 defines how the symptoms manifest themselves as defects, and so are called the *principal symptoms* or *common symptoms*. Whenever the causes for the principal symptom categories are "obvious" (i.e., all knowledgeable hands agree) from the nature of the symptoms, then an analysis can be made by basic cause categories. In still other cases where defects might be the result of any of several possible causes, it is nevertheless instructive to attempt to classify by basic cause categories.

Table 11-8   Defect Costs in a Foundry [2, p. 16-5]

Defect name	% of all defect costs		Annual cost $000
	This defect	Cumulative	
Pits	36	36	315
Light	9	45	78
Physical excess	8	53	73
Hard	5	58	41
Wide gaps	4	62	39
Thin face	4	66	32
Rough sides	3	69	30
Broken(foundry)	3	72	30
Casting	3	75	24
Broken(machining)	3	78	23
All others	22	100	186
Total	100	—	871

The example given in Figure 11-4 depicts symptoms that appeared during the operations of a sheet metal fabrications shop. Figure 11-4 is a true Pareto diagram because it is a bar graph showing the frequency of occurrence of various concerns, ordered with the most frequent ones first. [9, p. D-13]

The symptoms in Figure 11-4 were not sufficiently distributed to allow concentration on the vital few. So a special study was set up for a limited period, during which each rejection or error was carefully traced to its origin by a task force representing Engineering, Production, and Inspection. Based on the facts uncovered, the task force's members tried to agree on the cause classification. Figure 11-5 represents the Pareto analysis basic cause category for the sheet metal fabrication shop. The most promising direction for study appears to be the basic cause category "operator error," since operator errors (acknowledged as such by the operator in each case) are by a wide margin the single biggest class. [5, p. 45-19]

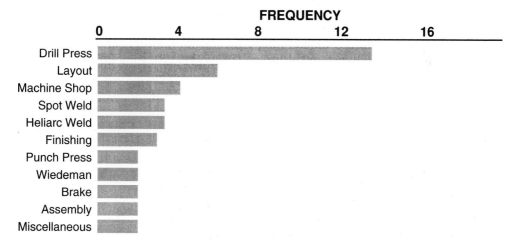

Figure 11-4 Symptoms Pareto diagram. [2, p. 45-19]

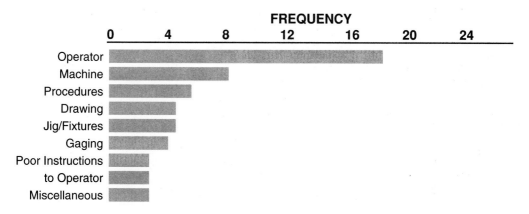

Figure 11-5 Basic causes Pareto diagram. [2, p. 45-19]

For computer software, some data of frequency of occurrence or errors is available. First, Rubey's "Quantitative Aspects of Software Validation" [10] data is presented. Table 11-9 shows the basic cause error categories. Then, for the major causes the common symptoms are shown in Tables 11-10, 11-11, 11-12, and 11-13.

SQA personnel can draw several inferences from the data in Table 11-9. First, there is no single reason for unreliable software, and no single validation tool or technique is likely to detect all types of errors. Chapter 20 discusses many possible ways to improve software reliability. Second, the ability to demonstrate a program's correspondence to its specification does not justify complete confidence in the program's correctness, since a significant number of errors could be due to an incomplete or erroneous specification, and the documentation of the program cannot always be trusted. Third, intentional deviation from specification and the violation of established programming standards more often leads to minor errors than to serious errors. On the other hand, invalid timing or improper handling of interrupts almost always results in a significant error.

Table 11-9 Basic Causes Error Categories for Software

ERROR CATEGORY	Total		Serious		Moderate		Minor	
	No.	%	No.	%	No.	%	No.	%
Incomplete or Erroneous Specification	340	28	19	11	82	17	239	43
Intentional Deviation from Specification	145	12	9	5	61	13	75	14
Violation of Programming Standards	118	10	2	1	22	5	94	17
Erroneous Data Accessing	120	10	36	21	72	15	12	2
Erroneous Decision Logic or Sequencing	139	12	41	24	83	17	15	3
Erroneous Arithmetic Computations	113	9	22	13	73	15	18	3
Invalid Testing	44	4	14	8	25	5	5	1
Improper Handling of Interrupts	46	4	14	8	31	6	1	0
Wrong Constants and Data Values	41	3	14	8	19	4	8	1
Inaccurate Documentation	96	8	0	0	10	2	86	16
TOTAL	1202	100	171	14	478	40	553	46

The data presented in Table 11-9 summarize the errors found in independent validations. In practice, however, the organization responsible for independent validation does not wait until the developer has completed program debugging. Instead, the independent validation organization often becomes involved at each program development phase to check that intermediate products (such as the program specification and program design) are correct.

The errors occurring in the categorization of Table 11-10, incomplete or erroneous specifications, indicate either deficiencies in, or the absence of, the verification of the program specification or program design, since there should be no errors in the final programs attributable to program specification if the preceding verification efforts were perfect. As shown in Table 11-10, 19 serious and 82 moderate errors have escaped the verification efforts and have been found only during the checking of the actual coding. In 239 additional cases, errors due to incomplete or erroneous specification are considered of minor consequence; this is largely because the coding had been implemented correctly even though the program specification is itself in error.

Table 11-10   Common Symptoms for Software Defects: Incomplete or Erroneous Specifications

ERROR CATEGORY	Total		Serious		Moderate		Minor	
	No.	%	No.	%	No.	%	No.	%
Dimensional Error	41	12	7	37	17	21	17	7
Insufficient Precision Specified	15	4	0	0	11	13	4	2
Missing Symbols or Labels	4	1	0	0	0	0	4	2
Typographical Error	51	15	0	0	0	0	51	21
Incorrect Hardware Description	7	2	3	16	3	4	1	0
Design Consideration Incomplete or Incorrect	177	52	8	42	47	57	122	51
Ambiguity in Specification or Design	45	13	1	5	4	5	40	17
TOTAL	340	100	19	6	82	24	239	70

Table 11-11   Common Symptoms for Software Defects: Erroneous Data Accessing

ERROR CATEGORY	Total		Serious		Moderate		Minor	
	No.	%	No.	%	No.	%	No.	%
Fetch or Store Wrong Data Word	79	66	17	47	52	72	10	83
Fetch or Store Wrong Portion of Data Word	10	8	10	28	0	0	0	0
Variable Equated to Wrong Location	10	8	4	11	6	0	0	0
Overwrite of Data Word	10	8	4	11	4	2	2	17
Register Loaded with Wrong Data	11	9	1	3	10	0	0	0
TOTAL	120	100	36	30	72	60	12	10

If all of the 239 minor erroneous or incomplete specification errors were faithfully translated into coding, the total number of serious errors in the resultant coding would be 84 and the total number of moderate errors would be 162. Only 94 of the 239 minor errors would remain minor errors, even if the coding implemented the erroneous specification. This would make the incomplete or erroneous specification error category in Table 11-9 the largest error source by a factor of two, and would increase the total number of serious errors by 38 percent and the total number of moderate errors by 12 percent. Verification of the program specification and design in advance of coding and debugging is a very beneficial activity, and indeed is probably essential if reliable software is desired. [11, pp. 7, 8]

Table 11-12   Common Symptoms for Software Defects: Erroneous Decision Logic or Sequencing

ERROR CATEGORY	Total		Serious		Moderate		Minor	
	No.	%	No.	%	No.	%	No.	%
Label Placed on Wrong Instruction/Statement	2	1	2	5	0	0	0	0
Branch Test Incorrect	28	20	10	24	15	18	3	20
Branch Test Set Up Incorrect	2	2	1	2	1	1	0	0
Computations Performed in Wrong Sequence	9	6	1	2	2	2	6	40
Logic Sequence Incorrect	98	71	27	66	65	78	6	40
TOTAL	139	100	41	29	83	60	15	11

Table 11-13 Common Symptoms for Software Defects: Erroneous Arithmetic Computation

ERROR CATEGORY	Total		Serious		Moderate		Minor	
	No.	%	No.	%	No.	%	No.	%
Wrong Arithmetic Operations Performed	69	61	12	55	47	64	10	56
Loss of Precision	9	8	1	5	6	8	2	11
Overflow	8	7	3	14	3	4	2	11
Poor Scaling of Intermediate Results	22	20	4	18	15	21	3	17
Incompatible Scaling	5	4	2	9	2	3	1	5
TOTAL	113	100	22	19	73	65	18	16

Another source of data for a cost by type analysis is provided in *Software Reliability*. [12] This book presents an extensive collection of analysis of error data performed at TRW. The data have resulted from the analysis of seven projects; characteristics of the projects are shown in Table 11-14. Note that project 5 is broken down into four subprojects. Each is a project unto itself because of the differing management, languages, development personnel, requirements, and so on.

Table 11-15 presents an analysis that is similar to the breakdown of the Rubey data. Although the definition of error types does not completely agree for the two studies, there is a striking similarity in the two sets of data: logic errors and data-handling errors rank first and second in the serious error category in the Rubey data, and they likewise rank first and second in the TRW data (in fact, their respective percentages are similar). [11, p. 8]

The TRW study further analyzes various subtypes of errors. For example, logic errors are divided into the following types:

- incorrect operand in logical expression
- logic activities out of sequence
- wrong variable being checked
- missing logic on condition test

It is very important, as well as interesting, to examine this more detailed analysis of the two most costly errors—logic and data handling. The results are shown for Project 5. Table 11-16 shows the results for logic errors and Table 11-17 the detailed data handling errors. These data indicate that the most frequent error subtype (according to TRW's data) and the most serious subtype (according to Rubey's data) is *missing logic or condition tests.* The second most frequent and serious error subtype is *data initialization done improperly.*

Table 11-14   Characteristics Breakdown of Projects Analyzed

Approach	Software Type	Operating Mode	Language	Development
Project 2	Command and Control	Batch	JOVIAL J4	Single Increment*
Project 3	Command and Control	Batch	JOVIAL J4	Single Increment*
Project 4	Data Management	Time-Critical Batch	PWS MACRO	Operational
Project 5	Applications Software	Real-Time	FORTRAN	Top-Down Multiple Increment
	Simulator Software	Real-Time	FORTRAN	Top-Down Multiple Increment
	Operating System	Real-Time	Assembly	Top-Down Multiple Increment
	PA Tools	Batch	FORTRAN	Single Increment*

* "Single increment" refers to a typical development cycle where each development phase is performed only once. This is in contrast to the top-down, multiple increment approach where the cycle is repeated several times, first for a system of stubs and subsequently for replacement of stubs with deliverable software.

Table 11-15   Percentage Breakdown of Code Change Errors into Major Error Categories

Project 5 Major Error Categories	Proj. 3 (%)	Proj. 4 (%)	Applications Software (%)	Simulator Software (%)	Operating System (%)	Project 5 PA Tools (%)
Computational (A)	9.0	1.7	13.5	19.6	2.5	0
Logic (B)	26.0	34.5	17.1	20.9	34.6	43.5
Data Input (C)	16.4	8.9	7.3	9.3	8.6	5.5
Data Output (E)						
Data Handling (D)	18.2	27.2	10.9	8.4	21.0	9.3
Interface (F)	17.0	22.5	9.8	6.7	7.4	0
Data Definition (G)	0.8	3.0	7.3	13.8	7.4	3.7
Data Base (H)	4.1	2.2	24.7	16.4	4.9	2.8
Other (J)	8.5	0	9.4	4.9	13.6	35.2

Table 11-16   Project 5 Detailed Error Category Breakdown

| Detailed Error Categories | Percent of Major Category | | | |
	Applications Software	Simulator Software	Operating System S/W	PA Tools
B000 Logic Errors	2.1	8.3	0	4.3
B100 Incorrect Operand in Logical Expression	21.3	6.2	7.1	4.3
B200 Logic Activities out of Sequence	17.0	29.2	10.7	10.6
B300 Wrong Variable Being Checked	4.3	8.3	14.3	2.1
B400 Missing Logic or Condition Test	46.8	39.6	60.7	76.6

Table 11-17   Project 5 Detailed Error Category Breakdown (continued)

| Detailed Error Categories | Percent of Major Category | | | |
	Applications Software	Simulator Software	Operating System S/W	PA Tools
D000 Data Handling Errors	10.0	21.1	11.8	70.0
D100 Data Initialization not Done	6.7	10.5	17.6	0
D200 Data Initialization Done Improperly	20.0	10.5	41.2	10.0
D300 Variable Used as a Flag or Index not Set Properly	20.0	5.3	23.5	10.0
D400 Variable Referred to by Wrong Name	6.7	21.1	0	0
D500 Bit Manipulation done Incorrectly	10.0	0	0	0
D600 Incorrect Variable Type	3.3	10.5	0	0
D700 Data Packing/Unpacking Error	10.0	5.3	0	10.0
D900 Subscripting error	13.3	15.7	5.9	0

Another interesting study performed by TRW was to analyze error types according to major error categories. A particular error will have its source in one of the following stages of development: requirements, specifications, design, or coding. TRW performed this detailed analysis for 23 major error categories during the design and coding stages of development for Project 3. The results are shown in Table 11-18.

Table 11-18   Project 3 Error Sources

MAJOR ERROR CATEGORIES		% of TOTAL CODE CHANGE ERRORS	PROBABLE SOURCES	
			% DESIGN	% CODE
Computational	(AA)	9.0	90	10
Logic	(BB)	26.0	88	12
I/O	(CC)	16.4	24	76
Data Handling	(DD)	18.2	25	75
Operating System/ System Support Software	(EE)	0.1	(1)	
Configuration	(FF)	3.1	24	76
Routine/Routine Interface	(GG)	8.2	93	7
Routine/System Software Interface	(HH)	1.1	73	27
Tape Processing Interface	(II)	0.3	90	10
User Requested Change	(JJ)	6.6	83	17
Database Interface	(KK)	0.8	10	90
User Requested Change	(LL)	0	(2)	
Preset Database	(MM)	4.1	79	21
Global Variable/ Compool Definition	(NN)	0.8	62	38
Recurrent	(PP)	1.3	(1)	
Documentation	(QQ)	0.8	(1)	
Requirements Compliance	(RR)	0.4	89	11
Unidentified	(SS)	1.0	(1)	
Operator	(TT)	0.7	(1)	
Questions	(UU)	1.1	(1)	
Averages			62%	38%

Notes: (1) Although errors in these categories required changes to the code, their source breakdown of design versus code is not attempted here. Those categories considered in all other categories encompass 95 percent of all code change errors. (2) For Project 3 product enhancements or changes to the design baseline were considered "out-of-scope" and, therefore are not present here.

The following observations are offered about the data in Table 11-18. The over-all result shown—62 percent of all errors being design errors and 38 percent coding errors—is representative of what other studies of similar data have shown. A rule-of-thumb used in the industry is that about 65 percent of all the errors will be design errors and 35 percent coding errors. The fact that 65 percent of all errors are design errors suggests why the average cost of an error is so high. Another point illustrated by Table 11-18 is the high cost of logic errors. Indeed, logic errors are the most frequent and, considering that 88 percent of logic errors are design errors, they contribute enormously to the cost of a given development. These data and this observation reinforce the point made by Rubey's data: logic errors are the most seri-ous error type. One of the implications of this result is that work done by SQA per-sonnel with specifications should be heavily concentrated in the areas of logic and data handling.

A further area to investigate is the identification of internal modules within a system that can result in high cost. That is, is there a way to identify the modules whose errors will have a large impact on the cost of the system? Specifically, a mod-ule's error becomes costly if that module has many affects on the rest of the modules in a system. A given module could be highly "coupled" with the rest of a system as a result of the parameters it passes, the global data it affects, the interrupts it can cause, or the modules it involves. If such a highly coupled module has errors, it can be very costly since erroneous assumptions made in the module can be spread throughout the rest of the system. The SQA personnel should look at module cou-pling to assure that it is minimized. It should be noted that the term module can be applied to any internal unit of a system.

The main references for this section are "Module Connection Analysis" [9] and *Applied Software Engineering Techniques.* [13]

Assume that a system is decomposed into N modules. These are N^2 pairwise relationships of the form

P_{ij} = probability that a change in module i necessitates a change in module j

Let P be the N by N matrix with elements P_{ij}. Let A be a vector with N ele-ments that corresponds to a set of "zero-order" changes to a system. That is, A is the set of immediate changes that are contemplated for a system without considering intramodule side effects. The total number of changes T will be much greater than A because of the coupling and dependency of the modules. An approximation of the total amount of changes T is given by:

$$T = A \ (I - P) - 1$$

where I is the identity matrix.

An example from a Xerox System will be used to illustrate. The Probability connection matrix P for the Xerox System is shown in Figure 11-6.

	1	2	3	4	5	6	7	8	9	10	11	12	13	14	15	16	17	18
1	.2	.1	0	0	0	.1	0	.1	0	.1	.1	1	0	0	0	.1	0	0
2	0	.2	0	0	.1	.1	.1	0	0	0	0	0	.1	.1	.1	0	.1	0
3	0	0	.1	0	0	0	0	0	0	0	0	0	0	0	0	0	0	0
4	0	.1	0	.2	0	.1	.1	.1	0	0	0	0	0	0	.1	0	.1	0
5	.1	0	0	0	.4	.1	.1	.1	0	0	0	0	0	0	0	0	.1	0
6	.1	0	0	0	0	.3	.1	0	0	.1	0	0	0	.1	0	0	.1	0
7	.1	0	0	.1	.2	.1	.3	.1	0	.1	0	0	0	.1	0	.1	.1	0
8	.1	.1	0	.1	.2	0	.1	.4	0	.1	0	0	0	.1	0	0	0	.1
9	0	0	0	0	0	0	0	0	.1	0	0	0	0	0	0	0	0	0
10	.1	0	0	0	0	.1	.1	.1	0	.4	.2	.1	.2	.1	.1	.1	.1	.1
11	.1	0	0	.1	0	0	0	0	0	.2	.3	.1	0	0	0	0	0	0
12	.2	0	0	0	0	.1	0	0	0	0	.2	.3	0	0	.1	.1	0	0
13	.1	.1	0	0	0	.1	.1	.1	0	.2	.1	0	.3	0	0	0	0	0
14	0	0	0	0	0	0	0	0	0	0	0	0	0	.2	0	0	0	0
15	0	0	0	0	0	0	0	0	0	0	0	0	0	0	.2	0	0	0
16	0	0	0	0	0	0	0	0	0	0	0	0	0	0	0	.2	0	0
17	0	0	0	0	0	0	0	0	0	0	0	0	0	0	0	0	.2	0
18	0	0	0	0	1	0	1	0	0	.1	0	0	0	0	0	0	0	.3

Figure 11-6 Probability connection matrix P.

Let us look at P_{48}; $P_{48} = 0.1$, indicating a 10 percent probability that if module 4 is changed then module 8 will also have to be modified.

Let us assume that a global change to the system is to be made that will result in modification to many of the modules. This global set of zero-order changes can be represented as a vector A (Table 11-19). (These are actual changes per module that were applied to the Xerox System during a specified period.)

Given A, one can now compute the approximation T of the total number of changes that will be required. This is done by computing

$$T = A (I - P)^{-1}$$

where I is the 18 × 18 identity matrix.

The results are shown in Table 11-20.

Table 11-19   Changes Per Module

A(1)	2	A(2)	8
A(3)	4	A(4)	6
A(5)	28	A(6)	12
A(7)	8	A(8)	28
A(9)	4	A(10)	8
A(11)	40	A(12)	12
A(13)	16	A(14)	12
A(15)	12	A(16)	28
A(17)	28	A(18)	40

Notice the factor of 10 increase of total work over the initial set of changes; this is caused by the ripple effect of a change through highly coupled modules. The approximation of 2963.85 is within 4 percent of what Xerox actually experienced. [9]

Table 11-20   Module Changes Required

Module	Xerox System: Initial & Final Changes	
	Initial Changes (A)	Total Changes $T = A(I - P)^{-1}$
1	2	241.817
2	8	100.716
3	4	4.4444
4	6	98.1284
5	28	248.835
6	12	230.376
7	8	228.951
8	28	257.467
9	4	4.4444
10	8	318.754
11	40	238.609
12	12	131.311
13	16	128.318
14	12	157.108
15	12	96.1138
16	28	150.104
17	28	188.295
18	40	139.460
TOTALS	296	2963.85

The results in Table 11-20 clearly indicate that modules 10, 1, and 7 are highly coupled with the rest of the system. Module 10, for example, initially has eight changes and ends up with 318 spillover cumulative changes in all modules. On the other hand, module 3 initially has four changes and ends up with only four changes.

The point is that by identifying the modules with the highest coupling (modules with maximum rows of probabilities in P) one can anticipate which modules are most dangerous to modify. Similarly, errors in these same modules will have an enormous impact on the rest of the system since the errors have to be removed not only from these modules but also from all the coupled modules. The errors made in these highly coupled modules will be the most costly. [11, pp. 17–21] It is clear from this that Pareto analysis helps by identifying the focus areas that cause most of the problems. Fixing these problems will usually give you the best return on investment. [14, p. 133]

11.6 Inspection

The Pareto Principle has been applied to the assembly line inspection process by Juran. He suggests setting up a special study to secure the data for the needed distribution. Trained inspection personnel of proven accuracy are assigned to audit each work station for a period of time long enough (about a month) to establish the station-to-station variability. (The alternative of planning all inspectors at the end of the line is a waste of inspection effort. It also increases the lag between operation and detection. In cases where prior operations are buried by later operations, no ready check is possible at the end of the line.) The operators are then classed A, B, and C, respectively. These classifications are then used, in accordance with the Pareto Principle, as an aid in planning the distribution of inspection effort among the assembly line stations. [5, p. 41-12]

Like the assembly line, the programming process has a series of operations, each operation having its own exit criteria (see Chapter 9 for further details). There must be some means of measuring completeness of the product at any point of its development by inspections or testing. Then, the measured data may be used by SQA personnel for controlling the process more effectively. It has not been found to get in the way of programming, but has instead enabled higher predictability then other means.

This section uses the principles discussed in Michael E. Fagan's "Design and Code Inspections to Reduce Errors in Program Development" [15] to guide the use of the Pareto Principle in the programming process (detailed analysis is made by James Dobbins in Chapter 9). For design inspection, participants, using the design documentation, literally do their homework to try to understand the intent and logic of the design. To increase their error detection in the inspection, the inspection team should first study the ranked distributions of error types found by recent design and code inspections, such as shown in Tables 11-21 and 11-22. This study will prompt them to concentrate on the most fruitful areas (what is called the vital few).

Table 11-21 Summary of Design Inspections by Error Type (Order by Error Frequency) [15, p. 192]

VP Individual Name	Inspection file				
	Missing	Wrong	Extra	Errors	Error %
LO Logic	126	57	24	207	39.8
PR Prologue/Prose	44	38	7	89	17.1
CD CB Definition	16	2	18		3.5 } 10.4
CU CB Usage	18	17	1	36	6.9
OT Other	15	10	10	35	6.7
MD More Detail	24	6	2	32	6.2
IC Interconnect Calls	18	9		27	5.2
TB Test & Branch	12	7	2	21	4.0
MN Maintainability	8	5	3	16	3.1
RM Return Code/Msg	5	7	2	14	2.7
IR Interconnect Reqts	4	5	2	11	2.1
PE Performance	1	2	3	6	1.2
RU Register Usage	1	2		3	.6
L3 Higher Lvl Docu.	1			2	.4
PD Pass Data Areas		1		1	.2
FS FPFS	1			1	.2
MA Mod Attributes	1			1	.2
ST Standards					
	295	168	57	520	100.0
	57%	32%	11%		

Copyright © 1976 IBM Corp.. Reprinted with permission from the *IBM System Journal*, Vol. 15, No. 3 (1976).

Tables 11-21 and 11-22 show the common symptoms for defects in the design and code respectively. From the defect identification section above, it is a logical extension to the basic causes for these defects. The basic causes are shown in Tables 11-23 and 11-24.

Table 11-22   Summary of Code Inspections by Error Type (Order by Error Frequency)[15, p. 192]

| VP Individual Name | Inspection file | | | Errors | Error % |
	Missing	Wrong	Extra		
LO Logic	33	49	10	92	26.4
DE Design Error	31	32	14	77	22.1
PR Prologue/Prose	25	24	3	52	14.9
CU CB Usage	3	21	1	25	7.2
CC Code Comments	5	17	1	23	6.6
IC Interconnect Calls	7	9	3	19	5.5
MN Maintainability	5	7	2	14	4.0
PU PL/S or BAL Use	4	9	1	14	4.0
PE Performance	3	2	5	10	2.9
FI		8		8	2.3
TB Test & Branch	2	5		7	2.0
RU Register Usage	4	2		6	1.7
SU Storage Usage	1			1	.3
OT Other					
	123	185	40	348	100.0

Copyright © 1976 IBM Corp. Reprinted with permission from the *IBM System Journal*, Vol. 15, No. 3 (1976).

One of the most significant benefits of inspections is the detailed feedback of results on a relatively real-time basis. Because there is early indication from the first few units of work inspected, the individual is able to show improvement, and usually does, on later work even during the same project. [15, p. 197]

Table 11-23   Basic Causes for Design Defects

	Errors	%	Cumulative %
Unclear Requirements	17	3	100
Missing Requirements	34	7	97
Design	307	59	59
Poor Standards	125	24	83
Miscellaneous	37	7	90

Table 11-24   Basic Causes for Code Defects

	Errors	%	Cumulative %
Unclear Design	84	24	91
Missing Design	117	34	34
Coder	115	33	67
Poor Standards	24	7	98
Miscellaneous	8	2	100

11.7   Statistical Techniques

The use of statistical analysis as an extension to Pareto analysis is discussed first in light of existing techniques, then extended to software techniques.

Figure 11-7 shows the frequency of errors of various types in a sampling of high volume claim documents. Figure 11-8 shows the same data arranged according to the Pareto analysis.

The design and code inspections defect distributions previously shown in Tables 11-21 and 11-22 were adapted from Fagan (Reference 15). Tables 11-25 and 11-26 show how they originally appeared in the article. So, Tables 11-21 and 11-22 are the result of arranging the data according to the Pareto analysis.

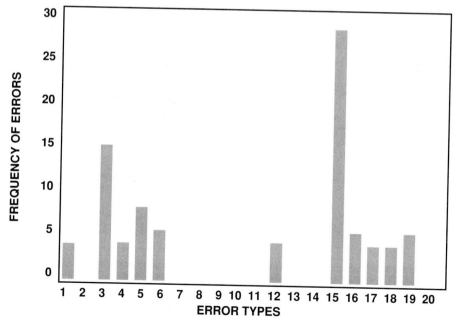

Figure 11-7   Frequency of error types in claim documents. [5, p. 46-11]

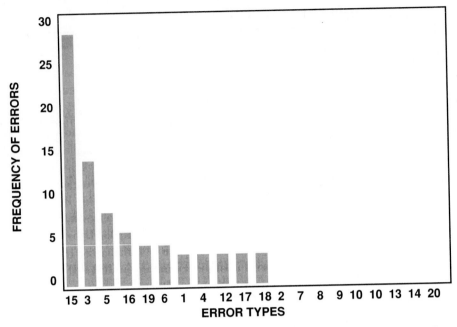

Figure 11-8   Pareto analysis of error types in claim documents. [5, p. 46-11]

In preparing bids, experienced managers know that a few major components are decisive; the rest can be thrown in as a percentage. In valuing a plant, the experienced engineer singles out the major pieces of equipment and values them individually. The rest he or she figures as a percentage, or studies a sample and applies the findings to all. [4, p. 50] In the preparation of software bids, the details required and desired are excruciatingly painful to supply. The rule of the trivial many especially applies here. The experienced manager should supply a software bid solidly based upon the vital few components with percentages taken for the trivial many components.

Table 11-25   Summary of Design Inspections by Error Type [15, p. 192]

VP Individual Name	Inspection file				
	Missing	**Wrong**	**Extra**	**Errors**	**Error %**
CD CB Definition	16	2	18		3.5 ⎫ 10.4
CU CB Usage	18	17	1	36	6.9 ⎭
FS FPFS	1			1	.2
IC Interconnect Calls	18	9		27	5.2
IR Interconnect Reqts	4	5	2	11	2.1
LO Logic	126	57	24	207	39.8
L3 Higher Lvl Docu.	1			2	.4

Table 11-25   (continued)

VP Individual Name	Inspection file				
	Missing	Wrong	Extra	Errors	Error %
MA Mod Attributes	1			1	.2
MD More Detail	24	6	2	32	6.2
MN Maintainability	8	5	3	16	3.1
OT Other	15	10	10	35	6.7
PD Pass Data Areas		1		1	.2
PE Performance	1	2	3	6	1.2
PR Prologue/Prose	44	38	7	89	17.1
RM Return Code/Msg	5	7	2	14	2.7
RU Register Usage	1	2		3	.6
ST Standards					
TB Test & Branch	12	7	2	21	4.0
	295	168	57	520	100.0
	57%	32%	11%		

Copyright © 1976 IBM Corp. Reprinted with permission from the *IBM System Journal*, Vol. 15, No. 3 (1976).

Table 11-26   Summary of Code Inspections by Error Type [15, p. 192]

VP Individual Name	Inspection file				
	Missing	Wrong	Extra	Errors	Error %
CC Code comments	5	17	1	23	6.6
CU CB Usage	3	21	1	25	7.2
DE Design Error	31	32	14	77	22.1
FI		8		8	2.3
IC Interconnect Calls	7	9	3	19	5.5
LO Logic	33	49	10	92	26.4
MN Maintainability	5	7	2	14	4.0
OT Other					
PE Performance	3	2	5	10	2.9
PR Prologue/Prose	25	24	3	52	14.9
PU PL/S or BAL Use	4	9	1	14	4.0
RU Register Usage	4	2		6	1.7
SU Storage Usage	1			1	.3
TB Test & Branch	2	5		7	2.0
	123	185	40	348	100.0

Copyright © 1976 IBM Corp. Reprinted with permission from the *IBM System Journal*, Vol. 15, No. 3 (1976).

Once a project is being executed, the job of controlling it in order to meet delivery schedules involves the Pareto Principle. For instance, to production control personnel, the "vital few" are the "bottlenecks." Formalized approaches—CPM (critical path method) or PERT (program evaluation and review technique)—for predicting bottlenecks in complex system planning have coined the term "critical path" as a label for the vital few. [4, p. 47] Many software projects have been controlled by CPM or PERT so there is nothing new here except the realization of it being another aspect of the Pareto Principle.

For software testing, a unique statistical methodology has been devised by Dr. C. K. Cho and is covered in Chapter 19. The input domain of a piece of software can be represented by a Symbolic Input Attribute Decomposition (SIAD) tree. The choice of input units using the SIAD tree is a statistical application of Pareto analysis since it is virtually impossible to use every input in the testing.

11.8　Pareto Chart Comparison

Quality improvement teams use the Pareto chart extensively to focus on the important causes of trouble. But what happens when a team needs to compare one Pareto chart against another? The answer, provided by Ron Kennett in "Making Sense Out of Two Pareto Charts," [16] is the M-test, which signals significant differences in the distribution of errors. The M-test indicates whether differences between two Pareto charts can be attributed to random variation or to special causes. Such a signal is crucial if one wants to determine the impact of changes in working procedures or of new engineering tools and techniques.

Without such a statistical tool, random differences can be mistakenly interpreted as improvements (or deteriorations) and real improvements ignored as just noise. For concreteness, the technique is explained based upon data from an article by D. E. Knuth on changes made in development of TEX, a software system for typesetting, during a period of ten years.

Knuth's logbook contains 516 items for the 1978 version, labeled TEX78, and 346 items for the 1982 version, labeled TEX82. These entries are classified into 15 categories (K = 15):

A = Algorithm	L = Language
B = Blunder	M = Mismatch
C = Cleanup	P = Portability
D = Data	Q = Quality
E = Efficiency	R = Robustness
F = Forgotten	S = Surprise
G = Generalization	T = Typo
I = Interaction	

The A, B, D, F, L, M, R, S and T classifications represent development errors. The C, E, G, I, P, and Q classifications represent "enhancements" consisting of unanticipated features that had to be added in later development phases. These enhancements indicate that the developers did not adequately understand customer requirements and, as such, can be considered failures of the requirements analysis process.

Taking the 516 reported errors in TEX78 as a standard against which the 346 errors in TEX82 are measured provides another opportunity to use the M-test. In this example, the categories are in alphabetical order to facilitate the comparison between TEX78 and TEX82. For Knuth's data $K = 15$ and for a significance level of 1 percent, one derives by interpolation in the M-test table that $C = 3.2$. Table 11-27 presents the various data and computations necessary to perform the M-test. An asterisk indicates a significant difference at the 1 percent level. TEX82 contains significantly more errors in the cleanup (C), efficiency (E), and robustness (R) categories than TEX78. Significantly fewer errors are found in blunder (B), forgotten (F), language (L), mismatch (M), and quality (Q).

The Pareto chart is an essential ingredient in any quality improvement effort. Most report packages on software error data include such charts. The M-test helps to compare different Pareto charts by pointing out what differences are indeed significant and therefore deserve further attention.

Table 11-27 Data and Computations Needed to Perform M-Test [16, p. 72]

Category	TEX78	Pi	TEX82	Ei	Si	Zi
A	23	0.04	14	15.42	3.84	-0.37
B*	42	0.08	7	28.16	5.09	-4.16*
C*	37	0.07	85	24.81	4.80	12.54*
D	36	0.07	19	24.14	4.74	-1.08
E*	17	0.03	23	11.40	3.32	3.49*
F*	50	0.10	13	33.53	5.50	-3.73*
G	60	0.12	48	40.23	5.96	1.30
I	74	0.14	59	49.62	6.52	1.44
L*	30	0.06	2	20.12	4.35	-4.16*
M*	25	0.05	0	16.76	3.99	-4.20*
P	10	0.02	12	6.71	2.56	2.06
Q*	54	0.10	14	36.21	5.69	-3.90*
R*	23	0.04	30	15.42	3.84	3.80*
S	24	0.05	20	16.09	3.92	1.00
T	11	0.02	0	7.38	2.69	-2.75

* Indicates differences significant at least at the 1 pecent level.

11.9   Conclusions

A broad survey of the Pareto Principle was presented. This included some historical perspective leading to the use of the Pareto Principle as an effective quality tool for detecting major error trends during the development of software projects. Extensions of the Pareto Principle to software have been drawn from the areas of defect identification, inspections, and statistical techniques.

In summary, the steps for the application of the Pareto Principle are given by Juran [4, p. 44] as follows:

1. Make a *written* list of all that stands "between us and making this change."
2. Arrange this list *in order of importance*.
3. Identify the *vital few* as projects to be dealt with individually.
4. Identify the *trivial many* as things to be dealt with as a class.

In software, as well as in general, the list of the vital few (through use of the Pareto Principle) does *not* come as a complete surprise to all concerned: some of the problems on the list have long been notorious. But, to be sure, some of the problems will come as a genuine surprise. Indeed, the big accomplishment of the Pareto analysis is rather that! In summary,

1. Some notorious projects are confirmed as belonging among the vital few.
2. Some projects, previously not notorious, are identified as belonging among the vital few.
3. The trivial many are identified. This is not new, but the extent is usually shocking.
4. The magnitudes of both the vital few and the trivial many are, to the extent practicable, quantified. Ordinarily, this is not done.
5. There is established a meeting of the minds as to priority of needs for breakthrough. This is the biggest contribution of all since the Pareto analysis sets the stage for action.

The Pareto analysis also provides an early check on the attitude toward breakthrough. If either the vital few or the trivial many look like good candidates for change, then the original hunch is confirmed, so far. If, on the other hand, the Pareto analysis shows that none of these is economically worth tackling, that is likely the end of the matter. [4, pp. 51, 52]

Much has already been done in the application of the Pareto Principle to software, but there is much more to work on. Emphasis on the vital few has produced a payoff, but there are always ways to improve the take. In fact, with the availability of the PC and its related software packages on the desk of every manager or analyst wanting to perform Pareto analysis, there is more reason for greater payoff. Some examples follow:

- Quality assurance departments in today's companies tend to rely heavily upon personal computers as tools to aid in preventing, detecting, and solving problems before or as they occur. PCs contain software packages that include Microsoft Office, Lotus 1-2-3, SQCpack, Netshell, Statgraphics, and WordPerfect word processing. SPCpack offers a Pareto charting option that enables the user to chart by count or cost, and to include percentage of total on the graph. [17, pp. 26–29]
- Another package is QA/S SPC software, developed by Hertzler Systems Inc. of Goshen, IN, that offers both a variable system with real-time charting and alarms, and an attribute, statistical process control (SPC) system with multilevel Pareto analysis. [18, pp. 111–114]
- Crystal Ball 3.0 adds sensitivity charts, which let you pick the most significant variables from a complex model—once your model contains more than a half dozen assumption distributions, you really need this feature. New distributions in version 3.0 include Pareto, etc. [19, p. 83]

The latest implementation is even at the personal level. Watts Humphrey has included Pareto analysis as an integral aspect of the process: "With PSP [Personal Software Process^{SM}] quality management and engineers track their own defects, find defect removal yields, and calculate cost-of-quality measures. Pareto defect analysis is used to derive personal design and code review checklists, which the engineers update with defect data from each new project." [20, pp. 3–6]

References

1. Arthur, Lowell Jay, "Quantum Improvements in Software System Quality." In: *Communications of the ACM*, Vol. 40, No. 6, June 1887.
2. Arthur, Lowell Jay, *Improving Software Quality: An Insider's Guide to TQM* (New York: John Wiley and Sons, Inc., 1993).
3. Dunn, Robert H., *Software Quality Concepts and Plans* (Englewood Cliffs: Reprinted by permission from Prentice Hall, Inc., © 1990).
4. Juran, J. M., *Managerial Breakthrough* (New York: McGraw-Hill Book Co, Inc., 1964).
5. Juran, J. M.; Gryna Jr., Dr. Frank M.; & Bingham Jr., R. S. (editors), *Quality Control Handbook* (3rd edition) (New York: McGraw-Hill Book Co, Inc., 1979).
6. McCabe, Thomas J., *SQA—A Survey* (Columbia: McCabe Press, 1980).
7. McCabe, Thomas J., *SQA—Seminar Notes* (Columbia: McCabe Press, 1980).

8. McCabe & Associates, Inc., *Phase I Report of Software Quality Assurance Project for the Federal Reserve Bank of New York*. General Purpose Computer Dept., July 29, 1982.

9. Haney, F. A. "Module Connection Analysis." In: *AFIPS Conference Proceedings*, Vol. 4, 1972 Fall Joint Computer Conference, AFIPS Press.

10. Portions reprinted, with permission, from Rubey, Dana and Biche "Quantitative Aspects of Software Validation." In: *IEEE Transactions on Software Engineering*, © June 1975, IEEE.

11. McCabe, Thomas J. "Cost of Error Analysis and Software Contract Investigation." In: *PRC Technical Note PRC 819-5*, 20 Feb. 1979, Contract No. DCA 100-77-C-0067.

12. Thayer et al, *Software Reliability* (New York: North-Holland Publishing Co., 1978).

13. McCabe, Thomas J., *Applied Software Engineering Technique*. Control Data Corp., 1975.

14. Kan, Stephen H., *Metrics and Models in Software Quality Engineering*, (extracted from pages 4, 7, 8, 47). © 1995 Addison-Wesley Publishing Company, Inc., Reprinted by permission of Addison-Wesley Longman Inc. (Reading: Addison-Wesley Publishing Company, 1995).

15. Fagan, Michael E. "Design and Code Inspections to Reduce Errors in Program Development." In: *IBM System Journal*, Vol. 15, No. 3, 1976. pp. 182–211.

16. Kennett, Ron S., "Making Sense Out of Two Pareto Charts." In: *Quality Progress*, May 1994, pp. 71–73.

17. Claussen, Lisa R., "PC Software is Vital Quality Assurance Tool at Speed Queen." In: *Industrial Engineering*, December 1988, pp. 26–31.

18. Carson, "Scrap, Defect Rates Cut by 50%." In: *Quality*, vol. 30, no. 4, April 1996.

19. Seiter, Charles, "Crystal Ball 3.0." In: *MacWorld,* Vol. 11, no. 10, October 1994.

20. Humphrey, Watts, "Making Software Manageable." In: *CrossTalk*, December, 1996, pp. 3–6.

General References

Samuelson, Paul A., *Economics, An Introductory Analysis* (New York: McGraw-Hill Book Co, Inc., 1951).

Miller, David W. and Starr, Martin K., *Executive Decisions and Operations Research* (2nd edition) (Englewood Cliffs: Prentice-Hall Inc., 1969).

Understanding the Capability Maturity Model (CMM^{SM}) and the Role of SQA in Software Development Maturity

Andreas Felschow
Technology and Process Consulting, Inc. (TPC)

This chapter introduces the reader to the Software Engineering Institute's (SEI) Software Capability Maturity Model (CMM) and discusses how implementing a software quality assurance program plays a role in the maturity of a software development organization.

12.1   Introduction to the CMM

The CMM was designed to help organizations initiate a program of process improvement through benchmarking their current software practices and then selecting strategies for orderly improvement of those issues where the organization recognized that the process could be improved. By focusing on a limited set of activities and working aggressively to achieve them, an organization can steadily improve its organizationwide software process to enable continuous and lasting gains in software process capability. Using the CMM helps instill a culture of software engineering and management excellence.

The CMM is based on a staged architecture similar to many of the principles of product quality that have existed for the last sixty years. In the 1930s, Walter Shewart promulgated the principles of statistical quality control. His principles were further developed and successfully demonstrated in the work of W. Edwards Deming [8] and Joseph Juran [5,6]. These principles, along with Philip Crosby's model [7] of the quality management maturity grid (Chapter 3) have been adapted by the SEI into a maturity framework that establishes a project management and engineering foundation for quantitative control of the software process, which is the basis for continuous process improvement.

---

^{SM} The CMM (Capability Maturity Model) is a service mark of the Software Engineering Institute.

12.2   Evolution of the CMM as a Framework for Continuous Process Improvement

In 1986, the SEI, with assistance from the Mitre Corporation, began developing a process maturity framework that would help organizations improve their software process. This effort was initiated in response to a request to provide the federal government with a method for assessing the capability of its software contractors. In September 1987, the SEI released a brief description of the process maturity framework and a maturity questionnaire [1,2]. The intention of the maturity questionnaire was to provide a simple tool for identifying areas where an organization's software process needed improvement. The questionnaire was a sampling of some of the key elements of the maturity framework. Unfortunately, in these initial stages, the maturity questionnaire was too often regarded as "the model" rather than as a vehicle for exploring process maturity issues.

After several years of using the framework and the preliminary version of the maturity questionnaire, the SEI evolved the software process maturity framework into the Capability Maturity Model for Software (CMM) [3]. As a result, the CMM further evolved from knowledge gained by conducting software process assessments and through extensive feedback from both industry and government.

The initial release of the CMM, version 1.0, was reviewed and used by the software community during 1991 and 1992 and was ultimately refined in April 1992. Version 1.1 [4] is the result of the feedback from workshops and ongoing feedback from the software community and is currently being used today. Associated with the release of version 1.1, a revised SEI maturity questionnaire was also released, which became extremely useful, since it was directly traceable to the goals and a sampling of the key practices of the CMM. Today, the questionnaire is used to "ballpark" an organization and allow the assessment team to focus on the key process areas identified as potential issue areas during the assessment. An essential point to remember is that the Capability Maturity Model, not the questionnaire, is the basis for improving the software process.

The obvious question many organizations ask is why use the CMM? The obvious answer is that it provides a framework for assessing and measuring an organization's software development capability. This allows organizations to compare results, if they so desire, and determine where their practices are in relationship to the CMM. Some of the true benefits of the CMM are that it is a benchmarking tool for the process, not the product. The focus of the CMM is to improve the process and, as a result of progress in process, the product will also improve.

One of the ideal characteristics of the CMM that makes it work for any organization is that it describes the software capability of an organization without prescribing the specific means for getting there. Basically, the CMM tells you what to do and the organization can define and document how to satisfy the "whats" of the CMM.

Therefore, the practices described are a well-founded expression of best practices independent of product/business lines. The use of the CMM facilitates identifying, importing, and adopting best practices from across the software community by use of standard language and goals. The CMM addresses practices that are the framework for process improvement in any software development environment. The CMM is not prescriptive; it does not tell an organization how to improve, which means that it

- does not limit the choice of life cycle
- neither requires nor precludes specific software technologies or language (e.g., prototyping, design method, coding, or testing practices)
- does not require that documentation conform to a particular set of standards (e.g., DOD-STD-2167A or IEEE)
- is the result of a national consensus of identifying practices that any organization should be practicing

Version 2.0 of the CMM, which is a continued elaboration of version 1.1, is expected to be released in 1998. Version 2.0 is a direct result from the SEI conducting CMM workshops and receiving feedback from the community as a whole.

12.3   Benefits of Using the CMM

After many years of unfulfilled promises about productivity and quality gains from applying new software methodologies and technologies, industry and government organizations began to realize that the fundamental problem was the inability to manage the software process. As a result of having conducted many software process assessments it was very evident that organizations attempting to mature through the use of better methods and tools could not successfully implement them due to the chaotic and undisciplined processes they were following. In many organizations, projects are often excessively late and double the planned budget. In such instances, the organization frequently is not providing the infrastructure and support necessary to help projects avoid these problems.

In an undisciplined organization, some software projects produce excellent results, however they tend to be the result of heroic efforts of a dedicated team, rather than through following a defined and repeatable process. In the absence of an organizationwide software process, repeating results depends entirely on having the same individuals available for the next project. Therefore, the success of new projects resides with the heroes or individuals, assuming they are available to work on the new projects. This concept provides no basis for long-term productivity and quality improvement throughout an organization. To achieve continuous improvement the organization must become focused and must commit to a dedicated effort towards building a process infrastructure of effective software engineering and management practices.

Setting sensible goals for process improvement requires understanding the difference between an immature and a mature software organization. In an immature software organization, software processes are generally improvised by practitioners and their management during the course of the project. Even if a software process has been defined or documented, it is typically not rigorously followed or enforced. The immature software organization tends to be reactionary with managers usually focused on solving immediate crises. Schedules and budgets are routinely overrun because they are not based on realistic estimates. Estimates are rarely based on any historical data. When hard deadlines are imposed, product functionality and quality are often compromised to meet the schedule.

Typically, in an immature organization, there is no objective basis for judging product quality or for solving product or process problems. Therefore, product quality is difficult to predict. Activities intended to assure quality, such as reviews and testing, are often cut short or even eliminated in order to meet the pressures of delivering a product on time.

In contrast, a mature software organization possesses an organizationwide ability for managing software development processes. The software process is routinely communicated to both existing staff and new employees, and work activities are carried out according to the planned process. The processes mandated are fit for use and consistent with the way the work actually gets done. These defined processes are updated when necessary, and improvements are developed through controlled pilot programs and/or cost benefit analyses. Roles and responsibilities within the defined process are clear throughout the project and across the organization.

In a mature organization, managers monitor the quality of the software products and customer satisfaction. As the organization continues to mature, there is a quantitative basis for judging product quality and analyzing problems with the product and process. Schedules and budgets are based on historical performance rather than personal experience and are typically realistic. The expected results for cost, schedule, functionality, and quality of the product are usually achieved in a timely manner. As a result, a disciplined process is consistently followed because of the buy-in of participants who were involved in the evolution of the process. As a result of being stakeholders they understand the value of following the process. Additionally, management willingly provides the necessary infrastructure required to support the process.

12.4   The Structure of the CMM

The CMM is organized into the five levels shown in Figure 12-1. The structure of the CMM prioritizes improvement actions for increasing software process maturity.

Capability Maturity Model

Level	Focus	Key Process Areas	Result
5 **Optimizing**	**Continuous** **Improvement**	Process Change Management Technology Change Management Defect Prevention	**Productivity** **& Quality**
4 **Managed**	**Product and** **Process** **Quality**	Software Quality Management Quantitative Process Management	
3 **Defined**	**Engineering** **Process**	Organization Process Focus Organization Process Definition Peer Reviews Training Program Intergroup Coordination Software Product Engineering Integrated Software Management	
2 **Repeatable**	**Project** **Management**	Software Project Planning Software Project Tracking & Oversight Software Subcontract Management Software Quality Assurance Software Configuration Management Requirements Management	
1 **Initial**	**Heroes**		RISK

Figure 12-1   The Capability Maturity Model.

In simple terms the five levels of the CMM can be described as follows:

Level 1: Initial

The software process is typically characterized as ad hoc, and occasionally even chaotic. Few processes are defined, and success depends on individual effort.

The organization typically does not provide a stable environment for developing and maintaining software. When an organization lacks sound management practices, the benefits of good software engineering practices are undermined by ineffective planning and reaction-driven commitment systems.

In a crisis, projects typically abandon planned procedures and revert to coding and testing. Often, many of the activities to assure the quality of the process are ignored in order to meet schedule. Success depends entirely on having an exceptional manager and a seasoned and effective software team. Occasionally, capable and forceful software managers can withstand the pressures to take shortcuts in the software process, but when they leave the project, their stabilizing influence leaves with them. Even a strong engineering process cannot overcome the instability created by the absence of sound management practices.

The software process capability of Level 1 organizations is unpredictable because the software process is constantly changing as the work progresses. Schedules, budgets, functionality, and product quality are generally unpredictable. Performance depends on the capabilities of individuals and varies with their innate skills, knowledge, and motivations. There are few stable software processes in evidence, and performance can be predicted only by individual rather than organizational capability.

Level 2: Repeatable

At Level 2 basic project management processes are established to estimate and track cost, schedule, and functionality. The necessary process discipline is in place to repeat earlier successes on projects with similar applications.

The organization puts policies for managing a software project in place and procedures to implement those policies are established. Planning and managing new projects is based on historical data, when available, rather than personal experience. An objective is to institutionalize effective management processes for software projects, which allow organizations to repeat successful practices developed on earlier projects, although the specific processes implemented by the projects may differ. An effective process can be characterized as practiced, documented, trained, enforced, and measured.

Projects at the Repeatable level have installed basic software management controls. Project commitments are based on the results observed on previous projects and on the requirements of the current project and tend to be more realistic. The software managers on the project track software costs, schedules, and functionality; problems in meeting commitments are identified when they arise. Software requirements and the work products developed to satisfy them are baselined, and their integrity is controlled. Software project standards are defined, and the organization ensures they are consistently followed. The software project works with its subcontractors, if any, to establish a strong customer-supplier relationship. If there are no subcontractors, the Subcontract Management Key Process Area can be considered to be not applicable to the organization and therefore, does not have to be included in a software process assessment.

The software process capability of Level 2 organizations can be summarized as disciplined, because planning and tracking of the software project is stable and earlier successes can be repeated. The project's process is under the effective control of a project management system, following realistic plans based on the performance of previous projects.

Level 3: Defined

The software process for both management and engineering activities is documented, standardized (where appropriate), and integrated into a standard software process for the organization. Projects use an approved, tailored version of the organization's standard software process for developing and maintaining software.

A standard process for developing and maintaining software across the organization is documented, including both software engineering and management processes, and these processes are integrated into a coherent whole. This standard process is referred to throughout the CMM as the organization's standard software process. The standard process does not have to be one process; the organizational process may consist of several different approaches to solving a particular process need. Processes established at Level 3 are used (and changed, as appropriate) to help the software managers and technical staff perform more effectively. The organization exploits effective software engineering practices when standardizing its software processes. There is a group that is responsible for the organization's software process activities, e.g., a software engineering process group, or SEPG [9]. An organization-wide training program is implemented to ensure that the staff and managers have the knowledge and skills required to fulfill their assigned roles. At Level 3 an organization understands its personnel's skill base which is contained in an organizational training plan.

Projects may tailor the organization's standard software process to develop their own defined software process, which accounts for the unique characteristics of the project. A defined software process contains a coherent, integrated set of well-defined software engineering and management processes. A well-defined process can be characterized as including readiness criteria, inputs, standards and procedures for performing the work, verification mechanisms (such as peer reviews), outputs, and completion criteria. Because the software process is well defined, management has good insight into technical progress on all projects.

The software process capability of Level 3 organizations can be summarized as standard and consistent because both software engineering and management activities are stable and repeatable. Within established product lines, cost, schedule, and functionality are under control, and software quality is tracked. This process capability is based on a common, organizationwide understanding of the activities, roles, and responsibilities in a defined software process.

Level 4: Managed
Detailed measures of the software process and product quality are collected. Both the software process and products are quantitatively understood and controlled.

The organization sets quantitative quality goals for both software products and processes. Productivity and quality are measured for important software process activities across all projects as part of an organizational measurement program. An organizationwide software process database is used to collect and analyze the data available from the projects' defined software processes. Software processes are instrumented with well-defined and consistent measurements. These measurements establish the objective foundation for evaluating the projects' software processes and products.

Projects achieve control over their products and processes by narrowing the variation in their process performance to fall within acceptable quantitative boundaries. Meaningful variations in process performance can be distinguished from random variation (noise), particularly within established product lines. The risks involved in moving up the learning curve of a new application domain are known and carefully managed.

The software process capability can be summarized as predictable because the process is measured and operates within measurable limits. This level of process capability allows an organization to predict trends in process and product quality within the quantitative bounds of these limits. When these limits are exceeded, action is taken to correct the situation. Software products are of predictably high quality.

Level 5: Optimizing

Continuous process improvement is enabled by quantitative feedback from the process and from piloting innovative ideas and technologies. Old technologies and methodologies can be successfully retired based on the quantitative understanding of the organization's processes.

The entire organization is focused on continuous process improvement. The organization has the means to identify weaknesses and strengthen the process proactively, with the goal of preventing the occurrence of defects. Data on the effectiveness of the software process is used to perform cost benefit analyses of new technologies and proposed changes to the organization's software process. Innovations that exploit the best software engineering practices are identified and transferred throughout the organization.

Software project teams analyze defects to determine their causes. Software processes are evaluated to prevent known types of defects from recurring, and lessons learned are disseminated to other projects.

The software process capability of the organization can be characterized as continuously improving because the organization is continuously striving to improve the range of their process capability, thereby improving the process performance of their projects. Improvement occurs both by incremental advancements in the existing process and by innovations using new technologies and methods.

12.5   Understanding Software Quality Assurance within the CMM

This section explores the implications that the CMM has placed on establishing fundamental software quality assurance practices. Software Quality Assurance is one of the six key process areas defined at the repeatable level of the CMM. The purpose of Software Quality Assurance, as described in the CMM, is to provide management with appropriate visibility into the process being used by the software project and of the products being built.

Software Quality Assurance involves reviewing and auditing the software products and activities to verify that they comply with the applicable procedures and standards and providing the software project and other appropriate managers with the results of these reviews and audits.

The CMM lists four goals that need to be achieved in order to satisfy the requirements for this key process area. The goals are stated as follows:

Goal 1—Software quality assurance activities are planned.

Goal 2—Adherence of software products and activities to the applicable standards, procedures, and requirements is verified objectively.

Goal 3—Affected groups and individuals are informed of software quality assurance activities and results.

Goal 4—Noncompliance issues that cannot be resolved within the software project are addressed by senior management.

Let us take a closer look at how these goals translate into a cultural style and a set of practices that the organization and projects must follow.

When SQA is referred to in the following text, it may be a group or an individual. The organization will have to determine whether the personnel performing the SQA tasks will be part-time or full-time personnel. This all depends on the number of projects and size of the organization.

The first and foremost step that any organization must commit to is the fact that software quality assurance is vital to the success of a project. Therefore, the organization needs to establish the infrastructure, which effectively provides the guidelines on how the projects are required to implement software quality assurance. Most organizations issue an organizationwide policy that addresses this infrastructure. Within the policy the organization provides guidance, which typically includes the following:

- An SQA function is in place on all software projects. This function is typically the responsibility of an independent group or person.
- The SQA group or person has a reporting channel to senior management that is independent of the project manager, the project's software engineering group, and other software-related groups.
- Adequate resources are provided to ensure that the SQA function is effectively carried through.
- Training is provided to the SQA personnel.
- Training is provided to the affected software engineering groups so they understand the role and responsibilities of the SQA group. This training should also include the value of SQA to the organization.

- Measurements are made and used to determine the cost, benefit, and status of the SQA activities.
- The SQA activities are reviewed with senior and project management on a periodic basis.
- Experts independent of the SQA group periodically review the activities and software work products of the project's SQA group.

To understand this infrastructure, senior management is committing to establishing an organization that will allow the SQA function to be somewhat independent. This is a very important concept since the independence will allow the individuals performing the SQA role with the freedom to be the "eyes and ears" of senior management on the software project. For many immature organizations, there is a lack of trust in the SQA personnel who are perceived to be there to act as the "process police" and will report the individuals to management. Senior management must instill a belief that the SQA personnel are there to verify compliance to the project's processes. If an organization is going to spend the energy to define, document, and train individuals on a process, it makes sense that there should be a mechanism in place to enforce that the process is being followed.

A second concept is that individuals performing the SQA role are protected from performance appraisals by the management of the software project they are reviewing. It would be very difficult for an individual to complete an objective review/audit of a process that is managed by their immediate supervisor. The impact of negative results from an SQA audit should never put the individual in an uncompromising position. This "second concept" is usually not a problem and often helps the SQA's supervisor in performing the performance review.

The SQA infrastructure should provide senior management with confidence that objective information on the process and products of the software project is being reported. This is usually accomplished by having an independent SQA group or function. With an independent review of the process and product, management would have an objective mechanism to verify that the process and product quality standards are being adhered to.

For the SQA personnel to be effective they will need special training. The training should include a good understanding of the following:

- software engineering skills and practices
- roles and responsibilities of the software engineering group and other software-related groups
- standards, procedures, and methods for the software project
- application domain of the software project
- SQA objectives, procedures, and methods

- involvement of the SQA group in the software activities
- effective use of SQA methods and tools
- interpersonal communications

   With an understanding of the infrastructure, the SQA organization must strategize, plan, and document the processes by which they will function on a project. For SQA to function effectively they need to be involved early in the planning stages of the project. It is important that they are involved in reviewing other project planning documents, and requirements. Following these steps will be fundamental in an organization with being compliant with the SQA key process area for Level 2.

   To best communicate their strategy on a project, SQA should issue an SQA plan. A procedure should be established by the organization providing specific guidance in what type of information the SQA plan should contain and the review and approval process for the plan. The following template may serve as an example of what typically goes into an SQA plan. By using this template an organization could satisfy the intent of CMM Level 2 for software quality assurance.

   A typical outline for an SQA Plan template is depicted in Figure 12-2. The type of information that should be included in the SQA plan is described below.

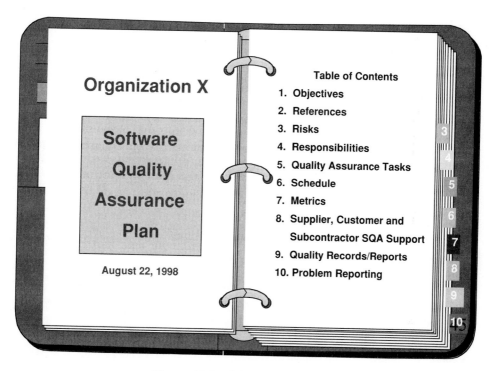

Figure 12-2   SQA plan outline.

Typical SQA Plan Contents

1. Objectives

This Software Quality Assurance Plan is based on procedure SQA-XXX (reference the procedure from which this SQA plan was written). This document calls out any procedures, plans, guidelines, or standards that are to be adhered to on this project. This plan has been reviewed and approved by senior and project management.

Specify quality objectives for the product. Express in measurable terms, if possible (i.e. all documentation reviewed and signed off, zero outstanding priority one problems, 100 percent code coverage during code inspections).

Provide an overview of the product and the project. If this is inappropriate, reference the document where the overview can be found.

2. References

Provide all references to other documents that are affected by SQA or the project that may be applicable to the SQA Plan.

3. Risks

State any risks or issues that are facing the SQA organization with respect to this project.

4. Responsibilities

Identify the responsibilities of the quality assurance manager, the project manager, personnel on the project and senior management with respect to the SQA Plan. State what the responsibilities of the SQA team are on this project and how they will interact with the other groups listed.

5. Quality Assurance Tasks

Identify the quality assurance tasks to be performed during the project and the responsible organizational groups (i.e. SQA, Engineering) for each of these tasks. Examples of quality assurance tasks are review documents, participate in document preparation, monitor project schedule, witness acceptance tests, and verify code review minutes. This section should identify the audits and reviews to be conducted by the SQA group. This section may also reference the project standards and procedures to be used as the basis for the SQA group's reviews and audits.

For each type of review, state how SQA will participate. Most projects have the following types of reviews:

- Contract Review
- Management Reviews
- Progress Reviews
- Technical Reviews
- Joint Reviews
- Software Development Plan and Planning Data Review

Identify any audits conducted by the quality group. These project audits determine compliance with contract requirements and project plans and procedures. Describe the procedure for handling nonconformances.

Describe the controls and process in place, which ensures that the overall project activities, as well as quality assurance activities, are being managed and tracked properly. This can include controls, such as:

- Program status meetings
- Review of program status reports
- Preparation of quality evaluation reports
- Quality audits
- Corrective action process
- Escalation of corrective action requests
- Operational software and support software
- Participation in the preparation and review of the project's software development plan, standards, and procedures
- Deliverable and nondeliverable products
- Software and nonsoftware products (e.g., documents)
- Product development and product verification activities (e.g., executing test cases
- Activities followed in creating the product

Describe or reference the process used to provide feedback to the project on SQA activities and the results of these activities.

6. Schedule for SQA activities

Provide a schedule of all SQA reviews and audits planned and any other appropriate milestones.

7. Metrics

The project metrics are typically captured in the project's Software Development Plan (SDP). The SQA metrics may be also included in the SDP, but at a minimum they should appear in the SQA plan and be referenced in the SDP.

Define the metrics that are to be collected during the project and describe their use. Product metrics should be reported and used to manage the development and delivery of the product. Examples of product metrics are number of defects, lines of new code, and lines of reused code. Process metrics should be reported and used to determine the quality of the development and delivery process. Examples of process metrics are the scheduled and actual duration of each development phase, estimated and actual project costs, and estimated and actual effort required for each phase.

Typically, the metrics associated for SQA at Level 2 are as follows:

- Completion of milestones compared to the SQA Plan
- The work completed
- Effort expended

Typical SQA Plan Contents (continued)

- Funds expended in the SQA activities compared to the plan
- Number of product audits and activity reviews compared to the plan
- Number of deviations noted by SQA

The rationale behind these measurements is to help the organization understand the cost of quality at this stage of maturity. The organization can then determine whether more funds should be allocated to SQA so they can perform more audits. In essence, the organization is trying to measure whether the funds expended for SQA are yielding a sufficient return on investment in terms of helping improve quality through their independent reviews. At Level 2 the requirement is not to have this analysis completed, but to collect the measures and to start to use the data to make those types of evaluations.

8. Supplier, Customer, and Subcontractor SQA Support

State the provisions for assuring that the supplier, customer, and the supplier's product meet established requirements. This may include reviews with subcontractors, and supplier or subcontractor audits.

9. Quality Records/Reports

Describe the documentation that the SQA group is required to produce. Identify the method and frequency of providing feedback to the software engineering group and other software-related groups on SQA activities.

Describe or list quality records that will be maintained on the project.

Describe the identification, collection, indexing, filing, storage, maintenance, and disposition of quality records.

10. Problem Reporting (Noncompliance Issues)

Describe procedures (or reference procedures) to be used to report, track, and resolve problems or defects identified in the software products. The appropriate procedures may be referenced, if applicable.

Describe procedures (or reference procedures) to be used to report, track, and resolve problems identified in the software development process. The appropriate procedures may be referenced, if applicable.

SQA should document or reference a procedure for handling deviations, which typically specifies that:

- Deviations from the software development plan and the designated project standards and procedures are documented and resolved with the appropriate software task leaders, software managers, or project manager, where possible.
- Deviations from the software development plan and the designated project standards and procedures not resolvable with the software task leaders, software managers, or project manager are documented and presented to the senior manager designated to receive noncompliance items.

- Noncompliance items presented to the senior manager are periodically reviewed until they are resolved.
- The documentation of noncompliance items is managed and controlled.

Describe the process to be used to detect and eliminate potential causes of problems or defects.

The plan will serve as the driving force for how the SQA organization will function on the project and what activities they will take in parallel with other software development activities. When new projects come along, the project will not have to reinvent the wheel and attempt to figure what goes into the plan. With time and experience the organization can learn valuable lessons from following the plan and improving the overall processes to make them more effective.

Once the plan is written it should be reviewed by the groups that are affected by the plan. The affected groups should be able to negotiate and ultimately have the plan officially approved by the project and the organization. Once the plan is approved, the SQA organization should manage according to the plan.

Once the SQA activities are identified in the plan, SQA should provide status to management. The primary purpose of periodic reviews with senior and project management is to provide awareness of and insight into software process activities at an appropriate level of abstraction and in a timely manner. The time between reviews should meet the needs of the organization.

Once the activities have been identified in the plan, the SQA group should implement the plan by conducting the approved tasks, reviews, and audits. Prior to initiating the reviews the SQA group verifies that plans, standards, and procedures are in place and can be used to review and audit the software project. The groups should provide consultation and review of the plans, standards, and procedures with regard to

- compliance to organizational policy
- compliance to externally imposed standards and requirements (e.g., standards required by the statement of work)
- standards that are appropriate for use by the project
- topics that should be addressed in the software development plan
- other areas as assigned by the project

At this point the SQA group now has the criteria for verifying compliance and may start the reviews of the software engineering activities to verify compliance. The activities are evaluated against the software development plan and the designated software standards and procedures. Once the processes have been reviewed the SQA group audits designated software work products to verify compliance. The intent is to have these reviews completed prior to the software products being delivered to the customer. The software work products are evaluated against the designated software standards, procedures, and contractual requirements.

As a result of the audits/reviews the SQA person has two possible actions to take. In the event an audit reveals a discrepancy, deviations are identified, documented, and tracked to closure. In this event the SQA group must also ensure that the corrections are verified. The deviations that are identified in the software activities and software work products are documented and the discrepancy/deviation report should be written following the documented procedure outlined in the SQA Plan.

Even for reviews/audits that result in no deviations being noted, the SQA group periodically reports the results of its activities to the software engineering group.

In keeping with the SQA activities progress, the SQA group should conduct periodic reviews of its activities and findings with the customer's SQA personnel. This should be done as appropriate, however the importance of this aspect of communication cannot be underestimated. Often times, the immature organization is dealing with an immature customer, who is not interested in paying for SQA. By communicating status to customer SQA personnel, the communication barrier is broken down, which is essential to the maturing organization. By communicating status and being open with the customer, they start to gain an understanding and respect for the rigor that the organization is going through to ensure quality. Once recognized, the customer tends to appreciate the efforts of SQA, often suggests more, and provides adequate funding to ensure that all their projects have the same level of quality assurance in place.

12.6   The Maturing QA Organization (Software Quality Management and the Quest for SQA Maturity)

In Section 12.5 we identified the basic practices that an SQA organization should establish in seeking maturity at the repeatable level. Typically, as the organization continues to mature, the SQA organization will also make great strides in terms of maturing their own capabilities. Usually the organization will have a sense of the value of SQA and will find that the efforts expended by the SQA organization to support the process are more than worth while. The maturing organization will typically expand the horizons of SQA by having the personnel involved in all phases of the development or maintenance life cycle.

The typical Level 2 project will have SQA review and/or audit a few of the processes of the life cycle. As the SQA organization expands its review capabilities, it will also begin to instrument many of its activities. Checklists will be established to simplify the reviews that SQA is to perform. As the checklists become institutionalized and understood by all project personnel the process reviews may begin to shift to the personnel on the project. This will allow SQA to review the most critical of activities, but with the implementation of the checklists, the organization has now educated itself on what quality means to the organization.

As the organization moves to Level 3, process checklists are quite common on all projects and the checklists are continuously being improved over time. There are no real "extra" criteria for an organization in terms of further establishing SQA standards at Level 3, with the exception of applying the same rigor of assuring quality through independent reviews and audits to the engineering processes. With the discipline established for the management processes the projects and organization are poised to accept software quality assurance practices as a part of the standard engineering processes. Also at Level 3 the results from the software quality assurance activities are being put into the process asset library. The result of this effort will be the source for all historical data associated with the organization's software quality assurance efforts. With the existence of historical data the organization can begin to think about measuring quality. In terms of additional measurements that are collected and used, the software quality assurance function will initiate the collection and use of defect data.

Associated with the measurements collected at Level 2 the organization can begin to understand the historical data collected and start to use it. With many organizations, schedule is the only measure of progress, so it is important for an organization that wishes to continue to mature and improve its capabilities to focus on quantitative quality measures. Within a Level 3 organization many of the measurements are still focused on status of activities. As the organization continues its journey to mature, the measurements focus turns to performance.

The purpose of Software Quality Management is to develop a quantitative understanding of the quality of the project's software products and processes. For a Level 4 organization the intent is to establish quality goals, establish mechanisms to quantitatively control the processes, and to ultimately achieve the goals that were estimated at the beginning of a project life cycle. It is important that the goals that are established meet the business goals established for the organization and the organization will have to establish a strategy and plans to accomplish these goals. Some of the aspects that the organization will have to consider include

- Establishment of the quality goals for the organization
- Definition of quality measures to define how the organization measures the progress towards meeting the quality goals
- Development of a Quality Plan
- Establishment of mechanisms to collect and analyze the measurements
- Establishment of a method to quantify metrics
- An understanding of the process tolerances
- Management of the process based on the established tolerances

With these principles in place the organization is in a position to achieve the quality goals that were established. To understand these principles let's take a closer look at each one.

One of the primary reasons senior management must be involved is to motivate the organization through action. In order to do this, senior management is usually in the best position to understand "quality" based on the customer's needs. Therefore they may be able to provide the most insight into what measures are the most reasonable. If numerical measures are not established at this point the effort may again take on the presence of just another management quality improvement initiative. If this is the case the quality program may not have a lasting impact, however usually organizations that have made it to this point are so focused on process and the desire to improve that this should not be a major issue. Some examples of quality goals that may and have been established for organizations are as follows:

- Lowering the number of defects/phase
- Reduction in number of defects impacting mission success
- Zero Defects
- Meeting customer's schedule
- Meeting budget estimates
- Reducing the cost to support a project
- Improving the productivity in terms of lines of code/complexity
- Simplifying software structure
- Improving software reliability and availability

The next step is to establish a mechanism for the measurements program. Figure 12-3 depicts a program for establishing a measurement program which is further defined in the Software Engineering Institute's technical report called *Measurement in Practice* (TR-16) [10].

When defining metrics it is not necessary to collect data on a large number of metrics to derive the business value from the data collected. One of the common pitfalls that many organizations fall into is that they attempt to make too many measurements at Level 4. It is important to collect information on a discrete set that can be analyzed effectively to improve the processes and products of the organization. A two-step process can be applied to choosing the appropriate metrics. First the organization needs to determine what business value exists for collecting the metric and secondly it is important to determine if the metric will be supported by the project and/or management. The metrics that are collected should be an indicator of process performance and process capability.

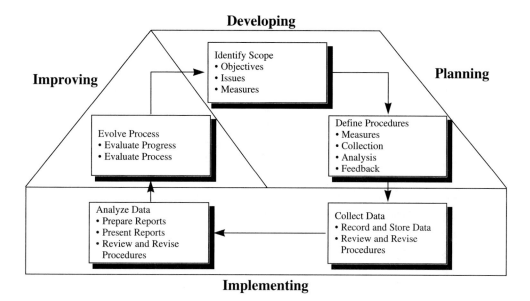

Figure 12-3   Program for establishing a Measurement Program.

When selecting measurements, the following criteria should be considered:

- Is the indicator used in measuring software process performance?
- Does the indicator help the project/organization understand overall process capability?
- Is the indicator an existing measure?
- Is the measurement hard to obtain?
- Does the organization have to derive the indicator based on complex algorithms?
- Is it easy to automate the collection and analysis of the measurement?
- To what extent can the value be changed by either a software development or maintenance action?
- Is the measurement available in a timely fashion to affect the software development or maintenance process?
- Can the measure collected be repeatedly used by various personnel?
- Can trends be established as a result of using the measurement over time?

Once a set of metrics is established, the organization must tie the goals and the metrics together. This is best achieved through the development of the Quality Plan.

This differs from the plan described earlier in the chapter. This plan should focus on the following aspects:

- Defining Quality for the Organization
- Measuring to represent quality
- Defining who your customers are and what their needs are
- Identifying and developing product features that meet customer needs
- Defining the processes that enable you to establish the product
- A strategy for putting this plan into action

With these concepts in place a mechanism must be established that will allow the organization to collect and analyze the metrics. The obvious approach would be to automate the collection and automation process, but that may not always be possible. It is important for the organization to think this effort through, or this may become one of the bottlenecks of the Level 4 process. When establishing the mechanism for collecting the metrics, the organization will have to understand whether the selected metrics will help

- determine how many dollars are saved versus the dollars invested
- increase productivity
- reduce defects
- move toward a reduction in error rates
- reduce problems during integration
- decrease the cost of rework
- translate the customers needs into a measure of quality
- reduce the time to market
- increase product quality
- increase process quality

These may be some of the goals that the organization looks at in terms of metrics at this time in the program. The key point is to establish a credible method for collecting the measure and having the ability to interpret what the measure means to the organization. If the analysis does not yield a meaningful metric, then it should be considered to be dropped from the program. Measures should be key indicators of performance that relate to the organization's quality goals.

With the completion of several product cycles, historical data should be available to begin to understand the process tolerances. By evaluating process tolerance the organization should be in a position to start to recognize if the performance measures are starting to push the limit of a defined tolerance level, then the appropriate management actions can be taken to bring the process into control. Essentially, the organization will be measuring the processes quality through these tolerance limits and putting corrective actions based on the ability of the organization to bring the process back under control. This is very valuable information to the organization since the data is now allowing the organization to start predicting the quality based on the measures that are being collected and analyzed.

The last aspect of this maturing quality program is for the organization to manage the program based on the measures it is collecting and analyzing. The organization will be able to start answering some tough questions like, is a particular process in the project within the defined parameters of a process based on historical data and, if not, what is causing the deviation? Another element to consider based on the management style is if a trend is developing based on the information being analyzed and does a process need to be adjusted to improve the process effectiveness? As more data is collected and analyzed the organization will begin performing root cause analysis of defects and take appropriate measures to prevent them from occurring.

As the organization continues its journey beyond Level 4 the effectiveness of the processes can be measured. The SQA organization will now have the capability to determine the cost, productivity, and quality of each of its activities. With this understanding the SQA organization can help determine which processes can be replaced by more efficient processes. Based on data gathered and interpreted, the organization will have the capability to prevent defects and will ultimately be in a proactive process and product quality program rather than in a reactive program, which is quite typical of Level 1 organizations. These concepts really have helped many organizations build quality into their development and maintenance processes, which is quite a contrast to those organizations that depend on quality to help discover the errors in the product and process as the project progresses.

In summary, the SQA organization goes through an education process by learning about the processes that the organization is using. Initially, the SQA organization is dependent on the software engineering organization to help understand the processes. With those processes defined, documented, and practiced the SQA organization has a mechanism for verifying compliance and for evaluating the infrastructure to be supported as a vital aspect of the project. As time goes on quality becomes a way of life for the entire organization and the project life cycles tend to operate more in harmony than the way they were several cycles before, when they were just beginning to learn about how to assure quality.

References

1. Humphrey, W. S., *Characterizing the Software Process: A Maturity Framework.* Software Engineering Institute, CMU/SEI-87-TR-11, ADA182895, June 1987.

2. Humphrey, W. S. and Sweet, W. L., *A Method for Assessing the Software Engineering Capability of Contractors*. Software Engineering Institute, CMU/SEI-87-TR-23, ADA187320, September 1987.

3. Paulk, M. C., Curtis, B., Chrissis, M. B., et al, *Capability Maturity Model for Software*. Software Engineering Institute, CMU/SEI-91-TR-24, ADA240603, August 1991.

4. Paulk, M. C., Weber, C. V., Garcia, S., Chrissis, M. B., and Bush, M., *Key Practices of the Capability Maturity Model,* Version 1.1, Software Engineering Institute, CMU/SEI-93-TR-25, February 1993.

5. Juran, J. M., *Juran on Planning for Quality*. (New York: Macmillan, 1988).

6. Juran, J. M., *Juran on Leadership for Quality*. (New York: The Free Press, 1989).

7. Crosby, P., *Quality is Free*. (New York: The New American Library, 1979).

8. Deming, W. Edwards, *Out of the Crisis*. (Cambridge, MA: MIT Center for Advanced Engineering Study, 1986).

9. Fowler, P. and Rifkin, S., *Software Engineering Process Group Guide*. Software Engineering Institute, CMU/SEI-90-TR-24, ADA235784, September, 1990.

10. Cox, C., Rifkin, S., *Measurement in Practice*. Software Engineering Institute, CMU/SEI-93-TR-16, July 1993

General References

Paulk, M. C., Curtis, B., Chrissis, M. B., et al, *Capability Maturity Model for Software*. Software Engineering Institute, CMU/SEI-91-TR-24, ADA240603, August 1991.

Paulk, M. C., Weber, C. V., Garcia, S., Chrissis, M. B., and Bush, M., *Key Practices of the Capability Maturity Model*, Version 1.1. Software Engineering Institute, CMU/SEI-93-TR-25, February 1993.

Report of the Defense Science Board Task Force on Military Software. Office of the Under Secretary of Defense for Acquisition, Washington, D.C., September 1987.

Humphrey, W. S., "Process Fitness and Fidelity." In: *Proceedings of the Seventh International Software Process Workshop*, 16–18 October 1991.

CHAPTER   1 3

SEI CMM^{SM} Level 5: Boeing Space Transportation Systems Software

Gary B. Wigle
Boeing Defense and Space Group

George Yamamura
Boeing Defense and Space Group

13.1   Introduction

The Space Transportation Systems (STS) organization within the Boeing Defense and Space Group (D&SG) in Seattle, Washington, has demonstrated that it is operating at a Level 5 using the Software Engineering Institute (SEI) Capability Maturity Model (CMM). This organization included a new start up launch vehicle program less than two years old and demonstrated successful deployment of high maturity processes. This chapter presents a case study associated with the experiences and challenges encountered on the road to process improvement certified at CMM Level 5. You will learn about the Boeing STS organization, its long history of process improvement, and the many obstacles it had to overcome to succeed. Also, you will learn about the measurable results directly attributable to process improvement, the measures associated with customer and employee satisfaction, and the potential impact on future business.

This accomplishment was achieved during the 1996 summer Olympics, and an analogy was immediately drawn that reaching Level 5 is like earning an Olympic Gold Medal in software development. After years of hard work and preparation (just like an athlete), this team demonstrated world class excellence and won the Gold Medal. Of more than 700 organizations worldwide that have been assessed according to SEI CMM criteria, fewer than 1 percent have achieved Level 5! By virtue of this accomplishment, Boeing STS became the first Department of Defense contractor organization to hold the Level 5 rating.

This chapter copyright © 1997 Boeing Company.

^{SM} The Capability Maturity Model (CMM) is a product of Software Engineering Institute at Carnegie Mellon University.

We thought the excitement would die down, but that did not happen. Rather, this achievement has acted as a catalyst to deploy Level 4 and 5 practices to other software organizations more quickly. And now, senior management is even thinking that the application of these concepts should go beyond software.

13.1.1 Boeing STS Organization

The Boeing STS organization supports space transportation for the Department of Defense (DoD) and National Aeronautics and Space Administration (NASA) through a variety of projects. These projects include main launch systems and upper stage boosters for multiple satellite payloads and planetary missions. At the time of the assessment, STS included three projects: the Inertial Upper Stage (IUS), the Avionics Obsolescence Activity (AOA), and a New Launch Vehicle Start Up Project. The STS organization is shown in Figure 13-1.

STS projects were in various life cycle stages including sustaining, full-scale development, and new start conceptual design. IUS was a highly successful 18-year old project in the sustaining phase. AOA was a development project using Integrated Product Teams (IPT), and was nearing completion at the time of the assessment. The project had performed requirements, design, code, and all associated testing. The New Launch Vehicle Start Up Project was in a Low Cost Concept Validation phase performing all front-end planning and requirements work under the new DoD acquisition reform procedures.

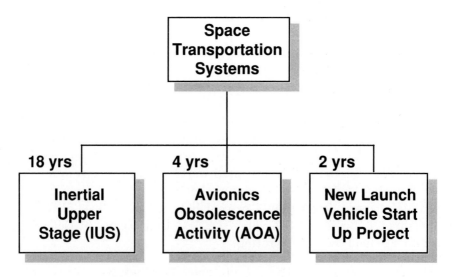

Figure 13-1   Boeing STS organization.

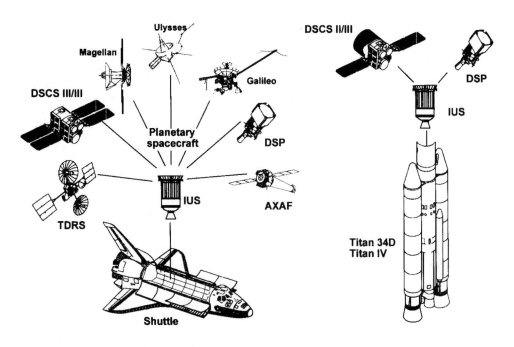

Figure 13-2   Integrated inertial upper stage.

Software development functions on these projects have included algorithm development, mission design, software-systems requirements, design, test, product assurance and integration, and mission operations support. STS products have been used to place many satellites into high altitude orbits, and to launch three planetary missions—Magellan, Ulysses, and Galileo. Figure 13-2 illustrates the many kinds of payloads deployed by one STS product, the IUS.

13.1.2 Process Focus

The establishment of the SEI and the subsequent development of the software CMM are part of an industry trend over the past several decades. In the 1960s and 1970s industry tended to focus on the technology that was under development. We all remember the effort to put a man on the moon. Costs and schedules were only a minor concern. Many great technological innovations were developed during that time. However, the concerns shifted in the 1980s with the emphasis being placed on cost control. There had been numerous cost and schedule overruns, and costs associated with DoD projects underwent a high level of scrutiny, a trend that continues today. As part of the solution, the focus now has been directed to the processes that are used to develop complex products. We believe that this focus will improve the cost, schedule, and quality of our products with predictability, and deliver more customer value. During this evolution to a process focus, STS had emphasized process improvement as a priority for many years, as you will see later in this chapter.

13.1.3 Assessment Process

Boeing D&SG has adopted the SEI CMM (see Chapter 12 for further details) as a framework for assessing the software development capability of its organizations, including the STS organization. The STS assessment was conducted using the CMM-Based Appraisal for Internal Process Improvement (CBA IPI) method. This method is a more stringent approach requiring specific evidence of institutionalization to be provided for all software development activities. The assessment was conducted over the standard two-week period, including on-site preparation. There was more than fifteen years worth of process-related data to review! This data was captured in a process library that included more than one hundred notebooks. The measurement data spanned the full eighteen years of the project. This process data was reviewed in a detailed presentation to the assessment team, followed by a further review of the data and interviews to confirm institutionalization.

13.2 STS Process Improvement History

STS has a long history of software process improvements, spanning more than fifteen years. Most of these processes and improvements were in place before the CMM was developed, as illustrated in Figure 13-3. Several frameworks for process improvement were used along the way, with each one providing a more complete structure than the previous one. These frameworks included the Boeing software standards (which provided process definition), a process management method, continuous quality improvement (CQI) techniques, and now the SEI CMM. The CMM is not a process improvement model, but rather an assessment framework. SEI has defined the IDEAL process improvement model—Initiating, Diagnosing, Establishing, Acting, and Leveraging—which is the model that STS had implemented. The maturity criteria used to measure progress, though, are contained in the CMM.

The following paragraphs discuss the four major areas shown in Figure 13-3.

13.2.1 Process Definition and the Boeing Software Standards

In the early 1980s, the STS organization documented its software processes. This was the first step in defect analysis and prevention. The processes needed to be defined and documented as a basis for improvement to eliminate future occurrences of defects. The core set of STS metrics was also defined primarily to measure status. STS participated with other Boeing organizations and the D&SG Central Software Engineering group to develop a companywide embedded software development

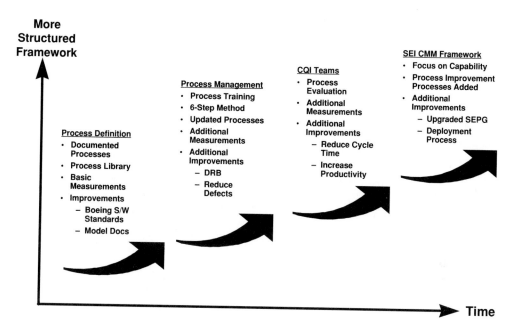

Figure 13-3   STS history of process improvement.

standard. This standard was used by Boeing representatives to various industry organizations to form a basis for comments directed towards DOD-STD-2167 and DOD-STD-2168. Training in these standards was developed and made available to all software personnel.

The Boeing software standard was more than 350 pages in length and contained requirements for the "largest project that we could think of." The team thought that it would be easier to tailor out what you don't need than to tailor in what you don't know. This standard defined the Boeing software development processes and associated products. Much of the input for this standard came from the STS organization. Although the STS organization was "grandfathered" because its projects were already in place before the standard was implemented, STS used the standard as a basis to identify further processes to capture. This initial version of the Boeing software standard did not address the goals of the processes, and also did not include measures to assess progress towards satisfying the standard. However, it provided the first formalized structure for Boeing projects to use as a basis for improving software processes and products.

13.2.2 Process Management

In the late 1980s, an organizationwide process improvement effort was initiated using a six-step method for process management. This method was applied to all parts of the STS organization, including software development, and consisted of the following steps:

1. Define the mission: The bridge from the current process to the future process.
2. Define the process parameters: Understand the process requirements, boundaries, and satisfaction criteria.
3. Develop a schedule for steps: Manage the improvement activities.
4. Develop process flow diagrams: Understand the current process steps.
5. Define measurements: Use facts and data to make decisions.
6. Analyze, improve, and monitor: Implement the process improvements.

At this time, the documented software processes were evaluated, and bottle-necks and error-prone steps identified. As an example, the peer review process was not uniformly effective in defect detection due to reviewer inconsistency, especially during a high turnover rate of software engineers. A core team of reviewers was identified, usually the key domain experts who were also trained in detailed inspection procedures. Effective checklists were developed to be used by this team. This formal inspection process was called the Design Review Board (DRB) process. Measurements taken showed dramatic improvements in defect reduction, as will be shown later in this chapter.

A four-step defect corrective action process was also implemented, reducing the recurrence of the most common errors. This process is still in place today and includes the following steps:

1. Fix the defect.
2. Fix the process that allowed the defect to occur.
3. Check the updated process.
4. Check for any other similar occurrences.

These steps are normal in most production lines. However, Levels 1 and 2 (see Chapter 12; Figure 12-1) software development processes seem to tolerate applying only step 1 in most organizations and, therefore, allow repetition of the same defects. You will see a great similarity in this process to the Defect Prevention Process in the CMM (at Level 5). Yet, this process was implemented years before the CMM was developed!

13.2.3 CQI Techniques

In the early 1990s, continuous quality improvement (CQI) methods were implemented organizationwide. These methods are well documented in literature and we will not define the specific steps here. Suffice it to say that CQI teams were formed and, again, the software processes were evaluated and updated accordingly. Evaluation forms were used for each process, and were retained for lessons learned. Simpler interfaces and user friendliness were important factors in the survey results used to evaluate the processes. Cycle time reduction was the key focus with 50 percent efficiency realized in some processes. The CQI methods provided a more formal structure for process improvement than the previous standards and methods. The software processes that had been documented years earlier were, once again, updated and streamlined using another process improvement framework.

13.2.4 SEI CMM Framework

In the past three years, the SEI software CMM has been used as a framework to support process improvement. This framework is specifically designed for software and provides a much more complete set of criteria to assess maturity. Much of the activity has been to correlate existing STS processes to the CMM framework, as a way of measuring where the organization stood. Most of the practices at Levels 2–5 were already institutionalized in the STS organization! The biggest problem that STS encountered during this activity concerned interpretation of the Level 4 and 5 Key Process Areas (KPA). This issue will be discussed later in this chapter as part of the challenges faced.

In an organization with a common product line, such as STS, most of the processes can be managed at the organization level rather than the project level. This provides a major savings for new start projects in the organization, since they can use an existing set of common processes with trained personnel. Metrics become just another data point added to the organization's capability baseline, rather than becoming an initial set of measures for new processes. The lessons learned are fed back into the processes rather than starting from scratch again.

Figure 13-3 should not be viewed as a road map to Level 5; it simply shows that process improvement has been occurring in STS over many years and that the best practices were used during each period of time. Each framework or method used provided more structure and knowledge to the process improvement activities than the previous one. A project starting out today could use the SEI CMM along with the IDEAL process, and achieve the same kind of improvements in a much shorter time period.

13.3 Challenges

Throughout the STS process improvement activities, there have been many challenges to overcome. The first and foremost of these is sponsorship, with which most of you are familiar. Not so obvious are the many other challenges that can equally cause setback or failure in the process improvement activities. Some of the key challenges that the STS organization faced on its road to Level 5 are discussed in the following paragraphs. Many of these challenges will be familiar to you, especially if you are working on software process improvement activities.

13.3.1 Sponsorship

Sponsorship begins with an organizational commitment to quality, with an immediate connection to one of the strategic business goals: to be a leader in customer satisfaction. Sponsorship is usually sought from senior management, as is appropriate. However, an organization must also have sponsorship at all mid-levels of management, and at the first line supervisor level. The key champions need to be at the lowest levels of management to be able to fully implement process improvement. The upper levels of management need to embrace the concept, with an understanding of the benefits that will be attained in time. However, a lack of sponsorship at any of these levels of management can significantly hinder success. STS obtained strong sponsorship at all levels of management, which was a key factor in its success.

The issue of sponsorship must be resolved before significant activity begins. Preliminary planning of process improvement tasks should occur in parallel with the task of obtaining sponsorship. But work beyond this should be limited until sponsorship has been attained. An opposing view says that process improvement should be implemented and that, eventually, senior management will come around and support it. Most efforts that we have seen take this route have failed over time, because they are the first to get cut when funding resources become tight. Without a commitment from someone who can ensure the availability of a budget, the effort is unlikely to succeed.

A key task to succeed in obtaining sponsorship is educating senior management about software process improvement. Having facts and data from a successful project also helps. Establishing realistic goals can then be achieved. With facts and data, you can avoid questionable goals such as "We will demonstrate a Level 3 maturity in six months." STS senior management had to make a long-term commitment, including the funding, before they realized any downstream benefits.

13.3.2 Benefits Realization

This challenge had to do with the time it takes organizational personnel to see the benefits of process improvement. There may be a few gains initially, but the benefits will seem small compared to the investment. Boeing experiences seem to show that only small benefits will be realized while progressing toward a Level 2 maturity. More benefits will be realized as the organization approaches a Level 3 maturity;

however, the majority of the benefits from process improvement are realized when the organization has progressed to Levels 4 and 5 maturity.

Based on current industry data, the average time to progress to Level 2 is 18–24 months, with the same amount of time required to progress to Level 3. This means that it may be three to four years before significant benefits appear in most organizations! How many organizations are patient enough to await the benefits? This links directly back to the issue of sponsorship. STS was fortunate to have such management with necessary long-term vision. The emphasis was on "fire prevention" rather than "fire fighting." As the earlier STS data showed, process improvement had been ongoing for more than fifteen years, and the benefits have been realized. But everyone on a new project must be prepared to make the long-term commitment, since most benefits are downstream in the life cycle. Once again, realistic expectations need to be established.

13.3.3 The SEPG

The most common mistake associated with establishing the Software Engineering Process Group (SEPG) is that the SEPG is set up and chartered to prepare for and support an assessment (or series of assessments). When the assessment is completed, the SEPG falters because it does not know what to do next. The solution, of course, is to charter an SEPG that is based on continuous process improvement and provide it real authority to make a difference. The STS SEPG was established based on these concepts, and the processes that it performs are shown in Figure 13-4.

Figure 13-4 shows the SEPG processes at Level 5; however, we train SEPGs to begin these processes at the earliest stages of a project possible. The capturing of processes is the focus of Process Definition. Once these processes are captured, they need to be managed through Process Change Management. Process Improvement Support collects measurement data and lessons learned from the projects, has a repository for these, and provides access to the data to a variety of users. Assessment support begins with the first assessment, and we strongly recommend that this activity be managed like any other project in the organization, with the proper level of visibility reporting. Training activities also begin early in a project, and should be assigned to the SEPG. At Level 3, additional focus is placed on a formal training program with a training plan and tracking of training accomplished. Technology Insertion activities include maintaining visibility of new technologies, identifying candidate technologies to pursue, piloting projects when appropriate, and implementing those that meet success criteria. Process Evaluation uses quantitative data to analyze processes for potential problems that may not be identified through other techniques. The impact of candidate changes to the processes can be evaluated using measurement data.

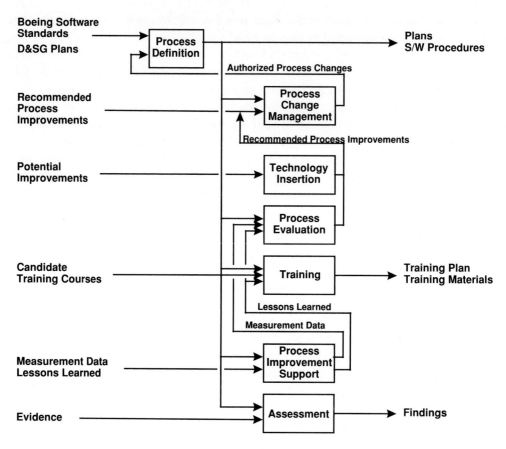

Figure 13-4   Boeing STS SEPG processes.

Some organizations have argued that many of these processes can be performed by people or groups other than the SEPG. We find that the process activities in these organizations are not well coordinated, and visibility is marginal. Having all of the right people involved in process decisions reduces conflict, optimizes schedules, and provides optimal visibility. We find that an SEPG empowered to perform these tasks satisfies these concerns, and supports higher maturity processes much better.

The second most common mistake with SEPGs is an SEPG that is set up as an "outside group" separate from the project engineers. These kinds of SEPGs consist of full-time process people who often do not understand the processes being performed in the organization. They "tell" the engineers what the processes will be. The solution to this problem is to assign members to the SEPG that include the key leads and domain experts from the projects in the organization. Institutionalization occurs quickly when the process owners make the decisions about their processes.

STS has had some form of an SEPG active for many years. In the earlier years, it took the form of a lead engineers group or the DRB. More recently, it was restructured into a more formal SEPG and renamed as such. Its tasks and responsibilities were expanded to include the processes shown in Figure 13-4. The current STS SEPG consists of the following process owners:

- Chairman & Space Transportation Systems Software Functional Manager
- Space Transportation Systems & Inertial Upper Stage SEPG Focal Point
- New Project SEPG Focal Point
- Space Transportation Systems Software Configuration Management (SCM) Manager
- Space Transportation Systems SCM Lead
- Space Transportation Systems Software Quality Assurance Lead
- Inertial Upper Stage & Avionics Obsolescence Activity Software Requirements Lead
- Inertial Upper Stage & Avionics Obsolescence Activity Flight Design Lead
- Inertial Upper Stage & Avionics Obsolescence Activity Software Design Lead
- Inertial Upper Stage & Avionics Obsolescence Activity Software Test Lead
- Avionics Obsolescence Activity Software Lead
- New Project Flight Software Lead
- New Project Ground Software Lead

13.3.4 Cultural Change

Cultural change presents the most frustration to those involved in process improvement. It is a challenge that must be recognized so that it can be managed. The key concerns encountered in STS were:

- "The SEPG focal point is an outsider" (the focal point was a senior software engineer with process skills brought in from another organization).
- "Someone is going to come in and tell me how to do my job better?"
- "They want me to document my job so that anyone (translation: lesser experienced/paid) can do it."
- "This task means that I am going to have to do a lot more work on an already tight schedule."
- "Process improvement is just a side job necessary to fill a square."

These perceptions cannot be taken lightly. The SEPG lead worked with STS engineers to help them understand that processes do not replace people. Most real engineering work is creative by nature and is seldom captured in a process. However, an engineer's time is filled with many other daily tasks. It is those tasks that were initially captured so that the engineers would not have to think about them. They could spend more time doing what they love most—engineering! They began to see that process improvement could help them. Everyone in the organization (including senior management) understood that great processes with inexperienced people could still produce poor quality products.

Eventually, this new way of thinking was institutionalized, causing a breakthrough in overcoming the primary cultural challenges. Consequently, as STS progressed to CMM Level 5, attitudes changed and evolved to the following:

- "Process improvement starts with me and is part of my normal work."
- "We own the processes!"
- "Great processes do not replace experienced people."
- "I am freed up to do more of the real engineering work now."
- "Process improvement has saved me time and improved my products."

When people truly believe these principles, process improvement ideas readily flow from everyone in the organization.

13.3.5 Process Knowledge

Those of us working in process improvement often go into a new organization and make a fatal assumption: that everyone understands what we mean by processes and process improvement. Remember back to the early years of software development, when all you knew were flow charts. Then along came Hierarchical Input Process Output (HIPO) charts, Chapin charts, state diagrams, control flow charts, and then, finally, a variety of system modeling techniques. Now, you may talk about behavior models, architectural models, control models, or objects! However, most of the engineering workforce has not been trained in these methods.

It is similar in process improvement. Yes, there are many process modeling techniques that have been developed. However, most of the engineers have not been trained in those techniques. Having them go through a two- or three-day course in the SEI CMM does not teach them about processes. Yet, we often assume that the understanding is there upon completion of the CMM training. Process training must be ongoing and cumulative. It should start out simple and evolve to the more complex concepts over time as the organization matures. This training must begin at the start of process improvement. STS incorporated process training into SEPG meetings, staff meetings, all-hands meetings, and any other meeting where it made sense.

13.3.6 Capturing Processes

This challenge is tied to the issue of process knowledge. When beginning process improvement, the organization must capture its processes. It must do this in order to have a baseline from which to improve. STS defined a template for software process procedures that included only the basics, and allowed the process owner to define the steps of the process in whatever format was easiest. The time was not right to teach advanced process modeling techniques to them. This decision was very successful, and it resolved issues concerning the processes that had been documented previously.

Many organizations start out today by defining a process template that includes requirements to describe the process in a graphical format using techniques such as behavior or control modeling. Then they add the requirements for entry and exit criteria, and finish it with requirements for including process measures, process effectiveness, and tailoring options. Remember that you are trying to capture the existing process in terms people understand now. Keep it simple! This task can be made more difficult than it should be. Capture the existing processes, and then look at improving them.

A simplified process description template can include the following items:

- Identification, Title, and Date
- Purpose—an explanation of what this process accomplishes and when it is performed.
- Process Resources—this may include inputs (data, reports, memos, etc. used in the performance of the process), outputs (product or service that results from performing the process), and optional special resources (information, data, tools, computer resources, etc. used in accomplishing the tasks).
- Process Steps—a brief description of the basic steps of the process, including identification of any authority needed to do the work, decisions to be made, who is responsible for doing each step, and identification of any reviewers involved in the process and the point at which they are involved. Significant entry or exit events associated with the process not discussed in the steps above should be discussed. A graphical representation may be included if it enhances the understanding of the process user.
- Process Measures (optional)—process metrics may be included, but only if they are derived from the organizational measurement program.
- Revision History—date and reason for each change.

The question always arises as to what processes should be captured. We established three criteria. If a process met any one of these criterion, it was captured at the organizational level. These criteria are:

- Is the process important to the business objectives of the organization?
- Do multiple people perform the process, and is a common way preferred?
- If a process is performed by only one person, is it important that any follow-on person perform the process the same way?

13.3.7 Process Evidence

Although an organization may have performed processes defined by the CMM for years, evidence of these activities is necessary to support an assessment. One of the lessons learned from our process improvement work was to think about evidence early on. Not only was this approach useful for an assessment, but it helped us to better define the data associated with our processes. Our challenge was to capture the evidence from so many years ago. As seen in earlier challenges, nothing is quite as easy as it seems.

About three years ago, Boeing initiated a program called "5S"—Sorting, Simplifying, Sweeping, Standardizing, and Self-discipline. In the first three steps, teams are required to sort through their work areas, remove the unnecessary, and establish a basis for efficient area organization. During the next step, work groups define and document safe and reliable methods. Work groups that complete the last step are able to demonstrate ongoing self-discipline in keeping their work areas clean and safe, and have documented and improved their processes. The key phrase in the preceding is "removing the unnecessary." Everyone was to review their data and either destroy it or archive it, if they had not used the data in the last two to three years. Some STS personnel had performed this task before our attention became focused on the evidence issue. Some historical data was lost, but fortunately, most was recognized in time to avoid its loss. Since much of our evidence concerned tasks accomplished over the last ten to fifteen years, electronic forms of the data were often not available (or no longer readable by current tools). All data is now reviewed from the evidence perspective, in addition to frequency of use, before it is removed from the organization.

13.3.8 Team Environments

STS uses a structure of Analysis and Integration Teams (AIT) and Integrated Product Teams (IPT) to manage and build products. An AIT is a team assigned to perform program-level tasks that involve more than one IPT. The AIT has the delegated authority and the allocated budget required to perform the assigned work tasks defined in its team charter. The AIT integrates the efforts of the IPTs by conducting system and subsystem requirements analysis and ensuring integration of lower level IPT products. The IPT is a team chartered with a program product responsibility. The IPT is composed of members from the appropriate functional disciplines and is assigned authority and an allocated budget to perform the assigned work defined in their team charter. The use of a team-oriented product development approach reduces costs, shortens schedule flow time, and improves product quality. Equally important is the improvement in people's attitudes when they are involved in a team environment. An example AIT/IPT structure for an STS project is illustrated in Figure 13-5.

Although STS has transitioned to a team environment, all software personnel report administratively to an STS Software Engineering Manager. This structure enables software personnel to be assigned to IPTs based on the skills required for a specified period of time. It also permits certain software functions, such as the SEPG, to operate at the STS organizational level.

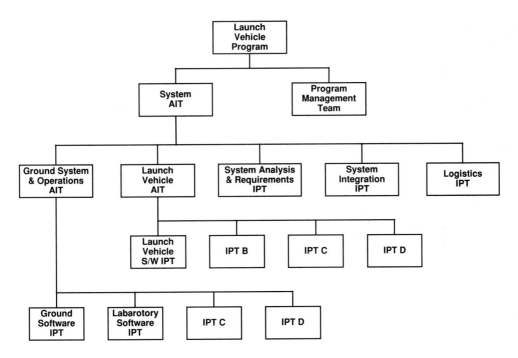

Figure 13-5   Example project team structure.

The position of the STS Software Engineering manager became very important to the success of this effort. New projects at Boeing are being organized using the AIT and IPT structure, without the traditional software manager role. STS discovered during the process improvement activities that this organizational structure posed a significant problem. Many of the process (and technical) decisions that need to be made affect all software development in the system, which is managed by many of these AITs and IPTs. Without a single software team or software manager in place with the authority to make these decisions, it is very difficult to implement the decisions across the project. The current CMM seems to expect a project software manager to be in place to take care of such decisions. Fortunately, the STS organization was in transition to AITs/IPTs from the traditional stove pipe functional organization of the past, and the STS Software Engineering manager role was retained.

This problem appears to stem from the current implementation of AITs and IPTs. These teams have been defined to implement the engineering processes on the project. The business processes (including certain management responsibilities) are to be defined in the future and overlaid on the engineering processes. The result of this staggered implementation is a gap in the project processes that is the likely cause of the problem described above.

13.3.9 Interpreting CMM Levels 4 and 5

Implementing processes defined through CMM Level 3 was mostly straightforward and required minimal interpretation. We were told that if you are at Level 3, you will know it. We found that to be basically true. However, Levels 4 and 5 are quite another story with most of the problematic interpretations involving Level 4 KPAs. As you might have guessed, Quantitative Process Management (QPM) is the biggest hurdle. Many process people believe that QPM requires rigorous statistical process control methods like those defined in the manufacturing areas. This can only be done when a process is clearly bounded and repetitive; key attributes of the inputs, process, and outputs can be defined and measured; and quantifiable relationships of the key attributes of the inputs and processes to the key attributes of the outputs can be determined (i.e., a change in an input parameter has a known impact on the output product). Applying these principles to software engineering processes (or any engineering process) is questionable at best, and more often an exercise in futility. This occurs due to the creative nature of engineering processes. There may be some elements of statistical process control that could be applied to engineering processes, but they are not those currently applied to the manufacturing processes. We can solve this problem by referring to statistical control methods, which means that statistical techniques of some kind are used on the historical data to assist in the control of the processes.

Such statistical techniques are under study, but have not been validated on a wide range of software engineering applications. There are issues associated with small sample sizes for small projects to deal with (small projects should not be prevented from achieving Level 4), along with concerns associated with the validity of statistical techniques on an ever changing process (after all, we are doing continuous process improvement and each iteration may be different). Suffice it to say that there is still much to learn about these concepts before they are explicitly required in the CMM. The state of practice today is quantitative management, not statistical management.

Quantitative management means that historical data is available from which estimates can be generated with a higher confidence level, the data is sufficient to establish upper and lower variances using either statistical techniques or engineering judgment, and there are predefined actions that will be taken when the variance (upper or lower) is exceeded. We have encountered many assessment team members who insist that statistical process control techniques can be used to satisfy the goals of the QPM KPA. This simply has not been observed as STS has demonstrated. Over time, and especially with version 2.0 of the CMM, this may change.

Other areas of significant interpretation include Software Quality Management (SQM) and Process Change Management (PCM). One interpretation of SQM is that quality factors (defined in a quality metrics framework) must be used to measure and control the quality of your products (they are used as an example in the CMM). Boeing was involved in the definition of quality metrics via contracts sponsored by Rome Air Development Center. [1] Quality metrics can be useful in the requirements domain, but they do not reflect an agreed upon definition of software quality. They were developed so that DoD customers could specify certain attributes of software in the requirements, and then measure conformance to those requirements. The only quality factor that might be of value to SQM is reliability, as it is derived from defects. Defects that affect mission performance appear to be the primary customer concern related to quality, and establishing value-added quality criteria should be derived from this concept.

The issue related to PCM concerns the extent to which processes are "analyzed" to identify potential improvements. Organizations are managing changes to their processes at Levels 2, 3, and 4. However, the lack of process measurement data at Levels 2 and 3 prevents the process changes from being quantitatively managed. With process measurement data, you can identify areas in the life cycle that need to be improved, and predict the impact of the changes.

The interpretations associated with Levels 4 and 5 can be minimized once the organization makes a connection between its software activities and the business goals of the organization.

13.3.10 Deployment to a Start Up Project

The STS organization included a new launch vehicle start up project. Deployment of a Level 5 capability would be a challenge to any organization; however, this is where the real benefits of process improvement are demonstrated! Sponsorship was obtained immediately at all levels of management (after seeing facts and data). Training was performed to bring new engineers up to speed rapidly on all aspects of their tasks. And due to domain commonality, many processes and products could be used without change. This significantly reduced the time required to prepare plans and procedures. More time was available for the engineering requirements and design work. The fact that most of the organizational processes could be deployed directly to the new project was the single reason for this success.

There were some exceptions to the processes that could be deployed, such as the requirements and design methodologies. The organizational methodologies in these areas were based on older methods from established projects, primarily focusing on sustaining tasks. The SEPG was asked to form a team to identify more appropriate methodologies for the new project. This effort was successfully completed in a matter of weeks. A Level 5 organization can admit when a specialized process is not defined, because it knows that processes are in place to successfully resolve the issue quickly.

13.3.11 More Challenges

There were also several smaller challenges to overcome. One of these concerned organizational policies that reflect the commitment to process improvement. Boeing D&SG had recently streamlined its command media so that redundant project policies were combined into higher level policies at the D&SG level. The SEI CMM requires organizational policy covering most project activities addressed by the KPAs. We examined the D&SG policy to determine how much could be satisfied by reference to it. It was lacking in many areas when viewed against the CMM, especially concerning Levels 4 and 5 processes. We also saw the need for such policy to define and provide authority for the SEPG, which also was absent from the D&SG policy. STS decided to supplement the D&SG policy with an expanded STS policy.

Another challenge concerned standards compliance. With foresight, our organizational software standards included process improvement processes. In the early 1990s, the Boeing Software Standards were updated to include two sets of processes: software development processes and process improvement processes. The process improvement processes are very close to the processes assigned to the SEPG in Figure 13-4, and that was quite deliberate. There is one exception—the compliance process. Compliance responsibility is not assigned to the SEPG. The SEPG should never be put into the position of being a "policeman." The STS SEPG reviews project software plans and comments on them, but the SEPG does not have sign-off authority. Compliance responsibility needs to be assigned to a steering committee or software functional manager at the organizational level. At CMM Levels 4 and 5, compliance becomes less of an enforcement function as the processes are institutionalized and sustainable.

The transition from the Software Process Assessment (SPA) method to the CBA IPI method was another challenge. The SPA method permitted many subjective decisions to be made and, of course, a team may rate itself more optimistically than would an external team. The CBA IPI placed more stringent requirements on the issues of evidence and institutionalization, and therefore, motivated us to capture some processes in a more formalized way. But once that had been done, the engineers saw the value—a better basis for communication was developed, processes were reaffirmed as correct, and the ability to provide training was enhanced. These "captured" processes also provided a means of visibility to management on what work was being performed.

As described earlier in this chapter, the STS organization documented many of its processes almost fifteen years ago. One more challenge was how to make this process data widely available when only a hard copy was available with which to work. The SEPG undertook a task to have the older process procedures scanned in. The scanned files were edited and updated. A decision was then made to make this data available via the organizational intranet. This decision caused two additional problems. First, a Web site had to be established, and all of the learning that goes with it had to occur. Second, placing all of the process procedures (and plans) on the intranet would make them available to anyone at a Boeing work station (including non-Boeing personnel). Security became a major issue and is still a limiting factor in making this data widely available within the company.

13.3.12 Challenges Revisited

We have covered many of the challenges faced on the road to software process improvement; however, there are others not mentioned. Recognizing the many challenges that you will face and managing them will lead to success. At each level of maturity, there are additional challenges. But they can be managed better at each higher level when a solid process improvement foundation is established during the preceding levels of maturity. When you overcome these challenges and operate at a higher level of maturity, benefits are realized as described in the next section.

13.4   Process Improvement Results

Data in the STS organization has demonstrated many of the benefits of the process improvements that have been implemented. There is not sufficient space here to present all of the data, but a sampling is provided to give you some insight into what can be expected from projects that reach CMM Level 5.

13.4.1 Software Defects

Software defects are a key indicator to process improvement success. They are tracked and analyzed on a continuous basis. In the early years, most defects were found in testing: 70 percent in verification, 19 percent in validation, and the remainder in other activities. The STS organization has significantly reduced the number of defects and moved the detection earlier in the life cycle, as shown in Figure 13-6. This reduction has been primarily accomplished by use of multiple layers of checklists and formal inspections.

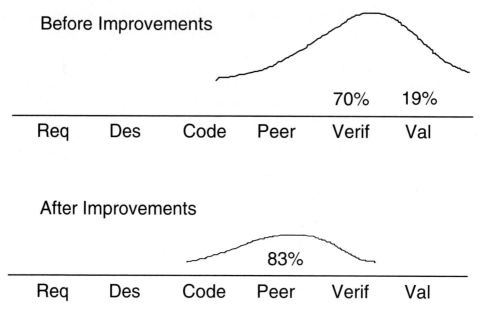

Figure 13-6   Life cycle shift in defect detection.

Checklists are used by software designers, the design review board, software testers, and software configuration management staff. The reduction in defects greatly reduces the rework effort to produce the final operational product. STS is currently working to move this defect prevention even earlier in the life cycle to the requirements and design phases, although problems found in those earlier phases before release are called errors (the term "defect" is used after release to software configuration management).

Software defects and errors are categorized based on severity, using the following definitions:

- Catastrophic—The problem prevents the operation of the system.
- Severe—The problem seriously degrades the operation of the system with no known alternative work-around solution.
- Major—The problem seriously degrades the operation of the system, but a known alternative work-around solution exists.
- Minor—The problem is an operator inconvenience or annoyance or does not affect a required operational or mission essential capability.
- Other—All other problems. These problems have no effect on the operational capability of the system.

With such a low rate of defects, defect prevention activities are focusing more on errors (problems found prior to release). Errors found in a recent STS software review by the DRB are categorized as shown in Figure 13-7. As a result of process improvement activities, the severity of these errors has been reduced significantly to where nearly three-fourths of them are in the "other" category, with no catastrophic errors reaching the DRB in this software release.

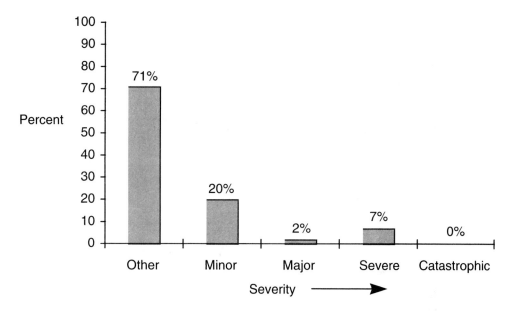

Figure 13-7   Error severity in recent software release.

The cumulative defect profile in Figure 13-8 shows the effect of the defect prevention activities implemented within STS. The initial slope is high, but becomes more shallow as process improvements have been implemented. With the implementation of the DRB inspection, there is a dramatic reduction in the defect rate to almost flat.

Boeing STS has also measured the effectiveness of its processes related to defect prevention. Initially, 89 percent of the defects were found before release from the software teams. Additional defects were found by System Test and Vehicle Test and Stress Testing. This improved to 94 percent and now nearly 100 percent of defects are eliminated before release as shown in Figure 13-9.

The STS defect data shows that in a Level 5 organization, defects/errors are found earlier in the life cycle, the severity of defects/errors found is reduced, the number of new defects is reduced, and fewer escapes from the software processes occur.

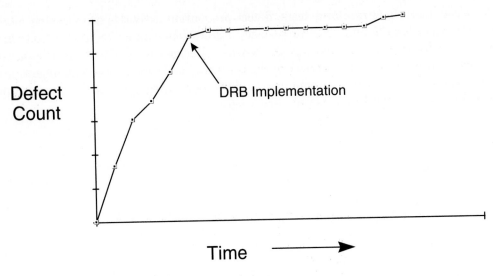

Figure 13-8   Cumulative defect count.

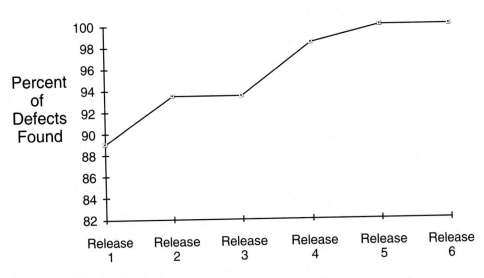

Figure 13-9   Defects found before release outside software teams.

13.4.2 Cost/Benefit Data

Data has been collected to determine the cost:benefit ratio associated with process improvements. One example of this data is the implementation of the DRB. Figure 13-10 illustrates the effort that was required for the life cycle of a software product. The bottom bar shows the initial effort for each phase, while the top bars show the rework effort originally required. Implementation of the DRB required 4 percent additional effort during the design phase, but reduced rework efforts in the last three phases where we normally spent much of our time. As you can see in Figure 13-10, STS benefited with a 1 to 7 return on investment. This data is consistent with similar results reported elsewhere in industry.

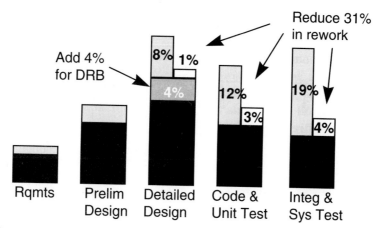

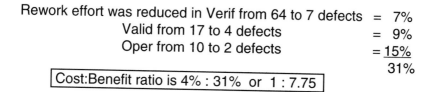

Implementing DRB increased design effort by 4%

Rework effort was reduced in Verif from 64 to 7 defects = 7%
Valid from 17 to 4 defects = 9%
Oper from 10 to 2 defects = 15%
31%

Cost:Benefit ratio is 4% : 31% or 1 : 7.75

Figure 13-10   Cost:benefit ratio for DRB.

13.4.3 Software Productivity

Software productivity is one of those terms that is not well defined in industry. So, rather than focus on absolute values that tend to get us side-tracked, we want to simply show you that productivity will increase with process improvements. Based on the STS method of measurement, we have increased our productivity by 240 percent over the years, as shown in Figure 13-11. The message is clear: Regardless of how you measure software productivity, you can expect to see improvements directly attributable to process improvements. Our challenge now is to deploy these improved processes faster on new projects so that these gains can be realized much quicker.

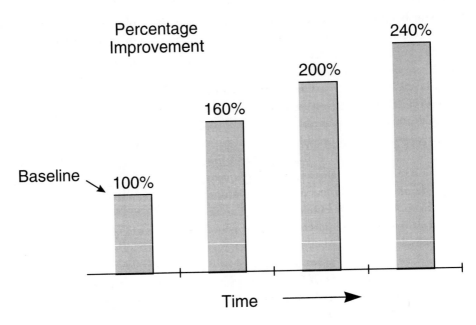

Figure 13-11   Software productivity improvement.

Process improvements within the STS organization have saved the projects millions of dollars through software cost underruns. Two significant cost underruns have been recognized by the STS organization. Although we cannot include the specific details here, it is these kinds of facts and data shown in the previous figures that have given credibility to the assertion that process improvement does provide an organization with significant benefits in terms of cost and quality.

13.5   Customer and Employee Satisfaction

An organization at a higher level of maturity should be able to demonstrate a high level of customer and employee satisfaction. We will now look at some of the results of the measures for customer and employee satisfaction that STS uses. Customer measures consist of customer evaluations, an award fee, and an incentive fee; and employee measures consist of results from surveys.

13.5.1   Customer Satisfaction

One customer review evaluates our performance in eight separate areas, including software. Although we cannot go into detail here, STS has exceeded its goal for about eight years now. Another customer review is performed by the Defense

Contract Management Command (DCMC) representatives. This review is a monthly review that has resulted in a "green" (highest) rating in all areas, including those with software. This review has shown a green rating for many prior years.

Another measure of customer satisfaction is the award fee shown in Figure 13-12. This fee is based on cost and schedule performance. Performance in these areas should be excellent, if we have achieved predictability in our processes. Figure 13-12 shows that STS has exceeded its goal of 95 percent for at least the last five years, often reaching 99–100 percent.

Another measure of customer satisfaction that we use is the incentive fee, which is based on the booster insertion accuracy. The insertion accuracy is a measure of how close the booster delivers the payload to the desired position in space. This accuracy is measured by the spacecraft fuel expended to achieve final position. The less fuel burned, the more propellant that remains in the spacecraft for station keeping and mission life. That is why this measure is called an incentive fee. The circle on the left in Figure 13-13 represents the amount of propellant burn associated with the percent of incentive fee received. The inner circle represents 100 percent and is enlarged on the right. As you see, the IUS booster has performed in the inner 20 percent of that circle.

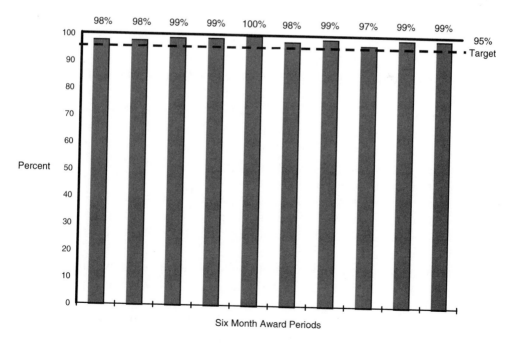

Figure 13-12   Award fee measure.

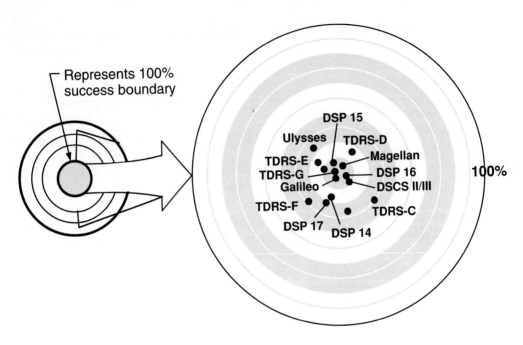

Figure 13-13   IUS incentive fee measure.

13.5.2 Employee Satisfaction

Another STS goal is to have a motivated and skilled workforce. This results in very satisfied and productive employees. An informal survey was taken of software engineering personnel in STS before and after major process improvements. Before improvements, the development environment was ad hoc and somewhat chaotic with constant tiger teams and fire fighting. The results showed 26 percent were dissatisfied with a mean near a neutral value. After process improvements and implementing a structured, disciplined development approach with clear goals, the satisfaction percentage jumped to 96 percent, showing a very satisfied workforce. This data is consistent with experiences that SEI personnel shared with us. Employees in a higher maturity level organization find it difficult to go back to an organization that is functioning at a Level 1 or 2.

The informal surveys also identified employee needs and how important each was to the individual. As you look at the needs below, you will see why morale in a Level 5 organization is high. Process improvement in higher maturity organizations ensures that the most important employee needs are satisfied. Employee needs, identified in order of importance to the individual, are:

- Achievement and recognition
- Work assignments and levels of responsibility

- Opportunity for advancement and growth
- Security
- Salary
- Work environment
- Relationships to others in the organization
- Supervision

13.6   Implication for Future Business

The real value of Levels 4 and 5 comes from a paradigm shift in the way the team thinks. The business goals of the organization are understood by everyone in the organization, and everyone understands how what they do affects those goals. The process and product data that are key to Level 4 provide the capability to estimate with highly predictable results. This data also is used to determine the impact of changes. The business goals that evolve at Level 5 establish the criteria against which decisions are made. At Level 5, these data and criteria are used to make decisions that are right for the organization, and everyone understands why!

A Level 5 organization is not perfect, but it is in a position to be more competitive. Boeing STS is an organization that wants to be competitive in order to grow and obtain more business. The Level 5 maturity provides some key attributes that can significantly impact the future business of the organization; these are discussed in the following paragraphs.

13.6.1 Capability Baselines

The Boeing STS capability baseline is determined by the processes implemented in its existing projects. This capability baseline has a fundamental role in supporting organizational new business goals, as it defines the basis for estimates used in new business proposals. The data in the "Results" section above shows that process improvements reduced defects, reduced cycle time, increased productivity, and resulted in high customer satisfaction. These are key elements of the STS organization's capability baseline that make us more competitive. Having quantifiable data to support these claims increases the customer's confidence level in STS proposals, and this provides STS with a competitive advantage.

When STS began to operate at Levels 4 and 5, we began to fully understand how activities relate to the organization's business goals. STS manages decisions concerning process improvement activities to ensure that the highest leverage changes are implemented. STS can prevent the kind of short term decisions often made on projects that hurt the organization in the long run. As our capability improves, we win more business, and growth in the organization continues.

13.6.2 Effect on SDCEs and SCEs

Software Development Capability Evaluations (SDCE) and Software Capability Evaluations (SCE) occurred even when STS reached a higher maturity level. However, operating at this higher maturity level directly contributed to our ability to respond faster and better to a recent SDCE requirement. The STS Level 5 operations provided several advantages in this effort. First, all key processes were defined, which makes responding to the questions much easier. We could summarize the processes and then include specific documented references. In one area where we did not have a specific process already defined, we described the SEPG process in place that would ensure that this new process would be defined in a timely manner. Second, estimates required for tasks described in the SDCE were based on the STS capability baseline. Having the data readily available provided for rapid responses when time was critical. Third, the quantitative data associated with STS processes and products allowed us to better estimate the impact of changes to some processes necessary for the new project. And fourth, operating at this level of maturity ensured that STS had a process in place to capture a new process (preparing a SDCE response) that had not been done before in this organization. This SDCE process has now been deployed to other organizations within D&SG.

13.6.3 Customer Expectations

Although contracts are not awarded based on single issues, software development is viewed as a very important part of the decision process. Leaders in DoD have said in the past few years that demonstration of higher software development maturity will be required to even bid on DoD contracts, and certainly to have any chance of winning them. The DoD appears to be transitioning in that direction. A recent Request for Proposal included the following statement: "If the technical division of the corporation developing the [deleted] proposal has a rating from the Software Engineering Institute (SEI) outlining the assessment of the contractor against the Capability Maturity Model (CMM), they may provide this rating AND the report substantiating this rating for consideration."

It is clear that our customers are focusing on process improvement both internally and externally. They are encouraging contractors to attain a Level 3 capability, while at the same time adopting the CMM internally for military software organizations. A briefing on the STS achievements was given to DoD personnel at the Pentagon Department of Defense for Acquisition, as the first DoD contractor organization demonstrating a Level 5 capability. Other military organizations, Federal Aviation Administration (FAA) executives, and international business executives have requested briefings. Customers want a higher level of confidence in all new start up projects. Our Level 5 achievement will help us accomplish that much faster.

13.7 Conclusions

The Boeing STS organization operates with world class practices that provide the highest quality products, impressive performance unmatched in accuracy and dependability, high employee morale, and excellent customer satisfaction. These results were achieved because the organization knew the right things to do and was committed at all levels to improve. We faced and embraced the challenges with determination, and successfully addressed each one. Now, employees are motivated, the teams have ownership, significant improvements continue, and processes are institutionalized and maintained.

An organization should implement process improvement with the primary goal of improving its effectiveness, whether it is to improve the big four (cost, schedule, quality, and performance) or to support its marketing business. A great emphasis is now placed on achieving a specific SEI CMM level, due to the visibility from customers. Customers have indicated the importance of using assessed capability as a factor in future contract awards. However, it can be easy to lose sight of the real goals of process improvement and be directed to achieve a particular SEI level. Each organization must look at what business goals are right for them, and then chart a course for success.

The ultimate measure of success is still customer satisfaction as measured in terms of cost, schedule, software quality, and software performance. To achieve this success, STS has applied proven concepts aptly called "Yamamura's Formula for Success." First, make sure you are doing the right thing. Sometimes general processes do not fit a project quite right. Second, take small steps. Some efforts try to implement everything all at once. Look for the highest value added in the near term. Third, keep it simple. There are too many academic solutions being applied without validation of the value added. And fourth, make sure the time is right. Often, we try to force implementations when the environment is not ready. Applying these principles will enhance your probability of success. The formula to remember for value-added success is RSST:

- Right thing
- Small Steps
- Simple
- Timing

Manage with facts and data, manage to your business goals, and manage with common sense (Yamamura's Formula for Success). When all of these come together, you will be ready to go for the Gold Medal in software development.

References

1. Bowen, T.P.; Wigle, G.B.; and Tsai, J.T. *Specification of Software Quality Attributes*, RADC-TR-85-37 (3 Volumes), February 1985.

## CHAPTER 14

Software Quality Assurance CASE Tools

James I. McManus
Northrop Grumman Corporation,
Electronic Sensors and Systems Division

14.1 Introduction

Software tools have become commonplace in today's development environment. Tools exist for every phase of the life cycle. In this regard, tools support program management, risk analysis, cost analysis, requirements management, software development, configuration management, software quality, specific metrics, software evaluations, reliability, test and maintenance, etc. Many tools are commercial off-the-shelf (COTS) provided through a variety of vendors and many tools are home-grown to meet a unique set of requirements or purportedly to cut cost.

There are several reasons for today's increased tool use. Three key reasons are availability, fitness, and productivity. The *availability* of tools is almost endless. Tools are advertised almost everywhere—through direct marketing, symposia, conferences, computer software and quality magazines, through professional organizations, and on the Internet. *Fitness* is a function of how well a tool meets the user's need. The problem here, in many cases, is not in finding a tool, but in selecting one from a variety of tools all professing to do the same job. *Productivity* is a measure of how well we perform our tasks, both singly and collectively. If an engineer can do the same job in less time with fewer mistakes, this benefits the company, equating to reduced *cost*, reduced *schedule,* and reduced *risk*; the improvement ultimately defines a better *process*, and in the end this yields a higher quality *product*.

When used properly, tools can provide a reliable way to increase productivity on the job. Through tools, productivity improves in two ways. First, the right tool can provide a *quick, reliable* way to help produce and/or evaluate a product. Without the tool, the user would spend many more hours on the job to achieve the same result.

Second, the tool provides *consistency*. Once the tool is qualified it can be used repeatedly to perform the same process over and over. If you use a qualified tool as part of your process, you have built-in consistency and reliability.

This chapter focuses on the emerging awareness of CASE tools as a means of improving the quality of the process of software development. Section 14.2 discusses the origins of CASE and the environment for using CASE tools. Section 14.3 discusses the importance of CASE technology to the software development process and to software quality assurance (SQA), in particular. Section 14.4 discusses the applicability of tools from a user's point of view. Section 14.5 summarizes where to find tools in a dynamically changing market. Section 14.6 presents a look ahead.

14.2   Environment for CASE

14.2.1 What is CASE?

Over the past several years there has been an explosion in what is known as CASE technology. CASE stands for Computer Aided Software Engineering and refers to an integrated collection of tools designed to aid the life cycle process of developing compliant software products.

One of the first uses of the acronym CASE occurred in 1979. The application was specifically intended for distributed systems and stood for Computer Assisted Software Engineering. [1] Today CASE takes on a broader meaning for software. Its applications range from centralized systems to distributed client server networks, from the stand-alone personal computer to large, complex, real-time, embedded software systems. [2] CASE can also take on the broader scope of software systems and in this sense is defined as Computer Aided Software/Systems Engineering.

14.2.2 Software Engineering Environments (SEE)

A Software Engineering Environment (SEE) also refers to an integrated collection of tools. However, the concept behind the SEE is characterized by the following additional attributes: [2]

- The environment enforces processes and methodologies (such as those required for requirements management, configuration management, automated test, and project management)
- processing is distributed but linked across different sites and across phases of the life cycle
- the environment supports automated documentation and organizes information into documentation templates

- the environment provides checks across development and project management activities
- the environment is expandable and supports software reusability
- the environment is user friendly and may use an expert system
- the environment contains powerful, automated, integrated tools to support software development

Currently no one environment contains all of these characteristics.

Both industry and government have promoted SEEs. Examples include:

- Compaq Computer's (formerly Digital Equipment Corporation's) COHESION, [3] which supports multiple platforms and integrated tools sponsored by DEC and third party vendors
- the National Aeronautics and Space Administration's (NASA) software support environment Space Station Freedom (NASA SSF) [4]
- the Department of Defense's (DoD) SLCSE (pronounced slice), which stands for Software Life Cycle Support Environment. SLCSE was originally defined by the U. S. Air Force at the Rome Air Development Center (RADC) to support DOD STD 2167A programs under development [4]

CASE, then, is a subset of a SEE. As part of the support environment, CASE is the set of integrated tools within the environment. This implies restricting the use of CASE tools to function within the set of enforceable processes defined by the SEE.

With the commercialization of standards requirements occurring within the DoD, strides have been made to provide CASE environments that support integration of multiple tools from multiple vendors. The use of client-server networks with open systems architecture (OSA) has opened the door to a new generation in CASE technology.

14.3 The Case for CASE

With the power of CASE, significant improvements to both process and product can be realized by software engineering and software quality.

14.3.1 Benefits of CASE

Benefits anticipated from application of CASE technology include cost benefits, reduced rework, automated support for the user, better managed processes, improved product performance, increased confidence going into development, predictability, and more standardization in software development processes.

14.3.2 CASE-Related Concerns

The need for a fully integrated CASE environment is also supported by several concerns.

- the cost of software
- the quality of software
- consistency and confidence

The Cost of Software.   The cost of software continues to escalate in today's environment. Witness the rise in costs of contracts let by various Government agencies. The days of cost plus contracts have, for all practical purposes, disappeared, forcing companies to weigh very carefully their profit margins and price-to-cost ratios.

Even the daily news carries events of major cost impact, as noted by the following past announcements:

- a news article about a government stop work order for an Air Force program
- a TV broadcast that DoD terminated one of its state-of-the-art programs; congressional auditors estimated that delays and projected changes would probably push costs to at least five billion dollars over budget, if bailed out by the government
- *The Washington Post* reported major cost overruns for an FAA program, the troubled division finally being bought out by another company

From another perspective, several contractors have been hit with the news of government cutbacks in production numbers, limiting the profit potential of the affected companies. And of course there is the overall reduction in the defense budget initiated under the Clinton Administration.

On the commercial side, costs are just as severe. According to a 1997 source, "73 percent of the software projects in corporate America were canceled, over budget, or late." [5] Consider the liability costs associated with the following possibilities:

- the cost of radioactive cleanup and containment due to a software failure at a nuclear power plant
- the case where a cancer treatment device delivers an overdose of radiation to unsuspecting patients
- a software failure causes an airliner full of passengers to crash
- and, of course, the Year 2000 problem, which, for many of us, will still be with us after the year 2000

The Quality of Software.   The quality of software has also suffered as a result of the way that software is developed. The complexity of large software programs is on the rise, making it more difficult than ever to know what is actually going on during development. Development today makes use of many concurrent processes that must all come together for the first time during the software integration phase and later during the systems integration phase of the life cycle. Visibility needs to be exploited on the front end of software development, specifically where errors are introduced into the process.

Consistency and Confidence.   How do we know what we are building, when we are in the middle of the building process? What is there to tell us if we are—or even if we are capable of—building software right the first time, as originally proposed by Philip Crosby [6] and now by the more recent Total Quality Management (TQM) approach for software? [7] Is most of software development subject to trial and error? What is there that provides a method of standardization and consistency that managers and engineers can rely on time and time again? How can we know and assess the real risks during the software development process? What is a true measure of progress? What is the true measure of performance?

These and other concerns are of increasing importance to the software community at large and to the customer. We can no longer afford to be at risk, vulnerable to the point where vital programs can be swept away by the tide of noncompliance and delays. Witness the ripple effect through the economy of so many jobs lost in key industries across the country following the announcement of DoD program cutbacks and terminations. Not only are the prime contractors hurt but also the subcontractors, the vendors, and the individual.

14.3.6 Using CASE to SQA Advantage

Software quality assurance has the primary role of assuring that software is developed to perform as specified by the customer. In today's environment this includes tasks at the project level and tasks at the division level or higher. In this broader, total quality role, SQA has opportunities not available a few years back. This broader perspective offers SQA a way to add value to both the project and the company. In today's value-added climate, the days of black box monitoring only at the end of the process are over. SQA needs to know what's going on inside the development process and in one form or another to be a part of that process. To prevent problems, you must be involved in the process from the beginning.

The fact that these value-added changes are being implemented is supported by the following real life examples:

1. **Peer inspections** (see Chapter 9 for details) mandate formal role playing for every member of the inspection team. In many companies the role of moderator is often assigned to SQA, making SQA a major part of the process. CASE tools used by SQA in support of peer inspections include a projectwide database for entering and recording the status of inspection data. Value-added roles for SQA are both short term and long term.

   - Short term: SQA evaluates the effectiveness of finding/fixing problems confined to the project. Problems found here are preventative since they do not propagate to code and test. Whether moderator or not, SQA should use the database to generate metrics on the number of problems found (i.e., prevented) versus the time spent in inspections. These problems also need to be categorized, via the database, to support Pareto analyses (see Chapter 11) which are needed to identify the worst case problems and to define in what phase and in what modules the most serious problems are being found. This information is value-added information, important to both the team and to project management. The advantage is that prevention occurs in-phase (i.e., errors are not propagated to the next phase). These errors are the least costly to fix.
   - Long term: Statistics on problems found using preventive techniques, such as the peer inspection process, need to be collected from multiple projects over time. These kinds of data define trends and improvements (or the lack thereof) in targeted trends. This visibility is extremely significant and supports use of metrics common among SEI Level 4 companies. These long term metrics define not only where the company is strong, but also where the company needs to improve versus the competition and targets areas for benchmarking. Since these longer term metrics and trends span multiple programs, they are not likely to be supported by engineers and managers buried in the day to day battles within their project. Consequently, this is an excellent area of opportunity for SQA to step forward and take the lead—advantage SQA. A companywide database is required here to capture the data from the various projects. CASE tools needed are those that support sharing of data between various project databases and the companywide database. Additional CASE tools needed are those that generate key process area metrics and at the same time easily interface with the companywide database. Selection of CASE tools should consider minimizing duplication of data and use of symbolic referencing so that a change to a project database is automatically reflected in the companywide database.
   - The role of SQA here, to capture and maintain data that defines long term trends, also supports establishing an independent organization

within the company, such as a Software Engineering Process Organization (SEPO). Organizations like SEPO value such information on trends because this kind of data provides direction in their efforts to target processes for improvement and also provides a measure of those improvements in time. Where successful, improvements in processes lead to improved companywide procedures. This information is also valuable for assessing the degree of consistency practiced among the various projects throughout the company. The point here is that SEI Level 1's are ad hoc, Level 2's and beyond are repeatable.

2. **Requirements definition.** Although a systems engineering task, there is a nice role here for SQA, one worth fighting for. As opposed to the traditional role of evaluating the set of performance, operational, and functional requirements at the end of the functional baseline process, the value-added way for SQA to participate in this process is for SQA to maintain the database of requirements. This has several advantages for SQA:

- Up-front assessment of requirements validation. This is critical to the role of assurance. Long before validating the product (a post-task activity reserved for the end of the program), the single most critical role for SQA on the front-end of the program, a role which distinguishes SQA from any other disciplines on the program, is to assure us that we are building the right product. [8] Of course, any decision of this magnitude will involve the customer. If no one can assure that we are building the right product, it's time to stop, regroup, and rethink the requirements. We do not want to find out, near the end of the program, that the product does not meet customer expectations.

  Getting involved with requirements on the front end of the program provides early insights into understanding what the product must do. Consequently, maintaining the requirements database is a good hands-on value-added way for SQA to become familiar with requirements. CASE tools here may be a relational database, such as the Requirements & Traceability Management tool (RTM) from GEC Marconi Limited (c/o Marconi Systems Technology, 4115 Pleasant Valley Road, Suite 100, Chantilly, VA 22021), or an object-oriented database such as the System Level Automation Tool for Engineers (SLATE) (c/o TD Technologies, Inc., 2425 N.Central Expressway, Suite 200, Richardson, TX 75080, 972 669-9937, info@tdtech.com, www.tdtech.com).

  Note: the reference to CASE tools here comes from the built in interface these databases have with existing tools such as Cayenne Software's Teamwork (formerly Cadre's Teamwork), FrameMaker, etc. and their compatibility with some sort of File Transfer Protocol (FTP), which permits easy transfer of files to and from the database (i.e., from a UNIX environment to a PC environment hosting, for example, Microsoft Office running under Windows 95 or NT).

- Assessment of readiness to baseline. In maintaining the requirements database, SQA observes firsthand any and all changes to requirements. The volatility of change is a good indication of whether or not the set of requirements is ready to baseline. If not, SQA may recommend delaying the baseline task until the set of requirements can be firmed up through additional trade studies and customer meetings.

- Customer Visibility. Changes to requirements are often customer driven. SQA, as a prime user of the database, has the option of tagging requirements changes as customer driven or contractor initiated. Such data may become important later. As keeper of the database, SQA will most likely have the advantage of participating in customer meetings conducted to define requirements.

  Once requirements have been baselined, the database can be used to track requirements volatility, a metric reserved to track the number of changes to baselined requirements. Changes to requirements are important since these changes adversely impact schedule and progress, resulting in more and more rework the further into the life cycle the project progresses.

3. **Test.** The traditional role of SQA here is to verify requirements at test. However it is interesting to note that the real role of SQA is behind the scenes as opposed to just witnessing the actual test. In order to have confidence in the results, everything leading up to the actual test must be in place and correct. This entails what are considered test readiness activities. In section 14.2 we introduced the notion of a software engineering environment (SEE). Readiness for test requires two mini software engineering environments: the test environment itself and the configuration control environment.

   The test environment includes
   - Documentation: The test plan (defines overall test strategy, levels of test, test coverage, constraints, etc.), test procedures (defines actual test steps with expected results), verification cross-reference index or matrix (traces each approved testable requirement to a test procedure).
   - Test Support Software/Tools: Approved commercial off-the-shelf (COTS) software tools, certified simulations, calibrated equipment, etc. data recording and reducing software package.

The configuration control environment includes

- Software: Configured version of the application software under test, any required but approved input data and media for reading/accessing such data, embedded controlled COTS software that is deliverable and therefore subject to test, configured certified support tools and simulations, etc.
- Documentation: All of the above configured documentation listed under the test environment above plus any open software problem reports (SPR) that impact the test outcome, any approved work arounds, and minutes of the Test Readiness Review.

Given the above two mini SEEs, the role of SQA here is not so much the use of any particular tool for SQA, but the certification of the CASE tools for the proposed test environment and certification of CASE tools for the proposed configuration control environment prior to their use.

Note: an independent role for SQA during the test phase is to track the number of new problems found at test and compare this against the number and kinds of errors found during the peer inspection process. This provides some measure of feedback to assess the effectiveness of the peer inspection process in attempting to eliminate errors prior to test. A worthwhile goal is to note the worst case problems found at test and to target improvements in the peer inspection process to eliminate these problems on the next future project. This task is best sponsored by organizations like SEPO to provide improvements companywide. Again the tool of preference here is a relational or object-oriented database.

We have discussed the role of SQA and the corresponding advantages of using CASE tools in three key process areas: peer inspections, requirements definition, and test. A concern for all three processes areas is risk assessment. It is specifically in the area of high risk where CASE technology can play a major role. The use of better control (both front end and back end), widespread automated integration throughout a program, and high visibility are what is needed to reinforce up front project management and technical decision making. These are but a few of the potential rewards awaiting use of CASE technology.

14.4   Applicability of Tools

An important thing to remember about tools is that they are not an end unto themselves; tools are only a means to an end. This is significant. Tools are only as good as the user(s) behind them. The user must therefore carefully define

- what process the tool will support

- how the tool will be used
- what the expected benefit will be

Note, in this sense, that use of the term user is not limited to one person. Frequently the objectives of a proposed process and selection of an appropriate tool are often the careful deliberation of a users' group such as a process improvement team or an Integrated Product Team (IPT).

The tool then, as an instrument of implementation, becomes a reflection of the process. The tool therefore supports and even becomes a standard part of a specified process to yield the anticipated benefits noted above; i.e., lower costs, shorter schedules, less risk, an improved process, and a better product.

In today's environment, these anticipated benefits are expected; just ask management. The relative importance of tools and reasons to fund their purchase are tied to their ability to support the following: to increase profitability; to maintain a competitive edge in the marketplace, to maintain a leadership role in the industry, to provide cost-effective products, and to support internal process improvement goals. This last item supports corporate objectives to attain or maintain the International Organization for Standardization's (ISO) certification and to achieve compliance with acceptable, capability maturity levels as defined by the Software Engineering Institute's (SEI) Capability Maturity Model (CMM) (see Chapters 12 and 13).

14.5   Where to Find Tools

The literature is filled with advertisements for many tools. To assist the reader in researching the latest in tool technology and tool vendors, this section provides a list of sources. Key sources are professional organizations, conferences and symposia, magazines, and the Internet. Note, the approach taken here deviates somewhat from the approach taken in the previous edition of this *Handbook*, noting that any list of tools, no matter how current, will soon be obsolete. The more practical approach, taken here, is to present the reader with a way to find the most current tools, today, tomorrow, next year, and beyond.

14.5.1 Professional Organizations

Many professional organizations have access to tools and vendors that support the industry represented by the professional society. Following is a list of several professional organizations as well as various ways to contact or join them:

The American Society for Quality (ASQ):

address: ASQ, P.O. Box 3066,
                      Milwaukee, WI 53201-3066

phone:	(800) 248-1946 or (414) 272-8575
fax:	(414) 272-1734
Web site:	http://www.asq.org
magazines:	*Quality Progress* (primary magazine)
	Software Quality (software chapter)

The Association for Computing (ACM):

address:	ACM Member Services
	Church Street Station, P.O. Box 12114
	New York, NY 10257-0163 USA
phone:	(800) 342-6626 (U.S. & Canada)
	(212) 626-0500 (Outside U.S.)
fax:	(212) 944-1318
e-mail:	orders@acm.org (to join or to order)
	acmhelp@acm.org (for questions)
Web site:	http://www.acm.org
magazine:	*Communications of the ACM*

DPMA: The Association of Information Technology Professionals:

address:	Association of Information Technology Professionals
	315 South Northwest Highway, Suite 200
	Park Ridge, IL 60018
phone:	(800) 224-9371
fax:	(847) 825-1693
magazine:	*Information Executive* (monthly)

The American Institute for Aeronautics and Astronautics (AIAA), Inc.:

address:	American Institute for Aeronautics and Astronautics. Inc.
	Suite 500
	1801 Alexander Bell Dr.
	Reston, VA 20191-4344
phone:	(703) 264-7500
	(800) 639-2422
fax:	(703) 264-7551
e-mail:	majordomd@frymulti.com
netscape\mail:	webmaster@aiaa.org
Web site:	http://www.aiaa.com
magazine:	*AIAA Journal*

The Institute of Electrical and Electronics Engineers (IEEE), Inc.:

address: IEEE Computer Society
                      10662 Los Vaqueros Circle
                      P.O. Box 3014
                      Los Alamitos, CA 90720-1314
phone: (714) 821-8380   or   1 (800) 678-4333
fax: (714) 821-4641   or   (732) 562-6380
Web site: http://www.ieee.org
                      http://www.computer.org (IEEE Computer Society)
e-mail: webmaster@ieee.org
                      membership@computer.org (IEEE Computer Society)
magazines: *Spectrum* (primary magazine)
                      IEEE Software (software chapter)

Note: the above addresses, phone numbers, Internet addresses, etc. are subject to change.

If you belong to a professional organization, you have access to the latest symposia and conferences. Often the symposium or conference is cosponsored by more than one professional organization or may be cosponsored by one or more government agencies. Additionally, your membership entitles you to at least one or more monthly periodicals. Between the symposia, conferences, and the periodicals you should have more than enough information to begin a search of the latest tools related to your field of interest.

14.5.2 Conferences and Symposia

Professional organizations sponsor or cosponsor annual conferences and symposia—some local to your area. If you're fortunate enough that your company requires training for employees, you might request attending one or more conferences in your field as a means of satisfying training requirements. If all goes well, you can take full advantage and investigate first hand the latest methods and tools available today. Many conferences sponsor tool exhibitions, providing a separate place and time during the course of the conference, for vendors to demonstrate the latest tools they have on the market.

The author attended two such conferences [9,10] in his local area. The latter conference, Automated Software Test & Evaluation, [10] cosponsored by the Society for Software Quality (SSQ) followed this exact format, offering both the presentation format and a separate tool exhibit.

The well-noted magazine, *Quality Progress*, [11] sponsored by the ASQ, also lists conferences [11, pp. 80–88] for Quality Engineers, such as ASQ's "Annual

Quality Congress & Exhibition." This conference also reserves one or more blocks of time over a three-day period for tools and methods.

It is also worth mentioning that not only is this a good way to meet peers in your industry; this is also an avenue for benchmarking. Peers attending conferences may offer first hand knowledge of tools they have used and may also be able to compare such tools with those of the exhibitor.

14.5.3 Magazines

Magazines are another resource for tools. The company or public library is a good place to start. The latest month's periodicals are most likely on display for easy reference.

As noted above, professional societies offer a variety of magazines that advertise tools. For example, when you join ASQ you receive *Quality Progress*. [12] Table 14-1 represents a snapshot of some of the quality tools found in this magazine.

Table 14-1 Sample List of Tools in *Quality Progress* [12]

Software Tool	Company / Owner of Tool	Phone/Internet Address	Function Performed
SQCpack® for Windows™	PQ Systems Dayton, Ohio	(800) 777-3020 (737) 885-2252 fax http://www.pqsystems.com	Converts data to charts for Pareto analysis, SPC, etc.
PathMaker®	SkyMark™ 7300 Penn Ave. Pittsburgh, PA 15208	(800) 826-7284 (412) 371-0681 fax www.pathmaker.com	Quality management tool; supports quality improvement via SPC.
Procedure Design™	MEGA International	(800) 920-6342 www.mega.com	Software package for writing and accessing procedures online.
JMP®	SAS Institute, Inc. JMP® Sales Dept. SAS Campus Dr. Cary, NC 27513	(919) 677-8000 (919) 677-4444 fax www.JMPdiscovery.com	Statistical tools; link graphs & statistics; interactive.
QMX	DPI Services	(800) 374-2140 www.qmx.com	Quality Management and ISO compliance software; automated processes.
QFD Scope™ 1.1 for Windows™	Integrated Quality Dynamics, Inc.	(800) 870-4200 (310) 540-6392 fax www.iqd.com	Quality function deployment toolset.

Note: the above versions, addresses, phone numbers, etc. are subject to change.

It is also worth noting that many magazines today are free to the reader practically for the asking, with some exceptions: *Datamation* is one well known example. A second magazine, also free to the public, since the magazine is funded by the government, is *CrossTalk, The Journal of Defense Software Engineering*. [13] *CrossTalk* is quite unique, since this magazine covers tool evaluations and provides this information, upon request, to those individuals working DoD programs. Others may also be able to request *CrossTalk*. Tools are evaluated by the Software Technology Support Center (STSC) at Hill Air Force Base, Ogden, Utah. To subscribe, a request form is accessible via the Internet at the following url:

http://www.stsc.hill.af.mil

The company library may also subscribe to electronic library services, such as a CD-ROM service, which offers the latest listings of vendors and tools by category of interest. These services are usually updated monthly. If your company does not provide this service, your public library may.

The CD-ROM service is an excellent resource. A list of tool/tool summaries can be quickly generated by user-defined parameters to include product category and application. For example, the author generated a list of tools using the CD-ROM service provided by Information Access Company, Inc. [14] Tools were searched under the listing for: 'Software/Systems/Application Development/System Design.' The following categories were searched:

- Application Development Environment   711 tools found
- Debug and Test   454 tools found
- Design Analysis Management Tools   478 tools found
- Documentation Generation / Aids   55 tools found
- Program Generation   61 tools found
- Program Utilities   857 tools found
- Simulation   64 tools found
- Software Engineering / CASE Tools   181 tools found
                                             2861 total

Table 14-2 provides a sample of tools from the list of Software Engineering/CASE Tools.

Using the same CD-ROM [14] service the author conducted a second search for CASE tools under quality with the following results:

Under: Software Product Specifications (includes tools)   44,679 items

searching for: 'CASE' 'software quality'   866 items
searching for: 'CASE' 'quality'   63 items

Table 14-2 Sample List of Software Tools from CD ROM Service Provided by Information Access Company, Inc. [14]

SW CASE Tool	Company	Phone	Function Performed
Maestro II (V2.2) $10,000/workstation Sold 30,000	Softlab, Inc. 1000 Abernathy Rd. Suite 1000 Atlanta GA 30328-5613	(770) 668-8811 (770) 668-8812 fax	Allows users to maintain mainframe legacy systems and identify mainframe components for re-use in client/server & other architectures. Includes scanning capability for PL/1,COBOL, SQL, CICS, DL/I, IMS DB/DC.
AppBridge Professional (V3.0)	Software Development Tools, Inc. 60 State St. Ste 700 Boston, MA 02109	(617) 854-7454 (617) 371-2950 fax	Automated code generator for legacy to Windows applications. The tool set migrates to 3D of client/server; error free C code and compiled C/C++ Windows programs.
BPSimulator$300	Technology Economics, Inc. (TEI) 11212 Stephalee Lane Rockville, Md. 20852	(301) 984-1334 (301) 984-0816 fax	Part of Business Process Re-engineering (BPR) Suite. Simulation tool designed for BPR—provides statistics, I/O analysis, animation for visual demos.
TeamWare Flow (V1.1) $495/user	TeamGROUP 3055 Orchard Dr. San Jose, CA 95134	(408) 432-1300 (408) 456-7272 fax	Enables teams to plan, execute, participate, track and manage business processes. Includes Graphical Planner, Viewer, and Forms Builder. Does document management with version control. Includes API and scripting for customization.
Softest (V5.1) $2500 Sold 400	Bender & Associates, Inc., 484 Magnolia Ave. PO Box 849 Larkspur, CA 94939	(415) 924-9196 (415) 924-3020 fax	Test CASE design tool. Formats test cases in batch mode (for batch jobs) and in script (for online interactive systems). Generates a decision table for the entire test suite and a matrix showing which part of system's functionality has been tested.

Note: the above versions, addresses, phone numbers, etc. are subject to change.

Table 14-3 lists a sample of the software quality CASE tools found using the corporate CD-ROM service.

Table 14-3   Sample List of SQA CASE Tools from CD ROM Service Provided by Information Access Company, Inc. [14]

SQA CASE Tool	Company	Phone	Function Performed
Analyzer	Case Consult Corp. 945 Concord St. Framington, MA 01701	(800) 288-9510 (508) 620-4531 (508) 620-4532 fax	Ensures comprehensiveness of test data providing test coverage for COBOL programs. Compatible with Windows 95, NT and 3.X, PC-MS/DOS, IBM/MVS, OS/2, AS/400, Unisys, XENIX.
Q/Artisan Version 2.5	Case Consult Corp. 945 Concord St. Framington, MA 01701	(800) 288-9510 (508) 620-4531 (508) 620-4532 fax	Rule-based COBOL transformation tool that rewrites COBOL to create reliable, readable, transportable COBOL programs. Improves code quality. Rewrites code that falls outside the user-set rules. Windows 95, NT, 3.X, PC-MS/DOS, IBM/MVS, OS/2.
PureDDTS (Release 3.3)	Pure Atria 1309 S. Mary Ave. Sunnyvalle, CA 94087	(800) 353-7873 (408) 720-11600 (408) 720-9200 fax	Tracks known defects, enhancement, and change requests. Provides change management control. Stores info for check in/out per defect. Has SQL & Oracle Database support. Offers UNIX, WEB, Command line & e-mail interfaces.
Teamwork/SD Version 7.0	Cayenne Software, Inc. 8 New England Executive Park Burlington, MA 01803	(800) 528-2388 (617) 273-9003 (617) 229-9904 fax	Creates/edits graphic verifiable SW designs via Structure Charts, DFDs, Module Specs, Data Dictionary. Checks design specs for cohesion, coupling, quality, accuracy, completeness, syntax, and balancing. Automates Yourdon-Constantine Structured Design method.
AISLE/QualGen & CISLE/QualGen	Software Systems Design 3627 Padua Ave. Claremont, CA 91711	(909) 625-6147 (909) 626-9667 fax	Analyzes code and produces over 200 metrics and 30 reports to view tabular and graphic metrics. Use AISLE for Ada code.Use CISLE for C code.

Table 14-3 *(continued)*

SQA CASE Tool	Company	Phone	Function Performed
ABLE (Asset Based Lending Environment)	Computer and Software Enterprises, Inc. P.O. Box 5207 San Luis Obispo, CA 93403	(805) 544-5821	Portfolio Management SW for asset-based and corporate finance lending. Handles structuring/monitoring of complex loan relationships, letters of credit, online approval/availability and trend analysis.
Quality Management	a4 Health Systems 5501 Dillard Dr. Cary, NC 27511-9234	(800) MSA-DATA (919) 851-6177 (919) 851-5991 fax	Allows QA directors to consolidate, report, track departmental and hospitalwide problems. Monitors indicators required by JCAHO to perform medical staff QA including drug use evaluation, surgical case review, clinical department monitoring.
SPSS Base for Windows Version 7.5	SPSS Inc. 444 N. Michagan Ave. Chicago, IL 60611-3962	(800) 543-2185 (312) 329-2400 (312) 329-3668 fax FORTRAN & C++	Statistical Data Analysis Package. Includes statistical routines, data management, plots, graphs, conjoint, correspondence, time-series analysis routines & presentation tables. Includes Chart Editor. Modules include SPSS Trends, SPSS Chaid, MapInfo and QIAnalyst.

Note: the above versions, addresses, phone numbers, etc. are subject to change.

14.5.4 The Internet

The Internet is also an excellent resource. With the Internet everything is essentially at your fingertips. The major organizations now have a Home Page on the Internet, as noted above for IEEE, ASQ, and ACM.

Sources of technical magazines are also easy to find; however the search for magazines that describe tools and their applications is more involved and time consuming. Again, a good place to start is through the professional organizations and the magazines they sponsor.

One service on the Internet rated the top 100 magazines in software. "Internet Valley," found under Yahoo! (http://www.yahoo.com/News/Magazines), provides a brief synopsis of each of the top 100 software magazines rated. The Internet also has an Electric Library which lists magazines alphabetically and provides a search capability by keywords. These are too numerous to mention here and better left to the reader.

Note, however that if you provide the name of the tool vendor, your search becomes a lot easier. This makes a legitimate case for attending conferences and symposia that sponsor tool exhibitions. Table 14-4 presents a partial list of vendors that participated in the tool exhibition at one of the Automation and Software Test Evaluation (ASTE) conferences. [10]

Table 14-4   Partial List of Vendors Attending Tool Exhibition at ASTE Conference 1997 [10]

1. From "Reducing Costs and Schedules with Automated Unit Level Testing," William K. McCaffrey, Vector Software, p. 260; [10]
   - Vector*CAST*—intelligent test tool

2. From "Automating the Testing of Web Based Products," Jeffrey Payne & Janathon Beskin; Reliable Software Technologies, p. 279; [10]
   - http://www.rstcorp.com   (703) 404-9293
   - http://www.rstcorp.com/hotlist.html   has links to tool vendors
   - http://www.rstcorp.com/tools.htm
      - WhiteBox DeepCover   for JAVA code
      - WebSpider   tests links, validates html
      - WebCapture   tests web servers for load

3. From "Effective Use of Automated Test Tools," Uri G. Lichtman, Bellcore, p. 292; [10]
   - Efficient Data Analyzer (EDS)   adapted to Telecommunications Software & client/server distributed computing
   - Automatic Efficient Test   tests System, Unit, and Protocol
     Generation (AETG)

4. From "Driving GUI Based Applications," Jason M Selvidge; Software Engineering Technology, Inc., p. 319; [10]
   - http://www.toolset.com   (423) 637-1333 x229   fax (423) 637-0802
                                         methodology to test Graphical User Interfaces

You can search the Internet by defining one or more keywords using a search engine, such as Yahoo! The author found 50 matches using the following keywords: software, quality, and tools. The search produced the following command:

http://search.yahoo.com/bin/search?p=software+quality+tools

The Internet results were presented in short brief statements with a heading category, the company name and a description for each tool found. The searched keywords words were also highlighted. Examples of software quality tools found on the Internet are shown in Table 14-5:

Table 14-5   Sample of Software Quality Tools found on the Internet using the
Yahoo Search Engine

Business and Economy: Companies: Construction: Software

- Quality Plans and Software, Inc.—Tools for building professionals.

Business and Economy: Companies: Computers: Software: Programming Tools: Testing

- Quality Checked Software, Ltd.—A provider of real-world software testing solutions
- RadView Software Ltd., on the Web—Designs, develops and markets tools for enhancing software quality. The company is a member of the RAD group.
- Eastern Systems Software Testing Solutions—Establishes a "Test Life Cycle" plan in order to recommend the best tools to improve the quality of the software and software-based systems of each customer.

Business and Economy: Companies: Computers: Software: Scientific

- Jandel Scientific Software—A full line of software tools to enhance and improve the quality of your research.

Business and Economy: Companies: Quality: ISO: Consulting

- International Quality Management—IQM offers ISO 9000 quality management, Deutscher Qualitaetsmanagement server, software tools, Kostenloser Download Musterhandbuch 20 QM elemente und Verfahrensanweisungen, Kostenlose Beratung via e-mail. Okoaudit (German).

Business and Economy: Companies: Computers: Software: Programming Tools: Development:

- Centerline Software—Software quality automation tools and services, including programming, error checking, coverage testing, widget-based GUI testing, error simulation, post-deployment monitoring.

Business and Economy: Companies: Computers: Software: Scientific: Data Collection and Analysis

- OOO Software, Inc.—Tools for cross-tabulation, data analysis, statistics and report writing. Produce publication-quality output from Oracle, Sybase or Ingres databases and sequential files.

Business and Economy: Companies: Quality: Consulting

- Consulting, training, and software to help improve business competitiveness: TQM, Hoshin, DOE, QC tools.

Business and Economy: Companies: Computers: Software: Databases

- Woll2Woll Software—Specializing in the creation of high quality, professional and easy to use tools for database application developers and end-users. Four tools—EzDoc, EzTools, EzDialog for Paradox, and InfoPower for Delphi.

14.5.5 Vendors

With regard to tools, vendors are of two types; vendors who provide existing COTS tools available to the general public and vendors who specialize in building prototype one-of-a-kind tools for specified limited unique use. Examples of vendors selling COTS tools to the general public are Microsoft (Windows NT), Motorola (Power PC), Sun Microsystems (JAVA), AT&T (UNIX), Compaq Computer (Digital Equipment's VMS). Examples of companies building unique applications would be any company you hire (IBM, CSC, Motorola, etc.) under a subcontract to develop software in accordance with a unique set of requirements as defined in a subcontractor's specification.

Vendors can be located using resources such as those noted in Tables 14-1 and 14-2. Another good resource for finding software vendors is the Annual Quality Software Directory. The Quality Software Directory is published every year in the ASQ magazine *Quality Progress* [15]. The Software Directory lists vendors in alphabetical order and highlights their field(s) of expertise.

14.6   A Look Ahead

CASE technology has come a long way in the last few years. Many tools today have built in hooks that provide a direct interface to other tools like RTM and Teamwork or SLATE and FrameMaker (Section 14.3). Advances in local and wide area networks (LAN/WAN) have improved to the point where tools from different vendors can be interfaced together on the same network to access the same data. The Open Systems Architecture (OSA) and client server network have opened the door to new advances in tool integration. The pace for future advancements is on the increase. High technology companies are on the move with an eye toward the future, in an effort to not be left behind, as today's tools become tomorrow's has-beens.

The Internet also has a part in this. Information is now at you fingertips. Access to information on the latest vendors and software quality CASE tools is making its way on to the Internet through direct marketing, advertising by professional societies for upcoming conferences, magazines, etc. The lists are growing.

Finally, both ISO and SEI continue to influence the industry. ISO, with its objective to pursue standardization throughout the software industry on an international scale, and SEI, with its goal to push that standard to the highest level of maturity on an ever increasing scale, are gaining wider and wider acceptance throughout the software community. These changes are pushing the limits of the software process and are opening the door to the next generation of CASE tools and results. As standardization and improvement take hold, new CASE tools will fall in line with this new direction. The new tools will be more adaptable to the software process and will more readily support the anticipated standardization and expected improvements.

References

1. Amey, W., *The Computer Assisted Software Engineering (CASE) System*. Proceedings Fourth ICSE, September, 1979.

2. Fedchak, Elaine, "An Introduction to Software Engineering Environments." In: *Proceedings of COMPSAT 1986, the IEEE Computer Societies' 10th Annual International Computer Software and Applications Conference*, pp. 456–463, IIT Research Institute, IEEE, (Chicago, IL: October 8–10, 1986). (Note: Material is reprinted with permission of IEEE.)

3. *The Digital COHESION Environment for CASE, Digital Equipment Corporation*, 1990. (Note: Copyright © 1990, Digital Equipment Corporation. All rights reserved. Reprinted by permission.)

4. McKeehan, David, "Avionics Software Development for PAVE PILLAR & PAVE PACE Architectures." SEI-90-SR-15, July 1990. (Note: Material reprinted with permission of the Software Engineering Institute, Carnegie Mellon University, Copyright © 1990, SEI.)

5. Vecchio, Dale, "A Strategy of Time" (A WHITE PAPER), Viasoft Inc. (Supplement to *Software Magazine*) 1997.

6. Crosby, Philip B., *Quality Without Tears*, (New York: McGraw-Hill Book Co., 1984).

7. Schulmeyer, G. Gordon, and McManus, James I., *Total Quality Management for Software*, (New York: Van Nostrand Reinhold Co., 1992).

8. Boehm, Barry W., *Software Engineering Economics*, (Englewood Cliffs, NJ: Prentice Hall, 1981).

9. *Software Acquisition Management, The Third Annual Conference on*; sponsored by: the Education Foundation of the Data Processing Management Association; Conference Management by: Technology Training Corporation; Oct. 7–8, 1996.

10. *Automated Software Test & Evaluation (ASTE '97), The 7th Annual Conference and Tools Exhibition on*, Washington D.C.; sponsored by: the Education Foundation of the Data Processing Management Association; Conference Management by: Technology Training Corporation; March 20–21, 1997.

11. *Quality Progress*, Volume 31, No 3. The American Society for Quality (ASQ), March 1998.

12. *Quality Progress*, Volume 31, No 6. The American Society for Quality (ASQ), June 1998.

13. *CrossTalk, The Journal of Defense Software Engineering*, Ogden AALC/TISE, 7278 Fourth St., Hill AFB, UT 840556-5202, 1997.

14 Data Services Report, CD ROM Service, Information Access Company, 1997.

15. *Quality Progress*, Volume 31, No 4. The American Society for Quality (ASQ), April 1998.

General References

1. ISO 9000, *Quality Management and Quality Assurance Standards—Guidelines for Selection and Use*. (Geneva, Switzerland: International Organization for Standardization (ISO), Case Postale 56, CH-1211 Geneve 20, Switzerland, 1991.)

2. ANSI/ISO/SQC Q9001-1994. *Quality Systems—Model for Quality Assurance in Design, Development, Production, Installation, and Servicing*. (Milwaukee, WI: ASQC, 611 East Wisconsin Ave., Milwaukee, Wisconsin 53202, 1994.)

3. ISO 9000-3, *Quality Management and Quality Assurance Standards—Part 3 Guidelines for the Application of ISO 9001 to the Development Supply and Maintenance of Software*. (Geneva, Switzerland: International Organization for Standardization (ISO), Case Postale 56, CH-1211 Geneve 20, Switzerland, 1991.)

Software Quality Assurance Metrics

G. Gordon Schulmeyer
PYXIS Systems International, Inc.

15.1 Introduction

What is the difference between a measure, a metric, and an indicator? Before traveling into the details of software quality metrics, an understanding of these differences is in order. *A **measure** (Figure 15-1) is to ascertain or appraise by comparing to a standard. A standard or unit of measurement encompasses the following: the extent, dimensions, capacity, etc. of anything, especially as determined by a standard; an act or process of measuring; a result of measurement.* Without a trend to follow or an expected value to compare against a measure gives little or no information. It especially does not provide enough information to make meaningful decisions. *A **metric** (Figure 15-2) is a quantitative measure of the degree to which a system, component, or process possesses a given attribute. It is a calculated or composite indicator based upon two or more measures.* A metric is a comparison of two or more measures—in Figure 15-2 see body temperature over time—or defects per thousand source lines of code. *An **indicator** (Figure 15-3) is a device or variable that can be set to a prescribed state based on the results of a process or the occurrence of a specified condition.* An indicator generally compares a metric with a baseline or expected result. This allows the decisionmakers to make a quick comparison that can provide a perspective as to the "health" of a particular aspect of the project. [1, p. 29]

The purpose of software quality metrics according to the IEEE *Standard for a Software Quality Metrics Methodology*, [2, p. 4] is to make assessments throughout the software life cycle as to whether the software quality requirements are being met. The use of metrics reduces subjectivity in the assessment of software quality by providing a quantitative basis for making decisions about software quality. However, the use of metrics does not eliminate the need for human judgment in software evaluations. The use of software quality metrics within an organization or project is expected to have a beneficial effect by making software quality more visible.

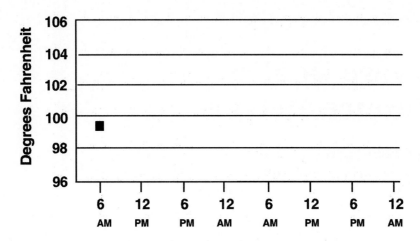

Figure 15-1   Measure sample. [1, p. 29]

One should note that the quality management models and metrics emerged from the practical needs of large-scale development projects and draw on principles and knowledge in the field of quality engineering (traditionally being practiced in manufacturing and production operations). For software quality engineering to become mature, a systematic body of knowledge should encompass seamless links among the internal structure of design and implementation, the external behavior of the software system, and the logistics and management of the development project. [3, p. 336]

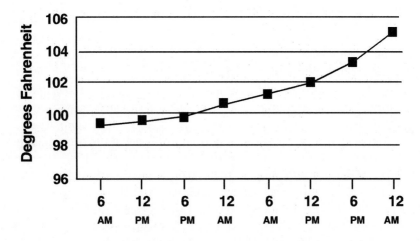

Figure 15-2   Metric sample. [1, p. 29]

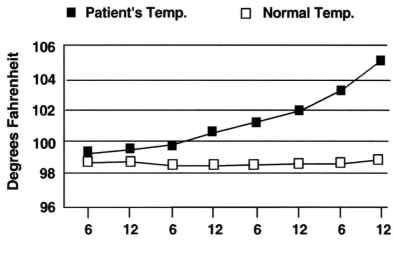

Figure 15-3   Indicator sample. [1, p. 29]

Software quality assurance metrics have taken on various guises over the years. This chapter introduces those used most. Also, to introduce a few relevant concepts, there is a brief review of an interesting software quality survey. This is followed by discussions of data collection methods and the idea of validating metrics.

There is a section devoted to an explanation of various methodologies for the capture and presentation of software quality metrics. That is followed by a section on what is being called the "omnibus" software quality metrics that derived from the work of McCall and Boehm. Software quality indicators have been published and a brief survey of their intention and use is covered.

Next, there are a number of examples illustrating various practical implementations of SQA metrics. That section covers Hewlett-Packard's experiences, Basili and Rombach's quantitative SQA, Walker Royce's TRW pragmatic quality metrics, The Carman Group's MIL/SOFTQUAL, Fairley's technical performance measurements, effectiveness measurement, Humphrey's personal software process, AT&T's and Bellcore's implementation, software process improvement measurement, software quality metrics prediction, and Microsoft's software quality metrics set.

15.1.1 Software Quality Survey

Some interesting metric information relating to software quality is contained in a software quality survey [4] conducted by the Software Quality Technical Committee of the American Society for Quality (ASQ). The survey is based upon 108 responses from industries that had 50 percent representation from aerospace/electronics and banking/financial, and the remaining 50 percent from other diverse industries.

Quality metrics, defined in the survey as a technique used to quantify the attributes of software quality through hard numbers, on average is used by 13 percent of those responding.

A little over 12 percent of the survey population employed metrics as an indicator of software reliability. The following three indicators were cited for this quality attribute: error rate, error density, and error severity. The metrics used for these are error rate—errors/month and errors/release; error density—errors/KSLOC (thousands of source lines of code) and number of problem reports; error severity—errors/category and number of rejections

Less than 4 percent of the survey population employed metrics to bound the complexity, maintainability, and/or testability of their software. The most cited metric for these quality goals are for complexity (4 percent)—cyclomatic number; maintainability (2 percent)—number of maintenance requests; and testability (1 percent) —coverage.

Only an average of 4 percent of those surveyed used a metrics analyzer, which is defined as an automated tool used to collect, analyze, and report the results of metrics quantification and analysis activities. [5]

15.1.2 Data Collection

A three-stage procedure for implementing a data collection scheme is:

1. Set the goals (why are you collecting the data, what reports do you want to see and when?)
2. Model the production process and the data (what data do you need to collect and when?)
3. Devise a collection scheme and put it in place (how do you make it happen?)

As a result of significant data collection the following important lessons were learned:

- Recording large volumes of data on paper is useless
- A scheme starts by transcribing data, not collecting it
- Define the process model, then the metrics
- Technology changes during a long term collection project
- Target and prediction data is not the same as *actual* data

As a part of this data collection exercise, it was found that subjective metrics (subjective complexity, quality, and the like) are unreliable for preliminary identification of anomalies but very useful when diagnosing their causes. [4, pp. 80, 81, 85]

Experience has shown that software developers do not mind quality criteria targets and the collection of data to achieve their goal as long as they participate in setting those goals and agree with them. But when data collection and interpretation are hidden from them, they will wonder whether the ground rules have been changed without their being informed. [6, p. 32]

So, quality can be measured throughout the software engineering process or after the software has been released to the customer and users. Metrics derived before the software is delivered provide a quantitative basis for making design and testing decisions. Quality metrics in this category include *program complexity, effective modularity,* and overall *program size.* Metrics used after delivery focus on the number of defects uncovered in the field and the *maintainability* of the system. It is important to emphasize that *after-delivery measures (correctness, maintainability, integrity,* and *usability)* of software quality present managers and technical staff with a post-mortem indication of the effectiveness of the software engineering process. [7, pp. 51–53]

15.1.3 Validation of Metrics

The validation of software quality measures are of interest here. There are two levels of validation necessary, referred to as *internal* and *external*. A software quality measure is internally valid if, in the sense of measurement theory, it provides a numerical characterization of some intuitively understood attribute. In all cases one must know for which aspect of the product (or process) a given measure is defined and whether there is a formal model for such definition (ensuring no ambiguity). Thus, for example, a valid measure of the attribute of modularity of designs requires a formal model for designs and a numerical mapping which preserves any relations over the set of designs intuitively imposed by the attribute of modularity. Thus, the proposed measure of modularity should indeed measure precisely, that if it is generally agreed that D_1 has a greater level of modularity than design D_2, then any measure m of modularity must satisfy

$$m\ (D_1) > m\ (D_2)$$

A software quality measure is externally valid if it can be shown to be an important component or predictor of some behavioral software quality attribute of interest. For example, if it could be demonstrated that modularity of designs is an important factor in subsequent ease of maintenance of the implemented code, then it could be said that modularity is a validated indicator of maintainability.

Proponents of software quality measurement have said that we cannot control what we cannot measure. It is equally true that we cannot *predict* what we cannot measure, but this viewpoint has rarely been articulated or understood. It seems strange that so much effort has been placed on externally validating metrics that predict attributes like cost, errors, changes, and certain external "quality" attributes, when there are not yet agreed upon standards for their definition nor the ability to identify (let alone measure) these attributes properly after they have occurred! Unless this is done there is no hope for true validation of predictive metrics.

Thus, in the absence of any standards for their definition and means of measurement, the use of historical data for defects, changes, costs, etc. as a means of external validation should be treated with extreme caution.

There is another reason why one should be far more careful in the approach to predictive metrics, which can never be effectively validated without an explicit life cycle model. In the absence of a generally agreed upon model, the use of even a validated predictive metric may be limited, except possibly in "conservative" areas like predicting specific code or maintenance attributes from code measures, or code attributes from measures of the detailed design. This would be particularly true in the case of current trends such as *evolutionary* design by rapid prototyping, where "traditional" life cycle views are irrelevant. [8, pp. 75, 76]

At a software engineering lab described in reference 9, each project spends on average 3 percent of its budget on data collection and validation. The organization spends an additional 4 to 6 percent on off-line data processing and analysis. However, one should expect a higher investment up front to build a new program. [9]

15.2   Software Quality Metrics Methodology

In this section on the rules for successful measurement, we are highlighting the methodology (process—see rule 3 below) for software quality measurement.

1. Make measurement beneficial for the person collecting the data.
2. Make measurement flexible to respond to custom requirements.
3. **Define the process first, then the measurement.**
4. Measure processes and verify them through feedback.
5. Define recognition, reward, and advice procedures for people who measure. [10, pp. 136, 137]

15.2.1 IEEE

This section is abstracted from the IEEE *Standard for a Software Quality Metrics Methodology*. [2] The software quality metrics methodology is a systematic approach for establishing quality requirements and identifying, implementing, analyzing, and validating software quality metrics for a software system. It spans the entire software life cycle and is comprised of five steps, which are:

- establish software quality requirements
- identify software quality metrics
- implement the software quality metrics
- analyze the software quality metrics results
- validate the software quality metrics

15.2.2 Establish Software Quality Requirements

The methodology starts by identifying quality requirements that may be applicable to the software system. Use organizational experience and required standards or regulations to create this list. Also, list other system requirements that may effect the feasibility of the quality requirements. Consider acquisition concerns, such as cost or schedule constraints, warranties, and organizational self-interest. Focus on direct metrics instead of predictive metrics. A direct metric value is a numerical target for a factor to be met in the final product. Whereas a predictive metric value is a numerical target related to a factor to be met during system development. It is an intermediate requirement that is an early indicator of final system performance.

Rate each of the listed quality requirements by importance. Importance is a function of the system characteristics and the viewpoints of the people involved. To determine the importance of possible quality requirements survey all the involved parties, and create an agreed upon final ordered list of quality requirements.

For each factor, assign a direct metric to represent the factor, and a direct metric value to serve as a quantitative requirement for that factor. For example, if "high efficiency" was one of the quality requirements, the direct metric "actual resource utilization/allocated resource utilization" with a value of 90 percent could represent that factor. This direct metric value is used to verify the achievement of the quality requirement. Without it, there is no standard to tell whether or not the delivered system meets its quality requirements.

15.2.3 Identify Software Quality Metrics

Create a chart of the quality requirements based on the hierarchical tree structure found in Figure 15-4. Only the factor level should be complete at this point. Now, decompose each factor into subfactors for as many levels as are needed until the subfactor is complete. Then, decompose the subfactors into metrics using the software quality metrics framework.

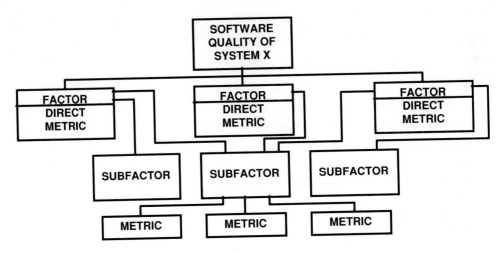

Figure 15-4   Software quality metrics framework. [2, p. 6]

The software quality metrics framework (Figure 15-4) begins with quality factors which represent management-oriented views of system quality. Associated with each factor is a direct metric, which serves as a quantitative representation of the quality factor. For example, a direct metric for the factor reliability could be faults/KLOC. Each factor must have an associated direct metric and a target value, such as 1 fault/KLOC, that is set by project management. Otherwise, there is no way to determine whether the factor has been achieved.

At the second level of the hierarchy are quality subfactors, which represent technically-oriented concepts. These are obtained by decomposing each factor into measurable software attributes. Subfactors are independent attributes of software, and therefore may correspond to more than one factor.

At the third level of the hierarchy the subfactors are decomposed into metrics used to measure system products and processes during the development life cycle. Direct metric values (factor values) are typically unavailable or expensive to collect early in the software life cycle. For this reason, metrics on this level are used, either collectively or independently, to estimate factor values.

For each validated metric on the metric level, assign a target value that should be achieved during development. To help ensure that metrics are used appropriately, only validated metrics (i.e., either direct metrics or metrics validated with respect to direct metrics) shall be used to access current and future product/process quality. Nonvalidated metrics may be included for future analysis, but shall not be included as a part of the system requirements. Each metric chosen must be documented on the form shown in Table 15-1.

Table 15-1   Metrics Set [2, p. 10]

TERM	DESCRIPTION
Name	Name of the metric
Metric	The mathematical function used to compute the metric
Costs	The costs of using the metric
Benefits	The benefits of using the metric
Impact	An indication of whether a metric may be used to alter or halt the project
Target Value	Numerical value of the metric that is to be achieved to meet quality requirements
Factors	Factors that are related to this metric
Tools	Software or hardware tools that are used to gather and store data, compute the metric, and analyze the results
Application	A description of how the metric is used and its area of application
Data Items	The data items (i.e., input values) that are necessary for computing the metric values
Computation	An explanation of the composition of the metric (i.e., steps involved in the composition)
Interpretation	An interpretation of the results of the metrics computation
Considerations	Metric assumptions, appropriateness (e.g., Can data be collected for this metric? Is the metric appropriate for this application?)
Training Required	Training required to implement or use the metric
Example	An example of applying the metric
Validation History	The names of projects that have used the metric and the validity criteria the metric has satisfied
References	References for further details on understanding or implementing the metric. List of projects, project details, etc.

After the software quality metrics framework is applied, a cost-benefit analysis is to be performed. Identify all the costs associated with the metrics in the metrics set. For each metric, estimate and document the following impacts and costs: metrics utilization costs, software development process change costs, organizational structure change costs, special equipment, and training. Then, identify and document the benefits that are associated with each metric in the metrics set. Finally, view the costs versus benefits and adjust the metrics set accordingly.

15.2.4 Implement the Software Quality Metrics

For each metric in the metric set, determine the data that must be collected and assumptions made about the data (e.g., random sample, subjective, or objective measure). The flow of data should be shown from point of collection to evaluation of metrics. Describe when and how tools are to be used. Identify the organizational entities that will directly participate in data collection. Describe the training required for this metric.

Test the data collection and metric computation procedures on selected software. Determine the cost of this prototype effort to further refine the cost estimates. Select the appropriate set of tools (manual or automated) to satisfy the requirements for data collection and metrics computation. Collect and store the data at appropriate times in the life cycle. Compute the metric values from the collected data.

15.2.5 Analyze the Software Metrics Results

The results should be interpreted and recorded against the broad context of the project as well as for a particular product or process of the project. Software components that appear to have unacceptable quality are identified. During development validated metrics are used to make predictions of direct metric values. Predicted values of direct metrics shall be compared with target values to determine whether to flag software components for detailed analysis. Direct metrics are used to ensure compliance of software products with quality requirements during system and acceptance testing. Software components and process steps whose measurement deviate from the target values are noncompliant.

15.2.6 Validate the Software Quality Metrics

The purpose of metrics validation is to identify both product and process metrics that can predict specified quality factor values, which are quantitative representations of quality requirements. Remember, metrics validation is addressed in the introduction to this chapter. If metrics are to be useful, they must indicate accurately whether quality requirements have been achieved or are likely to be achieved in the future. To be considered valid, a metric must demonstrate a high degree of association with the quality factors it represents (Section 15.3 discusses quality factors). This is equivalent to accurately portraying the quality condition(s) of a product or process. A metric may be valid with respect to certain criteria and invalid with respect to other criteria.

Metrics validation shall include the following steps: (1) identify the quality factors sample, (2) identify the metrics sample, (3) perform a statistical analysis, and (4) document the results. Additionally, it is necessary to revalidate a predictive metric each time it is used. Metrics validation is a continuous process. Confidence is not a static, one-time property. Confidence in metrics increases over time with a variety of projects. As metrics are validated, the metrics database increases and sample size increases.

To the extent practicable, metrics validation shall be undertaken in a stable development environment, and there shall be at least one project in which metrics data have been collected and validated prior to application of the predictive metrics.

15.2.7 Process-Based

For an organization to measure in a purposeful way it is necessary that it

1. Specify the goals for itself and its projects.
2. Trace those goals to the data that are intended to define these goals operationally.
3. Provide a framework for interpreting the data in order to understand the goals.

Thus, it is important to make clear, at least in general terms, what informational needs the organization has, so that these needs can be quantified whenever possible, and the quantified information can be analyzed to determine whether or not the goals are being achieved. [11, p. 24]

Like any top-down approach to problem solving Goal-Question-Metric (GQM) assumes that the problem to be solved is sufficiently well-defined to be decomposed into smaller units, which can be readily solved. This method of problem reduction is generally considered to be well-suited to mature and well-understood problem areas but less well-suited to new and undefined areas. In software, we often do not have an adequate understanding of the properties of the product being produced or the process used to produce it. We should not therefore be surprised that the application of a top-down view to measurement should encounter limitations. [12, p. 61]

From a knowledge of the process (per the capability maturity model, Chapters 12 and 13), one knows that once the process has been defined and successfully measured, the opportunity to optimize the process is achievable. What follows is a discussion of a cyclic activity that provides for a continuous optimization of the process that involves the practical use of metrics. Once the process is defined, the process improvement cycle to be defined should consist of

1. Defining the goals and objectives.
2. Defining and collecting data that provides information relative to the goals and objectives.
3. Making quantitative assessments.
4. Learning from successes and failures.

     5. Packaging successes for future use.
     6. Providing information for the next cycle.

    The first step requires that goals and objectives be established, with the related issues identified, ranked, and prioritized. In this next phase, the source(s) of data are identified, collected, organized, and saved for quantitative assessment.

    Match measurements to the prioritized objectives. Select measurement methods and tools to carry them out with minimal amount of effort. An automated measurement is better than a manual one, and a manual measurement is better than none at all. [10] During the assessment process, measurements versus identified data are analyzed, performance indicators are reviewed with process improvement results being documented and reported. Relative to lessons learned, the following three activities are necessary for continuous process improvement:

     1. Document the measurement experiences.
     2. Determine if the initially identified issues are satisfied.
     3. Determine if new issues for process improvement are needed.

    Once lessons learned are completed, successes for process improvement need to be packaged and reported for future optimization opportunities. During this process, improvement recommendations are identified and documented for subsequent program usage. Finally, a report of the recommendations is made and presented to top management. [13, pp. 166, 167]

15.3   Omnibus Software Quality Metrics

There have been several attempts to quantify the elusive concept of software quality by developing an arsenal of metrics which quantify numerous factors underlying the concept. The most well known of these metric systems are those developed by Boehm, Brown, Kaspar, Lipow, MacLeod, and Merrit [14], Gilb [15], and those developed by McCall, Richards and Walters [16]. The Boehm et al. and McCall et al. approaches are similar, although differing in some of the constructs and metrics they propose. Both of these systems have been developed from an intuitive clustering of software characteristics which are illustrated in Figure 15-5.

    The higher level constructs in each system represent (1) the current behavior of the software, (2) the ease of changing the software, and (3) the ease of converting or interfacing the system. Here, we will stay with the McCall et al. set of metrics. McCall et al. identified eleven quality factors, and beneath them there are 25 criteria. For example, *self-descriptiveness* underlies a number of factors included under the domains of product revision and transition.

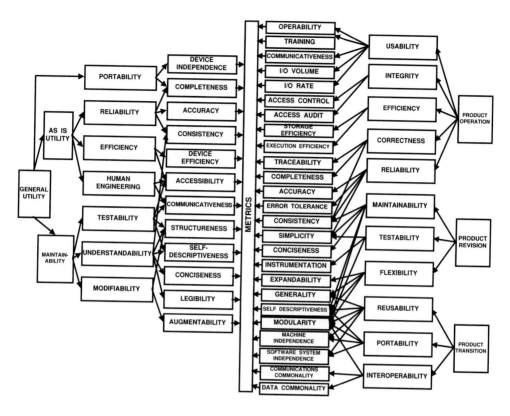

Figure 15-5 Software quality models. [17]

Primitive constructs and criteria are operationally defined by sets of metrics that provide the guidelines for collecting empirical data. There are 41 software metrics consisting of 175 specific elements.

No project can stay within a reasonable budget and maximize all of the quality factors. The nature of the system under development will determine the proper weighting of quality factors to be achieved in the delivered software. [17, pp. 204, 205]

Factors (Table 15-2) in software quality provide a framework for the acquisition manager to quantify concerns for the longer life cycle implications of a software product. For example, if the system is in an environment in which there is a high rate of technical breakthroughs in hardware design, the portability of the software should take on an added significance. If the expected life cycle of the system is long, finding and fixing errors as effectively as possible (maintainability) becomes a cost-critical consideration. If the system is an experimental system where the software specifications will have a high rate of change, flexibility in the software product is highly desirable. If the functions of the system are expected to be required for a long time, reusability is of prime importance in those units that implement the major functions of the system. Because of many networks available today, more systems are being required to interface with other systems, so interoperability is very important. [18, p. 130]

Table 15-2   Software Quality Factors [18, p. 129]

Correctness	Extent to which a program satisfies its specifications and fulfills the user's mission objectives.
Reliability	Extent to which a program can be expected to perform its intended function with required precision.
Efficiency	The amount of computing resources and code required by a program to perform a function.
Integrity	Extent to which access to software or data by unauthorized persons can be controlled.
Usability	Effort required to learn, operate, prepare input, and interpret output of a program.
Maintainability	Effort required to locate and fix an error in an operational program.
Testability	Effort required to test a program to insure it performs its intended function.
Flexibility	Effort required to modify an operational program.
Portability	Effort required to transfer a program from one hardware configuration and/or software system environment to another.
Reusability	Extent to which a program can be used in other applications—related to the packaging and scope of the functions that program performs.
Interoperability	Effort required to couple one system with another.

Each software system is unique in its software quality requirements relative to specific levels of quality. There are basic system characteristics which affect the quality requirements and each system must be analyzed for its fundamental characteristics. Examples of these fundamental characteristics and the associated quality factors follow.

Characteristic	Quality Factor
Human lives affected	Reliability Correctness Testability
Long life cycle	Maintainability Flexibility Portability

Characteristic	Quality Factor
Real-time application	Efficiency Reliability Correctness
Classified information processed	Integrity
Interrelated with other systems [19, p. 144]	Interoperability

The above quality factors take a management perspective to software quality. To introduce a dimension of quantification, this management orientation must be translated into a software-related viewpoint. This translation is accomplished by defining a set of criteria for each factor (Table 15-3). These criteria further define the quality factor and help describe the relationships between factors since one criterion can be related to more than one factor. The criteria are *independent attributes* of the software, or the software production process, by which the quality can be judged, defined, and measured.

Table 15-3   Criteria Definitions for Software Quality Factors [18, pp. 133, 134]

Criterion	Definition	Related Factors
Access Audit	Those attributes of the software that provide for an audit of theaccess of software and data.	Integrity
Access Control	Those attributes of the software that provide for control of the access of software and data.	Integrity
Accuracy	Those attributes of the software that provide the required precision in calculations and outputs.	Reliability
Communications Commonality	Those attributes of the software that provide the use of standard protocols and interface routines.	Interoperability
Communicativeness	Those attributes of the software that provide useful inputs and outputs which can be assimilated.	Usability
Completeness	Those attributes of the software that provide full implementation of the functions required.	Correctness
Conciseness	Those attributes of the software that provide for implementation of a function with a minimum amount of code.	Maintainability
Consistency	Those attributes of the software that uniform design and implementation techniques and notation.	Correctness Reliability Maintainability
Data Commonality	Those attributes of the software that provide the use of standard data representations.	Interoperability

Table 15-3   *(continued)*

Criterion	Definition	Related Factors
Error Tolerance	Those attributes of the softwarethat provide continuity of operation under non-nominal conditions.	Reliability
Execution Efficiency	Those attributes of the software that provide for minimum processing time.	Efficiency
Expandability	Those attributes of the software that provide for expansion of data storage requirements or computational functions.	Flexibility
Generality	Those attributes of the software that provide breadth to the functions performed.	Flexibility Reusability
Instrumentation	Those attributes of the software that provide for the measurements of usage or identification of errors.	Testability
I/O Rate	Those attributes of the software that provide for the measurement of the speed of acquired inputs and sending outputs.	Usability
I/O Volume	Those attributes of the software that provde for the measurement of the number of inputs arriving at the system and the number of outputs leaving the system.	Usability
Machine Independence	Those attributes of the software that determine its dependency on the hardware system.	Portability Reusability
Modularity	Those attributes of the software that provide a structure of highly independent modules.	Maintainability Flexibility Testability Portability Reusability Interoperability
Operability	Those attributes of the software that determine operation and procedures concerned with the operation of the software.	Usability
Self-Descriptiveness	Those attributes of the software that provide explanation of the implementation of a function	Flexibility Maintainability Testability Portability Reusability
Simplicity	Those attributes of the software that provide implementation of functions in the most understandable manner. (Usually avoidance of practices which increase complexity.)	Reliability Maintainability Testability

Table 15-3 *(continued)*

Criterion	Definition	Related Factors
Software System Independence	Those attributes of the software that determine its dependency on the software environment (operating systems, utilities, input/output routines,etc.)	Portability Reusability
Storage Efficiency	Those attributes of the software that provide for minimum storage requirements during operation.	Efficiency
Traceability	Those attributes of the software that provide a thread from the requirements to the implementationwith respect to the specific development and operational environment.	Correctness
Training	Those attributes of the software that provide transition from current operation or initial familiarization.	Usability

Quality metrics can be established to provide a quantitative measure of the attributes represented by the criteria. The measurements, represented by the quality metrics, can be applied during all phases of development to provide an indication of the progression toward the desired product quality. The measures themselves are predictive, and are of two types. The first, like a ruler, is a relative quantity measure; and the second is a binary measure (present or absent). Figure 15-6 provides example metric collection sheets. [18, p. 130-136]

Gerald Murine reports on some results from Japan using the omnibus software quality metrics with a customized program called SQMAT (software quality measurement and assurance technology). Motoei Azuma and others at Nippon Electric Company reported the following in 1985. Four pilot projects were undertaken that spanned a range of application, size, programmer experience level, and other parameters. Each produced interesting results (Table 15-4) and the following conclusions:

- "The quality target can be concretely established because of the qualifying quality."
- "Quality can be assessed objectively because of small differences between reviewers' scores."
- "Visual management can be put into practice through displaying quality graphically."
- "Software Quality Measurement and SQMAT are necessary technologies to measure quality quantitatively for managing software quality . . ."
- "This methodology contributes to management engineering from a standpoint of not only controlling quality but also managing software development by means of quality." [20, pp. 40, 41]

Factors(s) Reliability, Maintainability, Testability

CRITERION/ SUBCRITERION	METRIC	REQMTS Yes/No 1 or 0	Value	DESIGN Yes/No 1 or 0	Value	IMPLEMENTATION Yes/No 1 or 0	Value
Data and control flow complexity	S1.3 Complexity measure (by module, see para. 6.2.2.6)			☐		☐	
	System metric value: Sum of complexity measures for each module / # modules			☐		☐	

Factor: Correctness

CRITERION/ SUBCRITERION	METRIC	REQMTS Yes/No 1 or 0	Value	DESIGN Yes/No 1 or 0	Value	IMPLEMENTATION Yes/No 1 or 0	Value
Completeness	CP.1 Completeness checklist:	☐		☐		☐	
	1. Unambiguous references (input, function, output).	☐		☐		☐	
	2. All data references defined, computed, or obtained from an external source.	☐		☐		☐	
	3. All defined functions used.	☐		☐		☐	
	4. All referenced functions used.	☐		☐		☐	
	5. All conditions and processing defined for each decision point.	☐		☐		☐	
	6. All defined and referenced calling sequence parameters agree.	☐		☐		☐	

Figure 15-6   Example metrics. [12, p.137]

Table 15-4   Nippon Electric Co. SQMAT Results [20, p. 41]

PROJECT	A	B	C	D
SOFTWARE TYPE	Operating System (Assembly)	Cost Control (COBOL)	Application (COBOL)	Telephone EXC (PL1)
PHASES	All	Design	Code Design	Code Test
FACTOR(S)	Usability	Correctness Reliability	Correctness Reliability	Correctness Reliability
# ELEMENTS	28	15(D), 22(C)	9(D), 8(C)	3
SQM STAFF	4	3	1	Not Complete
COST	25%	20.8%	12.7%	Not Complete
RESULTS	Reduce Spec 25% Reduce Cost 33%	Reduce Test 50.8%	Reduce Code 46.2%	Not Complete

15.4   Software Quality Indicators

Scientific Systems Inc., under a contract to the Air Force Business Research Management Center, developed a set of software quality indicators (Table 15-5) to improve the management capabilities of personnel responsible for monitoring software development projects. The quality indicators address management concerns, take advantage of data that is already being collected, are independent of the software development methodology being used, are specific to phases in the development cycle, and provide information on the status of a project.

Eleven quality indicators are recommended:

1. *Progress*; measures the amount of work accomplished by the developer in each phase.
2. *Stability*; assesses whether the products of each phase are sufficiently stable to allow the next phase to proceed.
3. *Process Compliance*; measures the developer's compliance with the development procedures approved at the beginning of the project.
4. *Quality Evaluation Effort*; measures the percentage of the developer's effort that is being spent on internal quality evaluation activities.
5. *Test Coverage*; measures the amount of the software system covered by the developer's testing process.

6. *Defect Detection Efficiency*; measures how many of the defects detectable in a phase were actually discovered during that phase.

7. *Requirements Traceability*; measures the percentage of the requirements that have been addressed by the system.

8. *Defect Removal Rate*; measures the number of defects detected and resolved over time.

9. *Defect Age Profile*; measures the number of defects that have remained unresolved for a long period of time.

10. *Defect Density*; detects defect-prone components of the system.

11. *Complexity*; measures the complexity of the design and code.

These quality indicators have certain characteristics. Quality measures must be oriented toward management goals. One need not have extensive familiarity with technical details of the project. Quality measures should reveal problems as they develop and suggest corrective actions that could be taken. Quality measures must be easy to use. They must not be excessively time consuming, nor depend heavily on extensive software training or experience. Measures that are clearly specified, easy to calculate, and straightforward to interpret are needed. Quality measures must be flexible. [21, pp. 1, 2, 7]

Table 15-5   Quality Indicators by Development Phase [21, p. 25]

	Software Requirements Analysis	Preliminary Design	Detailed Design	Code and Unit Testing	CSC Integration and Testing	CSCI Testing
PROCESS INDICATORS						
Management Concern:						
Progress	Requirements Volume	Top Level Design	Detailed Designs	Units Completed	Tests Accomplished	Tests Accomplished
Stability	System Requirements Stability	Software Requirements Stability	Top-Level Design Stability	Detailed Design Stability	Software Stability	Software Stability
Compliance	Process Compliance	<——>				
Quality Effort	Quality Evaluation Effort	<——>				
Defect Detection:						
1. Test Coverage				Percentage of Paths Executed	Percentage of Paths Executed	Percentage of Paths Executed

2. Defect Detection Efficiency	Defect Detection Efficiency	<———————————————————————————————>		

PRODUCT INDICATORS

Completeness	System Requirements Traceability	Software Requirements Traceability		
1. Defect Removal Rate	Open and Closed Problem Reports	<————————————————————————————>		
2. ACI Profile	Problem Report Age Profile	<————————————————————————————>		
3. Defect Density	Defect Density	<————————————————————————————>		
Complexity	Requirements Complexity	Design Complexity	Design Complexity	Code Complexity

15.5   Practical Implementations

15.5.1 Hewlett Packard

At Hewlett Packard (H-P) there has been a history of software quality improvement efforts that have been reported at various conferences. The following is a timeline of H-P companywide efforts:

1980   Management awareness training for every General Manager and above.

1980   Developed FURPS (Functionality, Usability, Reliability, Performance, and Supportability) to describe software quality attributes, which was later revised to FURPS+ to include localization, predictability, and portability.

1981   Created the function of Productivity Manager in each Research & Development division.

1982   Formed a metrics council of interested engineers and managers, explored/collected many metrics from divisions, highlighted in the 1986 book, *Software Metrics: Establishing a Company-wide Program.*[22] H-P has kept very detailed records of software defect data after product release for years, but only recently have they had some divisions analyze the causes of defects found prior to release. [22, p. 22]

1983   Set up the Software Engineering Laboratory in corporate engineering for tools and methods.

1984   Started the Software Engineering Productivity Conference, an internal forum with over 800 attendees, where practical implementations of productivity and quality improvements are discussed.

1985   Established a corporate software quality manager.

1986   Established the Software 10X improvement goal: John Young, H-P CEO, stated, "I want us to achieve a tenfold improvement in two key software quality measures in the next five years."

1987   A high management level software 10X task force reaffirmed the magnitude of the issues, and the need for focus on software.

1987   The BET (Break Even Time) metric was introduced. This focuses on getting the right product to market in a timely manner. The goal is to cut the Break Even Time in half in five years.

1990s   Robert Grady's books and articles describing software metrics applied to inspections, maintenance, and software quality assurance.

Companywide measures at H-P are very few and very focused. They serve as drivers for division efforts and programs which are resulting in a set of best practices at the divisions. [23, pp. 8B-41, 8B-42]

15.5.2 Quantitative SQA

Following the process-based software quality metrics methodology of Basili discussed above. Basili and Rombach suggest a model for quantitative SQA that consists of three phases:

1. Define quality requirements in quantitative terms. Select the quality characteristics of interest, define priorities among and relations between those quality characteristics, define each characteristic by one or more direct measures, and define the quality requirements quantitatively by assigning an expected value.

2. Plan quality control through adequate actions to assure fulfillment of the defined quality requirements, control the proper execution of these actions, and evaluate the results.

3. Perform quality control which consists of: (1) measurement, in which the methods and techniques specified during the planning phase are applied to gather actual values for all defined measures, and (2) evaluation, in which the direct measurements are compared to the quality requirements and indirect measurements are interpreted to explain or predict the values of direct measures. Evaluation also involves deciding if the requirements were met for each quality characteristic and for the entire set of project requirements.

The quantitative SQA model considers the importance of the process, not just the product. One reason quality and productivity are perceived as conflicting is that process quality is often neglected, at least until the ISO 9000 standards were released. It is believed that productivity increases if a high quality development process is employed.

The quantitative SQA model also accounts for the equal importance of analytic and constructive SQA activities. The term "assurance" (as opposed to analysis) indicates that the objective is both to determine if quality requirements are met (the analytic aspect) and, when they are not met, to suggest corrective action (the constructive aspect).

The model covers all phases of software development so that effective software quality corrective action may be suggested.

Finally, the model stresses the importance of separating responsibilities for development and SQA. It is not important *who* performs the measurement part of quality control as long as it is planned for and evaluated by development-independent personnel. [24, p. 8]

15.5.3 Pragmatic Quality Metrics

Walker Royce at TRW Space and Defense calculated metrics on real time Ada projects. Simplicity is achieved by keeping the number of statistics to be maintained in a Software Change Order (SCO) database to five (type, estimate of damage in hours and SLOC, actual hours, and actual SLOC to resolve) along with the other required parameters of an SCO. Furthermore, metrics for $SLOC_C$ (configured source lines of code) and $SLOC_T$ (total source lines of code) need to be accurately maintained.

An SCO constitutes a direction in which to proceed when changing a configured software component.

The metrics described here were easy to use by personnel familiar with the project context. Furthermore, they provide an objective basis for discussing current trends and future plans with outside authorities. Table 15-6 provides raw data definitions for source lines, errors, improvements, and rework. Table 15-7 shows the in-progress indicator definitions of rework ratio, backlog, and stability. Table 15-8 defines the end-product quality metrics of rework proportions, modularity, changeability, and maintainability; as well as some values determined from real projects.

There are enough perspectives that provide somewhat redundant views so that misuse should be minimized. The possibility of misinterpretation exists, and so it would be beneficial to obtain more experience to evaluate where misinterpretation is most likely. [25, pp. 5, 17, 18]

Table 15-6   Raw Data Definitions [25, p. 8]

Statistic	Definition	Insight
Total Source Lines	$SLOC_T$ = Total Product SLOC	Total effort
Configured Source Lines	$SLOC_C$ = Stand alone Tested SLOC	Demonstrable Progress
Errors	SCO_1 = No. of Open Type 1 SCOs SCO_1 = No. of Closed Type 1 SCOs SCO_1 = No. of Type 1 SCOs	Test Effectiveness Test Progress Reliability
Improvements	SCO_2 = No. of Open Type 2 SCOs SCO_2 = No. of Closed Type 2 SCOs SCO_2 = No. of Type 2 SCOs	Value Engineering Design Progress
Open Rework	B_1 = Damaged SLOC Due to SCO_1 B_2 = Damaged SLOC Due to SCO_2	Fragility Schedule Risk
Closed Rework	F_1 = SLOC Repaired after SCO_1 F_2 = SLOC Repaired After SCO_2	Maturity Changeability
Total Rework	$R_1 = F_1 + B_1$ $R_2 = F_2 + B_2$	Design Quality Maintainability

Table 15-7 In Progress Indicator Definitions [25, p. 9]

Indicator	Defintion	Insight
Rework Ratio	$RR = \dfrac{R_1 + R_2}{SLOC_C}$	Future Rework
Rework Backlog	$BB = \dfrac{B_1 + B_2}{SLOC_C}$	Open Rework
Rework Stability	$SS = (R_1 + R_2) - (F_1 + F_2)$	Rework Trends

Table 15-8. End-Product Quality Metrics Definitions [25, pp. 11, 14]

Metric	Definition	Insight	Value
Rework Proportions	$R_E = \dfrac{Effort_{SCO_1} + Effort_{SCO_2}}{Effort_{Total}}$	Productivity Rework	6.7%
	$R_S = \dfrac{(R_1 + R_2)_{Total}}{SLOC_{Total}}$	Project Efficiency	13.5%
Modularity	$Q_{mod} = \dfrac{R_1 + R_2}{SCO_1 + SCO_2}$	Rework Localization	54 SLOC / SCO
Changeability	$Q_C = \dfrac{Effort_{SCO_1} + Effort_{SCO_2}}{SCO_1 + SCO_2}$	Risk of Modification	15.7 Hrs / SCO
Maintainability	$Q_M = \dfrac{R_E}{R_S}$	Change Productivity	0.49

15.5.4 MIL/SOFTQUAL

A software quality tool for assisting in metric evaluation is MIL/SOFTQUAL produced by The Carman Group, Inc. MIL/SOFTQUAL takes inputs based on development phases and subphases, it calculates Costs of Quality by project, phase, and subphases (Departments), and provides 145 different output charts. The MIL/SOFTQUAL outputs include:

- Cost of Quality
  - Project
  - Phase
  - Department
- Defects
  - Pareto
    - Project

- Phase
  - Department
- Defect Costing
- Liability
- Relational—Cost of Quality
  - Budget
  - Operating Expenses
  - Headcount
  - Lines of Code [26, p. 15, 16]

15.5.5 Technical Performance Measurement

Technical Performance Measurement (TPM) is used to: (1) measure planned vs. actual values of technical parameters during system development, and (2) predict the variance between specified and delivered values of technical parameters. The importance of TPM for software is:

- We do not know how to design software systems to required levels of technical performance or quality.
- Allocation of technical parameters to system components and periodic demonstration of planned vs. actual values during system development is the only means we have for controlling software quality.
- Incremental development and binary tracking provide the mechanism for measuring and controlling technical parameters in software.

TPM tracking works as follows:

- Technical parameters are allocated to the incremental builds.
- When an increment is completed, demonstrated values are compared to planned values.
- A performance index is computed and compared to the allowed demonstrated technical variance.
- A contingency plan is invoked if the demonstrated technical variance is greater than allowed or if the predicted technical performance is too great (Figure 15-7).

Some Technical (Quality) Parameters for Software:

- Throughput
- Response time

- Memory utilization
- Defect density
- Mean time between failures
- Accuracy of computations
- Direct access transfer rate
- Effective communication bandwidth

The following values are specified and measured for each technical parameter of interest:

- Planned values at various demos and tests
- Demonstrated values in various demos and tests
- Demonstrated technical variance between planned and demonstrated values in various demos and tests
- Specified requirement for the delivered value of the parameter
- Current estimate of the parameter value at delivery
- Predicted technical variance between current estimate and the specified requirement [27, pp. 2-28 to 2-31]

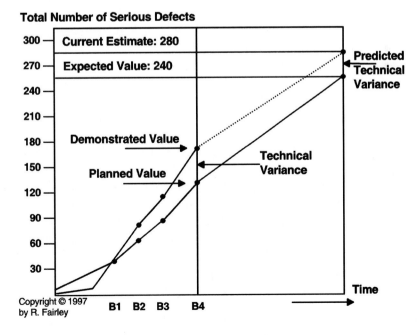

Figure 15-7 Profile of a TPM parameter: Tracking of expected vs. actual defects. [27, p. 2-30]

TPM requires the use of binary tracking. With binary tracking, we can be sure that work products have been completed and meet their pre-specified completion criteria. Lowest level tasks are 0 percent or 100 percent complete; percent completion of higher level activities is the ratio of completed lower level to total lower level: **5 / 15 = 33 percent complete**.

It is better to be 100 percent complete with 50 percent of the work than to be 50 percent complete with 100 percent of the work.

Binary tracking of rework: A new work package is opened and charged to rework when an accepted work product is later found to be defective. Rework is then calculated as the ratio of effort required for rework work packages completed to effort for total work packages completed: **36 / 140 = 26 percent rework**. [27, p. 2-23]

Norm Brown coordinates the Software Program Managers Network, which provides cogent questions for the software program manager. This is particularly applicable to the software quality aspect of the program as can be seen by the following questions concerning binary quality gates or binary tracking:

1. Do you use binary quality gates on your project? (Quality gates are checkpoints that ensure the quality and integrity of products before they are used in the next step of development.)
2. How many quality gates are in your development plan?
3. Do quality gates serve as checkpoints for product quality at discrete points in the project schedule prior to product release for general use?
4. How are you assured that your criteria and requirements are flowing down to the quality gate level?
5. Describe your requirements traceability mechanism. How are you tying it to your quality gates and their criteria?
6. List five representative quality gates for the project.
7. How many defects were discovered for products that have previously passed quality gates?
8. What quality gates have you established that ensure proof of concept (i.e., early deliveries, demos, time on machine)?
9. What is your definition of inch pebbles? Do you use them on your project? What are the lowest level tasks on your activity network?
10. Give an example of the lowest level tasks on your activity network?
11. How many tasks do you have at the lowest level of the work breakdown structure?
12. What is the longest duration of the lowest level task?
13. What is the highest cost item of your lowest level task?
14. What is the average cost and duration of the lowest tasks of the work breakdown structure?

15 What provisions exist in the plan for tasks that have yet to be determined or decomposed?

16. What type of reviews are conducted to access the quality of all engineering products before they are released for project use? [28, p. 11]

15.5.6 Effectiveness Measure

Measuring the effectiveness of individual quality assurance procedures and of the entire program is an important component of quality control. Robert Dunn's [29] simple effectiveness measure for individual activities is:

$$E = \frac{N}{N + S}$$

where E = effectiveness of activity
       N = number of faults (defects) found by activity
       S = number of faults (defects) found by subsequent activities

This measure can be tuned by selecting only those faults (defects) present at the time of the activity and susceptible to detection by the activity [29]. Testing effectiveness (the percentage of all errors found in testing that were found in system testing) is one important such measure. The development manager needs to know how the testers are doing as well as how the programmers are doing. Like error rate, testing effectiveness can be analyzed with a control chart. Establishing a chain of effectiveness measures spanning the life cycle also supports process improvement goals.

The percentage of effort spent in rework provides the best measure of the overall effectiveness of a quality assurance program. Estimates of rework in software development range from 30 to 50 percent (i.e., 30 to 50 percent of the total effort is spent on corrective problems.) More errors means more rework. More rework means lower productivity. An effective quality assurance program will decrease rework effort over time. Unfortunately, most software enterprises are very sensitive about measuring rework effort because it tends to be a measure of "failure" rather than of "success." [30, pp. 88, 89]

15.5.7 Personal Software Process (PSP)

A principal PSP objective is to apply proven quality principles to the work of individual software engineers. The expectation is that this will give software work more of an engineering flavor and make it more manageable.

A basic principle of quality management is that "If you don't demand quality work, you are not likely to get it." With PSP quality management, engineers track their own defects, find their defect removal yields, and calculate cost of quality measures. Pareto defect analysis (Chapter 11) is used to derive personal design and code review checklists, which the engineers update with defect data from each new project. [31, pp. 3, 5]

If you're measuring personal performance, be sure that you ask the people who know. [32, p. 141]

15.5.8 AT&T and Bellcore

The standard software quality metrics provide useful information to project and corporate management. The metrics permit the evaluation of trends and the quantifiable analysis of quality, starting with system test. The measurements quantify:

- the number of faults in generic software, normalized by software size
- the responsiveness of development and customer support organizations in resolving customers' problems
- the impact of software field fixes on customers

Descriptions of these measurements follow:

- Cumulative fault density found internally—faults found internally depict the faults found by the development organization normalized by the total software size in the system test phase.
- Cumulative fault density found by customers—faults found by customers depict the faults found by customers in the normal operation of released software, normalized by the total size of the released software.
- Total serious faults found—provides the number of serious faults found and the status of those faults—open (uncorrected) or closed (corrected)—as of the report date.
- Mean time to close serious faults—provides a measure of the responsiveness of the development and customer support organizations by showing the average time that serious faults remain open.
- Mean time still open for serious faults—provides a value for each month of the mean length of time that the serious faults, open at the end of the current month, have been open.
- Total field fixes—provides a measure of the impact of software field fixes on customers. [33, pp. 113-118]

Bellcore's general model is concerned with a number of customer releases of a certain software product and the underlying trend of software quality. In order to give a numerical illustration of the application of the methodology, consider a problem involving R = 3 releases of a software product. The number of lines of code in the three releases are:

$L_1 = 160,000$
$L_2 = 150,000$
$L_3 = 155,000$

Initially, the variances for the three releases were calculated as:

Release	Variance
# 1	0.04
# 2	0.03
# 3	0.02

But, the use of a formulation based upon the Quality Measurement Plan for tracking the quality of manufactured hardware, used to predict the faults detected by customers for each release, proved to be a better predictor than the assumption of exponentially distributed fault discovery times: [34, pp. 665–676]

Release	Variance
# 1	0.003
# 2	0.012
# 3	0.093

15.5.9 Measuring Software Process Improvement

Many organizations are setting goals for software process improvement based upon the Software Engineering Institute's CMM for software (Chapters 12 and 13). Therefore, a need exists for the measurement of where an organization is in relation to those goals. Motorola [35] has instituted an internal progress assessment process to have a better understanding of where they in relation to where they want to be.

When conducted quarterly, these progress assessments are summarized as shown in Figure 15-8 for the key process areas. To arrive at the results shown in Figure 15-8, a summary of each key process area must be captured, such as shown in Figure 15-9. That summary captured in Figure 15-9 requires a definition of the scoring, which is shown in Figure 15-10.

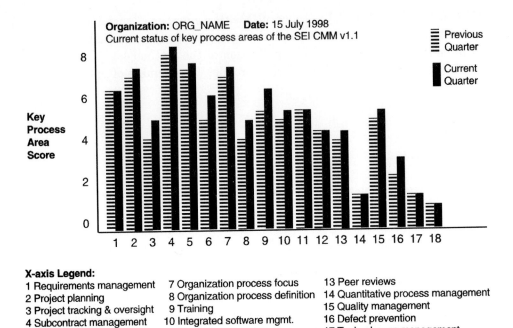

Figure 15-8   Summary key process areas status adapted from [35, p. 20].

Motorola also uses Kiviat representations for their software process status, but another similar example is provided here based upon the NORAD System Support Facility. [36, p. 44] To provide a clear view of multiple factors, such as the key process areas of the CMM Level 2, the Kiviat graph (Figure 15-11) from NORAD is a good example.

15.5.10 Predicting Software Quality

Basic models for predicting software quality include:

Akiyama $D = 4.86 + 0.018\, L$

Gaffney $D = 4.2 + 0.0015\, L^{3/4}$ where D: defects; L: lines of code
                      (optimum module size 877 LOC)

Compton and Withrow $D = 0.069 + 0.00516\, L + 0.00000047\, L^2$
                      (optimum module size 83 Ada LOC)

The problems with models such as these are that:

- defects are not solely caused by design complexity or size
- models ignore complexity of problem
- if you do not test you do not find defects
- component people produce "better " designs
- we cannot trust defect density figures

SEI Level 2 CMM v1.1 **Organziation:** ORG_NAME **Date:** 07/15/98											
KPA: Software project tracking and oversight **Average score**: 4											
List of key activities:	0	1	2	3	4	5	6	7	8	9	10
1. A documented software development plan is used for tracking software activities and communicating status.							X				
2. The project's software development plan is revised according to a documented procedure.			X								
3. Senior management reviews and approves all commitments and commitment changes made to individuals and groups external to the organization.	X										
4. Approve changes to software commitments or commitments affecting software activities are explicitly communicated to the staff and managers of the software engineering group and software related groups.				X							
5. The project's software size is tracked and corrective actions are taken.							X				
6. The project's software costs are tracked and corrective actions are taken.	X										
7. The project's critical target computer resources are tracked and corrective actions are taken.					X						
8. The project's software schedule is tracked and corrective actions are taken.								X			
9. Software engineering technical activities are tracked and corrective actions are taken.				X							
10. The software technical, cost, resource, and schedule risks are tracked throughout the life of the project.					X						
11. Actual measured data and replanning data for the project tracking activities are recorded for use by software engineering staff and managers.								X			
12. Software engineering staff and managers conduct regular reviews to track technical progress, plans, performance, and issues against the development plan.			X								
13. Formal reviews, to address the accomplishments and results of project software engineering, are conducted at selected project milestones and at the beginning and completion of selected stages.		X									

Figure 15-9 Sample scoring worksheet adapted from [35, p. 19].

SCORE	Key activity evaluation dimensions		
	Approach	Deployment	Results
Poor (0)	No management recognition of need. No organizational ability. No organizational commitment. Practice not evident.	No part of the organization uses the practice. No part of the organization shows interest.	Ineffective.
Weak (2)	Management has begun to recognize the need. Support items for the practice start to be created. A few parts of organization are able to implement the practice.	Fragmented use. Inconsistent use. Deployed in some parts of the organization. Limited monitoring/verification of use.	Spotty results. Inconsistent results. Some evidence of effectiveness for some parts of the organization.
Fair (4)	Wide but not complete commitment by management. Road map for practice implementation defined. Several supporting items for the practice in place.	Less fragmented use. Some consistency in use. Deployed in some major parts of the organization. Monitoring/verification of use for several parts of the organization.	Consistent and positive results for several parts of the organization. Inconsistent results for other parts of the organization.
Marginally qualified (6)	Some management commitment; some management becomes proactive. Practice implementation well under way across parts of the organization. Supporting items in place.	Deployed in some parts of the organization. Mostly consistent use across many parts of the organization. Monitoring/verification of use for many parts of the organization.	Positive measurable results in most parts of the organization. Consistently positive results over time across many parts of the organization.
Qualified (8)	Total management commitment. Majority of management is proactive. Practice established as an integral part of the process. Supporting items encourage and facilitate the use of the practice.	Deployed in almost all parts of the organization. Consistent use across all parts of the organization. Monitoring/verification of use for almost all parts of the organization.	Positive measurable results in almost all parts of the organization. Consistently positive results over time across almost all parts of the organization.
Outstanding (10)	Management provides zealous leadership and commitment. Organizational excellence in the practice recognized even outside the company.	Pervasive and consistent deployment across all parts of the organization. Consistent use over time across all parts of the organization. Monitoring/verification for all parts of the organization.	Requirements exceeded. Consistently world-class results. Counsel sought by others.

Figure 15-10　Guidelines to rate CMM activities adapted from [35, p. 18].

The solution involves a need to better reflect "difficulties" of quality management. Synthesize partial quality models to (1) include elements from each approach, (2) explain existing empirical results, and (3) be consistent with "good" sense. There is a need to cope with uncertainty and subjectivity. These solutions are addressed by the Bayesian Belief Networks (BBNs). BBNs consist of three major components: (1) graphical models, (2) conditional probability tables which model prior probabilities and likelihoods, and (3) Bayes' theorem applied recursively to propagate data through the network. The graph topology models the cause-effect reasoning structures. A BBN is a graphical network that represents probabilistic relationships among variables. BBNs enable reasoning under uncertainty and combine the advantages of an intuitive visual representation with sound mathematical basis in Bayesian probability. With BBNs, it is possible to articulate expert beliefs about the dependencies between different variables and to propagate consistently the impact of evidence on the probabilities of uncertain outcomes, such as "future system reliability." BBNs allow an injection of scientific rigor when the probability distributions associated with individual nodes are simply "expert opinions." A BBN will derive all the implications of the beliefs that are input to it; some of these will be facts that can be checked against the project observations, or simply against the experience of the decisionmakers themselves. There are many advantages to using BBNs, the most important being the ability to represent and manipulate complex models that might never be implemented using conventional methods.

At a general level we can see how the use of BBNs and the defect density model provide a significant new approach to modeling software engineering processes and artifacts. The dynamic nature of this model provides a way of simulating different events and identifying optimum courses of action based on uncertain knowledge. These benefits are reinforced when we examine how the model explains known results, in particular the "Is bigger better?" dilemma. Our new approach shows how we can build complex webs of interconnection between process, product, and resource factors in a way hitherto unachievable. We also should see how we can integrate uncertainty and subjective criteria into the model without sacrificing rigor and illustrate how decisionmaking throughout the development process influences the quality achieved.

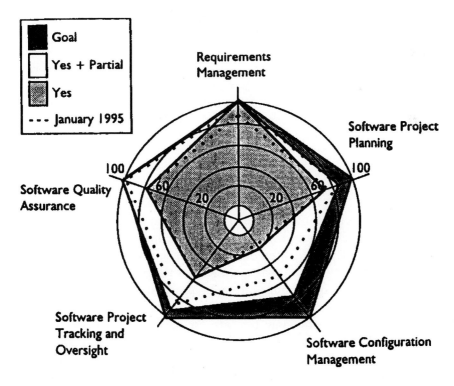

Figure 15-11   Sample Kiviat graph for process improvement. [37, p.23]

The benefits of this new approach are

- it is more useful for project management than other analysis and classical statistics
- it incorporates current research ideas and experience
- it can be used to train managers and enable comparison of different decisions by simulation and what-if analyses
- it integrates a form of cost and quality forecasting [38, pp. 219, 223]

15.5.11 Microsoft

Useful metrics for overall quality:

- total number of defects
- number of defects in each routine
- average defects per thousand lines of code
- mean time between failures
- compiler-detected errors [39, p. 545]

Unless results of a quality assurance plan are measured, one will have no way of knowing whether the plan is working. Measurement tells you whether your plan is a success or a failure and also allows you to vary your process in a controlled way to see whether it can be improved. Measurement has a second, motivational, effect. People pay attention to whatever is measured, assuming that it's used to evaluate them. Choose what you measure carefully. People tend to focus on work that is measured and to ignore work that is not.

15.6   Conclusion

Traditionally, most of our business measurement processes have been financially based—produced by accountants, designed for accountants (or regulators), not by or for managers. Measures come in the form of balance sheets, monthly profit and loss statements, and ROIs. They are often damage reports, telling us nothing about what we do today or tomorrow. We can extrapolate from them, but we know how dangerous that is. Nor do most of our measurement processes tell us about those other objectives that a reengineer wants to constantly scrutinize, such as cycle time and quality, or if they do, reports come too late for us to take action. On the whole, today's measurement processes do not really help us manage. [32, p. 122]

Although the idea of measuring quality by surveying users is novel in software engineering, it is not at all unusual in reviewing other products. Reviews are by experts, who rely for their credibility primarily on the reputation of the organization, not on their personal qualifications. Such reviews are published for many kinds of products: audio equipment, cameras, automobiles, and personal computer software, to name a few.

We have argued that measuring quality is not just for quality assurance. We have suggested that it is wise to break free from narrow notions of what constitutes quality. From a user's perspective, we have indicted the importance of software multiple releases. We have asserted that subjective assessment of quality can be useful, and that objective measures should be used to support subjective assessment. [40, p. 9]

There are many software quality assurance metrics to choose from and many are being used rather successfully by various companies. Personal experience has shown that any metrics program is very time consuming to implement and difficult to define. I have chaired a software metrics working group for the past two years. The progress shown by the working group has been slow, and seemingly every software metric needs to be redone for a myriad of reasons.

It is interesting to note that IEEE/EIA 12207, *Information Technology - Software Life Cycle Processes* [41], section 7.1.2.1 has the following to say concerning quality metrics.

The manager shall prepare the plans for execution of the process. The plans associated with the execution of the process shall contain descriptions of the associated activities and tasks and identification of the software products that will be provided. These plans shall include, but are not limited to, the following:

. . . g) Quality control measures to be employed throughout the process . . .

Software Technology Support Center (STSC) has proposed a metrics capability maturity framework, which is highlighted here, even though it is not specifically directed at software quality metrics. The software metrics capability maturity framework includes the following (not all inclusive) characteristics (Table 15-9 expands on these characteristics for maturity Levels 1 through 3):

- Level 1: Initial—No consistent metrics.
- Level 2: Repeatable—Project metrics implemented. Some basic infrastructure to support tracking and retention of project data.
- Level 3: Defined—Product metrics integrated in projects. Product database standardized across projects.
- Level 4: Managed—Process measured and controlled. Process database exists. Evidence of quality improvement.
- Level 5: Optimizing—Focus on improving software development products and processes based on quantitative data from historical databases. [42, pp. 16]

Table 15-8   Themes and Levels of Software Metrics Capability Maturity [42, p. 17]

Theme	Level 1 Initial	Level 2 Repeatable	Level 3 Defined
1. Formalization of development process.	Process unpredictable. Project depends on seasoned professionals. No or poor process focus.	Projects repeat previously mastered tasks. Process depends on experienced people.	Process characterized and reasonably understood.
2. Formalization of metrics process.	Little or no formalization.	Formal procedures established. Metrics standards exist.	Documented metrics standards. Standards applied.
3. Scope of metrics.	Occasional use on projects with seasoned people or not at all.	Used on projects with experienced people. Project estimation mechanisms exist. Metrics have project focus.	Goal/Question/Metric package development and some use. Data collection and recording. Specific automated tools exist in the environment. Metrics have product focus.
4. Implementation support.	No historical data or database.	Data (or database) available on a per project basis.	Product-level database. Standardized database used across projects.
5. Metrics evolution.	Little or no metrics conducted.	Project metrics and management in place.	Product-level metrics and management in place.
6. Metrics support for management control.	Management not supported by metrics.	Some metrics support for management. Basic control of commitments.	Product-level metrics and control.

While metrics remain controversial, that controversy is diminishing as research results show their usefulness, as issues of software reliability and safety become part of the public consciousness, and as government and industry realize the growing dependence on software and the concomitant need to measure software's functionality, reliability, cost, and schedule. Remember: You can't control what you can't measure. [43, p. 16]

Finally, listen to Andy Grove, CEO of Intel: "What gets measured, gets done."

References

1. Ragland, Bryce, "Measure, Metric, or Indicator: What's the Difference?" In: *CrossTalk*, Vol. 8 No. 3, March 1995. STSC, Ogden, pp. 29–30.

2. Institute for Electrical and Electronics Engineers, Inc., *Standard for a Software Quality Metrics Methodology P-1061* (New York: IEEE, 12 March 1993) Copyright (c) 1993 by IEEE, Inc., Reprinted by permission.

3. Kan, Stephen H., *Metrics and Models in Software Quality Engineering* (extracted from pages 4, 7, 8, 47). © 1995, Addison-Wesley Publishing Company Inc., Reprinted by permission of Addison-Wesley Longman Inc. (Reading: Addison-Wesley Publishing Company, 1995).

4. Portions reprinted with permission from Niall, Ross, "Using Metrics in Quality Management." In: *IEEE Software,* © July 1990, IEEE.

5. Reifer, Donald J., Richard W. Knudson, and Smith, Jerry, *Final Report: Software Quality Survey,* prepared for American Society for Quality Control, 20 November 1987.

6. Portions reprinted with permission from Grady, Robert B., "Work-Product Analysis: The Philosopher's Stone of Software?" In: *IEEE Software,* © March 1990, IEEE.

7. Pressman, Roger S., *Software Engineering: A Practitioner's Approach* (3rd edition) (New York: McGraw-Hill Book Co., 1992).

8. Portions reprinted with permission from Fenton, Norman E., "Software Metrics: Theory, Tools and Validation." In: *IEEE Software Engineering Journal,* © January 1990, IEEE.

9. Portions reprinted with permission from Rombach, H. Dieter, "Design Measurement; Some Lessons Learned." In: *IEEE Software,* © March 1990, IEEE, p. 20.

10. Arthur, Lowell Jay, *Improving Software Quality: An Insider's Guide to TQM* (New York: John Wiley and Sons, Inc., 1993).

11. Basili, Victor R., "Applying the Goal/Question/Metric paradigm in the experience factory." In: *Software Quality Assurance and Measurement: A Worldwide Perspective*, Fenton, Norman, Whitty, Robin and Iizuka, Yoshinori (editors), (Boston: International Thomson Computer Press, 1995).

12. Bache, Richard and Neil, Martin, "Introducing metrics into industry: a perspective on GQM." In: *Software Quality Assurance and Measurement: A Worldwide Perspective*, Fenton, Norman, Whitty, Robin and Iizuka, Yoshinori (editors), (Boston: International Thomson Computer Press, 1995).

13. Carey, David and Freeman, Donald, "Quality Measurements in Software." In: *Total Quality Management for Software,* Schulmeyer, G. Gordon and McManus, James J., eds. (New York: Van Nostrand Reinhold Co., Inc., 1992).

14. Boehm, B. W. et al., *Characteristics of Software Quality* (Amsterdam: North Holland, 1978).

15. Gilb, T., *Software Metrics* (Cambridge: Winthrop, 1977).

16. McCall, J. A., Richards, P. K., and Walters, G. F., *Factors in Software Quality*, General Electric, Command & Information Systems Technical Report 77CIS02, Sunnyvale, CA, 1977.

17. Curtis, Bill, "The Measurement of Software Quality and Complexity." In: *Software Metrics,* Perlis, Alan J., Sayward, Frederick G., and Shaw, Mary , eds., (Cambridge: The MIT Press, 1981).

18. McCall, James A., "An Introduction to Software Quality Metrics." In: *Software Quality Management*, Cooper, John D., and Fisher, Matthew J., eds. (New York: A Petrocelli Book, 1979).

19. Walters, Gene F., "Application of Metrics to a Software Quality Management (QM) Program." In: *Software Quality Management,* Cooper, John D., and Fisher, Matthew J., eds. (New York: A Petrocelli Book, 1979).

20. Murine, Gerald E., "Integrating Software Quality Metrics with Software QA." In: *Quality Progress,* American Society for Quality Control, November 1988.

21. MacMillan, Jean and John R. Vosburgh, *Software Quality Indicators* (Cambridge: Scientific Systems, Inc., 1986).

22. Grady, Robert B. and Deborah L. Caswell, *Software Metrics: Establishing a Company-Wide Program* (Englewood Cliffs: Reprinted by permission from Prentice-Hall, Inc., © 1987).

23. Ward, T. Michael, "Software Measures and Goals at Hewlett Packard." In: *Juran Institute Conference Proceedings*, 1989.

24. Portions reprinted with permission from Basili, Victor R. and H. Dieter Rombach, "Implementing Quantitative SQA: A Practical Model." In: *IEEE Software,* © March 1990, IEEE.

25. Royce, Walker, "Pragmatic Quality Metrics for Evolutionary Software Development Models." Private paper, May 1990.

26. Mandeville, William A., "Defects and Software Quality Costs Measurements." In: *NSIA Fifth Annual National Joint Conference Tutorial Notes,* 28 February 1989.

27. Fairley, Richard E., PhD, *Software Quality Engineering, An ACM Professional Development Seminar* (Washington, D.C., 1997).

28. Brown, Norm, *How Do You Know? What Do You Mean? Can You Show Me?* (Software Program Managers Network, 1996).

29. Dunn, Robert H., "The Quest for Software Reliability." In: *Handbook of Software Quality Assurance*, Schulmeyer, G. Gordon and McManus, James I., eds. (New York: Van Nostrand Reinhold, 1987), pp. 137–177.

30. Card, David N. and Glass, Robert L., *Measuring Software Design Quality* (Englewood Cliffs: Reprinted by permission from Prentice Hall Inc., © 1990).

31. Humphrey, Watts S., "Making Software Manageable." In: *CrossTalk*, STSC, Ogden, December 1996, pp. 3–6.

32. Champy, James, *Reengineering Management: The Mandate for New Leadership* (New York: Harper Collins Publishers, Inc., 1995).

33. Inglis, James, "Standard Software Quality Metrics." In: *AT&T Technical Journal*, Vol. 65 Issue 2, March/April 1986, pp. 113–118.

34. Portions reprinted with permission from Weerahandi, Samaradasa and Hausman, Robert E., "Software Quality Measurement Based on Fault-Detection Data." In: *IEEE Transactions on Software Engineering,* © 1994, IEEE.

35. Portions reprinted with permission from Daskalantonakis, Michael K., "Achieving Higher SEI Levels." In: *IEEE Software*, © July 1994, IEEE, pp. 17–24.

36. Hollenbach, Craig, Young, Ralph, Pflugrad, Al and Smith, Doug, "Combining Quality and Software Improvement." In: *Communications of the ACM*, Vol. 40, No. 6, June 1887.

37. Wakulczyk, Capt. Marek, "NSSF Spot Check: A Metric Toward CMM Level 2." In: *CrossTalk,* Ogden, STSC, July 1995, pp. 23–24.

38. Martin, Neil and Fenton, Norman, "Predicting Software Quality Using Bayesian Belief Networks." In: *Twenty-First Annual Proceedings of the Software Engineering Workshop Proceedings*, Goddard Space Flight Center, Software Engineering Laoratory Series, SEL-96-002, December 1996, pp. 217–224.

39. McConnell, Steve, From: *Code Complete* (Redmond: by Microsoft Press, 1993) Reproduced by permission of Microsoft Press. All rights reserved.

40. Gentleman, W. M., "If Software Quality is a Perception, How Do We Measure It?" (Ottawa: Institute for Information Technology, National Research Council of Canada, 1996).

41. IEEE/EIA 12207.0, *Software life cycle processes*, March 1998.

42. Budlong, Faye C., and Peterson, Judi A., "Software Metrics Capability Evaluation Methodology and Implementation." In: *CrossTalk*, STSC, Ogden, January 1996.

43. Portions reprinted with permission from Mills, Harlan D. and Peter B. Dyson, "Using Metrics to Quantify Development." In: *IEEE Software*, © March 1990, IEEE.

Practical Applications of Software Quality Assurance to Mission-Critical Software

James H. Heil
Telos Corporation

16.1 Special Concerns with Mission-Critical Software

Mission-critical software has been defined by the U.S. Department of Defense (DoD) to be software that is used in weapon systems or real-time sensor systems, and also in Command and Control, Communications, and Intelligence Systems. Mission-critical software is characterized as having a direct effect on the operational success or failure of a military mission, usually involving significant risk to human life. Examples of software of this type include ground-based systems to detect and track Inter-Continental Ballistic Missiles (ICBMs) and Submarine-Launched Ballistic Missiles (SLBMs), and satellite-based systems to detect military activity of various kinds (and transmit specific messages back to command and control nodes). Other examples include airborne avionics systems for communications/navigations, defense electronics counter-measures, and flight control.

Certain mission-critical software systems are large, with over one million executable source lines of code (SLOCs), and reside on large mainframe computers or networks. Other systems are relatively small, and may be only 20,000 to 100,000 SLOCs. These smaller systems usually reside on embedded microcomputer systems, which may have limited memory and addressing capability. In the early years, most of the real-time embedded applications were written in Assembly language because of the very limited memory available (frequently 64K words or less). However, the capabilities of microcomputers have greatly expanded, and memory size and processing speed have really improved. Furthermore, many applications are now written in higher-order languages, such as Ada.

For certain real-time systems, there is a critical need to execute certain program paths in a few milliseconds to meet system performance requirements. In the last twelve years, the author has been involved primarily with small, embedded, real-time systems of this general type. However, it is important to note that software and microcomputer technology are improving rapidly, and software for such embedded systems can now be written in higher-order languages with some selective use of Assembly language for critical time-sensitive kernels.

Most mission-critical software for the U.S. Air Force and Navy is still being developed per MIL-STD-498, Software Development and Documentation, dated 5 December 1994. The U.S. Army (with a few exceptions) does not allow the use of MIL-STDs but has not actively endorsed the use of the comparable industry standard (IEEE Std P1498/EIA IS 640, J-STD-016, Software Development: Acquirer-Supplier Agreement, dated 15 July 1995). In 1994, William J. Perry, then Secretary of Defense, issued *DoD Policy on the Future on MILSPEC* that said: ". . . use performance and commercial specifications and standards in lieu of military specifications and standards unless no practical alternative exists to meet the user's needs. . . ." As of 1998, the following is the situation with regard to commercial standards being available for use on DoD mission-critical projects. There are available the following three related standards under consideration for use on software-intensive mission-critical systems:

- IEEE/EIA 12207.0-1996 *Software Life Cycle Processes*, March 1998
- P12207.1 draft *Software Life Cycle Processes; Implementation Considerations,* February 1997 (focuses on work products)
- IEEE/EIA 12207.2-1997 *Software Life Cycle Processes; Implementation Considerations*, April 1998 (focuses on processes)

As may be seen from the list, P12207.1 is still in draft stage, so the set of commercial standards as desired by the DoD is not yet readily available. Therefore, projects already started and even fairly recent startup projects are still following MIL-STD-498.

MIL-STD-498 evolved as a joint industry/government effort to update the earlier DOD-STD-2167A, Defense System Software Development, dated 29 February 1988. Although a few critics of DOD-STD-2167A noted that several of the figures suggested or implied a "waterfall" process (despite the statements in the Foreword and the Software Development Process, paragraph 4.1.1), one of the valuable benefits in DOD-STD-2167A was the simplified model in Figure 16-1 that provided a comprehensive overview of the activities, products, and reviews, etc., and how they interrelate. The essence of this figure is provided as Figure 16-1 with several additional annotations, and with several of the preliminary documents tailored out. Figure 16-1 indicates the nominal software development activities across the top of the diagram. The

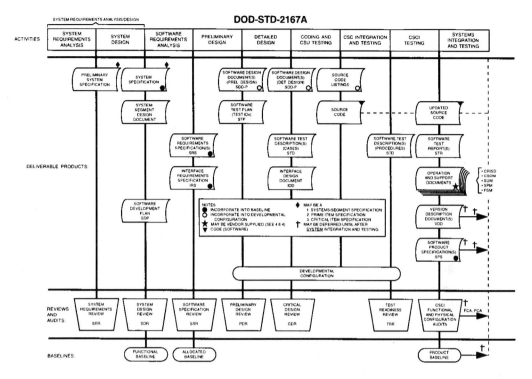

Figure 16-1 Deliverable products, reviews, audits, and baselines (based on Figure 2 in DOD-STD-2167A).

deliverable products, which normally are produced by each activity unless tailored out of the contract, are indicated in the middle of the diagram. Six different formal reviews with the customer (plus the final Functional and Physical Configuration Audits) are indicated near the bottom of the diagram. Finally, the three baselines used for formal government configuration management are shown at the bottom. For simplicity, no recursions nor iterations are indicated and only a single iteration or build is indicated.

MIL-STD-498 made changes to reflect the lessons learned from the use of DOD-STD-2167A, and also merged the two standards for mission-critical software and Automated Information Systems (AISs) software into a single standard. MIL-STD-498 further deemphasized the waterfall development paradigm, and sought to facilitate the use of incremental and evolutionary development paradigms (strategies). Unfortunately, the single overview diagram disappeared, and four separate diagrams were used in an Appendix of MIL-STD-498 to illustrate the Grand Design, Incremental, Evolutionary, and Reengineering program strategies/paradigms. The

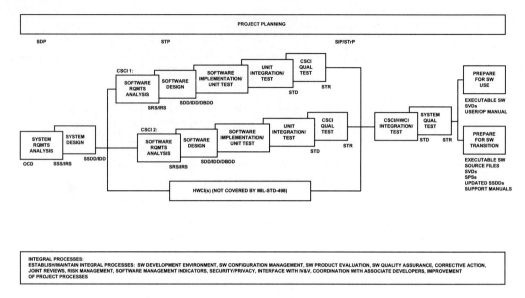

Figure 16-2 One possible way of applying MIL-STD-498 to the Grand Design program strategy (based on Figure 9 in MIL-STD-498).

simplest diagram, the Grand Design, is included here as Figure 16-2. Two separate computer software configuration items (CSCIs) are displayed (each with different schedules, and each with a certain overlap of activities). CSCI/Hardware Configuration Item (HWCI) integration has been added prior to the system-level testing. Preparation for software use and for software transition also have been added. MIL-STD-498 deemphasizes the documentation products as part of the move away from a document-driven software development process. The names of several of the documents have also changed. Project planning is shown as a pervasive function throughout the development period. The DOD-STD-2167A formal joint reviews and the baselines have been removed from the bottom of the MIL-STD-498 figure. Finally, MIL-STD-498 explicitly adds the integral processes or activities across the bottom of the diagram (activities such as Software Quality Assurance (SQA), corrective action, software product evaluation, etc.). The document products (or data items) shown in short form in the diagram are listed in Table 16-1 in order of their appearance in MIL-STD-498.

Note that MIL-STD-498 allows the IRS, IDD, and DBDD also to be used at the system level. Similarly, MIL-STD-498 allows the test documents (STP, STD, STR) also to be used at the system level.

Table 16-1 Data Item Descriptions in MIL-STD-498

Reference Para (498)	Data Item Description (DID) Title
5.1.1	Software Development Plan (SDP)
5.1.2, 5.1.3	Software Test Plan (STP)
5.1.4	Software Installation Plan (SIP)*
5.1.5	Software Transition Plan (STrP)
5.3.2	Operational Concept Description (OCD)
5.3.3	System/Subsystem Specification (SSS)
5.3.3, 5.5	Interface Requirements Specification (IRS)
5.4.1, 5.4.2, 5.13.5	System/Subsystem Design Description (SSDD)
5.4.1, 5.4.2, 5.6.1, 5.6.2, 5.6.3	Interface Design Description (IDD)
5.5	Software Requirements Specification (SRS)
5.6.1, 5.6.2, 5.6.3	Software Design Description (SDD)
5.4.1, 5.6.1, 5.6.3	Database Design Description (DBDD)*
5.9.3, 5.11.3	Software Test Description (STD)
5.9.7, 5.11.7	Software Test Report (STR)
5.12.1, 5.13.1, 5.13.2, 5.13.4	Software Product Specification (SPS)
5.12.2, 5.13.3	Software Version Description (SVD)
5.12.3.1	Software User Manual (SUM)
5.12.3.2	Software Input/Output Manual (SIOM)*
5.12.3.3	Software Center Operator Manual (SCOM)*
5.12.3.4	Computer Operation Manual (COM)
5.13.6.1	Computer Programming Manual (CPM)
5.13.6.2	Firmware Support Manual (FSM)

* DIDs based on the AIS standard DOD-STD-7935, dated 31 October 1988.

16.2 Embedded Mission-Critical Software

The mission-critical software used in most embedded systems is characterized by tight constraints on memory, processing power (millions of instructions per second [MIPS]), input-output capability, and, in several cases, by the instruction set of the microprocessor. Of course, the capabilities of the assembler or compiler used for the source language can influence the performance of the delivered code, which can make a significant difference for several embedded systems.

Embedded computer systems are frequently composed of several microprocessors, rather than just one. Different functions are allocated to each microprocessor and its software. This functional allocation serves several purposes, including executing several aspects of the total processing job in parallel to meet time deadlines.

Usually, software residing within a single microprocessor is controlled as a separate CSCI for project management, configuration management (CM), documentation, and cost purposes. Certain CSCIs may have multiple instances (copies) to handle the load requirements for a system. It should be noted that two to four instances are reasonably common, and one system had over 40 instances of the same software. There may be cases where each instance of software is slightly different because of the need to identify itself in its outputs.

The microprocessors in a system of multiple microprocessors may be arranged in different patterns, and communicate in different ways. The architectures of federated, multiple microprocessor systems can be quite diverse. The following discussion considers three main types. The simplest form is a multiple, independent channel system (see Figure 16-3[a]). Each microprocessor is separate and independent, and interfaces only with its own channel; it is not a "federated" system in the normal sense.

A second architecture is where several microcomputers are attached to a single bus, and each microcomputer has its own address or ID. The microcomputer only processes those messages that have its address, or an acceptable address or code. A message goes down the entire bus, and is usually processed only by the intended microcomputer(s) (see Figure 16-3[b]). A broadcast message with a particular broadcast code may be processed by all of the microcomputers, for various systems func-

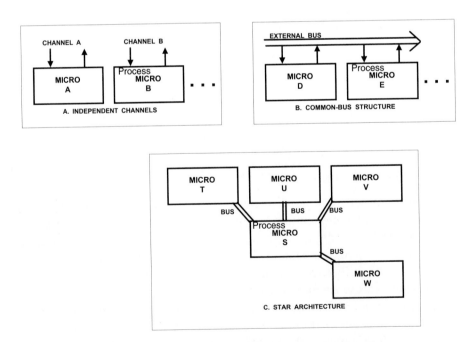

Figure 16-3 Some simple federal system architectures.

tions, etc. In certain cases, the bus may be in a ring structure, hence the term "ring architecture."

Another form of architecture is the star pattern of microprocessors. In this system, a single microprocessor acts as the central supervisor or controller at the hub of the star. A bus then goes to each satellite processor from the supervisor (see Figure 16-3[c]). In a classic star architecture, there is no communication directly between the satellite processors (T, U, V, etc.). The supervisor handles all communications with the other processors, and may task the processors to do certain work or may interrupt the processors. The supervisor will also initialize the system, and oversee the Built-In Testing (BIT) at initialization and other times. In larger systems, there may be secondary supervisors, each with their own cluster of satellite processors; the secondary supervisor would communicate directly with the main supervisor.

16.3   The Special Development Life Cycle for Mission-Critical Software

Mission-critical software usually goes through several cycles of software development (along with the overall system). The final stage of development, formerly called the Full-Scale Development (FSD) phase, is now called the Engineering and Manufacturing Development (EMD) phase, and the intent of this phase is to develop the final software (and system) that will be deployed for operational use. However, prior to the EMD phase, there is frequently a Program Definition and Risk Reduction (PDRR) Phase, where an initial version of the software and system is developed, as a prototype, to reduce risk in an effort considerably smaller than EMD. A PDRR effort may be 10 to 50 percent of the EMD, assuming the go-ahead is given to proceed into EMD. In certain cases, a Concept Exploration phase may precede the PDRR phase. Software may go through three or more macro cycles (or project phases), and the "Spiral Model" [1] for software development is one way to characterize these multiple macro cycles.

The planning for the SQA program (described in DOD-STD-2168) is usually considered a full-blown effort for the EMD phase. Typical SQA efforts for EMD phases run approximately 9 to 12 percent of the software engineering effort, exclusive of software documentation. For the PDRR effort (if there is one), the SQA percentage of the smaller effort is normally in the 6 to 9 percent range, exclusive of software documentation. If there is a Concept Exploration phase at the front end, the SQA requirements imposed by contract are usually tailored out, and only the contractor's procedures guide the level of SQA effort, which could range from 0 to 5 percent of the software engineering effort. A typical progression for a hypothetical project might be similar to the values indicated in Table 16-2. DOD-STD-2168, although now superceded and no longer used on new contracts, is a valuable SQA source. An ISO Guidebook, ISO 9000-3, provides "Guidelines for the Application of ISO 9001 to the Development, Supply, and Maintenance of Software."

Table 16-2   Typical Relationships Between Software Engineering and SQA Efforts

	Concept Exploration Phase	Program Definition and Risk Reduction (PDRR) Phase	Engineering and Manufacturing Development (EMD) Phase
Software Engineering Effort (Person-years)	30	60	200
SQA Effort (Person-years)	0.9 (3%)	4.5 (7.5%)	20 (10%)

The nominal activities discussed in DOD-STD-2167A, MIL-STD-498, or J-STD-016 may not be fully adequate, particularly for embedded mission-critical software. As noted in paragraph 4.1.1 of DOD-STD-2167A (or paragraph 4.1 of 498), the software development process actually used shall include certain major activities, but may also include additional ones. The nominal software development activities from MIL-STD-498 are provided in Figure 16-4, which is the *folded waterfall chart* used extensively by Dunn [2], Niech, Heil, and others. More complicated versions indicate the relationships for other development paradigms (e.g., incremental, evolutionary). Software quality is primarily concerned with the internal reviews (verification milestones) and the subsequent formal customer reviews (joint technical reviews).

For embedded systems, the process starts with the system requirements analysis. The output of this process is the top-level system specification, usually an "A-Spec" or a "B1" Prime Item Development Specification (System Specification), referred to as an SSS in MIL-STD-498 and J-STD-016 (IEEE 1498). Then, the system design is developed based on the "black box" requirements for the system. This system design normally takes the design down one level, usually to system elements that end up as critical items. These critical items are typically major elements of the system that will have to be defined further, usually in a subsequent Critical Item Design Specification (a "B2" Specification). The critical items, when defined, usually contain both hardware and software elements, each of which will require still further system design. It is usually at these levels that software is synthesized, and become one or more CSCIs. Several of the critical item's functions are allocated to the software, and interfaces between each CSCI and other system elements are defined or postulated. The external definition of the CSCI is analyzed and iterated, and finally is hardened into a version that is presented in an internal design review for the critical item. Typically, Systems Engineering, Software Engineering, Quality Engineering, and SQA participate in this review. At this time, SQA and Software Engineering are concerned primarily with external definition of the CSCI(s) and the reasonableness of this definition.

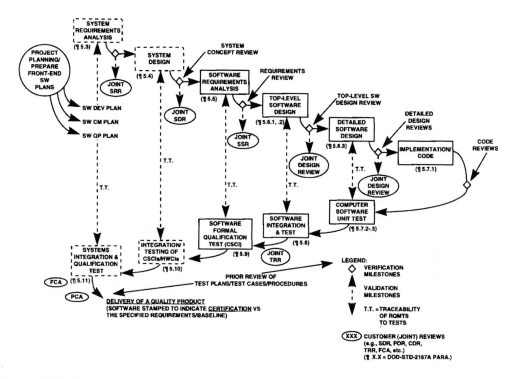

Figure 16-4 Nominal software development activities (showing internal reviews and customer reviews).

It should be noted that (at this point) the detailed definition asked for in the SRS does not exist, just external, black-box definitions exist for the CSCIs. After the completion of the critical item's design reviews, and the resolution of any action items, the revised external definition of the CSCI serves as the basis for the Software Requirements Analysis phase, which is the next activity. Certain large systems may even have additional intervening levels, e.g., distinct subsystems, each made up of several critical or prime items.

The subsequent phases of Software Top-Level Design and Detailed Design are similar to what is described in MIL-STD-498 (paragraph 5.6). However, on occasion, an incremental build approach is applied to the design, code, and test phases, such that each build is treated as a separate entity until the later stages of integration and test. Coding and computer software unit (CSU) testing for embedded systems are also similar to MIL-STD-498.

Computer software component (CSC) integration and testing (I&T) (a term introduced in DOD-STD-2167A) may be different in two ways. First, the CSC integration may be broken into two activities, the first of which is on a host development machine.

The second activity is the integration of several of the CSCs in a hardware environment that includes the new target computer, actual hardware interfaces, and other real hardware from the newly designed system. This second phase is different because the new software is tested with the new hardware to see whether it works together and to find as many errors as possible. This activity is called hardware-software integration, and may start with only one (or two) CSC(s), particularly, with a top-down, partial-build implementation strategy. The second way that CSC I&T can be different is that multiple builds may be used, and extensive testing may be done with only part of the software, before other software is incrementally added for additional testing.

CSCI testing may involve a considerable amount of integration and testing for embedded systems. Where multiple, partial builds are utilized, the integration aspects can be complex and extensive. In certain cases, all the integration and testing may be done on the host development machine. In any case, the final CSCI testing is usually done on the target microcomputer with the other real hardware.

From a "pure software" viewpoint, the final steps are the qualification or acceptance testing of the CSCI on the target hardware, etc. Partial software builds may have several informal sell-offs, one for each build. At a certain point, the complete CSCI is built and the entire CSCI is tested, culminating in a final sell-off of the entire CSCI that is witnessed by SQA and customer representatives.

Finally, once the software CSCIs have been tested and accepted, the several levels of system testing begin. This usually includes line replaceable unit (LRU)—or weapon repairable assembly (WRA)—level testing, followed by subsystems and systems testing.

After qualification and acceptance testing of the entire system (hardware and software), there are usually two additional phases. The first phase is the development testing (DT), where the software and testing are controlled by the contractor. The second is the operational testing (OT), where the government controls the tests and any changes to the software. Each of these phases could take from three to nine months. After all approved changes have been made, based on DT and OT, then the system may be approved to go into production and to be deployed for operational use.

16.4   The Role of SQA for Mission-Critical Software

Various government standards and specifications have mandated SQA, as fully explained in Chapter 4. DOD-STD-2168 set the software quality program for all DoD software, as noted in the foreword of 2168:

> "This standard implements the policies of DOD 4155.1, Quality Program, and provides all the necessary elements of a comprehensive quality program applicable to software development and support. This standard interprets the applicable requirements of MIL-Q-9858A, *Quality Program Requirements*, for software."

The provisions of DOD-STD-2168, plus the software product evaluation and formal qualification testing subsections of DOD-STD-2167A, provided a framework for an organization's software quality program, and now provide a valuable (but voluntary) source of information. From 1988 to 1994, there was no choice about establishing an SQA program (see Chapter 5) if you developed software for DoD. In this sense, SQA in the DoD Software community is more mature than in the commercial area (see Chapter 17), although there are several notable exceptions. Institute of Electrical and Electronics Engineers (IEEE) standards in the software quality area have existed for several years, but their implementation in the commercial area has been largely voluntary. Standardization efforts in the international area have recently intensified, and many U. S. companies are interested in qualifying (becoming certified) to the new international standards (such as ISO 9001 noted earlier) so that they can compete in various overseas markets in the coming years. In late 1994, DOD-STD-2168 was canceled, and is no longer used on new DoD contracts. MIL-STD-498 included subsections in Software Quality Assurance, Product Evaluation, Corrective Action, Qualification Testing, and Test Planning and covered approximately 70 percent of the topics in DOD-STD-2168 (although some at a general level). In July 1995, IEEE P1498/EIA 640 was issued as a commercial standard that could be used instead of MIL-STD-498 and became an ANSI standard (J-STD-016) in January 1995. This commercial standard was similar to MIL-STD-498 from a software quality perspective, and has the same topics covered in a similar way (except that any military language and military-unique requirements have been removed). ISO 9000-3 has a similar paragraph on the "Quality Plan" (paragraph 4.2.3) for a particular project.

For mission-critical software, contractors must have a comprehensive SQA Program in place if they want to successfully compete for new business. The software quality program must cover deliverable and most classes of nondeliverable software. The software quality program also must address the software-intensive firmware, related to the deliverable and nondeliverable software noted in the previous paragraphs. The contents of the firmware device are the computer software or data that must be carefully controlled. For production, exact copies of the correct versions must be "burned" into the firmware devices and then verified. For embedded systems, all of the software eventually gets burned into firmware devices of one kind or another during production. Even an error as small as one bit can cause a system to fail in a life-critical situation. Suffice it to say that if 200 or 300 systems are built, the firmware copies in each system must be verified as a natural part of the production quality process.

The SQA program must also ensure the quality of nondevelopmental software—software not developed under the particular contract. This software may be commercial off-the-shelf (COTS) software, or it may be furnished by the government or another third party. Or the software may have been developed by the contractor's organization for an earlier contract or project. The software that is reused without modification may have been developed under different standards or documented in a different manner or to different Data Item Descriptions (DIDs). For mission-critical software, there can be no "trust me, it works"; the quality of all nondevelopmental software also must be verified.

Most contractors (developers) find it advantageous to have a full set of generic SQA procedures written and approved. The procedures should cover all of the requirements in the various standards, such as DOD-STD-2168 and DOD-STD-2167A and the newer MIL-STD-498 and IEEE 1498, as well as the key process areas of the Capability Maturity Model (see Chapter 12). Certain contractors will find it necessary (or desirable) to also satisfy the requirements in ISO 9001 and the related software guidebook, ISO 9000-3. A single set of these procedures defines how a company or division runs its Software Quality Program. It is too expensive and confusing to have several different sets of procedures within an organization. These procedures should be reviewed and updated on an annual cycle.

The intent of the above stated standards is not to tell a contractor how he will meet the quality program requirements, just what he has to meet. The company or division SQA procedures tell how the requirements will be met. Each company's procedures will, of course, be different. Further, certain procedures will be fairly general, and others will be quite specific. At one contractor, for example, there is a Policy and Standard Practice for SQA, which provides a ten-page overall product assurance policy. At a more detailed level, there is a family of operating instructions that describe, in greater depth, each of the SQA tasks, responsibilities, and procedures. These operating instructions are grouped into areas as follows:

- Internal Reviews
- SQA Planning
- Testing and Certification, etc.

Blocks of numbers were assigned to each area, and several blank numbers exist for possible future growth. The SQA operating instructions are set up as illustrated in Table 16-3.

Table 16-3 Sample SQA Operating Procedures

Internal Reviews	
2.10.001	System-Level Concept Review (Internal)
2.10.002	Software Requirements Review (Internal)
2.10.003	Top-Level Software Design Review (Internal)
2.10.004	Detailed Software Design Review (Internal)
2.10.005	Software Code Inspections and Audits
2.10.007	Documentation Reviews (Internal)

SQA Planning

2.10.021	Software Quality Plan and SQA Program Management

Testing and Certification

2.10.032	Unit Testing
2.10.034	Software Integration and Testing
2.10.036	Software Formal Qualification/Acceptance Testing
2.10.037	Software Certification and Product Delivery

Software Configuration Management

2.10.051	Software Change Control Board
2.10.052	Software Configuration Control and Software Library Audits
2.10.054	Firmware Configuration Control

SQA Reporting and Record Retention

2.10.062	SQA Record Retention
2.10.063	Software Quality Reporting
2.10.067	Software Quality Assurance Inspection Reports
2.10.069	Software Quality Assurance Checklists

SQA Analysis

2.10.061	Software Defect Collection, Analysis and Reporting
2.10.065	Software "Cost-of-Quality" System

SQA Corrective Action and Control

2.10.071	Software Quality Assurance Corrective Action and Control

Software Installation, Field Test and Production

2.10.081	Software Installation and Checkout
2.10.082	Software Field Testing (SQA Activities)
2.10.083	Control of Software in Production (SQA Activities)

Support Software

2.10.091	Software Tools (SQA Activities)
2.10.092	Nondeliverable Software (SQA Activities)

External Interfaces

2.10.101	Subcontractor Surveys, Surveillance and Control (SQA Activities)
2.10.102	Commercially Available/Reusable/Government Furnished Software (SQA Activities)
2.10.111	V&V Interface
2.10.112	DCMC Coordination
2.10.113	Customer Technical Meetings (SQA Activities)

Formal Reviews and Audits

2.10.121	Customer Formal Reviews
2.10.122	Customer Formal Audits – FCA/PCA

Note: There are some gaps in the Procedure Numbers to allow for possible future growth.

With a generic software quality program documented and in place, and people trained in implementing the program, the next step is to document how this company software quality program will be applied to meet a specific contract's requirements. The Software Quality Program Plan (SQPP) or the SDP are normally used to document how these procedures will be applied to a particular contract. The SQPP can be a stand-alone document, per DOD-STD-2168 DID DI-QCIC-80572, or it can be incorporated into the SDP (such as the SDP for DOD-STD-2167A per DID-DI-MCCR-80030A or MIL-STD-498 DID DI-IPSC-81427, or the IEEE 1498 product description for an SDP in Annex E).

The author's experience is that it is very helpful to have a model SQPP ready to use, which represents the SQA state-of-the-art at your organization. Conceptually, a copy of this model SQPP can be "redlined" for a particular project, thus saving a lot of time under a tight deadline. If it is adequate, a new SQPP may then become one of a family of model SQPPs kept in the SQA department's library. An outline (sample) for an SQPP is described in Table 16-4. The sections that will vary significantly from one project to another are marked with an asterisk.

Section 4 of the SQPP may present several problems because it is organized into three broad headings (e.g., Procedures, Tools, and Quality Records), rather than by the specific requirements in DOD-STD-2168.

One way to solve this problem in the SQPP and still be fully compliant with the DID is to add a Section 4.4, which is a cross-reference matrix to the specific DOD-STD-2168 requirements. Each DOD-STD-2168 requirement (or other requirements) can be listed in order as a line item in the matrix (or database). In concept, there are three columns: one for procedures, one for tools, and one for the software quality records for each quality activity or requirement. The SQPP paragraph number or item number can be entered into the matrix. Any omission becomes very obvious. If a requirement is tailored out of the contract, it should be "flagged," even if one is voluntarily complying with the requirement. Obviously, the first time you prepare the matrix, it will take some time, but it is a worthwhile investment.

Table 16-4   Sample Outline of a Software Quality Program Plan (for DOD-STD-2168)

1.0   Scope

   1.1   Identification (of system)*

   1.2   System Overview (purpose of system and software function)*

   1.3   Document Overview (summarize purpose and contents on SQPP)

   1.4   Relationship to other Plans (e.g., to SDP, Quality Program Plan [QPP], etc.)

2.0   Referenced Documents

   (List all documents referenced or cited in the SQPP—include document number, title, revision, date)

Note: Government Specs, Standards, Handbooks are listed first; then other Government documents, drawings, publications; then contractor publications/ standards; then contractor forms.

3.0 Organization and Resources

3.1 Organization (include authority and responsibilities of each organization; include an organization chart showing proper relationships)

3.2 Resources (used for Software Quality)*

3.2.1 Facilities and Equipment (desired for equipment software, tool and services to be used for SQ Program)

3.2.2 Government Furnished Facilities, Equipment, Software, and Service

3.2.3 Personnel (Describe number and "skill levels" of personnel who will do SQ Program activities)

3.2.4 Other Resources

3.3 Schedule* (for SQ Program activities, plus key milestones—e.g., formal Reviews and Audits, Key Meetings, document reviews, Qualifications or Acceptance Tests, etc.)

4.0 SQPPs, Tools, and Records

4.1 Procedures should be in Section 2 (to be used in the SP Program) (Identify and map to requirements to which they apply) (Do NOT include the procedure details on Revision and Date)

4.2 Tools (to be used in the SQ Program) Identify, description of tool, how used, in the SQ Program, and status (of development).

4.3 Software Quality Records Plans for preparing, verifying, maintaining, and accessing for reviews the records. Indicate forms (and data content) "such as" to allow for improvements. Indicate Software Quality Reports to be extracted from the records

4.4 Cross-Reference Matrix for DOD-STD-2168 Requirements** (vs. Procedures, Tools, and Records in SQ Program Plan)

5.0 Notes

General information, background information or details, glossary for terms, acronyms, abbreviations, etc.), Appendixes (if needed)

A. (Sections 10.1, 10.2, etc.)

B. (Sections 20.1, 20.2, etc.)

C. (Sections 30.1, 30.2, etc,)

---

* These sections vary considerably from one project to another.

** Requirements of DOD-STD-2168 are contained only in Section 4 and 5 of the Standard. If the requirement is tailored, indicate it.

An interesting question arises when a contract does not require you to do something that you normally do. The contract *requirements* may be tailored, but should your software quality program be tailored? Should one yield to the temptation to try to save time and money, possibly at the risk of quality? Is your normal way of doing business somewhat flexible? As discussed earlier, do you handle a Program Definition project in the same manner as an EMD project? To reduce the variability due to different development phases, first consider whether you should perform the standard software quality tasks for all EMD projects, even if the contract doesn't require them. To a great extent, it depends on how you accomplished the proposal (which is an implied promise), and also on what you promised to do in the SQPP delivered after contract start.

The cost or budget of the software quality program could be a function of the perceived risk. A high-risk project may be funded for higher levels of SQA effort to reduce the risk. Also, it may be desirable to focus more effort on certain crucial elements of software.

Utilization of the SDP to document the SQPP (rather than a stand-alone SQPP document) is not very direct. There are several existing sections in the DOD-STD-2167A SDP DID that can be used (to varying degrees) including the following:

3.10	Corrective Action Process
3.11	Problem/Change Reports
4.1	Organizational Structure—Software Engineering (and relationship to the organizations, etc.)
4.2	Software Development Techniques and Methodologies (e.g., design and coding standards, qualification testing)
5.1	Organization and Resources—formal qualification testing
5.1	Test Approach/philosophy
6.1	Organizational Structure—software product evaluations
6.2	Software Product Evaluations Procedures and Tools
6.4 (and 6.5)	Software Product Evaluation Records.

The MIL-STD-498 SDP DID has sections and paragraphs that exactly track the requirements in the standard itself (e.g., 5.16 is the SDP paragraph to discuss SQA). However, many topics covered in DOD-STD-2168 (such as "Evaluations of the processes . . .," "Evaluation of the Software Development Library," etc.) are not really addressed in DOD-STD-2167A and the SDP. Several of these topics can be addressed in a new Section 6.6 of the SDP. A hybrid approach can be useful, with a page or so of text on the Software Quality Program in a new Section 6.6, with a reference to the stand-alone SQPP. In any event, most contracts will call for a deliverable SDP document, but certain contracts will not call for a deliverable SQPP.

The author's experience suggests that, at the very least, an informal SQPP must be prepared so that project management and the SQA department knows what its plan is, even if it is only a redlined version of a model SQPP with a new cover attached. Even in this case, the preparer should sign and date the SQPP, and the SQA manager should review it and sign it when it is approved.

The software product evaluations are a key part of the software quality program, but are not the exclusive province of the SQA department. Modern practice is that both the software development and the software quality groups are involved directly in product evaluations. To ensure that product evaluations are considered an in-line part of the software development process, these product evaluations were inserted in each of the activity phases in DOD-STD-2167A (while MIL-STDs-498 and -1498 treat product evaluations separately, but with reference to the specific paragraph of the activity). Using the nominal paradigm indicated in Figure 16-2 of DOD-STD-2167A, all of the software (or documentation) items to be evaluated from each activity phase are shown in a consistent series of matrix-like tables. The criteria to be used in the evaluations for each item or product are included in the matrixes. Although one may debate a few points here and there, the guidance provided by these sections of DOD-STD-2167A and the corresponding matrix tables is reasonably complete, and serves as a good basis for developing systems for product evaluations for your own special needs and software development processes. Table 16-5 summarizes the product evaluation requirements distributed throughout the various activity phase subsections in Section 5 of the DOD-STD-2167A. Note that the results of the product evaluations are organized by activity phase (or nominal activity phase), and are to be presented at (or before) a joint review. Certain general requirements for software product evaluations are presented in Section 4.4 of DOD-STD-2167A, and in Section 5.15 of MIL-STD-498, and in Section 5.15 of the recent IEEE 1498/EIA 640. The paragraphs on Independence, Final Evaluations, and Evaluation Records in DOD-STD-2167A are particularly important to the Software Quality Program evaluations.

The tasks covered in DOD-STD-2168 and DOD-STD-2167A provide a good basis for preparing a set of SQA procedures. Several of the products are not tightly coupled to the phase, and their timing may be modified when the development process is defined (e.g., STP, STDs). Most software development organizations analyzed these standards to identify each requirement and task, then used traceability techniques to ensure that all requirements were covered in their SQA procedures. Both MIL-

STD-498 and IEEE 1498/EIA 640 have excellent paragraphs on Software Product Evaluation (both paragraph 5.15), plus additional detailed guidance in Appendixes (Appendix D and Appendix L, respectively), but they are not organized by activity phase; they are organized, instead, by product to allow flexibility in the timing of the process (see Table 16-6).

Table 16-5 Product Evaluations in DOD-STD-2167A

Activity Phase	Software Product Evaluations and Products	Results of Product Evaluations
5.1 System Requirements Analysis and Design	5.1.4 (Figure 16-4) SSDD, SDP	(SRR*, SDR**)
5.2 Software Requirements Analysis	5.2.4 (Figure 16-5) SRS, IRS	Summarize at SSR(s)
5.3 Preliminary Design	5.3.4 (Figure 16-6) SDD IDD, STP, CSC test requirements	Summarize at PDR (s)
5.4 Detailed Design	5.4.4 (Figure 16-7) SDD, IDD, STD (cases), CSU test requirements and test cases, CSC test case, contents of CSU and CSC SDFs	Summarize at CDR(s)
5.5 Coding and CSU Testing	5.5.4 (Figure 16-8) source code, CSU test procedures and test results, CSC test procedures, contents of CSU and CSC SDFs	—
5.6 CSC I&T	5.6.4 (Figure 16-9) STD (test procedures), CSC Integration test results, updated source code, contents of updated SDFs	Summarize at TRR
5.7 CSCI Testing	5.7.4 (Figure 16-10) STR updated source code	(FCA, PCA)
5.8 System I&T	5.8.4 (Figure 16-10) updated design document, updated source code	(FCA, PCA)

* SRR reviews Preliminary SSS
** Preliminary SRSs and IRS may be tailored out, so SDR will focus on the System/SubsystemDesign

Table 16-6 Product Evaluations in MIL-STD-498 and J-STD-016 (Organized by Product, Not by Activity Phase)

Software Product	Paragraph No. in MIL-STD-498 and J-STD-016	Information per DID
Software Development Plan	5.1.1	SDP*
Software Test Plan	5.1.2, 5.1.3	STP*
Software Installation Plan	5.1.4	SIP*
Software Transition Plan	5.1.5	STrP*
Operational Concept	5.3.2	OCD*
System Requirements	5.3.3	SSS, IRS
Systemwide Design	5.4.1	SSDD, IDD, DBDD
System Architectural Design	5.4.2	SSDD, IDD, DBDD
CSCI/Software Item Requirements	5.5	SRS, IRS
CSCI/Software Itemwide Design	5.6.1	SDD, IDD, DBD
CSCI/Software Item Architectural Design	5.6.2	SDD, IDD
CSCI/Software Item Detailed Design	5.6.3	SDD, IDD, DBDD
Implemented Software	5.7.1	N/A
CSCI/Software Item Qualification Test Descriptions	5.9.3	STD
CSCI/Software Item Qualification Test Results	5.9.7	STR
System Qualification Test Description	5.11.3	STD*
System Qualification Test Results	5.11.7	STR
Executable Software	5.12.1, 5.13.1	N/A
Software Version Description	5.12.2, 5.13.3	SVD
Software User Manuals	5.12.3.1	SUM*
Software Input/Output Manuals	5.12.3.2	SIOM*
Software Center Operator Manuals	5.12.3.3	SCOM*
Computer Operation Manuals	5.12.3.4	COM*
Source Files	5.13.2	N/A
"As Built" CSCI/Software Item Design	5.13.4	SPS*
"As Built" System Design	5.13.5	SSDD, IDD, DBDD
Computer Programming Manuals	5.13.6.1	CPM*
Firmware Support Manuals	5.13.6.2	FSM*
Sampling of Software Development Files (SDFs)	5.7.2, 5.7.3, 5.8.1, 5.8.4, 5.9.4, 5.10.1, 5.10.4, 5.11.4	N/A

* Timing (and number of versions) may be flexible

16.5   The Role of SQA During the System Requirements and System Design Phases

At the start of a contract or project, a preliminary System-level Specification is normally appended to the contract's statement of work (SOW). One of the first tasks is the analysis of the specification and the development of a revised specification for the customer. SQA, systems engineering, quality systems software engineering, and other interested parties must review the revised System-level Specification in an internal technical review before sending it to the customer. After the review and finalization, this revised Specification is sent back to the customer, and the joint System Requirements Review is then scheduled (usually for one or two months later). The System-level Specification typically does not have a lot of detail on software. There may, however, be certain constraints in place, such as the target processors to be used, the source language to be used, and sometimes the software support environment that must be used to support the software after the system is deployed. If any constraints exist, their impact on the project must be assessed; if the impact is major, it should become the subject of certain tradeoffs and discussions with the customer.

The feasibility of handling the input-to-output transformation with the available information, within the allowable time, and with the required accuracy and precision represents the single-thread performance of the system. These requirements have to be addressed for feasibility, and will become the basis for several of the system-level acceptance tests. The rates that the system has to handle under high-traffic conditions present another level of complexity and will ultimately affect the size of the embedded computer resource segment. Most of these issues are the province of the system engineers, and there should be a few senior software engineers on the team to provide the software expertise.

When the system design task starts, postulations of the various major components of the system are made. Usually, these system designs are based on extensive experience with prior systems in the same domain. At a certain level in the design hierarchy, CSCIs are postulated, and tasks assigned to them as black boxes. At the CSCI level, it is possible to make an initial assessment of the loading under different scenarios to establish the worst case loading(s). The feasibility of the processor loadings during peak periods can be assessed at least on a preliminary basis. Particularly for "unprecedented" systems, the margin for processing power to allow for uncertainties should be significant, based on an agreed-upon margin. The memory utilization for embedded systems, in terms of the Read-Only Memory (ROM) for the program and the dynamic Random Access Memory (RAM) should also be sized to ensure that the estimated memory is below the target utilization. The suitability of the microprocessors selected, if there is a potential speed or memory problem, has to be addressed. It may also be necessary to have multiple processors (and therefore multiple instances of a CSCI) to do a particular function at full load for the system. Note that several of the CSCIs may be system-level databases.

The external requirements for the CSCI(s) are then analyzed and reviewed. SQA ensures that all of the appropriate factors are considered and that any problems are identified and resolved as quickly as possible. SQA participates in the internal system design reviews for the software elements and records the results of any action items on the SQA inspection report (SQAIR). Other elements such as safety, reliability, BIT (built-in test), initialization/reinitialization, ease of modifying software, etc., must also be considered. Areas of high-technical risk or schedule risk related to the embedded computers and software must be identified. The results of the internal reviews are then reflected in the System/Subsystem Design Description (SSDD) or its equivalent that are presented to the customer. For a pure software system, an SSDD may be used to capture the system design information. Preliminary versions of the SRSs and IRS may not be required at system design time to avoid interfering with the System Design effort. The system design is reviewed by the customer, and usually a joint technical review is then held to discuss findings and issues. The developer has a reasonable time to resolve all of the issues, and revise the System Design. The developer's quality and software quality groups must participate in the internal review of the revised System Design to ensure all of the issues are resolved in a reasonable manner, prior to the release of the revised System Design to the customer and others.

At system requirements time or design time, the SDP is also prepared and reviewed internally by engineering and SQA. The SDP has become an increasingly important plan in the newer standards (MIL-STD-498 and J-STD-016) and in actual practice. When the SDP is acceptable, and all of the problems are resolved, then the SDP is transmitted to the customer for review. As discussed in the prior section of this chapter, a stand-alone SQPP may also be a required deliverable document at this time for the System Design Review or for a separate SDP/SQPP Review.

16.6　SQA During the Crucial Software Requirements Phase

The Software Requirements Analysis phase is geared to producing two kinds of outputs: An SRS (one for each unique CSCI) and an IRS (for all of the CSCIs). These documents are very important because they are the foundation on which the whole software development effort is built.

The SRS contents and format are defined by MIL-STD-498 DID DI-IPSC-81433 or the J-STD-016 equivalent. Any deviations or additions to the SRS must be discussed and agreed to by Software Engineering, Systems Engineering, and SQA near the beginning of this phase. When the internal technical review for each CSCI's SRS is held, SQA should first verify that all of the contents (as agreed) are included in the draft SRS. Approximately five working days must be allowed for each technical reviewer to read and analyze the draft SRS before the scheduled review meeting.

A second task is for SQA to review the requirements traceability. The system design material is reviewed to develop a list or database of all requirements allocated (mapped "down") to the particular CSCI. Then, the SRS is reviewed to see whether all of these requirements have been picked up in the SRS. There should be no gaps in the downward traceability of higher-level requirements (ultimately from the System Specification requirements) down to the SRS (or IRS).

Another aspect of the traceability analysis is to identify the basis for each software requirement in the SRS. To do this, a unique number should be assigned to each SRS requirement (if not already assigned) and then the basis for each of these requirements should be determined. Normally, most of the SRS requirements will be traceable to a requirement in the higher-level requirement specification immediately above the SRS in the specification hierarchy. It is a concern to SQA if an SRS requirement has no apparent predecessor or basis. In this case, this requirement must be flagged, and a determination must be made if the SRS requirement is a valid implicit requirement or a derived requirement. If the SRS requirement is neither of these, it is an invalid requirement with no basis, and no justifiable reason for being there. "Do not do it, if nobody wants it"—the principle of parsimony in software development. Such an invalid requirement is sometimes referred to as an "alien" requirement and should be eliminated.

Note that certain requirements unique to data processing are introduced for the first time at the SRS level in the specification tree, e.g., initialization, reinitialization. These requirements are not always covered in the higher-level specifications, although one could argue that they should be. These may constitute valid requirements, which must be introduced in the SRS (if not before) to provide a comprehensive requirements base for software design. Any such valid implicit requirements should be flagged in the SRS (as valid but implicit). The result would be the mapping of the SRS requirements back up to the higher-level requirements in the SSS or a flag indicating a valid implicit requirement with no predecessor. This traceability analysis lends itself to a database, which can be printed out as an Appendix to the SRS.

If multiple (incremental) builds are to be used, the mapping of requirements to each build should be documented in some form in the SRS, or a companion document.

As noted earlier in this chapter, evaluation criteria for each product are shown in the various standards. The SRS evaluation criteria in Figure 16-5 of DOD-STD-2167A include internal consistency and understandability.

MIL-STD-498 adds "meets SOW," "meets CDRL," "follow SDP," "feasible," "testable," and coverage of the requirements allocated to each particular CSCI (J-STD-016 is very similar to MIL-STD-498).

In addition, the SRS should be consistent with the other SRSs and the IRS, which are at the same level in the Specification hierarchy tree. SQA must also check the appropriateness (not always yes or no) of the allocation of sizing and timing requirements to the CSCI. Special areas related to safety, security, and design constraints must also be reviewed explicitly by SQA.

The adequacy of quality factor requirements [3] (e.g., maintainability, portability) must be evaluated, but this is an emerging area that is not widely understood. However, the contractor may define other quality factors to apply to either the system or CSCI level. Human performance and human engineering requirements must also be reviewed for correctness, traceability, and feasibility. For certain embedded systems, the user merely pushes an ON button and notes whether the ON indicator stays on, and all of the other functions far transcend human capabilities and speeds.

The adaptation requirements (if any) must also be reviewed for completeness and correctness. Most technical reviews deal with the completeness and correctness of the capability or functional performance requirements, the interfaces outside of the CSCI, and for data elements internal to the CSCI.

The test coverage of the requirements can be determined by reviewing sections 4.1 and 4.2 of the DOD-STD-2167A SRS or Section 4 of MIL-STD-498 or J-STD-016. However, analysis of the database that indicates each requirement (by requirement number and SRS paragraph) makes it easy to see how many of the requirements will be demonstrated or tested, or be qualified by analysis or inspection. The SDP should give a value of functional test coverage that must be met, e.g., 90 percent of all SRS requirements not qualified by analysis or inspection must be qualified by demonstration. SQA can analyze the SRS qualification section to determine if the agreed-upon target has been met (should any CSCI requirements be left unvalidated?).

SQA must also review the SRS for the following: are the requirements explicit and unambiguous; and are they testable against a specific, feasible criteria with a well-defined pass-fail value or threshold?

SQA prepares its list of discussion items for the internal software requirements review and raises each point at the appropriate time. Any items that are not resolved on the spot are recorded as action items with a target date and a responsible person. SQA will write up an SQAIR, indicating the results of the review, including all action items. When all action items are resolved and validated by SQA, the SRS can be updated and issued to the customer for review (usually at least 30 days before the joint Software Requirements Review). Based on this joint review, the customer will agree on (or ask for) certain changes to the SRS, and the SRS will be updated and reissued. SQA will review the revised SRS before it is released. This revised SRS becomes part of the allocated baseline for the system once the SRS is approved and signed by the customer's representative. A practical problem is getting an agreement and signature from the customer for the SRS within a reasonable number of days (e.g., 30 days) to preclude delays to the project schedule.

16.7   SQA During the Top-Level Design Phase

Top-level design is the bridge between software requirements and the actual design of the software. The software requirements usually are the responsibility of the systems engineering group, although the importance of software engineering participation is well known. If this bridge is correctly handled, the software will be off to a good start. Otherwise, the problems that can be created during this phase will be very pervasive, and can be very expensive and time-consuming to fix. Few people would argue that a good software engineering development process would not be valuable at this phase, and would tend to consistently produce good software designs. In the broad sense, a mature software quality "process" is part of the larger software development process, and can contribute to producing a high-quality software design that will not be beset by many problems in the future.

The software quality process must be concerned with the underlying *process* of software design, as well as looking at the products of software design. Errors of omission are usually more difficult to detect, unless there is a comprehensive framework available. It is important to remember that the SDP may tailor, modify, or augment the generic process and procedures for the particular project; therefore, the SDP must be the basis for comparisons and process compliance checking. To a great extent, good SQA procedures (processes) and supporting checklists can be helpful. It is even more helpful if the software developers have copies of the SQA procedures and checklists so there are no surprises. The developers want to do a good job, and if they understand the expectations, they will try to deliver a product that meets these expectations, rather than knowingly produce a product that will not pass.

The SQA procedure for top-level design reviews is not the only "command media" that deals with System Design Reviews (SDRs). A Policy and Standard Practice that deals with the engineering aspects has been very helpful. One such Engineering Standard Practice deals with all kinds of reviews, not just software reviews; however, it includes the various internal software design reviews, including top-level and detailed software design reviews. The inclusion of software design reviews, which is in essence an evaluation of an interim product during the development process, in the Engineering Standard Practice makes quality an integral part of engineering responsibilities, rather than only a quality assurance concern. The description in the Engineering Standard Practice is very brief, but is of the form shown in Table 16-7. Attendance at this top-level software design review shall be established in the procedures, and should include:

- Principal Software Designer (Originator)
- Software Engineering Section Head (or a Software "peer" if run as a peer review)

- Electronics Engineering Representative*
- Digital Engineering Representative*
- Software Quality Assurance
- Systems Engineering

---

* not necessary for "pure" software systems

Table 16-7　A Sample Engineering Standard Practice for the Top-Level Software Design Review

Top-Level Software Design Review

A.　Objective

　1)　Assure that all requirements allocated to each CSCI are adequately covered by the Top-Level Design.

B.　Topics To Be Covered

　1)　CSCI Top-Level Design

　　Functional Performance requirement

　　Memory, input/output, and real-time estimate

　　Design and Programming conventions

　　Database design CSC performance

　　Executive control methodology

　　Family tree (Software)

　　Configuration management

　2)　Preliminary Software Integration Plan

　3)　Preliminary Hardware/Software Integration Plan

　4)　CSCI Qualification Test Plan

　5)　Test Requirements/Plans for lower-level software elements

C.　Documentation

　1)　CSCI Top-Level Design Specification (SDD-Part I)

　2)　Preliminary IDD

　3)　Preliminary Software Integration Plan

　4)　Preliminary Hardware/Software Integration Plan*

　5)　Software Test Plan

　6)　Software Development File (SDF) Information on Test Requirements/Plans (for CSCI and lower-level software elements)

D.　Responsibility. This review shall apply to each CSCI, and shall occur when the CSCI software architecture has been designed to the point where it can serve as a baseline for detailed design. This review shall be scheduled by the responsible software engineer with the design review coordinator.

---

* not essential for "pure" software systems

SQA should spotcheck the top-level design process to see whether software engineering is proceeding in accordance with the SDP, the detailed software engineering procedures, and any special contractual requirements. This suggests SQA must initially prepare a profile of any and all special contractual requirements for software quality. Depending on the risks and what was promised in the SQPP, one check for each CSCI is usually sufficient. If problems are uncovered, follow-up process audits should be scheduled in that area. Each audit must be documented (in an SQAIR, or equivalent).

Other reviews or audits are usually not done until the top-level design is considered ready by the responsible lead software engineer. Then, that lead software engineer schedules a design review with the engineering design review coordinator, usually for five working days in the future. Sufficient lead time must be allowed for the reviewers to study the design package and identify any problems or questions. The logistics of getting a large design package to each of the various five or six reviewers can be challenging, particularly if the design package is classified. Access to electronic media can help speed up the process, but there may still be certain elements in paper form that must be physically distributed. The meeting announcement must also be very clear on the scope, agenda, ground rules, classification levels, and the time and location of the meeting. Through trial and error, it has been found that if a person cannot attend, they must promptly tell the design review coordinator who will be their substitute. This allows a new schedule to be established, but only if most of the principals cannot attend that day.

SQA examines the design review in a slightly different way than the other attendees. SQA is concerned primarily with the quality of the design, but not directly with the cost or schedule. Therefore, the question becomes simply whether the quality level is fully acceptable; not the question of a cost or schedule tradeoff versus quality. SQA must insist that the quality be fully acceptable!

For the top-level software design, the SQA analysis of the design package usually starts with a quick reading of the SDD material for familiarity, e.g., what's there and what's missing. Then, a detailed review of all of the requirements allocated to the CSCI is done, based on the contents in the previously reviewed SRS, per the SRS requirements traceability section. This SRS section will either contain a list of all of the allocated requirements, or will refer to an SRS Appendix, which has a printout from the requirements traceability database. SQA shall determine how and where each requirement is actually handled in the top-level design, one requirement at a time. The analysis must systematically address every requirement in the SRS, which can be in the hundreds. Because SQA is asking whether all of the requirements are covered, all of the SRS requirements must be listed. Without a computer database system, this gets very tedious if the CSCI has over 100 requirements. A listing could be developed (by computer or manually) that resembles Figure 16-5. As required by DOD-STD-2167A, every requirement should have a project unique requirements ID. The following format could be used for CSCI-level requirements IDs:

AA	R	NNNN

SRS RQMT. ID*	SRS PARAGRAPH*		TLCSC(S)	OK
(AA-R-NNNN) ■ ■ ■	(3.2.X)			
(AA-R-0072)	3.2.14		3	Y
(AA-R-0073)	3.2.4	Process	4, 5	Y, Y
(AA-R-0074)	3.2.21		2	N
(AA-R-0075)	3.2.23		99**	gap

*Based on SRS data

**99 = cannot be found (in Top-Level Design)

Figure 16-5   Representative list for CSCI requirements analysis.

The AA field would be a two-alpha field to identify the CSCI. The "R" literal simply identifies this as a requirement entity. The NNNN field would be the number of the requirement within that CSCI, normally starting with "0001." This CSCI Requirement ID and the SRS paragraph is based on the SRS. The SQA reviewer would identify which Top-Level CSC (TLCSC) in the design handles this requirement, and enter the TLCSC number or ID into the database or form. When the TLCSC seems to adequately handle the requirement, a yes "Y" code could be entered into the database. If it is not adequately handled, a no "N" code could be entered (see Figure 16-5). In the top-level design package, if the organization is similar to the format of the SDD, each CSC will be described in a unique subsection. There is something to be said for numbering the CSCs and the subsections such that CSC Number 1 is in subsection 3.2.1, etc. A rational numbering system for any Lower-Level CSC (LLCSC) or units would also help, as illustrated in Figure 16-6.

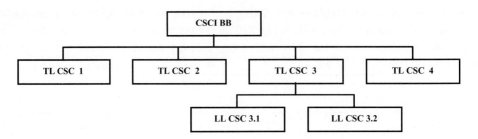

Figure 16-6 Sample CSCI top-level architecture chart (a partial family tree).

When the requirements traceability analysis is done, any gap or uncovered SRS requirements will be obvious. It will save time to call the lead software engineer before the review meeting about any potential gaps. Remember, SQA may have missed them in the design package. The questions regarding not adequately handling the requirement are not quite as severe, and perhaps could wait until the design review meeting.

The review of the relevant portions of the IDD must be done in concert with the SDD for the particular CSCI. The interfaces for that CSCI must be reviewed, even if the IDD was covered before as an entire document. It should be noted that the IDD is normally a single document for all CSCIs in the system or for a major subsystem/segment similar to the requirements IRS. In certain cases, there may be no Preliminary IDD required by the contract because it was tailored out. In any event, a certain level of detail of information on CSCI interfaces is still required for the SDD. This information must be reviewed for consistency with the interface information in the SRS and the IRS. If there are any inconsistencies or omissions, they must be identified at the internal top-level design review.

After the analysis of the CSCI-level design, SQA should then address the internal design of CSCI, down to the TLCSCs or equivalent design elements. It should be noted that the requirements traceability analysis already determined the requirements mapping to the TLCSCs. The actual mapping of requirements should then be compared with the information in the design package for that CSC because sometimes the two are not identical. The data flow into and out of each CSC should match the processing needed to meet the functional requirements. The data elements for each requirement or function should be checked. Are there any extra or missing data inputs or outputs? Is the execution control adequate, reasonable, and fast enough to meet requirements? Use of nondevelopmental software should also be reviewed for risk and adequacy.

The memory, processing time, and input/output allocations for the CSCI should be reviewed for reasonableness and consistency with hardware and software capabilities. The total used should still provide an adequate reserve of design margin, consistent with the contract and SOW. If the contract does not mandate a required margin, design standards should be used. If no standards are available, the project should define and document them. A 35 to 40 percent margin is suggested, and this margin is normally eroded by the time of acceptance tests by requirement changes and add-ons. At this time, the budgets are just budgets or allocations that hopefully can and will be met. Hopefully, the totals for the CSCI provide reasonable margins within the available capacities.

At the top-level design review for the CSCI, other items are normally covered, although sometimes a separate meeting may be scheduled to avoid an overly-lengthy single meeting. DOD-STD-2167A required that the STP for the CSCI (or group of CSCIs) be prepared at this time, and presented at the Preliminary Design Review (PDR), but more modern practice is to review the STP at a separate joint technical meeting (see MIL-STD-498 or IEEE 1498/J-STD-016). SQA will have to review the draft of the STP at about the same time as the SDD-Top-Level Design. The STP is for the qualification tests for the CSCI, and most of the qualification tests are done at the CSCI level. For certain embedded systems, this means the qualification tests are at the end of the Hardware/Software Integration phase with the actual (target) digital hardware and microcomputer. In a few cases, the qualification tests are conducted in the target system with a complete system. In any event, the CSCI qualification tests are not necessarily for every requirement in the SRS, but should address the most important and most critical functions. The functional test coverage of the SRS requirements should normally be at the 70- to 80-percent level, as defined in the SDP (or as required in the contract).

In reviewing the Test Plan, [4] SQA should compare the STP against the SRS qualification sections (section 4), particularly for those requirements that were to be tested versus requirements to be validated by analysis or inspection. Any discrepancies have to be identified and resolved.

Special classes of tests such as stress tests (100 percent of load requirements), overload tests, boundary/corner tests, erroneous input tests, etc., may also test several of the same requirements again, but from a different perspective. The types of data to be recorded, and the related data reduction and analysis writeups must be reasonable for each test. The test schedule should be feasible for the number of test teams to be used; if they are artificially tight, quality may suffer. It is important to note that the STP is not very detailed. It is the STD that details out each test into test case descriptions; the STD is an output of a later phase.

The preliminary Software Integration Plan for the CSCI and the preliminary Hardware/Software Integration Plan describe the test and integration for both activities, and must be reviewed for reasonable tests at each level of software integration. The sequence and schedule must also be reviewed for reasonableness and completeness. Neither plan is specifically discussed in DOD-STD-2167A, MIL-STD-498, or IEEE 1498/J-STD-016.

The CSC test requirements, based on the requirements mapped to the CSC, and the interfaces with that CSC (as defined in the SDD) are important areas. The CSC test requirements are analogous to the CSCI STP. It should be noted that CSC test cases with the details for testing each CSC is normally an output of the later detailed design phase. There is no DID for the CSC test requirements information, so this must be defined in the internal Software Procedures. SQA should review the CSC test information, CSC test requirements at this time for completeness against the CSC requirements, design, and interfaces, plus testing standards and the definitions for the CSC test requirements.

At this point, the updated support software and hardware requirements must be reviewed to ensure that all elements required for development are identified and will be available, and an SQA checklist is helpful here. If a Computer Resources Integrated Support Document (CRISD) or parts of a Computer Resources Life Cycle Management Plan (CRLCMP) is under contract, a similar update and review cycle for this document that plans for the support environment for post-deployment support will also be needed, and should be reviewed together with the development environment information.

The SDP may require several additional updates at this time. Therefore, a review of the revised SDP is necessary. The SDP should be compatible with the other informal plans and the development environment. Hopefully, the SDP changes will not be extensive, but this plan is a living document that is likely to change over the development period as everyone gets smarter.

To make the reviews of these various outputs more modular, it is suggested that separate SQAIRs be used for each one. This is especially important if the reviews extend over a period of time, or are performed by several SQA engineers.

At the internal review meeting(s), each item is briefly discussed but not resolved. Each action item is given a number, a due date, and assigned to a particular person. When all the action items are closed, the SQAIR can be closed out and considered complete. Then, that item can be prepared as a final deliverable document if required by the contract. The schedule should allow for the internal review of the draft documents. An SQA scheduling parameter of reviewing (technical level) five to six pages per hour seems acceptable. The completed document should be reviewed in its entirety, rather than in fragments. Document review forms (paper or electronic) should be used to document the comments. It saves time if the SQA person discusses any areas of disagreement with the document author face-to-face, and a resolution is sought. When all issues are resolved, SQA can approve the publication of the document.

The customer will then review the "delivered" document and present formal comments, either by letter or at a review meeting. SQA (and others) normally will review the comments, and then the revised document to ensure it meets the customer's valid comments. An SQAIR and document review form are usually used for the revised document, too. When all items have been resolved, SQA can approve the revised document for shipment. It is a good practice for SQA to keep a copy of the document in its files, along with the customer's comments and the SQAIRs. If there are any agreements or clarifications from the customer, copies of these letters must also be retained in the SQA files.

16.8 SQA During the Detailed Design Phase

The Software Detailed Design phase not only expands the Software Design to greater levels of detail down to the unit or data element, but it also refines the top-level design because of new insights. The top-level design is very rarely finished or perfect at the end of the top-level design phase, and is modified to a certain degree, as a result of additional design effort during the detailed design phase. Barring any significant changes in requirements, the top-level design should be final by the end of the detailed design phase. However, in the real world, sometimes external factors may necessitate requirements changes even if there is a significant cost and/or schedule impact. The result in this case is a new functional baseline and a new allocated baseline, which then can ripple down into the software design.

The products of the Detailed Design phase are:

- Revised SDD for each CSCI, with the addition of detailed design sections
- IDD

In addition, it may be necessary to update the STP in order to keep it current and valid. An STD may also be prepared during this phase (or the next phase) to define the test cases to test each software requirement in the SRS (for CSCI qualification testing).

Other information that may be produced at this phase is:

- the test cases for CSCs or equivalent units
- the test requirements for the units
- the test cases for the units

This latter information should reside in the appropriate SDFs, which usually are not treated as deliverable data. However, a specified percentage of the SDFs should be evaluated by SQA during this phase; the required percent is normally specified in the SDP, and may also be specified in a stand-alone SQPP if one exists. As discussed for prior phases, SQA shall review or evaluate these various products during the detailed design phase.

A separate SQA operating procedure has been found useful to provide guidance for the software detail design reviews. The design parts of the reviews deal with the design of one or a few related CSCs. In certain cases, the detailed design of an entire

TLCSC can be handled in one review meeting, which has several advantages over fragmenting the review into several smaller design reviews. The SQA procedure (out of self-defense) also stresses that the design package must be distributed and received at least five working days before the scheduled review to allow enough time to prepare. If the design package deals with a software TLCSC that is likely to exceed 10,000 SLOC, more than five days is recommended, unless a small modification to nondevelopmental software is to be used.

With the design review for a CSC or TLCSC, the comparable parts of the IDD must be reviewed. Each CSCI external interface that relates directly or indirectly to the CSCs shall be considered, but it should be remembered that external interfaces do not necessarily interface directly with the CSC under review. The interfaces between the CSCs in a CSCI are described in the SDD. The interfaces between units are also covered in the SDD.

A separate review meeting dealing with the IDD is recommended because this document details the interfaces between the CSCI and other configuration items, and is not directly related to the design of a particular TLCSC.

The SQA procedure for detailed design reviews should also be supported by a detailed SQA checklist. For the detailed design reviews, several checklists are helpful:

- CSC Design Checklist
- CSCI Interface Design Checklist
- STD—Test Cases Checklist
- CSC and CSU Test Cases Checklist
- CSC and CSU Test Requirements Checklist

In addition, SQA checklists for the audits of the CSC and Unit SDFs are useful at this phase of the development cycle.

The detailed design review is scheduled by the software engineer responsible for the CSC design. The lead software engineer also must distribute the CSC detailed design package in time to allow five days for analysis.

Attendees at the detailed design review should include:

- Lead software engineer for the CSC
- Software Engineering section head (or a software "peer" if run as a peer review)
- Electronics engineering representative (for certain CSCs)*
- Digital Engineering representative*
- Software Quality Assurance
- Systems Engineering

---

* not necessary for "pure" software systems

Representation at the design review is mandatory, and a delegate must be sent if the primary person cannot attend.

The description of the detailed design review in the Engineering Standard Practices is of the form indicated in Table 16-8. As previously noted, there are advantages in breaking out the review of the STD of the CSCI because it is really a CSCI-level global matter, not directly related to any one CSC. The schedule may be the only common theme; they may both be produced in the detailed design phase.

Table 16-8 A Sample Engineering Standard Practice for the Detailed Software Design Review

Detailed Software Design Review

A. *Objectives*

    1) Assure that the design of the individual software modules (in one or more CSCs) is compatible with the top-level design and CSCI requirements.

    2) Audit the algorithms and the real-time processing and memory estimates.

B. *Topics To Be Covered*

    1) Review of detailed design of each module within the CSC Interface designs

    2) Detailed memory and real-time processing estimates

    3) STD—of Test Cases (CSCI)**

    4) Software Integration Plan (for CSCI)**

    5) Hardware/Software Integration Plan (for CSCI)**

    6) Test Cases for the CSC

    7) Test Requirements & Test Cases for the units

C. *Documentation*

    1) CSCI Software Design Document—Parts I and II

    2) IDD

    3) Software Test Description—Test Cases**

    4) Revised Software Integration Plan (CSCI)**

    5) Revised Hardware/Software Integration Plan (CSCI)

    6) Test Cases for the CSC

    7) Test Requirements for the units

    8) Test Cases for the units

D. *Responsibility*

This review shall be held when the CSC software design stage is completed. The responsible Software Design Engineer schedules this review with the Design Review Coordinator after completion of the detailed software design.

** Separate technical reviews of the CSCI STD (for qualification testing), the Software Integration Plan (for the CSCI), and the Hardware/Software Integration Plan (for the CSCI) are recommended.

The STD—Part I describes the test cases to test the CSCI requirements, which are consistent with SRS Sections 4.1 and 4.2. In fact, almost all of the requirements in the SRS that are to be qualified by a test or demonstration should be covered in the STD by at least one test case. The STD is also built on, and is traceable back to, the STP and the various levels and classes of tests defined there. The CSCI test cases should provide the functional test coverage for the desired percent of requirements that are not otherwise qualified by analysis or inspection.

For test traceability purposes, SQA must review the STD to see which requirements are, in fact, tested. A simple list or database can be built from the STD test descriptions, as follows:

SRS Requirement ID	Test Case ID
AA-R-NNNN	AA-T-NNNN
•	•
•	•
•	•
AA-R-0074	AA-T-0308
AA-R-0075	AA-T-0381
•	•
•	•
•	•

(The "T" indicates a test entity in the Test Case ID column.)

The requirements actually tested in accordance with the STD shall be checked against the STP and SRS. Any anomalies must be documented and addressed at the review meeting for the STD. Also, the total number of requirements tested versus the total requirements not otherwise qualified are calculated as a percentage.

For example:

310	Total requirements for the CSCI
− 48	Requirements to be qualified by either inspection or analysis
262	Requirements addressable by testing (potentially)
203	Actually tested, per the Software Test Description

Percent of functional test coverage (Net):
203/262 = 78 percent

Percent of functional test coverage (Gross):
203/310 = 66.5 percent

Percent untested/unvalidated:
59/310 = 19 percent

The net test coverage percentage is more useful since it eliminates the intervening variables of the numbers of requirements handled by analysis or inspection. If the target value required for net coverage was 80 percent, then the number of requirements to be tested should be: $0.80 \times 262 = 209.6$, or 210 requirements should be tested. For this example, seven more "testable" requirements that are important in some sense should be tested. A scale for identifying the important and critical requirements is needed so that these requirements are tested. If you can only test 80 percent, test the critical 80 percent, not the trivial 80 percent.

For each test case, the information required is shown in the STD-DID (see Section 4.X.Y of MIL-STD-498 DID); preparations for the test are to include information per Section 3.X.2. SQA must ensure that the information is complete and reasonable for each test case. SQA must also review the definition of the CSCI-level regression test set, but this is normally defined outside the STD (usually the source is defined in the STP).

The CSC test cases for the complete CSC is similar to the problem of reviewing the CSCI test cases. A "requirements first" approach can be taken down to the CSC, if the SRS requirements are mapped to the CSC, and there is high functional cohesion within the CSCs.

Net functional test coverage for the CSC can similarly be determined, and compared with the target percent. "White-box" test planning techniques should be utilized to make certain that all of the execution controls and subroutine calls are exercised, which are other kinds of test coverage that transcend intraunit structural coverage.

The unit test requirements, followed by the unit test cases, are normally outputs during the detailed design phase. However, in most cases, these cannot be done meaningfully until the unit is designed. The detailed, internal design of the unit can be considered the most detailed level of design, and is done prior to the actual coding. However, the use of prototyping makes this distinction fuzzy. The general sequence of these steps is indicated in Figure 16-7. The timing of the review(s) can be flexible. One variation used in the past by the author was that a separate review was held for the unit-level design, followed immediately by a second review (part 2) on the test requirements to test the unit (based on the design logic). Because 100 percent structural testing was strongly encouraged, units tended to be noncomplex, so they usually could be completely path-tested with less than ten test cases. Boundary cases and error cases were additional. There were no subsequent reviews of the detailed test cases, but the coding seemed to go very well, and the unit testing progressed well, even with the virtually complete path testing. The number of coding errors discovered in later test stages was strikingly low.

The person who designed the unit and defined the unit test requirements also did the coding/implementation and unit testing in approximately 80 percent of the cases, so there was a high knowledge carryover from the unit design and test requirements steps.

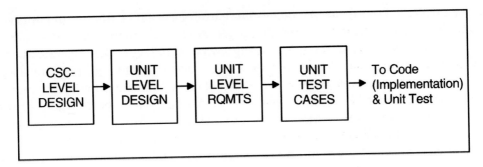

Figure 16-7 Detailed design phase steps for CSU-level activities.

The SDP defines how the software development will be performed, and if a good case is made for a variation from the nominal process in DOD-STD-2167A or MIL-STD-498, approval to try it will probably be received.

SQA, in any event, will analyze the various products, and prepare for the design reviews. All action items assigned at the review meeting are documented in an SQAIR, along with the due date and the responsible person. When all of the action items have been resolved and verified by SQA, then the design review(s) can be considered complete for the particular unit(s). SQA must track the status and closure of all of the action items, and report when they are all closed. When all of the CSCs for that CSCI have been completed, then the SDD detailed portion (plus the updates to the top-level design) can be documented or completed and published. The SDD is normally sent to the customer 30 to 60 days before the scheduled detailed design review. Normally, the customer reviews the SDD prior to the review, and should be prepared to discuss it at the joint technical design review. When all issues raised at the joint design review are finished and coordinated, a revised SDD can be published for final customer approval and authentication. It is in everyone's interest to try to resolve these issues quickly because usually the developer has to start the coding/implementation and unit test (at the developer's risk) to meet the schedules and also to not have a big gap where everyone is just waiting for customer approval of the SDD.

SQA should also do a process audit in certain selected areas for the detailed design phase. The audit is to ensure that the activities are being done properly, in accordance with the SDP and the referenced Software Engineering Procedures, plus any special contractual requirements. If people are doing the right things in the right way, the consensus is that the software design will tend to be good. This is the underlying concept for the Software Engineering Institute (SEI) software process maturity model (see Chapter 12) developed by Watts Humphrey and others. Furthermore, the process audits tend to keep everyone on their toes, so that no one is tempted to cut corners or get sloppy. Results of the audit are documented in an SQAIR. SQA must identify any adverse trends and initiate correction action.

Returning to the product reviews, SQA tracks the action items uncovered at the various reviews, and determines whether there are an unusually large number of any particular kind of errors, e.g., requirements errors, top-level design errors, detailed design errors. Boris Beitzer [5] has developed a very detailed and comprehensive structure for error types and related statistics. Whatever system of error types are used, the point is to see whether a larger-than-expected number of errors were introduced during a certain phase, or perhaps that the defect removal process at a particular point was not effective, and the errors were not found until a later phase when their removal could be much more costly. Getting statistics for a particular project can be very useful.

A simple illustration for requirements errors might be helpful. The hypothetical requirements errors found at each stage are shown in Table 16-9. In this illustration, 126 requirements errors were found during development. It is not known how many more errors exist, and of those, how many would be found in DT or OT versus operational use. Experience suggests that a few more errors would be found during DT and OT. Without estimating the not-yet-found errors, we can say there were 126 requirements errors found so far, 61 of which were found in requirements reviews. In other words, approximately 48 percent of the requirements errors were found in the internal software requirements review. From a quality perspective, does this mean that this review was effective? What about the detailed design reviews where only 3 percent of the errors were found? Should detailed design reviews find more requirements errors, or are they geared primarily for finding design errors? The author thinks the latter is true.

Other important questions are: Is the software requirements process itself within acceptable limits or norms since it produced at least 126 requirements errors? What is an acceptable error density? For a system with 2,000 software requirements, would 126 requirements errors be acceptable? For a small system with only 100 unique software requirements, 126 requirements errors would seem excessive, and something is probably wrong with the requirements process. In the illustration, the effectiveness of the requirements review process (48 percent) seemed to be within normal limits based on widely published values, based largely on the work of T. Capers Jones [6] and others. Table 16-10 indicates these acceptable values for all kinds of defects (not just requirements errors) and implies that certain defects will remain in the software at delivery time. Normal values of two to three defects per thousands of Source Lines of Code (KSLOC) of delivered source executable code are typical of current practice, but several higher quality cases exist with less than one defect per KSLOC. Quality targets of less than one defect per delivered KLOC may be necessary if the United States is to maintain its competitive edge. For a system with 1,000,000 lines of source code, i.e., 1,000 KSLOC, even one defect per KSLOC (i.e., 1,000 errors in the delivered software) does not seem that great! For a life-critical system, 1,000 errors would be a serious concern.

From a quality standpoint, what should the target be for normalized error injection, for residual errors in delivered code, and for the removal effectiveness of various reviews tools and series of tests? More specifically, what should the target be for your particular process? Would certain projects need more stringent targets?

Table 16-9   Requirements Errors Found at Different Points in the Development Process

	Number of Errors Found
Software Requirements Reviews	61
Top-Level Design Reviews	34
Detailed Design Reviews	4
Code Inspections	0
Static Analysis	0
Unit Test	1
CSC Integration & Test	4
CSCI Integration & Test	16
System Integration Test	6
Total Requirements Errors Found:	126
Total Requirements Errors Not Found:	?

Table 16-10   Defect Removal Effectiveness

	From	**To**
Requirements Reviews	20%	50%
Top-Level Design Review	30%	60%
Detailed Design Reviews	30%	70%
Code Inspections	20%	75%
Static Analysis	20%	75%
Unit Test	10%	50%
SW Integration Test	25%	60%
SW Qualification Test	25%	65%

(From T.C. Jones and Others) [6]

16.9 SQA During the Coding and Unit Test Phase

The Coding/Implementation and Unit Test phase is the point in the software development cycle where the design is finally implemented in something physical. The time and effort spent in this phase is a small part of the total effort for mission-critical software. This effort is approximately 20 to 25 percent of the effort from software design through hardware/software integration and CSCI qualification testing.

The products from the Coding/Implementation and Unit Test phase are:

1. source code— for each unit (or database)
2. CSC-level test procedures (for the next phase)
3. unit test procedures
4. unit test results

Source listings are not separate products, but are just one representation of the source code, which may be viewed on a computer display screen or printed out whenever desired, based on the source code files (see item 1, above) resident in the computer.

The SDFs shall be evaluated on a sample basis, in addition to the four products listed in the above paragraph. The SDFs are not usually considered products, although certain information and artifacts in them are important. The sample percentage of SDFs evaluated in this phase need not be the same as that used in other phases, and may vary with the type of software.

For unit-level SDFs, the contents of the SDF should include:

1. The source code for each unit (latest two or three versions).
2. The relocatable object code for each unit, and information of which version of the compiler or assembler was used to produce it. If there are special compiler instructions used, these instructions should be captured in the SDF.
3. The unit test procedures—these are generally not needed* because of the skill levels of the personnel in this domain, and because of the test tools used.
4. The unit test results for the last few sets of test runs. If any Software Problem Reports (SPRs) were generated, they should be cited in the test results. The version and date of the CSU that was tested are also important.
5. The unit test requirements, test cases, and the test data (inputs).
6. Design information, data, constraints, and other design considerations.
7. Schedule and status information.

---

* If not needed, make sure this is documented in the SDP. Note that the SPRs are not normally generated during unit test or code inspection, mainly due to the number of problems uncovered and fixed. However, it may be desired to collect the data for process improvement purposes.

Information on several related units (or objects) can be put into one SDF but this can also cause several complications. A system of SDFs that match the unit reference numbers from the software architecture chart (software family tree) can simplify the use of one SDF for one CSU. The CSCI architecture chart shown earlier in the Top-Level Design subsection (16.7) should be expanded down to the unit level, although for a large CSCI, this chart may be too complex for a single diagram. Alternatively, if just one TLCSC (TLCSC3) is taken, and expanded down for each level until all of the units are enumerated, the structure and numbering could look like that shown in Figure 16-8. The unit SDFs for this TLCSC (TLCSC3) would, conceptually, be organized in the equivalent numerical sequence, as follows:

USDF 3.1.1.1
USDF 3.1.1.2
USDF 3.1.1.3
USDF 3.1.2.1
USDF 3.1.2.2
USDF 3.1.2.3
USDF 3.2.1
USDF 3.2.2

(where USDF = Unit SDF).

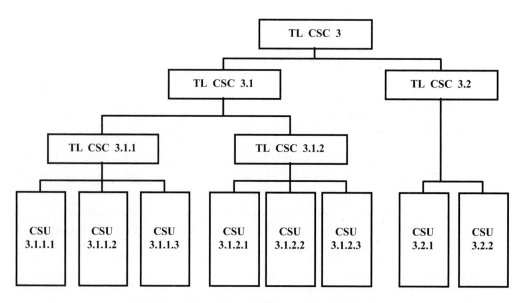

Figure 16-8   Software family tree for TLCSC3.

The Unit SDFs for TLCSC4 would follow those for TLCSC3 in the database, etc. Other CSCIs would be treated similarly, and Unit SDFs can be added or declared replaced, as needed. It is not a good idea to actually delete an SDF if a unit is dropped from the design.

The product evaluation of the source code usually takes the form of either a code review or a code inspection. The code inspection is a very rigorous, structured procedure, originally developed and codified by Michael E. Fagan [7] (see Chapter 9). In addition to the quality benefits, Fagan claimed a new improvement in productivity of 94 hours per KLOC.

The code review or code inspection, in either case, is done before the unit is tested by execution on a computer using various test cases (dynamic testing). One reason for this sequence is that code inspections can more economically and more quickly find errors than path testing for all seven categories of defects (computational, logic, input-output, data handling, interface, data definition, and database). Therefore, the code inspection is a good way to remove many defects before actual testing begins. However, subsequent testing will usually find a few errors that were not found by the code inspection, mainly because of a different perspective or approach.

The code inspection (or the less rigorous code review) is a product evaluation of one kind. The participants in this review meeting are the coder, one or two technical experts in the application software domain ("peers"), an SQA engineer, an inspection leader, and a recorder. Others may be added, if necessary. Visitors and noncontributors should be discouraged. Managers may inhibit the free discussion and candor needed to flush out all the problems.

A code inspection may be scheduled to handle several closely related units, particularly if they are all coded by the same programmer.

What is evaluated at a code inspection? There are six main areas, as follows:

1. **Code functionality.**
   Does the unit code meet the specific requirements allocated to it (refer to the SDD)? Does the unit do things it should not do, or that are not required? Also, is the code reasonable in terms of code efficiency, run time, memory utilization, and error control/error handling?

2. **Unit interfaces.**
   Do the unit interfaces match the expectations of the other units, etc.? Are the conventions and data definitions the same? (e.g., 1 = YES or 0 = NO, Least Significant Bit = 15, High Altitude = 1, or Low Altitude = 0.) Are error condition exits handled correctly? Are all interfaces handled on the other side of the interface?

3. **Data.**
   Is all data set or used by the unit the same? Are there any data conflicts? Is the data initialized or reinitialized properly? Is the data redundant? Is the

precision of the data sufficient? Are the data descriptions clear and unambiguous? Is there any data validation required? How often is the data used or set?

4. **Specification conflicts.**

Does the unit have any conflicts with the SRS requirements or the SDD design?

5. **Prologues and comments.**

Is the prologue adequate to describe the processing, inputs and output, any subroutine calls, and configuration and data information? Are the comments in the code adequate to describe how the program works, and any anomalies or special considerations. Is configuration, author, and date information included?

6. **Programming conventions.**

Does the unit adhere to the programming standards and conventions referenced in the SDP, and any special contractual requirements?

Example:
a. Structured coding constructs
b. Unit size limits (executable source statements, memory requirements)
c. Unit entry/exit limitations
d. Nesting conventions and limits
e. Prologue and comment requirements
f. Labeling and naming conventions
g. Prohibition of execution-time self-modification of the code
h. Limits on McCabe [8] cyclomatic or essential complexity or equivalent (see Chapter 15)

At the risk of stating the obvious, the source language should be acceptable for this contract.

It is also useful to revisit the unit test cases, and analyze the paths tested by each test case. If the McCabe cyclomatic complexity is relatively low (10 or less), then it is feasible to path-test every path through the unit. Code that is not complex is not expensive to completely test, and is generally easier to maintain or modify over its operational life (and during testing). Once the code has been reviewed and any problems resolved, it is useful to see whether all of the code paths are tested by the set of test cases developed earlier (based on the design and the requirements). The actual code may be somewhat different than the detailed design logic was at design time. The set of test cases may not test all of the paths of the actual code, so a glass-box view of these test cases and their path coverage is useful. Whenever possible, the test cases should exercise all of the paths in the current design logic (this will find any inadvertent omissions in the code).

If there are redundant test cases, the redundant test cases should be eliminated so each path is tested exactly once. Also, look at the boundary case test cases from an input space viewpoint. Are all boundary cases covered? Finally, look at the error cases; are all the errors tested (or at least the critical ones)? In several of these cases, the analysis of the code is sufficient based on each test case. Dr. Harlan Mills [9] makes an interesting point in his "Clean Room" approach that unit testing may not be necessary at all if the code is thoroughly inspected by the programmer (or by a reviewer) for each test case. To implement the test case inspections (even with certain unit testing retained), SQA and software engineering procedures would need to be modified from today's versions. Another related method of looking at the input space of test cases is covered in Chapter 19 by Dr. Cho.

Static analysis of the source code can be utilized to find additional problems prior to test execution (dynamic analysis). As Dunn and Ullman [10] point out, compilers, such as C and Ada, have been doing static analysis for many years. Dunn lists typical outputs of static analysis, e.g., unused variables, uninitialized variables, cross-reference lists for operands, etc. The software engineering process and SQA process should capitalize on these capabilities, which vary with the compiler (or other tools) actually used. Use of these "static analyzers" should be encouraged, preferably before the unit test.

If there is no shortage of computer power (particularly during off-hours), it is not wise to insist that the code inspections be done before compilation because the compiler or other static analysis tools may quickly detect problems that can be fixed by the programmer before the code inspection, thus saving time for everyone. It may be hard to prevent programmers from using these tools before the inspection, even if you want to; most programmers want to look good at the inspection. In fact, several organizations require an error-free compilation before the code inspection. SQA does not have to concern itself with this static analysis process, but may want to spotcheck certain units and run them through the static analysis toolset to see whether there are still problems after the inspection or after code changes; this spotcheck may encourage programmers to use the available tools to improve quality.

The next main activity in the Coding/Implementation and Unit Testing phase is the unit testing activity. The product of the unit testing activity is revised source code, and a lot of unit test results. The goal is to end up with a version of the unit (by version and date) that has passed all of the test cases and the test results (data, and PASS/FAIL indications) retained in the unit SDF. SQA can audit the process by witnessing the unit tests and auditing the unit SDF and documenting the results in an SQAIR. A final audit should be done on a sample of completed, released units to ensure that all of the tests have been run on the final version of software, and that all the test data actually mean a PASS for all the test cases. Release of a unit without successfully testing all of the test cases would be a serious matter, and not only would an SQAIR be written, but a more fundamental *Corrective Action Request* would be sent to software engineering regarding the apparent breakdown in the process. "We ran out of time and couldn't test everything" is not considered acceptable!

After a unit is released to the CSC I&T library, it should still be maintained in the development library so that future problems can be addressed and fixed by the developer, without playing around with the copy in the CSC I&T Library.

Tracking the status of the units completed provides good overall information on the coding/implementation and unit testing phase (e.g., of 394 units, 168 have completed Implementation and Unit Testing). Tracking the individual problems, and CSU test case completions is usually left to the developer and the lead software engineer to prevent micromanagement. SQA would track only serious breaches in the Unit Code/Test process, such as not completing the agreed-upon test cases or not properly recording the test results in the SDF, or making sub-rosa changes to the software-under-test.

16.10   SQA During the Software Integration and Testing Phase

The Software I&T phase usually has several subphases for embedded mission-critical software. Software integration of several units within a CSC would normally occur first. This integration can be done in two main ways: bottom-up or top-down. Later, several CSCs (after they have completed CSC integration) can be integrated and tested as part of the CSCI. Most or all of the CSCI I&T is done in a simulated environment on a host development computer. At the planned point, the CSCI testing moves to a Hardware-Software Integration phase where the software runs on the actual target microcomputer and interfaces with real, usually newly-designed, hardware. The task is to test the new software and the new hardware, and resolve any problems and incompatibilities.

At the end of the Hardware-Software Integration activity, the CSCI is completely built and tested, and Acceptance Testing of the complete CSCI (or a preplanned partial build of the CSCI) begins in the "real hardware" environment. When the software seems to work 100 percent correctly as per the STD Acceptance Test Specification, SQA is called to witness a final dry run test. When the dry runs are successfully completed (which may take several attempts before everyone including SQA is satisfied), customer and government representatives (e.g., Defense Contract Management Command [DCMC] Quality in-plant personnel) are notified and the Formal Acceptance Test is scheduled. You do not want any surprises or embarrassments in front of the customer, nor do you want to waste their time and create resentment. CSCI level testing is discussed further in subsection 5.11.

The products of the CSC-level integration and testing phase are the updated code built into various CSCs and the updated STD, including any detailed test procedures and any refinements to the Test Case Descriptions developed earlier. For certain embedded systems, the test procedures part of the STD is not needed, and is tailored out because the people running the CSCI tests (reference section 16.11) are experts who do not need the procedures.

For certain embedded systems, the human interactions at this level of testing are virtually zero, and one particular signal is injected on top of background noise. This is far different from a large command and control system, where there are normally extensive human interactions and many carefully scripted "threat" and "environmental" (simulated or real) inputs.

Another output of the CSC integration phase is the CSC integration test results for each CSC test case. These test results for the current CSC software version for all of the test cases shall be contained in the CSC-level SDF.

The above products are subject to product evaluations by engineering, SQA, and others. As with several of the prior phases, the updated SDFs for the CSC are subject to evaluation on a sample basis.

The activity of CSC I&T is subject to process evaluations by SQA to ensure that the methods and procedures promised in the SDP and its references are being properly followed, and that all other contractual requirements for these activities are being met. For example, are the tests being conducted properly and completely; are all of the test case results being recorded properly and accurately; are Software Problem Reports (SPRs) being written promptly for any observed anomalies; are changes to the software being controlled properly in the developmental configuration; are any unauthorized software changes being made; is the software design documentation being kept current (at least weekly) with the software changes?

A fundamental question relates to the CSC integration approach. Should the CSC be integrated all at once or in an incremental approach? The incremental approach seems to work well for most situations in the embedded system arena. This incremental approach is planned around the major software functions and is briefly described as follows:

1. Design, code, and test one unit
2. Add another unit to the CSC
3. Test the collection of the two units (a "partial build" of the CSC)
4. Repeat steps 2 and 3 for additional units, until all the units have been incorporated and tested

One advantage of this incremental approach from a software quality viewpoint is that only a few new units are added to the CSC build at one time, thus tending to isolate potential problems to either the few new units, or to interfaces with these units. This self-focusing approach can be helpful in isolating and finding the causes of problems. Furthermore, it is easy to back up to the prior build and do special testing, whenever necessary. This incremental approach is also compatible with a top-down implementation approach, which is very useful in many kinds of systems, particularly embedded Mission-Critical systems. The CSC builds should be functionally coherent to allow several units to work together to produce an overall result or output. Stubs may be necessary to substitute for real units until they are available. Whichever approach is used, SQA will periodically spotcheck the CSC integration and test, and document the findings in an SQAIR.

When the CSC testing is reported to be complete, all of the units for that CSC should be included in the build, and this complete aggregate of software should have successfully passed all the CSC-level test cases. SQA shall be notified of the completion; SQA should then validate completion of the CSC testing, using the results in the CSC-level SDF. On certain projects, the SDP may also call for a small CSC Test Review Meeting, involving the tester, the lead software engineer, and SQA.

The other product of the CSC I&T Phase is the updated STD—to be used in the next phase for CSCI-level qualification testing. In certain cases, the qualification testing may be done at other levels than the CSCI-level, but this is not too common. The test procedures may be added to the STD at this time in the development process. If test procedures are required for the qualification tests (i.e., have not been tailored out of the contract), then this information is added to the STD.

The required content (test execution procedures) of each STD Test Procedure subsection (per MIL-STD-498) are indicated in Table 16-11, and these contents must be reviewed and evaluated by Engineering and SQA before the document is published.

In addition, the qualification test preparations (Section 3 of the STD) are to be added for each of the tests at this time (Section 3 for the first test, etc.) The specific contents for these STD sections are shown in Table 16-12.

SQA must also review the document to ensure the customer comments on the earlier STD are adequately resolved. SQA will review the completed draft of the updated STD, and write up any comments via an SQAIR before the document is published. If there are any disagreements or questions on the SQA comments, it is essential to meet promptly, discuss only these SQA comments in question, and resolve these open comments. The normal evaluation criteria of internal consistency and understandability apply. The test procedures have to be traceable back to the test cases in the STD. When the last comment is resolved, SQA can sign off for the publication of the document. The document is then printed and distributed with copies to the customer and others, including SQA. It is important that the customer respond promptly on the STD because it must be used in the next phase, CSCI Testing. There is little alternative but to allow 30 days for customer comments, and then proceed as is if no comments are received by then; however, it is necessary to tell the customer that you must proceed at the end of 30 days to preclude a schedule impact. Also, recognize the customer comments may take up to two weeks to analyze and address, so that an STD with problems can delay the CSCI Testing phase (particularly if the comments are received on Day 29). On the other hand, a good STD will tend to prevent schedule impacts and reduce the rework effort.

Table 16-11   Software Test Description Test Procedure Information

4.X.Y.6   (Test Case Name) Test Procedure—for Test Case Y of Test X

Arranged as a series of sequentially numbered steps. For each step:

- Step Number
- Test Operator actions, and equipment operation required
- Expected Result
- Evaluation criteria (as applicable)
- Actions, in case of a program stop or indicated error
- Data Reduction and analysis procedures
- In addition, the scripted time of the desired test operator action, either in absolute test time from T = O, or from some prior event. Also, special data recording instructions may be needed.

Table 16-12   Software Test Description Test Preparation Information

3.X   (Test Name) Pretest Procedures—for Test Case X

3.X.1   Hardware Preparation

- Specific hardware to be used (by name and number)
- Diagrams to show hardware, interconnecting control, and data paths
- Switch settings and cabling (identify by name and location)
- Step-by-step instructions for placing hardware in a "ready state"

3.X.2   Software Preparation (for the CSCI, and any support software)

- Specific Software to be used
- Storage medium of CSCI, and step-by-step instructions for loading the CSCI
- Storage medium of any support software, and step-by-step instructions for loading the support software
- When the support software is to be loaded
- Instructions for CSCI and support software initialization (common to more than one test case)

3.X.3   Other Pretest Preparations

A significant formal review called the Test Readiness Review (TRR) can be held at the end of this phase. The requirements of this review were spelled out in MIL-STD-1521B, but are streamlined in MIL-STD-498. Sometimes, this review is tailored out of the contract if the development effort is considered low risk. One practical reason for this review was the very large time gap between the Detailed Design Review and the software qualification tests. Apparently, the government was getting too many surprises when they came in to witness the CSCI acceptance tests; the TRR was added to DOD-STD-2167 and -2167A as an intermediate checkpoint, i.e., an opportunity for midpoint corrections. The TRR is retained as an optional review in MIL-STD-498.

16.11   SQA During the CSCI Test Phase

The CSCI Testing phase is the culmination of the main part of the software development effort. The various CSCs (or equivalent) that comprise the CSCI are integrated and tested, preferably one or two at a time. When the CSCI is complete, the entire CSCI can be tested as an entity, leading up to the CSCI acceptance or qualification testing. As indicated in Figure 16-4, each software qualification test is based on the CSCI requirements captured in the SRS and the test cases described in the STD. The test cases in the STD are traceable back to the SRS, and are specifically covered in the SRS qualification section (Section 4). All of the requirements to be addressed directly by testing are covered as demonstration/test items in the SRS. The mapping or verification of the requirements (by ID number) to the test cases (by test case ID) was discussed earlier in subsection 16.8 as an SQA work product. The advantages of including a verified printout from the test traceability database in the STD are significant. Every requirement is listed, even those that were deleted in subsequent changes approved for the SRS (allocated baseline). This listing is very useful to SQA, product management, and to the customer. This requirements list could take the form indicated in Table 16-13.

The direct products of the CSCI Testing phase are:

The updated source code for all of the units in the CSCI
The STRs for the qualification testing, primarily at the CSCI level

Several of the other products that were shown in DOD-STD-2167A as products of the CSCI Testing phase are now deferred (refer to MIL-STD-498). The reason for deferring these documents (such as the operation and support documents) and the Software Product Specifications is that the software usually undergoes additional changes as a result of system-level I&T. To reduce expense and the drawdown of project talent, these documents are normally finalized just once, after the dust has settled. Usually, these documents are still subject to several comments from the customer or from an independent verification and validation (IV&V) contractor supporting the customer, but the time and energy to resolve these comments is normally modest with computerized documentation/publishing systems. In any event, these operation and support products must be thoroughly reviewed by all parties (including SQA) before they are finalized and shipped to the customer.

Table 16-13   Complete Requirements List For CSCI AA

Requirement ID	Requirement Name	SRS Paragraph	SRS Qualification Method (A, D, I)	STD Test Case ID
AA-R-0001	Change modes, per User Input	3.2.1	D	AA-T-0006
AA-R-0002 • • •	Automatic Mode Change	(deleted: ECN 0212)		–
AA-R-0074	Determine Pulse Repetition Interval	3.2.38	D	AA-T-0308

Qualification Methods:
   A = Analysis
   D = Demonstration (Test)
   I = Inspection
Note: All requirements are shown for completeness, arranged by Requirement ID.

     The Software Version Description (SVD), as defined in DID DI-IPSC-81442, is used when a new version of the software is established based on a revised allocated baseline in the SRSs. The SVD describes the changes incorporated since the last version, and lists the media and related documentation for this software release. The SVD is delivered to the customer with the software media for the particular version. Because the software itself is not considered final until at least the completion of systems-level test, the SVD is normally not published at the completion of CSCI Testing, but is deferred.

     Incremental CSCI Testing (using incremental builds of the CSCI) has been found to be very effective especially for embedded software. The early builds allow debugging of the test facilities and test procedures and facilitate learning. If a separate test team is used for CSCI Testing, the early builds allow the team to get started and learn on a smaller problem, which facilitates the initial phases of CSCI Testing. The CSCI integration plans included in Table 16-5 are in addition to the CSCI STD. The software integration plans cover the integration and testing done in a software environment on a host development machine. Although there may be advantages in going directly to the real hardware and target computer, the new hardware may not be available in time. Therefore, certain meaningful testing can be done, and usually must be done, to meet schedules in a software environment with simulations of the real hardware.

The Hardware/Software Integration plan covers the CSCI I&T done on the real hardware and target microcomputer. The circuit board with the computer and memory and other hardware elements is set up in a test cage with other interfacing equipment, signal generators to provide certain inputs, and waveform analyzers to examine the outputs.

It is time-consuming to reburn Programmable Read-Only Memories (PROMs) each time a problem is fixed and a software change is made, so test console systems to replace the PROMs and read the software from floppies or hard disks are used. Any software changes can be made and saved (at least temporarily) during this process. At least weekly, these changes would be submitted to the software change control system, and would be formally released to the software library, once approved. SQA is a member of the Software Change Control Board for each project, along with Software Engineering, Software Configuration Management, and the System Engineering group.

SQA will do in-process audits of the CSCI testing to ensure that engineering test logs are properly kept, test data are correctly recorded, and that the CSCI-level SDFs and related data are maintained in correct and current form. SQA will prepare an SQAIR for each spotcheck audit, even if no problems are found.

When the CSCI integration testing is completed, and the CSCI is considered ready for the CSCI acceptance tests, a dry run is scheduled. The SQA operating procedure dealing with software test and validation simply states: "SQA shall witness dry runs of all qualification and acceptance tests involving software."

The entire STD is followed in the dry run, and any anomalies are identified. If any anomalies require changes to the STD, several telephone calls with the customer to discuss the necessary STD changes are recommended. The STD changes can be redlined onto a master copy, or a revisions mode can be used with an electronic version. SQA and engineering must both be assured that the CSCI satisfactorily and fully passes all of the test cases in the STD. The dry-run test results are stored in the CSCI SDF. SQA keeps a summary of the test results (by test case) and documents the results of the dry run in an SQAIR. If there are any problems, they must be fixed and a new revision of software processed through the Software Change Control Board, etc., and the full qualification test dry run must be rerun with the new software version.

Finally, when the software is 100 percent ready, and SQA concurs, the customer can be notified and the acceptance (qualification) test scheduled for the government representatives to witness. Even if customer representatives are on-site, it may take several days before everyone can be available for the actual qualification test.

Although certain tests may take only a day or two, larger tests can take several weeks. For the illustrative CSCI case discussed in subsection 16.8, 203 requirements of a potential 262 addressable by testing will be tested in the qualification test. The mapping of requirements to test cases varies, but if the average is two requirements per test case, approximately 100 test cases will be run. If each test case requires a different input signal, data recording and reduction, plus an average of one hour of analysis and discussion, then two hours per test case is not unreasonable. For 100 test cases, this means approximately 200 hours of actual testing work. With at least four hours of introductory briefings, etc. on the front-end, and possibly four to six hours of summary briefings on the last day, the elapsed time totals approximately 26 normal work days. The customer should be a party to planning so that the time commitment is known well in advance. If the test might take more than two weeks, two test teams and two-shift test operations could be considered.

In one case, two test teams were used, but they alternated the use of the facilities and equipment with only light contention (from approximately 7:30 AM to 7:00 PM). Each team had two software engineers, one system engineer, one SQA engineer, and one or two customer representatives.

Not every customer sends a team to witness the qualification testing of each CSCI. In certain cases, the customer will delegate the local government people to witness the testing for them. In other cases, they rely on the developer's SQA group to witness and certify the testing and validate the test results.

During the acceptance test, SQA keeps a separate test log, and records each event, the time, any anomalies, pass/fail information, and any other key data. This is in addition to the engineering test log. At the end of each day, the test log is carefully reviewed for any gaps, problems, etc., by the test team. However, if a major phase completes, the review will be held at that time. Any additions or clarifications are discussed and entered in the log, along with initials and the time of the changes. When everyone agrees that this log represents a complete and accurate picture of the day's testing, all of the parties sign and date each of the pages for that day. Copies of these signed pages are then given to the government representatives and to SQA. The customer seems to appreciate the procedures and has a feeling of confidence that things are being done professionally. The customer also appreciates that no changes can be made afterwards to the test results or any other information in the test logs. SQA then locks up the master log books and other test materials for the night. SQA unlocks the test materials and log on the next morning in the government's presence, and everyone take a few minutes to review yesterday's results before the plan for the current day is established. If any changes have to be made to the STD, a master copy is redlined and each change is initialed and dated, and changes are noted in the test log. The redined copy of the STD becomes a new revision and copies are made after the test, with copies going to the customer, to SQA, and to Software Configuration Management (SCM) for release to the software library.

Because of the dry runs, it is unlikely that there will be any surprises or problems during the qualification testing. Therefore, there should be no reason to stop and modify the software under testing during the formal test. If a glitch is observed, it is usually better to just record the anomaly and continue the testing. This approach gives time to address any problems off-line while testing continues. The anomaly is usually isolated in a day or two. In this case, where the glitch is minor, the test will usually be considered by the customer as a conditional acceptance, conditional on the software being fixed and retested in the next couple of weeks.

At the end of the testing, a final out-briefing is held to summarize customer's view of the testing, and whether there were any problems or action items.

The STR is a formal, deliverable document that uses the information from the STD, the test logs, the recorded test data, and the results summarized in the test out-briefing. It normally takes several weeks after the completion of the testing to complete the document, and for SQA to review it. The heart of the STR is the Test Results section, Section 4.

In the STR, each test has a separate major section (e.g., 4.1, 4.2, etc.). Within each test, the results for each test case within that group is given, Section 4.X.Y. For each Test Case, three subsections are provided:

4.X.1 (Test Case Name) Test Results Summary
4.X.2 (Test Case Name) Problems Encountered
4.X.3 Deviations from Test Cases/Procedures (if any)

STR Section 5 contains a copy of the test logs.

An executive summary of the test is to be provided in Section 3.1 for each test group. Although not required, the use of a test results summary table is suggested. A sample of such a test results summary table for all of the test cases in a test is indicated in Table 16-14.

The STR DID is not very detailed, and each development organization should prepare a more detailed template for their standard model of an STR. Based on this model, SQA should prepare a detailed checklist to serve as a tool to guide the SQA review of the draft STR before it is published.

SQA should also review the updated code to make certain it meets all of the coding standards, including current configuration information. SQA should particularly review the units affected by SPRs to ensure that the SPRs are properly incorporated.

Table 16-14   Sample Test Results Summary Table (for all test cases in a given test)

Test Case ID	Success (P = Pass)	Failure and Step No. (S)	Software Problem Reports (SPRs)	Remarks
•				
•				
•				
BB-T-0032	P			
BB-T-0033		F	SPR-018	Minor Problem
BB-T-0034		Step 8		
•		F		
•		Step 10	SPR-032	Response Time Problem*
•		Step 22	SPR-033	Minor Problem

Note:
   CSCI: Time Domain Pulse Sorter (Code BB)
   Test: Single Threats, Light Noise Background
   Test Class: Basic Performance
   Level: CSCI
*Needs correction for full approval

   Similarly, the design documentation (primarily the SDD) should be reviewed by SQA to ensure that it is current for all approved Software Problem Reports that change the design, and therefore change the design documentation. If the contract does not call for a formal delivery of the updated SDD, at least a master copy of the SDD should be redlined and keep current by the lead software engineer for internal use. SQA should review this copy to ensure that all design-related changes have been incorporated.

   As each CSCI completes testing, it should be promoted to the system-level testing library.

16.12   The Role of SQA During the Subsystem and System Integration Test Phase

For embedded mission-critical software, the testing does not end with the CSCI-level testing, even though this testing is a qualification test for each CSCI. The software is embedded in a hardware system, and the total entity is a new design and must work together to meet a higher-level system specification. Normally, there are between one to three levels of system integration and test, depending on the size and complexity of the system. For example, there could be testing at the line replaceable unit (LRU) level, then several LRUs could be integrated into a subsystem, and finally, several subsystems would be integrated to make up the entire working system.

At each level of testing, problems will be noticed, several of them traceable to the software. In other cases, the cause of the problem may not be in the software, but the solution will be to change the software to resolve the problem. In either event, SQA will be concerned with the software aspects of the system testing. Anomalies or problems tracked to the software must be assigned an SPR number. Software changes approved by the Software Change Control Board will be cut into the source code and CSCI run-load files, as soon as possible. Each new software version/revision must identify the SPRs that are being incorporated in the new software release. At the various system levels of testing, the released software is normally burned into some type of PROM, so there are several additional steps where SQA must verify (basically) that the firmware is correct.

Hopefully, the number of software changes per week will not be too great. Where possible, new compilations will be made and then a new build made with the revised software, using the project's link/editor tools. It is a good idea to try to make a new build each week so that the changes do not accumulate. This way, if there are any problems encountered during regression testing, the number of new changes in the new load file(s) are limited, and the source of the problem is bounded to just the few modified units and their interfaces.

During system testing, it may be necessary to temporarily patch the run-load with a temporary fix, and retest to see whether the patch really solves the problem. If it does, at least system testing can proceed in the meantime; software engineering should be working in parallel on the corresponding change to the source code. The software engineering practices usually have guidelines on the maximum number and size of patches, and other guidance for software patches. SQA should track the maximum amount of memory used for patches and the number of patches, and help ensure that a new source code build will be used before the limits are exceeded. The original Navy software standard, MIL-STD-1679, limited the number of patches to one-half a percent of the total software memory, but this was relaxed in MIL-STD-1679A and also is not explicitly covered in DOD-STD-2167A, MIL-STD-498, and IEEE 1498. Therefore, the organization's internal standard practices will have to set the groundrules for patches. Certain standard practices also limit the maximum size of a single patch to reasonable values, e.g., 50 words maximum. Certain organizations do not allow patches except in very limited, temporary situations. Retaining patches as part of the software product is not recommended.

The software products of the System I&T phase are the updated source code and the updated design documentation, as discussed in the prior subsection.

In addition, any changes to the software after the CSCI qualification tests must be carefully documented, and the tests for those changes shall be documented as addenda to the STD. The test must be witnessed and certified by SQA and documented in an SQAIR, and addenda to the appropriate STRs must be prepared. The test results shall be available within the CSCI SDFs. These changes will have to be addressed later in the software Functional Configuration Audit (FCA) and Physical Configuration Audit (PCA).

The system-level acceptance/qualification test is supported by SQA for the software-related items. SQA must certify the correct version and revision of each CSCI under test, and the related firmware contents and labeling. SQA will ensure that any software anomalies are documented and addressed, and that no unauthorized changes are made to the software. If the customer is to witness the system-level qualification test, a prior dry run is essential to ensure that everything works properly.

After the system test is completed, the various operation and support documents, the SVD, and the SPS can be finalized, reviewed by SQA, and then shipped to the customer for review and approval.

16.13   Functional and Physical Configuration Audits for Software

The FCA and PCA are the two final audits held for each configuration item (including Software Configuration Items) before going into production. These audits were described in MIL-STD-1521B, Appendixes G and H, and later in MIL-STD-973 "Configuration Management." However, these standards have now been cancelled, and the exact words must be added to the SOW if either the FCA or PCA (or both) is required.

16.13.1 Functional Configuration Audit

For software, the FCA is used to determine and verify that each CSCI actually meets the requirements in the SRS and IRS. This is done primarily by reviewing the test results in the STR(s) for all of the CSCI's requirements. To facilitate this process, an output from the SRS requirements traceability database would be helpful, showing each SRS/IRS requirement and the test case ID (or inspection/analysis case ID) where it is validated, and the test results may be found. In addition, the completed operation and support documents are reviewed at the FCA to ensure that they are adequate to support the system once it is deployed. These user/support documents are shown in Table 16-15 for both DOD-STD-2167A and the counterparts in MIL-STD-498 and IEEE 1498.

To be able to conduct the FCA, the software requirements (SRS and IRS) must have been previously approved and authenticated for the correct version. These requirements form the allocated baseline for each CSCI. The STR for each CSCI's qualification testing should also have been made available for customer review prior to the FCA. The SPS, which describes the as-built CSCI that completed the qualification testing and system testing, is also needed by the customer prior to the FCA. In the "real world," the SPS may not be available much ahead of the FCA.

Table 16-15   Software Operation and Support "Documents"

DOD-STD-2167A	MIL-STD-498/IEEE 1498
Computer System Operator's Manual (CSOM)	Computer Operation Manual (COM)
Software User's Manual (SUM)	Software User Manual (SUM)
Software Programmer's Manual (SPM)	Computer Programming Manual (CPM)
Firmware Support Manual (FSM)	Firmware Support Manual (FSM)
Software Product Specification (SPS)	Software Product Specification (SPS)
*	Software Center Operator Manual (SCOM)
*	Software Input/Output Manual (SIOM)

* No counterpart in DOD-STD-2167A (only in MIL-STD-7935A for Automated Information Systems)

All of the CSCIs for the system should be scheduled for one FCA, whenever practical. The contractor must notify the customer of the FCA agenda, including which items are to be covered, and the following specifics for each CSCI:

- Nomenclature of the CSCI
- Specification number(s) of SRS and IRS
- Configuration item number and ID for the exact version/revision of software to be audited
- A complete list of deviations and waivers and their status
- Status of any software test tools used in the CSCI qualification testing

It is a good idea to also indicate the document numbers and status of the STRs and SPSs for each CSCI.

Because of the importance of the FCA—basic acceptance of the software for production and deployment (or not)—internal planning meetings and an abbreviated dry run by the contractor is recommended. SQA must ensure that all items needed for the formal audit are identified, are compatible, and are made ready for the FCA. These items include:

- The SRS for each CSCI
- The IRS
- The SPS* for each CSCI
- The Software Test Plan
- The STD for each CSCI
- The STR for each CSCI
- A list of all approved Engineering Change Proposals (ECPs)

- Approved minutes of the joint design reviews
- Briefing materials on the CSCI requirements and design (minimal)
- Briefing materials on the CSCI testing and the test results (minimal)
- Requirements traceability from SRS/IRS requirements "down" to the test case ID

* The SPS includes the updated Software Design Document and references to the associated source code files.

SQA, software engineering, SCM, and the project management office are the principal parties in the FCA planning and preparation. SQA must verify that all of the necessary information is, indeed, available and it is all the correct version.

The FCA dry run is an internal walkthrough of all of the activities that must be done before the formal FCA. These activities include:

- Briefings on each CSCI and the testing.
- Discussion of any requirements not met, along with proposed solutions.
- Discussion of any Engineering Change Proposals (ECPs) incorporated and test results.
- Highlights of the test results, both problem areas and successful accomplishments.
- Audits of the STPs, down to the test descriptions/procedures, and the STRs, for consistency and traceability, and versus the actual recorded test data and test log data. Also, the completeness and accuracy of the actual test data and test logs must be checked.
- Audits of all approved ECPs to ensure they are incorporated correctly and completely.
- Consistency of all of the technical documents in the document set.
- Audit of the joint design review minutes to ensure that all findings and action items have been fully incorporated.
- Audit of the interface testing against the IRS.
- Audit of the final memory and storage allocation versus the requirements and margins for delivery time; also, the actual processing timing (including processor loading, path lengths, etc.) and input/output port loadings versus requirements and margins.
- Audit of the as-built database characteristics versus requirements and design.
- Adequacy of human interfaces, workloads, and human factors.
- Adequacy of the operation and support documents.
- Audits of the quality program records for those requirements qualified by analysis or inspection.
- Other tasks, as determined by the FCA planning group.

The results of the FCA dry run should be documented, any deficiencies should be noted, and action items should be assigned to specific individuals with a due date. SQA should document the dry-run results in an SQAIR, track all of the action items, and highlight the items due each week and any overdue items.

When all action items are resolved, then the real FCA can be held with the customer. For the real FCA, the activities are the same as for the dry run. A person on the contractor's FCA team must be the recorder, and take careful minutes each day. A useful idea is to publish a draft of the FCA minutes each day for everyone to review and to ensure good sharing of information. If there are any problems, they should be addressed that day (or early the next morning) to keep things moving ahead smoothly.

The final result of the FCA is that each CSCI is either accepted as is, or certain items must be fixed before the CSCI can be accepted. In certain cases, noncritical deficiencies can be mapped into a future update because the initial capability is considered adequate for now. These points all have to be discussed and documented at the end of the FCA, and the customer has the final decision. There should be a good understanding of the final results and of the customer's feelings regarding acceptance (or not) for each CSCI.

The developer's FCA team prepares the formal minutes of the FCA, and submits them to the customer for approval. A draft should be compiled and coordinated for all of the days (with the possible exception of the last day) for informal review on the last day. The customer's contracting agency reviews the formal minutes, may ask for additional data, and ultimately determines one of three possible outcomes for each CSCI:

1. Approval
2. Contingent Approval—not approved until satisfactory completion of the indicated action items
3. Disapproval—the FCA was not adequate

With the timely formation of an internal FCA team and a certain amount of reasonable planning and preparation, the outcome should be either 1 or 2. The dry run will tend to ensure that the results are full approval if the dry run discrepancies are addressed seriously. SQA should act as a surrogate customer and play the customer's role during the FCA dry run. These efforts are not free, but they do help make for a successful FCA and will enhance the reputation and success of your company with the customer, which will be considered for future business.

If sufficient test data is not available at the FCA, it is necessary to hold a separate review in the near future (sometimes called a Formal Qualification Review [FQR]), usually after both the FCA and PCA. However, the practice now is to have a single combined FCA, which obviates a separate FQR just to review the test results against the requirements. Commercial projects usually do not conduct formal PCAs, but it is a good practice to review the test results against all of the SRS requirements.

16.13.2 Physical Configuration Audit

The PCA for software is the audit and formal examination of the actual as-built software product versus the design documentation and user/support manuals. The PCA is done after the FCA.

The key items for a Software PCA include the following:

- The SPS for each CSCI. The SPS includes the updated software design description and the comparable final source code.
- The software version description.
- The appropriate software operation and support manuals (e.g., CSOM, Software User Manual, CPM, Firmware Support Manual, etc.).
- The SRS for each CSCI.
- The IRS.
- FCA minutes for each CSCI.
- Findings/status of the quality assurance program for the software.
- The coding standards used for the project.
- A listing of all of the project's software (CSCIs or equivalent).

The planning and preparation for the PCA should be done by a designated PCA team, including representatives from Software Engineering, SQA, and SCM. The agenda has to be prepared and coordinated with the customer. SQA must verify that all of the necessary materials have been collected and organized in advance.

A dry run PCA should be held with SQA acting as the surrogate customer. All action items from the dry run must be documented, resolved, and verified before the formal PCA with the customer.

The PCA itself consists of a series of steps:

1. Review the SPS components for format, correctness, completeness, and compatibility.
2. Review the FCA minutes for any discrepancies, and the corresponding actions that must be taken.
3. Review the design descriptions in the SPS for proper entries, symbols, labels, tags, references, and data descriptions.
4. Compare the top-level software component design descriptions with their lower-level software components for consistency.

5. Compare the lower-level component design description with the actual software code for consistency, accuracy, and completeness.
6. Check the various user manuals for completeness, consistency, and correctness with the final version of code.
7. Examine the CSCI delivery media for conformance with SRS packaging/labeling requirements and special contract requirements, e.g., media characteristics and format, classification marking, etc.
8. Review the annotated listings (if any required) for compliance with the approved coding standards for the contract.

In preparing for the PCA, SQA should take care to ensure that all recently approved STRs have been fully and consistently included in both the code and the documentation set. Furthermore, SQA should verify that these code changes meet all of the coding standards.

After completion of the PCA, the contractor must prepare, review, and submit copies of the formal minutes and the attachments to the customer for review and the ultimate decision. The customer then either accepts, or rejects the PCA for each CSCI.

When both the FCA and PCA are approved for a given CSCI, that CSCI is then accepted for production and deployment. This approval defines the product baseline for production. SQA can play a significant role in the planning, preparation, and actual conduct of the software PCA, and contribute to the success of the PCA. A rejection of one or more CSCIs is costly to resolve and impacts the deployment schedule.

Subsequent changes to the product baseline are possible via ECPs. Any such changes will ultimately create a new set of baselines (functional, allocated, and product) for that ECP, starting with a given effectively point (e.g., effective serial number 122 and subsequent). Units already in the field also may have to be retrofitted with the software change. New baselines (with new requirements) will normally have mini-FCAs and mini-PCAs to ensure they are correct and complete before deployment.

16.14   Development and Operational Testing (The "Real World")

For most embedded, real-time systems (particularly systems for DoD), extensive testing is done outside the development laboratory after the System Acceptance Test. The purpose is to test the systems extensively in realistic environments, which usually are not practical in the contractor's development laboratory. These test sites are usually at government installations, such as test ranges or extensive simulation facilities.

The field test team that supports the testing normally consists of several systems engineers and a few software engineers. Usually, there is not an on-site SQA person or any SCM person. The testing may be at one site for a few weeks, and then may move to another test site for additional testing, sometimes with a week or two gap in between testing.

Because of project-critical schedule and expensive test ranges costs, the test schedule for each test flight must be met, if at all possible. For testing systems for aircraft, the flight schedule may, for example, call for flights every Monday, Wednesday, and Friday, starting at approximately 7:00AM. The software must be ready to go, which can mean fixing a problem that was observed on the last test, testing it on a test bench system of some sort, and then reburning PROMs with the change and installing them on the board, and reinstalling the black box back into the aircraft and retesting the system. The total time to do this, from touchdown of one test to takeoff for the next test, is usually a little under 48 hours.

The activity starts with a debriefing on the completed test based on observations, test logs, and "QUICK-LOOK" data reduction. Problems (if any) are highlighted. A more detailed analysis, supported by more thorough data reduction, then occurs to examine all relevant parts of the test. A master list of any problems and anomalies from the test is assembled for control and tracking purposes. This process may only take a few hours, or could run six to eight hours, depending on the complexity of the test, and the amount of analysis required to determine what really happened and where are the "root cause" problems.

Problems that potentially are due to software are assigned to one of the software engineers as the principal investigator. A software problem report (SPR) number is assigned at this point, and an SPR is created. The software engineer must try to repeat the error, based on similar inputs and other conditions. Analysis of the recorded data may reveal what the software really does, given this set of inputs. If the error can be duplicated and confirmed, then it must be addressed further.* There is no way to estimate how long it will take to duplicate and isolate the problems; some problems take only an hour or two; but some problems take days.

The problem (once found) must still be fixed. Usually, this takes some careful analysis and desk-checking, because there is not time to do it twice. It is usually a good idea to bounce the proposed solution off a second person as a double-check.

After the proposed change has been checked, then the change to the code is usually done as a binary patch to the run-load file for the CSCI if there is no time to develop new source code and recompile. Very careful records of the patches must be kept in a field test patch log. Each patch is assigned a number in the patch log (consistent with the Software Engineering standard practices), and the SPR number is referenced. The exact changes (both the "FROM" and the "TO") and the

---

* If the error cannot be duplicated, the SPR is closed out as a "can not duplicate."

address for each WORD changed is noted. The patch could be a simple change in place to a few consecutive instructions or to a single data value, or it may involve putting in a JUMP to a previously unused address where a significant number of new instructions can be added, followed by a JUMP, usually back to next instruction in the original program. These patch logs must be verified, and signed by both the originator and the on-site reviewer. Copies of the patch log pages must be mailed or faxed back to Software Engineering and to SQA and SCM at least once a week for review and archiving. Each set of new patches creates a new run load file, which receives a new file number. SCM back at the laboratory keeps track of all of the patches assigned to each run-load file, and of the various revisions and dates to the run-load files for each CSCI. For a sizable field test, a hundred or so patches may be made, a few of which may later get removed or replaced by other patches. If there are three flights a week for eight weeks, approximately 24 versions of the set of run-load files will probably be needed. However, not every CSCI will change for each flight, and several CSCIs will not change very often over the test period. Normally, one or two CSCIs will receive more changes that the others. Also, CSCIs that contain data elements that are "tunable" like a software trimpot will receive tuning changes to try to optimize thresholds, limits, timing values, weighting factors, etc.

Back at the laboratory, SQA should review the batch of new patch log pages to ensure no pages are missing (numbered and dated pages are highly recommended), and to ensure that the patch log contents are complete and consistent. If there is a problem, SQA should get on the telephone immediately and try to correct the matter. Software Engineering in the laboratory should validate that the change will do what it is supposed to do, but it is not always possible to predict whether the patch will solve the problem, and also not create new problems. After the next flight test where that test case is rerun with the new patch, it is possible to tell whether the patch worked. Patches that seem to fully solve a problem get a big checkmark, and may be resourced. Each verified patch is assigned to a programmer back at the laboratory to resource as soon as possible, referencing the original SPR number. To provide support from the laboratory, each CSCI is assigned to one or more software engineers such that each person has responsibility for approximately 10,000 to 15,000 executable source lines. Certain CSCIs are less than 10,000 source lines while others are greater than 50,000 source lines and will need to be split among several support people.

If the number of patches in the field grows so large that patches are on top of patches, etc., the patched software can be difficult to maintain, and at a certain point will be virtually impossible to maintain. It is necessary to preclude this problem by periodically developing and validating new source code baselines, recompiling and relinking, and sending a clean resourced load file to the site.

The new source run-load file will first have to be tested at the laboratory, and the testing shall be witnessed and certified by SQA. Modifying the source code does introduce several risks; therefore, regression testing should be done using a significant subset of the test cases for each CSCI, plus any test cases that are specific to the changes. A practical problem is obtaining time on the system to do regression testing at the system level; the modified CSCIs must work with the other hardware and software elements in the system. Usually, the system assets are very scarce, and test time is very hard to get. The problem is one of allocating time to a less-than-optimal number of test cases to get the most value of the limited test time available. This is a classic tradeoff of time versus risk; the more test time available, the lower will be the risk. Automated test tools can help productivity in this case (by running the regression tests overnight). When the testing is completed, and revised source code is formally released, the software design description also has to be updated, and sometimes the STD.

SQA must track and verify patches and their related SPRs. Each time a new software release of source code is prepared using a Software Engineering Release Notice (SERN) (or equivalent), the release must be checked to make certain all of the necessary patches have been included. Furthermore, no unapproved patches should be included in the software release. The release is normally handled at the CSCI level at this stage. Each SERN lists the patch numbers and related SPR numbers that have been incorporated to advance the CSCI to the next configuration level. In certain cases, an SPR may be included but there was no field patch related to it. SQA will ensure that all the differences between the prior revision's source files and the new revision's source files are for approved SPRs, and that all approved SPRs are fully implemented.

A coding convention that highlights the changed code for an SPR with an initial comment line and a final comment line can be very helpful when reviewing the source code file or the corresponding source listing. These comment lines could look like the following:

```
"****** SPR #288 START******"
```

at the front of the change, and a trailing comment line at the end of the change, such as:

```
"****** SPR #288 END ******"
```

and would be useful for highlighting the modified source code for each SPR. Certain software engineering standards also require the SPR number for the current changes to be included as part of the configuration information in the prologue (header) for the affected units.

After all of the field testing is finished, there will still need to be a final cleanup of the last patches. These patches must be cut into the source code, recompiled and relinked, and a final set of software and system tests run to make certain that the clean software works properly. If the software is mature, the last group of patches should not be too large (perhaps under ten or so), due to a low defect discovery rate with the mature code. In this sense, mature means that virtually all of the latent defects have been found and fixed, and discovery of any of the new remaining defects will be a relatively rare event. This is analogous to saying that the mean time between failures is quite large, and the Software Reliability (see Chapter 20) has grown to a respectable value, which can be independently estimated using various reliability models. [11] The result is software that is sufficiently mature and reliable to deploy, and meets the performance requirements under a wide variety of realistic conditions (including stress and error tests). Public law requires that DoD Systems be tested by an independent operational test group within the service department (Army, Navy, or Air Force). The objective is to acquire an objective evaluation of the system (including the software). The system must be considered suitable for the stated purpose/objectives and be effective. Usually, the software coming out of Development Testing and Evaluation (DT&E) is cleaned up (via ECPs, etc.), and all known problems are resolved. The resulting improved software proceeds into OT, sometimes called Operational Testing and Evaluation (OT&E), where the contractor and the project manager (PM) do not see it until testing is completed. A test report is written by the service's OT&E group, which basically states whether or not the system is ready to deploy.

The software may be considered acceptable, but several changes may be cut in for the production baseline. Of course, the contractor must ensure the changes are correct and do not cause other problems.

If the system is not considered acceptable, the system will go back to the developer to have the problems resolved, if possible. In several ways, OT is equivalent to beta testing at a customer site in the commercial world.

If a significant number of DT or OT changes have occurred since the FCA/PCA audits, a mini-FCA and a mini-PCA should be held to cover these additional changes that are now in the product baseline. These versions of the CSCIs would be the configuration of the software released to production; an illustrative sample of the CSCIs for a system is indicated in Table 16-16. This release would be for production lot I, and SQA should review the release to ensure the correct software versions and their systemwide compatibility. A new release would be used for lot II, and the software VERSIONS/REVISIONS might be different for lot II, at least for several of the CSCIs.

Table 16-16   Systemwide Configuration of Software CSCIs to be Released to Production

Subsystem	CSCI	Version/Revision	SERN* and Release Date
Alpha	AA	03.07	288-8/14/97
	BB	03.03	279-8/09/97
	CC	02.04	201-6/05/97
	DD	02.05	218-7/01/97
Gamma	SA	03.24	289-8/15/97
	SB	03.06	246-7/17/97
	SC	03.04	247-7/17/97
Omega	WB	04.08	271-8/02/97
	WK	03.34	290-8/16/97
	WW	03.03	231-7/08/97
	WZ	03.08	248-7/18/97

* SERN = Software Engineering Release Number for the project

SQA can thus contribute to the quality of the software and related products throughout the development activities and phases, and thus lower the overall program risk as well as lower software rework costs.

References

1. Boehm, B., "A Spiral Model of Software Development and Enhancement." In: *ACM SIGSOFT*, Vol. 11, August 1986, pp. 14–24.
2. Dunn, R. H., and Ullman, R.S., *Quality Assurance for Computer Software* (New York: McGraw-Hill Book Co., 1982) p. 159.
3. Bowen, T. P., Wigle, G. B., Tsai, J. T., *Specification of Software Quality Attributes*. Boeing Aerospace Company, RADC-TR-85-37 (Volume I), February 1985.
4. Heil, J. H., "Ensuring Good Test Plans and Test Descriptions." Automating Software Test & Evaluation Conference, Educational Foundation—Data Processing Management Association, Washington, D.C., May 1991.
5. Beitzer, B., "Bug Taxonomy and Statistics." Appendix, *Software Testing Techniques*, second edition (New York: Van Nostrand Reinhold, 1990).
6. Jones, T. C., "Technical Report: Program Quality and Programmer Productivity." *TR 02.764*, IBM General Products Division, January 1977.
7. Fagan, M. E., "Design and Code Inspections to Reduce Errors in Program Development." In: *IBM Systems Journal*, Vol. 15, No. 3, 1976, pp. 182–211.
8. McCabe, T., "A Complexity Measure." In: *IEEE Transactions on Software Engineering*, Vol. SE-2, No. 4, December 1976, pp. 308–320.

9. Mills, H., "Engineering Discipline for Software Procurement." In: *Proceedings of NSIA QRAC Fall Joint Conference on Software Quality*, 30 Sept.–2 Oct. 1987, p. 88, NSIA, Washington, D.C., 1987.

10. Dunn, R. H., Ullman, R. S., *Quality Assurance for Computer Software* (New York: McGraw-Hill, 1982) pp. 166–168.

11. Heil, J. H., Gorenflo, F. M., Cannon, J., and Polizzano, J., "The Use of Software Reliability to Measure Software Quality Improvement." In: *Proceedings of NSIA QRAC Sixth Annual Software Quality and Productivity Conferences*, April 17–19, 1990, NSIA, Washington, D.C., 1990.

General References

DoD Documents

MIL-STD-498, *Software Development and Documentation*, Dept. of Defense, Washington, D.C., 5 December 1994.

MIL-STD-973, *Configuration Management, Dept. of Defense*, Washington, D.C., 17 April 1992, plus Notice 1, 1 December 1992.

MIL-STD-1521B, *Technical Reviews and Audits for Systems*, Equipments and Computer Software, Dept. of Defense, Washington, D.C., June 4, 1985.

DOD-STD-2167A, *Defense System Software Development*, Dept. of Defense, Washington, D.C., February 29, 1988.

DOD-STD-2168, *Defense System Software Quality Program*, Dept. of Defense, Washington, D.C., April 29, 1988.

DIDS: DID-MCCR-80030A, *Software Development Plan*, DoD, Washington, D.C., February 29, 1988.

DI-QCIC-80572, Software Quality Program Plan, DoD, Washington, D.C., April 29, 1988.

Military Handbooks

Mission-Critical Computer Resources Software Support—Military Handbook MIL-HDBK-347, Dept. of Defense, May 1990.

IEEE Documents

IEEE P1498/EIA IS 640, *Standard for Information Technology Software Life Cycle Processes*, Software Development, Acquirer-Supplier Agreement, July 15, 1995 (ANSI J STD-016).

IEEE Standard for Software Quality Plans, ANSI/IEEE Standard 730.1-1989, October 1989.

IEEE Standard Glossary of Software Engineering Terminology, IEEE Standard 729-1983, February 1983.

International Standards Organization (ISO) Documents:

ISO 9001, Second Edition, *Quality Systems—Model for Quality Assurance in Design, Development, Production, Installation and Servicing*, 1994.

ISO 9000-3, *Part 3: Guidelines for the Application of ISO 9001 to the Development, Supply, and Maintenance of Software*, 1991.

Other General References

Bersoff, E., "Elements of Software Configuration Management." In: *IEEE Trans. Software Engineering*, Vol. SE-10, January 1984.

Bersoff, E., Henderson, V., Siegal, S., "Software Configuration Management: A Tutorial." In: *IEEE Computer Society Magazine*, Vol. 12, No. 1, January 1979.

Boehm, B., *Software Engineering Economics* (Englewood Cliffs, NJ: Prentice-Hall, 1981).

Boehm, B. et al, "A Software Development Environment for Improving Productivity." In: *IEEE Computer*, June 1984, pp. 30–44.

Charette, R.N., "Software Risk Management from Theory into Practice." In: *Proceedings of Automated Software Test & Evaluation Conference*, pp. 240–259, Washington, D.C., March 20-21 1997

Cooling, J.E., *Software Design for Real-Time Systems* (London and New York: Chapman and Hall, 1991).

DeWeese, P.R., "U.S. National Software Standards—Transition to Commercial Standards." In: *Proceedings of Software Acquisition Management Conference*, pp. 260–280, Washington, D.C., October 7–8, 1996.

Deutsch, M., *Software Verification and Validation: Realistic Project Approaches* (Englewood Cliffs, N.J: Prentice-Hall, 1982).

Dunn, R. H., *Software Defect Removal* (New York: McGraw-Hill Book Co., 1984).

Dunn, R. H., *Software Quality—Concepts and Plans* (Englewood Cliffs, N.J: Prentice-Hall, 1990).

Endres, A., "An Analysis of Errors and their Causes in System Programs." In: *1975 International Conference on Reliable Software*, IEEE Cat. No. 75CH 0840-7CSR, pp. 327-336.

Gannon, C., "Error Detection Using Path Testing and Static Analysis." In: *IEEE Computer*, IEEE Computer Society Magazine, Vol. 12, No. 8, August 1979, pp. 26–31.

Halstead, M., *Elements of Software Science* (New York: Elsevier-North Holland, Inc., 1977).

Humphrey, W. S., *Managing the Software Process* (New York: Addison-Wesley Publishing Co., 1989).

Kafura, D., and Reddy, G., "The Use of Software Complexity Metrics in Software Engineering." In: *IEEE Trans. Software Engineering*, Vol. SE-13, March 1987, pp. 335–343.

Jones, T. C., *Assessment and Control of Software Risks* (Englewood Cliffs, NJ: Yourdan Press/Prentice-Hall, 1994).

Lipow, M., and Thayer, T. A., "Prediction of Software Failures." In: *Proceedings 1977 Annual Reliability and Maintainability Symposium*, IEEE Cat. No. 77CH 1161-9RQC, pp. 489–494.

McGarry, John, NUWC/JLC-JGSE, "Practical Software Measurement." In: *Proceeding of Software Acquisition Management Conference*, pp. 92A et subseq., Washington, D.C., October 7–8 1996.

Meyers, W., "An Assessment of the Competitiveness of the United States Software Industry." In: *IEEE Computer*, March 1985, pp. 81–92.

Musa, J., "SOFTWARE ENGINEERING: The Future of a Profession." In: *IEEE Software*, January 1985, pp. 55–62.

Musa, J., "Software-Reliability-Engineered Testing." *Proceedings of Automated Software Test & Evaluation Conference*, pp. 139–154, Washington, D.C., March 20–21 1997

Petschenik, "Practical Priorities in System Testing." In: *IEEE Software*, Vol. 2, September 1985, pp. 18–23.

Walston, C.E., and Felix, C. P., "A Method of Programming Measurement and Estimation." In: *IBM Systems Journal*, Vol. 16, 1977, pp. 54–73.

Wegner, P., "Varieties of Reusability." *Proceedings—Workshop on Reusability in Programming*, Newport, R.I., September 1983, pp. 30–45.

CHAPTER   17

Practical Applications of Software Quality Assurance to Commercial Software

Lawrence E. Niech
Automatic Data Processing (ADP)

17.1   Introduction—SQA Principles Applied

Previous chapters of this book discussed specific techniques, methodologies, and philosophies that contribute to a successful software quality assurance (SQA) program. The next step is to address the practical application of these topics.

This chapter provides insight through experiences and lessons learned regarding how to successfully implement SQA programs related to commercial software applications. Specific issues that are addressed include: quality's role in the commercial software sector, SQA program philosophies, software testing within the quality framework, the key attributes of a successful software quality program, and the similarities and differences between quality activities involving mission-critical and commercial software.

17.2   Commercial Software Defined

The category of commercial software immediately excludes software that is produced for a government agency (e.g., NASA, DoD, FAA, etc.) where the software development process traditionally has been subject to strictly enforced standards and contractual requirements. Although, more recently, as pointed out in Chapter 4, there is a specific trend to use commercial standards. Typically, this class of software is known as mission-critical software (although many are now applying this "mission-critical" or "mission" term to some commercial software).

Commercial software includes software produced in the nongovernment sector, targeted for a competitive consumer market and intended for multiple distribution (as opposed to "one of a kind" solutions). Examples of commercial software or products containing commercial software include:

- Payroll/Personnel Systems (paychecks, employee profiles, taxes)
- Telecommunications Systems (voice mail, switches)
- Consumer Applications (word processing, games, tax filing, organizers)
- Business/Management Software (finances, spreadsheets)
- Industrial Systems (robots, queuing devices)
- Software Development Aids (code generators, compilers, debuggers)

17.3   Software Quality's Role in the Commercial Sector

One philosophy is to view any quality assurance (QA) program (software or hardware) as the last line of "quality defense" between a company and its customers. That is, the QA program should encompass the necessary methodologies and processes to ensure product quality prior to shipment. Essentially, the quality program provides the necessary and last opportunities to decide a product's market worthiness in terms of a company's reputation and future. Simply stated, if product quality is defined as "delighting the customer," the QA program should provide the necessary activities and assessments to continuously measure progress against that goal.

Businesses and corporations are created to produce a product that meets a consumer's need while generating a profit. The overall business objective is to identify the areas of greatest need in order to maximize a profit. Since the upper bound of a commercial company's profits are not regulated, the potential for success, measured in dollars, is unlimited (Microsoft's performance, for instance). Although it is in the best interest of a business to produce quality software, quality programs in the commercial software sector are strictly voluntary (unlike the military contracting segment). Consequently, companies that are considering a formalized software quality process must embrace two concepts:

- the approach to quality will not erode expected profits
- the approach to quality will in fact provide a substantial return on investment (ROI)

Short of running two prototype software projects in parallel, one with a quality program, the other without, it is usually quite difficult to provide quantitative evidence to justify a formalized software quality process prior to its implementation in terms of the two above criteria. Any such quantitative data would focus on anticipated rework, mistakes, and "unplanned" risks. Activities "we all know we can avoid."

Consequently, organizations typically initiate a formal software quality process only after they have felt the aftershocks of a poor (or absent) software quality program. Thus, many companies tend to see quality as a defensive mechanism rather than an offensive weapon.

If viewed from the defensive perspective, there are several measurable advantages to implementing an effective formal quality program that addresses software. Similar to a quality program for hardware, if the SQA program is ineffective, the results could be disastrous, leading to:

- slippage in project schedules/deliveries
- loss of revenue
- damage to company image
- loss of future business
- loss of market leadership

The problems outlined above are some of the primary reasons for many commercial organizations initiating or enhancing SQA programs.

Once the commitment has been made to implement an SQA program, the scope and ground-rules of the process must be established. An effective approach to planning, implementing, and enhancing any SQA program involves providing services that are:

- incorporated into each phase of the software product life cycle
- consistent with software industry standard techniques
- planned, structured, and documented
- repeatable and automated
- measurable

17.4 Commercial vs. Mission-Critical SQA Programs—An Overview

Why is it important to address mission-critical SQA in a chapter on commercial SQA? For one thing, the discipline of SQA has its beginnings deeply rooted in the mission-critical (i.e., military/government) software development segment (see Chapter 16). The SQA philosophy encompasses everything from management style and standards to development/quality techniques and processes. Because government contractors' early attempts at software development and management were lacking, the military decided to define and mandate an approach that they believed would lead to a quality software product. As software became more prevalent in military applications, the typical characteristics of a software-intensive contract were:

- the product was delivered well beyond the scheduled completion date
- total actual costs exceeded estimated costs
- maintenance was a nightmare

Some of the factors contributing to these problems included poor project control methodologies and undefined software development processes. Thus, government standards and specifications covering everything from the software development process and configuration management to specification practices and quality assurance programs were born. [1]

Some software professionals believe that the commercial sector is lucky that it does not have to contend with the document-driven approach and regulations imposed by the government on software developers. Some insist that government standards negatively impact quality. The argument has been that the government's mandated methodologies and overwhelming documentation requirements are cost drivers and thus other product development areas are affected by the need to scrimp and save on overall product cost. However, if the intent of the various government standards and methodologies are understood with a concomitant movement to a relaxation of the "overwhelming" documentation to a more reasonable level, they can be invaluable in any SQA program.

Which brings us to the second reason for considering military SQA programs. Commercial SQA programs can benefit from reviewing, tailoring, and implementing many of the processes defined in the government software standards and specifications. Later in the chapter a summary of which SQA techniques can successfully be transferred from the military to the commercial environment will be outlined. Also, the fundamental differences that exist between SQA programs in commercial companies and SQA programs in military contractors are examined.

17.5   SQA Program Implementation Philosophy

The term *software quality assurance* (or SQA) often conjures up a vision of a department of people. Until the early 1980s, the military sector traditionally forced (via standards and contracts) the responsibility for quality upon a single organization. The commercial sector, unlike the military software environment, has always been free to define the organizations, roles, responsibilities, techniques, etc. necessary to achieve a quality software product. However, as noted below, to successfully produce quality software, organizational mindsets and philosophies must be considered.

Example 1: The military's pioneer standard for software quality (see Chapter 4) was MIL-S-52779A (SQA Program Requirements). As a result of the independence requirement stated in MIL-S-52779A, most software quality organizations sprang up within the Quality/Product Assurance Department. Consequently, the quality responsibility was perceived to rest within the Quality Department and the Software Engineering Department only had to convince the software quality "auditor" that all was well.

Example 2: An actual incident at a major defense contractor's manufacturing facility further illustrates how quality is sometimes perceived to be owned by one organization. The contractor, shut down due to poor quality, formed an investigative team to determine the causes of their problems. The team's finding was "that 'quality' was centered in a large quality assurance organization that inspected parts after they were built. Accordingly, no one on the production line felt responsible for quality; everyone felt it was quality assurance's job." [2]

The "lesson learned" is that the SQA task must be considered in broader terms. Commercial companies want to maximize product sales and (hopefully) the resulting profit. Inevitably, commercial organizations are going to exercise their freedom to define the proper mix of project roles and responsibilities in order to reduce cost, improve quality, and ultimately maximize profit. More often than not, companies discover that the best quality role/responsibility mixture can be derived from the often repeated statement: "quality is everyone's business."

The sharing of the responsibility for software quality is a common key attribute in the commercial market. Since the average commercial software shop can not afford to fund a full time quality organization to police quality, employees find themselves wearing many hats and tasked with many diverse responsibilities. Sharing responsibility also suggests that commercial organizations are more apt to practice "true" SQA. This concept is further illustrated in the three characteristic statements outlined below. Software Quality Assurance is:

- the approach which assures the effectiveness of a software quality program (it does not assure the quality of software)
- an integral part of all software development, test and maintenance activities
- the set of activities that make up the software quality program [3]

The above characteristics imply that SQA is not meant to be a department; instead, it must be a program/team approach involving various software professionals, each with his own area of expertise. In short, SQA is a managed set of activities utilized to achieve a quality software product. Thus, companies that have developed processes to improve software quality within the commercial market have probably developed true SQA *programs* without even realizing it. That is, the SQA concept was developed from a project team approach and not via defined organizational responsibilities. A more detailed discussion of SQA programs is in Chapter 5.

17.6 Testing within the Software Quality Framework

A common trait among commercial software organizations is that software testing is assigned to organizations outside and independent of the software development group. It is quite common in the commercial environment that software testing is assigned to the QA Department. Regardless of the name of the organization that performs software testing, assigning responsibility for product validation to a group other than the developers themselves is a sound philosophy. "The use of organizationally independent testers is often thought, correctly, to be a technique for reducing the risk of delivering software of poor quality." [4] Additionally, " . . . test groups represent the attitude of the potential users of the software. Handing the system—or in the case of integration testing, its parts—to another organization is tantamount to bridging the gap from chiefly technical concerns to those of the marketplace or the user community." [5]

As noted, the objectives of software testing can vary greatly. Usually the objectives vary with the level of testing that is being performed or the maturity of the software (i.e., how much of the software or system is available). For example, the typical levels or types of tests performed on commercial software include:

- unit
- hardware/software integration
- performance
- stress/capacity
- functional
- software integration
- acceptance
- regression
- usability
- documentation

Commercial tests must also consider various user environmental and platform concerns. Consequently, the role of *diverse* testing to measure and improve product quality plays a vital role in an effective commercial SQA program. Examples of situations that involve environmental, platform, or installation diversity concerns include:

- multiple available versions of software operating systems
- multiple available versions of network operating systems and topologies
- multiple hardware product types (including clones) of personal computers, modems, printers, etc.
- multiple system connectivity (PC, laptop, Client/Server, mainframe)
- third party software usage and connectivity

17.7 Implementing the Commercial SQA Program: The Keys to Success

17.7.1 A General Framework

Organizational Re-engineering. The term "re-engineering" has become a common phrase with regard to organizational development. Often it is meant to indicate an effort to provide organizational services that should have always existed. If the implementation of an SQA program is to have any chance of succeeding it must be preceded by changes (or re-engineering) in organizational cultures, skills sets and management styles.

The vision, mission, and objectives of the SQA program must be carefully defined and effectively communicated throughout the entire organization. Examples of a typical SQA program's vision, mission, and objectives are outlined in Table 17-1.

Table 17-1   SQA Program Example: Vision, Mission, and Objectives

Vision

The premier provider of high quality applications by providing effective and timely quality services that are:

- Incorporated into each phase of the software life cycle
- Consistent with software industry standard techniques
- Planned, structured, and documented
- Automated and repeatable
- Measurable

Mission

- Represent the company and its customers' interests to assure product quality
  (via conformance to customer requirements and prevention of software defects)
- Provide outstanding customer service via increased software reliability and maintainability
- Increase customer service and QA personnel productivity via aggressive automation
- Implement programs that measure software successes (and failures) to provide the overall quality process
- Operation in evaluation/test environments which reflect the changing needs and preferences of our customers
- Promote customer retention through product satisfaction

Business Objectives

- Improve product time-to-market
- Reduce product development and maintenance costs (early detection)
- Improve customer satisfaction and retention via increased software (not product) quality
- Develop a culture that fosters state-of-the-industry skill sets
- Increase productivity through standardized processes and improved skill sets and abilities

Once the general direction of the group has been outlined, the short term and overall needs of the SQA program should be assessed. An example of immediate initiatives that produce deliverables to form a consistent SQA framework may be as outlined in Table 17-2.

Table 17-2 Initial SQA Program Initiatives

Initiative	Purpose/Objective
Define Process with Supporting Standards and Procedures	Develop a common quality process that can be "tailored" for individual project needs. Develop support procedures and documented methodologies to provide process guidance. Includes Terminology Guide.
Provide Quality/Test Education	Develop a quality and test curriculum for employees. Includes suggested courses and skill sets. Modify job descriptions if necessary. Establish Technical Library and suggested reading references.
Obtain Equipment and Establish Test Environments	Address obtaining standardized equipment (i.e., workstations, manuals, etc.) to support employee efforts. Address obtaining standardized test environments and needed test lab requirements. Address planned integrated testing by multiple groups on same projects.
Obtain Quality and Test Tools	Propose, acquire, develop, and implement common quality and test tools that span the entire software life cycle.
Define Quality Metrics Program	Develop a supporting metrics program to provide quantitative status and completion criteria.
Develop Implementation: Process Assessment	Develop strategies to assess development and quality processes, measure activities, and improve approaches. Develop strategies to validate newly proposed approaches on actual projects.
Define Project Management and Administration Activities	Support tasks necessary to implement and administer the SQA program.

Product Life Cycles. As noted previously, the implementation of a formal software quality process will require changes to many embedded organizational practices and capabilities. Another key area that must be considered when fostering change in software quality is the software/product development approach. First and foremost, the most significant change in development philosophy that must occur is the acceptance and formalization of a well-defined software product life cycle (PLC) approach to producing a software product.

The implementation of a software PLC aids the software quality effort because it allows the SQA program to utilize *review hooks* or *assessment windows* during the software production process in order to assess the progress and quality of the product under development. These hooks are most effective when mapped upon the software life cycle model. While there are many definitions of software PLCs (and its overlapping partner—the *waterfall model*) a typical software PLC may include the phases and activities as depicted in Figure 17-1. [6] The review milestones denoted by the diamonds in Figure 17-1 are typical examples of review hooks or assessment windows.

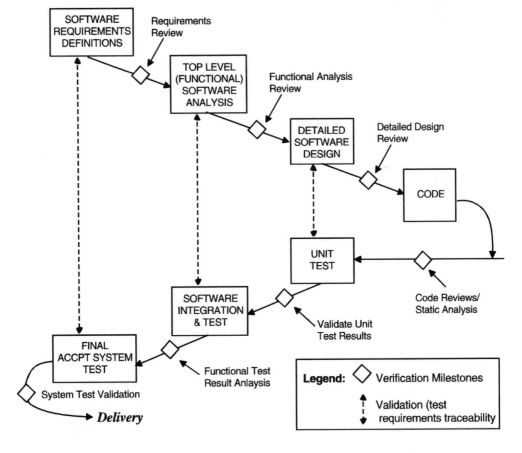

Figure 17-1 Typical software product life cycle (and major milestones).

The orderly development process promoted by the PLC approach also complements the SQA program's prime activity—verification and validation (V&V). Verification is the process of determining whether or not the product at a given phase of the PLC fulfills the requirements established during the previous phase. Examples of verification activities in Figure 17-1 include ensuring that:

- the top-level software analysis/design is traceable back to the software requirements definition
- the detailed software design is traceable back to the top-level software analysis/design

Validation is the process of evaluating software at the end of the software development cycle to ensure compliance with the software requirements. Examples of validation activities (denoted by the dotted vertical lines) in Figure 17-1 include performing:

- unit testing to ensure that all detailed design requirements are met
- software final acceptance system testing to ensure that all software requirements are met

Because of new development tools (CASE analysis), platform technologies (Graphical User Interface—GUI), and time-to-market-with-quality pressures, many companies have progressed beyond the ordinary waterfall and simple PLC approach to software development. However, many of the newer product development approaches (i.e., the iterative approach) still have a foundation based upon the tried and true PLC. Experiences with tools, technologies, and time-to-market are discussed later in the chapter.

SQA Program Roles.   As previously noted, software quality assurance is essentially a management approach, not a department of personnel. As such, the implementation of the managed process can involve personnel from various organizations and disciplines. For example, a typical SQA project program for a Client/Server–based payroll system (i.e., commercial software) may involve the organizations and roles outlined in Table 17-3.

Quality Personnel within the SQA Program.   The role of the personnel involved in the software quality process depends upon several factors: industry requirements, organizational structures, the product being developed, etc. Generally, software quality personnel are members of independent quality groups who monitor technical activities and provide product assessments. As Dunn points out, quality personnel can assume numerous roles in order to reach similar objectives: [7]

- The Peacekeeper—ensure process standards and project plans are met, including audits of reviews/walkthroughs, documents, libraries, and tests
- The Surrogate—perform defect removal via independent testing
- The Data Collector—perform measurements, collect project data
- The Analyst—assess project status and progress via collected data
- The Planner—develop and document the project quality plan

Generally, the Surrogate role is quite common in commercial SQA Programs because of the test role played by quality personnel. Since quality auditing/reviewing are very weak methodologies (i.e., management is not willing to fund) in commercial software programs, quality personnel in commercial SQA programs do not often have the chance to fulfill the Peacekeeper role. The remaining roles, Data Collector, Analyst, and Planner, are at best only addressed by most commercial quality personnel.

Table 17-3 SQA Program Roles

Organization	Roles
Marketing	• Research market activity and needs
	• Define market/customer requirements
	• Assess success/failure of delivered product
Payroll Analysis Group	• Translate Marketing requirements into software requirements and the top-level design based upon knowledge of existing systems
Software Product Development Group	• Formulate detailed software design based upon payroll analysis information
	• Generate code
	• Perform unit and integration testing
Quality Assurance and Test Group	• Assess the activities during the PLC process
	• Perform functional integration, system integration, and final acceptance system testing
Documentation Group	• Create user documentation, tutorials, and online "wizards" based upon software requirements and design specifications
Software Support	• Assist customers after product roll-out
	• Provide input to the development process based upon customer experience
Implementation Group	• Plan and coordinate beta testing of developed software product
	• Plan an orderly "general availability" of the product

The role of software quality personnel also depends upon the responsibilities and capabilities of the other personnel participating in the SQA program. Examples of the roles that software quality personnel can fulfill within a SQA program are discussed in a case study later in this chapter.

Now that we've established the framework for an SQA program, the next section will discuss techniques for ensuring that the program is successful.

17.7.2 Experience and Inside Tips

Deutsch and Willis utilize a planning outline of over a dozen important aspects for addressing the needs of an effectively planned software quality (engineering) process. [8] The intent of the outline is to provide quality program planners with a summary of key implementation questions and considerations. Because the outline transcends the entire software PLC, it is also an excellent vehicle for presenting a list of SQA Program implementation successes. Summarized in Table 17-4 are personal experiences and inside tips which should be considered when planning a SQA Program. These experiences should help you expedite the subject task and/or help make an applicable quality requirement more effective.

Table 17-4   SQA Program Experiences

Area	Experience
Quality Requirements	• define a solid set of project requirements (the cornerstone of the SQA program)
	• establish SQA program requirements via vision, mission, objective, and goal statements
Effective Plans	• create standardized software plans (development, quality, configuration management); tailor plans to the needs of each project
	• plan to "build quality into the product"
	• plan the SQA Program as if you really mean it
	• share, communicate, and educate via established plans; partner with other affected organizations to create plans in order to obtain "buy in"
Organization	• promote intra-organization communication: set up planning/coordination meetings with other organization well in advance of tasks to be completed/ coordinated (publicize project expectations as soon as possible)
	• hire personnel based upon projects needs
	• avoid being the organizational dump of problem employees
	• ensure that the quality and test personnel are as capable as the software development personnel
	• utilize low cost personnel (clerks, technicians) to free up senior personnel when possible
Training	• establish internal formal training programs based upon the project needs (i.e., languages, computer platforms, databases, networks, quality processes, testing, etc.)

Table 17-4 *(continued)*

Area	Experience
Standards	• expose personnel to software industry advances via seminars, periodicals, texts, professional organizations, etc.
	• cross-pollinate groups within departments via staff presentations
	• develop software standards based upon the customer environment (are IEEE, FDA, etc. standards required?)
	• utilize published guidelines (e.g., standards developed by the IEEE, DoD, NASA, etc.) to tailor a process to your needs/product when standards are not required
	• distribute standards and staff actions to affected groups
Reviews	• include requirements, design, code, test, documentation, and process reviews
	• establish written procedures; designate a review chairman [key guidelines: advanced notice and data, concentrate on design not designer, don't solve every problem in the review—take action items]
Testing	• test development should coincide with software development
	• test personnel should be involved in all requirements, design, and code reviews
	• plans, specifications, cases, reports are a must
	• automate where possible
People	• estimate staff size based upon experience; utilize cost/sizing models; collect, retain, analyze historical costs based upon each project task
	• avoid percentage staffing (i.e., quality or test staff as a percentage of the development staff)
Procedures	• develop procedures based upon required standards and product environment
	• disseminate procedures, follow-up on concurrence and implementation
Tools	• investigate aids to expedite the software process or to measure quality
	• ensure that internally developed tools are subject to a defined quality assurance process ("practice what you preach")
Facilities	• plan for resources well in advance of their need
	• provide support personnel (quality, test, field, etc. groups) with the same equipment capability as the personnel developing the software
Subcontractor Controls	• don't allow your subcontractor to do any less than you would have your own personnel do (implement your SQA program on their project)
	• establish points of contacts; conduct frequent status meetings
	• establish contractual measurable software milestones
Measurements and Feedback	• remember, you can't improve what you can't measure
	• utilize data to locate both the problem and the source; perform appropriate corrective action
Configuration Controls	• establish libraries, error reporting systems, review boards, version control methodologies, documented procedures, etc.
	• consider that even if the other 13 points are exceeded in their implementation, if there is no configuration control, there is no identifiable product

17.8   Implementing an SQA Program: Problems, Payoffs, and Lessons Learned (A Case Study)

17.8.1 Objective

The previous sections outlined the activities and implementation techniques that lead to a successful SQA program. The next sections examine the experiences associated with the *actual start-up and enhancement* of an SQA program within the commercial sector. The following case study involves a fictitious company (MPA) that produces a fictitious product—an Auto Parts Management (APM) software package (parts tracking, location identification, accounts receivable, accounts payable, over-the-counter sales). The experiences, solutions, and results are real (only the names have been changed to protect the innocent!).

17.8.2 The Setup—Defining the Product Environment

The product environment includes Client/Server–based users of the APM software. The average software program is GUI-based with a relational database and takes approximately one year from analysis to beta testing. The Client/Server system also interfaces with a mainframe for data collection and major processing tasks. The target application is executed in various operational environments including:

- various workstations including clones
- multiple versions of stand-alone and network operating systems
- multiple types of peripherals (including clones)
- multiple and unique organizational configuration

Key organizations participating in the SQA program and their designated roles include:

- Marketing: participate in requirements reviews and project status meetings. Define market/customer requirements
- Software product development: analyze requirements, create software design, generate code, perform unit testing, perform/support integration testing; conduct all requirements and design reviews
- Quality Assurance /Test group: assess all software activities during the PLC (attend reviews/walkthroughs, review documentation), perform functional and system integration testing, perform performance and acceptance testing, oversee configuration/disaster controls, maintain/analyze project metrics and trends
- Software support: assist customers after product general release; provide inputs to the software product via PLC reviews based upon customer experiences

17.8.3 The Approach—Setting the Stage for Improvement

MPA management immediately realized that up-front planning and a skillfully laid quality program framework were the keys to installing an effective software quality process. Consequently, MPA personnel focused their attention on two key tasks during the early phases of planning the SQA program:

- defining the SQA Program mission (based upon the software/user product environment)
- establishing the SQA Program objectives

The MPA SQA Program was viewed as a service mechanism attending to the needs of MPA software development personnel and MPA customers. The following MPA SQA Program charter (i.e., mission) was established to help define the SQA Program's direction and future growth:

- represent MPA and its customers' interests to assure product quality via conformance to customer requirements and prevention of software defects
- provide outstanding customer service via increased software reliability and maintainability
- increase customer service and software personnel productivity via aggressive automation
- implement techniques and methodologies that measure software successes and failures to improve the overall quality process
- operate in evaluation/test environments that reflect the changing needs and preferences of MPA customers
- promote customer retention through product satisfaction

The following SQA program objectives were established to meet MPA's charter:

- emphasize defect prevention as well as defect removal
- prevent defects by embedding quality procedures into all phases of the PLC
  - controlled development process
  - conformance to standards
  - implementation of verification & validation techniques
- detect and remove defects early in the product life cycle
- implement an effective metrics program
- plan structured and documented organizational procedures consistent with successful software industry standard techniques

The ultimate goal was to develop and maintain an SQA program that utilized state-of-the-industry, in-process, software PLC activities to evaluate software product quality. An overview of the QA in-process (i.e., spanning the entire PLC) activities of an ideal quality program (the goal), consistent with the previously stated SQA Program charter is summarized in Table 17-5.

Table 17-5   The "Ideal" SQA Program (In-Process Activities)

A. Quality Program Characteristics
- Effective defect prevention and defect removal techniques
- Embedded validation & verification techniques in each phase of the software product life cycle
- Extensive metrics program
- Planned, automated, structured, and documented

B. Quality Program Details
- Introduce QA tools, techniques and methods
  - test case generators
  - test analyzers
  - commercially available tools
  - quality and test standards
  - CASE tools
- Oversee divisional configuration control
  - software duplication/production control
  - off-site software storage
  - error collection systems
  - software baseline development and control (Librarian)
  - code management systems
  - departmental software library (Golden Masters)
- Develop, implement, and monitor quality metrics
  - error tracking and trends
  - error review boards
  - complexity
  - tagging and seeding
  - baseline stability/improvement
  - modeling
- Perform software verification and validation via

- Passive QA techniques
  - Requirements review
  - Design reviews/walkthroughs
  - Code reviews/walkthroughs
  - Static tests (reviews/formal analysis, symbolic execution)
- Dynamic/active QA techniques
  - Unit test (white box)
  - Path tests, breakpoints/diagnostic traces, assertion testing)
  - Integration test (glass/gray box)
  - System/functional/scenario tests (black box)
  - Special tests (LAN, random, stress, capacity, timing, baseline, etc.)
- Develop and maintain quality and test documentation
  - Quality program plans/procedures
  - Test plans, specifications, cases, and reports

17.8.4 The Need—Why Improve the Software Quality Process?

Why did MPA management choose to improve the software quality process? Although MPA's software products consistently provided users with the desired results (e.g., part locations, over-the-counter prices, inventory status) they believed that the software development, test, and maintenance processes could be improved to further increase software product quality and reliability. A review of the MPA software development, test, and deployment process revealed that the following improvement objectives could provide significant dividends:

- eliminate the presence of latent defects
- prevent ambiguous and changing requirements
- provide structure and definition to current nonrigorous testing approaches (i.e., "what/how much has been tested")
- improve the release decision making process (i.e., metrics usage)
- remove configuration ambiguity (e.g., what version has been tested, various authorized versions, disaster controls, etc.)

MPA management believed that improvements in the above areas would increase the satisfaction levels of their customer base. However, in order to improve the above processes, MPA management needed to understand what caused the subject areas to be judged inadequate. Several of the contributing negative factors uncovered by MPA management were:

- *Staff makeup:* quality process review personnel and test personnel were heavily weighted with analytical skills; minimal programming knowledge; minimal formal training in quality or test techniques.
- *Software Methodologies:* ad-hoc, limited/informal procedures; elementary product life cycle; software quality effort backend-loaded; limited configuration/disaster controls. Also: quality personnel accustomed to debugging (vs. verification & validation role); minimal quality involvement (processes or personnel) in the up-front development process; minimal data gathering to support product deployment decisions.
- *Test Approach and Environment:* minimal automated test equipment in use; testing performed under "ideal" conditions.

Consequently, MPA management concentrated on the above five improvement objectives by focusing attention on correcting the above three areas. The following section discusses how the negative elements in the three subject areas were corrected and how the resulting change significantly improved the software development and quality process.

17.8.5 Problems, Payoffs, and Lessons Learned

Quality Staff Makeup.   The roles of the QA/Test group were previously outlined as follows:

- assess all software activities during the PLC (attend reviews/walkthroughs, review documentation, signoff on key deliverables)
- perform functional, system, performance and acceptance testing
- oversee configuration/disaster controls
- maintain/analyze project metrics and trends

Key responsibilities of the QA/Test group are outlined in Figure 17-2.

MPA management felt that of all the difficult changes that they had made, reorganizing and adjusting the staff makeup was perhaps the most arduous task. Staff adjustments were necessary in order to complement the strengths or to fill the voids within the QA/Test group. The successful planning and implementation of the QA/Test group essentially consisted of the following activities:

- utilizing software consultants
- utilizing temporary and college personnel
- adding permanent staff with complementary backgrounds and knowledge
- centralizing key support services within the QA/Test group

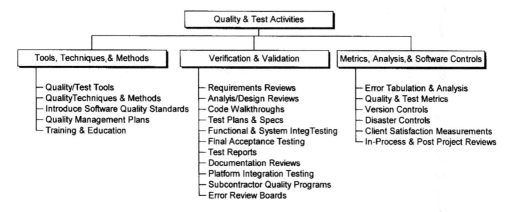

Figure 17-2   Responsibilities of the QA/Test group.

Outlined below (in no order of importance) are some lessons learned from the QA/Test staffing experiences:

Personnel Knowledge and Background. It was evident in the early phases of the improvement efforts that if the QA/Test staff consists of "x" personnel, you do not need "x" QA/Test personnel who are only "product experts" (i.e., only analysts or only test executors). Personnel with specific knowledge of testing, quality assurance, networks, specification writing, and programming were needed. The QA/Test group needed a proper mix of analysts, testers, programmers, and clerks. However, the importance of knowing the product or "subject" under test should not be diminished. While it is impossible to require every QA/Test candidate who walks off the street to know MPA inventory or accounts receivable concepts, it was important to find ways to educate QA personnel with regard to MPA products. Training methodologies included off-site seminars, tutorials given by in-house experts, on-site courses, and the videotaping of key chalkboard sessions.

Permanent Staff and Consultants. Consultants were brought in to complement the existing staff's product knowledge with quality methodology, programming, and test tool knowledge and to alleviate the intensive labor requirements associated with the start-up of an automated test process.

The use of consultants reinforced the above points regarding knowledge background. MPA needed to employ a QA/Test staff that was familiar with the many facets of the programming and MPA product world. Many of the cost saving tools (described later) that were built during the SQA program enhancement period were implemented by consultants based upon needs and requirements identified by QA/Test analysts. Several benefits were realized from employing consultants:

- the utilization of programming skills found an important and necessary niche within the QA/Test group (including implementing code walkthroughs)
- tools developed for quality process and test evaluation purposes were use by the QA/Test group were also used by development and support (field) personnel
- the extra labor force expedited the test automation progress

Many of the consultants contributed extremely cost-effective quality and test solutions and were later hired and made a part of the full-time QA/Test staff. Additionally, the increase in programming knowledge that occurred within the QA/Test group also increased the Software Product Development group's confidence in and respect for the QA/Test group.

Temporary / College Assistance. As tests were planned and documented, low cost clerk and college level intern (computer science and engineering students) personnel supported the quality and test efforts. Clerks and students were used to:

- collect/retain metric data utilizing simple database, spreadsheet, and graphic programs which they developed
- document existing procedures and processes
- document (and then automate) existing tests
- execute (repeatedly) automated tests
- perform simple edits of automated tests
- generate quality reports for management

Miscellaneous Support / Overhead. During the enhancement period, the increase in quality and test services and associated responsibilities also brought an increase in the need for additional administrative help. Activities such as regression testing (re-executing several dozen tests on each release of software), configuration management, error reporting/tracking, LAN administration, and documentation/software version control all required dedicated clerk-type assistance. Some of the above services were replicated in numerous software product development groups. MPA was able to transfer some of the underutilized clerks from the development groups to the QA/Test group and centralize many of the duplicated services.

Organizational Structure. After realigning the makeup of the QA/Test group, MPA implemented an organizational structure that took advantage of the improvements and diversity in the QA/Test staff. An example of the current QA/Test group is outlined in Figure 17-3. The responsibilities of each of the groups and the skill sets utilized are outlined below:

➤Quality and Test Programs. These groups perform verification & validation on both mainframe and PC/Client/Server products. The groups employ analysts, programmers, clerks and include a college co-op program. Their responsibilities include: requirements reviews, design reviews, code reviews/walkthroughs and various levels of testing (functional, system, acceptance) including development of test plans, specifications, and cases and test execution, analysis, and reporting. Also, PC/Client/Server to mainframe interface issues: PC/Client/Server software product to mainframe compatibility and PC/Client/Server to mainframe test interfaces.

➤Quality Assurance/Test Central Services and Support Groups. These groups support the groups responsible for the Quality and Test programs. The groups employ configuration management analysts, librarians, programmers, clerks, technicians, LAN administrators, documentation writers and include a college co-op program. Their responsibilities include:

- Divisional configuration and data control
  - Software duplication/production control
  - Off-site software storage
  - Error collection systems
  - Software baseline development and control (librarian)
  - Code management systems
  - Departmental software library
- Release management
  - Coordinate release content
  - Identify customer needs
  - Audit release content between transition phases
- Test tools and automation
  - Develop unique application aides
  - Procure off-the-shelf solutions
  - Develop tool and automation standards
- Test environments and testbeds
  - Create and maintain mainframe and PC/Client/Server QA testbeds: typical/atypical (clone) PCs, modems, printers, multiple software products, multiple LAN configurations
- Standards/procedures and process improvements
  - Develop, introduce, and enforce quality and test standards, methodologies, and documentation

- Develop, implement, and monitor quality metrics
- Conduct post project reviews
• LAN administration
- Maintenance of PC product release, QA test files, QA application software, QA LAN hardware configuration
- Technical library

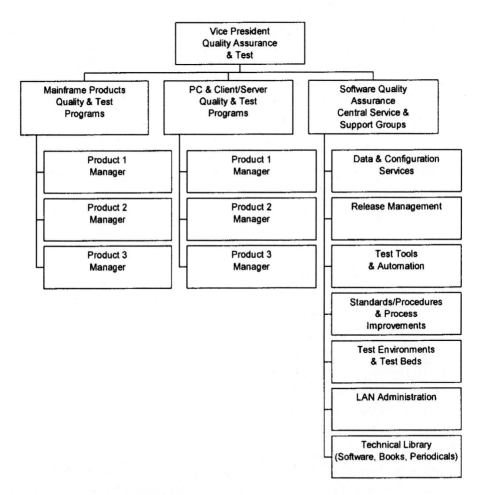

Figure 17-3   MPA quality assurance/test organization.

Organization and Staffing Payoffs. Summarized in Table 17-6 are the resulting benefits (payoffs) as a result of the changes that were made in the QA/Test group.

Table 17-6 MPA QA/Test Program Payoffs

Opportunity	Action
Not all QA personnel needed to be analysts	• Employed a mix of programmers, technical assistants, and clerks • Created separate, but equal, career paths for analysts and programmers • Established right jobs for the right personnel • Ensured cost effectiveness: clerks for repetitive jobs • Utilized co-op students to infuse new technologies and assist with programming and test tasks
Lack of formal QA or test training	• In-house and off-site seminars were offered • Utilized available training or arranged for education in the areas of tool usage, networks, company products, quality and test techniques, operating systems, database products
Programming not utilized as an effective quality tool	• Hired consultants and "temps" with programming knowledge to meet short term milestones • Alleviated intensive and nonrecurring automation start-up labor burden • Designed and developed key software-based tools to validate application software • Complemented the existing staff's product knowledge
Lack of support staff synergism: many configuration and metric activities resided within several development groups	• Implemented standard processes for metric activities • Reduced resources via centralized shift to QA/Test group • Implemented activities included: error tracking, version control, software baseline builds for quality testing

Software Methodologies.   One of the key requirements of an effective SQA program is a software PLC. MPA management realized the need for a PLC and therefore drafted and implemented a PLC. The successful implementation of the PLC included activities such as: organizational reviews of draft approaches, companywide approval of the final PLC, dissemination of the PLC methodologies to all the affected personnel, and conducting PLC training courses. The PLC documentation described several life cycle phases:

- Analysis and Requirements Definition
- Design
- Coding and Development Testing
- Functional Integration Testing
- Systems Integration Testing
- Final Acceptance System Testing
- Customer Installation Testing
- Field Beta/Pilot
- General Release
- Final Analysis/Lessons Learned

The Life Cycle methodologies also included the:

- goals for each phase
- requirements necessary to complete a phase
- project team participants/responsibilities
- mechanisms for promoting project team communications (peer reviews, standardized documents, etc.)

Changes were also made to various software development and quality processes. Summarized in Table 17-7 are the methodologies that required enhancement and the resulting benefit (payoff).

Table 17-7   MPA Development and Quality Methodology Payoffs

Opportunity	Action
Limited procedures, plans, and specifications	• Developed standardized QA Plans and Configuration Management Plans
	• Created standardized test plan, specification and procedure data item templates
	• Documented various levels of testing
	• Implemented as part of the PLC
	• Utilized published standards from the IEEE and DoD as guidelines
Limited concern for configuration/disaster controls	• Implemented a full complement of configuration/disaster controls
	– master library

	– post production process (duplication) checkout
	– automated version control
	– off-site storage
Testing was performed under ideal conditions	• Creation of a dynamic test environment
	• Procured clone and multiple brand PC's, modems, printers
	• Began testing on multiple operating systems and network configurations
Testing was a manual, time-consuming process	• Utilized automated test tools
	• Spanned the entire test environment (white, gray, black box testing)
	• Freed up QA analysts
	• Reduced product release time
	• Allowed for measurable testing coverage
No quality involvement in the up-front development process	• Participated in specification reviews and code walkthroughs throughout the PLC
No techniques in place to gather the data needed to convince management that a product was not ready for shipment	• Implemented a simple metrics program (error trending, development/test progress, etc.)
	• Issued reports to management
Need programming expertise and tools to test software	• Developed a QA tools group
	• Analyzed/procured tools
	• Developed (programmed) internal tools
	• Tested products below screen level (i.e., database and code knowledge)
	• Developed tools which were also used by the support staff

Test Approach and Environment. The process turnaround that paid the largest dividends was in the area of software testing. The challenge to enhance the test automation and test measurement programs was formidable because of the complexity of multiple workstation hardware configurations and the corresponding inventory and accounting software applications. Typical inventory and accounting PC applications are characterized by large numbers of data elements, relationships, and processes. The challenge will continue to grow as many applications previously confined to mainframe and minicomputers are ported to workstations and Client/Server platforms.

MPA management addressed the challenges described above by outlining the following objectives:

- Improve test coverage by exercising a greater percentage of code.
- Improve the accuracy of testing by having precisely defined and reproducible test cases.
- Improve the utilization of current resources by allowing QA analysts to concentrate on the creation of tests instead of the implementation of tests.

Testing Tools, Automation and Metrics. The verification of a design's implementation involves many combinations of data and permutations of logical flow. Script writing and manual testing are perceived to provide an unsatisfactory percentage of functional test coverage (typically less than 50 percent). Automatic software testing is intended to increase the test coverage for the same (or lesser) cost as manual testing. Automatic testing also increases the quality of testing by exactly defining each test and making each test reproducible. Additionally, tests may be run 24 hours a day, needing no human intervention once constructed. Test automation systems can check the contents of a screen, file, or other I/O subsystem to verify conformity.

Initially, the MPA Quality/Test group's test tool set was made up of test aids which promoted automated and regressive execution of product test suites. Consequently, MPA decided to enhance the quality of their software products and broaden the capabilities of the QA/Test group through the acquisition and development of software metrics and code analysis tools. The tools allowed the group to effectively measure the quality of software during the evaluation process of the software development and testing phases. These software development and test measurements provided a proactive approach to improving product quality, increasing development productivity and reducing software PLC maintenance costs.

MPA management was guided by software industry studies demonstrating that employing techniques such as software metrics (including improvement feedback) and code analysis result in increased productivity and fewer defects. The use of predictive metrics and code analysis also have been shown to be much more cost-effective than utilizing only conventional black box testing software testing techniques.

Previously, the MPA QA/Test Group had concentrated only on removing defects during the final System Acceptance Test phase of the software life cycle. A software metrics and code analysis program was developed as an effective approach to removing defects in earlier phases of the software life cycle.

MPA found that an additional benefit of software analysis tools is the ability to identify software defects earlier in the software life cycle. Early error identification reduced overall development costs and also led to a reduction in software maintenance activities. MPA's results were consistent with Barry Boehm's widely published studies which demonstrated that errors exposed earlier in the software life cycle can be repaired at a fraction of the cost associated with allowing the defect to propagate into the post development phases of the cycle. MPA's experiences were also consistent with other studies which noted that greater than 50 pecent of software life cycle costs are spent after a system is deployed. Thus, MPA's goal was to reduce software maintenance (i.e., corrective, adaptive, and perfective activities) by reducing the number of defects present in each PC product deployed to the field.

MPA management believed that the software metrics and code coverage analysis approach yielded the following benefits:

- provided significant cost savings due to defect prevention and the resulting decrease in software maintenance costs
- reduced rework due to the elimination of ripple effect errors
- allowed more efficient testing
- provided faster response (turnaround) time on product rollouts
- yielded a higher quality software product

General Test Approach. MPA's QA/Test department had members from differing backgrounds: engineers, programmers, product support specialists, data processing operations, etc.. MPA's newly implemented test automation and analysis cycle utilized these diverse backgrounds and expertise. For example, personnel were organized into specialist groups:

DESIGN	*Quality Assurance Analysts* utilize their product expertise to create actual tests.
CODE	*Programmers* utilize their skills to construct the test tools.
TEST	*Testers* automate and execute the tests and produce the results.
ANALYSIS	*Quality Assurance Analysts* review results to verify conformance and to check test coverage.

Figure 17-4 depicts key elements of the MPA test process, which encompasses the design, code, test, and analysis activities.

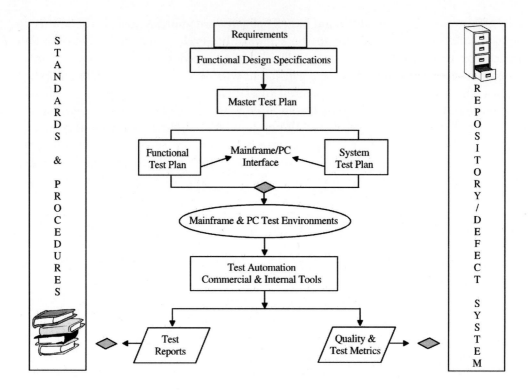

Figure 17-4   Overview of the MPA test process.

MPA management realized that the production and selection of the correct test tools was crucial. They also believed that self-sufficiency in tool technology allowed customization to exact needs. Generally, MPA's test tools were intended for two purposes: testing/analysis and debugging. MPA's test tools also fell into three functional categories:

- Black box testing (e.g., record/playback)
- White box testing (e.g., database analysis, report compare, code analysis)
- Metrics (e.g., code and test analysis, benchmarking, status, management reports)

MPA's tools complemented each other during the QA/Test group's repetitive test cycle. An example of MPA's typical automated test approach is depicted in Figure 17-5. Outlined below are the classes of test tools which were either developed or procured by the MPA Quality/Test group during the enhancement period. For further details on SQA CASE tools refer to Chapter 14.

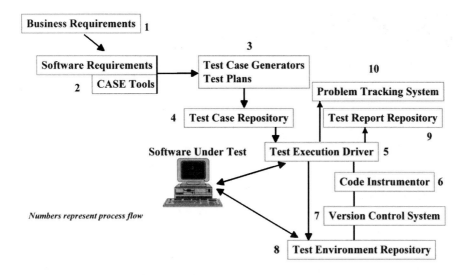

Figure 17-5   Overview of MPA's automation approach.

Automatic Test Execution Tools
- Provides record and playback capabilities.
- Features: Keystroke replay, screen capture, and comparison with expected results. Dynamic flow and control of tests according to results found.
- Uses: Unit testing, functional verification, system testing, capacity, performance, regression testing

Static (Quality Analysis) Systems
- Analyzes source code to improve code quality and maintenance activities.
- Features: Identifies source structure (diagrams), measures structured programming attributes, determines module complexity.
- Fundamentals of Operation: Submit source to Analyzer.
- Uses: Analysis of source code and psuedo-code during the requirements, design, code, and unit test phases.

Dynamic (Test Coverage Analysis) Systems
- Executes tests on "instrumented code" to measure and improve test coverage.
- Features: Identifies modules, branch points, assignments.
- Fundamentals of Operation: Instrument source, generate audit trails, process trails to produce reports.
- Uses: Analysis of coverage by automated functional verification and system tests.

Dynamic Analysis / Database Analysis Tools
– Outputs the physical contents of a database to a file before and after a test. Comparison allows identification of changes to database, both expected and unexpected.

Test Automation / Measurement Payoffs. Summarized below are the benefits (payoffs) and lessons learned from the changes made to MPA's test approach and environment:

- Testing now performed at white, gray, and black box levels.
- Metrics are defined for each test phase.
- Analysts analyze, programmers program, and clerks run tests.
- Automated tools in use:
  - playback/regression
  - database analyzer
  - coverage measurement
  - complexity measurement
  - custom programs (which utilize the design of software under test)
  - CASE tools to generate test specs
- Test types: unit, functional/system integration, acceptance, concurrent locks, performance, security, capacity.

Benefits:
- Test cases and data sets are accumulated assets.
- Code coverage increased with every release.
- Regression testing, once perfected, was very easy, low in cost and 100 percent accurate.
- Automatic tests ran 24 hours/day, seven days/week.
- Test cases were held in an easily maintained database and fed directly to the test tool.
- Exact test data and sequence causing a failure was known.
- Product differential over competitors was created by allowing development and testing of far more complex software in a shorter time.
- Greater certainty and confidence levels were obtained regarding what has been tested.

Possible Disadvantages:
- Caveat to regression testing (see above). Some of the playback and record tools would not allow an automated test to be constructed until the application was error-free.

- There were significant costs associated with the initial equipment setup and the addition of specialist staff/skills.

Future Directions:
- Obtain good manual procedures before automating to prevent an automated mess.
- Store all test data in a central database.
- Plan test data sets and automatic software testing methodology with database administrators and integrate into CASE strategy/methodology.
- Try to produce generic test tools and methodologies that can be applied across your whole product line.
- Continued management support is paramount since automated software testing can be very expensive.
- Insist that testing is performed by a group independent of the software development group.
- Plan how to store, process, evaluate, and report on the data; test automation, once in place, generates mountains of data.
- Plan on putting hooks into products to allow redirection of I/O for test analysis.

First Year Successes of the MPA SQA Program.   Outlined below is a partial list of SQA Program accomplishments and enhancements achieved by the MPA Corporation:

QA / Test Process Definition and Documentation
- Defined metrics
- Created QA and test methodology standards
- Developed QA and test documentation standards
- Implemented duplication/release/storage controls
- Increased the emphasis on critical product utilities
- Emphasized white box testing as well as black box testing

Test Automation
- Planned, documented, and utilized:
  - Incoming Acceptance Tests
  - Functional Integration Tests
  - System Integration Tests
  - Final Systems Acceptance Tests

– Capacity and Volume Tests

– Training Manual Tests

QA Support Tool Development

• Procured and built cost effective automation tools

• Developed in-house database analyzers

• Developed various test measurements (e.g., code/test coverage, application performance, product stability, etc.)

The enhancements to the SQA program allowed MPA to make significant improvements in the overall software development, quality, test, and management process. For example, some of the notable successes during the SQA program implementation and enhancement period are outlined below:

• Built-up test coverage via automation and measurement

• Established simple metrics for release decisions

• Avoided major disasters via configuration control and in-process production testing

• Educated top management on the "science of testing"

• Attracted software developers to a more technical QA/Test group

• Reduced the overall software test/release period

• Increased morale and job satisfaction

Future SQA Program Evolution and Goals.   The ultimate goal of MPA management is to develop an SQA program that utilizes state-of-the-industry, in-process, full product life cycle activities to evaluate software product quality. An overview of MPA's SQA program's evolution which is currently in phase 3 and its future direction is outlined in Table 17-8.

17.9   Additional Practical Applications

17.9.1 Adaptive Quality and Test Strategies

New technologies and development processes force the existence of adaptive software quality programs. Examples of technology challenges and how they affect quality and test initiatives include:

• Object-oriented technology: iterative and incremental development and testing.

• Client/Server technology: design and test considerations include concurrency, time-outs, stress, configuration, compatibility, database integrity, performance, and security.

Table 17-8 MPA SQA Program Evolution

Phase/Emphasis	Description	Key Quality/Techniques
0 Initial State	• Perform QA and Support • Investigate QA in other· organizations/companies • Describe formal QA program	• Ad Hoc
1 Start Up	• Selling the QA function • Staffing • Investigating automation	• Black Box testing using product experts • Random, manual testing • Automated black box
2 QA Implementation and Automation	• Initial automation • Training the QA staff: programming, testing, products • Introducing programming and tools as aids to QA analysts • Basic metrics (error trends) • QA and test standards • Structured test methodology • Configuration Control • Basic testbed • Product release control	• Some tools to perform limited white box testing • Initial development of test specs and standards • Control of software: internal duplication and field • Some error trending • Testbed design
3 Advanced Implementation and Automation	• Advanced metrics • Enhancing the QA staff • Full test phase coverage • Enhanced field/customer relations • Advanced testbed • Common test environment • Increased design involvement	• Full black, gray, and white box testing • Advanced measurement tools • QA with programming knowledge • Common testbed for all products • Analyze customer use/experience • Design and code reviews • Documentation and Specification reviews
4 Refined QA	• Automation, etc. • Automated test documentation • Test requirements traceability • Release modeling integrated design, code, test	• Statistical QA • CASE tools

- Graphical User Interfaces (GUI): global consistency and usage issues, window level attributes, field level validation, various control mechanisms.
- Evolutionary/iterative deliverables: requires more planning and realistic schedules for all teams, increased technical overhead, enhanced communication, increased co-ordination of effort, team performance improves with each iteration.

An example of a QA/Test program adaptive to new technology involves a project developing GUI software on a Client/Server with iterative deliverables. Through the staging of deliverables (with incremental capability), overlapping phases and the sharing of project test roles and test responsibilities, product time-to-market was considerably reduced. Figure 17-6 is an overview of the testing process while Figures 17-7 to 17-10 provide test phase details.

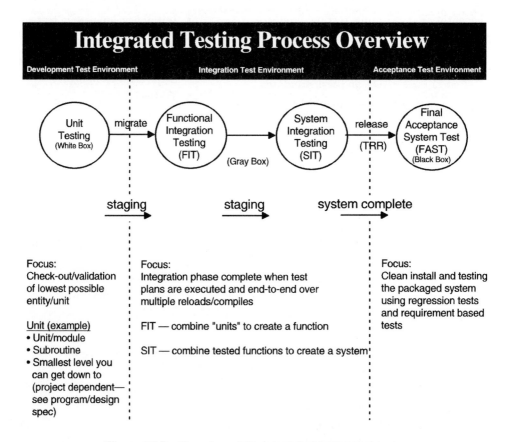

Figure 17-6   Overview of the integrated testing process.

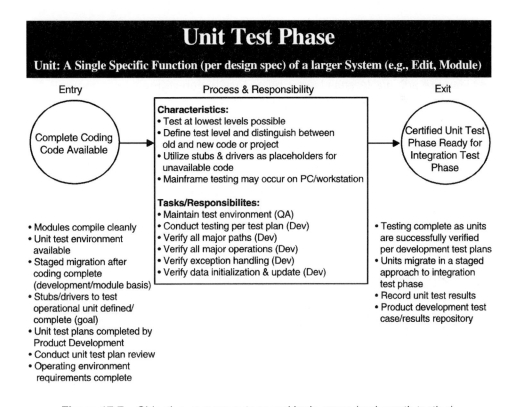

Figure 17-7 Objective: remove sytnax and logic errors (major path testing).

17.9.2 Post-Project Reviews, Lessons Learned

Once an SQA program has been implemented, it is important to continue to build a learning organization. Organizations must encourage the continuos improvement of project practices while ensuring that good experiences are built upon and bad practices are eliminated. Typically, post-project reviews are utilized to improve the efficiency and effectiveness of all functional groups involved in the PLC through the application of lessons learned. Key elements of a lessons learned program include:

- Establish/maintain "experience repository" of reference material
- Establish measurement criteria for lessons learned
- Identify lessons learned
  - practices/activities to promote
  - practices/activities to eliminate

- Identify areas for improvement
- Assign improvement action items
- Implement measures for improvement action plan implementation
- Compare against lessons learnt repository to determine regression
- Identify and publish lessons learned

17.10   Commercial vs. Mission-Critical SQA Programs— A Final Comparison

The following summary of the differences and similarities between military and commercial SQA programs is based upon experiences in both types of programs. The experiences were the result of performing a wide range of roles regarding SQA programs (e.g., manager, implementer, outside reviewer/auditor, and consultant).

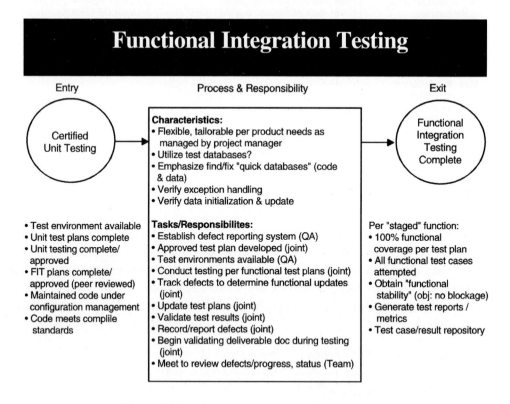

Figure 17-8   Objective: remove functional defects.

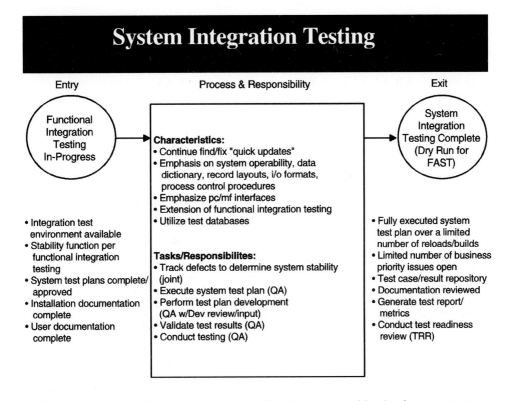

Figure 17-9   Objective: remove defects as functions are combined to form a system.

17.10.1 Unique Characteristics

Commercial Sector

• Quality programs are generally not mandated by customers; must "sell" SQA programs to management

• No consensus on the optimal software project reporting structure

• Emphasis on test role allows continuity/objectivity

• Total Quality Management (TQM), a DoD "buzzword" has been an industry trait

• Similar to the DoD's Independent Validation & Verification (IV&V) role

• Most quality personnel actually *assure software* (see below)

• Quality personnel better equipped and trained due to their test roles

• Software procedures/methodologies may be in place but not followed (no outside enforcement or compliance auditing)

• Few paper requirements

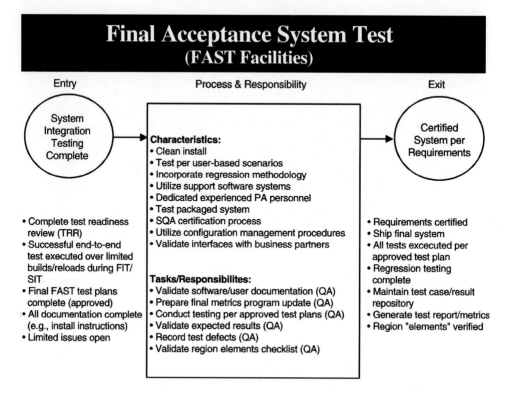

Final Acceptance System Test
(FAST Facilities)

Entry	Process & Responsibility	Exit

Entry: System Integration Testing Complete

Characteristics:
- Clean install
- Test per user-based scenarios
- Incorporate regression methodology
- Utilize support software systems
- Dedicated experienced PA personnel
- Test packaged system
- SQA certification process
- Utilize configuration management procedures
- Validate interfaces with business partners

Tasks/Responsibilites:
- Validate software/user documentation (QA)
- Prepare final metrics program update (QA)
- Conduct testing per approved test plans (QA)
- Validate expected results (QA)
- Record test defects (QA)
- Validate region elements checklist (QA)

Exit: Certified System per Requirements

Entry details:
- Complete test readiness review (TRR)
- Successful end-to-end test executed over limited builds/reloads during FIT/SIT
- Final FAST test plans complete (approved)
- All documentation complete (e.g., install instructions)
- Limited issues open

Exit details:
- Requirements certified
- Ship final system
- All tests exceucted per approved test plan
- Regression testing complete
- Maintain test case/result repository
- Generate test report/metrics
- Region "elements" verified

Figure 17-10   Objective: execute regression- and requirements-based system tests of the to-be-shipped, packaged software.

Military Sector (Mission-Critical)
- Quality programs are required
- Frameworks for software project reporting structures are provided
- Software procedures/methodologies are monitored by both internal and external agencies
- Many paper requirements
- Quality personnel are tasked with assuring the SQA program
- Stresses documentation and requirements verification/traceability
- Emphasizes management of the Quality program to assure effectiveness and monitor technical activities

17.10.2 Common Characteristics

- Use of design/test reviews

- Use of automated configuration controls
- Need for tools and automation
- Not enough emphasis on formal training

Many of the tools, techniques, and methodologies required on military contracts can be used successfully in the commercial sector. Table 17-9 outlines actual examples of techniques used in commercial SQA programs that were borrowed from mission-critical SQA programs.

Table 17-8   Mission-Critical SQA Program Methodologies Successfully Utilized on Commercial SQA Programs

Management	*Test*
• Peer Reviews/Guidelines	• TRR's (Release Reviews)
• Project Life Cycles	• Test Reports
• Documentation Standards	• Acceptance Tests
• Defection Prevention	• Incoming Tests
• Standardization	• Baseline Verification
• Cost Estimation Models	
Requirements / Design / Code	*Metrics*
• Requirements Traceability	• Error Severity/Priority
• Code Walkthroughs	• Trending/Cost of Quality
• Engineering/QA Notebooks	• Complexity
• Work Certification	• QA Sampling/SPC
Configuration Management	
• Change Control Boards	
• FCA/PCA Concepts	
• Version Description Type Documentation	
• Configuration Controls	

While commercial and mission-critical SQA programs differ regarding organization role and project implementation requirements, there is one common point of agreement. Generally, after obtaining the necessary commitments (i.e., management, customer, finances, etc.) both SQA programs have the same objective: meeting the customer's requirements and needs.

17.11   A Word About SEI CMM and ISO 9001

Organizations utilizing the techniques discussed in the case study will find their organizations utilizing repeatable and defined processes (per the SEI Process Maturity Models). As an example, quality and test program elements that are typical "Level 2" or repeatable processes include:

- Automated tests for repeatable measurement and improvement
- Release criteria (e.g., no critical defects, consider performance, usability, functionality)
- Defect tracking system
- Defect metrics
- Error review boards
- Prioritized changes only
- Documentation templates
- Review, critique and sign-off specs
- Defined product release cycles
- Requirements management (stated, verifiable/testable)

The question of whether an organization should utilize the SEI Model or the ISO 9001 Standard for guiding their Quality program development is left to the reader. As an example, the highlights of the comparisons from Paulk [9, 10] are provided in Chapter 4.

17.12   Summary

This chapter outlines the philosophy, framework, personnel roles, successes, benefits, and lessons learned for a SQA program in the commercial sector. Keys to the successful implementation of an effective SQA program are:

- Obtaining commitment from management
- Meeting customer requirements/needs
- Providing/participating in full software life cycle coverage
- Providing accountability (via measurements)
- Acquiring customer/user confidence

References

1. Dunn, Robert H, *Software Quality Concepts and Plans* (Englewood Cliffs, N.J.: Prentice Hall, 1990), p. 254.

2. Deutsch, Michael and Willis, Ronald, *Software Quality Engineering* (Englewood Cliffs, N.J.: Prentice Hall, 1988), p. 273.

3. Dunn, Robert H., op cit, pp. 11, 255.

4. Ibid, p. 135.

5. Ibid, p. 135.

6. Dunn, Robert and Ullman, Richard, *Quality Assurance for Computer Software* (New York: McGraw-Hill, 1982), p. 159.

7. Dunn, Robert H., op cit, pp. 159–173.

8. Deutsch, Michael and Willis, Ronald, op cit, p. 272.

9. Paulk, Mark, "How ISO 9001 Compares with the CMM." In: *IEEE Software*, January 1995, pp. 74–82.

10. Paulk, Mark, "A Comparison of ISO 9001 and the Capability Maturity Model for Software." In: Software Engineering Institute, *Technical Report*, July 1994.

General References

Hetzel, William, *The Complete Guide to Software Testing* (Wellesley, Massachusetts: QED Information Sciences, 1984).

Niech, Lawrence E., "Implementing an Effective Commercial Testing Program Utilizing DOD Software Experiences." Washington, D.C., *EDPMA Technical Conference Transactions* (1991).

Niech, Lawrence E., "The Pitfalls and Payoffs of Implementing a QA Program for Software." Washington, D.C., *NSIA Technical Conference Transactions* (1991)

Niech, Lawrence E., Cheetham, Richard S., "Starting Up an Automated Test Group: Problems and Payoffs." San Francisco, CA., *Quality Week Conference Transactions* (1991).

Niech, Lawrence E., Shaikh, Fareed Z., " Testing Experiences (and Inexperiences) with New Technologies and Industry Initiatives." Washington, D.C., *5th Annual Automated Software Test and Evaluation Conference Transactions* (1995).

Schulmeyer, G. Gordon and MacKenzie, Garth R., Mansucript for *Verification and Validation of Modern Software-Intensive Systems* (Englwood Cliffs, N.J.: Prentice Hall, Inc., 1999).

## CHAPTER 18

Effective Methods of Information Services Quality Assurance

William E. Perry, CQA, CSTE
Quality Assurance Institute (QAI)

18.1   What Is Quality Assurance?

Quality assurance has been a rapidly growing part of data processing. Organizations establish quality assurance to improve their applications, processes, and image. It is one of the cornerstones of an effective Information Services function.

Quality assurance begins with the definition of quality standards, methodology, and procedures; in other words, bringing order and control to the environment. Some systems analysts feel that a quality assurance group is an impediment by management to hinder them from doing their job on time. This may be true if the function is established and operated incorrectly. If the quality assurance process itself is burdensome, it may not work.

Quality must be a routine habit in the department. It can't be imposed upon people at particular points in time. The quality assurance group must continually build a quality environment. Looking at a single application will not improve data processing productivity. However, in looking at several applications, the symptoms of problems in the environment can be identified and analyzed, upon which recommendations can be made to improve the whole of quality within the data processing function.

To see where Quality stands in the Information Services industry, the Quality Assurance Institute surveyed its membership in mid-1998. Highlights of this annual survey are presented in the following report: "1998 Information Services Quality Practices and Salary Survey Report." *

---

* Copyright © 1998 by Quality Assurance Institute ®. Suite 350, 7575 Dr. Phillips Blvd., Orlando, FL 32819-7273, Telephone: 407-363-1111, FAX: 407-363-1112

Quality Assurance Institute

1998 INFORMATION SERVICES QUALITY PRACTICES AND SALARY SURVEY REPORT

ABOUT THE SURVEY

This survey was conducted during the Quality Assurance Institute's (QAI) Annual International Information Technology Quality Conference, held April 15–17, 1998, in Orlando, Florida. Approximately 40 percent of the attendees responded to the survey.

The purpose of the survey was to collect and provide feedback on quality functions operating in I/S organizations and the status of quality practices/programs/initiatives and salaries in those organizations. This report may be used to compare your organization's quality practices to those of others, and to gain insight from the strengths and problems that the participating organizations shared with us concerning current quality practices and corresponding compensation levels.

The survey results were compiled and interpreted by the QAI's professional staff. Data from previous QAI surveys were used, in part, for comparisons and trend identification and have been included in this report.

SIGNIFICANT FINDINGS

1. Sixty percent of the survey participants said management delegates quality initiatives to the QA function for implementation. (Reference: I/S Management's Attitude, Fig. 18-3.) Likewise, 61 percent felt management support positively impacted the I/S QA function. (Reference: What conditions impact your I/S QA function?, Fig. 18-18.) However, conditions negatively impacting the I/S QA function included lack of support, resources not available, and staff resistance. Although management is supporting quality, there may not be appropriate measurement and feedback to indicate these initiatives are being supported at lower levels of the organizations.

2. Ninety-nine percent of the respondents indicted their organizations were addressing the Year 2000 problems. (Reference: Addressing The Year 2000 Problem, Fig. 18-12.) Most companies are using in-house staff and contract programmers. Only 21 percent of the represented organizations projected target completion dates past June, 1999. Seventy-nine percent surveyed said one or more projects were late, over budget, canceled, or delayed during the past 12 months. (Reference: Project Results, Fig. 18-10.) Although half of the organizations are using special processes for Y2K work, their experience in non-Y2K project successes seem to indicate high risk in meeting targeted Y2K completion dates.

3. Almost 50 percent of the survey population stated their QA function performed both process- (definition, deployment, improvement) and product- (reviews, formal inspections, testing) related activities. (Reference: QA Functions Performed, Fig. 18-14.) This combination could be useful in coordinating metrics from testing for use in process improvement activities. Unless properly managed, this combination can be risky if schedule demands cause the use of all QA resources for testing activities.

4. Sixty-nine percent of the participants felt the most important new activity in which their I/S QA function will be involved during the next 12 months will be process improvement and methodology implementation. (Reference: Important New Activities, Fig. 18-19.) This may be the result of the increasing emphasis organizations are placing on the use of industry models and industry certification. (Reference: Use of Industry Models, Fig. 18-4.) Heightened awareness of Year 2000 was reported by 5 percent of the respondents as positively impacting the I/S QA function. Y2K projects may be providing feedback to management indicating the quality of their organization's current processes and need for making significant changes.

5. I/S QA salaries for nonmanagement (staff) remained similar to those reported in 1997, while salaries for management (ones with direct reports) increased over 20 percent. (Reference: QAI Salary Survey Trends, Fig. 18-20.) Average increase in salary was 7.9 percent, similar to that reported in 1997.

6. The most significant positive changes in I/S QA functions since the QAI 1997 I/S Quality Practices and Salary Report include more emphasis on the Year 2000 problem, identification and plans for process improvement, methodology implementation activities, and increased industry certification.

DETAILED SURVEY RESULTS

Part 1.   General Information

Over half of the survey population belonged to I/S organizations with over 200 employees as shown in Figure 18-1. The size of the organizations may be related to the fact that 58 percent reported performing review and testing functions. (Reference: QA Functions Performed, Fig. 18-14, p. 6.)

Seventy-five percent of the participants were from service companies (primarily finance, communications, healthcare, and consulting, as shown in Figure 18-2). Representation from government and manufacturing is considerably lower than those recorded since 1994.

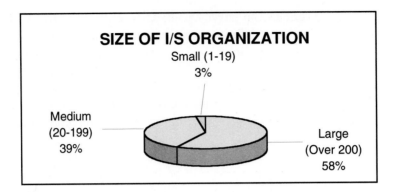

Figure 18-1   Size of I/S organization.

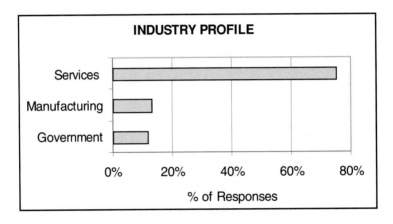

Figure 18-2   Industry profile.

Part 2.   The Information Services Organization

When respondents were asked, "In your organization, what is the definition of quality?" 72 percent responded. Those definitions most frequently stated were:

- Meet customer requirements and expectations (45 percent)
- Produce a quality product on time and within budget (20 percent)
- Deliver quality products to our customers (20 percent)
- Other (15 percent)

Thirty-seven percent of survey respondents categorized their management's attitude toward quality (Figure 18-3) as actively committed. These managers were described as providing budget and resources, communicating their commitment, and participating in quality activities. Sixty percent said their management delegates quality initiatives. The number of managers actively involved in quality initiatives increased by 5 percent over the 1997 survey results. Delegation increased 8 percent.

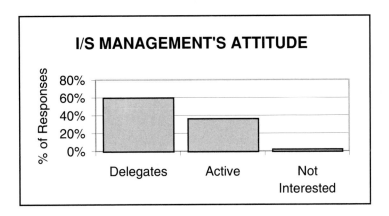

Figure 18-3 I/S management's attitude.

Fifty-one percent of all participants said their organizations are using one or more industry models (Figure 18-4) as a benchmark or baseline. This is almost 10 percent lower than responses in 1997 and 1996. Of those organizations using industry models, more than half are using the SEI (CMM) model. Almost 20 percent are using the ISO 9000 model. Seventeen percent of organizations using industry models have achieved industry certification.

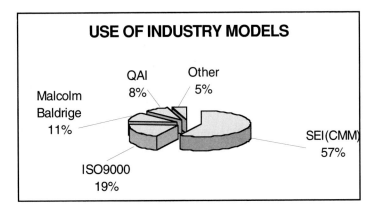

Figure 18-4 Use of industry models.

Eighty-two percent of the survey population said their organization used automated tools for project management (Figure 18-5). Almost 60 percent use MS Project. The other category included Multitrak, Plannet, Enterprise PM, Test Director, and Excel. The list below identifies the most commonly used software development tools by the respondents.

List of automated tools identified as most commonly used for software development by represented organizations

Client/Server	Mainframe	Object Oriented	PC
Powerbuilder	Hiperstation	JAVA	LANDESK
Oracle	File-Aid	C++	APS
Mercury WinRunner	Visual Age Generator	Clear Case	Web
C++			

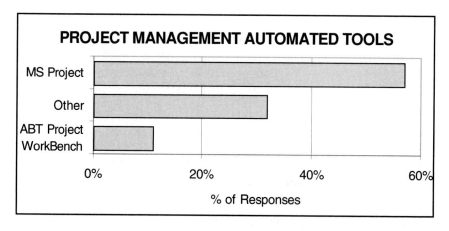

Figure 18-5   Project management automated tools.

Thirty-eight percent of the participants stated their organizations are using automated workflow diagramming tools, as shown in Figure 18-6. Visio and ABC Flowcharter have been consistently mentioned most often over the last several years. The "Other" category included Flow 4, Logic Works, AllClear, and System Archetect.

When asked, "What development/maintenance methodology is used in your organization?" over 50 percent answered with waterfall methodology. Several indicated (Figure 18-7) they were using multiple methodologies. Those identifying "Other" mentioned OO, Spiral, Oracle CDM, and in-house/hybrid.

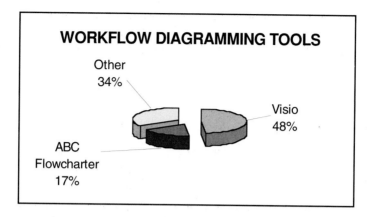

Figure 18-6 Workflow diagramming tools.

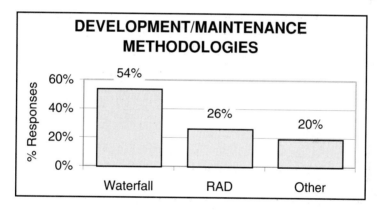

Figure 18-7 Development/maintenance methodologies.

Fifty-eight percent of the respondents said their I/S processes are well defined and governed through policies, standards, and procedures, as shown in Figure 18-8. This number has not changed since 1997. Fifty-one percent have an active standards committee in place, which is 18 percent higher than 1997. Most media used is paper. Other media utilized included Lotus Notes, an intranet, MS Word, and a LAN.

When asked, "Is there currently a measurement program deployed in your organization?", 49 percent answered positively, as depicted in Figure 18-9. This is 6 percent lower than the 1997 response. Other data mentioned included customer surveys and process defects.

Survey participants were asked to rank five common measurements in order of importance on a scale of 1–5 (1 highest, 5 lowest). Mean scores were: defects 3.41, productivity 3.33, budget 2.90, schedule 2.74, customer satisfaction 2.18.

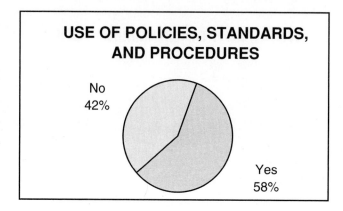

Figure 18-8   Use of policies, standards, and procedures.

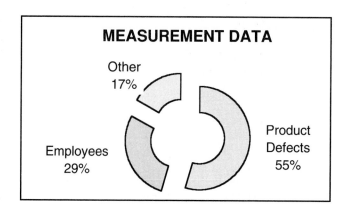

Figure 18-9   Measurement data.

Survey participants were asked if any projects in their organization were canceled, over budget, or late in the last 12 months. Seventy-nine percent said one or more projects were late, 64 percent over budget, 43 percent canceled, and 11 percent "Other" which included delayed, rescheduled, or scoped down as shown in Figure 18-10.

Fifty-seven percent of the survey population said their organizations were outsourcing some of their I/S functions (Figure 18-11). This response was similar to that from 1997. Frequently mentioned functions were: software development 47 percent, Y2000 projects 13 percent, maintenance/support 27 percent, and data center operations 13 percent.

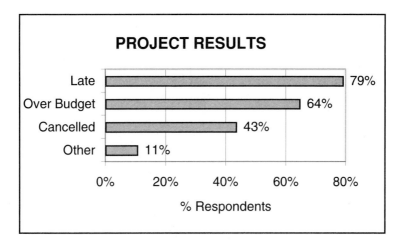

Figure 18-10   Project results.

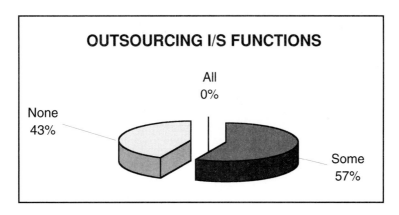

Figure 18-11   Outsourcing I/S functions.

Part 3.   The Year 2000 Problem

Ninety-nine percent of the entire survey population said their organizations were addressing the Year 2000 problem. Almost 10 percent are in multiple project phases. Figure 18-12 shows that seventy-five percent are in code and test, 14 percent in planning, and 13 percent in assessing. Seven percent have completed their Y2K projects.

Year 2000 projects are being managed by I/S middle management (59 percent), I/S executive management (24 percent), corporate executive management (11 percent), business management (4 percent), and vendor executive management (4 percent).

Eighty-seven percent of the companies are using in-house staff, 54 percent contract programmers, and 36 percent are using outside vendor resources. Of those indicating specific target dates, 5 percent estimated completion by June, 1998, 53 percent by December, 1998, 21 percent by June, 1999, and 21 percent by December, 1999.

Automated tools most frequently mentioned for Year 2000 projects were Hour Glass 2000, Hiperstation, and Compuware QA Suite. Half of the projects are using special processes for Y2K work.

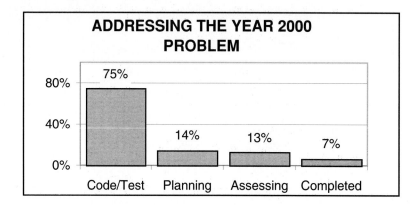

Figure 18-12   Addressing the Year 2000 problem.

Part 4.   The I/S Quality Assurance Function

Eighty-six percent of the participants had a QA function, as shown in Figure 18-13. This number has increased over previous QAI QA Surveys. Of those that do not currently have a QA function, 36 percent have never had one. Forty-four percent plan to have one in the future.

Within I/S organizations the QA function reports to:

- I/S middle management (50 percent)
- Other, e.g., director, president, etc. (23 percent)
- CIO (16 percent)
- I/S project management (11 percent)

When asked, "What function does your QA staff perform?" participants' responses (Figure 18-14) included:

- Both process and testing functions (49 percent)
- Process definition, deployment, improvement (22 percent)
- Other e.g., metrics, internal consulting (20 percent)
- Reviews, formal inspections, testing, etc. (9 percent)

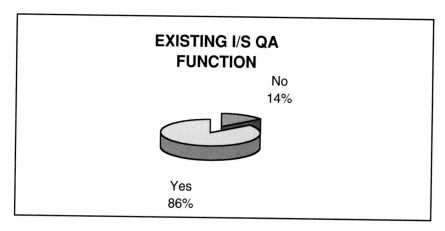

Figure 18-13   Existing I/S QA function.

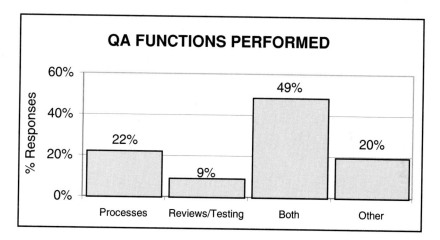

Figure 18-14   QA functions performed.

Thirty-one percent of the respondents reported their QA groups had just started. Thirty-eight percent of the groups were less than four years old and 31 percent were older than four years old, as shown in Figure 18-15. Seventy-two percent of the QA groups have fewer than 10 employees. These numbers are similar to those of 1997.

Twenty-seven percent of the survey population felt that the role of the QA function (Figure 18-16) is clearly understood throughout the organization. This is significantly higher than the 1997 response of 14 percent.

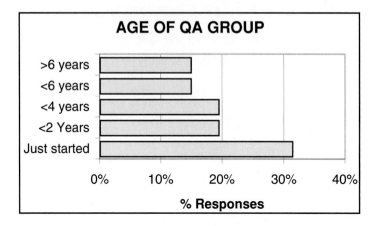

Figure 18-15   Age of QA group.

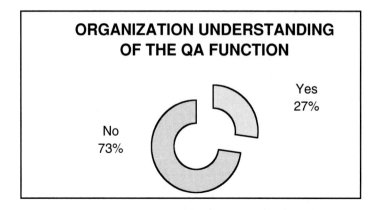

Figure 18-16   Organization understanding of the QA function.

Seventy-four percent of the survey participants reported they received training in the last 12 months, as shown in Figure 18-17. Those receiving training most often mentioned QAI conferences and seminars. Other quality training included SEI, project management, and tools. Courses unrelated to quality were not described.

Respondents were asked," What conditions impact your I/S QA function?"

Conditions positively impacting the I/S QA function:
1. Management support (61 percent)
2. Commitment of staff (7 percent)
3. Heightened awareness of Year 2000 (5 percent)

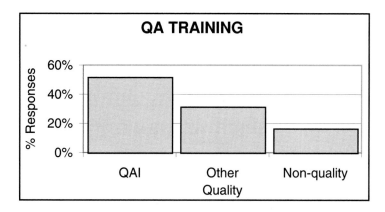

Figure 18-17 QA training.

Conditions negatively impacting the I/S QA function:
1. Lack of support (36 percent)
2. Resources not available (33 percent)
3. Staff resistance (15 percent)

Sixty percent of the participants said the most significant contribution made by the QA staff to the organization (Figure 18-18) was improvement of the quality of processes and methodologies. Processes mentioned included project management, formal inspections, and configuration management. This is an increase of over 20 percent from 1996 and 1997 QAI survey responses.

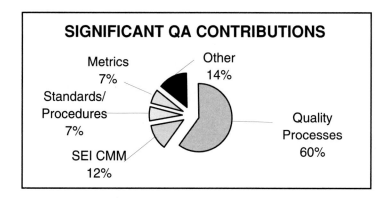

Figure 18-18 Significant QA contributions.

Respondents were asked, "What do you believe is the most important new activity in which your I/S QA group will be involved in the next 12 months?" Sixty-nine percent identified process improvement and methodology implementation, as shown in Figure 18-19. This response is 18 percent higher than that of 1997. Other activities cited included establishing a separate project office, evaluating vendors, expanding internet capabilities, and improving corporate communications.

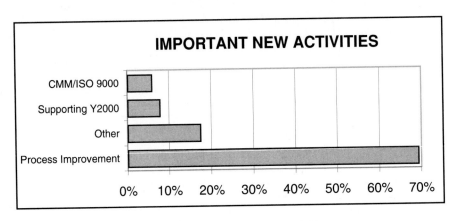

Figure 18-19   Important new activities.

Part 5.   Salary/Compensation

Survey respondents who identified themselves as managers (defined as ones with direct reports) outnumbered non-managers (staff) by 10 percent. The average salary reported for a management position was $74,109, while the average for staff was $58,602, as shown in Figure 18-20. The salaries have remained relatively flat since 1995, until this year when the managers' salaries increased by over 20 percent.

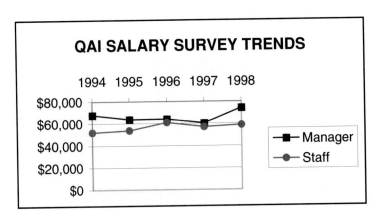

Figure 18-20   QAI salary survey trends.

Eighty-two percent of the survey population earned a four-year degree or higher, as shown in Figure 18-21. The education attainment level has steadily increased since 1992, except for 1997 when it decreased slightly.

The average salaries by education level were:
- Masters $76,909   • Bachelor $54,197
- High School $70,367   • Associate $55,000
- Doctorate $69,750

Seventy-three percent of those surveyed received a bonus or profit sharing in the last 12 months. Average increase in salaries was 7.9 percent.

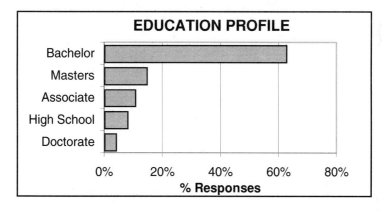

Figure 18-21   Education profile.

Sixty-two percent of the survey population said they held one or more professional certifications, as shown in Figure 18-22. This represents an increase of over 10 percent from the 1997 QAI survey results. Certification has been steadily increasing since 1994. Certifications other than QAI included CPA, CSQE, CDP, and PMP.

Part 6.   Comments

Respondents had several suggestions on what QAI can do to assist QA groups with quality improvement activities. The two most frequently mentioned were:

1. Provide more workshop and "how to" sessions; and
2. Assist as a reference source for QA topics in order to provide people-to-people contact.

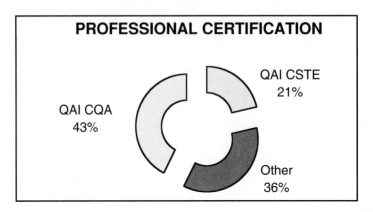

Figure 18-22   Professional certification.

18.2   Quality Assurance as a Facilitator to Improve Overall Information Services Quality

Experience has proven that an Information Services function needs a model (an approach) to follow in order to improve quality and productivity. These models are based on work processes to manage and produce deliverables. One of the better accepted Information Services models has been developed by the Quality Assurance Institute and is described below.

There are three basic approaches to doing work. These are to perform work as an art, a craft, or an engineering discipline. An artist can perform work in any manner desired, and usually experiments to find the most effective way for that individual to work. In a craft, an individual is taught skills and guidelines on how to perform work. In an engineering discipline, the process is detailed with required compliance, and skills are based on what is needed to follow the processes.

The QAI approach is built on the PDCA (Plan-Do-Check-Act) cycle. QAI has slightly changed the terms to be more consistent with information services technology, as shown in Figure 18-23.

Both the QAI strategic and tactical views incorporate this time-proven continuous improvement cycle.

QAI's Strategic Approach to Quality Management (see Figure 18-24) incorporates *manage by processes,* which implies that work will be performed as an engineering discipline. Since information services is a creative endeavor, it assumes that the professionals using those processes are properly skilled to use them. Thus, the processes are not defined to the same level of detail as one would expect in a manufacturing plant making thousands of the same product. The professional processes provide adequate checks and balances that enable individuals to be creative but still within the rigor imposed by the work processes.

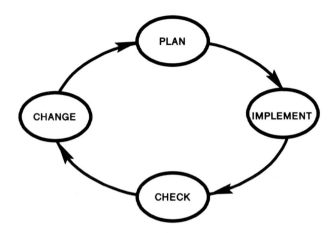

Figure 18-23   Continuous improvement cycle.

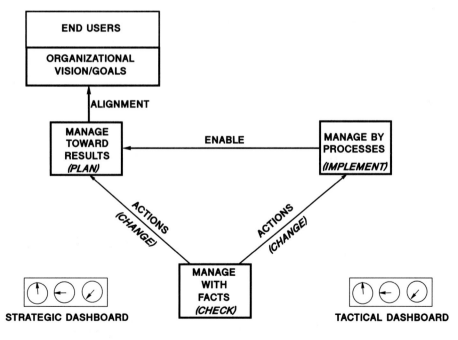

Figure 18-24   The QAI approach to quality management—strategic view—what to do.

The QAI Strategic Approach to Quality Management identifies *manage by processes* as one of the key strategies for quality management. Managing by processes is significantly different from managing an information services activity as an art or craft activity. The difference is that rigor, induced by the engineering discipline which provides consistency and reliability, produces the agreed to results, as well as the base upon which continuous improvement can be established.

18.2.1 How to Manage—The Strategic View of the QAI Approach

The relationship of the plan/implement/check/change cycle is illustrated in Figure 18-23. Some insight into how to use these management activities as an integrated strategic approach for managing information services follows.

Manage Toward Results.   Management must define the results that they hope to achieve. These can be quality results, such as implementing 100 percent of end-user requirements correctly; or they can be process or constraint results, such as implementing projects on time and within budget. The results need to be clearly and quantitatively stated. In addition, the number of results specified by management should be limited. Three to eight results are acceptable.

The difficulty in specifying too many results is that two or more specified results lead to compromise. In addition, if more than one result is specified they may be contradictory. For example, if the results are completed on time and have 100 percent of the requirements implemented, it may lead to a compromise on the number or extensiveness of the implemented requirements. In other words, to meet time constraints the project may have to compromise on the quality of implemented requirements. Likewise, if the specified results were easy-to-access systems, and highly secure systems, those results are in conflict. By opening up the system to make it easy to use, security, by definition, is compromised.

If more than one result indicator is specified, management should rank the desired results in importance. In our example of meeting schedule and having 100 percent of the requirements implemented, management would need to specify which was most important. If it was 100 percent requirements implemented, then a compromise would be made on a schedule; on the other hand, if schedule was most important, then compromise would be made on the number or quality of implemented requirements.

Manage by Processes.   Management must ensure that there are appropriate processes in place to enable the workers to meet the desired results. Without processes, there can be much variability and unpredictability to the job of meeting the results. For example, if you give a project leader the objectives to have 100 percent of the requirements implemented and meet schedule, but give that project leader no process, then the project leader must not only meet the results but must build the process to meet those results. Since each project leader would build a different process, the results would vary and the resources required would be unpredictable because the process has never been tried before. On the other hand, with proven and effective processes the results are highly predictable with minimum variability.

For repetitive jobs (i.e., job shop processes), the processes can be used, and even customized, to meet the results specified for similar jobs. On the other hand, if the results are new or unique, or involve new technology, then the processes need to be created before the workers can be expected to meet management's defined results.

The maturity of the process will affect the variability and predictability of results. In the SEI Capability Maturity Model (see the "Strategic View of How I/S Activities Mature Their Processes" in the section below), five levels of process maturity are defined. At Level 1 the processes are not well defined, and thus are subject to high variability and unpredictable outcomes. As the processes mature to Level 5, the variability reduces dramatically and the predictability of the process increases dramatically. Thus, it is important to have an effective process definition process.

Manage with Facts.   The specified results should be quantitative, and the processes should provide adequate quantitative data as a by-product of the process to determine whether or not the specified results are being achieved. If not, the management process must make adjustments to either the execution of the processes, or change the desired results so that at the conclusion of the work the results are met.

Management by fact involves three distinct activities, as follows:

- Establish a results (i.e., strategic) dashboard. These are the key results or key indicators established in the management toward results process.
- Establish a tactical dashboard. These are the measures and metrics that will be used to evaluate the quality of the product and performance of the process.
- Quantitative decisionmaking. Using the tactical and strategic dashboard, management must make decisions that lead to actions to make the necessary adjustments so that the processes meet the desired results, and/or remove defects from the products.

Let's look at a simple example of how this approach works. Let us assume the example of wanting 100 percent of the requirements implemented and the project completed on schedule. In our first process category, the manage toward results process category, two results have been specified. These two results become the strategic dashboard. Since software development is normally a repetitive process in an information services activity, we can assume that there is a software development process that enables employees to build software systems. These processes should enable the employees to meet management's defined results.

To manage a process effectively, a tactical dashboard needs to be established. To simplify the example, let's assume there are only three tactical dashboard indicators, which might be number of changes requested, number of project staff assigned, and number of requirements fully tested.

The project manager knows the desired results. To manage the project, the project manager watches the tactical dashboards. The project manager knows that if the number of changes is too high, the project cannot be completed on time while meeting 100 percent of the requirements. To manage with facts when the number of changes becomes too high either the number of changes requested by the end user has to be reduced or the process tactics have to change (for example, adding more people) or the results indicator must be adjusted to allow more time to implement the changes. Likewise, if the number of requirements tested is below expectations to meet the scheduled completion date, the project leader may have to take action such as initiating overtime or adding more testers to meet management-defined results.

18.2.2 Strategic View of How I/S Activities Mature Their Processes

Implementing the QAI Strategic Approach to Quality Management is a complex challenge. The challenge is building an organization capable of meeting the defined information results in an effective and efficient manner. This requires an organization whose processes are highly predictable and can change and innovate to ensure world-class quality, high productivity, and a high end user satisfaction level.

The base needed to build an information organization is its vision, principles, assumptions, and goals. The vision sets the direction in which the organization will move. The principles are the guiding rules that must be incorporated into the way work is performed. For example, principles that affect work include assuring that the integrity of the individual will not be compromised, that work will be performed in an excellent manner, and that the end user will be the primary focus of the organization. Assumptions about doing work exist and need to be documented, and confirmed or rejected. For example, an information activity may have the assumption that all changes submitted by the user have to be implemented. This type of assumption, if held by the management and staff, can greatly influence the work processes. Goals, both short term and long term, should quantitatively establish the work performance that the organization desires to achieve.

There are five levels in QAI's strategic view of process management. By definition, all organizations begin at Level 1. Maturity means moving to Levels 2 through 5. While organizations may do activities in several different levels concurrently, it is not practical to skip a level in the maturity process. The reason for this is that each level prepares the culture for movement to a higher level. To skip a level in the maturity process would be equivalent to skipping a grade level in a public education process.

The five strategic manage by processes levels are illustrated in Figure 18-25 and described below.

Level 1—Manage People.

This level results in an unstructured, inconsistent level of performance. At the manage people level, tasks are not performed the same way by different people or different activities. For example, one system development activity may use part of the system development methodology, but improvise other parts; another activity may select different parts of the same system development methodology to use, and decide not to perform tasks done by a previous activity.

At this level, management manages people and jobs. Management will establish goals or objectives for individuals and teams, and manage to those objectives and goals with minimal concern about the means used to achieve the goals. This level is normally heavily schedule-driven, and those who meet the schedules are rewarded. Since there are no standards against which to measure deliverables, people's performance is often dependent upon their ability to convince management that the job they have done is excellent. This causes the environment to be very political. Both management and staff become more concerned with their personal agenda than with meeting their organization's mission.

The emphasis that is needed to move from Level 1 to Level 2 is one of discipline and control. The emphasis is on getting the work processes defined, the people trained in the work processes, and implementing sufficient controls to assure compliance to the work processes and producing products that meet predefined standards.

Level 2—Manage Processes.

There are two major objectives to be achieved at Level 2. The first is to instill discipline in the culture of the information organization so that through the infrastructure, training, and leadership of management individuals will want to follow defined processes. The second objective is to reduce variability in the processes by defining them to a level that permits relatively constant outputs. At this level, processes are defined with minimal regard for skills needed to perform the process <u>AND</u> with minimal regard for the impact on other processes. At Level 2, the work processes are defined, management manages those processes, and uses validation and verification techniques to check compliance to work procedures and product standards. Having the results predefined through a set of standards enables management to measure people's performance against meeting those standards. Education and training are an important component of Level 2, as is building an infrastructure that involves the entire staff in building and improving work processes.

The emphasis that needs to be put into place to move to Level 3 is defining and building the information activity's core competencies.

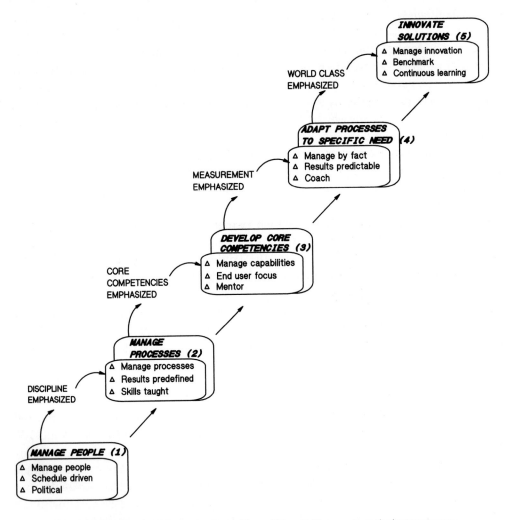

Figure 18-25   Strategic view of how I/S activities mature their processes.

Level 3—Develop Core Competencies.   At this level, an information organization defines its core competencies and then builds an organization that is capable of performing those core competencies effectively and efficiently. The more common core competencies for an information services organization include system development, maintenance, testing, training, outsourcing, and operation. The information activity must decide if it wants core competencies in fields such as communication, hardware and software selection, contracting, and so forth. Once the core competencies are determined, then the processes defined at Level 2 must be reengineered to drive the core competencies. In addition, the tasks are analyzed to determine what skills are needed to perform those processes. Next, a staff must be retrained, recruited, motivated, and supported to perform those core competencies in an effective and efficient manner. It is the integration of people and processes, coupled with managers with people management skills, that are needed to maintain and improve those core competencies. Lots of mentoring occurs at this level, with the more experienced people building skills in the less experienced. It is also a level that is truly end user focused, because both the information organization and the end user know the information activity's core competencies.

The managerial emphasis that is needed to move to Level 4 is quantitative measurement. Measurement is only a practical initiative when the processes are stabilized and focused on achieving management's desired results.

Level 4—Adapt Processes to Specific Needs. This level has two objectives. The first is to develop quantitative standards for the work processes based on performance of the Level 3 stabilized processes. The second objective is to provide management the dashboards and skillsets needed to manage quantitatively. The result is predictable work processes. Knowing the normal performance of a work process, management can easily identify problems through variation from the quantitative standards to address problems quickly to keep projects on schedule and budget. This level of predictability is one that uses measurement to manage as opposed to using measurement to evaluate individual performance. At this level, managers can become coaches to help people address their day-to-day challenges in performing work processes in a predictable manner. Management recognizes that obstacles and problems are normal in professional activities, and through early identification and resolution, professional work processes can be as predictable as manufacturing work processes.

The management emphasis that is needed to move to Level 5 is one of desiring to be world class. World class means doing the best that is possible, given today's technology.

Level 5—Innovate Solutions. At Level 5, the information organization wants to be a true leader in the industry. At this level, the organization is looking to measure itself against the industry through benchmarking, and then define innovative ways to achieve higher levels of performance. Innovative approaches can be achieved through benchmarking other industries, applying new technology in an innovative way, reengineering the way work is done, and by constantly studying the literature and using experts to identify potential innovations. This level is one in which continuous learning occurs, both in individuals and the organization.

18.2.3 QAI Tactical Approach: The Six Categories of Processes that Need To Be Managed

In an art/craft organization, management manages jobs, projects, and organizational entities such as projects, schedules, and budgets. In an engineering-oriented quality management organization, processes are managed. These processes become the core competencies of an information services organization.

QAI believes that the processes needed to manage an organization fall into six categories. The six categories of process management are illustrated in Figure 18-26. The organization's vision, principles, assumptions, and goals will shape and customize the individual processes used within each category.

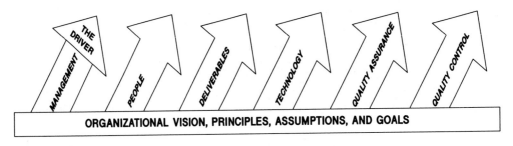

ORGANIZATIONAL VISION, PRINCIPLES, ASSUMPTIONS, AND GOALS

Figure 18-26   QAI's tactical approach to quality management process categories.

The six categories of processes that QAI has identified for the tactical approach for process management are:

- **Management.** The top levels of management within an information services function that are responsible for planning and managing the short- and long-term activities within that function, as well as assuring they are aligned with the organization's overall vision, mission, principles, and assumptions.

- **People.** The people management activities are governed by human resources, salary administration, and related activities within the organization.

- **Deliverables.** These are the activities within the information services function held accountable for developing and maintaining software. In some organizations, this function will be performed through contracting or purchase of software. The activity is responsible for the software operating capabilities and the data needed to support those capabilities.

- **Technology.** This primarily involves the computer operations activities, such as selection of hardware, communication, and operating software, environmental processes, security, and configuration management.

- **Quality Assurance.** The individuals, groups, and activities responsible for defining and improving work processes. In some organizations this responsibility falls under the standards committee and the subcommittees or work groups that develop individual standards and processes.
- **Quality Control.** These are the activities and individuals responsibile for the check and act components of the PDCA cycle. These activities include quality assurance, independent test, problem tracking, and other audit-type activities.

18.3 Quality Assurance as a Measurement Science

The key to a successful quality assurance group is to define and measure quality. This requires some reeducation of DP management and staff. What is needed by a QA group is a methodology for defining and measuring quality.

There has been an increased awareness in recent years of the critical problems that have been encountered in the development of large scale software systems. These problems not only include the cost and schedule overruns typical of development efforts, and the poor performance of the systems once they are delivered, but also include the high cost of maintaining the systems, the lack of portability, and the high sensitivity to changes in requirements.

Software metrics measure various attributes of software and relate to different aspects of software quality. The potential of the software metric concepts can be realized by their inclusion in software quality programs. They provide a more disciplined, engineering approach to quality assurance and a mechanism allowing a life cycle viewpoint of software quality. The benefits derived from their application are realized in life cycle cost reduction.

During the past decade, the evolution of modern programming practices, structured and disciplined development techniques and methodologies, and requirements for more structured, effective documentation has increased the feasibility of the effective measurement of software quality.

However, before the potential of measurement techniques could be realized, a framework or model of software quality had to be constructed. An established model, which at one level provides a user- or management-oriented view of quality, is described in the perspective of how it can be used to establish software quality requirements for a specific application.

The actual measurement of software quality is accomplished by applying software metrics (or measurements) to the documentation and source code produced during software development. These measurements are part of the established model of software quality and through that model can be related to various user-oriented aspects of software quality. (See Chapter 11 for an application of software metrics to the Pareto Principle in a practical case.) Metrics can be classified according to three categories:

- Anomaly-detecting
- Predictive
- Acceptance

Anomaly-detecting metrics identify deficiencies in documentation or source code. These deficiencies usually are corrected to improve the quality of the software product. Standards enforcement is a form of anomaly-detecting metrics.

Predictive metrics are measurements of the logic of the design and implementation. These measurements are concerned with form, structure, density, and complexity. They provide an indication of the quality that will be achieved in the end product, based on the nature of the application, and design and implementation strategies.

Acceptance metrics are measurements that are applied to the end product to assess its final compliance with requirements. Tests are a form of acceptance-type measurements.

The measurements described and used in this manual are either anomaly-detecting or predictive metrics. They are applied during the development phases to assist in identification of quality problems early on so that corrective actions can be taken early when they are more effective and economical.

The measurement concepts complement current quality assurance and testing practices. They are not a replacement for any current techniques utilized in normal quality assurance programs. For example, a major objective of quality assurance is to assure conformance with user/customer requirements. The software quality metric concepts described in this manual provide a methodology for the user/customer to specify life cycle–oriented quality requirements, usually not considered, and a mechanism for measuring how well those requirements have been attained. A function usually performed by software quality assurance personnel is a review/audit of software product produced during a software development. Software metrics add formality and quantification to document and code reviews. Metric concepts also provide a vehicle for early involvement in development since there are metrics that apply to the documents produced early in the development.

Testing is usually oriented toward correctness, reliability, and performance (efficiency). Metrics assist in the evaluation of other qualities like maintainability, portability, and flexibility.

18.3.1 Example of How Measurement is Used to Improve Software Quality

The primary purpose of applying software quality metrics in a quality assurance program is to improve the quality of the software product. In other words, rather than simply measuring, metrics exert a positive influence on the product in that they improve its development.

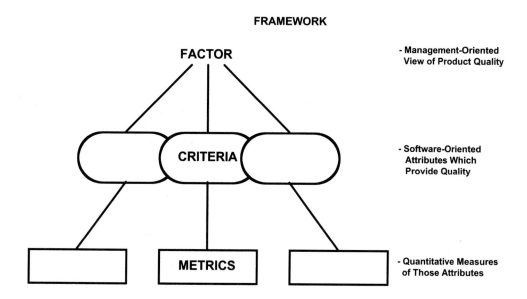

Figure 18-27 Hierarchical model of software quality.

The vehicle for establishing performance requirements is the hierarchical model of software quality. This model, shown in Figure 18-27, has at its highest level a set of software quality factors that are expressed as user/management–oriented terms and represent the characteristics that comprise software quality. At the next level for each quality factor is a set of criteria that provides the characteristics represented by the quality factors. These criteria are software-related terms. At the lowest level of the model are the metrics, which are quantitative measures of the software attributes defined by the criteria.

The procedures for establishing the quality requirements for a particular software system utilize this model and will be described as a three-level approach, the levels corresponding to the hierarchical levels of the software quality model. The first level establishes the quality factors that are important; the second level identifies the critical software attributes; and the third level identifies the metrics that will be applied and establishes quantitative ratings for the quality factors.

Once the quality requirements have been determined according to the procedures described in the subsequent paragraphs, they must be transmitted to the development team. If the development is being done internally, the quality requirements should be documented in the same form as the other system requirements and provided to the development team. Additionally, a briefing emphasizing the intent of the inclusion of the quality requirements is recommended.

18.3.2 Procedures for Identifying Important Quality Factors

The basic tool to be utilized in identifying the important quality factors will be the software quality requirements survey form shown in Table 18-2. The formal definitions of each of the quality factors are provided on that form.

A preliminary briefing should be given to the decisionmakers who will use the following tables and figures, prior to soliciting their responses to the survey. This should be done so that only meaningful quality factors will be measured for a project, i.e., with the avoidance of unnecessary measurements for less meaningful quality factors. The decisionmakers may include the acquisition manager, the user/customer, the development manager, and the QA manager. To complete the survey, the following procedures should be followed.

Table 18-2 Software Requirements Survey Form

---

1. The 11 quality factors listed below have been isolated from the current literature. They are not meant to be exhaustive, but to reflect what is currently thought to be important. Please indicate whether you consider each factor to be Very Important (VI), Important (I). Somewhat Important (SI), or Not Important (NI) as design goals in the system you are currently working on.

Response	Factors	Definition
_____	Correctness	Extent to which a program satisfies its specifications and fulfills the user's mission objectives.
_____	Reliability	Extent to which a program can be expected to perform its intended function with required precision.
_____	Efficiency	The amount of computing resources and code required by a program to perform a function.
_____	Integrity	Extent to which access to software or data by unauthorized persons can be controlled.
_____	Usability	Effort required to learn, operate, prepare input, and interpret output of a program.
_____	Maintainability	Effort required to locate and fix an error in an operational program.
_____	Testability	Effort required to test a program to insure it performs its intended function.
_____	Flexibility	Effort required to modify an operational program.
_____	Portability	Effort required to transfer a program from one hardware configuration and/or software system environment to another.

_____	Reusability	Extent to which a program can be used in other applications—related to the packaging and scope of the functions that programs perform.
_____	Interoperability	Effort required to couple one system with another.

2. In what type(s) of application(s) are you currently involved?

_____

3. Are you currently in:

_____ 1. Development phase

_____ 2. Operations/Maintenance phase

4. Please indicate the title which most closely describes your position:

_____ 1. Program Manager

_____ 2. Technical consultant

_____ 3. Systems Analyst

_____ 4. Other (please specify)

Consider Basic Characteristics of the Application. The software quality requirements for each system are unique and are influenced by system or application-dependent characteristics. There are basic characteristics which affect the quality requirements; therefore each software system must be evaluated for its basic characteristics. Table 18-3 provides a list of some of these basic characteristics.

For example, if the system is being developed in an environment in which there is a high rate of technical breakthroughs in hardware design, *portability* should take on an added significance. If the expected life cycle of the system is long, *maintainability* becomes a cost-critical consideration. If the application is an experimental system where the software specifications will have a high rate of change, *flexibility* in the software product is highly desirable. If the functions of the system are expected to be required for a long time, while the system itself may change considerably, *reusability* is of prime importance in those modules which implement the major functions of the system. With the advent of more computer networks and communication capabilities, systems are increasingly being required to interface with other systems and the concept of *interoperability* is extremely important. These and other system characteristics should be considered when identifying the important quality factors.

Table18-3   System Characteristics and Related Quality Factors

CHARACTERISTIC	QUALITY FACTOR
If human lives are affected	Reliability
	Correctness
	Testability
Long life cycle	Maintainability
	Flexibility
	Portability
Real time application	Efficiency
	Reliability
	Correctness
On-board computer application	Efficiency
	Reliability
	Correctness
Processes classified information	Integrity
Interrelated systems	Interoperability

   Consider Life Cycle Implications.   The 11 quality factors identified on the survey can be grouped according to three life cycle activities associated with a delivered software product. These three activities are product operation, product revision, and product transition, The relationship of the quality factors to these activities is shown in Table 18-4. This table also shows where quality indications can be achieved through measurement and where the impact is felt if poor quality is realized. The size of this positive impact determines the cost savings that can be expected if a higher-quality system is achieved through the application of the metrics. This cost savings is somewhat offset by the cost of applying the metrics and the cost of developing the higher quality software product as illustrated in Figure 18-28.

   This cost to implement versus life cycle cost reduction relationship exists for each quality factor. The benefit versus cost-to-provide ratio for each factor is rated as high, medium, or low in the right-hand column of Table 18-4. This relationship and the life cycle implications of the quality factors should be considered when selecting the important factors for a specific system.

Table 18-4 The Impact of Not Specifying or Measuring Software Quality Factors

Life-Cycle Phases Factors	Development			Evaluation	Post-Development			Expected Cost Saved vs. Cost to Provide
	Rqmts Analysis	Design	Code & Debug	System Test	Operation	Revision	Transition	
Correctness	^	^	^	X	X	X		High
Reliability	^	^	^	X	X	X		High
Efficiency	^	^	^		X			Low
Integrity	^	^	^		X			Low
Usability	^	^		X		X		Medium
Maintainability		^	^			X	X	High
Testability		^	^	X		X	X	High
Flexibility		^	^			X	X	Medium
Portability		^	^				X	Medium
Reusability		^	^				X	Medium
Interoperability	^	^		X			X	Low

Legend: ^ — where quality factors should be measured.

X — where impact of poor quality is realized.

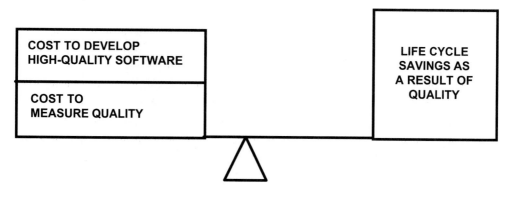

Figure 18-28 Cost vs. benefit tradeoff.

Perform Tradeoffs Among the Tentative List of Quality Factors.   As a result
of the first two steps, a tentative list of quality factors should be produced. The next
step is to consider the interrelationships among the factors selected. Figure 18-29
and Table 18-5 can be used as a guide for determining the relationships between the
quality factors. Some factors are synergistic while others conflict. The impact of conflicting factors is that the cost to implement will increase, which will lower the bene-
fit-to-cost ratio described in the preceding paragraph.

Provide Definitions.   The definitions in Table 18-6 also should be provided as
part of the specification. The relationship of these criteria to the quality factors is
discussed next.

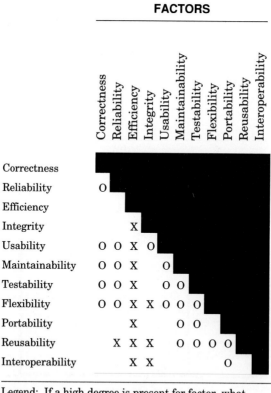

Legend: If a high degree is present for factor, what
degree of quality is expected for the other?

O = High   X = Low

Blank = No relationship or application-dependency

Figure 18-29   Relationships between software quality factors.

Table 18-5 Typical Factor Tradeoffs

Integrity vs. Efficiency	The additional code and processing required to control the access of the software or data usually lengthen run time and require additional storage.
Usability vs. Efficiency	The additional code and processing required to ease an operator's tasks or provide more usable output usually lengthen run time and require additional storage.
Maintainability vs. Efficiency	Optimized code, incorporating intricate coding techniques and direct code, always provides problems to the maintainer. Using modularity, instrumentation, and well-commented high-level code to increase the maintainability of a system usually increases the overhead, resulting in less efficient operation.
Testability vs. Efficiency	The above discussion applies to testing.
Portability vs. Efficiency	The use of direct code or optimized system software or utilities decreases the portability of the system.
Flexibility vs. Efficiency	The generality required for a flexible system increases overhead and decreases the efficiency of the system.
Reusability vs. Efficiency	The above discussion applies to reusability.
Interoperability vs. Efficiency	Again, the added overhead for conversion from standard data representations and the use of interface routines decrease the operating efficiency of the system.
Flexibility vs. Integrity	Flexibility requires very general and flexible data structures. This increases the data security problem.
Reusability vs. Integrity	As in the above discussion, the generality required by reusable software provides severe protection problems.
Interoperability vs. Integrity	Coupled systems allow for more avenues of access and for different users who can access the system. The potential for accidental access of sensitive data increases as the opportunities for deliberate access increase. Often, coupled systems share data or software, which further compounds the security problems.
Reusability vs. Reliability	The generality required by reusable software makes providing error tolerance and accuracy for all cases more difficult.

Table 18-6   Criteria Definitions for Software Quality

CRITERION	DEFINITION
Traceability	Those attributes of the software that provide a thread from the requirements to the implementation with respect to the specific development and operational environment.
Completeness	Those attributes of the software that provide full implementation of the functions required.
Consistency	Those attributes of the software that provide uniform design and implementation techniques and notation.
Accuracy	Those attributes of the software that provide the required precision in calculations and outputs.
Error Tolerance	Those attributes of the software that provide continuity of operation under nonnominal conditions.
Simplicity	Those attributes of the software that provide implementation of functions in the most understandable manner (usually avoidance of practices which increase complexity).
Modularity	Those attributes of the software that provide a structure of highly independent modules.
Generality	Those attributer of the software that provide breadth to the functions performed.
Expandability	Those attributes of the software that provide for expansion of data storage requirements or computational functions.
Instrumentation	Those attributes of the software that provide for the measurement of usage or identification of errors.
Self-Descriptiveness	Those attributes of the software that provide explanation of the implementation of a function.
Execution Efficiency	Those attributes of the software that provide for minimum processing time.
Storage Efficiency	Those attributes of the software that provide for minimum storage requirements during operation.
Access Control	Those attributes of the software that provide for control of the access of software and data.
Access Audit	Those attributes of the software that provide for an audit of the access of software and data.

Operability	Those attributes of the software that determine operation and procedures concerned with the operation of the software.
Training	Those attributes of the software that provide transition from current operation or initial familiarization.
Communicativeness	Those attributes of the software that provide useful inputs and outputs that can be assimilated.
Software System Independence	Those attributes of the software that determine its dependency on the software environment (operating systems. utilities, input/output routines, etc.).
Machine Independence	Those attributes of the software that determine its dependency on the hardware system.
Communications Commonality	Those attributer of the software that provide the use of standard protocols and interface routines.
Data Commonality	Those attributes of the software that provide the use of standard data representations.
Conciseness	Those attributes of the software that provide for implementation of a function with a minimum amount of code.

Procedures for Identifying Critical Software Attributes.   Identifying the next level of quality requirements involves proceeding from the user-oriented quality factors to the software-oriented criteria. Sets of criteria, which are attributes of the software, are related to the various factors by definition. Their identification is automatic and represents a more detailed specification of the quality requirements.

Table 18-7 should be used to identify the software attributes associated with the chosen critical quality factors. For example, using the relationships provided in Table 18-7, the criteria listed in Figure 18-30 would be identified as shown.

18.4   Moving QA from a Concept to a Reality

Quality assurance works if the concept of quality is implemented. It has taken many corporations years to develop a formula that makes quality assurance really effective (see Table 18-8). Although most corporations agree with quality assurance at the conceptual level, when faced with compliance with standards and increased productivity, they encounter many problems. A quality assurance analyst may feel that a system is not complying to standards, and the systems analysts often feel that in order to comply with standards the implemented system will be late and run over budget. Usually the decision is made to get it in on time and worry about quality later. The price corporations pay for this compromise is huge.

Table 18-7   Software Criteria and Related Quality Factors

Factor	Software Criteria	Factor	Software Criteria
Correctness	Traceability	Flexibility	Modularity
	Consistency		Generality
	Completeness		Expandability
Reliability	Error Tolerance	Testability	Simplicity
	Consistency		Modularity
	Accuracy		Instrumentation
	Simplicity		Self-Descriptiveness
Efficiency	Storage Efficiency	Portability	Modularity
	Execution Efficiency		Self-Descriptiveness
Integrity	Access Control		Machine Independence
	Access Audit		Software System Independence
Usability	Operability	Reusability	Generality
	Training		Modularity
	Communicativeness		Software System Independence
Maintainability	Consistency	Interoperability	Modularity
			Communication Commonality
			Data Commonality

Table 18-8   What Makes QA Actually Work?

• Must go from a CONCEPT to actual IMPLEMENTATION.

• Everybody agrees at the conceptual level.

• Needed:

  – An embodiment (organized set of QA procedures used as part of everyday routine).

  – Centralized function (someone who is responsible).

18.4.1 Defining and Enforcing QA as a Priority Activity

Excitement and enthusiasm over quality is a goal itself. Quality assurance personnel are marketing people—they have to sell their staffs on the fact that quality is important. Japanese automobile factory managers post on their walls the names of their workers and the number of defects reported from the field based on the parts made by the responsible workers. This policy could be adopted in data processing departments. If the names of erring programmers were put on a chart with check marks by their names for each problem inflicted on users, some different concerns about quality would evolve. One organization has bestowed the name "Captain Quality" on its quality assurance manager, who becomes excited over various concepts and gets the staff equally enthused.

The quality assurance examination can be compared to a medical examination. Certain tests must be done to determine if the "patient" is well or sick. There can be no guesswork on what quality is: quality must be predetermined and then checks made to assure it exists as specified. Resistance to change is a problem managers have in getting quality accepted. (See Table 18-9 for the typical QA implementation problems.) When people have done something a certain way and they are asked to change, they will fight the concept. Still, through its acceptance of all concerned the image of quality assurance simply as a policeman must be overcome.

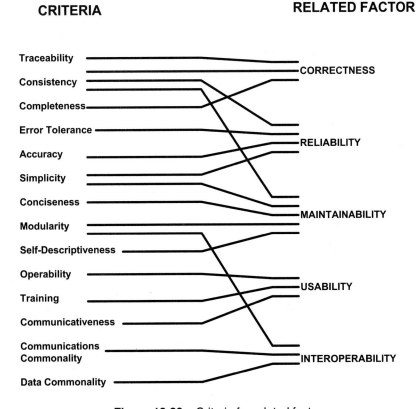

Figure 18-30 Criteria for related factors.

Table 18-9   Typical Problems in Implementing QA

PROBLEM	QA APPROACH OR SOLUTION
Resistance to change	Education, successful pilot project, some will never be converted.
Big brother	Education, QA works with PM, matters resolved at lowest level.
Not responsive	Skilled competent QA staff, QA must assist team.
No teeth	Approval authority, management follow-up.
Too burdensome	Less paper-driven, practical procedures, flexible.
Too conceptual	A prescribed routine, habit.

In order for a quality assurance group to function effectively, it must be backed by management. Management must make the staff aware of what it will and won't support. The systems analyst must be made to believe he or she is being judged on user satisfaction, and getting projects done on time and within budget. Failure to receive a salary increase when expected because of a system being poor in quality will unequivocally show the systems analyst the importance the company attaches to quality.

It is very difficult for many systems analysts to be enthusiastic about quality because a lot of other pressures take priority on their time. To implement quality concepts in their organizations, companies have devised several seemingly drastic means to assure quality is controlled. One company has given the production library and source library to quality assurance. If a systems analyst wants to place a compiled program into production, it first must be approved by quality assurance. Before programs can be placed into the source library, the data processing analyst must first write design specifications and submit them to quality assurance. Another company requires the systems analysts to sit in the computer room every time a program is run on which adequate operations documentation is not completed; the company schedules the run from midnight to 2:00 AM to get the point across. Still another company fails to promote or transfer people until their systems are certified by quality assurance.

18.4.2 Positioning the QA Manager

The QAI study revealed that the higher in the organization the centralization of the function reports, the more successful it is (see Table 18-10). If it is too low, it is ignored, and being too high can also cause problems; the person managing this activity—the QA manager—needs to be placed on a par with the other managers in the department. The study showed that pay grades for quality assurance managers range from three below a senior systems analyst to three above, which is a wide range in the organizational structure. The quality assurance manager must strive to get cooperation from other department and middle managers, to get involved in the operation and application of the program or user's system, and to get involved in the development of standards because quality problems occur throughout the organization.

Table 18-10 Centralized QA Function

- QA must he placed at high level in organization.

- If too low, it will be ignored.

- If too high, it may lose detailed, operational effectiveness.

- QA and project manager must strive for concurrence.

18.4.3 Opening Communications from Vendor to User

Some time ago, I ordered an animal trap through the mail. When it finally arrived, I eagerly ripped open the package only to find a lot of unassembled parts. I looked in vain for instructions to assemble the parts into an animal trap, but since the instructions were missing I worked with the parts until completely frustrated. The next morning I called up the company to request that they forward me the instructions for assembling the animal trap, only to be informed by a young lady on the other end that they were only in the business of making parts—they didn't make instructions. My next question to her was as to what kind of animal I could catch in the event I was lucky enough to get the trap put together. She quickly responded that I could catch anything I wanted with it—they didn't make decisions.

Many software products obtained from vendors come without instructions, like those parts in the box. There are things called controls and features, but nobody tells you how to put these together or how to optimize the software for your organization. This lack of communication between seller and buyer or developer and user forces many organizations to rely on the decisions of software programmers who are usually not familiar with the buyers' or users' business and may have no more than minimal loyalty to their own organizations. These software programmers have made major quality decisions with which each organization's quality assurance department is forced to understand and work.

18.4.4 Growth and Maturity of QA

The National Institute of Standards and Technology defines quality as a three-phase approach: (1) the development of the standards, procedures, and guidelines; (2) automating segments of the Information Services process; and (3) automating and integrating individual segments (see Table 18-11). Phase 1 includes the acquisition and use of a systems development life cycle. This phase has brought order out of some of the chaos that existed during the 1960s. Phase 2 involves improving quality by automating the individual pieces, such as data dictionaries and libraries. In Phase 3, the individual pieces are automated and integrated. For example, the data dictionary is integrated into the database management system; and high-level programming languages will unify the programs under one roof, i.e., make them relatively computer-independent, as well as speed their development. This integrated systems environment is very important in increasing productivity in a quality environment.

Quality assurance is a new, rapidly growing discipline implemented in hundreds of companies. While in many companies it is still a fairly small function, it is maturing and in some companies involves 50 or more people within data processing departments of 50–600. When it gets larger, quality assurance encompasses the disciplines of database administrations, education, production control, software programs, development of standards, compliance with standards, project review, project scheduling, tracking of projects, error analysis, and S.W.A.T.-team concepts to make data processing work. Two especially promising techniques to define and measure quality, supplementing the foregoing, are metrics and risk analysis,

A successful quality assurance function can be recognized as the group that does many of the nonproduction functions. These people, who are not building, maintaining, or operating systems, belong under the quality banner because the discipline of assurance in all functions is necessary, Stand-alone standards require real-world interaction with projects. Enforcing and tailoring standards give a different view from writing standards. Good standards are essential because systems analysts/programmers will not follow them if they are bad.

The effective quality assurance group increases productivity rather dramatically. As experience in the quality assurance group grows, the corporation experiences fewer problems, fewer user complaints, fewer requests for changes, quicker maintenance, and fewer hang-ups in the computer area. The quality assurance group that is able to focus on the concept of quality and productivity pays for itself over and over again.

With management support and good objectives, quality assurance is the solution to productivity in the 1980s and beyond. The quality assurance function in a data processing department makes its members visible within their corporation as a function that has done something positive to improve quality and productivity.

Table 18-11   Phases of Quality

PHASE 1
STANDARDS, PROCEDURES, GUIDELINES
PHASE 2
AUTOMATING SEGMENTS OF THE IS PROCESS
PHASE 3
AUTOMATING AND INTEGRATING INDIVIDUAL SEGMENTS

General References

Perry, William E., *The Hatching Trilogy*, Quality Assurance Institute, Suite 305, 7575 Dr. Phillips Blvd., Orlando, Florida 32819, 1986.
QAI Website: qaiusa.com

Statistical Methods Applied to Software Quality Control

C. K. Cho, Ph.D.
Computa, Inc.

19.1 Quality Control

The term "quality control" in the context of this chapter refers to a powerful and widely used tool to ensure product quality in modern manufacturing industries. It is a tool developed during World War II based on statistical methods including random sampling techniques, testing, measurements, inspection, defective cause findings, improvements, statistical inference, and acceptance sampling. During World War II, contracts for military procurement mandated that suppliers employ statistical quality control procedures in their processing and that random samples of finished goods be submitted for quality conformance inspection. Since then, the tool has been widely used in the United States and abroad and has become important to agencies of the federal government in enforcing production of quality products as well as to consumer groups. It also has become a competitive weapon enabling manufacturing organizations to survive in modern marketing. It is a simple extension to apply quality control to control software quality during software development.

Quality control activities in manufacturing industries may be summarized as follows from Cho: [7, 15]

1. *Set Quality Standard.* For each quality characteristic, a standard should be established as a product specification with which to compare the characteristic of the finished product. For example, the diameter and the acceptable tolerance variation of a steel ball to be used in a ball bearing should be specified, such as 0.25 +/– 0.001 in. If the diameter of a finished ball falls within 0.0249 to 0.251 in., then the diameter of the ball is considered as acceptable. Otherwise it is considered defective.

2. *Plan to Attain the Quality Standard.* The achievement of the product quality requires careful planning and engineering of manufacturing process and equipment, acquisition of good quality materials, training operators, and so on.

3. *Determine Preventive Methods to Control Manufacturing Process.* The old saying "it is better to prevent than to cure" holds true in quality control. During the manufacturing process all possible factors affecting the quality characteristics of the product must be carefully controlled. For example, the purity of raw materials, temperature, and pressure control can affect the diameter of a steel ball.

4. *Determine Conformance of Quality.* The determination includes
   a. interpretation of the product quality standard
   b. random sampling of product units for inspection
   c. inspection and measurements of the sampled product units
   d. comparisons of c with a for each sampled product unit
   e. judgment of conformance of quality of each product unit
   f. acceptance or rejection of the product lot by statistical methods
   g. documentation of the inspection data

It is from these principles that software quality control flows, especially in relation to steps a through g of item 4—Determine Conformance of Quality.

A manufacturing industry factory uses a process to make raw materials into useable products. It may be expressed mathematically as

$$U = F(R)$$

where R is a set of raw materials and U is a set of product units.

A factory possesses two major characteristics:

1. its raw materials are well defined; types and quality characteristics such as properties and chemical components of each material type are specifiedd
2. the product unit and product unit defectiveness, quality characteristics of each product unit are also well-defined.

These characteristics enable the application of quality control to ensure the quality of the products for the consumers.

The relationship between quality control and a manufacturing process, called the *quality cycle*, is depicted in Figure 19-1. The cycle starts with product concept formulation after human needs have been identified. The characteristics of the product are then determined. The product is designed for manufacturing; methods and engineering approaches are then devised to make the product; machinery and raw materials are procured; and equipment and instruments are installed. Finally, manufacturing begins. The products are then inspected to verify conformance of quality against the characteristics. Consumers buy and use the product with their experience being fed back to the cycle. The cycle then starts all over again.

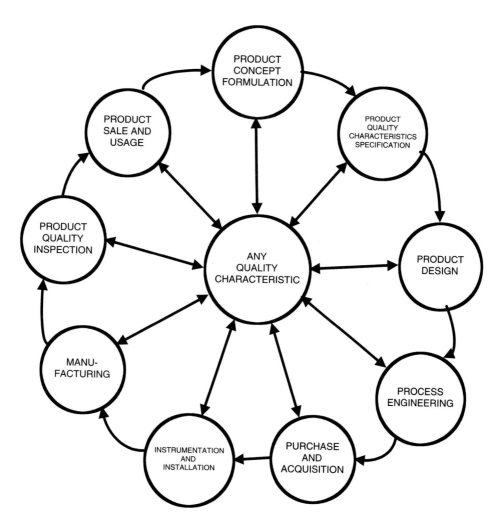

Figure 19-1 Manufacturing quality cycle. (From Cho, C. K., *An Introduction to Software Quality Control*, New York: John Wiley & Sons 1980. Copyright © 1980 by John Wiley & Sons, Inc. Reprinted by permission of John Wiley & Sons, Inc.)

Mass inspection of product units in determining quality conformance may not be feasible or economical due to the size of the product population. Therefore, statistical sampling inspection comes to play a major role here. Sampling inspection usually involves an estimate of the population defective rate θ. The rate is defined as $\theta = D/N$, where D is the number of defective units in the product population and N is the total number of product units in the population. The estimate of θ can be easily done by using the binomial distribution, important in the study of probability, statistics, and quality control. The application of the distribution often arises when sampling from a finite population consisting of a finite number of units with replacement, or from an infinite population consisting of an infinite number of units with or without replacement.

In any factory, it is hardly possible to produce a defect-free product lot, therefore, the conformance of product quality is usually measured by a defective rate less than an acceptable number, e.g., $\theta < 0.01$. With a statistical sampling method, a confidence level such as 95 percent certainty can be imposed on the conclusion of the defective rate.

There is another measure in determining acceptability of a product population, called the *acceptance sampling*. In this method, a sample of K units is taken and inspected. If the sample contains less than an acceptable number of defective units c, then the population is acceptable, else unacceptable. In this sampling, there are two types of risks involved in reaching a conclusion: the *producer's risk* and the *user's risk*. The former is the risk assumed by the producer in having a good quality product lot rejected by the sampling method. The latter is the risk assumed by the user in accepting a poor-quality product lot.

The details of the sampling techniques may be found in Cho [7] and Juran [8]. For the purpose of this chapter, only the sampling inspection for estimating the population defective rate will be discussed with examples.

19.2 Software Quality Control

An analogy can be drawn between a manufacturing factory and a piece of software. Software input and output are the raw materials and finished goods of a factory.

If the software output is defined in terms of "product unit," then the output is a collection of product units called the *output population* of the software. For any nontrivial program, the population contains a very large number of units. The goal of software testing is to find certain characteristics of the population such as the ratio of the number of defective units in the population to the total number of units in the population. The ratio may be called the defective rate of the population and may be imposed on the software as the *software quality index*. Clearly a mass inspection of the population to find the rate is prohibitive. An efficient method is through statistical random sampling. With statistical quality control, one can build confidence in the quality of the population in numerical terms.

With this concept, the quality of the data must be built in from the beginning of manufacturing to the hand of the user. Similar to a manufacturing process, there is a close relationship called the *software quality cycle* between quality control and development of the software, as shown in Figure 19-2. An examination of Figures 19-1 and 19-2 reveals a close parallelism.

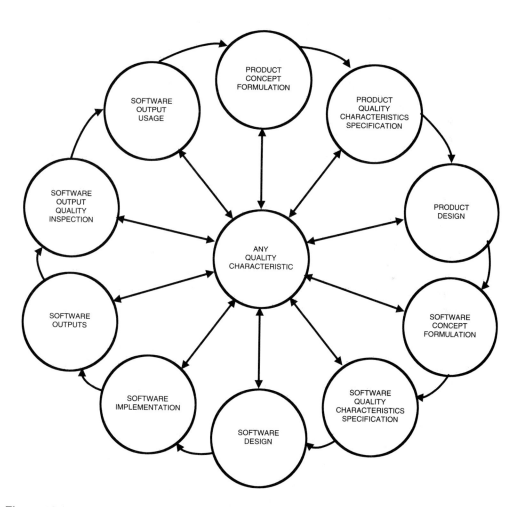

Figure 19-2 Software quality cycle. (From C. K. Cho, *An Introduction to Software Quality Control.* New York: John Wiley & Sons, 1980. Copyright © 1980 by John Wiley & Sons, Inc. Reprinted by permission of John Wiley & Sons. Inc.)

But if one investigates current software practices (Figure 19-3) in terms of the quality cycle in Figure 19-2, one would immediately notice three important ingredients missing: product concept formulation, product quality characteristics specification, and product design, including definitions of product units and product *unit defectiveness*. Because of these missing ingredients, as shown in Figure 19-3, the tool of quality control cannot be applied.

A methodology, called quality programming, incorporating the tool of quality control along with the software quality cycle of Figure 19-2 will be discussed with an example.

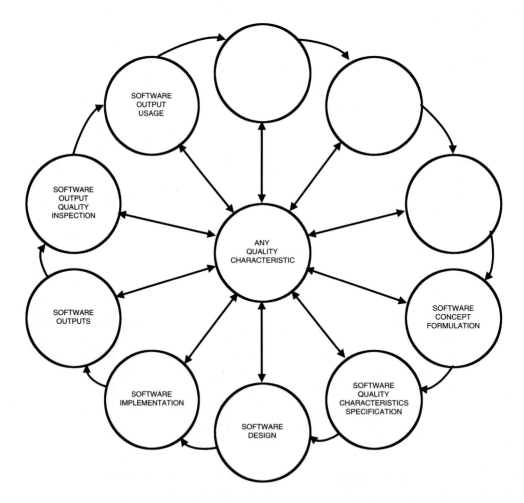

Figure 19-3   Incomplete software quality cycle, modified from Cho. [7]

19.3   Quality Programming

A software development process that implements the quality cycle of Figure 19-2 incorporating the tool of quality control is shown in Figure 19-4. Given a system to be developed, a model is developed to analyze and understand the "problem." The modeling activities may take several iterations (see backward arrow from modeling to problem in Figure 19-4 to thoroughly understand the problem. Models including a description of the problem and the product to be generated by the software are built to form the basis of product design and the concept of the software being developed.

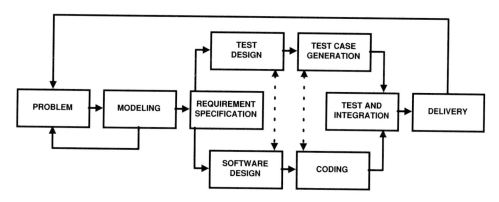

FIGURE 19-4   Quality programming life cycle.

Requirements are then generated as a result of the modeling activity. Included in the requirements are software and test requirements. Software requirements define the functions the software is to perform and the quality characteristics such as response time, throughput, understandability, and portability. Test requirements define the product units and product unit defectiveness for statistical sampling, sampling methods for estimating the defective rate of the software population with which to judge software quality, statistical inference methods and confidence level of software output population quality, the acceptable software defective rate, and test input unit generation methods.

With well-defined requirements, software development can be divided into two channels that can proceed concurrently: software design and implementation, and software test design and implementation. Top-down design, structured programming. and critical-module-first implementation methods are used in the software channel. The formulation of sampling plans for estimating software defective rate and population acceptability, the design of input units, and the implementation of the sampling plans are used in the test channel. During the design and implementation phases, interfaces between the channels are incorporated to ensure that quality is built into the software at every stage of development. The two channels meet at the time of testing and integration. Testing and integration are performed again on a most-critical-module-first basis to ensure that the software is integrated on a quality-spare-part basis. If the software passes the test satisfying the test requirements, delivery to the user takes place. The user employs the quality control tool to determine the acceptability of the software output population, in turn the basis for accepting or rejecting the software. With the user's experience, modification, enhancement, and maintenance start from the beginning of the cycle again.

19.3.1   I. Modeling

Modeling is the activity of understanding the problems under consideration. The following are the major tasks that must be done well before software development begins:

A. Problem Description

This is the description of what the software being developed must do. An exact, unambiguous, and complete description is essential to smooth the development of the software, and is an integral part of a document to be produced at the modeling stage.

B. Types of Raw Materials

Definitions of the types of raw materials required are an integral part of a plan in building a factory. For any factory, the types, quality characteristics, and sources of raw materials, and the means of transporting the materials to the factory, are well-defined before the factory is built. By analogy, the types of raw materials of a piece of software are the input variables. The variables possess certain quality characteristics, such as numerical including range, nonnumerical, or both. The source(s) of the raw materials can be a database, a terminal, or a real-time data acquisition system. An exact and complete definition of the raw materials constitutes an integral part of the modeling activity.

C. Characteristics of Raw Materials

Once the types and sources of all of the raw materials of a factory have been identified, the characteristics of each of the raw materials must also be analyzed: properties, chemical components, and so on. Are the characteristics of the materials suitable for the manufacturing? What side-effect does each characteristic have on the operations of the factory? Are there any constraints in using the materials? Is there any substitute for each of the materials? These are but some questions that should be answered before the use of these materials is finalized.

Similarly. the characteristics of the input variables of a piece of software to be developed should be analyzed. Is a variable assuming numerical values? What are the lower and upper bounds of the variable? If the variable assumes nonnumerical values, what kinds of data are to be assigned to the variable? What are the components of the variable? (e.g., if NAME is a variable containing people's names, the components would be FIRST NAME, MIDDLE NAME, and LAST NAME.) What are the characteristics of each of the components? (e.g., no numerical characters are to be in a FIRST NAME.)

D. Rules of Using Raw Materials

The order, and in many cases timing, in which raw materials are entered into a manufacturing process must be strictly followed. A variation of the rules may lead to poor-quality products, waste, or even disaster. Such rules must be defined before a factory is built.

Similarly, rules governing the use of data in a piece of software must be defined. For example, whether or not LAST NAME should precede FIRST NAME and MIDDLE NAME, or vice versa, in a database management system should be decided well in advance.

E. Definition of a Product Unit

The capacity of a factory can be measured in many ways. In the manufacturing of discrete products such as screws, nuts, and automobiles, capacity may be measured by the number of units produced per day. In the production of continuous products, such as gasoline and flour, measurement can be by volume or weight, such as gallons or tons, per day. The measurement unit (gallon or ton), may be considered as the product unit. With the definition of a product unit, product quality inspections using the quality control tool introduced in Section 19.1 can be conducted.

If a piece of software is viewed as a factory, the definition of product unit is necessary for software development. The quality of the software product population can be inspected using the same quality control tool. A piece of software is said to be of good quality only when it is able to produce a good-quality product population.

The lack of product unit definition in the software industry has been observed to be the root of many of the technical problems listed discussed throughout this *Handbook*. Product unit definition is crucial to solving these problems in developing high-quality and cost-effective software.

(The "product unit" produced by software should not be confused with the development unit produced by people. The latter is an entity such as a routine, module, or program which, as a productivity measure, is usually measured in terms of lines of code generated by programmers per day. The use of "product unit" in this chapter specifically refers to the output produced by software. analogous to the output of a factory.)

F. Definition of Product Unit Defectiveness

As the definition of product unit is the basis on which to apply the quality control tool, the definition of product unit defectiveness forms the basis on which to judge quality conformance of a product unit. The latter definition is generally difficult for a particular product. For example, an automobile is a product unit. The defectiveness of the unit may not be easily defined: it involves the identification of the quality characteristics of a car, such as weight, physical properties, chemical components of each spare part, gas mileage, tire life, the length of normal battery life, and so forth. It also involves the definition of defectiveness in terms of each of the characteristics. For example, gas mileage must be 30 miles per gallon on the highway; the mean time to failure of a battery is three years. The definitions become the quality standards that govern the manufacture of a product.

Similar observations can be made in viewing a piece of software as a factory. Without quality standards, it is difficult to attain the goal of developing high-quality and cost-effective software.

G. Methods of Manufacturing

Usually a product consists of many parts and more than one method can be used to produce a part. Therefore, many methods need to be investigated before determining which method to use to manufacture which part of the product. In addition, methods of assembling the parts into the product need to be studied to ensure smooth production.

Similarly, many methods can be used to solve a problem in software development. For example, there are many methods of finding the roots of equations of one variable, such as the bisection method, Newton's algorithm, secant method, fixed-point iteration, the modified regular falsi, Steffensen iteration method, and so on. As many methods as possible should be studied and documented at this point of development for later use.

H. Characteristics of Factory

The characteristics can be the production capacity, speed, size of the factory, types of buildings, materials used to build the factory, storage capacity for incoming raw materials, means of transportation within a factory, ways of handling materials in the factory, and so on. These characteristics should be well-planned before the factory is designed and built.

Similarly, the characteristics of a piece of software can be the output data generation capacity, speed, memory size, data storage capacity, data flows, and the like. They must be studied at this stage of software development.

I. Manufacturing Process

Since a product usually consists of many parts and the manufacturing of the parts requires many raw materials and some intermediate products fabricated within a factory, the flow of these materials and intermediate products constitutes a complex network. The smooth movement of the object is essential to efficient manufacturing of the product. When and how to inspect the quality of the raw materials and intermediate products to ensure that the finished goods are to be of good quality need to be studied at the beginning of this stage of development.

Similarly, the way the input data is flowing into a piece of software: the temporary storage of intermediate data, the way the data is structured to be processed before output data is produced should be analyzed to facilitate later development of the software.

J. Method of Building a Factory

While there are many ways of building a factory, the selection of one has a significant impact on how the building should be designed. Should the factory be built and installed on its site? Should it be fabricated somewhere else and transported to the site and then assembled? Should a model be built first? What effects will each building method have? Questions of this kind should be fully investigated.

The same questions can be asked of software development. Should the software be developed from scratch? Are there any existing software packages available? Should a software model be developed first? And so on. Answers to these questions will greatly facilitate the later software design stage.

19.3.2 II. Requirements Specification

The requirements for software development can be specified in two classes: software and test. The first includes the input domain, functions, and characteristics of the software being considered. The second consists of a test plan with which the software is to be tested and accepted. The document produced in the modeling stage is essential to this important software development task.

Software Requirements. Software requirements include input, processing, and output descriptions of the software. The input requirements consist of the types, and characteristics of raw materials and the rules governing the use of the raw materials. The process requirements contain exhaustive listings of the functions the software must have. The output requirements include man-machine interface and other characteristics of the products to be generated by the software. The following are the detailed descriptions of the requirements.

A. Input Domain

The input domain of a piece of software is the representation of all possible input data and the rules governing the construction of input to be processed by the software. With a well-defined input domain, random input units can be constructed to test the software. The input data used in daily production is in fact a subset of all of the possible input that can be generated from the domain. The input domain of a piece of software can be represented by a symbolic input attribute decomposition (SIAD) tree (a detailed description of the tree is given in Cho [7]). The following example is a demonstration of a SIAD tree representing mailing list software that maintains the accuracy of mailing addresses.

An address can be decomposed into name, street, city, state, and zip code. A name can be decomposed into first name, middle name, and last name. A first name can be either a full first name or a first initial. It is obvious that the decomposition of the components can be done into a number of levels. The results can be arranged in a tree, as shown in Figure 19-5.

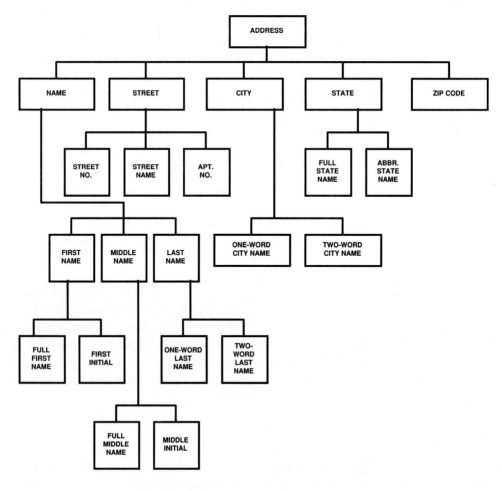

Figure 19-5   A tree structure of an address.

The tree may be represented in a SIAD tree, as in Table 19-1. The tree has four columns: index, tree symbol, tree element, and rule index. The indices are for sampling use. The tree symbols preserve the tree structure of the tree elements in Figure 19-5. A tree element is a node in Figure 19-5 with some explanation of the node. A rule index points to a rule that governs the use of the tree element in constructing an input unit.

Table 19-1 Example Nonnumerical SIAD Tree

INDEX	TREE SYMBOL	TREE ELEMENT	RULE INDEX
1	X1	ADDRESS, N1 alphanumeric characters	1 13
2	X1, 1	NAME, N2 alphabetic characters	2 12 13 14 16
3	X1, 1, 1	FIRST NAME, N3 alphabetic characters	3 13 14 15 16
4	X1, 1, 1, 1	FULL FIRST NAME, N3 alphabetic characters	3 13 14 15 16
5	X1, 1, 1, 2	FIRST INITIAL, N3 alphabetic characters	3 13 14 15 17
6	X1, 1, 2	MIDDLE NAME, N4 alphabetic characters	4 13 14 15 16
7	X1, 1, 2, 1	FULL MIDDLE NAME, N4 alphabetic characters	4 13 14 15 16
8	X1, 1, 2, 2	MIDDLE INITIAL N4 alphabetic characters	4 13 14 15 17
9	X1, 1, 3	LAST NAME, N5 alphabetic characters	5 13 1416
10	X1, 1, 3, 1	ONE-WORD LAST NAME, N5 alphabetic characters	5 13 14 17 19
11	X1, 1, 3, 2	MULTIWORD LAST NAME, N5 alphabetic characters	5 13 14 15 18
12	X1, 2	STREET, N6 alphanumeric characters	6 13 15 16
13	X1, 2, 1	STREET NO., N7 alphanumeric characters	7 13 16

(continued)

Table 19-1   *(continued)*

INDEX	TREE SYMBOL	TREE ELEMENT	RULE INDEX
14	X1, 2, 2	STREET NAME, N8 alphanumeric characters	8 13 15
15	X1, 2, 3	APARTMENT NO., N9 alphanumeric characters	9 13 15 17 19 20
16	X1, 3	CITY NAME, N10 alphabetic characters	10 13 14 15 17 19
17	X1, 3, 1	ONE-WORD CITY NAME, N10 alphabetic characters	10 13 14 17 19
18	X1, 3, 2	TWO-WORD CITY NAME, N10 alphabetic characters	10 13 14 15 19
19	X1, 4	STATE, N11 alphabetic characters	11 13 14 15 17 19
20	X1, 4, 1	FULL STATE NAME, N11 alphabetic characters	11 13 14 17 19
21	XI, 4, 2	ABBREVIATED STATE NAME, N11 alphabetic characters	11 13 14 15 17 19
22	X1,5	ZIP CODE, N12 numeric characters	12 13 15 17 19

The rules governing the use of tree elements in a SIAD tree can be listed as shown in Table 19-2. A rule index is used to identify a rule to be used. The rule description is the rule of interest. The subrule index points to a subrule to supplement the use of the rule, as shown in Table 19-3.

Examples of constructing input units using the SIAD tree are given in Section 19.3, subsection II, Requirements Specification, Sampling Methods.

The foregoing discussion involves the representation of a nonnumerical input domain by a SIAD tree. Similarly, a numerical input domain can also be represented by a SIAD tree. An example is given in Section 19.4, subsection II, Practical Examples, Reusable Software.

B. Process

In building a manufacturing factory, the process stage includes the description of all of the processes required to produce the goods that must be developed into real processes. Similarly, in developing software, a complete description of all the functions must be created and developed in real executable code. The information given in Section 19.3, Modeling, is to be incorporated into the process section of the requirements document.

C. Output

Software output requirements include man-machine interface, the characteristics of the products to be generated by the software, response time, data input-output format and contents, and interpretation of data produced by the software.

Table 19-2   Input Domain Rules for the SIAD Tree in Table 19-1

RULE INDEX	RULE DESCRIPTION	SUBRULE INDEX
1	$N1 = N3 + N4 + N5 + N7 + N8 + N9 + N10 + N11 + N12$	1 2 3 4 5 6 7 8 9
2	$N2 = N3 + N4 + N5$	1 2 3
3	$N3$	1
4	$N4$	2
5	$N5$	3
6	$N6 = N7 + N8 + N9$	4 5 6
7	$N7$	4
8	$N8$	5
9	$N9$	6
10	$N10$	7
11	$N11$	8
12	$N12$	9
13	Excluding characters + * / ' " $ & # @ / = : :) (! ? =] [% ¢	
14	Excluding characters 0 1 2 3 4 5 6 7 8 9	
15	Including one character . or space	
16	Including character -	
17	Excluding character -	
18	Including character ,	
19	Excluding character ,	
20	Including space	

Table 19-3   Example Subrules of the Input Domain Rules in Table 19-2

SUBRULE INDEX	SUBRULE DESCRIPTION	REMARK
1	$1 \leq N3 \leq 24$	Length of FIRST NAME
2	$1 \leq N4 \leq 24$	Length of MIDDLE NAME
3	$2 \leq N5 \leq 40$	Length of LAST NAME
4	$1 \leq N7 \leq 10$	Length of STREET NO.
5	$1 \leq N8 \leq 20$	Length of STREET NAME
6	$1 \leq N9 \leq 10$	Length of APARTMENT NO.
7	$2 \leq N10 \leq 20$	Length of CITY NAME
8	$2 \leq N11 \leq 20$	Length of STATE NAME
9	$5 \leq N12 \leq 9$	Length of ZIP CODE

Test Requirements.   Test requirements are specified as the criteria for software testing and acceptance upon completion. They consist of definition of product units, definition of product unit defectiveness, seven test methods (regular, weighted, boundary, invalid, special, efficiency, and stress performance tests), software acceptance criteria (producer's risk—risk assumed by the producer whose good products are rejected using the QP technology; buyer's risk—risk assumed by the buyer accepting poor quality products using the QP technology), sampling methods, and software reliability confidence level are among the test requirements.

A. Definition of a Product Unit

Once the modeling activities in Section 19.3 have been completed, the definition of product unit is transferred here into the requirement specification document. The information collected in Section 19.3, Modeling, paragraphs C, D, E, and F, is reviewed and refined to ensure that the definitions are correct.

B. Definition of Product Unit Defectiveness

The information obtained in Section 19.3, Modeling, paragraphs E and F, is entered into the requirement specification document.

C. Software Acceptance Criteria

With the definitions of product unit and product unit defectiveness. the acceptance of a piece of software is equivalent to that of the product population the software generates. Criteria are needed to determine the acceptability of the population. Such criteria can be divided into two classes: population defective rate estimate and population acceptance.

a. Population Defective Rate Estimate Criteria. The criteria are the values such as the *desired accuracy factor* and the *confidence level*. A sampling plan for estimating the defective rate of a population can be formulated, as explained in Cho. [7, 15]

One other criterion is required to decide the acceptability of the population—the acceptable defective rate. Intuitively, the output population defective rate must be 0 to be acceptable. But because of the size of the population, a mass inspection of it is not feasible. The sample size approaches infinity when the defective rate is 0. Therefore, after the defective rate has been estimated, the acceptability of the population is judged by the estimated defective rate being less than the acceptable defective rate.

b. Population Acceptance Criteria. There is another measure in determining acceptability of a product population, called the *acceptance sampling*. In this method, a sample of K units is taken and inspected. If the sample contains less than an acceptable number of defective units c, then the population is acceptable, else unacceptable. In this sampling, there are two types of risks involved in reaching a conclusion: the *producer's risk* and the *user's risk*. The former is the risk assumed by the producer in having a good quality product lot rejected by the sampling method. The latter is the risk assumed by the user in accepting a poor quality product lot. With these criteria, an acceptance sampling plan can be determined, i.e., the sample size and the acceptable number of defective units in the sample can be decided statistically to provide a fair protection to both of the parties. The details of the formulation of a plan may be found in Cho. [7, 15]

D. Sampling Methods

The purpose of defining a software product unit is twofold: testing and usage. When a piece of software is viewed as a factory, daily processing of input units into product units becomes conceptually equivalent to taking random product units from the software's population. If the product units in the population are all of good quality, then the units taken will be of good quality.

Since the software product population is extremely large, and may be considered infinite, generating of the entire population and then taking a random sample from the population for estimating the defective rate is impossible. An easy way is through random construction of input units from the SIAD tree of the software. The random sampling may be done in four ways:

1. *Regular Sampling.* Let $w_1, w_2, \ldots, w_t$ be the weights to be placed on the input variables $v_1, v_2, \ldots, v_t$ (or on the SIAD tree elements $e_1, e_2, \ldots, e_t$) of the software. If $w_1 = w_2 = \ldots = w_t$, then the sampling is called regular sam-

pling. In other words, each tree element in the SIAD tree has an equal chance of being taken from the tree for the construction of an input unit. This is a simulation of inputs in daily usage of the software.

2. *Weighted Sampling.* The sampling method is the same as basic sampling, except some of the weights $w_1, w_2, \ldots, w_t$ are not equal, e.g., $w_1 \neq w_5$.

3. *Boundary Sampling.* This method is the same as basic sampling, except that each numerical variable of a piece of software assumes either its lower or upper bound value. If there are s such variables, $u_1, u_2, \ldots, u_s$, then there are 2^s input units of 2^s product units in the population. For example, there will be 2^{31} or 2,147,483,648 units that can be generated if the number of numerical variables is 31. Clearly, inspecting 2,147,483,648 units exhaustively is uneconomical if not impossible. It is seen that random sampling of product units from the population is an easy and economical way of inspecting the quality of the population.

4. *Invalid Sampling.* This method is the same as regualar sampling, except that some of the variables $v_1, v_2, \ldots, v_t$ assumes some invalid data, e.g., assigning the value outside of the defined lower and upper bound of a numerical variable or embedding some invalid characters into the datum of a nonnumerical variable.

It is seen that a product population can be generated under each of the sampling methods. The software acceptance criteria given in the previous subsection can be imposed on each of the populations in the requirement specification document.

E. Software Quality Confidence Level

The user can impose the quality requirement on the object software, e.g., the population defective rate to be less than 0.001 with a confidence level of 95 percent and an accuracy factory of 0.01 for sampling purposes. For further details see Cho. [15]

19.3.3　III. Concurrent Software Design and Test Design

Software design and test design are two major tasks in the design stage of software development. With a well-prepared model and requirements specification documents, the tasks can proceed concurrently.

There are many software design methods in practice, such as structured design, [9] structured analysis and design technique, [10] and object-oriented design. [11] They may be classified into two groups: *function-oriented* and *object-oriented* methods. The first deals with general development of software using most programming languages, while the second is similar to the first but more suitable for developing software in the new Ada programming language. Since the second method requires the Ada language, only the function-oriented design method is discussed here. The object-oriented design with Quality Programming may be found in Cho. [15]

Software Design. The major design tasks of the quality programming method include:

A. Derivation of software functions from a software model.
B. Organizing the functions into a tree structure (each of the functions becomes a software module).
C. Generating input domain of each module in performing the function of the module.
D. Design of user interface.
E. Design of module interface.
F. Design of module.

The design tasks should be performed in that order and should be refined with test design upon completion.

A. Derivation of Software Functions from a Model
In any manufacturing, the building of a factory requires many blueprints. Each blueprint represents a portion of the factory that performs a specific function. In order to generate the blueprints, the functions of the factory must first be identified. The identification of such functions are the results of studying the model of the factory, as described in Section 19.3.

B. Organizing the Functions into a Tree Structure
After all of the functions have been identified, their interrelationships are defined. The functions are then organized into a tree structure to illustrate the relationships. Such a structure allows understanding of a complicated problem on a tree level-by-level basis. A function at a level in the tree is an abstraction of the subfunction(s) at a lower level and hides some detailed information from the subfunction(s). The resultant tree structure becomes the structure of the software being developed.

C. Generating Input Domain of Each Module in Performing the Function
Similar to a software system, the function of a module is to produce an output from an input. The input domain of a module must also be designed for module interfaces and can also be represented in a SIAD tree as described in Section 19.3, Requirements Specification. A module SIAD tree is required because:

- it insures testability of a module, since inputs to the module can be constructed from the tree to facilitate test design,

- it forms a convenient basis for module interfaces,
- it enables concurrent development of module design and module test design.

D. Design of the User Interface

User interface consists of input preparation and output interpretation. Human factors must be considered in designing such an interface. e.g., easy to use and difficult to misuse.

E. Design of Module Interfaces

The design is based on the SIAD tree of a module. The following factors should be considered in designing module interfaces:

- To avoid bad common coupling, two modules should not be "glued" together by the interface. A module, once developed, should be reusable. For example, a variable in an interface should be given a significant name within the module, instead of being tied to the name of the function or calling module.
- To avoid control coupling. the logic of a module should not depend on the logic of a calling module and vice versa.

F. Design of Module

A module consists of two parts: data structure and algorithm. There are many data structures and algorithms that can be developed to perform the intended function of a module. Design alternatives and simplicity should be considered in designing a module.

Module design can be expressed in a program design language (PDL). The PDL contains six major parts:

- Module name: for module identification.
- Level number: the level of detailed description of the module. (This level number should not be confused with the level of a tree structure.)
- Description: the description of the function or subfunction(s) of the module, the constraints on the module, and other information related to the module.
- Input: the description of the input domain of the module in terms of input variables with which data is to be passed to the module. The description includes the types and the structures of the variable and rules of constructing input data, and so forth.
- Output: the description of the output of the module, similar to that of the input variables.
- Process: the body of module design. It uses a program design language (PDL), which is simple English, to describe the constructs of module logic. The con-

structs include SEQUENCE, IF-THEN-ELSE, DO-WHILE, DO-UNTIL, and CASE, as described in Cho. [15]

The input and output part of the design is the interface of the module with the "outside world."

If a module is complicated, then the design can be developed by refining the PDL level by level, e.g., level-l, level-2, and level-3 PDL of a module. The level-l PDL is an abstraction of the level-2 PDL, hiding some detailed information from the level-2 PDL. Similarly, the level-2 PDL is an abstraction of the level-3 PDL, hiding some detailed information from the level-3 PDL; and so on. The lowest-level PDL is very close to the programming language to be used. The criteria in developing these levels of abstraction are shown in Table 19-4.

An example of a three-level PDL can be found in reference 15. The advantages of using the three-level approach are:

- After each level of PDL has been completed, a design review or walkthrough can be conducted to insure that nothing is missing from the PDL before the design of the next-level PDL.
- After the review, the design is refined and the result is a design document for that level.
- The level of abstraction in the PDL provides a top-down comprehension of the design, enhancing tremendously the readability of the software being developed.

Table I9-4   Three Levels of PDL

PDL	LEVEL		
	1	**2**	**3**
Input Variable	Basic description and how it is used.	Adding the structure of the variable.	Adding data type, lower and upper bounds, rules of using the variable.
Output Variable	Basic description and how it is to be used by other modules.	Adding the structure of the variable.	Adding data type, lower and upper bounds, rules of using the variable.
Process	Basic functions and the logical order in which the functions are to be performed.	Decomposing each basic function into subfunctions, with description of necessary initialization and constraints.	Decomposing each subfunction into smaller pieces, with detailed description of initialization and constraints.

Test Design.   The tasks of estimating the software defective rate using statistical quality control include:

A. Review of product unit definition for sampling.
B. Review of product unit defectiveness definition.
C. Design of a sampling plan.
D. Construction of random input units by a random procedure using a SIAD tree.
E. Analysis of test results.
F. Statistical inference on product population defective rate.

Tasks A, B, C, and D are design tasks which can proceed simultaneously with software design. Tasks E and F are implementation tasks to be performed after software coding and debugging has been completed, and are not further described.

A. Review of Product Unit Definition for Sampling
In any manufacturing industry, the definition of product unit is the basis on which to apply statistical quality control. As a piece of software can be viewed as a factory producing discrete outputs, so each of the outputs can be defined as a product unit. With this concept in mind, we can view accepting a piece of software as equivalent to accepting all of the product units the software generates.

B. Review of Product Unit Defectiveness Definition
This definition is essential to classify a product unit being defective or nondefective. Depending on the degree of seriousness, a defective unit may fall into one of four categories:

i.   Severely defective: it contains wrong and unusable results. The use of the results can cause severe damage to its user.
ii.   Seriously defective: it contains unusable results. The use of the results can cause serious difficulty to its user.
iii. Minor defective: it contains errors but will not affect its user.
iv.   Irregularly defective: it contains odd results. The use of the results will not affect its user.

A defective unit in categories iii and iv may be regarded as nondefective for economical reasons.

C. Design of a Sampling Plan
The design of a plan for estimating the defective rate of a software population includes the determination of sample size n, the number of product units to be taken randomly from the population. The value of n depends on two criteria:

1. the closeness of the accuracy between the population defective rate and the sample defective rate
2. the desired level of confidence.

The criteria should be given in the requirement specification document.

D. Construction of Random Input Units by a Random Procedure Using a SIAD Tree

The construction of a random input unit for testing begins with sampling from the tree elements of a software SIAD tree defined in a requirement specification document. Since there are three types of tree elements that can be specified in the tree — numerical, nonnumerical, and data value—the construction of a unit can be different.

These numerical, nonnumerical, and data value tree elements are used for regular sampling. The other three sampling methods—weighted, boundary, and invalid—as discussed in the test requirements in Section 19.3, paragraph II, Requirements Specification, Item D, may also be used to construct the input units for testing purposes.

19.3.4   IV. Software Implementation

As shown in Figure 19-4, software implementation consists of two major tasks: coding and test case generation with expected results of processing the input units. The tasks are simply the implementation of software design and test design respectively. Proper program constructs including SEQUENCE, IF-THEN-ELSE, DO WHILE or DO UNTIL, and MODULE should be used for algorithm coding for better understandability. In addition, proper data structures including VARIABLE, ARRAY, LIST, STACK, QUEUE, TREE, and NETWORK (or PLEX) should be used for efficiency of a particular algorithm. In the test case generation, n units should be generated using the design in the test design stage discussed in this section, where n is the sample size.

Although there are many methods of software implementation, such as top-down and bottom-up, it has been this author's experience that a good method is top-down design with critical-module and bottom-up implementation. This method is based on the concept of building on a "secured spare-part and assembly" basis. If bottom-up implementation cannot be done, then it means the software design is incomplete. Implementation of a software system with an incomplete design is asking for trouble!

A detailed description of software implementation methods is given in Cho. [15]

19.3.5   V. Testing and Integration

After software design and test design have been implemented, the individual modules are to be tested before it is integrated into the software. Testing and integration should be done from the modules at the bottom level to the modules at the top level in the software tree. This is like building a factory based on a "quality part" basis to avoid integrating a poor quality part into the factory. After each module has been tested and its output population defective rate satisfies a design criterion $\theta_i < c_i$ where i identifies a module and c_i is a given small number, the module is then integrated into the software. The module output population defective rate θ_i can also be estimated. After all of the modules have been tested and integrated, the software is then tested using the test input units implemented from the software's input domain and rules SIAD tree. Finally, the software product population defective rate e under each of the four sampling methods (regular, weighted, boundary, and invalid) discussed in the Test Requirements subsection of Section 19.3, is computed. If the estimated rates do not satisfy the requirement $\theta < c$ under at least one sampling method, then the software should not be delivered. The developer should improve the quality by correcting the error found during the test.

19.3.6   VI. Software Acceptance

If the developed software satisfies the quality requirement $\theta < c$, it is delivered to the user. The user can accept the software testing that the requirement $\theta < c$ has been met, or the user can verify the rate θ by conducting a test following the same techniques discussed. The quality control tool is seen to be a powerful weapon to protect the user from being a poor quality software victim.

19.4   Quality Programming Practical Experiences

Some practical experiences in applying the Quality Programming (QP) technology and tools to software development and testing to real world projects are illustrated in this section.

19.4.1   I. Application and Tool Experiences

The QP technology has been applied to many software entities, ranging from mainframe operating system components, PC and minicomputer database management to scientific applications since 1980, as illustrated below.

Software Applications.   The QP technology has been applied to numerous new and already-developed software systems and entities in the U.S. and other countries since the publication of references 7 and 15. The applications include:

- Air defense system
- Air traffic control system
- Large-scale defense systems

- Operating system
- Space decision support system
- Color graphics firmware system
- Printed circuit design system
- Multisensor tracking system
- Scientific systems
- Database management software

These systems were developed in the Ada, Assembly, COBOL, FORTRAN, and PL/M languages. Following the technology in developing a new system, software quality is automatically built into the system. The test of such software is fairly easy, as all of the ingredients necessary to the design and implementation of test have been built in the software along with the development process. [15] The major ingredients include the SIAD tree (input domain), definitions of product unit and product unit definitions, confidence in the test result, etc. [15]

Applying the Quality Programming technology to testing an existing system, developed using other software technologies, presents many difficulties. Many ingredients necessary to apply the technology to the design and implementation of test are missing. Therefore, those ingredients must be made available after the fact for testing and software use purposes. This is one reason why many software systems are of poor quality, even unusable!

Table 19-5 shows a number of existing software system/entity projects tested using the Quality Programming technology. Each of the entries was obtained by applying equation (5.3a) in Chapter 5 of reference 15, where the percent chance of getting wrong results is the sample defective rate in the equations. For example, the user would get wrong results 77 times out of 100 from using the Project 9 software during the operation of the system under the defined conditions (the conditions are not shown).

It is important to note that the entries in the column of "% chance of getting wrong results" should be interpreted strictly under the conditions of SIAD tree (input domain), product unit, product unit defectiveness and quality confidence level defined for the software. (None of these conditions is shown.) The chances of getting wrong results must not be generalized. In other words, each chance is valid only when the software is used under its defined conditions. Each system must be retested under a different set of conditions. For example, the chance of getting wrong results for Project 2 system is 0, meaning that it is 0 only under the conditions defined for the software to operate. The chance may not be 0 if the user is to use the system under another set of conditions. Similarly, the chance is 100 percent for Project 8. This does not mean that the system is not usable under another set of conditions. The chance must be obtained by retesting the system.

Table 19-5   The State of Health of, or Risks in using, the Software in 25 Projects

System		Number of Units tested	Number of Defective Units Found	User's Risks (% Chance of Getting Wrong Project Results)
1	OS/MAINFRAME	50	11	22.00
2		60	0	0.00
3		60	31	51.67
4		53	1	1.89
5		60	4	6.70
	TOTAL	283	47	16.60
6	DBMS/PC	30	0	0.00
7		38	2	5.30
8		12	12	100.00
9		122	94	77.10
10		30	29	96.70
	TOTAL	232	137	59.10
11	DBMS/HOL/MINI	380	8	2.10
12		380	8	2.10
13		2080	12	0.60
	TOTAL	2840	28	1.00
14	DBMS/HOL/MINI	77	43	56.00
15		36	(5 error)	*
16		88	(33 error)	*
17	SCIENTIFIC	36	4	11.11
18		55	6	10.91
19		55	9	16.36
20		112	14	12.50
21		30	8	26.67
22		30	2	96.70
23		30	16	53.33
24		30	8	26.67
25		30	30	100.00
	TOTAL	408	124	30.39

Note: The conditions under which each project was tested arc proprietary in nature and are not given.
* Only the number or errors were found in the text.
© Copyright by Computa. Inc., 1991. Reproduced by permission of Computa, Inc.

The software reliability measure using the Quality Programming technology is simply the value of $1 - d$, where d is the "% chance of getting wrong results" in using a system. For example, the reliability of Project 1 is $1 - 0.225 = 0.775$ in Table 19-5. The reliability value so obtained is independent of software test and operation clock time. Conventionally, the software reliability is measured by the "mean time to failure" which is dependent on the software operation clock time. However, the value of $1 - d$ is the "mean time to failure," where 'time' is the number of times a user uses the system under his defined conditions.

Tool Applications. A Software Certification System prototype (SCS 96) has been in development in Ada. Since Ada has the capability of interfacing with other languages, the SCS can be used to certify software developed in many languages, such as FORTRAN, COBOL, C, and Assembly. The use of earlier versions of the SCS prototype is illustrated below.

19.4.2 II. Practical Examples

The following are some experiences illustrating the effectiveness of the QP technology and some tools in real world software development and acquisition.

Commercial Firmware. The software was the VectorScan 512 graphics display controller.* The firmware had been in production and had been shipped to the market when this study was conducted. Before the study only one minor bug had been detected in the product's software.

The problems involved with fixing that bug in the software already in the field led to the deployment of the QP technology.

The software runs on an Intel 8085 microprocessor embedded in the device. It is 8 K of tightly coded assembly language burned into an EPROM in the device. Access to the internal variables or modules is precluded by the product.

Analytical techniques such as "proof of correctness" is very time consuming, error prone, and impractical. Factors such as the software is implemented in assembly language, rounding/truncation errors, and stack overflows rule out using these techniques.

The QP technology should be employed throughout the software life cycle to build quality into the software. In this study, only the test specification, design, implementation, and software acceptance were considered. This was because the product already had been developed and shipped to the consumers. The full power of the technology can be tapped during software modeling, requirements specification, software design and implementation stages. This was evidenced by the fact that the

---

* The technology being applied at that time was under the name "Software Quality Control."

original VectorScan 512 testing procedure was largely manual and many ingredients required by the QP technology were not available.

Often the end user does not have the opportunity to employ the QP technology during the entire software life cycle, unless under contractual requirements. There are several reasons for this. First, software development may have progressed significantly beyond the early stage of development before the user and developer are aware of the existence of the technology; secondly, the party performing the quality assurance and testing tasks has no control over the software developer's methodology.

In any case, there must be some set of standards against which existing software is tested. These can be requirements, software specifications, contract requirements, or a user's manual. Often the requirements are not explicitly stated. Rather, a system specification is given and the software is only one part that satisfies the system requirements.

Several ingredients crucial to development and quality assurance of the VectorScan 512 software were missing. These included: (1) a Symbolic Input Attribute Decomposition (SIAD) tree; (2) definitions of product unit and product unit goodness; and (3) software acceptance criteria, especially the producer's and buyer's risks. The SIAD tree represents software input domain, i.e. the specifications of the "raw materials," quality characteristics of the materials, and the rules and subrules of using the materials, etc. the Programmer's Manual of the firmware was used to reengineer these ingredients. This case study involved the following:

A. Requirement

Since the product was developed before this test, the SIAD tree did not exist and was reengineered. The tree was given in reference 5.

B. Test Design

This task included definitions of the product unit and product unit goodness to be generated by the software for the users' daily work. The firmware was divided into three functional parts for this test: vector, circle, and arc conversion and drawing. If the product was to be accepted, each part had to pass the QP test. There were three reasons: verification of the test was eased for its simplicity, buyer's risk could be assessed for each function based on the resources required to test the product, and the nature of the independent test easily allowed isolation of the problem area for easy maintenance.

Each of the three functions must pass the producer's and buyer's risks test. The product unit and product unit goodness were defined as follows:

- Vector Conversion: The product unit was a single vector drawn on the screen between two randomly chosen endpoints. The product unit goodness included: every pixel on the screen was within one pixel of the closest line between the two endpoints; there must be a pixel within each pixel on the ideal line; and the vector had to be continuous between the endpoints with the exact pixels represented by the endpoint coordinates.

- Circle Conversion: The product unit was a circle drawn on the screen, centered at a coordinate with a random radius. The circle was considered good if points drawn at one degree increments around the circle were within one pixel of the circumference.

- Arc Conversion: The unit was an arc centered at a screen coordinate with a radius. The arc had a random starting and ending angle, with a one degree resolution from 0 to 359 degrees. The arc was of good quality if the endpoints of the arc were within one pixel of the endpoints of the ideal arc.

C. Software Acceptance Criteria

With the input domain represented by the SIAD tree of the three functions and the product unit and product unit goodness defined above, the producer's and buyer's risks were determined for accepting the software: A 5 percent producer's risk at a 1 percent product unit population defective rate and a 5 percent buyer's risk at a 5 percent product unit population detective rate. Namely,

$$\alpha_1 = 0.05 \quad \theta_1 = 0.01$$

$$\alpha_2 = 0.05 \quad \theta_2 = 0.05$$

A single sampling plan, designated by (n, d), could be formulated with these risks. In this plan, a number of product units, n, were sampled from the product unit population, i.e., from the input. If the sample contained more than a specified number of defective product units, d, the software was rejected. The formulation of sampling plans is discussed in detail in references 7 and 15.

Four sampling plans can be formulated for each set of producer's and buyer's risks. In this case:

n = 137	d = 4
n = 155	d = 4
n = 183	d = 5
n = 197	d = 6

The four plans represent the best ones that can satisfy the producer's and buyer's risks. The final one is determined by examining the risks in each of the four plans. Table 19-6 depicts a summary of the four plans.

Table 19-6 A Comparison of Four Single Sampling Plans

Plan Number	Sample Size n	Number of Defective Product Units d	Producer's Risks		User's Risks	
			α_1	θ_1	α_2	θ_2
1	137	4	0.052	0.010	0.089	0.050
2	155	4	0.064	0.010	0.050	0.050
3	183	5	0.040	0.010	0.050	0.050
4	197	5	0.052	0.010	0.032	0.050

From the table, Plan 3, $(n, d) = (183, 5)$ is the one that meets the acceptance criteria the most and is chosen. In this plan, if a sample of 183 product units taken in testing a piece of software and the sample contains less than five detective units, the software is accepted. The acceptance sampling plan may seem loose for the user. In reality, a single plan can be formulated by selecting proper risks from the producer and buyer so that the plan $(n, 1)$ can be formulated. A "better" sampling plan requires more resources and must be carefully considered.

A word of caution must be given here. There are concerns in the software industry that no software is to be accepted with known errors. Since errors are reflected in the detective rate of the product unit population, no software is to be accepted with nonzero defective rate. In the QP technology, this means that the acceptance criteria are used for accountability. If the software meets the acceptance criteria, the developer has fulfilled his/her responsibility. Otherwise, the developer has not. In the former case, the buyer is responsible for correcting the software by paying the developer to remove the error, hence reducing the defective rate. In the latter case, the developer is responsible for correcting the software without payment from the user.

D. Test Implementation

Under the QP technology, up to seven test methods (regular, weighted, boundary, special, efficiency, and stress) are to be used to test and accept a piece of software. Only the regular test is illustrated here.

The vector, arc, and circle functions were tested independently. Each sample test was displayed on the screen. The test program prompted the operator to indicate a good or bad status After the status was input, the screen was erased and the next sample test was output The inspection of the product units was simplified by drawing reference patterns on the display. The three functions were tested as follows:

- Vector Function: The sampled vector was the first output on display in one of the four bit planes of the VectorScan 512. A sequence of points, the "ideal" vector for the end points, were output in another plane. The device map registers were set so that the points disappeared when the reference and ideal points coincided. If a pixel had only the test plane set, it appeared in low intensity. If only the reference level was set in a pixel, it was displayed in a higher intensity. A product unit was defective if two or more high intensity pixels appeared without low intensity pixel next to them, or if two or more low intensity pixels were displayed without high intensity pixel next to them. These cases represented the test vector being more than one pixel away from the reference.

- Circle Function: A sampled test circle was drawn in one plane. Then 360 reference points were drawn at a one degree space on the circumference of an "ideal" circle of the same radius in another plane. The circle was good only if the reference points were within one pixel of the test circle's circumference.

- Arc Function: This test drew arcs centered on the screen, with a radius and random starting and ending angles. Two reference vectors were drawn from the arc's center to the points that represented the start and end angles on the arc's circumference. If the endpoints were not within one pixel of the vector endpoint, the arc was considered defective.

The VectorScan 512 had a RS 232 communication line for test interface. A test driver program was developed for generating test data and interfacing with the firmware.

E. Test and Results

It took a total of two hours to complete the test. The arc test took about 15 minutes, the vector test took a half-hour, and the circle test took over an hour.

Since the VectorScan 512 had been working for almost a year when this study was conducted, no errors were expected. However, Table 19-7 represents the "surprise" test results.

Table 19-7 Test Results

Function Tested	Number of Product Units Tested n	Number of Defective Units Found d	Estimated Product Unit Population Defective Rate	Acceptance
Arc	183	13	0.0710	Reject
Circle	183	0	0.0000	Accept
Vector	183	3	0.0164	Accept

The acceptance sampling plan was (183, 5) for accepting each of the three functions. The arc function did not pass the test, or (183, 13). A major error was found in the function that determined when to stop and start plotting points in each octant. Although this function had been vigorously tested before the product was shipped to the market, this error had never been found. The error occurred in an average of one out of sixteen times, i.e., 0.0675. The rate found in this study was 0.0710 which was very close to 0.0675.

The circle function passed the acceptance test. i.e. no defective units were found, or (183, 0).

The vector function also passed the test, i.e. (183, 3).

The result in Table 19-7 indicated that the producer and buyer were responsible for the errors in the arc and vector functions, respectively, according to the plan. Note, had the producer's and buyer's risks been agreed upon to have a single sampling plan of (183, 1), then the producer would have to be responsible for the errors in both of the arc and vector functions.

Therefore. the acceptance criteria must be well planned for the accountability of the buyer and producer. (Since the VectorScan 512 was a commercial product. the responsibility was, of course, the producer's.)

F. Case Study Conclusion

The errors uncovered in this study indicate the effectiveness of the QP technology. The error would have to be corrected and retested using the QP test criteria to ensure that no new error was implanted in this error correction process.

The number of functions and that of test cases were severely limited due to resource constraints. For example, the inspection process was manual because the firmware was not designed to deploy an automatic verification process. This is one of the many difficulties of not using the QP technology throughout the development process. The following are crucial ingredients in applying the technology to developing and maintaining existing software:

- product unit acceptance criteria: producer's and buyer's risks
- product unit and product unit goodness definitions
- definition of software SIAD (and SOAD) tree

A potential financial disaster was prevented from happening because the QP tests were conducted early enough, before too many units had been shipped to the market and a major recall was required. The cost of conducting the acceptance test is negligible, as compared to that of 100 percent inspection or a recall of the products already shipped to the users.

Decision Support Software. This product was the PDM (product decision model) component of a decision support system. The quality assurance test was conducted as follows:

A. Requirements

a. An input domain was defined for the component, as represented in a SIAD tree in Tables 19-8a, 19-8b, and 19-8c.

Table 19-8a A PDM SIAD Tree

Index	Tree Symbol	Tree Element	Rule Index
1	x1	Year1	1
2	x2	Month1	2
3	x3	Year2	3
4	x4	Month2	4
5	x5	Year3	5
6	x6	Month3	6
7	x7	Months1	7
8	x8	Months2	8
9	x9	Months3	9
10	x10	Graphic Options	10

Table 19-8b A PDM SIAD Tree *(continued)*

Rule Index	Rule Description	Subrule Index
1	Year1 is 2-byte integer	1
2	Month1 is 2-byte integer	2
3	Year2 is 2-byte integer	3
4	Month2 is 2-byte integer	4
5	Year3 is 2-byte integer	5
6	Month3 is 2-byte integer	6
7	Months1 is 2-byte integer	7
8	Months2 is 2-byte integer	8
9	Months3 is 2-byte integer	9
10	Graphic options is 2-byte integer	10

Table 19-8c   A PDM SAID Tree *(continued)*

Subrule Index	Subrule Description	Remark
1	87 <= Year1	<= 99
2	1 <= Month1	<= 12
3	87 <= Year2	<= 99
4	1 <= Month2	<= 13
5	87 <= Year3	<= 99
6	1 <= Month3	<= 12
7	1 <= Months1	<= 60
8	1 <= Months2	<= 60
9	1 <= Months3	<= 60
10	7 <= Graphic Option	<= 9

b.   Product unit Definition

The product unit is defined as three start dates, project durations in months, and graphic options for data display. For example:

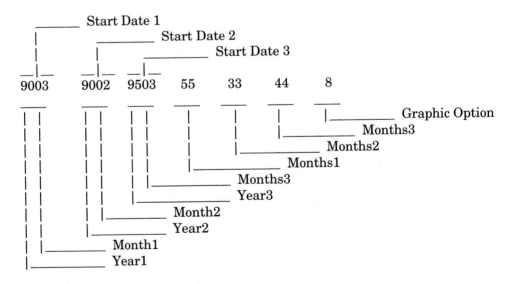

c.   Product Unit Defectiveness Definition

A PDM product unit is detective if any one of the conditions is met:

• a year 0 in output

• a month 0 in output

- wrong "smallest" date among the start dates
- wrong "largest" date among the end dates
- a start date plus duration month not equal to the end date

For example, the product unit is defective:

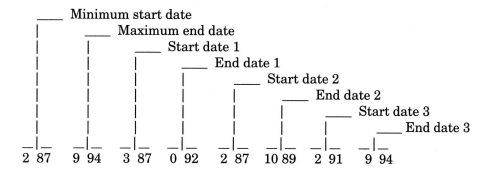

d.   Acceptance Requirement

The true quality of the PDM is better than 0.9900, i.e., 9,900 good product units per 10,000 units, at 95 percent confidence level.

(Originally, the requirement was not given for accepting this component. It is given here for reference only.)

B. Test Design

Many tasks were involved in designing the PDM test: selection of a random number generator, design of test data, expected product units to be generated and evaluation of product units actually generated by the PDM, dynamic test sufficiency decisionmaking, and tool development.

C. Test Implementation

The PDM test design was implemented as a driver in the same language as the PDM. The following are examples of test data, expected product units and evaluation of actual product units, and dynamic test sufficiency decisionmaking (equation 5.3a in reference 15):

```
8703   8702   9102  58   33   44   8

2       87    9          94     3    87   12   91   3   87   10   89   2   91   9   94
2       87    9          94     3    87   12   91   3   87   10   89   2   91   9   94
. . . . . . . .
```

9104	9609	9208	36	7	2	7								
4	91	3	97	4	91	3	94	9	96	3	97	8	92	5	94
4	91	3	97	4	91	3	94	9	96	3	97	8	92	5	94

ITERATION (I)	=	1
CONFIDENCE VALUE IN Z	=	1.9600
ACCEPTABLE THETA VALUE	=	0.1000
ACCURACY FACTOR	=	0.1000
NUMBER OF DEFECTS SO FAR	=	26
NUMBER OF SAMPLE UNITS SO FAR	=	30
SAMPLE DEFECTIVE RATE SO FAR	=	0.8667
SAMPLE SIZE N (I+1)	=	59

. . .

ITERATION (I)	=	2
CONFIDENCE VALUE IN Z	=	1.9600
ACCEPTABLE THETA VALUE	=	0.1000
ACCURACY FACTOR	=	0.1000
NUMBER OF DEFECTS SO FAR	=	49
NUMBER OF SAMPLE UNITS SO FAR	=	59
SAMPLE DEFECTIVE RATE SO FAR	=	0.8305
SAMPLE SIZE N (I+1)	=	78

. . .

ITERATION (I)	=	3
CONFIDENCE VALUE IN Z	=	1.9600
ACCEPTABLE THETA VALUE	=	0.1000
ACCURACY FACTOR	=	0.1000
NUMBER OF DEFECTS SO FAR	=	62
NUMBER OF SAMPLE UNITS SO FAR	=	78
SAMPLE DEFECTIVE RATE SO FAR	=	0.7949
SAMPLE SIZE N (I+1)	=	99

. . .

ITERATION (I)	=	4
CONFIDENCE VALUE IN Z	=	1.9600
ACCEPTABLE THETA VALUE	=	0.1000
ACCURACY FACTOR	=	0.1000
NUMBER OF DEFECTS SO FAR	=	75
NUMBER OF SAMPLE UNITS SO FAR	=	99
SAMPLE DEFECTIVE RATE SO FAR	=	0.7576
SAMPLE SIZE N (I+1)	=	122

. . .

ITERATION (I)	=	5
CONFIDENCE VALUE IN Z	=	1.9600
ACCEPTABLE THETA VALUE	=	0.1000
ACCURACY FACTOR	=	0.1000
NUMBER OF DEFECTS SO FAR	=	94
NUMBER OF SAMPLE UNITS SO FAR	=	122
SAMPLE DEFECTIVE RATE SO FAR	=	0.7705
SAMPLE SIZE N (I+1)	=	114

. . .

D. Test Results

Two sets of results were obtained, as shown in Table 19-9. One was under the SIAD tree in Table 19-8 (SIAD Tree 1). The other under the same SIAD tree, except the value of graphic options (Subrule 10) is from 1 to 10, inclusive (SIAD Tree 2).

A sample defective rate, d, in Table 19-9 is the user's risk in getting a defective product unit. The value of $1 - d$, the true quality of the PDM, is 0.2295 under SIAD tree 1. (or 0.0333 under SIAD Tree 2.). Therefore, the PDM should not be accepted for the intended application, as the acceptance requirement of the value is better than 0.99.

Table 19-9 PDM Test Results

SIAD Tree	Value of z	Value of a	No. of Iterations	Sample Size	No. of Defective Samples	Sample Defective Rate d
1	1.96	0.1	5	122	94	0.7705 (Reject)
1	1.96	0.1	1	30	29	0.9667 (Reject)

Reusable Software.   The product is the QROOT, a reusable package that finds roots to the quadratic equation:

$$A X ** 2 + B X + C = 0$$

This equation plays a very important role in many applications, such as in air defense and air traffic control systems. The true quality of the software is extremely critical to the reusability of the software, the use of which involves human life.

A. Requirements

The requirements of the QROOT are given in a SIAD tree, product unit definition, and product unit defectiveness definition, and acceptance criteria. (The requirements were not defined originally, and are given here for illustration only.)

a. SIAD Tree
A SIAD tree of the QROOT is shown in Tables 19-10a and 19-10b.

b. Product Unit Definition
The product unit is defined as the roots of the quadratic equation.

Table 19-10a   A QROOT SIAD Tree

Index	Tree Symbol	Tree Element	Rule Index
1	Y1	A, the coefficient	1
2	Y1, 1	LA, lower bound of A	1 2
3	Y1, 2	UA, upper bound of A	1 3
4	Y2	B, the coefficient	1
5	Y2, 1	LB, lower bound of B	1 2
6	Y2, 2	UB, upper bound of B	1 3
7	Y3	C, the coefficient	1
8	Y3, 1	LC, lower bound of C	1 2
9	Y3, 2	UC, upper bound of C	1 3

Table 19-10b   A QROOT SIAD Tree (continued)

Rule Index	Rule Description	Subrule Index
1	An input integer number, converted into a floating number.	0
2	L = 0	0
3	U = 500	0

c. Product Unit Defectiveness Definition

A product unit is defective if it fails to pass at least one of the frequency, serial, poker, and gap chi-square goodness-of-fit tests for the application, as defined in reference 15, Chapter 4.

d. Acceptance Requirement

The true quality of the QROOT for acceptance is better than 0.9999, i.e., 9,999 good units per 10,000 units generated, at 95 percent confidence level under the SIAD Tree and c = 0.0001.

(These are given here for illustration for a particular application only.)

B. Test Design

This includes input design that will yield a product unit, and generation of data for the coefficients A, B, and C from the SIAD tree. Namely, an input unit (A, B, C) is generated by:

$$A = [LA + (UA - LA) * R]$$
$$B = [LB + (UB - LB) * R]$$
$$C = [LC + (UC - LC) * R]$$

where R is a random number, $0.0 < R < 1.0$, and [Y] means truncation of the number Y into an integer.

The design also includes deciding the sample size, n. The number n is called the test sufficiency indicator. The decision on the value of n is dynamic during the test and is dependent on the true quality of the software (see equation (5.3a) in reference 15).

C. Test Implementation

The test of the QROOT has been automated with an earlier version of the SCS (Software Certification System). The output is illustrated as follows:

```
ID. OF MODULE/SYSTEM UNDER TEST : QROOT
CONFIDENCE LEVEL        =        9.50000E+01
z                       =        1.95995E+00
ACCEPTABLE RISK         =        1.00000E-02
ACCURACY FACTOR         =        1.00000E+00
ENTER STARTING SEED N, POSITIVE, ODD INTEGER
FOR RANDOM NUMBER GENERATION (1 ≤ N ≤ 32767) = 1357

STARTING SEED           =        1357

DEFECT                  =        0
SAMPLE DEFECTIVE RATE FOUND (THETA) = d / n = 0 / 1 = 0.000000

    .

    .

    .

DEFECT                  =        0
SAMPLE DEFECTIVE RATE FOUND (THETA) = d / n = 0 / 30 = 0.000000

CURRENT ITERATION NUMBER (I)                          =    1
CONFIDENCE LEVEL Z (NO. OF STANDARD DEVIATIONS)       =    1.959954E+00
DEFAULT DEFECTIVE RATE ( THETA0)                      =    1.000000E-02
TOTAL NO. OF DEFECTIVE UNITS FOUND SO FAR             =    0
TOTAL NO. OF UNITS TESTED SO FAR                      =    30
SOFTWARE POPULATION DEFECTIVE RATE FOUND SO FAR       =    1.000000E-02
TOTAL NO. OF UNITS REQUIRED TO TEST                   =    381
NO. OF ADDITIONAL UNITS TO TEST NEXT ITERATION        =    351
. . .

CURRENT ITERATION NUMBER (I)                          =    2
CONFIDENCE LEVEL Z (NO. OF STANDARD DEVIATIONS)       =    1.959954E+00
DEFAULT DEFECTIVE RATE ( THETA0)                      =    1.000000E-02
TOTAL NO. OF DEFECTIVE UNITS FOUND SO FAR             =    2
TOTAL NO. OF UNITS TESTED SO FAR                      =    381
```

SOFTWARE POPULATION DEFECTIVE RATE FOUND SO FAR   =   5.249344E-03
TOTAL NO. OF UNITS REQUIRED TO TEST   =   729
NO. OF ADDITIONAL UNITS TO TEST NEXT ITERATION   =   348
. . .

CURRENT ITERATION NUMBER (I)   =   3
CONFIDENCE LEVEL Z (NO. OF STANDARD DEVIATIONS)   =   1.959954E+00
DEFAULT DEFECTIVE RATE (THETA0)   =   1.000000E-02
TOTAL NO. OF DEFECTIVE UNITS FOUND SO FAR   =   5
TOTAL NO. OF UNITS TESTED SO FAR   =   729
SOFTWARE POPULATION DEFECTIVE RATE FOUND SO FAR   =   6.858710E-03
TOTAL NO. OF UNITS REQUIRED TO TEST   =   557
NO. OF ADDITIONAL UNITS TO TEST NEXT ITERATION   =   -172
. . .

TOTAL EXECUTION TIME   =   1313.77026 SECONDS

D. QROOT Test Results

Two sets of results were obtained, as shown in Table 19-11. One under the SIAD tree in Tables 19-10a and 19-10b (SIAD Tree 1). The other under the same SIAD tree, except that the value of U (Rule 3) in Table 19-10b is 100 in the same table (SIAD Tree 2).

The QROOT should not be used for the intended application, since the true quality is $(1.0 - 0.3) = 0.7$ which is not meeting the acceptance criteria (true quality better than 0.9999) under SIAD Tree 1 and $c = 0.0001$.

Table 19-11   QROOT Test Results

| SIAD Tree | Sample Defective Rates | | |
	c = 0.001	c = 0.0001	c = 0.00001
1	0.0069	0.3000	0.8667
2	< 0.01	0.0183	0.7333

Although the QROOT is not reusable for the intended application, it does not mean it cannot be used for other application as is. Selection of this package for reuse should be based on the requirements defined for that application. For example, if an application requires that the true quality be greater than 0.99, $(1 - 0.01)$, under SIAD tree 2 and $c = 0.0001$, then the QROOT is not reusable for that application either. However, if that application requires that the rate be greater than 0.98 under the same other requirements, then the QROOT is reusable (the true quality is $1.0 - 0.0183 = 0.9817$ under SIAD Tree 2 and $c = 0.0001$).

Random Number Generator.   The product of this test is an Ada random number generator. Random number generators play important roles in many real world applications. Every modern compiler has a random number generator in a compiler library.

The generator, Rand, in this example consists of two routines [25]:

- Procedure Set_Seed (x, y, z : in integer);

  It sets the seeds to the three integers x, y, and z. For the best results, these integers are generated by an independent non-constant function.

- Function Rand return Long_Float;

  It returns a uniform distribution random number between 0.0 and 1.0, exclusive. The routine Set_Seed has been called before this function is called.

A. Requirements

The requirements in selecting a random number generator are: efficiency, reproducibility, long period, and statistical acceptability. [15] Of these requirements, only the statistical acceptability needs testing.

a. SIAD Tree

The SIAD Tree is defined in Tables 19-12a and 19-12b for a selected application.

b. Product Unit Definition

The unit is defined as a sequence of 1,000 digits for a particular application, each digit being from 0 to 9 inclusive, computed from the numbers generated by the Rand with a set of X, Y, and Z seeds.

Table 19-12a A Rand SIAD Tree

Index	Tree symbol	Tree Element	Rule Index
1	X1	X for Set_Seed	1
2	X1, 1	LX for lower bound of X	2
3	X1, 2	UX for upper bound of X	3
4	X2	Y for Set_Seed	1
5	X2, 1	LY for lower bound of Y	2
6	X2, 2	UY for upper bound of Y	3
7	X3	Z for the coefficient	1
8	X3, 1	LZ for lower bound of Z	2
9	X3, 2	UZ for upper bound of Z	3

Table 19-12b   A Rand SIAD Tree *(continued)*

Rule Index	Rule Description	Subrule Index
1	A random integer number	0
2	LX = 1	0
3	UX = 32767	0

c.   Product Unit Defectiveness Definition

A product unit is defective if it fails to pass at least one of the frequency, serial, poker, and gap chi-square goodness-of-fit tests for the application, as defined in reference 15.

d.   Acceptance Criteria

The true quality of a random number generator for a particular application is better than 0.99, or 9,900 good product units per 10,000 units generated, at 95 percent confidence level.

B. Test Design

i.   The routine Set_Seed is called to initialize calling of the Rand.

ii. A product unit is designed to be 1,000 digits. A digit is obtained by:

$$I = [R * 10.0]$$

where R is a float number returned by the Rand, and $0.0 < R < 1.0$; the symbol [ ] means truncation of the multiplication result; and $0 \leq I \leq 9$.

C. Test Implementation

The test has been automated with an earlier version of the SCS (software certification system). The output is illustrated as follows:

```
ID OF MODULE/SYSTEM UNDER TEST  :  RAND
CONFIDENCE LEVEL                                    =        9.50000E+01
Z                                                  =        1.95995E+00
ACCEPTABLE RISK                                    =        1.00000E-02
ACCURACY FACTOR                                    =        1.00000E+00
ENTER STARTING SEED N,  POSITIVE,  ODD INTEGER
FOR RANDOM NUMBER GENERATION (1 ≤ N ≤ 32767)       =        9235

STARTING SEED          =       9235
SET SEED X Y Z         =       9231     5798     4562
```

SEQUENCE OF 1,000 RANDOM DIGITS:

16804	74918	41455	45065	09185	90653	60623	02731	97131	02315
57853	23135	03793	64964	32955	20177	23243	47755	27986	81346
74169	47513	26693	39015	10175	22693	02575	45833	49905	17511
61299	25346	79577	53093	42396	19217	51616	07029	22575	11091
19314	18426	69114	73337	93143	01788	46589	63059	13719	38977
61962	15097	70272	30494	58389	30278	83512	15850	34717	38787
25580	18524	60721	29123	49320	52034	34963	72685	44364	87993
61742	50559	25605	95497	82168	64400	00976	55436	90377	08364
16165	98406	96591	09282	92909	09680	57185	49825	49812	70018
85709	24909	65176	79349	02393	64947	80645	41965	17670	62734
49519	94410	58388	51646	42893	56211	42413	41605	46693	76901
78597	60672	76531	28837	99994	77358	63866	23958	03811	13026
11844	67483	25055	82887	07284	08454	38485	27596	68710	37398
65185	40220	95922	88212	91591	17164	72619	92141	34644	35267
75277	19051	99041	93461	01993	91816	57749	60849	57428	31029
80188	37008	54683	04283	08219	47852	88208	03149	89293	53535
02879	40632	42661	46980	41033	30187	95425	33780	49702	26335
78944	92384	63239	79485	96308	05919	28463	78088	61461	71713
63725	13557	06711	23152	29520	64722	06237	55671	88760	58190
75949	92113	41942	28187	84596	95864	57552	12707	85399	00267

MATRIX M

	0	1	2	3	4	5	6	7	8	9	TOTAL
0	6	10	13	8	6	12	10	5	9	11	90
1	9	11	9	11	9	6	12	13	13	16	109
2	7	11	8	13	5	10	10	10	12	10	96
3	12	10	8	8	15	10	8	13	9	7	100
4	5	12	10	8	7	8	14	10	4	19	97
5	8	14	12	9	13	10	3	11	11	14	105
6	8	12	5	9	13	11	6	10	7	10	91
7	11	12	10	6	6	13	8	10	13	10	99
8	11	6	8	11	12	15	7	9	11	7	97
9	13	11	13	17	11	10	13	8	8	12	116
TOTAL	90	109	96	100	97	105	91	99	97	116	1000

	FREQUENCY TEST	SERIAL TEST	POKER TEST	GAP TEST
COMPUTED CHI-SQUARE	5.78000E+00	8.35998E+01	4.17628E+00	7.60461E+00
EXPECTED CHI-SQUARE	1.69190E+01	1.13145E+02	7.81473E+00	9.48773E+00
DEFECT = 0				

SAMPLE DEFECTIVE RATE FOUND (THETA) = d / n = 0 / 1 = 0.000000

.

.

.

CURRENT ITERATION NUMBER (I)	=	1
CONFIDENCE LEVEL Z (NO. OF STANDARD DEVIATIONS)	=	1.959954E+00
DEFAULT DEFECTIVE RATE (THETA0)	=	1.000000E- 02
TOTAL NO. OF DEFECTIVE UNITS FOUND SO FAR	=	8
TOTAL NO. OF UNITS TESTED SO FAR	=	30
SOFTWARE POPULATION DEFECTIVE RATE FOUND SO FAR	=	2.666667E-01
TOTAL NO. OF UNITS REQUIRED TO TEST	=	12
NO. OF ADDITIONAL UNITS TO TEST NEXT ITERATION	=	-18

TOTAL EXECUTION TIME = 308.06982 SECONDS

D. Test Results

The test results shown in C above reveal that the sample detective rate of the Rand generator is 0.2667, i.e., the true quality of the Rand for the selected application is $1 - 0.2667 = 0.7333$. Thus the generator is not reusable for the application. (The result was listed in Table 19-5, Software Project 21.)

The test result should not be interpreted that the Rand cannot be used for other applications. It just means that it is not suitable for the intended application.

19.5   Proposed Solutions to Some Technical Problems in Software Engineering Project Management

An effective software development methodology based on statistical quality control has been proposed to help develop and acquire good quality and cost effective software. It is seen that the methodology provides some solutions to software engineering project management technical problems listed throughout this *Handbook*.

19.6   What Top Management Must Do

In his world-famous seminar on Japanese methods for productivity and quality, Dr. W. Edwards Deming, the father of modern Japanese quality control, points out 14 obligations that the top management of any manufacturing organization must carry out for the improvement of quality, productivity, and competitive position. [14] Since a piece of software is indeed a factory and the tool of quality control is applicable to ensure product quality of the software, the obligations Dr. Deming stresses are applicable to the software industry as well. The following are 12 of the 14 obligations (those with the most relevance to software) that the top management of a computer or software company must do to be responsible to software users:

1. To create a rigid goal toward improvement of software quality and productivity with a plan to become competitive and to stay in business. Top management is responsible to stockholders and to the general public as well.

2. To adopt a new philosophy. We are living in a new information age. We can no longer live with commonly accepted levels of delays. poor quality, and costly software.

3. To cease dependence on conventional software methods. Adapt, instead, statistical evidence to assure that quality is built into the software. Software managers have a new job and must learn it.

4. To end the practice of awarding software business on the lowest-bid basis. Instead, meaningful measures of quality along with price must be demanded. Software developers who cannot qualify with statistical evidence of quality must be removed.

5. To find problems. Everyone in a software organization must be provided with appropriate statistical methods by which to learn which software quality problems can be corrected "locally" and which belong to the system and require the attention of management. It is the management's job to work continually on the system (from requirement specification, design, implementation, testing, delivery, maintenance, improvement, to training supervision, and retraining).

6. To institute modern methods of training on the job, e.g., training software personnel with the method that uses the quality control tool.

7. To institute modern methods of supervision, e.g., award people with quality and quantity, rather than quantity alone. In the software industry, productivity is often measured by the number of lines of code produced per day. To require, instead, productivity as reducing the defective rate.

8. To drive out fear so that everyone within a software organization may work effectively.

9. To break down barriers between departments. People in software design and implementation must work as a team with people in software quality assurance to foresee problems of software quality that may be encountered in the development process.

10. To provide methods to measure software quality in meaningful numerical terms. (Cho [7] provides detailed discussions and may be used as a starting point.)

11. To institute a rigorous program of education and retraining.

12. To create a top management structure that will encourage and stimulate an everyday push on the above eleven action items.

The Quality Programming technology would be helpful in supporting implementation of these top management obligations.

19.7   Concluding Remarks

The Quality Programming technology has been developed, practiced, and proven effective in developing and acquiring quality software since 1980.

Unless top management in software developer and user organizations do something, the delivered defect-ladened software will continue and the whole software industry will continuously be victims of defective software practices.

Software technologies are readily available now that provide a statistical basis for deciding acceptable risk upon release of software. It is up to organizations to use or not to use the technologies in developing/deploying quality and cost effective software.

Acknowledgments

The author is indebted to Mr. Lance B. Jump and Mr. Robert Kondner for their help and kind permission to use the materials in the case study in Section 19.4. Also thanks to Dr. Raymond T. Yeh for his encouragement in developing this QP technology.

References

1. Thayer. R. H.; Pyster. A.; and Wood R. C., "The Challenge of Software Engineering Project Management." In: *IEEE Computer*, Vol. 13, No. 8 (August 1980) pp. 51—59.

2. Cho, C. K., *AERA Package 1 Test Bed Software Quality Assurance Tests of the Aircraft Data Manager*, Working Paper No. WP-81W00285, The MITRE Corp., June 1981.

3. Eagles, S. L., *SIAD Tree Experiments* (Control Data Corporation, November 1983).

4. Miller, C. R., *SIAD Tree Report* (Control Data Corporation, November 1983).

5. Jump, L. B., *Software Quality Control: A Case Study* (Applied Data Systems, December 1983).

6. Fultyn, R. V., *Computer Assisted Software Testing* (Maynard, MA: Digital Equipment Corporation, 1982).

7. Cho, C. K., *An Introduction to Software Quality Control* (New York: John Wiley & Sons, 1980).

8. Juran, J. M.; Seder, L. A.; and Gryna, E M., Eds., *Quality Control Handbook*, 2nd Ed. (New York: McGraw-Hill, 1962).

9. Yourdon, E. and Constantine, L. L., *Structured Design: Fundamentals of Discipline of Computer Program and System Design* (Englewood Cliffs, NJ: Prentice-Hall, 1979).

10. Ross, D. T.; Goodenough, L. B.; and Irvine, C. A., "Software Engineering: Process, Principles, and Goals." In: *IEEE Computer*, Vol. 8, No. 5 (May 1975) pp. 17–27.

11. Booch, G., *Software Engineering with Ada* (Menlo Park, CA: Benjamin/Cummins, 1983).

12. Ramamoorthy, C. V., and Bastani, E. B., "Software Reliability and Perspectives." In: *IEEE Transactions on Software Engineering*, Vol. SE-8, No. 4 (July 1982) pp. 354–371.

13. Nelson E., "Estimating Software Reliability from Test Data." In: *Microelectronics and Reliability*, Vol. 17(New York: Pergamon, 1978) pp. 67–74.

14. Deming. W. Edwards, *Quality, Productivity and Competitive Position* (Cambridge, MA: Center for Advanced Engineering Study, Massachusetts Institute of Technology, 1982).

15. Cho, C. K., *Quality Programming: Developing and Testing Software with Statistical Quality Control* (New York: John Wiley & Sons, Inc., 1987).

16. Cho, C. K., "Software Engineering with Statistical Quality Control." In: *Proceedings*, (METS), CIE/ROC and CIE/USA (Taiwan, Republic of China, 1986).

17. Cho, C. K., "Statistical Measurement and Software Warranty." In: *Proceedings, Software Cost & Quality Management*, The National Institute for Software Quality and Productivity, Inc., October 29–30, 1986, pp. C1–C34.

18. Cho, C. K., "Statistical Quality Control and the Software Warranty." In: *Proceedings, Software Cost and Quality Control*, The National Institute for Software Quality and Productivity, Inc., September 21–22, 1987, pp. CI–C17.

19. Cho, C. K., "Practical Experiences in Quality Programming." Computa, Inc., 1997.

20. Cho, C. K., "Statistical Methods Applied to Software Quality Control." In: *Handbook of Software Quality Assurance*, 2nd Ed., Schulmeyer, G. Gordon and McManus, J., eds., (New York: Van Nostrand Reinhold Co., 1992).

21. Cho, C. K., "The Statistical Software Quality Warranty: Buyer vs Seller Perspectives." In: *Proceedings, National Symposium on Improving the Software Process and Competitive Position via TQM for Software,* The National Institute for Software Quality and Productivity, Washington, D.C., May, 1991.

22. Cho, C. K., *Space Telescope Decision Support System (STDSS) Manager (VAX 2.4) Test Report on Software Reliability Using Statistical Quality Control*, General Sciences Corporation for National Aeronautics and Space Administration, Washington, D.C., April 30, 1987.

23. Cho, C. K., *Stress and Performance Test Methodology,* Volumes 1 & 2, Joint Data Systems Support Center Technical Report, Defense Communication Agency, Department of Defense, June 21, 1989.

24. Halberstam, D., "W. Edwards Deming, the Man Who Taught Japan about Quality, Believes Yes We Can!" *Parade* Publication, Inc., New York, July 8, 1984.

25. RR Software Inc., *Janus/Ada Compiler User Manual*, RR Software, 1988, pp. LIB-13.

26. Wohwand, H., "An Application of Statistical Sampling to Software Quality Measurement." Presented in the National Conference on Software Quality and Productivity, Sponsored by Department of Defense, National Security Industries Association, etc., Williamsburg, Virginia, 1985.

General References

Cho, C. K., *High Quality Software—An Introduction* (in Japanese). Translated and published by Kindai Kagaku Sha (Tokyo: 1982).

Cho. C. K., *Software Engineering and Quality Assurance.* Handout, Continuing Engineering Education Course No. 705, The George Washington University, December 1985.

Dahl. O. J.; Dijkstra, E. W.; and Hoare. C. A. R., *Structured Programming* (New York: Academic Press, 1972).

Handler. S. L., and King, J. C., "An Introduction to Proving the Correctness of Programs." In: *Computing Surveys*, ACM. Vol. 8. No. 3 (September 1976) pp. 331–353.

Myers, G. J., *Software Reliability—Principles and Practices* (New York: John Wiley & Sons, 1976).

Shooman, M. L., *Software Engineering* (New York: McGraw-Hill, 1983).

## CHAPTER 20

Software Reliability Management

James H. Dobbins, CQA
Defense Systems Management College

20.1   The Management of Software Reliability

In light of recent requirements for internal standardization in company processes for software development (ISO 9001—see Chapter 4, and the SEI Capability Maturity Model—see Chapter 13) and the need to measure those processes to more objectively evaluate the success of targeted improvements, this chapter provides insight into a set of 39 metrics. Although originally presented under the discipline of software reliability as Project 982, the set of metrics helps support the current need to evaluate processes for compliance with SEI Levels 3, 4, and 5 criteria. For this reason, the results of project 982 have value today. A subset of these metrics is presented in the appendix to this chapter.

The science of measurement and the practice of software quality assurance (SQA) have not always been bedfellows. They are still often considered diverse activities rather than companion disciplines. It is time that the practice of SQA and the discipline of measurement of software quality, in all aspects, merge and speak with a common voice. Quality cannot be assured if it cannot be measured. It is not enough to implement a technique or process. The result must be evaluated, and evaluation implies some form of measurement technique.

Attempts at the measurement of software quality have suffered from a lack of positive direction and this has led to a plethora of measurements of questionable utility. If it is understood that quality is an umbrella characteristic which covers many other selective aspects, such as reliability, then it is possible to begin to provide focus and direction on the measurement process and the intelligent selection and evaluation of the measurement applied. It is the purpose of this chapter to provide the framework for evaluation of one aspect of software quality, that of reliability, and do so in such a manner that reliability can be continually assessed and managed throughout the entire development life cycle. This assessment will allow the optimization of reliability, and this optimization will be seen to be the maximization of reliability within project constraints such as cost, schedule, resources, and the like.

20.2   Perspective

To ascertain the place at which this discipline has arrived, it is important to examine its brief and recent history.

The science of hardware reliability measurement has long been understood and practiced through the application of statistical models, usually either Bayesian or Poisson, by which the user can calculate how long a piece of hardware will operate in a given physical environment before it is likely to fail. The mean time between failure (MTBF) is an important characteristic to the user in determining the spare parts requirements, and certainly is a significant input to any consideration of system availability. These techniques have been proven over time and have been shown to be quite valuable.

Software reliability is a much more recent science which began with the assumption that the measurement of software reliability should be accomplished using the same techniques as are used for hardware reliability. During the 1970s, several models came into being; the majority fall into one of two fundamental categories: deterministic or seeding.

The deterministic models, which measure mean time between failure (MTBF) or mean time to next failure (MTTF), have certain inherent assumptions and each has its own set of considerations making it more or less applicable to a given environment. Deterministic models usually assume random testing and the recording of exact test-time periods, and random testing is generally not accomplished in a laboratory environment. The more usual case is the execution of predetermined test procedures at a specific time and for a specific period to test a given functional performance. Depending on the data collection needs of each particular model, [1] the model may or may not consider whether an error is serious or minor, within specification, or out of specification, or any of a number of other factors which are important to management or the user community.

Seeding models (see Chapter 11) have certain fundamental assumptions which are difficult or impossible to verify. These are usually those related to the types of errors seeded. It is assumed that seeded errors are the same types and in the same proportion as indigenous errors. On the basis of how many of the seeded errors are found during test, the models calculate the number of remaining indigenous errors left to be removed and, in some cases, approximately how much longer it will take to find them. If all of the seeded errors are found, one can allegedly infer that all the indigenous errors have been found and testing can cease.

A subtlety that is often overlooked in discussions of the accuracy or validity of software reliability models is the effect of the tests themselves. Any model depends heavily on the test data as input for the model. It necessarily depends on the robustness of the test and the accuracy of recording the ancillary parameters, such as the time period for which the test was conducted. The models also tend to presume that all of the software is being exercised continuously during the test period, and that is a largely invalid assumption. We have all seen numerous cases, especially for real-time systems, in which the total system is operating, but various functional subsystems may or may not be actively processing data, depending on whether the operator, or test conductor, has chosen to activate that function of the system.

When considering these elements, we must ask ourselves whether we are measuring the reliability of the software or the test. A test conductor can run two separate tests on the same software, one test being very robust and the other much less so. The results of the two tests may likely yield significantly different results in terms of errors detected. If the test data from the two tests are fed into any of the models, the result will be significantly different in terms of measured reliability, even though the software being measured by the two tests is identical. We tend to treat the results from the models as an inherent characteristic of the software being tested, and not think of it as indicative of the tests themselves. We also know that during tests of real-time systems, the operator has considerable control over which functions are being exercised at any time. If the MTBF is the desired reliability measure, and assuming perfectly robust tests and perfectly designed models, we would still have to keep completely accurate records of the time each functional subsystem is processing data, assuming that is even possible, in order to provide accurate and relevant data to the model. And, finally, we also know that software is data environment responsive, not physical environment responsive. Hardware is physical, and tends to break or wear out after being subjected to certain kinds of physical stress (friction, heat, etc.) for periods of time. But software is not physical, and it responds to data environments. The tests to date for a given suite of software may indicate that the software has a certain MTBF, but if the operator finds an environmental condition (data sequence, data type, data rate, etc.) that the system cannot respond to, then the operator can cause the system to fail on command, as often as he or she wants to create the condition. Conversely, once the condition is discovered, the operator can purposely avoid that condition. Either of these conditions will have a dramatic impact on the reliability measurement, but in either case the reliability measurement will not be indicative of the true operational reliability.

Without going into lengthy discussion on the many different models and their subtle differences, which can already be found in the literature, [2, 3] suffice it to say that the models, whatever their individual strengths or restrictions, generally require that the system be well into test before the necessary data can be collected and the model applied. Also, no one model has been identified by the professional community as that which should be used.

With these restrictions on the application of models, and the absence of a generally accepted model, there would seem to be no tool or set of measurements available for the software community to use any earlier than the test period itself. By this time, the software is developed, the design and implementation costs have been expended, and there is most likely to be an already established reliability for the software programs that will be altered very little (short of a redesign) by any activity during the later test phases. What is needed is a means to manage the reliability of the software from the conceptual phase all the way through to the operational phase.

20.3 The Fundamental Need

Hardware models give us reasonably accurate data on the time it will take hardware to break. However, software does not break; but it does respond to environmental stimuli. There is little sense to speak of an MTBF for software which does not break. Spare parts do not help since the spares will have the same defect. Whatever defect(s) the software has, it has had since the software has been in existence and the defect will remain thus until environmental conditions cause it to manifest itself; for example, an incorrect result is obtained or the software ceases to perform altogether. Then the opportunity is available to fix the problem, and once fixed, it should be fixed forever. When the software finally does fail, it does so because test conditions or user environmental conditions finally occur that force the software to execute in a manner it was not specified to handle or could not handle, either because of a hardware failure or inherent design inadequacy. During development, it is not so much the actual software failures that determine the results of any given software reliability model, but rather the effectiveness of the test plans and procedures in presenting a sufficiently thorough environment to allow software faults to manifest themselves as failures. If the test procedures are inadequate, the reliability measurement will look great because so few errors are being detected. If the test procedures are sufficiently comprehensive, the reliability measurement result may be quite poor because many errors are being found. In either case, the software is the same, and must therefore have the same inherent reliability.

Therefore, the true fundamental need is not a statistical model, but a means for managing the reliability of the software from concept to delivery. No single model or measurement will accomplish this. Reliability, if it is to be managed, must be maximized under conditions that account for cost, schedule, available resources, and the like. If reliability is so optimized, then there must be a series of measures that can be applied throughout the development process, which can provide an orthogonal view of the software at each development phase, and which will allow the development manager continuously to perform self-assessment and correction as the software progresses. At each phase, one must examine multiple aspects of the software to avoid being led astray by only one point of view of the product at any given time.

Equally important is the need to convert the data obtained from the measures into information that can be readily understood and utilized by management. In doing so, the measures and the information should be developed in light of three important characteristics: Primitives, Flexibility, and Graphics.

20.3.1 Primitives

Primitives are those things that are directly countable or observable. Some primitives may be measures. And some measures may be derived by mathematical manipulation of one or more primitives. Essentially, a primitive is a parameter that is a fundamental input to a selected measure. It may be the result of another measure or it may be a parameter that is directly measured rather than derived through the application of a formula or other technique. For example, temperature is a directly measurable parameter.

When establishing a database, the database should be constructed of primitives. If only the computational results producing measures are included in the database, the fundamental data upon which the measures are based is lost. The fundamental data from which to compute other additional measures is also lost. This also means that the ability to, at some time in the future, develop new measures based on some combination of these primitives cannot be accomplished with any historical perspective upon which a trend analysis might be performed.

20.3.2 Flexibility

Flexibility is the ability to respond to changing needs and conditions. The set of measures chosen at one point in time for the project may not be the same measures needed at a later time. The change in the measures may be due to the change in life cycle, or may be the result of a change in the condition of the project necessitating a different set of measures to evaluate the changed condition. This means that the database must be flexible enough to respond to these management needs, while retaining all of the requirements of rigorous database design. This can be done if the database is constructed from data consisting of primitives. In IEEE Standard 982.1 [4] and IEEE Guide 982.2, [5] the primitives are identified at the beginning as one set which satisfies the needs of all the measures described in the documents. Once the data, as described by the primitives, are collected, any measure in the standard can be computed.

20.3.3 Graphics

In converting any set of data into management information, it is highly recommended that the output be produced in the form of graphics. Graphics can convey a large amount of information very quickly, and if detailed background data is required for support, it can always be obtained directly from the database. Few managers have the time to spend pouring over reams of digital data trying to glean those bits of information needed to make the best decisions required for the life cycle management of software reliability.

20.4   Advantages

The advantages of such an approach to the task of measurement for reliable software are numerous. Such a measurement approach allows the development manager to apply a variety of measurements to the product rather than only one. The confidence level achieved when the variety of measures gives a consistent or at least understandable picture of the software at any point in time is necessary for the decision-making process. The visibility into the product status provided by the measurements is a necessary ingredient to these decisions. It is only through such measurements that effective self-assessment and correction can take place. The aspect of reliability being measured can be assessed, and the result will help determine whether the product proceeds to the next phase or remains in the present phase until the measurement is what is desired.

Without the measurement's availability, the decisions are made in a vacuum, largely as a result of gut-feeling or intuition based on some level of experience. The critical advantage of this measurement type of reliability management is the ability to perform the self-assessment and correction in real time. It is no longer necessary for reliability measurement, and reliability management, to be an after-the-fact process. Reliability management can now be based on a series of intelligently selected exit criteria which determine if and when the software will pass from one development phase to the next. Without the measurement availability, the exit criteria selection and evaluation are largely a process of whistling in the wind.

This is a conceptual leap that many will have difficulty adjusting to, partly because of the historical concepts and practices related to hardware reliability measurement which have been confined to an after-the-fact application of a statistical model.

But, it is no longer sufficient to learn what the reliability is; the manager must now also know what it will be, how to control it, and how to exercise that control through knowledge obtained from indicators of reliability measured at any point in time. Through the application of reliability management, the level of reliability will be determined and planned. If it is insufficient at any given phase, if the exit criteria are not being met, there will be a means for assessment to determine why, with the resultant opportunity to make the necessary corrections and reassess the product. In today's competitive environment, with the lives and safety of fellow citizens being ever more dependent on the reliability of the software products which so subtly affect them, the only approach that makes sense is to design and manage the reliability of the systems we produce. How to measure, and what measures to employ, are really the only questions that should remain.

20.5 Standardization

The literature is replete with measures of all types, each with its own data collection requirements and each more or less useful to the task facing the developer. Before any measurement selection process takes place, there should be some frame of reference through which discussion of candidate measures can be accomplished and which will afford some medium of evaluation.

The Institute of Electrical and Electronics Engineers (IEEE), through the Computer Society, recognized this need, and in 1982 initiated Project 982. This project was given the task of providing the community with a set of measures that could be used for the management of software reliability. This required that the members of the working group sort through the maze of measures discussed in the literature and select a candidate set to meet the project needs. This working group, made up of over 300 men and women, from industry, government and academia, and from many countries around the world, accomplished this task and submitted their candidate standard to the governing board in 1985. There was considerable discussion as to whether such a set of measures should be standardized. It was decided that standardization was necessary for an orderly development of this field. The work continued and the project was balloted, approved, and published by IEEE in 1988 in the form of IEEE Standard 982.1 and IEEE Guide 982.2.

There is no standardization imposed by the document regarding what measures the manager must utilize. This is clearly a matter of personal choice made by the developer. The standardization aspect comes into play once the selection has taken place. The document provides a set of 39 measures which may be used during development. The manager of a project is clearly free to choose any measure desired. However, if one of the measures contained in the IEEE document is selected, then the standardization governs how the measure is computed, when data is collected, and how the result is interpreted.

If application of the measures contained in the standard is consistent and uniform, then there is a basis for common discussion about the measures between professionals. However, if measures were applied in different ways and with different data collection requirements, there would be virtually no basis for common discussion.

Therefore, the standardization process is not applied to force the use of any one measure. In fact, the document is structured so that the set of measures may be modified as measurement science progresses. The set of measures is applied to increase communication and provide a firm basis for a common understanding of the application of measures, if the selection is made from the measures discussed in the document.

In order to accomplish this goal, each measurement section of the IEEE Guide 982.2 contains a common structure. This means that for each measure contained, the following should be known:

1. A description of what the measure does and for what it might be used.
2. An identification and definition of each of the primitives needed.
3. How the measure is to be implemented.
4. How the results are to be integrated.
5. Any special considerations related to that particular measure.
6. Any special training or experience required of one who applies the measure.
7. A specific example of the application of the measure.
8. A summary of the more important benefits of the measure.
9. The experience history in using the measure.
10. One or more published references on that measure.

By doing this, the developer is not left hanging with only a formula to apply. The entire framework for the measure is provided and the avenue for meaningful discussion is thereby created. The appendix to this chapter contains some of the sample measures from the final prepublication draft, which are virtually intact in the published version, of the IEEE Standard 982.1 and IEEE Guide 982.2. They are included here as examples of the type of information provided and the degree to which a measure has been discussed in the available literature. Some of the measures have had considerable evaluation reported in the literature and others, felt worthy of inclusion, may have had little publicly discussed evaluation but significant unpublished evaluation within one or more companies. It is hoped that their inclusion in IEEE Standard 982.1 and IEEE Guide 982.2 will result in significant public discussion of the results of application of each of the measures selected.

The factors that have contributed to the inclusion of the measures in the IEEE 982 documents are:

1. The ease with which the primitive data may be collected.
2. The relationship between the measurement results and eventual operational reliability.
3. The ease with which the results may be interpreted.
4. Usefulness of the results in the management of the aspect being measured.
5. The need for measurements of multiple aspects at each life cycle phase.

6. The ease of implementation.
7. The cost of implementation.

With these factors in mind, it should be clear that a considerable amount of evaluation has gone into the selection of the measures. This by no means implies that there are no other good or useful measures available. It simply means that the measures included in the document were found to serve the purposes and objectives for which the IEEE 982 documents were written. Attention to the foregoing list helps to shorten the selection process when measures are being evaluated. Since the document was written for general application and not directed to any one segment of industry, such as defense or nuclear power generation, it should be intuitively clear that no project should attempt to apply all of the measures in the document; each has its own requirements. Some measures require that a certain process be implemented, such as the inspection process. [6] If that requirement is not in place, then the measure cannot be applied.

In order to assist the manager, who may not be immediately familiar with the measurements that are available, a matrix is provided in the IEEE Guide 982.2 which gives a cross-reference between the general categories of the measures, the measures themselves, and the life cycle phases in which the measures may be applied. These matrices, when used in conjunction with the measure descriptions, should offer considerable assistance to the one responsible for selecting the measures to be applied on a given project.

20.6 Government Posture

The Joint Logistics Command (JLC) has actively participated in the standardization process and continues to provide industry with the challenge to increase the quality, and therefore reliability, of the products delivered under government contracts. The history and brief summary of the former software standard DOD-STD-2167A, the former software quality standard DOD-STD-2168, and the more recent MIL STD 498, EIA/IEEE J-STD-016, ISO/IEC 12207, and ISO 9000 Standards are provided in Chapter 4. The newer standards require that the contractor offer a specific software quality evaluation program and therefore a measurement program throughout the entire software development cycle. The standards also provide for specific tailoring, recommended by the contractor but subject to approval by the government.

In short, these standards force the contractor to scrutinize the project under development and select a set of measures which will allow the evaluation of quality, and therefore reliability, on a continuing basis and provide the customer with visibility into that process. They are driving the art of software quality assurance away from the arm-waving process of monitoring and inspecting, which has been tradition-al, and into the twenty-first century of effective measurement and analysis of the quality aspects of delivered products.

And so, we have a choice. We either evaluate and therefore measure ourselves in some intelligent fashion, or the customer will not approve our development pro-grams, with the resultant loss of business that will entail.

20.7   Application

Application of the measures advocated in the IEEE Project 982 standard requires an intelligent selection process. IEEE Standard 982.1 and IEEE Guide 982.2 contain 39 measures, which are not intended to be applied as a whole to any one project. The only way to select, intelligently, the measures which should be applied, is to choose those which meet a given project's specific goals and which can also be implemented within the project constraints of time, cost, schedule, manpower, experience, and the like. Clearly, if it would be necessary to delay a project in order to apply a particular measure, selection of that measure when the schedule is very ambitious is not in the best interest of the project.

20.8   Selection

Selection of a measurement base should always be the result of intelligent evalua-tion. The selection process is first dependent on experience. If experience in measure-ment is limited, one or a small number of measures should be selected and applied. As experience is gained, additional measures may be added to the base. The IEEE STD 982.1 and IEEE Guide 982.2 provide the software professional or project man-ager, or both, a basis for discussion with other professionals. Judicious use of the IEEE 982 documents will significantly shorten the learning curve in measurement technology. Certainly, familiarity with the P982 document and Guide will enable the software quality assurance person with expertise in software measurement to aid management significantly in the measurement selection process.

Selection is likewise dependent on the type of project under development. Each project type will require a different level of reliability when delivered and this will drive the set of measures selected to meet those goals. If the varied user base is examined, the differences may be readily seen. Such diverse projects as a nuclear power plant, a manned space flight series, commercial software for off-the-shelf use by multiple nonprofessional users, military weapons systems, financial industry applications, software games, and satellite communications systems applications will each have its own set of reliability requirements. Within each of these varied appli-cations will be found a unique set of project goals and constraints.

20.9 Optimizing Reliability

Examination of the project goals and constraints is a necessary prerequisite for the intelligent selection of the measures to be applied on a project. Many program managers become enthusiastic in their establishment of project goals, but the manager selecting the reliability measures must be cognizant of both the goals and the constraints. A few of these possible goals and constraints are:

- Develop the system for no more than x dollars.
- Develop using only entry-grade programmers.
- Develop within x months or years.
- Develop using no more than x programmers.
- Develop assuming the customer will do most of the software testing.
- Develop a system for use in millions of homes.
- Develop a critical life-dependent system.
- Develop for analysis of medical data.
- Develop a state-of-the-art weapons system.
- Develop for nonmilitary governmental use, such as the IRS or National Weather Service.
- Develop with a fixed specification.
- Develop with no available specification.
- Develop with a rapidly changing specification.
- Develop using one or more subcontractors.
- Modify an already produced product where the original may have been developed in-house or by another company.

These, and many others, make up the possible set of goals and constraints facing every development manager. A realistic evaluation of the full set of parameters aids in the proper selection of the measures to be applied, since the measures are only chosen to aid in the realization of those goals within those constraints. Measures inconsistent with these project parameters will be of little use to the program manager.

Assuming consistency with goals and constraints, measures should be selected for their ability to provide meaningful feedback to the developers. This feedback is in the form of an evaluation of the parameter under investigation, the intelligibility of the data derived, the correlation between the measure and a process required for its application, the ability to use the data to make a management decision to correct the product or process or to proceed with development, and the amount of additional information provided in light of information already being gathered. If complexity is already being measured, it may not be best to choose another complexity measure but rather a measure of some other aspect of the software so as to gain the maximum insight into the condition of the product. Through intelligent selection, based on identified existing criteria for each stage of development, the reliability of the product can be optimized.

20.10 Management

Reliability management will be achieved through continuous optimization during development. This requires that there be a clear commitment to the measurement process by the management team. To accomplish this, the management team must be willing both to apply the measures and to learn from the results of the measurements. Through educated use of the measurement results, the management team can gain sufficient visibility into the product to achieve the optimal software reliability.

A corollary is that managers must not use the measures as a club to hold over the heads of the individual programmers during performance evaluations. This does nothing to maximize reliability and will be detrimental to the collection of accurate data on the project. Any competent manager does not have to depend on the results of a few measurements to find out if a programmer or software test individual is performing properly. The objective of the measurements task is to optimize software reliability, a considerable task in itself.

Reliability management also requires periodic examination of the selected measures in light of results already achieved and possibly a change in goals or constraints or both. The required measures are also determined by whatever change may come about in the exit criteria previously identified for a given life cycle phase. A change in exit criteria may result from increased education in the selection and use of the measures, or it may come about from changes in the project itself.

20.11 Matrix Control

Inherent in the idea of reliability measurement selection and management is the idea of measurement control. Implementing this need requires that a set of measures be applied, and the results tracked throughout the application process. To accomplish this, a project application cross-reference matrix should be developed showing the measures selected, the phase or phases during which each can be applied, the goal or constraint affecting or affected by each, whether each has been actually applied, and the degree of satisfaction with the measurement result. This last point should not be confused with satisfaction with the condition of the software. The IEEE Guide 982.2 has various tables (two are provided in Tables 20-1 and 20-2) set up in matrix format which provide significant information regarding the measures. Some show all of the measures, and reflect the general categories of measure, process measure, or product measure, to which each belongs.

Table 20-1   Error/Faults/Failure Counting

Measures	LIFE CYCLE PHASE							
	Concepts	Requirements	Design	Implementation	Test	Installation & checkout	Operation & Maintenance	Retirement
1. Fault Density	^	^	^	^	^	^	^	^
2. Defect Density		^	^	^	^	^	^	^
3. Cumulative Failure Profile	^	^	^	^	^	^	^	^
4. Fault-Days Number	^	^	^	^	^	^	^	^
7. Requirements Traceability	^	^	^					
8. Defect Indexes		^	^	^	^	^	^	^
12. Number of Conflicting Requirements		^						
23. Requirements Compliance		^						

Table 20-2   Overall Risk/Benefit/Cost Explanation

Measures	LIFE CYCLE PHASE							
	Concepts	Requirements	Design	Implementation	Test	Installation & checkout	Operation & Maintenance	Retirement
5. Functional Test Coverage					^	^		
11. Man-Hours per Major Defect Detected			^	^	^	^	^	^
20. Mean Time to Remove Next K faults					^	^	^	
33. Rely	^	^	^	^	^	^	^	^
34. Software Release Readiness					^	^		

Other matrices are broken down by specific type of measure (e.g., Error, Faults, Failures (Table 20-1); Complexity; MTBF) and show in which life cycle phases each can be used. These matrices were included to assist the manager in selecting the measures which should be used on a given project, recognizing that many managers will not be familiar with most of the measures described. These matrices can be of considerable help on defense contracts now that the IEEE STD 982.1 has been included as a reference standard in several Request for Proposals (RFPs), and even more so since February 1991 when the new DOD Instruction 5000.2 was signed. The new DODI 5000.2 mandates the use of metrics on software projects.

When the reliability measurement program starts with a select few measures, and accurate records on the results achieved are kept, the selection and evaluation process is made much easier than it would be otherwise. If, for example, a selected measure turns out to be less utilitarian than anticipated, and if that is because the data the measure provides is really not important to the achievement of a particular result, then this information would suggest that it and similar measures be dropped from the set of selected measures. Such a tracking system will be a substantial aid in communications among those applying similar measures, particularly in deciding whether the measures should be retained, altered, or dropped.

20.12   Summary

Software reliability measurement is in its infancy, but is rapidly approaching puberty. As it progresses through puberty into maturity, the degree to which meaningful communication is achieved among those who practice this discipline will in large measure determine the direction it takes and the credibility it achieves in the reliability community. A great deal has to be accomplished in a short time to meet the rapidly developing needs of the market and of end users.

References

1. Duvall, L., Martens, J., Swearingen, D., and Donahoo, J., "Data Needs for Software Reliability Modeling." In: *Proceedings Annual Reliability and Maintainability Symposium*, 1980, pp. 200–208.

2. Farr, W H., *A Survey of Software Reliability Modeling and Estimation.* Technical Report NSWC TR 82-171 (Dahlgren, VA: Naval Surface Weapons Center, September 1983).

3. Schnick, G. J., and Wolverton, R. W., "An Analysis of Competing Software Reliability Models." In: *IEEE Transactions on Software Engineering*, Volume SE-4, No. 2 (March 1978), pp. 104–120.

4. IEEE Standard 982.1, 1988, June 12, 1989.

5. IEEE Guide 982.2, 1988, June 12, 1989.

6. Fagan, M. E., "Design and Code Inspections to Reduce Errors in Program Development." In: *IBM Systems Journal*, Vol. 15, No. 3 (July, 1976).

Appendix

**Sample Measures for Reliable Software
(From IEEE Guide 982.2; Published June 12, 1989)**

4.1 Fault Density

4.1.1 Application

This measure calculates the total faults per 1,000 source lines of code (KSLOC). It can be used to:

- Predict remaining faults by comparison with expected fault density.
- Determine if sufficient testing has been completed, based on predetermined goals for severity class.
- Establish standard fault densities for code type and programming organization to use for comparison and prediction.

4.1.2 Primitives

i = failure sequence number.
d_i = failure date.
S_i = severity of failure.
Cl_i = class of failure.
C_i = type of fault.
$KSLOC$ = source lines (e.g. executable) of code, in thousands.

4.1.3 Implementation

The implementation steps are:

- Establish a classification scheme for severity and class of failure.
- Observe and log each failure.
- Determine the severity and class of failure.
- Determine the program fault(s) that caused the failure. Additional faults may be found resulting in total faults being greater than the number of failures observed. Or one fault may manifest itself by several failures. Thus, fault and failure density may both be measured.
- Determine total lines of source code.
- Calculate the fault density (n_f):

$$N_T = \sum_i n_i = \text{the total faults found, where}$$

n_i = the number of faults found per failure i.

$n_f = N_T/\text{KSLOC}$.

4.2 Defect Density

4.2.1 Application

The defect density measure can be used after design and code inspections. If the defect density is outside the norm after several inspections, it is an indication that the inspection process requires further scrutiny. This measure is a variation of the fault density measure [see 4.1]. It is considered a separate measure because it focuses on the inspection process rather than the software product.

4.2.2 Primitives

i = inspection sequence number.

D_i = total number of defects detected during the ith design or code inspection process.

n = total number of inspections.

$KSLOC$ = source lines (e.g. executable) of code, in thousands, which have been inspected to date.

4.2.3 Implementation

At each inspection meeting, record the total lines inspected and the total defects. After several inspections have been completed on about 8–10 KSLOC, the total product volume and the total defects are summarized. The computation should be performed often (weekly) during design and code phases. If the design is not written in a structured design language, then this measure can be applied only during the code phase. The measure is computed as follows:

$$\text{Defect Density } (DD) = \frac{\sum_{i=1}^{n} D_i}{KSLOC}$$

4.3 Cumulative Failure Profile

4.3.1 Application

This is a graphical method used to:

- Predict reliability through the use of failure profiles.
- Estimate additional testing time to reach an acceptably reliable system.
- Identify modules, subsystems, etc., that require additional testing.

4.3.2 Primitives

i	= failure sequence number.
d_i	= failure date.
t_t	= failure time.
S_i	= severity of failure.
Cl_i	= class of failure.
C_i	= type of fault.

4.3.3 Implementation

Establish severity, class of failure, and fault types. Failure classes might include I/O, user, incorrect output, etc. Fault types might include design, coding, documentation, initialization errors, etc. Observe and log failures (severity and class) and the time of failure. Determine fault(s) causing each failure. Plot cumulative failures versus a suitable time base. Calculate the failure rate and plot versus time.

4.6 Cause and Effect Graphic

4.6.1 Application

Cause and Effect graphing aids in identifying requirements that are incomplete and ambiguous. This measure explores the inputs and expected outputs of a program and identifies the ambiguities. Once these ambiguities are eliminated, the specifications are considered complete and consistent.

Cause and Effect graphing can also be applied to generate test cases in any type of computing application where the specification is clearly stated (i.e. no ambiguities) and combinations of input conditions can be identified. It is used in developing and designing test cases that have a high probability of detecting errors that exist in programs. It is not concerned with the internal structure or behavior of the program.

4.6.2 Primitives

List of causes: a distinct input condition.

List of effects: an output condition or system transformation (an effect of an input on the state of the system).

A = number of ambiguities in a program.

4.6.3 Implementation

A Cause and Effect graph is a formal translation of a natural language specification into its input conditions and expected outputs. The graph depicts a combinatorial logic network. To begin, identify all requirements of the system and divide them into separate identifiable entities. Carefully analyze the requirements to identify all the causes and effects in the specification. After the analysis is completed, assign each cause and effect a unique number. To create the Cause and Effect graph:

- Represent each cause and effect by a node identified by its unique number.
- Interconnect the cause and effect nodes by analyzing the semantic content of the specification and transforming it into a Boolean graph. Each cause and effect can be in one of two states: true or false. Using Boolean logic, set the possible states of the causes and determine under what condition each effect will be present.
- Annotate the graph with constraints describing combinations of causes and/or effects that are impossible because of syntactical or environmental constraints.
- Identify as an ambiguity any cause that does not result in a corresponding effect, any effect that does not originate with a cause as a source, and any combination of causes and effects that are inconsistent with the requirement specification or impossible to achieve.

The measure is computed as follows:

$$CE = 100\% \left(1 - A_{existing} / A_{total}\right)$$

where $A_{existing}$ = number of ambiguities remaining to be eliminated.
                 A_{total} = total number of ambiguities identified.

To derive test cases for the program, convert the graph into a limited entry decision table with "effects" as columns and "causes" as rows. For each effect, trace back through the graph to find all combinations of causes that will set the effect to be TRUE. Each combination is represented as a column in the decision table. The state of all other effects should also be determined for each such combination. Each column in the table represents a test case.

4.7 Requirements Traceability

4.7.1 Application

This measure aids in identifying requirements that are either missing from, or are in addition to, the original requirements.

4.7.2 Primitives

R_1 = number of requirements met by the architecture.
R_2 = number of original requirements.

4.7.3 Implementation

A set of mappings from the requirements in the software architecture to the original requirements is created. Count each requirement met by the architecture (R1) and count each of the original requirements (R2). Compute the traceability measure:

$(R_1 / R_2) \times 100\%$

4.8 Defect Indexes

4.8.1 Application

This measure provides a continuing, relative index of how correct the software is as it proceeds through the development cycle. Application is a straightforward phase-dependent, weighted, calculation that requires no knowledge of advanced mathematics or statistics. This measure may be applied as early in the life cycle as the user has products that can be evaluated.

4.8.2 Primitives

For each phase in the life cycle:

i	= phase indicator.
N_i	= total number of defects found.
S_i	= number of serious defects found.
M_i	= number of medium defects found.
T_i	= number of trivial defects found.
$KSLOC$	= source lines (e.g. executable) of code, in thousands.
W_1	= weighting factor for serious defects (default 10).
W_2	= weighting factor for medium defects (default 3).
W_3	= weighting factor for trivial defects (default 1).

4.8.3 Implementation

The measure is generated as a sum of calculations taken throughout development. It is a continuing measure applied to the software as it proceeds from design through final tests. At each phase of development, calculate the following expression, P_i, associated with the number and severity of defects found.

$$P_i = W_1 \times (S_i / N_i) + W_2 \times (M_i / N_i) + W_3 \times (T_i / N_i)$$

The Defect Index (DI) is calculated at each phase by cumulatively adding the calculation for P_i as the software proceeds through development:

$$DI = \sum_{I=1}^{n} i \times P_i / KSLOC = (P_1 + 2P_2 + 3P_3 + ...) / KSLOC$$

where each phase is weighted such that the further into development the software has progressed, such as phase 2 or 3, the larger the weight (i.e., 2 or 3, respectively) assigned, and the sum of calculations is normalized according to program size, $KSLOC$.

The data collected in prior projects can be used as a baseline figure for comparison.

4.9 Error Distribution(s)

4.9.1 Application

The search for the causes of software errors involves the error analysis of the data collected during each phase of the software development. The results of this analysis can be best depicted by plotting error information to provide the distribution of errors according to different criteria.

4.9.2 Primitives

- Error description.
- Pointer(s) to fault(s) originated by the error.
- Cause of the error.
- Error classification of the phase (date) when the error was introduced.
- Error weight: assignment due to severity/delay in error revelation.
- Steps to prevent the error.
- Reasons for earlier nondetection of faults.

4.9.3 Implementation

The information for each error is recorded and the errors are counted according to the criteria adopted for each classification. The number of errors are then plotted for each class. Examples of such distribution plots are shown in Figures 20A-1 through 20A-3. In these three examples, the errors are classified and counted by phase, by the cause, and by the cause for deferred fault detection. Other similar classifications could be used such as the type of steps suggested to prevent the reoccurrence of similar errors or the type of steps suggested for the early detection of the corresponding faults.

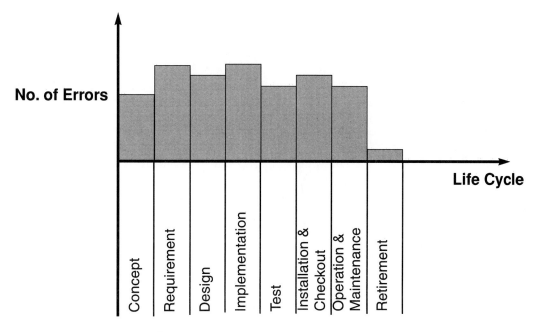

Figure 20A-1 Error analysis—Error distribution by phase.

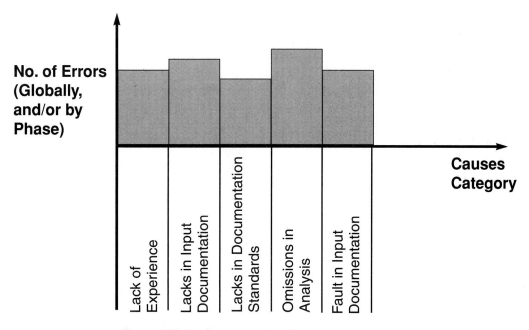

Figure 20A-2 Error analysis—Error by cause category.

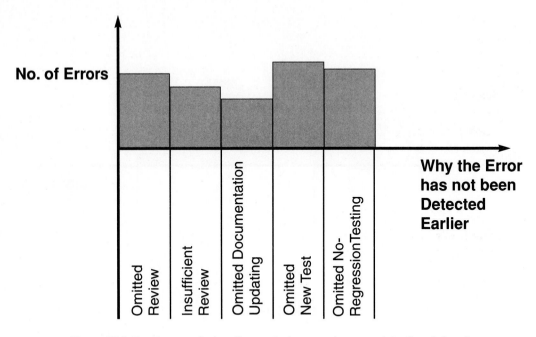

Figure 20A-3   Error analysis—Suggested causes for error detection deferral.

4.10 Software Maturity Index

4.10.1 Application

This measure is used to quantify a software maturity index for a software delivery, based on the functions (modules) that include changes and additions from the previous delivery. The primitives counted may either be functions or modules.

4.10.2 Primitives

M_T = number of software functions (modules) in the current software delivery.

F_c = number of software functions (modules) in the current delivery that include internal changes from a previous delivery.

F_a = number of software functions (modules) in the current delivery that are additions to the previous delivery.

F_{del} = number of software functions (modules) in the previous delivery that are deleted in the current delivery.

4.10.3 Implementation

The software maturity index (SMI) may be calculated in two different ways depending on the available data (primitives).

4.10.3.1 Implementation #1. For the present (just delivered or modified) software release, count the number of functions (modules) that have been changed (F_c). For the present software release, count the number of functions (modules) that have been added (F_a) or deleted (F_{del}). For the present software release, count the number of functions (modules) that make-up that release (M_T).

Calculate the maturity index:

Maturity Index   =

$$
\text{Number of Current Functions (Modules)} - \frac{\left|\begin{array}{ccc} \text{Number of Current} & \text{Number of} & \text{Number of Current} \\ \text{Release Functions} & \text{Functions} & \text{Release Functions} \\ \text{(Modules) that} + \text{(Modules)} + \text{(Modules) that} \\ \text{have been Added} & \text{Changed} & \text{have been Deleted} \end{array}\right|}{\text{Number of Current Release Function (Modules)}}
$$

i.e., $SMI = \dfrac{M_T - (F_a + F_c + F_{del})}{M_T}$

Notice that the total number of current release functions (modules) equals the number of previous release functions (modules) plus the number of current release functions (modules) that were added to the previous release minus the number of functions (modules) that were deleted from the previous release. In the maturity index calculation, the deletion of a function (module) is treated the same as an addition of a function (module).

4.10.3.2 Implementation #2. The Software Maturity Index may also be calculated as the ratio of the number of functions (modules) that remain unchanged from the previous release to the total number of functions (modules) delivered in the present release, but this method of calculation is more appropriate.

$$SMI = \frac{M_T - F_c}{M_T}$$

The change and addition of functions (modules) is tracked and the maturity index is calculated for each release. Problem reports that would result in a software update subsequent to the tracking period are included in the maturity analysis by estimating the configuration of the subsequent releases.

## CHAPTER 21

Software Safety and Its Relation to Software Quality Assurance

Kenneth S. Mendis
Roche Carolina, Inc.

21.1   Introduction

Software safety is an issue that has gained some prominence in the software community today. On the positive side, software managers and developers are becoming more aware of the need to consider safety as a design factor. On the negative side, the news media occasionally carry stories reflecting the impact of not adequately designing for safety. In either case, safety issues are not yet treated with the desired level of competence and consistency that one would expect of a mature organization. One probable cause for this is the way safety requirements are presented to the designer; i.e., in too general a fashion and in too stand-alone a manner. In order to assure that software safety issues receive adequate consideration up front in the life cycle, support must come from within. This is where software quality comes in.

For all practical purposes, safety is a quality concern. Consider the following; whenever delivered software products cause bodily harm or system damage, either directly or indirectly, we have not delivered a quality product. Consequently there is an ever increasing need to examine the function or discipline of Software Safety Assurance.

Software Safety Assurance is comprised of activities performed on safety critical systems during the software development life cycle. The objective of this effort should be to eliminate and/or reduce potential safety risks that are associated with software critical systems. Software Safety Assurance includes activities such as Software Security Assurance, Software Integrity Assurance, and Software Hazard-Free Assurance. Of particular importance in a Software Safety Assurance program is the fact that the requirements for Software Safety Assurance can be effectively addressed only as an integrated activity of the software development process.

Software Safety Assurance, therefore, should be concerned with reducing the potential risks associated with software and computers in safety-critical software systems applications. This effort is best performed by individuals who are trained in software safety measures and who have the organizational support to assure their proper implementation.

The standard for safety-related software systems is defined by Underwriters Laboratory, Inc., the National Aeronautics and Space Administration, the Institute of Electrical and Electronics Engineers (IEEE), the Organization of International Standardization (ISO), the Code of Federal Regulations (CFR), and the Department of Defense (DoD). All stipulate safety-related requirements for system software in terms of hazard avoidance. How these are interpreted and implemented is discussed in this chapter.

In Chapter 4, Schulmeyer's Table 4-5, which compares requirements that have appeared in various software quality standards, shows the intersection of the "safety analysis" requirements with a number of those standards.

21.2   Software-Caused Accidents

The number of accidents relating to poor software safety practices, that have resulted in death and/or serious injury to people and damage to other systems and the environment, is constantly increasing as our control systems become more and more software intensive. Robert Sibley, a staff writer for *The Citizen*, a Texas newspaper, reported that software errors in a linear particle accelerator–based cancer radiation therapy machine caused the machine to deliver lethal overdoses of radiation to several patients, five of whom died. Another article in *World News* reported that a nuclear power fuel-handling machine, containing a software error which was introduced into the computer system approximately four years earlier, caused a radioactive heavy water spill at the Ontario Hydro's Nuclear Power facility in Ontario, Canada. An error in the design of a blood data bank program allowed over 1,000 pints of blood that may have been contaminated with Acquired Immune Deficiency Syndrome (AIDS) to be distributed. Instrument failure, which caused the crash of a SAAB JAS39 Gripen fighter plane, was traced to a safety-related software issue. A Patriot missile system shutdown during the Gulf War, which left unprotected the U.S. barracks that was hit by a SCUD missile killing 27 and wounding 97 others, was caused by a software error. Finally, it is interesting to note that many of the incidents, both publicly and privately known, involving critical software, did not take place immediately following the release of the new software. All too often, the problem within the software had existed for some time before it resulted in an accident. Typically, software-caused accidents are time-independent. Many software errors have gone undetected because they were not found using standard validation and verification techniques.

Lawsuits are commonplace as a result of death or injury caused by unsafe software. Most of these cases are settled out of court, often on the condition that the injured person keep silent about the accident, the lawsuit, and the settlement. An emerging legal theory, which deals with software engineering malpractice and imposes new legal liability on software engineers and software developers for errors in software, has companies scrambling to implement preventive measures.

21.3   The Confusing World of Software Safety

The dispute between reliability and safety can best be answered by providing some key definitions.

Safety—the freedom from those conditions that can cause death, injury, illness, damage to or loss of equipment or property or environmental harm. Safety attempts to assure no accidents, whereas reliability attempts to ensure that no failures will exist within the software. The expectation is that a system is safe when it does not, under defined conditions, lead to a state in which human life, health, property, or the environment is endangered.

Reliability—it is appropriate to restate the definition of *software reliability* from Chapter 1—*the ability of the software to perform its required function under stated conditions for a stated period of time.* Using these definitions, reliability and safety are not the same. A reliable system can be unsafe and a safe system can be unreliable.

Hazard Analysis—an interactive process composed of identification and evaluation of hazards to enable them to be eliminated or, if that is not practical, to assist in the reduction of the associated hazard to an acceptable level. The term has often been associated with Failure Modes and Effects Analysis (FMEA) and with Fault Tree Analysis. It also at times applies to various forms of analysis stipulated by standards such as MIL-STD-882.

Critical Analysis—a procedure by which each potential failure mode is ranked according to the combined influence of severity and probability.

Fail Safe—safety-critical software which remains in or moves to a safe state after a failure.

Fail Soft—a methodology applied to a safety failure in which the system continues operation either with reduced performance and/or functionality.

Safe System—a system that prevents unsafe states from producing safety failures. In other words, the system never produces an output that will transform the state into an unsafe state.

Safety-Critical Software—Software whose use in a system can result in unacceptable risk. Safety-critical software includes software whose operation or failure to operate can lead to a hazardous state, software intended to recover from hazardous states, and software intended to mitigate the severity of an accident (*IEEE Standard for Software Safety Plans*, IEEE STD 1228-1994).

21.4   Standards, Guidelines, and Regulations

Are there too many standards, guidelines, and/or regulations? Do they help reduce the number of deaths? Are the regulatory bodies necessary? The argument that software is different from hardware in that its only failure modes are through design faults rather than from physical mechanisms, such as aging, makes applying safety standards difficult. Many potential software-caused accidents remain dormant, while others can be very difficult to diagnose. Another reason why we have not seen more software-caused accidents is because we normally use the systems in accordance with how they are tested and how they are supposed to be used. We can attribute our success in avoiding software-caused accidents to the manner of our training to use these systems. Software-caused accidents are awaiting the unusual and uncommon caused input. Therefore, we must address this when developing a software safety program.

The standards most frequently referenced are:

1. IEEE Standard for Software Safety Plans, IEEE STD 1228-1994
2. International Standard on System and Software Integrity Levels, ISO JCt/SC7 Project 7.30 1995-06-20
3. The Motor Industry Software Reliability Association (MISRA) Development Guidelines for Vehicle Based Software
4. National Aeronautics and Space Administration, Software Safety Standard, NSS 1740.13 Interim June 1994
5. Underwriters Laboratories Inc., Standard for Safety Related Software UL
6. Software System Safety Design Guidelines and Recommendations, Naval Surface Warfare Center, AD-A209-832
7. MIL-STD-882C System Safety Program Requirements

All of these standards have one theme in common: they make a convincing case for the fact that most of the safety-critical errors found in software systems are design-related errors. These errors arise from a variety of sources that include a lack of understanding of how a system is to be used, errors in assumptions of how the software and hardware work together, and unclear design requirements. Therefore, a significant part of the software system safety effort should be focused on eliminating design errors and testing the system with the understanding that the system should be capable of operating in environments that are not traditional "what if" conditions. Finally, it is important to consider that the development of the system with specific accident avoidance requirements should be taken into account.

21.5 What Does It Take to Develop a Software Safety Assurance Program?

Within the organization, software safety assurance involves three maturity levels. First, the development of a company culture aware of software safety–related issues. That is, qualified developers working to a standard set of development rules and these rules being consistently applied. Second, implementing a development process that involves safety assurance reviews and hazards analysis as a means of identifying and eliminating safety-critical conditions before they are designed into the system. This includes reviews and analysis of the human-computer interface (HCI). HCI is an important design consideration in many of today's products to assure that operators do not easily fatigue under stressful situations and that data is clear and easily understood. HCI affects airlines pilots, radar system operators, nuclear power control system specialists, health care administrators, etc. Third, and finally, is utilizing a design process that documents the results and implements continuous improvement techniques to keep safety-critical errors out of the system software. The chronology of a software safety program is shown graphically in Figure 21-1. It requires establishing a safety prevention program that influences design through safety engineering and a planned safety program. [1] The use of recognized software hazard analysis and mitigation techniques can reduce software safety faults anywhere from 40 to 70 percent. [2]

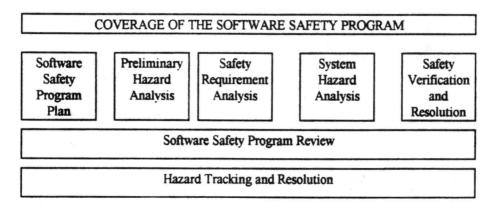

Figure 21-1 Software safety program.

The problem with software is that "safe" software is a difficult concept for which to design. It is an attribute that can only be tested. The goal then is to ensure that software can execute within a potentially hazardous system without causing or contributing to unacceptable risk or loss such as death. Items to consider when implementing such a program are the following:

- Software system safety requirements are established and specified as part of the organization's design policy.
- Software system safety requirements are consistent with contract-specific requirements and are designed into the system.
- Human-computer interface requirements are consistent with contract-specific requirements and are designed into the system.
- Software system safety is quantifiable to a defined risk level using standard measurement tools.
- Software system safety is addressed as a team effort involving management, Engineering, and Quality Assurance.
- Hazards associated with the software system are identified, tracked, evaluated, and eliminated as required.
- Changes in design, configuration, or mission requirements are accomplished in a manner that maintains an acceptable risk level.
- Historical software safety data, including lessons learned from other systems, are considered and used in future software development efforts.

Organizations concerned with safety assurance must be able to determine what needs to be done in order that the Software System Safety program will satisfy applicable contractual standards. The implementation of these requirements in a Software Safety Assurance Plan makes the process go smoothly. The IEEE 1228-1994 Standard For Software Safety Plans defines the minimum acceptable requirements for the contents of a software safety plan. [3] Such a plan must address the following:

1.0 Purpose
2.0 Definitions, Acronyms, and References
3.0 Software Safety Management
    3.1 Organization and Responsibilities
    3.2 Resources
    3.3 Staff Qualification and Training
    3.4 Software Life Cycle
    3.5 Documentation Requirements
    3.6 Software Safety Program Records
    3.7 Software Safety Configuration Management Activities

3.8 Software Quality Assurance Activities

3.9 Software Verification and Validation Activities

3.10 Tool Support and Approval

3.11 Previously Developed or Purchased Software

3.12 Subcontractor Management

3.13 Process Certification

4.0 Software Safety Analysis

4.1 Software Safety Analyses Preparation

4.2 Software Safety Requirements Analyses

4.3 Software Safety Design Analyses

4.4 Software Safety Testing Analyses

4.5 Software Safety Change Analyses

5.0 Post-Development

5.1 Training

5.2 Release and Use

5.3 Monitoring

5.4 Maintenance

5.5 Retirement and Notification

The minimum acceptable requirement for such an assurance plan must be defined, and it must apply to the software safety assurance requirements associated with development, procurement, maintenance, and the retirement of safety-critical software. In essence, the software safety assurance program must:

- assure that safety is designed into the system in a timely and cost-effective manner
- assure that hazards associated with each system are identified, evaluated, and eliminated or reduced to an acceptable level
- capture historical safety data and lessons learned from other systems for continuous improvement
- seek minimum risk when accepting and using new designs, materials, and production and test techniques
- minimize retrofit actions required to improve safety through the timely inclusion of safety features during R&D
- accomplish changes in design configuration or user requirements in a manner that maintains an acceptable risk level
- documents significant safety data as lessons learned, and submit as proposed changes to applicable designs

21.6 Organizational Requirements and Responsibilites

In Chapter 5, *Software Quality Program Organization*, Emanuel Baker and Matthew Fisher outline the organizational boundaries for implementing a software quality program. It is through such an organizational boundary that software safety issues should be addressed. Organizations that have used existing Reliability departments to perform this function have not created the impact to develop a serious awareness among the software developers to assure that software safety assurance is integrated into the development process. Since the requirement for software safety originates with the end-user organization and flows down to the development organization, Software Quality Assurance possesses the essential ingredients to best carry out the role of identifying, documenting, controlling and reducing software safety risk. Many of the roles the QA organization can expect to fulfill in this capacity are the following:

- Establishing the operational safety policy identifying acceptable risks and operational alternatives to hazardous operations.
- Chairing operational safety review panels and defining requirements for the conduct of these reviews.
- Determining safety criteria for system acceptance and assuring that the requirements flow down to the developer.
- Planning, developing, conducting, and approving the results of safety testing before the system is released.
- Documenting, investigating, evaluating, and resolving reported safety-related operational mishaps.
- Conducting regular safety reviews and audits of operational systems to assure continued operational adherence to established safety requirements.
- Defining the operational concept, operational doctrine, and user safety requirements.

21.7   Hazard Avoidance and Mitigation Technique

To avoid hazards, the system design must be analyzed in order to identify potential hazards that affect system safety. This can be accomplished by employing a technique known as hazard analysis. From this, safety risks can be defined and used to establish a risk mitigation plan. The best method to evaluate potential safety hazards is by using either Fault Tree Analysis or Failure Modes and Effects Analysis and by documenting the resulting hazards in an Event Probability and Occurrence Matrix similar to the one shown in Table 21-1.

Table 21-1   Event Probability and Occurrence Matrix

Event Occurrence	Event Probability
(A) Frequent	Likely to be continually experienced
(B) Probable	Likely to occur often
(C) Occasional	Likely to occur several times
(D) Remote	Likely to occur sometime
(E) Improbable	Unlikely, but may occur under exceptional conditions

In order to develop an approach to reduce the probability of event occurrence, the concept of risk must be used. The risk from a system is the condition of the event probability and its consequence. The risk assessment is developed from the Event Probability and Occurrence Matrix. See Table 21-2 for Risk Classification interpretation.

Table 21-2   Risk Classification

Risk Class	Interpretation
Category I—Catastrophic	Intolerable—Will cause death or severe injury to personnel and could result in system damage and loss.
Category II—Critical	Undesirable—Will cause personnel injury or major system damage.
Category III—Marginal	Tolerable—Can be countered or controlled without resulting in personnel injury or major system damage.
Category IV— Negligible	Acceptable—Will not result in personnel injury or system damage.

The safety risk is the combination of the Probability of Occurrence and the severity of the incident, which results in the hazard risk assessment index as shown in Table 21-3.

The aim is to eliminate all category I safety-critical exposures and to minimize category II exposures. Each hazard can be assigned a numerical rating that dictates the level of action required to satisfy the user requirements. This hazard analysis results from the foundation of documentation known as a Risk Assessment Report. [4, 5]

Table 21-3   Risk Index

Event Occurrence	RISK CLASS			
	I	II	III	IV
(A) Frequent	1	1	4	3
(B) Probable	1	1	3	4
(C) Occasional	1	2	3	4
(D) Remote	2	3	4	5
(E) Improbable	3	4	5	5

where:

Hazard Risk Index		Acceptance Criteria
1–2	=	Intolerable
3	=	Undesirable, decision
4	=	Tolerable with review and approval
5	=	Tolerable without review

12.8   Recommendations

Software System Safety Assurance is becoming more and more important and gaining acceptance in today's environment. The fact that a high reliability program does not mean high safety is cause for concern. As a result, design, development, test, and quality assurance disciplines need to consider the objectives of software safety as an integral part of their tasks during the development effort and maintain compliance with the imposed, applicable, software safety standards. It is hoped that the above discussion of software system safety assurance has provided adequate direction and awareness for the reader to create a comprehensive Software System Safety Assurance Program that can be integrated into the existing software development process. The result being that the Software System Safety Program will not be treated as a stand-alone, reactive task, but rather as an integrated, proactive process.

References

1. Leveson, Nancy G., *Software Safety in Embedded Computer Systems* (Communication of the CAN), February 1991/Vol. 34. No 2 .
2. Smith, Steven D., "What is Software Quality?" In: *SESG Newsletter*, August 1995.
3. Raytheon Company, *Cobra Dane System Modernization ADP Security Plan Rev 3*, CRTL 0131, Contract No. F19628-90-0070, January 1991.

4. Keene, Jr.. Samuel J., *Assuring Software Safety*, (Proceedings Annual Reliability and Maintainability Symposium), 1992.
5. Voas, Jeffrey, Morell, Larry, Miller, Keith, *Predicting Where Faults Can Hide from Testing*, (IEEE Software), March 1991.

Interesting Reading

Digital Woes: Why We Should Not Depend on Software
Lauren Ruth Smith Wiener
Addison-Wesley, 1993.

Computer Related Risks
Peter G. Neumann
Addison-Wesley, 1995.

Fatal Defects: Chasing Killing Computer Bugs
Ivars Peterson
Times Books, 1995.

Glossary of Acronyms

5S	Sorting, Simplifying, Sweeping, Standardizing, and Self-discipline
AA	Associate of Arts
ABEND	Abnormal Ending
ACM	Association for Computing (formerly Association for Computing Machinery)
ADP	Automated Data Processing
ADPA	American Defense Preparedness Association
AIAA	American Institute of Aeronautics and Astronautics
AIDS	Acquired Immune Deficiency Syndrome
AIS	Automated Information Systems
AIT	Analysis and Integration Teams
AITP	Association of Information Technology Professionals
ANSI	American National Standards Institute
AOA	Avionics Obsolescence Activity
APM	Assistant Project Manager
APM	Auto Parts Management
AQAP	Allied Quality Assurance Publication
ASQ	American Society for Quality (formerly ASQC—American Society for Quality Control)
ASTE	Automation and Software Test Evaluation

AT&T	American Telephone and Telegraph Corp.
BBN	Bayesian Belief Networks
BET	Break Even Time
BS	Bachelor of Science
CAD	Computer Aided Design
CAM	Computer Aided Manufacturing
CASE	Computer Aided Software Engineering
CBA-IPI	CMM-Based Appraisal for Internal Process Improvement
CCB	Configuration Control Board
CD	Computer Disk
CDP	Certificate in Data Processing
CDR	Critical Design Review
CE	Cause and Effect metric
CEO	Chief Executive Officer
CFR	Code of Federal Regulations
CI	Configured Item/Configuration Item
CICM	Certified International Configuration Manager
CM	Configuration Management
CMM	Capability Maturity Model
COQ	Cost of Quality
COTS	Commercial Off The Shelf
CPA	Certified Public Accountant
CPM	Critical Path Method
CPU	Central Processing Unit
CQA	Certified Quality Analyst
CQI	Continuous Quality Improvement
CRISD	Computer Resource Integrated Support Document
CRM	Computer Resources Management
CSC	Computer Science Corporation
CSC	Computer Software Component
CSCI	Computer Software Configuration Item
CSDM	Computer System Diagnostic Manual

CSOM	Computer System Operator's Manual
CSQE	Certified Software Quality Engineer
CSU	Computer Software Unit
D&SG	Defense and Space Group
DBDD	Database Design Document
DCMC	Defense Contract Management Command
DD	Defect Density metric
DEC	Digital Equipment Corporation
DI	Data Item
DI	Defect Index metric
DID	Data Item Description
DLA	Defense Logistics Agency
DoD	Department of Defense
DOD	Department of Defense
DODD	Department of Defense Directive
DODI	Department of Defense Instruction
DP	Data Processing
DRB	Design Review Board
DSMC	Defense Systems Management College
EDP	Electronic Data Processing
EIA	Electronics Industries Association
ESD	Electronics System Division (Air Force)
ETVX	Entry criteria, Task, Validation, Exit criteria
FAA	Federal Aviation Administration
FCA	Functional Configuration Audit
FDA	Food and Drug Administration
FMEA	Failure Modes and Effects Analysis
FSM	Firmware Support Manual
FTP	File Transfer Protocol
FURPS	Functionality, Usability, Reliability, Performance, and Supportability
GQM	Goal, Question, Metric (paradigm)
GUI	Graphical User Interface

HCI	Human Computer Interface
HDBK	Handbook
HOL	High Order Language
H-P	Hewlett Packard
I/O	Input/Output
I_0	High-Level Inspection
I_1	Low-Level Inspection
I_2	Code Inspection
I^2V&V	Internal, Independent Verification and Validation
IBM	International Business Machines, Inc.
ICBM	Intercontinental Ballistic Missile
ICCP	Institute for Certification of Computing Professionals
IDD	Interface Design Document
IDEAL	Initiating, Diagnosing, Establishing, Acting, and Leveraging
IEC	International Electrotechnical Commission
IEEE	Institute of Electrical and Electronics Engineers
IPT	Integrated Product Team
IR	Incident Report
IR	Information Resources
IRS	Interface Requirements Specification
IS	Information Systems/Information Services
ISO	Organization of International Standardization
IT	Information Technology
ITT	International Telephone and Telegraph
IUS	Inertial Upper Stage
IV&V	Independent Verification and Validation
J	Joint
JCG	Joint Coordinating Group
JCL	Job Control Language
JLC	Joint Logistics Command
JUSE	Union of Japanese Scientists and Engineers
KLOC	Thousand Lines of Code
KSLOC	Thousand Source Lines of Code

LAN	Local Area Network
LOC	Lines of Code
MAA	Mathematical Association of America
MBA	Master of Business Administration
MCCR	Mission-Critical Computer Resource
MIL	Military
MIS	Management Information System
MISRA	Motor Industry Software Reliability Association
MPA	Fictitious company name
MS	Master of Science
MSAC	Management of Software Acquisition Course
MTBF	Mean Time Between Failures
MTTF	Mean Time To Fail
NASA	National Aeronautics and Space Administration
NATO	North Atlantic Treaty Organization
NSA	National Security Agency
OCD	Operational Concept Document
OS/1	Operating System 1
OS/2	Operating System 2
OSA	Open Systems Architecture
PC	Personal Computer
PCA	Physical Configuration Audit
PCM	Process Change Management
P-D-C-A	Plan-Do-Check-Analyze
PDL	Program Design Language
PDM	Product Decision Model
PDR	Preliminary Design Review
PERT	Program Evaluation and Review Technique
PLC	Product Life Cycle
PM	Program/Project Manager
PSP	Personal Software Process
PSQM	Project Software Quality Manager
PTR	Problem Trouble Report

Q	Quality
QA	Quality Assurance
QAI	Quality Assurance Institute
QC	Quality Circle
QC	Quality Control
QFD	Quality Function Deployment
QP	Quality Program
QPM	Quantitative Process Management
QROI	Quality Return On Investment
R&D	Research and Development
R_0	Requirements Documents Inspection
RADC	Rome Air Development Center
RFP	Request for Proposal
ROI	Return On Investment
ROM	Read Only Memory
RSST	Right thing, Small steps, Simple, Timing
RTM	Requirements Traceability Matrix
S/N	Signal to Noise
SA-CMM	Software Acquisition-CMM
SAIF	Software Acquisition Improvement Framework
SCE	Software Capability Evaluations
SCM	Software Configuration Management
SCMP	Software Configuration Management Plan
SCMPR	Software Configuration Management Plan Review
SCO	Software Change Order
SDCE	Software Development Capability Evaluations
SDD	Software Design Document
SDDD	Software Detailed Design Document
SDF	Software Development File
SDP	Software Development Plan
SEE	Software Engineering Environment
SEI	Software Engineering Institute
SEPG	Software Engineering Process Group

SEPO	Software Engineering Process Organization
SIAD	Symbolic Input Attribute Decomposition
SIP	Software Installation Plan
SLATE	System Level Automation Tool for Engineers
SLBM	Sea-Launched Ballistic Missile
SLCSE	Software Life Cycle Support Environment
SLOC	Source Lines of Code
SMI	Software Maturity Index metric
SOAD	Symbolic Output Attribute Tree
SPA	Software Process Assessment
SPI	Single Process Initiative
SPICE	Software Process Improvement and Capability dEtermination
SPIN	Software Process Improvement Network
SPM	Software Programmer's Manual
SPR	Software Problem Report
SPS	Software Product Specification
SQA	Software Quality Assurance
SQAM	Software Quality Assessment and Measurement
SQC	Statistical Quality Control
SQE	Software Quality Engineer
SQE	Software Quality Evaluation
SQEP	Software Quality Evaluation Plan
SQM	Software Quality Management
SQM	Software Quality Manager
SQMAT	Software Quality Measurement and Assurance Technology
SQP	Software Quality Program
SRR	Software Requirements Review
SRS	Software Requirements Specification
SSDD	System/Subsystem Design Description
SSF	Space Station Freedom
SSPM	Software Standards and Procedures Manual
SSQ	Society for Software Quality
SSS	System/Subsystem Specification

STD	Software Test Description
STD	Standard
STLDD	Software Top-Level Design Document
STP	Software Test Plan
STPR	Software Test Procedure
STR	Software Test Report
STrP	Software Transition Plan
STS	Space Transportation Systems
STSC	Software Technology Support Center
SUM	Software User's Manual
SVVP	Software Verification and Validation Plan
SVVPR	Software Verification and Validation Plan Review
SVVR	Software Verification and Validation Report
SW	Software
SWIT	Software Integration and Test
T & E	Test and Evaluation
TicklT	✓ Information Technology
TLCSC	Top-Level Computer Software Component
TPM	Technical Performance Measurement
TQM	Total Quality Management
UL	Underwriters Laboratories, Inc.
V & V	Verification and Validation
VCRI	Verification Cross-Reference Index
VCRM	Verification Cross-Reference Matrix
VDD	Version Description Document
VHSIC	Very High Speed Integration Circuits
VLSI	Very Large Scale Integration Circuits
VMS	Virtual Memory System
WAN	Wide Area Network
WWMCCS	World Wide Military Command and Control System
WWW	World Wide Web
Y2K	Year 2000

Index

PRENTICE HALL

Professional Technical Reference
Tomorrow's Solutions for Today's Professionals.

www.phptr.com

Keep Up-to-Date with
PH PTR Online!

We strive to stay on the cutting-edge of what's happening in professional computer science and engineering. Here's a bit of what you'll find when you stop by **www.phptr.com**:

Special interest areas offering our latest books, book series, software, features of the month, related links and other useful information to help you get the job done.

Deals, deals, deals! Come to our promotions section for the latest bargains offered to you exclusively from our retailers.

Need to find a bookstore? Chances are, there's a bookseller near you that carries a broad selection of PTR titles. Locate a Magnet bookstore near you at www.phptr.com.

What's New at PH PTR? We don't just publish books for the professional community, we're a part of it. Check out our convention schedule, join an author chat, get the latest reviews and press releases on topics of interest to you.

Subscribe Today! **Join PH PTR's monthly email newsletter!**

Want to be kept up-to-date on your area of interest? Choose a targeted category on our website, and we'll keep you informed of the latest PH PTR products, author events, reviews and conferences in your interest area.

Visit our mailroom to subscribe today! **http://www.phptr.com/mail_lists**